# MORALITY TO ADVENTURE: MANCHESTER POLYTECHNIC'S COLLECTION OF CHILDREN'S BOOKS 1840–1939

A thrilling moment from the Wonder Book of Aircraft.

J-7184

# MORALITY TO ADVENTURE: MANCHESTER POLYTECHNIC'S COLLECTION OF CHILDREN'S BOOKS 1840–1939

W.H. SHERCLIFF

Published by
MANCHESTER POLYTECHNIC LIBRARY
in association with Bracken Books and Studio Editions

Published by
MANCHESTER POLYTECHNIC LIBRARY
in association with Bracken Books and Studio Editions 1988


ISBN 0 901276 18 9



Printed and bound in the
German Democratic Republic

## FOREWORD

As a collector and dealer in the history and literature of childhood I welcome this important catalogue. It is one of only a few printed catalogues of children's book collections in the United Kingdom, and the collection is large and varied, containing important old and newer books of great significance for the study of the many different patterns that can be made of children's literature. The Osborne collection catalogues from Toronto list books published prior to 1910, and the great Baldwin catalogues of the University of Florida library end in 1900. Although the Baldwin catalogue is extremely useful for books published during the last fifty years of the nineteenth century, it is by no means complete, and this new catalogue from Manchester Polytechnic provides many complementary entries. But for the period after 1910 it is indispensable, covering as it does a period very rich in children's writing and especially of illustrated books. It is the illustrated book which up to now has had to play second fiddle to the writing in children's books, and I hope that this catalogue will be the first of many such catalogues of collections, which will be adequately and completely catalogued, which will help to redress this balance, and which those outside the owner institutions will find increasingly useful.

Many of the public collections of children's books in this country are in the hands of local authorities including such early ones, for which catalogues have been published, as those at Preston and Bedford. Many serve a teaching need, which is admirable as it means that the books are used, and a developing amount of research work is being done upon them. But the difficulties of the ordinary reader wishing to read such works is very real. Few public libraries possess such collections (Wandsworth in London, and the Hertfordshire County Library collections are exceptions), and it is impossible for the general reader to secure copies to read of much out of print children's literature, particularly fiction, which cannot usually be borrowed on inter-library loan through the public library system.

Manchester Polytechnic is to be congratulated on the thoroughness with which it has pursued its ideals of classification, description, and indexing, which enables the reader of this catalogue to find many new references previously hidden from us, and to make fresh patterns with the material included. It will form a very useful contribution towards a union catalogue covering children's literature in this country which I hope it will be possible to fund within the next decade, and of which the collections in the Victoria and Albert Museum (including the Renier collection), and at the British and Bodleian libraries, will form a major part.

It is still not realised how important and basic are children's books to our existence. Set against the dynamics of childhood suggested by such books as Ivy Pinchbeck and Margaret Hewitt's CHILDREN IN ENGLISH SOCIETY (London, 1969, 1973) children's books are a part of our collective consciousness, added to a kind of inner myth that lives on in all of us. As children, as parents, and as grandparents many of us have a unique and continuing contact with children's literature. This catalogue will help us all immeasurably.

Peter Stockham

## ACKNOWLEDGEMENTS

I should like to acknowledge the help given in the early discussion about this project by Dr Ian Rogerson, the Polytechnic Librarian, and David Good of the Department of Library and Information Studies and author of a similar catalogue, namely that of the Spencer Collection of Children's Books at Preston Public Library. Cheryl Cooper, while working on a STEP Project, assisted for several months, mainly in cataloguing children's fiction, and much help was given in typing by Gaynor Worthington and Gladys Forristal.

W.H. Shercliff

# CONTENTS

## COLOURED ILLUSTRATIONS

# INTRODUCTION

Four main strands have been woven together to form the total collection of children's books in Manchester Polytechnic Library. The oldest historically is the group originally part of the Library of Art and Design which became part of the Polytechnic in 1970. These have been added to since then and are assembled chiefly because of their interest from the point of view of graphic design, illustration, binding and typography. The books are housed in special glass fronted shelving as part of the Book Design collection for reference only, referred to as C BD in this catalogue.

Second is the collection of children's books still at the Didsbury Library, which until 1977 was the largest College of Education Library and had a deep involvement with the study of children's literature as part of its teacher education courses. These books form about half of the Morten-Dandy Collection which includes also historic books on education in the widest sense from the beginning to 1949. The original nucleus of this collection is the 400 or so books given in 1968 to Didsbury College of Education Library by Miss Madge Dandy of Chester, a friend of Miss Q. E. Millichamp, then Head of the Infant Method Department. These were mainly rare nineteenth century children's books collected over a long period, including, for example, early editions of the works of such important authors as Mrs Burnett, Mrs Ewing, Rudyard Kipling, Mrs Molesworth, Edith Nesbit and Jules Verne. Other children's books were subsequently added including gifts from Eric J. Morten, Bookseller of Didsbury and from members of staff and parents of students. This collection was added along with the rest of the Didsbury Library stock to the Polytechnic Library following the merger of the two institutions in 1977.

The Didsbury Morten-Dandy Collection grew up to illustrate by good examples not only the historical development from the earliest times of fiction and imaginative writing for children, but also the development of didactic books of all kinds for all age groups including subject text books, readers and picture books. In the last twenty years has developed writing and publishing of the highest quality in this field and the interest in children's literature has grown enormously – the subject being one of the most popular options in the Bachelor of Education courses at Didsbury. These books are marked with the symbol Y SC (Didsbury, Morten-Dandy Special Collection) in this catalogue and are mostly available for loan.

The third and smallest group of books were acquired by Elizabeth Gaskell College of Education, which in 1977 with two other colleges became the City of Manchester College of Higher Education and are housed as a special collection in the former College building in Hathersage Road, Victoria Park. This institution was also merged with the Polytechnic in 1983, bringing all teacher education into one institution. These books, similar in character and purpose to the Morten-Dandy Collection, but on a smaller scale, are marked M CHILDREN'S COLLECTION in this catalogue and are for reference only.

The fourth and largest group of books have been acquired mainly in the first ten years of the Polytechnic Library, ie from 1970, in response to the interest of students of librarianship, of graphic design and teachers in training. This collection is especially strong in nineteenth and early twentieth century children's stories, and all periodicals in the collection are included here. These books are marked C in this catalogue and are housed in the Special Collections Room on the second floor of the Central Library, being for reference use only. There is not very much overlap between the four elements now brought together to form a significant collection within a very large Polytechnic Library. There are over 3000 items numbered in this catalogue, about two-thirds of which are housed in the Children's Books Special Collection at Central, about six per cent in the Book Design Collection at Central, about one-quarter in the Morten-Dandy Collection at Didsbury and about three per cent at Hathersage Road. The preservation for study of children's books of earlier eras has not been undertaken by many libraries. Because of heavy use in their lifetime many titles have now totally disappeared. It is hoped that this catalogue will make more widely known one of the larger collections.

The main strength of the combined collection is in the full coverage of the most popular mid and also late nineteenth century authors such as Ballantyne, Brereton, Fenn, Henty, Kingston, Reid, Stables, Verne and Westerman. For example, forty-four of Fenn's titles are included. (There are about 160 titles in the British Museum Catalogue.) Many of these titles are not listed in the catalogues of other well-known children's collections, eg the Osborne Collection at Toronto and the Spencer Collection at Preston. The books include many first editions, fine examples of the illustrator's art, typical original bindings of the different periods, and examples of the most heavily used early and later textbooks starting with the compendious approach, eg John Aikin's *Evenings at home . . . a book for the instruction and amusement of young persons* in 1857, through the highly factual approach to subjects such as geography, history and the early readers and mathematics text books, to the later more humane and interest based text books of the 1920's and 1930's. A large collection of eighty-nine periodical titles intended for use by families and children has been built up including long runs of many titles. These show the development from moralising tracts to the presentation of information in response to a child's sense of wonder, and fiction in response to a sense of adventure and humour.

In the Morten-Dandy Collection there are some manuscript examples of writing, drawing, grammar, and mathematical, historical and geographical exercises of the nineteenth century. The catalogue includes these in its last miscellaneous section. The collection also includes a fine example of a Victorian loose leaf scrapbook of cuttings, prints, pictures and letter headings entitled the Beehive. Some of these are hand coloured for the period 1830–1870 and must indeed represent the work of many people in a family pastime using scissors and paste.

Because the greatest strength of the whole collection lies in the period 1840–1939 this period of 100 years has been chosen for the printed catalogue. Facsimile editions of books printed in this period have been included. A children's book has been regarded as one which a child could read himself or have read to him without the need of intervening instruction. Books which teachers might use for their own guidance and books on teaching method are excluded.

With a collection such as this it is possible to study the development of children's literature through its moralising and didactic phases to the child-centred non-patronising literature of authors such as Nesbit, Lofting, Ransome, Grahame and Milne. There are many examples of minor authors' works as well as successive editions with illustrations of the children's classics, which show the improvement in interest and typography, and changes in binding and illustration over the period. The interesting development of books of fairy tales, legends, fables, poetry and nursery rhymes as well as the blossoming of picture books from the Kate Greenaway, Walter Crane, Randolph Caldecott era to the early modern developments made by, for example, Jean de Brunhoff, H.M. Brock, William Nicholson, Leslie Brooke, Marjorie Flack and Edmund Dulac are both well illustrated.

The collection of subject text books makes it possible to study their development in the light of the changing pattern of education as it evolved through various Acts of Parliament and codes in response to improved understanding of the process of education and child psychology and development. There are fascinating studies waiting to be written on this development in individual fields, eg mathematics, history, English composition and grammar, science and natural history. The social aspect of the collection is also important as the books tell the story of the adult–child relationship, their text, illustrations and many advertisements illuminate family life, the exploitation of children in mines or match factories, the Victorian Sunday, school life, costume and the clothing worn by the poor, and the adventures of exploration and of human and wild life in foreign parts.

Special attention has been given to examples of children's books published or printed locally or those such as Hesba

Stretton's Pilgrim Street which describe the local life of families in rich or poor circumstances, or the Wood Street stories written by Alfred Alsop, the Superintendent of a Mission for neglected boys in Manchester which showed what slum life was like and to those awarded as prizes by local schools and Sunday Schools – many of them containing special bookplates.

The catalogue has been arranged in 21 sections which are broadly similar to those used in the two Volumes of the catalogue of the Osborne Collection at Toronto Public Library and which reflect the way that writers on the history and literary value of children's books have devised their categories. Picture books have been gathered together as a separate section since from the point of view of the study of illustration, and the nature of material suitable to read with the very youngest children they are an important separate group which came to full flower, however, after the end of our period. The children's stories are divided into two parts (sections 17 and 18) 1840–1899 and 1900–1939, this point of division being chosen since it roughly marks the change from the older patronising and moralising stories to the newer child centred and more naturalistic books of authors such as Edith Nesbit. It seemed valuable to isolate into a separate section the collections of stories by different authors assembled in volumes as they are worthy of separate attention. Children's stories including picture books represent about two-thirds of the total items in this catalogue.

In the subject categories drama has been placed with poetry, biography with history and travel, and description with geography. In a Polytechnic section 16 dealing with applied technology in the form of inventions, health and medicine and the various practical arts and crafts is an important one, supported by the various approaches to giving instruction and entertainment by expounding the wonder of science and nature in section 10.

The history of recreation and leisure pursuits by children is becoming more important, so the small groups of books in this field and in songs and music are given separate categories. Books of general advice and instruction, section 6, include the compendia of etiquette and social behaviour as well as the early encyclopaedias and very general books of instruction.

The last section 21 includes any item which does not fall into the earlier categories together with books intended for children about children's authors and the manuscript collection already mentioned.

American and English books are intermingled but together with books translated from foreign languages can be distinguished by the different Dewey classification numbers used for fiction of different countries, in some cases also by place of publication. Books of instruction in the classical and foreign languages have been excluded. Within each section items are arranged alphabetically by author, or title, if no author. As almost all books are also included in the classified as well as the name catalogues of the Polytechnic Library and the remainder are in process of being included, it is possible to make a more detailed subject approach through the Subject Index and Classified Catalogue and to trace adult books by the same authors or illustrators through the Name Catalogue.

Brief notes are necessary to understand the nature and arrangement of catalogue entries. The main arrangement in each section is by author's name – the name used being that by which he or she is normally known, either given on the title page of the book or discovered by research with added entries for real names if pseudonyms have been used. Thus in some cases married surnames, in others, pre-marriage names of authors, are used. The names are given with as full forenames as possible within the limitations of time for research. Some entries are for books not to be found in the British Museum or US National Union Catalogues. The dates of authors are not included as these are for the most part available in the Osborne catalogues or the many books on children's literature. Normally all editions of the same title, eg Robinson Crusoe, are placed together in the section appropriate to when the book was originally written in date order but if editions are only in stock for a later period they will be placed in sections 17 or 18 according to the date of publication of the earliest edition held. If the date of publication of an author's works spread either side of the dividing line at 1900 he or she will be included in both sections, eg G. M. Fenn. Where no edition pre-1940 exists of a title, even if it is a classic and the library has a post 1939 edition, it will be omitted.

The title is for the most part given in full and in the upper or lower case as used on the title page. In a few cases unhelpful and tedious detail is abbreviated and this is indicated by dots.

After the title follows a bibliographical description which includes the country if other than Great Britain, the publisher's name, the first place of publication mentioned, the date and then a description of pagination, illustration and binding. Dates which after investigation cannot be obtained are estimated to the nearest decade from internal evidence and inscriptions of ownership, brackets being used and a question mark to show these are estimates. Since many popular books were reprinted many times and no date was printed on them the estimated date given refers to the general appearance and binding of the book. The original date of publication of an edition in English is added for the more important classics, unless the copy in the catalogue is a first edition.

Where catalogues of a publisher's list are included in the book the pages devoted to this are listed and especially interesting advertising matter is described. Much valuable information may thus be found. To aid the study of illustration and binding, details of colour and other plates and decorative features of the interior and exterior are included together with the form of binding. Any whole page illustration has been regarded as a plate. Lettering on covers and spine in gold or other single colours is not distinguished but the use of several colours is mentioned as well as gilt edges. Conventional abbreviations are used in the bibliographic description, eg front = frontispiece; col. = coloured; pub. cat. = publisher's catalogue.

A purely descriptive not critical annotation is included to provide a brief indication of the contents of the book if this cannot be deduced from the title, or to high light an interesting feature if this would not otherwise be known, for example, references to local life.

There follows at the end a note of the location of each item within the Polytechnic's classified sequences of books on the shelf. The terms used first describe the book's present site location, C = Central Library; Y = Didsbury Library; M = Elizabeth Gaskell Library. At the Central Library books can be assumed to be in the Children's Book Collection in the Special Collections Room on the second floor unless the letters BD are added. C BD books are in the locked glass cases of the Book Design Collection on the ground floor – apply for keys at the service desk. In the description of books at the Didsbury Library the letters SC refer to the Morten-Dandy Collection housed on the second floor. The Children's Collection at Elizabeth Gaskell is housed in a Special Collection Room on the second floor, apply for key at the counter. Where no class number is given to an entry it can be assumed to be the same as the preceding entry(ies). There is no location number for periodicals as they are shelved alphabetically by titles in the Central Library.

The index is in two parts. First there is an alphabetical sequence of all authors and titles where appropriate together with names of additional authors, and editors or translators when important, also the titles of series. The second part lists in alphabetical order all illustrators and engravers, together with printers and publishers where local. Reference is made in the entry to the number of the item in the catalogue. The main author entry for a title includes the title, but the subsidiary entries, eg those for subsidiary authors, translators, editors etc. mostly do not. Separate index entries are made to different editions of the same work but not to copies which only differ in a minor way such as a different coloured binding. Where there are different versions of a title used, eg for Gulliver's Travels these are all listed under the best known title.

A few subject entries and place name entries are included but the arrangement in broad subject categories should enable the reader to make a subject approach to the catalogue. Sets of text books or readers, and multi volume works are given one number in the catalogue. Where a person is both author and illustrator, eg Beatrix Potter, entries are made in both indexes.

Illustrators who only contributed illustrations are included solely in the second index.

In the arrangement of entries in the index, authors consisting solely of initials come first in the sequence, otherwise the broad principle of filing has been "nothing before something", eg De La Mare comes before Dean. Where a word is both an author's name and has another connotation, eg White, its use as an author's name followed by initials takes precedence.

Because some titles were added after the main numerical sequence and index had been compiled, some entries are marked with a number and the letters A, B, C, etc so that correct filing order could be maintained without renumbering. Because of changes in position of entries there are a few gaps in the sequence of numbers used. The closing date for additions was 15 June 1984.

For a particular name in the first index there may be three sequences of items, first, items to which he made a minor contribution; secondly, items of which he was the author which include the title; thirdly, items to which he made an important contribution as editor or illustrator.

Finally, may I urge my fellow librarians to take good care to preserve the excellent children's books which have been produced in this country since the Second World War, when the skill of writers, illustrators and book designers came to its full flowering, as well as the older children's books.

W.H. SHERCLIFF

# 1 FABLES

1 **AESOP.**
THE FABLES OF AESOP ILLUSTRATED WITH 25 DRAWINGS IN COLOR BY EDWARD J. DETMOLD. LONDON: HODDER AND STOUGHTON, limited edition of 750 copies, 1909. Unpaginated: 25 col. plates. Bound in red cloth with embossed decorative cover. Signed by the author.
CBDQ 398.21 AES

2 **AESOP'S FABLES.**
Illustrated by HARRY ROUNTREE. GLASGOW: THE CHILDREN'S PRESS, (193–?). Unpaginated: col. front., vignette on title page, 2 col. plates, ill. Bound in cream paper with coloured pictorial covers and matching dust cover.
CBD 398.245 AES

3 **CROXALL, SAMUEL** *(Translator)*.
THE FABLES OF AESOP. TRANSLATED INTO ENGLISH BY SAMUEL CROXALL, D.D. With new Applications, Morals, Etc. BY THE REV. GEO. FYLER TOWNSEND. With Eighty Original Illustrations. LONDON: FREDERICK WARNE AND CCO., (187–?). VIII, 152p.: front., ill., have been hand coloured by the owner. Bound in blue cloth, with embossed pictorial/ decorative covers.
YSC 398.2 AES

4 **CROXALL, SAMUEL** *(Translator)*.
THE FABLES OF AESOP; WITH instructive applications: by SAMUEL CROXALL. ILLUSTRATED WITH ONE HUNDRED ENGRAVINGS. HALIFAX: WILLIAM MILNER, 1847. XVIII, 296p.: folded front., ill. Bound in red cloth with embossed decorative cover and spine, printed in very tiny print.
C 888.0108 AES

5 **JACOBS, JOSEPH** *(Translator)*.
THE FABLES OF AESOP, SELECTED, TOLD ANEW AND THEIR HISTORY TRACED. By JOSEPH JACOBS. DONE INTO PICTURES BY RICHARD HEIGHWAY. LONDON: MACMILLAN AND CO., 1894. XXV, 222p. + 4p. pub. cat.: front., decorative title page, 42 plates, ill. Bound in black cloth with embossed pictorial cover and spine, with gilt edges.
CBD 398.21 AES

6 **JAMES, THOMAS** *(Translator)*.
AESOP'S FABLES: A NEW VERSION, CHIEFLY FROM ORIGINAL SOURCES. BY THE REV. THOMAS JAMES, M.A. WITH MORE THAN ONE HUNDRED ILLUSTRATIONS DESIGNED BY JOHN TENNIEL. LONDON: JOHN MURRAY, 1848. XXV, 232p.: ill. Bound in cream vellum with coloured decoration.
CBD 398.21 AES

7 **Another copy.**
1848. XX, 148p. + 32p. pub. cat.: ill. Quarter bound in red leather and pink cloth.

8 **Another copy.**
1868. Limp bound in green cloth with embossed decorative cover and spine.
C 888.0108 AES

9 **JONES, V.S. VERNON** *(Translator)*.
AESOP'S FABLES. A NEW TRANSLATION BY V.S. VERNON JONES WITH AN INTRODUCTION BY G.K. CHESTERTON AND ILLUSTRATIONS BY ARTHUR RACKHAM. LONDON: WILLIAM HEINEMANN, 1912. XXIX, 224p.: col. front., decorative title page, 12 col. plates, 19 plates, ill. Bound in green cloth with decorative cover and spine.
CBD 398.21 AES
Another copy.
In olive cloth with coloured pictorial dust jacket.
C 398.21 AES

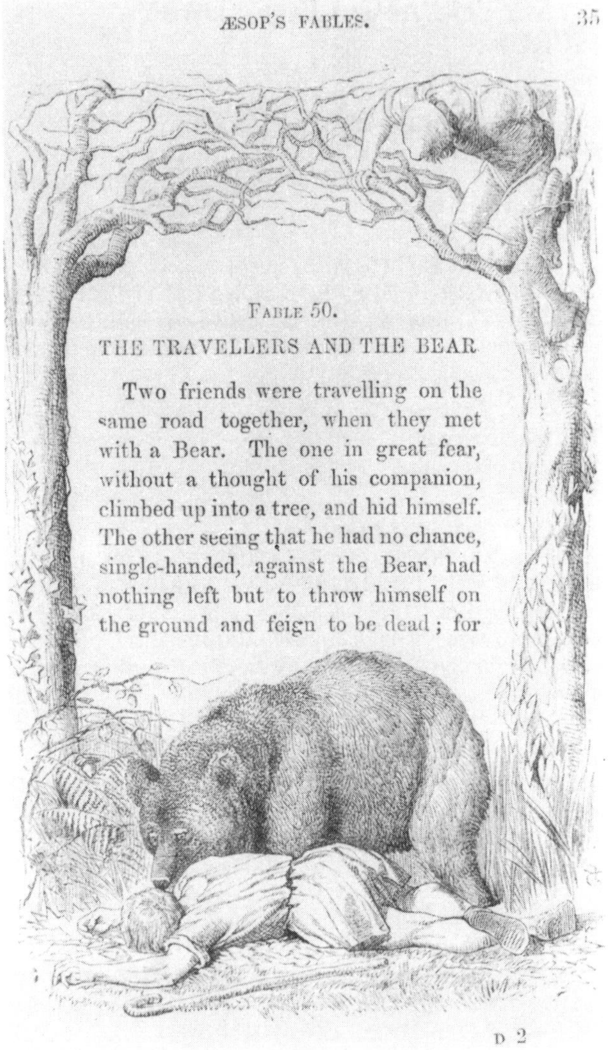

ÆSOP'S FABLES. 35
Fable 50.
THE TRAVELLERS AND THE BEAR
Two friends were travelling on the same road together, when they met with a Bear. The one in great fear, without a thought of his companion, climbed up into a tree, and hid himself. The other seeing that he had no chance, single-handed, against the Bear, had nothing left but to throw himself on the ground and feign to be dead; for
D 2

8

10 **LESTRANGE, ROGER** *(Translator)*.
A HUNDRED FABLES OF AESOP FROM THE ENGLISH VERSION OF SIR ROGER LESTRANGE, WITH PICTURES BY PERCY J. BILLINGHURST AND AN INTRODUCTION BY KENNETH GRAHAME. LONDON: JOHN LANE THE BODLEY HEAD, 1903. 201p. + 2p. pub. cat.: front., 100 plates. Bound in buff cloth with coloured pictorial cover and spine.
C 888.0108 AES

11 **LA FONTAINE, JEAN DE LA.**
The Fables of JEAN DE LA FONTAINE. Translated into English Verse by EDWARD MARSH. With Twelve Reproductions from Engravings by STEPHEN GOODEN. LONDON: WILLIAM HEINEMANN LTD., 1933. LXXI, 469p.: 12 plates. Bound in brown cloth with cream paper jacket.
CBD 841.4 LAF

12 **THORNBURY, WALTER** *(Translator)*.
THE FABLES OF LA FONTAINE TRANSLATED INTO ENGLISH VERSE BY WALTER THORNBURY. WITH ILLUSTRATIONS BY GUSTAVE DORÉ. LONDON: CASSELL, PETTER AND GALPIN, 2 VOLS. (188–?) LXIV, 839p.: front., 88 plates, ill. Bound in green leather with decorative cover and spine, with gilt edges.
CBD 841.4 DOR/LAF

13 **SMYTH, A.M.**
A BOOK OF FABULOUS BEASTS. Old Stories retold by A.M. SMYTH: Illustrations by DOROTHY FITCH. OXFORD: GEOFFREY CUMBERLEDGE, OXFORD UNIVERSITY PRESS, 1939, 80p.: 4 plates, ill. Bound in decorative coloured paper with matching dust jacket. Chameleon Books.
CBD 398.469 SMY

## 2 MYTHS AND LEGENDARY HEROES

14 **BAKER, MARGARET.**
TALES OF ALL THE WORLD. LONDON: OXFORD UNIVERSITY PRESS, 1936. 255p. Bound in pink cloth, with embossed decorative cover.
YSC 398.2 BAK

15 **BULFINCH, THOMAS.**
THE AGE OF FABLE. LONDON: J.M. DENT AND SONS, LTD., 1910. X, 371p.: decorative title page. Rebound in brown quarter leather. Everyman's Library edited by Ernest Rhys. For Young People.
C 398.2 BUL

16 **Another copy.**
Bound in blue cloth.
Y 398.2 BUL

17 **CANTON, WILLIAM.**
A CHILD'S BOOK OF WARRIORS. BY WILLIAM CANTON. ILLUSTRATED BY HERBERT COLE. LONDON: J.M. DENT & SONS LTD., (1912). X, 319p.: col. front., vignette on decorative title page, 2 col. plates, 13 plates, ill. Bound in green cloth with coloured pictorial cover and spine.
C 823.8 CAN and CBD 398.22 CAN

18 **CLARK, KATE McCOSH.**
MAORI Tales & Legends. COLLECTED AND RETOLD BY KATE McCOSH CLARK. WITH ILLUSTRATIONS BY ROBERT ATKINSON. LONDON: DAVID NUTT, 1896. X, 186p.: front., 5 plates, ill. Bound in pink cloth with black decorative cover and spine.
C 398.210993 CLA

19 **CLAY, BEATRICE.**
STORIES OF KING ARTHUR AND THE ROUND TABLE. BY BEATRICE CLAY. ILLUSTRATED BY DORA CURTIS. LONDON: J.M. DENT AND SONS LTD., 1905. XXVIII, 322p. + 6p. ill. pub. cat.: col. front., vignette title page with col. decorative border, 19 plates, ill. Bound in white cloth, with coloured, pictorial cover and decorative spine.
C 823.912 CLA

20 **COLUM, PADRAIC.**
The Children of Odin. By Padraic Colum. Illustrations by Willy Pogany. LONDON: GEORGE G. HARRAP AND COMPANY LTD., 1922. VIII, 282p.: col. front., vignette on title page, 2 col. plates, 3 plates, ill., decorative endpapers. Bound in blue cloth, with pictorial cover and decorative spine.
C 291.13 COL

21 **CRESWICK, PAUL.**
ROBIN HOOD AND HIS ADVENTURES BY PAUL CRESWICK. ILLUSTRATED BY T.H. ROBINSON. LONDON: ERNEST NISTER, (192–?). 312p.: col. front., vignette on title page, 3 col. plates, 8 plates, ill., pictorial endpapers. Bound in grey cloth with coloured pictorial cover and spine.
CBD 823.912 CRE

22 **CUTLER, URIEL WALDO.**
STORIES OF KING ARTHUR AND HIS KNIGHTS. RE-TOLD FROM MALORY'S "MORTE D'ARTHUR". BY U. WALDO CUTLER. LONDON: GEORGE G. HARRAP AND CO. LTD., 1905. XIX, 236p.: front., 7 plates. Bound in grey cloth, with pictorial cover and spine.
C 823.9 CUT

23 **DARTON, FREDERICK JOSEPH HARVEY.**
A WONDER BOOK OF OLD ROMANCE. BY F.J. HARVEY DARTON. ILLUSTRATED BY A.G. WALKER, SCULPTOR. LONDON: WELLS GARDNER DARTON & CO. LTD., 1907. XXIII, 424p. + 24p. ill. pub. cat.: front., vignette on title page, 39 plates, ill. Bound in maroon cloth with gold pictorial cover and spine.
C 398.2 DAR

24 **DICKSON, MAIDIE.**
THE SAGA OF THE SEA-SWALLOW. WITH THE STORY OF GREENFEATHER THE CHANGELING. TOLD BY MAIDIE DICKSON. ILLUSTRATED BY J.D. BATTEN AND HILDA FAIRBAIRN. LONDON: A.D. INNES AND CO., 1896. 159p.: front., 3 plates, ill. Bound in green cloth, with gilt pictorial cover and gilt top.
YSC 823.8 DIC

25 **EGAN, PIERCE.**
ROBIN HOOD AND LITTLE JOHN OR THE MERRY MEN OF SHERWOOD FOREST BY PIERCE EGAN. LONDON: W.S. JOHNSON, 1850. VIII, 280p. in 2 columns.: front. (signed etching-portrait of PIERCE EGAN) pictorial title page, 3 plates, ill. Additional title page: (AUTHORS' OWN EDITION). ROBIN HOOD AND LITTLE JOHN. OR, the Merry Men of Sherwood Forest. BY PIERCE EGAN THE YOUNGER. front., vignette. In 3 books – Authors large edition. Illustrated by W.B. THWAITES. Engraved by John Wall. Bound in black cloth.
C 398.22 EGA

26 **FARJEON, ELEANOR.**
MIGHTY MEN FROM ACHILLES TO HAROLD. By Eleanor Farjeon. Pictures by Hugh Chesterman. OXFORD: BASIL BLACKWELL, (1925?). X, 223p.: col. front., 19 plates. Bound in blue cloth with orange decorative cover and spine.
C 398.22 FAR

27 **FENN, GEORGE MANVILLE.**
Young Robin Hood. By G. Manville Fenn. Illustrated by Victor Venner. LONDON: ERNEST NISTER, 1899. (Printed in Bavaria). 68p.: front., 6 plates, ill. Bound with coloured pictorial cream paper cover and blue cloth spine.
823.8 FEN

28 **GILBERT, HENRY.**
KING ARTHUR'S KNIGHTS. THE TALES RETOLD FOR BOYS AND GIRLS. By Henry Gilbert. With Twenty-one Illustrations by Walter Crane and T.H. Robinson. LONDON: THOMAS NELSON AND SONS LTD., (1911). XII, 309p. + 3p. pub. cat.: col. front., 4 col. plates, 16 plates. Bound in red cloth.
C 398.22 GIL

29 **GILBERT, HENRY.**
ROBIN HOOD AND HIS MERRY MEN. By Henry Gilbert: with 8 illustrations in colour by Walter Crane. LONDON: T.C. & E.C. JACK, LTD. (191–?). VIII, 168p.: col. front., 7 col. plates. Bound in grey cloth with coloured pictorial cover and spine. IN DAYS OF OLD SERIES.
C 823.912 GIL

30 **GILBERT, HENRY.**
ROBIN HOOD AND THE MEN OF THE GREENWOOD. By Henry Gilbert. With Twenty-four illustrations in Colour and Line by Walter Crane and H.M. Brock. LONDON: THOMAS NELSON AND SONS, LTD. (1912). 372p. + 12p. pub. cat.: col. front., 23 plates. Quarter Bound in blue cloth on spine with paper covers. THE NELSONIAN LIBRARY (NO. 6). Bound in blue cloth.
C 823.912 GIL

30A **Another copy.**
With 16 plates. LONDON: T.C. AND E.C. JACK, 1912. XI, 360p. Rebound in green cloth.
CBD 398.22 GIL

31 **GREGORY, LADY AUGUSTA.**
GODS AND FIGHTING MEN: THE STORY OF THE TUATHA DE DANAAN AND OF THE FIANNA OF IRELAND, ARRANGED AND PUT INTO ENGLISH BY LADY GREGORY. WITH A PREFACE BY W.B. YEATS. LONDON: JOHN MURRAY, 1904. XXVIII, 476p. Bound in grey cloth, with paper covers.
YSC 398.2209415 GRE

32 **HARE, CHRISTOPHER.**
BAYARD: THE GOOD KNIGHT WITHOUT FEAR AND WITHOUT REPROACH. BY CHRISTOPHER HARE (pseud. for Mrs. Marian Andrews). WITH COLOURED ILLUSTRATIONS BY HERBERT COLE. LONDON: J.M. DENT AND SONS LIMITED, (191–?). 127p.: col. front., decorative title page, 7 col. plates. Bound in blue cloth, with coloured pictorial label on cover, and embossed decorative cover and spine. TALES FOR CHILDREN FROM MANY LANDS. EDITED BY F.C. TILNEY.
C 823.912 HAR

33 **Another copy.**
Bound in green cloth, with coloured pictorial label on cover, and embossed decorative cover and spine.
C 823.912 HAR

34 **HAZLITT, WILLIAM CAREW** *(Editor).*
TALES AND LEGENDS OF NATIONAL ORIGIN OR WIDELY CURRENT IN ENGLAND FROM EARLY TIMES. WITH CRITICAL INTRODUCTIONS BY W. CAREW HAZLITT. LONDON: SWAN SONNENSCHEIN AND CO., 1892. XV, 486p. + 4p. pub. cat.: vignette on title page. Bound in maroon cloth with gilt edges.
C 298.20942 TAL

35 **HERBERTSON, AGNES GROZIER.**
HEROIC LEGENDS, THE STORIES OF ST. GEORGE AND THE DRAGON, ROBIN HOOD, RICHARD AND BLONDEL, AND OTHER LEGENDS. RETOLD BY AGNES GROZIER HERBERTSON. Illustrated with Sixteen Coloured Plates by HELEN STRATTON. LONDON: BLACKIE AND SON LIMITED, 1908. 253p.: col. front., 15 col. plates. Bound in red cloth with decorative cover and gilt edges.
C 398.22 HER

36 **HUTCHINSON, WINIFRED MARGARET LAMBART.**
THE SUNSET OF THE HEROES, LAST ADVENTURES OF THE TAKERS OF TROY. BY W.M.L. HUTCHINSON. Illustrated by Herbert Cole. LONDON: J.M. DENT AND SONS LTD., 1911. 281p.: col. front., vignette on decorative title page, 7 col. plates, ill. Bound in green cloth, with decorative/pictorial cover and spine.
C 398.22 0938 HUT

37 **KEARY, ANNIE.**
The Heroes of Asgard. TALES FROM SCANDINAVIAN MYTHOLOGY. BY A. AND E. KEARY. ILLUSTRATED WITH DRAWINGS BY C.E. BROCK. LONDON: MACMILLAN AND CO. LTD., 1930. VIII, 222p.: col. front., pictorial title page, 15 col. plates, ill. Bound in green cloth, with two-colour decorative cover and coloured pictorial endpaper. Originally published in 1870.
C 398.20948 KEA

38 **KINGSLEY, CHARLES.**
THE HEROES; OR, GREEK FAIRY TALES FOR MY CHILDREN. BY CHARLES KINGSLEY. ILLUSTRATED. LONDON: MACMILLAN AND CO., 1879. XXII, 255p. + 4p. pub. cat.: front., 5 plates. Bound in blue buckram. Vol. VII of the Works. Originally published 1856.
YSC 398.2 KIN

39 **Another copy.**
ILLUSTRATED WITH DRAWINGS BY H.M. BROCK. LONDON: MACMILLAN AND CO. LTD., 1928. IX, 212p.: col. front., 15 col. plates. Bound in green cloth, with two-colour decorative cover.

40 **KNOWLES, SIR JAMES** *(Editor).*
THE LEGENDS OF KING ARTHUR AND HIS KNIGHTS. COMPILED AND ARRANGED BY SIR JAMES KNOWLES KCVO. (J.T.K.) ILLUSTRATED BY LANCELOT SPEED. LONDON: FREDERICK WARNE AND CO., NINTH EDITION, 1912. XX, 308p.: col. front., 7 col. plates, 12 plates. Bound in green cloth with decorative cover and spine.
CBD 398.22 KNO

42 **LANG, ANDREW** *(Editor).*
THE BOOK OF ROMANCE. EDITED BY ANDREW LANG. WITH NUMEROUS ILLUSTRATIONS BY H.J. FORD. LONDON: LONGMANS, GREEN, & CO., 1902. IX, 384p.: col. front., vignette on title page, 7 col. plates, 35 plates, ill. Bound in blue cloth with gold pictorial cover and spine.
C 398.2 LAN

43 **LANG, ANDREW.**
CUSTOM AND MYTH. BY ANDREW LANG, M.A. NEW EDITION. LONDON: LONGMANS, GREEN, AND CO., 1893. X, 312p. + 24p. pub. cat.: ill. Bound in maroon cloth.
C 291.13 LAN

44 **LANG, JEAN.**
A BOOK OF MYTHS. BY JEAN LANG (MRS. JOHN LANG). WITH TWENTY ORIGINAL DRAWINGS IN COLOUR BY HELEN STRATTON. LONDON: T.C. & E.C. JACK LTD., 1915. XV, 340p.: col. front., vignette on title page, 15 col. plates. Bound in green cloth with black decorative cover and spine.
C 398.22 LAN

45 **LANG, JEAN.**
STORIES FROM THE ODYSSEY. TOLD TO THE CHILDREN BY JEANIE LANG. With pictures by W. Heath Robinson. LONDON: THOMAS NELSON & SONS LTD. (192–?). VII, 118p.: col. front., 7 col. plates. Bound in blue cloth. TOLD TO THE CHILDREN SERIES (ed. by LOUEY CHISHOLM).
C 883.1 ROB/HOM

46 **LANG, LEONORA BLANCHE.**
THE RED BOOK OF HEROES. BY MRS. LANG. EDITED BY ANDREW LANG. WITH 8 COLOURED PLATES AND NUMEROUS ILLUSTRATIONS BY A. WALLIS MILLS. LONDON: LONGMANS, GREEN, AND CO., 1909. XIV, 368p.: col. front., vignette title page, 7 col. plates, 17 plates, ill. Bound in red cloth, with embossed pictorial cover and spine, and gilt edges.
C 920.02 LAN

47 **LITTLEWOOD, SAMUEL ROBINSON.**
Valentine and Orson, The Twin Knights of France. Retold from the Original by S.R. Littlewood. LONDON: SIMPKIN, MARSHALL, HAMILTON, KENT AND CO. LTD., 1919. XI, 143p.: col. front., 7 col. plates by Florence Mary Anderson, pictorial endpapers. Bound in red cloth, with coloured pictorial label on cover.
C 823.91 LIT

48 **MALORY, SIR THOMAS.**
MORTE D'ARTHUR. Sir Thomas Malory's Book of King Arthur and his Noble Knights of the Round Table. The Original edition of Caxton revised for modern use, WITH AN INTRODUCTION BY SIR EDWARD STRACHEY, BART. SECOND EDITION. LONDON: MACMILLAN AND CO., 1868. XXXVII, 496 + 4p. pub. cat.: vignette on title page. Bound in green cloth.
YSC 398.2 MAL

49 **MASON, EUGENE.**
FRENCH MEDIEVAL ROMANCES. From the Lays of Marie de France. Translated by Eugene Mason. LONDON: J.M. DENT AND SONS LTD., (193–?). XIX, 216p. Bound in blue cloth. EVERYMAN'S LIBRARY.
YSC 398.2 MAS

50 **MERSON, A.J.**
A BOOK OF CLASSICAL STORIES. LONDON: GEORGE G. HARRAP AND CO. LTD., 1930. 220p. Bound in orange cloth.
YSC 870 MER

51 **MORRIS, WILLIAM.**
STORIES FROM THE EARTHLY PARADISE. RETOLD FROM WILLIAM MORRIS BY MAGDALEN EDGAR, M.A. LONDON: GEORGE G. HARRAP AND CO., 1906. 239p.: front. by Chas. P. Samton, 15 plates by Gertrude Demain, Evelyn Paul and Sir E.J. Poynter. Half-bound in orange leather, with green cloth decorative cover.
YSC 398.2 EDG

52 **NEWBOLT, HENRY.**
THE BOOK OF THE HAPPY WARRIOR. BY HENRY NEWBOLT. WITH 8 COLOURED PLATES, AND 25 OTHER ILLUSTRATIONS BY HENRY J. FORD. LONDON: LONGMANS, GREEN AND CO., 1917. XIV, 284p.: front., 8 col. plates, ill. Bound in blue cloth.
C 398.22 NEW

53 **OUTRAM, MARY FRANCES.**
IN THE VAN OF THE VIKINGS; OR, How Olaf Tryggvason Lost and Won. BY M.F. OUTRAM. With Illustrations by J.A. Symington. LONDON: THE RELIGIOUS TRACT SOCIETY, (191–?). 316p. + 18p. pub. cat.: col. front., 3 plates. Bound in grey cloth, with coloured pictorial cover and spine.
C 823.912 OUT

54 **PYLE, HOWARD.**
The Story of Sir LAUNCELOT and his Companions. By HOWARD PYLE. LONDON: CHAPMAN AND HALL LTD., 1907. XVIII, 340p.: front., pictorial title page, 29 plates, ill. Bound in grey cloth with decorative cover.
CBD 398.22 PYL

55 **PYLE, HOWARD.**
The Story of the Grail and the Passing of Arthur. By HOWARD PYLE, LONDON: BICKERS AND SON LIMITED, 1910. XVIII, 258p.: front., pictorial title page, 22 plates, ill. Bound in red calf with gilt edges.
CBD 398.22 PYL

56 **ROYDE-SMITH, NAOMI GWLADYS.**
UNA AND THE RED CROSS KNIGHT AND OTHER TALES FROM SPENSER'S FAERY QUEENE. BY N.G. ROYDE-SMITH. ILLUSTRATED BY T.H. ROBINSON. LONDON: J.M. DENT AND SONS LTD., 1905. XX, 264p.: col. front., col. vignettes on title page, 22 plates, ill., pictorial endpapers. Bound in cream cloth, with coloured pictorial cover and spine.
C 823.912 ROY

57 **TILNEY, FREDERICK COLIN.**
ROBIN HOOD AND HIS MERRY OUTLAWS. RETOLD BY F.C. TILNEY. WITH COLOURED ILLUSTRATIONS BY IONE RAILTON. LONDON: J.M. DENT AND SONS LIMITED, (191–?). 128p.: col. front., decorative title page, 7 col. plates. Bound in maroon cloth with coloured pictorial label on cover and embossed decorative cover and spine.
C 823.912 TIL

57A **Another copy.**
Bound in green cloth with coloured pictorial label on cover and embossed decorative cover and spine.

## 3 NURSERY STORIES AND FAIRY TALES

58 **ANDERSEN, HANS CHRISTIAN.**
ANDERSEN'S FAIRY STORIES. Illustrated by Anne Anderson. LONDON: CHILDREN'S PRESS, (1924?). 128p.: col. front.: vignette on title page, 7 col. plates, ill. Bound in blue cloth with coloured pictorial paper cover.
C 839.8316 AND

59 **ANDERSEN, HANS CHRISTIAN.**
DANISH FAIRY TALES AND LEGENDS. BY HANS CHRISTIAN ANDERSEN. With a Memoir of the Author AND With Sixteen Illustrations by W.H. Robinson. LONDON: BLISS, SANDS AND CO., 1907. 332p. + 20p. pub. cat.: front., 15 plates. Bound in red cloth with pictorial cover and spine.
CBD 839.8136 AND and C839.8136 AND

59A **ANDERSEN, HANS CHRISTIAN.**
FAIRY TALES BY HANS CHRISTIAN ANDERSEN. ILLUSTRATED BY MONRO S. ORR. LONDON: GEORGE G. HARRAP AND CO. LTD., 1925. 309p.: col. front., vignette on title page, 7 col. plates. Bound in buff cloth with coloured pictorial cover and spine.
C 839.8136 AND

59B **ANDERSEN, HANS CHRISTIAN.**
Fairy Tales and Legends by HANS ANDERSEN. Illustrated by Rex Whistler. LONDON: THE BODLEY HEAD, 1935. 470p.: vignette on decorative title page, 10 plates, headpieces, tailpieces, ill. Bound in cream cloth with decorative covers and spine, with matching paper jacket.
CBD 839.8136 AND

60 **ANDERSEN, HANS CHRISTIAN.**
FAIRY TALES. A NEW TRANSLATION. BY MRS. H.B. PAULL. WITH A SPECIAL ADAPTATION AND ARRANGEMENT FOR YOUNG PEOPLE. With Original Illustrations. A NEW EDITION. LONDON: FREDERICK WARNE AND CO. (187–?). VIII, 671p.: front., 8 plates. Bound in brown cloth with embossed decorative cover and spine.
C 839.8136 AND

61 **Another copy.**
WITH ORIGINAL ILLUSTRATIONS. LONDON: FREDERICK WARNE AND CO., (188–?). 383p.: col. front., 2 col. plates, 6 plates, ill. Bound in blue cloth with embossed pictorial cover and spine.

62 **ANDERSEN, HANS CHRISTIAN.**
FAIRY TALES FROM HANS ANDERSEN. With introduction by Edward Clodd. Illustrations by Gordon Browne. LONDON: WELLS GARDNER, DARTON AND CO., 1901. XX, 420p. + 7p. pub. cat.: front., decorative title page with vignette in black and red, 14 plates, ill. Bound in yellow cloth with coloured pictorial covers and spine.
C 839.8136 AND and CBD 839.8136 AND

63 **ANDERSEN, HANS CHRISTIAN.**
FAIRY TALES from HANS CHRISTIAN ANDERSEN TRANSLATED BY E. LUCAS WITH TWELVE ILLUSTRATIONS BY T.H., C. AND W.H. ROBINSON. LONDON: J.M. DENT AND COMPANY, 1901. VIII, 312p.: col. front., col. decorative title page, 11 plates. THE TEMPLE CLASSICS FOR YOUNG PEOPLE.
C 839.8136 AND

63A **ANDERSEN, HANS CHRISTIAN.**
FAIRY TALES from Hans Christian Andersen. Translated by Mrs E. Lucas and illustrated by Thomas, Charles and William Robinson. LONDON: J.M. DENT AND CO., 5th edition, 1901. XIV, 539p.: col. front., col. decorative title page, 30 plates, ill. Bound in green cloth with coloured pictorial cover and spine.
C 839.8136 AND

64 **ANDERSEN, HANS CHRISTIAN.**
HANS ANDERSEN. FORTY STORIES. NEWLY TRANSLATED FROM THE DANISH BY M.R. JAMES, O.M. PROVOST OF ETON. LONDON: FABER AND FABER LIMITED, 1930. 466p.: vignette on title page, 24 col. plates by Christine Jackson. Bound in red cloth with small picture embossed on cover.
C 839.8136 and YSC 398.4 AND

65 **ANDERSEN, HANS CHRISTIAN.**
Hans Andersen's Fairy Tales. Illustrated by A. Duncan Carse. LONDON: ADAM AND CHARLES BLACK, 1912. XV, 373p. + 12p. pub. cat.: col. front., 11 col. plates, ill. Bound in blue cloth with coloured pictorial covers and spine. With an introduction by Gordon Home.
C 839.8136 AND

65A **Another copy.**
1912. VIII, 248p.: col. front., 7 col. plates. Bound in blue cloth with coloured pictorial cover and spine.

66 **ANDERSEN, HANS CHRISTIAN.**
HANS ANDERSEN'S FAIRY TALES WITH ILLUSTRATIONS BY W. HEATH ROBINSON. NOTTINGHAM:

BOOTS THE CHEMISTS, (192–?). 320p.: col. front., decorative title page, 15 col. plates, 34 plates, ill. Bound in red cloth with pictorial/decorative cover.
CBD 839.8136 AND

66A **ANDERSEN, HANS CHRISTIAN.**
Hans Andersen's Fairy Tales. WITH MANY ILLUSTRATIONS IN COLOUR AND IN BLACK-AND-WHITE BY HELEN STRATTON. LONDON: BLACKIE AND SON LIMITED. 1925. VII, 380p.: col. front.: vignette on title page, 15 col. plates, 17 plates, ill. Bound in blue cloth with pictorial paper cover and coloured pictorial spine.
C 839.8136 AND

66B **ANDERSEN, HANS CHRISTIAN.**
HANS CHRISTIAN ANDERSEN'S FAIRY TALES. Illustrated by MABEL LUCIE ATTWELL. LONDON: RAPHAEL TUCK AND SONS LTD, (192?). 288p. + 8p. pub. cat.: 5 col. plates, ill. (crayoned by owner). Bound in green cloth with coloured pictorial paper cover.
C 839.8136 AND

67 **ANDERSEN, HANS CHRISTIAN.**
STORIES AND FAIRY TALES BY HANS CHRISTIAN ANDERSEN. TRANSLATED BY H. OSKAR SOMMER, Ph.D. WITH 100 PICTURES BY ARTHUR J. GASKIN. VOLUMES 1 and 2. LONDON: GEORGE ALLEN, 1893. XI, 398p. XII, 426p.: fronts, 3 plates, 3 plates, ill., decorative initials. Bound in green cloth with pictorial/decorative cover.
C 839.8316 AND and CBD 839.8316 AND

68 **ANDERSEN, HANS CHRISTIAN.**
STORIES FROM HANS ANDERSEN. WITH ILLUSTRATIONS BY EDMUND DULAC. LIVERPOOL: LEWIS'S LTD. (192–?) 159p.: col. front., 6 col. plates. Bound in red cloth with decorative cover, with blue paper jacket and coloured pictorial cover.
CBD 839.8136 AND

69 **ANDERSEN, HANS CHRISTIAN.**
TALES AND FAIRY STORIES BY HANS CHRISTIAN ANDERSEN. TRANSLATED BY MADAM DE CHATELAIN. LONDON: GEORGE ROUTLEDGE AND SONS, (187–?). VI, 401p. + 10p. pub. cat.: front. Bound in brown cloth, with pictorial/decorative cover and spine. Happy Home Series.
YSC 398.4 AND

70 **THE ARABIAN NIGHTS.**
Illustrated by Charles Folkard. LONDON: ADAM AND CHARLES BLACK, 1913. XII, 411p. + 8p. pub. cat.: col. front., 11 col. plates. Bound in brown cloth with coloured pictorial cover and spine.
C BD 398.210953 ARA

71 **THE ARABIAN NIGHTS.**
With about One hundred and thirty Illustrations by W. Heath Robinson, Helen Stratton and others. LONDON: SELFRIDGE AND CO. LTD., 1911. XV, 435p.: col. front., col. pictorial title page, ill. Bound in brown cloth with pictorial cover and spine.
C 398.210953 ARA

72 **THE ARABIAN NIGHTS.**
With illustrations by Rene Bull. LONDON: CONSTABLE AND CO., LTD, (193–?). VIII, 299p.: col. front., 9 col. plates, ill. Bound in green cloth with decorative cover including inserted coloured pictorial label.
CBD 398.210953 ARA

73 **(ARABIAN NIGHTS).**
ALADDIN; OR, THE WONDERFUL LAMP. SINBAD, THE SAILOR; OR, THE OLD MAN OF THE SEA. ALI BABA; OR, THE FORTY THIEVES. Revised by M.E. BRADDON. ILLUSTRATED BY GUSTAVE DORÉ AND OTHER ARTISTS. LONDON: JOHN AND ROBERT MAXWELL, (1880). 96p. 1 double plate, 4 plates, ill. Bound in purple paper, with decorative covers.
YSC 398.4 BRA

74 **ARABIAN NIGHTS.**
DALZIELS' ILLUSTRATED ARABIAN NIGHTS ENTERTAINMENTS. The Text Revised and Emendated throughout by H.W. Dulcken, Ph.D. WITH UPWARDS OF TWO HUNDRED ILLUSTRATIONS BY EMINENT ARTISTS. ENGRAVED BY THE BROTHERS DALZIEL. LONDON: WARD LOCK AND TYLER, (187–?). XVI, 822p.: front., vignette on title page, ill. Bound in red cloth with embossed decorative cover.
CBD 398.210953 DAL

76 **ARABIAN NIGHTS.**
FAIRY TALES FROM THE ARABIAN NIGHTS, EDITED AND ARRANGED BY E. DIXON. ILLUSTRATED BY J.D. BATTEN. LONDON: J.M. DENT, 1893. 267p.: front., 4 plates, ill., decorative endpapers. Bound in green cloth with decorative covers and spine.
C 398.210953 FAI

77 **ARABIAN NIGHTS.**
THE MAGIC HORSE FROM THE ARABIAN NIGHTS. ILLUSTRATED WITH DESIGNS BY CERI RICHARD. LONDON: VICTOR GOLLANCZ LTD., edition limited to 495 copies, 1930. 27p.: vignette on title page, 5 col. plates, col. ill. Bound in black calf.
CBD 398.210953 ARA

78 **ARABIAN NIGHTS.**
STORIES FROM THE ARABIAN NIGHTS. Edited for Young People by FRANCES J. OLCOTT. Illustrated by MONRO S. ORR. LONDON: GEORGE G. HARRAP AND COMPANY LTD., 1933. 125p.: col. front., 2 col. plates. Bound in brown cloth with col. paper cover.
C 398.210953 STO

79 **ARABIAN NIGHTS.**
Stories from The Arabian Nights. Retold by Laurence Housman. With Drawings by Edmund Dulac. LONDON: HODDER AND STOUGHTON, 1907. No. 26 of a limited edition of 350 copies. XVI, 133p.: col. front., 49 col. plates. Bound in white vellum with decorative cover and spine.
CBD 398.210953 ARA

80 **ARABIAN NIGHTS.**
TALES FROM THE ARABIAN NIGHTS, ADAPTED BY F.C. TILNEY WITH COLOURED ILLUSTRATIONS BY T.H. ROBINSON AND DORA CURTIS. LONDON: J.M. DENT AND SONS LIMITED, 1914. 128p.: col. front., 7 col. plates, ill. Bound in green cloth with embossed decorative cover, with coloured pictorial label, and spine.
C 398.210953 ARA

81 **ARABIAN NIGHTS.**
(TALES FROM THE ARABIAN NIGHTS) (Edited by STEPHEN SOUTHWOLD). (LONDON: COLLINS, (193–?)) Title page missing. 255p.: 20 plates, ill. Bound in blue cloth.
YSC 398.4 SOU

82 **ARABIAN NIGHTS.**
The Thousand and One Nights COMMONLY CALLED IN ENGLAND THE ARABIAN NIGHTS' ENTERTAINMENTS. TRANSLATED FROM THE ARABIC BY EDWARD WILLIAM LANE. LONDON: SANDS AND CO., 1901. 508p. + 4p. pub. cat. Bound in red cloth.
YSC 398.4 LAN

82A **THE ARABIAN NIGHTS' ENTERTAINMENTS.**
ARRANGED FOR THE PERUSAL OF YOUTHFUL READERS BY THE HON. MRS. SUGDEN. LONDON: GEORGE ROUTLEDGE AND SONS, LTD, (189–?). VII, 501p.: col. front., 4 col. plates. Bound in blue cloth with decorative cover and spine.
CBD 398.210953 ARA

83 **THE ARABIAN NIGHTS ENTERTAINMENTS.**
Four Coloured Engravings on Steel. LONDON: GALL AND INGLIS, (187–?). 704p.: col. front.: 3 col. plates. Bound in green cloth, with decorative cover and spine, and gilt edges.
YSC 398.4 ARA

84 **Another copy.**
With Six Coloured Engravings on Steel. EDINBURGH: GALL AND INGLIS, (187–?). Bound in purple cloth, with decorative cover and spine, and gilt edges.
YSC 398.4 ARA

85 **THE ARABIAN NIGHTS ENTERTAINMENTS.**
CONSISTING OF One Thousand and One Stories. HALIFAX: MILNER AND SOWERBY, 1863. 416p.: front., additional vignette title page, 5 plates. Bound in brown cloth with embossed decorative cover and spine, with gilt edges.
CBD 398.210953 ARA

86 **ARABIAN NIGHTS ENTERTAINMENTS.**
RETOLD FOR YOUNG FOLKS. LONDON: COLLINS CLEAR TYPE PRESS, (191–?). 136p., col. front., col. title page with vignette, 7 col. plates, 12 plates. Bound in red cloth, with coloured paper label on cover and coloured pictorial endpapers with gilt edges.
C 398.210953 ARA

87 **THE ARABIAN NIGHTS ENTERTAINMENTS.**
SELECTED AND EDITED BY ANDREW LANG. LONDON: LONGMANS, GREEN, AND CO., 1898. XVI, 424p.: front., 32 plates, ill., by H.J. Ford. Bound in blue cloth, with pictorial cover and spine, and gilt edges.
C 398.210953 ARA

88 **THE ARABIAN NIGHTS' ENTERTAINMENTS.**
WITH ONE HUNDRED AND FIFTY ORIGINAL ILLUSTRATIONS DRAWN BY THOMAS B. DALZIEL. LONDON: GEORGE ROUTLEDGE AND SONS, 1889. 796p. + 8p. pub. cat.: col. front., vignette on title page, 3 col. plates, 2 plates, ill. Bound in blue cloth with coloured decorative cover and spine, with gilt edges.
C 398.210953 ARA

89 **THE ARABIAN NIGHTS ENTERTAINMENTS.**
WITH SEVERAL HUNDRED ILLUSTRATIONS BY W.H. ROBINSON, HELEN STRATTON, A.D. McCORMICK, A.L. DAVIS AND A.E. NORBURY. (LONDON): GEORGE NEWNES LTD., 1899. VIII, 472p. Bound in green cloth with coloured pictorial cover.
C 398.210953 ARA

90 **ASBJØRNSEN, PETER CHRISTEN.**
EAST OF THE SUN AND WEST OF THE MOON. OLD TALES FROM THE NORTH. ILLUSTRATED BY KAY NIELSON. LONDON: HODDER AND STOUGHTON, (1914). 206p.: col. front., 24 col. plates, ill., decorative endpapers. Bound in blue cloth with decorative cover and spine.
CBD 398.2109481 EAS

91 **ASBJØRNSEN, PETER CHRISTEN.**
NORWEGIAN FAIRY TALES TRANSLATED BY ABEL HEYWOOD FROM THE COLLECTION OF P. CHR. ASBJØRNSEN AND JORGEN MOE. ILLUSTRATED BY BESSIE DU VAL. LONDON: GEORGE ROUTLEDGE AND SONS LIMITED, 1895. IX, 295p.: front., 20 plates, ill. Bound in red cloth with coloured pictorial cover and spine, with gilt edges.
C 398.210948 ASB

91A **ASBJØRNSEN, PETER CHRISTEN.**
TALES from the FJELD, a series of Popular Tales from the Norse of P.Ch. Asbjørnsen. By Sir GEORGE DASENT, D.C.L. A New Edition with more than a HUNDRED ILLUSTRATIONS BY MOYR SMITH. LONDON: GIBBINGS AND COMPANY LIMITED, 1890. XX, 403p. + 16p. ill. Bound in green cloth with coloured pictorial cover.
M 398.2 DAS CHILDREN'S COLLECTION

91B **ATKINSON, (J.C.).**
SCENES IN FAIRYLAND OR MISS MARY'S VISITS TO THE COURT OF FAIRY REALM. BY CANON ATKINSON, ILLUSTRATED BY C.E. BROCK. LONDON: MACMILLAN AND CO., 1892. X, 246p. + 44p. pub. cat.: front., pictorial title page, 3 plates, ill. Bound in green cloth with pictorial cover.
C 823.8 ATK

92 **AULNOY, MARIE CATHERINE, COUNTESS D'.**
FAIRY TALES. BY THE COUNTESS D'AULNOY. TRANSLATED BY J.R. PLANCHÉ. WITH SIXTY ILLUSTRATIONS BY GORDON BROWNE. LONDON: GEORGE ROUTLEDGE AND SONS, 1888. XII, 468p.: front., vignette title page, 9 plates, ill. Bound in green cloth, with coloured pictorial cover and spine.
YSC 398.4 DAU

93 **Another copy.**
1894. XII, 468p.: col. front., 11 col. plates, 4 plates, ill. Bound in blue cloth with coloured decorative cover and spine and gilt edges.
CBD 398.210944 LAM

93A **AULNOY, MARIE CATHERINE, COUNTESSD'.**
THE FAIRY TALES OF MADAME D'AULNOY, NEWLY DONE INTO ENGLISH. WITH AN INTRODUCTION BY ANNE THACKERAY RITCHIE, ILLUSTRATED BY CLINTON PETERS. LONDON: LAWRENCE AND BULLEN, NEW EDITION, WITH ADDITIONAL ILLUSTRATIONS, 1895. XXI, 535p.: 15 plates. ill. Bound in green cloth with decorative cover and spine.
C 398.210944 AUL

94 **BAIN, R. NISBET** *(Editor).*
COSSACK FAIRY TALES AND FOLK-TALES. SELECTED, EDITED AND TRANSLATED BY R. NISBET BAIN. ILLUSTRATED BY E.W. MITCHELL. LONDON: LAWRENCE AND BULLEN, 1894. XII, 290p.: front., vignette on title page, 7 plates, ill., decorative initials to chapters. Rebound in green cloth with green decorative cover.
C 398.2039171 BAI

95 **BAIN, R. NISBET.**
RUSSIAN FAIRY TALES FROM THE SKAZKI OF POLEVOI BY R. NISBET BAIN. ILLUSTRATED BY C.M. GERE. THIRD EDITION. LONDON: A.H. BULLEN, 1901. VIII, 274p.: front., 5 plates. Bound in green cloth.
C 398.20947 GER/BAI

96 **BARING GOULD, SABINE.**
A BOOK OF FAIRY TALES RETOLD BY S. BARING GOULD WITH PICTURES BY A.J. GASKING. LONDON: METHUEN AND COMPANY, Second Edition, 1895. IX, 244p. + 40p. pub. cat.: pictorial title page, 3 plates, ill. Bound in blue cloth with pictorial cover and decorative spine.
C 398.21 BAR

97 **BARKER, MRS. SALE.**
LITTLE WIDE-AWAKE. A Story Book for Little Children. BY MRS. SALE BARKER. WITH FOUR HUNDRED ILLUSTRATIONS. LONDON: GEORGE ROUTLEDGE AND SONS, 1877. 379p.: col. front., 20 plates, ill. Bound in brown cloth with embossed decorative cover and spine and inserted coloured label.
C 823.8 BAR

97A **BIG BOOK OF FAIRY TALES.**
EDITED BY WALTER JERROLD AND ILLUSTRATED BY CHARLES ROBINSON. LONDON: BLACKIE AND SON LIMITED. 1911. XVIII, 344p.: col. front., 34 plates, some col., ill. Bound in red cloth with pictorial cover and coloured pictorial endpapers.
C 398.21 BIG

97B **BROCK, HENRY MATTHEW** *(Illustrator).*
THE BOOK OF FAIRY TALES. Comprising PUSS IN BOOTS, JACK and the BEANSTALK, HOP O' MY THUMB, BEAUTY and the BEAST. Pictured by H.M. BROCK. LONDON: FREDERICK WARNE AND CO. LTD. 1914. Unpaginated: vignette on title page, 24 col. plates, ill. Bound in buff cloth with coloured decorative cover.
M 398.2 BRO CHILDREN'S COLLECTION

97C **BROCK, HENRY MATTHEW** *(Illustrator).*
THE OLD FAIRY TALES. Comprising HOP O' MY

THUMB and BEAUTY and the BEAST. Pictured by H.M. BROCK. LONDON: FREDERICK WARNE AND CO. LTD. (1913). Unpaginated: col. front., vignette on title page, 11 col. plates, ill. Bound in brown cloth with coloured pictorial paper cover.
M 398.2 BRO CHILDREN'S COLLECTION

98 **BROWNE, FRANCES.**
GRANNY'S WONDERFUL CHAIR, AND ITS TALES OF FAIRY TIMES. BY FRANCES BROWNE. WITH ILLUSTRATIONS BY KENNY MEADOWS. LONDON: GRIFFITH AND FARRAN, 1857. VI, 169p. + 16p. ill. pub. cat.: col. front, 3 col. plates, ill. Bound in red cloth with gold embossed pictorial cover and spine and gilt edges.
YSC 823.8 BRO

99 **Another copy.**
WITH SIX ILLUSTRATIONS. LONDON: S.W. PARTRIDGE AND CO. LTD., (191–?) 202p. + 32p. pub. cat.: front., 5 plates by K.M. Roberts. Bound in blue cloth, with coloured decorative cover and spine.
C 823.8 BRO

100 **CALLOW, EDWARD.**
THE PHYNODDERREE AND OTHER LEGENDS OF THE ISLE OF MAN. BY EDWARD CALLOW. WITH SIXTY ILLUSTRATIONS, Drawn expressly for this work, and engraved on wood, by W.J. WATSON. LONDON: J. DEAN AND SON, (188–?). XV, 115p. + 12p. ill. pub. cat.: front., coat of arms on title page, 9 plates, ill. Bound in green cloth with embossed pictorial cover and spine.
C 398.204289 CAL

101 **CANTON, WILLIAM** *(Editor).*
The True Annals of Fairy-Land. Edited by William Canton. Illustrated by Charles Robinson. The Reign of King Herla. LONDON: J.M. DENT AND CO., (1900). XIX, 367p.: col. front., 18 plates, ill. Bound in blue cloth with decorative cover and spine, with decorative endpapers, with gilt edges.
C 398.21 TUR

102 **CHAPIN, ANNA ALICE.**
THE EVERYDAY AND NOW-A-DAY FAIRY BOOK By ANNA ALICE CHAPIN. With 8 Illustrations in colour by JESSIE WILLCOX SMITH. LONDON: J. COKER AND CO. LTD., (1922). Unpaginated: col. front., 7 col. plates. Bound in orange cloth with col. pictorial paper cover.
C 813.52 CHA

103 **THE CHILD'S OWN STORY BOOK.**
WITH COLOURED ILLUSTRATIONS BY T. PYM (pseud. Clara Creed). THIRD EDITION. LONDON: WELLS, GARDNER, DARTON & CO. (188–?). 135p. + 8p. pub. cat.: col. front., 3 col. plates. Bound in lilac cloth with coloured pictorial cover and spine.
C 823.8 PYM

104 **CHRISTMAS TALES OF FLANDERS.**
ILLUSTRATED BY JEAN DE BOSSCHÈRE. LONDON: WILLIAM HEINEMANN, 1917. XII, 145p.: col. front., col. pictorial title page, 11 col. plates, 12 plates in 2 colours, 15 plates, ill., col. pictorial endpapers. Bound in yellow cloth with decorative cover and spine.
C 398.209493 CHR

105 **CLARK, ELIZABETH.**
MORE STORIES TO TELL AND HOW TO TELL THEM. BY ELIZABETH CLARK. ILLUSTRATED BY NINA K. BRISLEY. LONDON: UNIVERSITY OF LONDON PRESS, LTD., 1928. 168p.: ill. Bound in blue linson, with coloured pictorial paper dust jacket.
YSC 823.912 CLA

106 **CLARK, ELIZABETH.**
TALES FOR JACK AND JANE. BY ELIZABETH CLARK. Illustrated by NINA K. BRISLEY. LONDON: UNIVERSITY OF LONDON PRESS LTD., 1936. 190p.: ill. Bound in green linson, with coloured pictorial paper dust jacket.
YSC 823.912 CLA

107 **(CRAIK, DINAH MARIA).**
THE FAIRY BOOK. The Best Popular Fairy Stories SELECTED AND RENDERED ANEW BY THE AUTHOR OF "JOHN HALIFAX, GENTLEMAN". WITH SIX ILLUSTRATIONS BY AGNES STRINGER. LONDON: S.W. PARTRIDGE AND CO., LTD., (189–?). 319p. + 32p. pub. cat.: front 5 plates. Bound in brown cloth with coloured decorative cover and spine. Originally published in 1863.
C 398.21 CRA

108 **Another copy.**
With 32 illustrations in colour by Warwick Goble. LONDON: MACMILLAN AND CO., 1913. 378p.: Bound in blue cloth with decorative cover and spine.
CBD 398.21 CRA

109 **Another copy.**
WITH 16 ILLUSTRATIONS IN COLOUR BY WARWICK GOBLE. MACMILLAN AND CO., LIMITED, 1926. VI, 232p.: 15 col. plates. Bound in red cloth with decorative cover.

110 **CROKER T. CROFTON.**
Fairy Legends AND TRADITIONS OF THE SOUTH of Ireland. BY T. CROFTON CROKER. A NEW AND COMPLETE EDITION EDITED BY THOMAS WRIGHT ESQ. M.A., F.S.A., ETC. . . . LONDON: WILLIAM TEGG, (1862). XXX, 366p.: some pictorial chapter headings. Bound in green cloth with decorative cover and spine. Originally published in 1834.
C 398.2109417 CRO

111 **Another copy.**
With illustrations BY MACLISE AND GREEN. LONDON: W. SWAN SONNENSCHEIN AND CO., (189–?). 352p.: decorative title page, decorative initial letters to chapters, ill. Bound in blue cloth with embossed decorative cover and spine, with gilt edges.
C 398.2109415 CRO

112 **THE CRUIKSHANK FAIRY-BOOK.**
FOUR FAMOUS STORIES: I. PUSS IN BOOTS, II. JACK AND THE BEANSTALK, III. HOP-O-MY-THUMB, IV. CINDERELLA. WITH FORTY ILLUSTRATIONS BY GEORGE CRUIKSHANK. LONDON: G.P. PUTNAM'S SONS, THE KNICKERBOCKER PRESS, 1897. VIII, 216p. + 2p. pub. cat.: front., vignette title page, 24 plates. Bound in maroon cloth, with embossed pictorial/decorative covers and spine, and gilt edges. Originally published in 1865.
YSC 398.4 CRU

112A **CRUIKSHANK, GEORGE.**
GEORGE CRUIKSHANK'S FAIRY LIBRARY. HOP-O'-MY-THUMB. JACK AND THE BEANSTALK. CINDERELLA. PUSS IN BOOTS. LONDON: BELL AND DALDY, (1870). 30, 32, 31, 40p.: front., decorative title page, 24 plates by G. Cruikshank. Bound in red cloth with embossed decorative covers and spine.
C398.21 GEO

113 **DARTON, FREDERICK JOSEPH HARVEY** *(Editor).*
A WONDER BOOK OF BEASTS. EDITED BY F.J. HARVEY DARTON. WITH ILLUSTRATIONS BY MARGARET CLAYTON. LONDON: WELLS, GARDNER, DARTON AND CO. LTD., (1909). XVIII, 402p. + 24p. ill. pub. cat.: col. front., col. pictorial title page, 22 plates, ill. Bound in green cloth, with embossed pictorial/decorative cover and spine, and gilt top.
YSC 398.4 DAR

114 **DAWSON, V.M.**
The Old Sundial. LONDON: DEAN AND SON LTD., (190–?). p. 31–58: col. front., 1 col. plate, ill. Bound in paper, with coloured pictorial cover. Twilight Series, 1d.
YSC 823.912 DAW

gets the Golden Hen, away from the Giant,


112

115 **DOUGLAS, SIR GEORGE** *(Editor)*.
SCOTTISH FAIRY AND FOLK TALES. SELECTED AND EDITED WITH AN INTRODUCTION BY SIR GEORGE DOUGLAS, BART. TWELVE ILLUSTRATIONS BY JAMES TORRANCE. LONDON: E.P. PUBLISHING LIMITED, 1977. (FACSIMILE OF 1896 EDITION PUBLISHED BY WALTER SCOTT, LTD.) XXXI, 301p.: 12 plates. Bound in blue cloth with blue pictorial paper dust cover.
C 398.209411 SCO

116 **DULAC, EDMUND**
EDMUND DULAC'S FAIRY-BOOK. FAIRY TALES OF THE ALLIED NATIONS. LONDON: HODDER AND STOUGHTON, (1916). 169p.: col. front., decorative title page, 14 col. plates, decorative endpapers. Bound in buff cloth with coloured decorative cover and spine.
C BD 398.21 DUL

117 **EDWARDSON, E.**
THE COURTEOUS KNIGHT AND OTHER TALES. BORROWED FROM SPENSER AND MALORY BY E. EDWARDSON. ILLUSTRATED BY ROBERT HOPE. LONDON: T. NELSON AND SONS, 1899. 172p.: front., vignette title page, 8 plates, ill. Bound in brown cloth with pictorial/decorative cover and spine.
C 823.8 EDW

118 **ELLIS, F.S.**
THE HISTORY OF REYNARD THE FOX WITH SOME ACCOUNT OF HIS FRIENDS AND ENEMIES TURNED INTO ENGLISH VERSE BY F.S. ELLIS. WITH ILLUSTRATIVE DEVICES BY WALTER CRANE. LONDON: DAVID NUTT, 1897. 289p.: front., additional decorative title page, headpieces. Bound in cream buckram.
CBD 398.2452974442 ELL

119 **EWING, JULIANA HORATIA.**
OLD-FASHIONED FAIRY TALES. BY JULIANA HORATIA EWING. LONDON: SOCIETY FOR PROMOTING CHRISTIAN KNOWLEDGE, (189–?). 169p. Quarter bound in brown cloth with decorative paper covers. Originally published in 1883.
C 398.21 EWI

120 **THE FAIR ONE WITH THE GOLDEN LOCKS.**
LONDON: GEORGE ROUTLEDGE AND SONS, (187–?). 6p.: 1 double col. plate, 4 col. plates. Mounted on linen and bound in yellow card with coloured pictorial cover.
CBD 823.8 FAI

121 **FORTUNE'S FAVOURITE, AND OTHER FAMOUS FAIRY TALES.**
With Illustrations by Richard Doyle. LONDON: DEAN AND SON, (186–?). 112p.: col. front. 1 plate. Bound in red cloth, with coloured pictorial label on cover, embossed decorative covers and spine, and gilt edges.
YSC 398.4 FOR

122 **FRANCE, ANATOLE.**
BEE, THE PRINCESS OF THE DWARFS. RETOLD IN ENGLISH BY PETER WRIGHT. (LONDON): WILLIAM GLAISHER LTD., (192–?). VIII, 128p.: decorative title page, coloured pictorial labels inserted above some chapter headings, ill. Bound in green cloth, with decorative cover and spine.
YSC 843.8 FRA

123 **FRYER, ALFRED C.**
BOOK OF English Fairy Tales FROM THE NORTH-COUNTRY BY ALFRED C. FRYER, PH.D., M.A. LONDON: W. SWAN SONNENSCHEIN AND CO., 1884. 143p.: front., vignette title page, 7 plates. Bound in green cloth, with coloured pictorial cover and spine, and gilt edges.
YSC 398.4 FRY

124 **GARSLIN, NORMAN.**
The Suitors of Aprille. By Norman Garslin. Illustrated by Charles Robinson. LONDON: JOHN LANE THE BODLEY HEAD, 1900. 212p.: front., decorative title page, 14 plates, ill. Bound in grey cloth with coloured decorative covers and spine.
CBD 823.8 GAR

125 **GASK, LILIAN.**
FOLK TALES from MANY LANDS. RETOLD BY LILIAN GASK. ILLUSTRATIONS BY WILLY POGANY. LONDON: GEORGE G. HARRAP AND COMPANY LIMITED, 1910. 255p. decorative title page, (front. missing), 3 col. plates, 19 plates, ill. Bound in brown cloth, with coloured pictorial cover and spine.
YSC 398.4 GAS

126 **GIBBON, JOHN MURRAY** *(Editor)*.
THE TRUE ANNALS OF FAIRY LAND. OLD KING COLE. ILLUSTRATED BY CHAS. ROBINSON. EDITED BY J.M. GIBBON. LONDON: J.M. DENT AND SONS LTD, 1911. XVII, 338p.: col. front., col. decorative title page, 16 plates, ill. Bound in cream cloth, with coloured pictorial cover and decorative spine.
YSC 398.4 GIB

127 **GRAVES, ALFRED PERCEVAL.**
THE IRISH FAIRY BOOK BY ALFRED PERCEVAL GRAVES. ILLUSTRATED BY GEORGE DENHAM. LONDON: T. FISHER UNWIN, (191–?). X, 310p.: col. front., 9 plates. Bound in grey cloth with coloured pictorial cover and spine.
C 398.2109415 GRA

128 **GRIERSON, ELIZABETH W.**
The Scottish Fairy Book By Elizabeth W. Grierson. With one hundred illustrations by Morris Meredith Williams. LONDON: FISHER UNWIN, 1910. XIII, 384p.: col. front., ill. and decorative initial letters in red and black, decorative purple endpapers. Bound in red cloth with coloured decorative cover and spine.
C 309.210941 GRI

128A **GRIERSON, ELISABETH, W.**
TALES FROM SCOTTISH BALLADS. BY ELISABETH

W. GRIERSON. WITH FOUR FULL-PAGE ILLUSTRATIONS IN COLOUR FROM DRAWINGS BY ALAN STEWART. LONDON: A. AND C. BLACK LTD. NEW ED., 1916. VII, 326p. + 2p. pub. cat.: col. front., 3 plates. Bound in blue cloth with coloured pictorial cover and spine: originally published in 1906.
C 823.912 GRI

129 **GRIMM, JAKOB LUDWIG KARL AND GRIMM, WILHELM KARL**
FAIRY TALES BY THE BROTHERS GRIMM. ILLUSTRATED WITH WOODCUTS BY FRITZ KREDEL. INTRODUCTION BY HARRY HANSEN. GERMANY: OFFENBACH a. M. WILH. GERSTUNG FOR LIMITED EDITIONS CLUB, 1931. Limited Edition of 1500 copies. XI, 96p.: col. ill. Bound in brown calf.
CBD 398.210943 GRI

130 **GRIMM, JAKOB LUDWIG KARL AND GRIMM, WILHELM KARL.**
GRIMM'S FAIRY TALES TRANSLATED BY MRS. H.B. PAULL. With Original Coloured Illustrations AND NUMEROUS WOODCUTS. LONDON: FREDERICK WARNE AND CO., (188–?). XII, 522p. + 6p. pub. cat.: col. front., 14 col. plates, 21 plates, ill. Bound in blue cloth with coloured pictorial/decorative cover and spine. First published in England in 1823.
C 398.210943 GRI

131 **Another copy.**
CAREFULLY CHOSEN FROM THE COLLECTION BY THE BROTHERS GRIMM WITH TWELVE ILLUSTRATIONS BY A. RACKHAM. LONDON: S.W. PARTRIDGE AND CO., (190–?). Expurgated edition. VII, 302p. + 32p.: front, 11 plates. Bound in red cloth with coloured pictorial cover and spine.

132 **Another copy.**
With an introduction by John Ruskin. Illustrated by Charles Folkard. LONDON: ADAM AND CHARLES BLACK, 1911. XIV, 331p.: col. front., 11 col. plates. Bound in cream cloth with coloured pictorial covers and spine.

133 **Another copy.**
LONDON: JOHN F. SHAW AND CO. LTD. n.d. No pagination: col. front. Bound with red cloth spine and coloured paper covers.

134 **Another copy.**
Illustrated by ANNE ANDERSON. LONDON: THE CHILDREN'S PRESS, (193–?). No pagination: col. front., ill. Bound in cream paper with coloured pictorial covers.

135 **Another copy.**
LONDON: CASSELL AND COMPANY LTD., 1908. 409p. + 2p. pub. cat.: decorative front. and title page. Bound in green cloth, with decorative spine. THE PEOPLE'S LIBRARY.
YSC 398.4 GRI

136 **Another copy.**
GRIMM'S FAIRY TALES FOR CHILDREN AND THE HOUSEHOLD. COLLECTED BY THE BROTHERS GRIMM. TRANSLATED BY BEATRICE MARSHALL. WITH COLOURED PLATES. LONDON: HARPER AND BROTHERS, 1912. 637p.: 7 col. plates by Ethel K. Burgess. Bound in brown cloth, with coloured pictorial cover and spine.

137 **GRIMM, JAKOB LUDWIG KARL AND GRIMM, WILHELM KARL.**
GRIMM'S HOUSEHOLD TALES EDITED AND PARTLY TRANSLATED ANEW BY MARIAN EDWARDES WITH ILLUSTRATIONS BY R. ANNING BELL. LONDON: J.M. DENT AND SONS LTD., 1901. XVI, 400p.: front., 14 plates, ill. Bound in cream cloth with coloured pictorial cover and spine.
C 398.210943 GRI

138 **GRIMM, JAKOB LUDWIG KARL AND WILHELM KARL.**
HANSEL AND GRETEL AND OTHER TALES BY THE BROTHERS GRIMM. ILLUSTRATED BY ARTHUR RACKHAM. LONDON: CONSTABLE AND CO., LTD., 1920. X, 160p.: col. front., 19 col. plates, 4 plates, ill. Bound in blue cloth with decorative cover and spine.
CBD 398.210943 GRI

139 **GRIMM, JAKOB LUDWIG KARL AND GRIMM, WILHELM KARL.**
HOUSEHOLD STORIES FROM THE COLLECTION OF THE BROTHERS GRIMM. TRANSLATED FROM THE GERMAN BY LUCY CRANE AND DONE INTO PICTURES BY WALTER CRANE. LONDON: MACMILLAN AND CO., 1882. X, 269p. + 2p. pub. cat.: col. front., decorative title page, decorative title pages to each story, ill. Bound in olive green cloth with decorative cover and spine.
CBD 398.210943 GRI

139A **GRIMM, JAKOB LUDWIG KARL AND GRIMM, WILHELM KARL.**
SNOWDROP AND OTHER TALES BY THE BROTHERS GRIMM. ILLUSTRATED BY ARTHUR RACKHAM. LONDON: CONSTABLE AND CO. LTD., 1920. XII, 165p.: col. front., pictorial title page, 19 col. plates, ill. Bound in blue cloth with pictorial cover.
M 398.2 GRI CHILDREN'S COLLECTION

140 **GRIMM, JAKOB LUDWIG KARL AND GRIMM, WILHELM KARL.**
TALES FROM GRIMM. Freely translated and illustrated by WANDA GAG. LONDON: FABER AND FABER LIMITED, 1937. 247p.: col. front., vignette on title page, 3 plates, ill. Bound in red cloth with green paper dust cover incorporating coloured picture.
YSC 398.4 GRI

141 **HALL, MRS A.W.**
THE TWO BROTHERS, A FAIRY TALE. BY MRS. HALL. LONDON: GRIFFITH FARRAN OKEDEN AND WELSH, 1889. 76p.: front., 1 plate, ill. Bound in blue cloth with decorative cover.
C 398.210941 HAL

142 **HALL, MRS A.W.** *(Editor).*
ICELANDIC FAIRY TALES. Translated and Edited by Mrs A.W. Hall. With original illustrations by E.A. Mason. LONDON: FREDERICK WARNE AND CO., (188–?). 317p. + 2p. pub. cat.: front., 6 plates, ill. Bound in blue cloth, with embossed pictorial cover and spine.
YSC 398.4 HAL

143 **HAMER, S.H.**
THE LITTLE FOLKS FAIRY BOOK. BY S.H. HAMER. ILLUSTRATED. LONDON: CASSELL AND COMPANY LIMITED, 1905. 190p. + 8p. ill. pub. cat.: col. front., 21 plates, ill. Bound in red cloth, with coloured pictorial paper cover.
C 823.912 HAM

144 **HARRIS, JOEL CHANDLER.**
NIGHTS WITH UNCLE REMUS. BY JOEL CHANDLER HARRIS. WITH ILLUSTRATIONS BY J.A. SHEPHERD. LONDON: CHATTO AND WINDUS, 1925. VIII, 367p.: col. front., vignette on title page, 7 col. plates, 13 plates, ill. Bound in red cloth, with embossed vignette on cover.
C 813.4 HAR

145 **HARRIS, JOEL CHANDLER.**
UNCLE REMUS AND NIGHTS WITH UNCLE REMUS BY JOEL CHANDLER HARRIS. WITH SIXTY-FIVE ILLUSTRATIONS. LONDON: GEORGE ROUTLEDGE AND SONS, LIMITED, (188–?). XXI, 248p.: front., ill. by A.T. Elwes: VIII, 312p.: front., 13 plates by Church. Bound in red cloth with coloured pictorial cover and spine.
C 813.4 HAR

146 **Another copy.**
Additional col. front. and title page, vignette title page. WITH FIFTY ILLUSTRATIONS BY A.T. ELWES. Bound in green cloth.

147 **HARRIS, JOEL CHANDLER.**
UNCLE REMUS OR MR. FOX, MR. RABBIT, AND MR. TERRAPIN. BY JOEL CHANDLER HARRIS. WITH FIFTY ILLUSTRATIONS BY A.T. ELWES. LONDON: ROUTLEDGE AND KEGAN PAUL LTD., (1905). XXXI, 248p.: front., vignette title page, 4 plates, ill. Bound in blue linson with coloured pictorial paper jacket.
YSC 813.4 HAR

148 **Another copy.**
WITH ILLUSTRATIONS BY J.A. SHEPHERD. LONDON: CHATTO AND WINDUS, 1901. XXXI, 288p.: col. front., vignette on title page, 8 col. plates, 9 plates, ill. Bound in red cloth, with embossed vignette on cover.
C 813.4 HAR

149 **Another copy.**
LONDON: GRANT RICHARDS, 1901. Bound in green cloth with coloured pictorial cover.

149A **HARRISON, JANE.**
THE BOOK OF THE BEAR. Being Twenty-one Tales newly translated from the Russian by JANE HARRISON and HOPE MIRRLEES. The pictures by RAY GARNETT. With a preface and Epilogue. LONDON: THE NONESUCH PRESS, 1926. XIII, 108p.: col. front., decorative title page, col. ill. Bound in buff buckram with coloured decorative covers.
CBD 398.210947 HAR and M 823 HAR CHILDREN'S COLLECTION

150 **HARTLAND, EDWIN SIDNEY** *(Editor).*
ENGLISH FAIRY AND OTHER FOLK TALES. SELECTED AND EDITED, WITH AN INTRODUCTION, BY EDWIN SIDNEY HARTLAND. LONDON: THE WALTER SCOTT PUBLISHING CO., LTD., (190–?). XXVI, 282p. Bound in green cloth.
C 398.210942 ENG
Another copy bound in red cloth with decorative cover, (192–?).

151 **HAWTHORNE, NATHANIEL.**
TANGLEWOOD TALES, A WONDER BOOK FOR BOYS AND GIRLS. BY NATHANIEL HAWTHORNE. Illustrations by WILLY POGANY. LONDON: T. FISHER UNWIN, (192–?). 320p.: col. front., vignette on title page, 3 col. plates, 24 plates, headpieces, tailpieces, decorative initials. Bound in red cloth with coloured decorative cover and spine.
CBD 813.3 HAW

152 **HAWTHORNE, NATHANIEL.**
A WONDER BOOK AND TANGLE-WOOD TALES. BY NATHANIEL HAWTHORNE. LONDON: J.M. DENT AND SONS LTD., 1906. 404p.: decorative front and title page. Bound in blue cloth, with decorative spine. Everyman's library for Young People, No.5.
YSC 398.4 HAW

153 **HAWTHORNE, NATHANIEL.**
WONDER BOOK FOR GIRLS AND BOYS BY NATHANIEL HAWTHORNE. WITH 60 DESIGNS BY WALTER CRANE. LONDON: OSGOOD, MCILVAINE AND CO., 1892. X, 210p.: col. front., col. decorative title page, 20 col. plates, ill., including headpieces and tailpieces, decorative endpapers. Bound in buff cloth with decorative cover and spine (worn).
CBD 398.20938 HAW

154 **Another copy.**
WITH ILLUSTRATIONS BY MILO WINTER. LONDON: DUCKWORTH AND CO., 1914. 254p.: col. front., 15 col. plates, pictorial end papers. Bound in blue cloth with embossed decorative cover and spine.
C 398.20938 HAW

155 **HENDERSON, B.L.K.**
WONDER TALES OF OLD JAPAN. BY B.L.K. HENDERSON AND C. CALVERT. ILLUSTRATED BY CONSTANCE E. ROWLANDS. LONDON: PHILIP ALLAN AND CO., 1924. VIII, 229p. col. front., 7 col. plates, 9 plates, ill. Bound in blue cloth, with embossed decorative cover.
YSC 398.4 HEN

156 **INGELOW, JEAN.**
MOPSA The Fairy. BY JEAN INGELOW. LONDON: J.M. DENT AND SONS LTD., (191–?). XII, 208p.: decorative front. and title page, 8 plates, ill., by Dora Curtis. Bound in brown cloth and quarter leather. EVERYMAN'S LIBRARY FOR YOUNG PEOPLE. Originally published 1869.
C 823.8 ING
Another copy, bound in blue cloth, with embossed decorative spine. EVERYMAN'S LIBRARY FOR YOUNG PEOPLE.

157 **INGELOW, JEAN.**
STORIES TOLD TO A CHILD. BY JEAN INGELOW. Illustrated. LONDON: WELLS, GARDNER, DARTON AND CO., 1900. 214p.: front., 3 plates by H. Petherick. Rebound in quarter red cloth and marbled yellow paper with curved corners.
C 823.8 ING

158 **JACOBS, JOSEPH** *(Editor).*
CELTIC FAIRY TALES, SELECTED AND EDITED BY JOSEPH JACOBS. ILLUSTRATED BY JOHN D. BATTEN. LONDON: DAVID NUTT, 1892. XV, 267p.: front., red vignette on title page, 7 plates, ill., decorative initials. Bound in green cloth with embossed decorative cover and spine.
C 398.210941 CEL

159 **JACOBS, JOSEPH** *(Editor).*
MORE ENGLISH FAIRY TALES, COLLECTED AND EDITED BY JOSEPH JACOBS, EDITOR OF "FOLK-LORE". ILLUSTRATED BY JOHN D. BATTEN. LONDON: DAVID NUTT, 1894. XIV, 243p. + 2p. pub. cat.: vignette on title page, 6 plates, ill. Bound in blue cloth with decorative cover and spine.
C 398.21 JAC

160 **JACOBS, JOSEPH** *(Editor).*
THE MOST DELECTABLE HISTORY OF REYNARD THE FOX. EDITED WITH INTRODUCTION AND NOTES BY JOSEPH JACOBS. DONE INTO PICTURES BY W. FRANK CALDERON. LONDON: MACMILLAN AND CO., 1895. XXXVII, 260p. + 4p. pub. cat.: front., 7 plates, ill. Bound in black cloth with decorative cover and spine, with gilt edges.
CBD 398.2452974442 REY

160A **JAMES, GRACE.**
GREEN WILLOW AND OTHER FAIRY TALES. BY GRACE JAMES WITH FORTY ILLUSTRATIONS IN COLOUR BY WARWICK GOBLE. LONDON: MACMILLAN & CO., LIMITED, 1910. 281p. + 2p. pub. cat.: col. front., 39 col. plates. Bound in blue cloth with pictorial cover.
CBD 398.21 JAM

161 **JAMES, MRS. T.H.**
THE PRINCES FIRE-FLASH AND FIRE-FADE. Told to Children by Mrs. T.H. James. LONDON: GRIFFITH, FARRAN AND CO., n.d. Unpaginated: 3 col. plates, col. ill. and printed on folded crepe paper. Bound with coloured pictorial paper covers. JAPANESE FAIRY TALE SERIES, No. 14.
YSC 398.4 JAM

162 **KAVANAGH, BRIDGET.**
THE PEARL FOUNDATION AND Other Fairy Tales. BY BRIDGET AND JULIA KAVANAGH. WITH THIRTY ILLUSTRATIONS BY J. MOYR SMITH. LONDON: CHATTO AND WINDUS, 1876. 245p.: front., 10 plates, ill. Bound in blue cloth, with embossed pictorial/decorative cover and spine.
YSC 398.4 KAV

163 **KEIGHTLEY, THOMAS.**
THE FAIRY MYTHOLOGY ILLUSTRATIVE OF THE ROMANCE AND SUPERSTITION OF VARIOUS

COUNTRIES. BY THOMAS KEIGHTLEY. LONDON: G. BELL AND SONS, 1900. X, 560p. + 32p. pub. cat.: front. Bound in brown cloth. BOHN'S LIBRARIES.
C 398.21 KEI

164 **KINCAID, C.A.**
DECCAN NURSERY TALES OR FAIRY TALES FROM THE SOUTH BY C.A. KINCAID, C.V.O. INDIAN CIVIL SERVICE. ILLUSTRATIONS BY M.V. DHURANDHAR. LONDON: MACMILLAN AND CO., LIMITED. 1914. XIII, 135p.: col. front., 7 col. plates. Bound in blue cloth with decorative cover and spine.
C 398.210954 KIN

165 **KING, VIOLET.**
The City of Enchantment. Monday's child. "Monday's Child is Fair of Face." Told by Violet King. LONDON: GALE AND POLDEN LIMITED, (193–?). 63p.: col. front. Quarter bound in purple cloth with coloured pictorial paper covers.
C 398.21 KIN

166 **KING, VIOLET.**
The Island of Shadows. Wednesday's Child. "Wednesday's Child is full of Woe." Told by Violet King. LONDON: GALE AND POLDEN LIMITED, (193–?). 64p.: col. front. Quarter bound in grey cloth with coloured pictorial paper covers.
C 398.21 KIN

167 **KING, VIOLET.**
Peggy's Adventure. Friday's Child. "Friday's Child is Loving and Giving." Told by Violet King. LONDON: GALE AND POLDEN LIMITED, (193–?). 64p.: col. front. Quarter bound in brown cloth with pictorial paper covers.
C 398.21 KIN

168 **KING, VIOLET.**
The Persian Tapestry. Tuesday's Child. "Tuesday's Child is full of Grace." Told by Violet King. LONDON: GALE AND POLDEN LIMITED, (193–?). 63p.: col. front. Quarter bound in maroon cloth with coloured pictorial paper covers.
C 398.12 KIN

169 **KING, VIOLET.**
The Phantom Ships. Saturday's Child. "Saturday's Child works hard for its Living." Told by Violet King. LONDON: GALE AND POLDEN LIMITED. (193–?). 63p.: col. front. Bound in brown cloth with coloured pictorial paper covers.
C 398.21 KIN

170 **KING, VIOLET.**
The Touching Stone. Thursday's Child. "Thursday's Child has Far to Go." Told by Violet King. LONDON: GALE AND POLDEN LIMITED, (193–?). 64p.: col. front. Quarter bound in blue cloth with coloured pictorial paper covers.
C 398.21 KIN

171 **KING, VIOLET.**
Woods Where Stories Grow. Sunday's Child. "But the Child that is born on a Sabbath Day is Loving, and Bright, and Good, and Gay." Told by Violet King. LONDON: GALE AND POLDEN LIMITED, (193–?). 64p.: col. front. Quarter bound in green cloth with coloured pictorial paper covers.
C 398.21 KIN

171A **KNOWLES, HORACE J.**
PEEPS INTO FAIRYLAND. WRITTEN AND ILLUSTRATED BY HORACE J. KNOWLES. LONDON: THORNTON BUTTERWORTH LTD, 1924. 90p.: col. front., decorative title page, ill. Bound in buff cloth with decorative cover.
M 398.2 KNO CHILDREN'S COLLECTION.

172 **KUNOS, IGNACZ** *(Editor).*
Forty Four Turkish Fairy Tales. Collected and translated by Dr Ignacz Kunos with illustrations by Willy Pogany. LONDON: GEORGE G. HARRAP AND CO., 1913. XI, 363p.: col. front., decorative title page, 14 col. plates, 16 plates, ill., pictorial end papers. Bound in buff cloth with coloured decorative cover and spine.
CBD 398.2109561 KUN

173 **LANG, ANDREW** *(Editor).*
BEAUTY AND THE BEAST AND OTHER STORIES FROM THE BLUE, BROWN, GREEN, VIOLET AND YELLOW FAIRY BOOKS. EDITED BY ANDREW LANG. WITH A COLOURED FRONTISPIECE AND NUMEROUS ILLUSTRATIONS BY H.J. FORD. Illustrated Library of Fairy Tales. LONDON: LONGMANS, GREEN AND CO., 1909. 254p.: col. front., 14 plates, ill. Bound in orange cloth with embossed decorative cover and spine, and decorative end papers.
C 398.21 BEA

174 **LANG, ANDREW** *(Editor).*
THE BLUE FAIRY BOOK. EDITED BY ANDREW LANG. WITH NUMEROUS ILLUSTRATIONS BY H.J. FORD AND G.P. JACOMB HOOD. SIXTH EDITION. LONDON: LONGMANS, GREEN AND CO., 1893. 390p.: front., vignette title page, 7 plates, ill. Bound in blue cloth with pictorial cover and spine, with gilt edges.
C398.21 LAN and CBD 398.21 LAN

175 **LANG, ANDREW** *(Editor).*
THE BROWN FAIRY BOOK. EDITED BY ANDREW LANG. WITH EIGHT COLOURED PLATES AND NUMEROUS ILLUSTRATIONS BY H.J. FORD. NEW IMPRESSION. LONDON: LONGMANS, GREEN AND CO., 1919. XIII, 350p.: col. front., vignette title page, 7 col. plates, 22 plates, ill. Bound in brown cloth, with embossed pictorial/decorative cover and spine. Originally published 1904.
YSC 398.4 LAN

176 **LANG, ANDREW** *(Editor).*
THE CRIMSON FAIRY BOOK. EDITED BY ANDREW LANG. WITH EIGHT COLOURED PLATES AND NUMEROUS ILLUSTRATIONS BY H.J. FORD. LONDON: LONGMANS, GREEN AND CO., 1903. XI, 371p.: col. front., 7 col. plates, 35 plates, ill. Bound in red cloth, with pictorial/decorative cover and spine.
YSC 398.4 LAN and CBD 398.21 LAN

177 **LANG, ANDREW** *(Editor).*
THE GREEN FAIRY BOOK. EDITED BY ANDREW LANG. WITH NUMEROUS ILLUSTRATIONS BY H.J. FORD. EIGHTH IMPRESSION. LONDON: LONGMANS, GREEN AND CO., 1909. XI, 366p.: front., vignette title page, 11 plates, ill. Bound in green cloth, with embossed pictorial cover and spine. Originally published 1892.
YSC 398.4 LAN

178 **LANG, ANDREW** *(Editor).*
THE GREY FAIRY BOOK. EDITED BY ANDREW LANG. WITH NUMEROUS ILLUSTRATIONS BY H.J. FORD. LONDON: LONGMANS, GREEN AND CO., 1910. XII, 387p.: front., vignette title page, 31 plates, ill. Bound in grey cloth with pictorial cover and spine.
CBD 398.21 LAN & YSC 398.4 LAN

179 **LANG, ANDREW** *(Editor).*
THE LILAC FAIRY BOOK. EDITED BY ANDREW LANG. WITH 6 COLOURED PLATES AND NUMEROUS ILLUSTRATIONS BY H.J. FORD. NEW IMPRESSION. LONDON: LONGMANS, GREEN AND CO., 1910. XV, 369p. + 2p. pub. cat.: col. front. 5 col. plates, 20 plates, ill. Bound in lilac cloth with embossed pictorial cover and spine.
CBD 398.21 LAN

180 **LANG, ANDREW** *(Editor).*
THE PINK FAIRY BOOK. EDITED BY ANDREW LANG. WITH NUMEROUS ILLUSTRATIONS BY H.J. FORD. NEW IMPRESSION. LONDON: LONGMANS, GREEN AND CO., 1916. VIII, 360p.: front., vignette title page, 22 plates, ill. Bound in pink cloth, with embossed pictorial cover and spine. Originally published 1897.
YSC 398.4 LAN

181 **LANG, ANDREW** *(Editor).*
THE VIOLET FAIRY BOOK. EDITED BY ANDREW LANG. WITH NUMEROUS ILLUSTRATIONS BY H.J. FORD. LONGMANS, GREEN AND CO., 1902. XII, 388p.: col. front., vignette title page, 7 col. plates, 25 plates, ill. Bound in violet cloth with pictorial cover and spine, with gilt edges. Originally published in 1901.
C 398.21 VIO and YSC 398.4 LAN

182 **LANG, ANDREW** *(Editor).*
THE YELLOW FAIRY BOOK. EDITED BY ANDREW LANG. WITH NUMEROUS ILLUSTRATIONS BY HENRY J. FORD. LONDON: LONGMANS, GREEN AND CO., 1933. XVI, 321p.: front., vignette title page, 21 plates, ill. Bound in yellow cloth with embossed pictorial cover. Originally published in 1894.
C 398.21 YEL and YSC 398.4 LAN

183 **LAUSCH, ERNST.**
Kurge Geschichten für kleine Leute. Von Ernst Lausch. Ausgabe für Mädchen. GERMANY, LEIPSIG: ALFRED DEHMIGTE'S VERLAG, (189–?). 64p.: 4 plates. Bound in red cloth, with pictorial paper cover.
YSC 398.210943 LAU

184 **LAVERTY, KITTY.**
OUT OF BED THE WRONG SIDE. BY KITTY LAVERTY. EDITED BY LADY KATHLEEN. LONDON: THE ALDINE PUBLISHING COMPANY, LTD. 44p.: ill. Bound in cream paper with pictorial cover. 1d. TALES FOR LITTLE PEOPLE NO 256.
YSC 823.912 LAV

185 **LEAMY, EDMUND.**
IRISH FAIRY TALES. BY EDMUND LEAMY, M.P. DUBLIN: M.H. GILL AND SON, (189–?). 167p.: front., 6 plates, ill. Bound in green cloth.
YSC 398.4 LEA

186 **LEE, HOLME.**
HOLME LEE'S FAIRY TALES. A NEW REVISED EDITION. With original illustrations. LONDON: FREDERICK WARNE AND CO., 1892. VII, 511p. + 6p. pub. cat.: front., 10 plates. Bound in blue cloth with embossed decorative cover and spine.
C 398.21 LEE

187 **LEE, HOLME.**
LEGENDS FROM FAIRYLAND. BY HOLME LEE. With Illustrations. LONDON: FREDERICK WARNE AND CO., (1868). VII, 239p. + 10p. pub. cat.: front., additional vignette title page, 5 plates. Bound in blue cloth with embossed decorative cover and coloured paper vignette, and decorative spine.
C 392.21 LEE

188 **LEE, HOLME.**
Legends from FAIRY LAND NARRATING THE HISTORY OF PRINCE GLEE AND PRINCESS TRILL, THE CRUEL PERSECUTIONS AND CONDIGN PUNISHMENT OF AUNT SPITE, THE ADVENTURES OF THE GREAT TUFLONGBO AND THE STORY OF THE BLACK CAP IN THE GIANT'S WELL. BY HOLME LEE. WITH ILLUSTRATIONS BY REGINALD L. KNOWLES AND HORACE J. KNOWLES AND AN INTRODUCTION BY EFFIE H. FREEMANTLE. LONDON: S.J. FREEMANTLE, 1907. XXVI, 276p.: front., decorative title page, 16 plates, ill., head and tail pieces, decorative initial letters and marginal decorations, decorative endpapers. Bound in green cloth with embossed decorative cover and spine.
CBD 398.21 LEE

189 **LEMON, MARK.**
The Enchanted Doll, A Fairy Tale for Little People. By MARK LEMON. With Illustrations by Richard Doyle. LONDON: ALEXANDER MORING, THE DE LA MORE PRESS, 1903. XI, 74p.: front., additional vignette title page, 12 plates, ill. Bound in green cloth with paper-covered boards, with pictorial cover.
C 823.8 LEM

190 **MACDONALD, GEORGE.**
THE DAY BOY AND THE NIGHT GIRL. The Fairy Tales of GEORGE MACDONALD. Edited by GREVILLE MACDONALD. (Vol. V). LONDON: ARTHUR C. FIFIELD, 1904. 75p.: pictorial title page, 1 plate from the original pen and ink drawing by Arthur Hughes. Bound in buff paper, with pictorial cover.
YSC 398.4 MAC

190A **MACDONALD, GEORGE.**
FAIRY TALES. BY George MacDonald. Edited by Greville MacDonald with title page and illustrations by Arthur Hughes. LONDON: ARTHUR C. FIFIELD, 1906. 435p. + 7p. pub. cat.: pictorial title page, 13 plates. Bound in blue cloth.
M 398.2 MAC

191 **MACDONALD, GEORGE.**
The Giant's Heart and the Golden Key. The Fairy Tales of GEORGE MACDONALD. Edited by GREVILLE MACDONALD. VOL. II. LONDON: ARTHUR C. FIFIELD, 1904. 87–169p.: pictorial title page, 3 plates from the original pen and ink drawings of Arthur Hughes. Rebound.
YSC 398.4 MAC

192 **MACDONALD, GEORGE.**
THE LIGHT PRINCESS. The Fairy Tales of GEORGE MACDONALD, Edited by GREVILLE MACDONALD. VOL. I. LONDON: ARTHUR C. FIFIELD, 1904. VII, 82p.: pictorial title page, 5 plates from the original pen and ink drawings by Arthur Hughes. Bound in buff paper, with pictorial cover.
YSC 398.4 MAC

193 **MARIE, QUEEN OF ROUMANIA.**
THE DREAMER OF DREAMS By THE QUEEN OF ROUMANIA ILLUSTRATED BY EDMUND DULAC LONDON: HODDER AND STOUGHTON, (193–?). 181p.: col. front., decorative title page, 5 col. plates. Bound in grey cloth with decorative cover and spine.
CBD 859.332 MAR

194 **MARIE, QUEEN OF ROUMANIA.**
THE STEALERS OF LIGHT, A LEGEND. BY MARIE, QUEEN OF ROUMANIA. LONDON: HODDER AND STOUGHTON, 1906. 190p.: col. front., 1 col. plate by Edmund Dulac. Bound in blue cloth with decorative cover and spine.
CBD 859.332 MAR

195 **MARKS, JEANNETTE.**
THE CHEERFUL CRICKET AND OTHERS. ILLUSTRATED BY EDITH BROWN. LONDON: GEORGE ALLEN, 1907. Unpaginated: col. decorative title page, decorative border on each page, some col. Bound in blue cloth, with coloured pictorial/decorative cover.
C 813.52 MAR

196 **MARSH, LEWIS.**
TALES OF THE HOMELAND. LONDON: HENRY FROWDE, HODDER AND STOUGHTON (191–?). VIII, 199p.: col. front., 5 col. plates, 8 plates, ill., by T.H. Robinson. Bound in buff buckram with coloured pictorial cover and spine.
C 398.2 MAR

197 **MERCER, JOYCE** *(Illustrator).*
THE JOYCE MERCER EDITION OF ANDERSEN AND GRIMM. ILLUSTRATED with Sixteen Colours and over two hundred and fifty black and white drawings. LONDON: HUTCHINSON AND CO. (PUBLISHERS) LTD., (193–?). 252p.: col. front., vignette on title page, 15 col. plates, ill. Bound in blue cloth, with pictorial sepia end papers.
C 398.2109489 AND

198 **MOLESWORTH, MARY LOUISA.**
FAIRIES – OF SORTS. BY MRS. MOLESWORTH. WITH ILLUSTRATIONS BY GERTRUDE DEMAIN HAMMOND. LONDON: MACMILLAN AND CO. LIMITED, 1908. IX, 249p. + 2p. pub. cat.: front., 7 plates. Bound in blue cloth, with embossed decorative cover and spine, and gilt

From Puss in Boots in the Book of Nursery Tales, Warne, 1934.

From Story of Aladdin, Black, 1913.

From Rapunzel in Grimm's Hansel and Grethel and other tales, Constable, 1920.

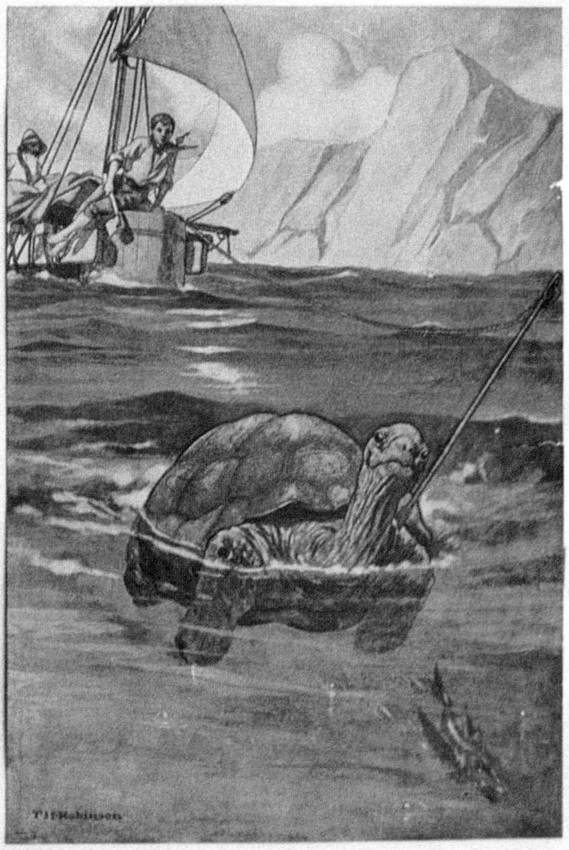


From Swiss Family Robinson, OUP, n.d.

"A ROMANY IN THE FIELDS"
BY
G. BRAMWELL EVENS
(THE TRAMP)

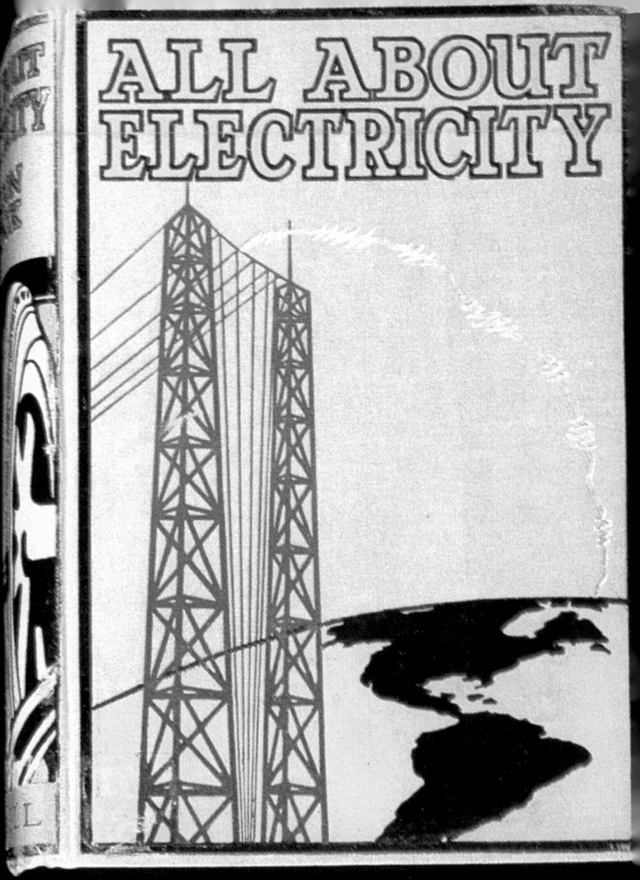
ALL ABOUT ELECTRICITY

THE BOY'S OWN BOOK OF NATURAL HISTORY
REV. J.G. WOOD

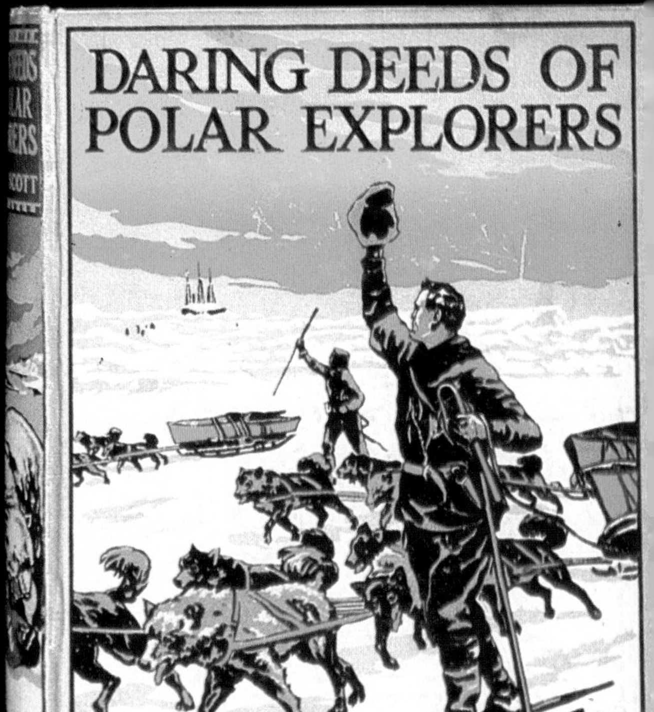
DARING DEEDS OF POLAR EXPLORERS

edges. Contains four stories: The Groaning Clock, Those Green Ribbons, The Bunnies' Home, and The Toy-less Visit.
C 823.8 MOL

**Another copy.**
Title page missing. Bound in blue cloth, with coloured decorative cover and spine.
YSC/F MOL

199 **MOLESWORTH, MARY LOUISA.**
LITTLE MISS PEGGY: ONLY A NURSERY STORY. BY MRS. MOLESWORTH. WITH PICTURES BY WALTER CRANE. LONDON: MACMILLAN AND CO., 1887. VIII, 195p. + 36p. pub. cat.: front., pictorial title page, 12 plates. Bound in orange cloth with pictorial/decorative cover and spine.
C 823.8 MOL

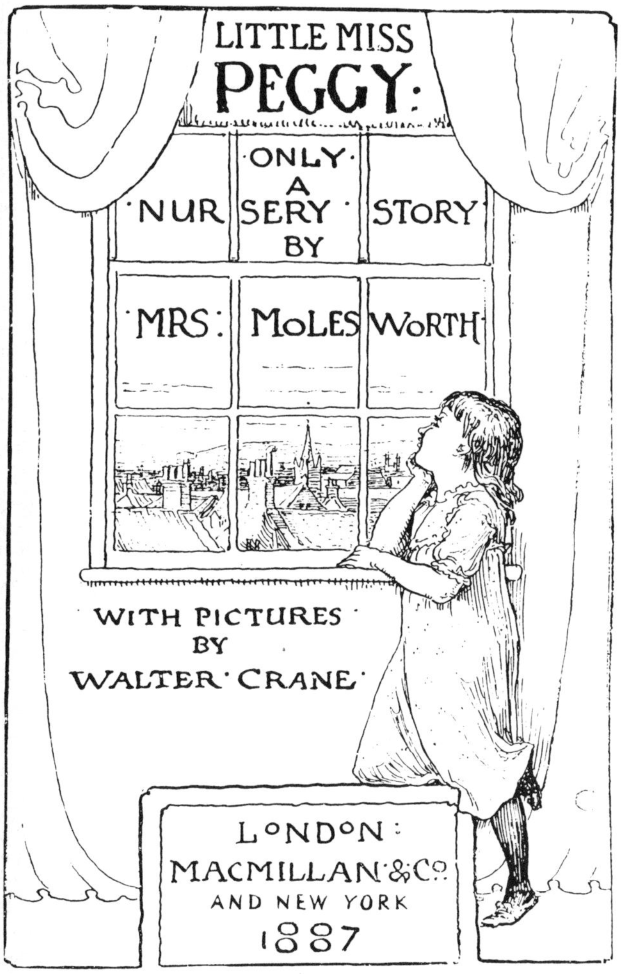

199

200 **MORRISON, SOPHIA.**
MANX FAIRY TALES. LONDON: DAVID NUTT, 1911. VIII, 186p.: front., by Ruth Cobb. Bound in yellow cloth with pictorial cover and spine.
C 398.21094279 MOR

201 **MURRAY, HILDA.**
FLOWER LEGENDS FOR CHILDREN, BY HILDA MURRAY. PICTURED BY J.S. ELAND. LONDON: LONGMANS GREEN AND CO. (189–?). 64p. col. front., col. pictorial dedication and col. pictorial title page, 13 col. plates, ill., some col. Bound in brown cloth with coloured pictorial paper covers.
C 398.242 MUR

202 **NODIER, CHARLES.**
THE WOODCUTTER'S DOG. TRANSLATED FROM THE FRENCH OF CHARLES NODIER. ILLUSTRATED BY CLAUD LOVAT FRASER. LONDON: DANIEL O'CONNOR, 1921. 18p.: col. front., col. vignette title page, col. ill. Bound in green.
C 843.912 NOD

203 **ORIENTAL FAIRY TALES, OR FANCY'S WANDERINGS IN THE EAST.**
WITH THIRTY-TWO ILLUSTRATIONS, BY WILLIAM HARVEY, ENGRAVED BY THE BROTHERS DALZIER. LONDON: GEORGE ROUTLEDGE AND CO., 1857. 338p.: front., additional pictorial title page, 6 plates, ill. Bound in blue cloth with embossed decorative cover and spine.
CBD 398.21095 ORI

204 **(PERRAULT, CHARLES).**
CINDERELLA, RETOLD BY C.S. EVANS AND ILLUSTRATED BY ARTHUR RACKHAM. LONDON: WILLIAM HEINEMANN, 1919. 110p.: col. front., col. decorative title page, 2 double col. plates, ill. in black silhouette. Bound in brown cloth with coloured pictorial paper cover.
CBD 398.210944 EVA

205 **PERRAULT, CHARLES.**
FAIRY TALES. By CHARLES PERRAULT. Illustrated by CHARLES ROBINSON. LONDON: J.M. DENT AND SONS LTD., 1913. 128p.: col. front., 7 col. plates. Bound in cream cloth, with coloured pictorial paper label on cover.
YSC 398.4 PER

205A **PERRAULT, CHARLES.**
HISTORIES OR TALES OF PAST TIMES TOLD BY MOTHER GOOSE WITH MORALS. Written in French by M. Perrault, and Englished by G.M. Gent. Newly edited by J. Saxon Childers. LONDON: THE NONESUCH PRESS, Limited Edition of 1250 copies, 1925. 128p.: hand col. front., decorative title page, hand col. headpieces to chapters by W.M.R. Quick. Bound in blue cloth with coloured decorative covers.
CBD 398.21 PER and M 823.08 MOT CHILDREN'S COLLECTION

205B **PERRAULT, CHARLES.**
OLD TIME STORIES told by MASTER CHARLES PERRAULT translated from the French by A.E. Johnson with illustrations by W. HEATH ROBINSON. LONDON: CONSTABLE AND CO. LTD., 1921. XII, 200p.: col. front., vignette on title page, 5 col. plates, 26 plates, ill. Bound in red cloth with pictorial vignette on cover and pictorial spine.
C 843.4 PER

205C **PERRAULT, CHARLES.**
TALES OF PASSED TIMES WRITTEN FOR CHILDREN BY MR PERRAULT AND NEWLY DECORATED BY JOHN AUSTEN. LONDON: SELWYN AND BLOUNT LTD., LIMITED EDITION OF 200. 1922. 64p.: col. front., col. ill. Bound in vellum with coloured pictorial cover. Signed by John Austen.
C 843.4 PER

206 **PITMAN, NORMAN HINSDALE.**
A CHINESE WONDER BOOK. BY NORMAN HINSDALE PITMAN. ILLUSTRATED BY LI CHU-T'ANG. LONDON: J.M. DENT AND SONS LTD., 1919. 219p.: col. front., 11 col. plates, decorative chapter headings. Bound in green cloth with grey paper cover, title in red and black.
C 398.210951 PIT

207 **PYLE, HOWARD.**
The WONDER CLOCK or Four and Twenty marvellous Tales, being one for each hour of the day; written and illustrated By Howard Pyle. Embellished with Verses by Katharine Pyle. U.S.A. NEW YORK: HARPER AND BROTHERS, 1906. XIV, 318p.: pictorial decoration to headings and initial letters of chapters, ill. Bound in buff cloth with decorative cover.
C 813.4 PYL

208 **QUEEN MAB'S FAIRY REALM.**
ILLUSTRATED by H. COLE, A. GARTH JONES, H.R. MILLAR, A. RACKHAM AND R. SAVAGE. LONDON: GEORGE NEWNES LTD., 1901. XII, 310p.: col. front., col. pictorial title page, 27 plates, ill. Bound in blue cloth, with coloured pictorial cover and spine. Fifteen European fairy tales by a variety of different authors.
YSC 398.4 QUE

THE SEVEN WITCHES

208

209 **QUILLER-COUCH, SIR ARTHUR THOMAS.**
The Sleeping Beauty and other fairy tales retold by Sir Arthur Quiller-Couch, illustrated by Edmund Dulac. LONDON: HODDER AND STOUGHTON, (191–?). 165p.: col. front., 14 plates, ill. Bound in blue cloth with blue dust jacket including coloured pictorial paper insert.
CBD 398.21 QUI

210 **RHYS, ERNEST.**
ENGLISH FAIRY TALES. BY ERNEST AND GRACE RHYS. WITH COLOURED ILLUSTRATIONS BY HERBERT COLE AND R. ANNING BELL. LONDON: J.M. DENT AND SONS, LIMITED, (191–?). 128p.: col. front., 7 col. plates, ill. Bound in red cloth with decorative cover and inserted coloured paper label.
CBD 398.20942 RHY

211 **RHYS, ERNEST** *(Editor).*
FAIRY GOLD, A BOOK OF OLD ENGLISH FAIRY TALES CHOSEN BY ERNEST RHYS, ILLUSTRATED BY HERBERT COLE. LONDON: J.M. DENT AND CO., 1906. XVI, 474p.: col. front., col. decorative title page, 11 col. plates, 25 plates, ill., decorative endpapers. Bound in buff cloth with coloured decorative cover and spine.
C 398.210942 FAI

212 **RHYS, GRACE** *(Editor).*
THE FAIRY GIFTS AND TOM HICKATHRIFT. ILLUSTRATED BY H. GRANVILLE FELL. LONDON: J.M. DENT AND CO., 1895. 61p.: front., vignette on title page, 16 plates, ill., with decorative endpapers. Bound in buff cloth with embossed pictorial cover and red tie band.
C 398.21 HIS

213 **RHYS, GRACE** *(Editor).*
THE HISTORY OF ALI BABA AND THE FORTY THIEVES, PICTURED BY H. GRANVILLE FELL. LONDON: J.M. DENT AND CO., 1895. 63p.: front., vignette on title page, ill., with decorative end papers. Bound in buff cloth with embossed pictorial cover and red tie band.
C 398.21 HIS

214 **RHYS, GRACE** *(Editor).*
THE HISTORY OF CINDERELLA OR THE LITTLE GLASS SLIPPER AND THE HISTORY OF JACK AND THE BEANSTALK. LONDON: J.M. DENT AND CO., 1894. 63p.: front., vignette on title page, ill., decorative endpapers. Bound in buff cloth with decorative embossed cover and red tie band.
C 398.21 HIS

215 **RHYS, GRACE** *(Editor).*
JACK THE GIANT KILLER AND BEAUTY AND THE BEAST ILLUSTRATED BY R. ANNING BELL. LONDON: J.M. DENT AND CO., 1894. 82p.: front., vignette on title page, 12 plates, ill., decorative endpapers. Bound in buff cloth with pictorial embossed cover and red tie band.
C 398.21 HIS

216 **RHYS, GRACE** *(Editor).*
LITTLE RED RIDING HOOD AND THE HISTORY OF TOM THUMB ILLUSTRATED BY H. ISABEL ADAMS. LONDON: J.M. DENT AND CO., 1895. 57p.: front., decorative border to title page, 8 plates, ill., decorative endpapers. Bound in buff cloth with embossed pictorial cover and red tie band.
C 398.21 HIS

217 **RHYS, GRACE** *(Editor).*
THE SLEEPING BEAUTY AND DICK WHITTINGTON AND HIS CAT. ILLUSTRATED BY R. ANNING BELL. LONDON: J.M. DENT AND CO., 1894. 60p.: front., vignette on title page, 7 plates, ill., decorative endpapers. Bound in buff cloth with embossed pictorial cover and red tie band.
C 398.21 HIS

218 **RINDER, FRANK.**
Old-World Japan. Legends of the Land of the Gods. Retold by Frank Rinder. With Illustrations by T.H. Robinson. LONDON: GEORGE ALLEN, 1895. XII, 195p.: 14 plates, ill., col. decorative endpapers. Bound in green cloth with decorative cover and spine.
CBD 398.20952 RIN

218A **ROSCOE, THOMAS.**
THE PLEASANT HISTORY OF REYNARD THE FOX. TRANSLATED BY THE LATE THOMAS ROSCOE. ILLUSTRATED WITH NEARLY ONE HUNDRED DESIGNS BY A.T. ELWES AND JOHN JELLICOE. LONDON: SAMPSON LOW, MARSTON, LOW AND SEARLE, 1873. XV, 136p.: front., vignette on title page, 12 plates, ill., decorative chapter numbers and initials, tailpieces. Bound in brown cloth with embossed decorative cover and spine, with gilt edges.
C 398.245 ROS

219 **ROUSE, WILLIAM HENRY DENHAM.**
Tom Noddy the Noodle WITH OTHER FOOLS AND WISE MEN NOT A FEW. BY W.H.D. ROUSE. ILLUSTRATED BY CONSTANCE ROWLANDS. LONDON: J.M. DENT AND SONS LTD., 1928. XI, 200p.: front., vignette title page, 9 plates, ill. Bound in beige cloth, with coloured pictorial cover and spine.
C 823.912 ROU

220 **RUSKIN, JOHN.**
THE KING OF THE GOLDEN RIVER; OR, THE BLACK BROTHERS. A Legend of Stiria. BY JOHN RUSKIN, M.A. ILLUSTRATED BY RICHARD DOYLE. TWENTY-FOURTH THOUSAND. LONDON: GEORGE ALLEN, 1901. 64p.: front., additional pictorial title page, ill., engraved by G. and E. Dalziel and others. Bound in green cloth, with embossed vignette on cover.
C 823.8 RUS

221 **Another copy.**
TWENTY-NINTH THOUSAND. LONDON: GEORGE ALLEN, 1904. 64p.: front., additional pictorial title page, ill., engraved by G. and E. Dalziel and others. Bound in green paper.

222 **Another copy.**
Thirty second thousand (191–?). Col., front., additional col. pictorial title page.
CBD 398.21 RUS

223 **RUSKIN, JOHN.**
THE KING OF THE GOLDEN RIVER. And Other Stories. BY JOHN RUSKIN, Etc. etc. LONDON: THOMAS NELSON AND SONS, (190–?). 159p. + 2p. pub. cat.: col. front., 7 col. plates. Bound in green cloth, with decorative covers. Includes also: The Golden Touch, by Nathaniel Hawthorne; Ten Pieces of Gold, told by Mrs. Craik; and The Golden Apples of Lough Erne, told from traditional sources.
YSC 398.4 RUS

224 **THE SILVER FAIRY BOOK.**
COMPRISING STORIES BY VOLTAIRE . . . AND OTHERS. WITH 84 ILLUSTRATIONS BY H.R. MILLAR. LONDON: HUTCHINSON AND CO., (189–?). VIII, 312p.: front., 6 plates, ill. Bound in blue cloth, with coloured pictorial cover.
YSC 398.4 SIL

225 **SMITH, CHARLES H.**
FAIRY TALES FROM CLASSIC MYTHS FOR BOYS AND GIRLS. TOLD BY CHARLES H. SMITH. PICTURED BY ALFRED JONES. MANCHESTER: JOHN HEYWOOD, (191–?). 72p.: pictorial title page, 14 plates in sepia, decorative initials, ill. Bound in blue cloth with pictorial paper cover.
C 398.22 SMI

226 **SOUTHWART, ELIZABETH.**
THE PASSWORD TO FAIRYLAND, BY ELIZABETH SOUTHWART WITH DRAWINGS BY FLORENCE MARY ANDERSON. LONDON: SIMPKIN, MARSHALL, HAMILTON, KENT AND CO., LTD., (192–?). 187p.: col. front., col. pictorial title page, 11 col. plates (some hand coloured), ill., hand coloured, col. pictorial endpapers. Bound in buff cloth with decorative cover and spine.
CBD 823.912 SOU

227 **STEEL, FLORA ANNIE** *(Editor).*
TALES OF THE PUNJAB. TOLD BY THE PEOPLE. BY FLORA ANNIE STEEL. WITH ILLUSTRATIONS BY J. LOCKWOOD KIPLING, C.I.E. AND NOTES BY R.C. TEMPLE. LONDON: MACMILLAN AND CO., 1894. XVI, 359p.: front., 4 plates, ill. Bound in black cloth with decorative cover and spine.
CBD 398.2109545 STE

228 **(THACKERAY, WILLIAM MAKEPEACE).**
THE ROSE AND THE RING; OR, THE HISTORY OF PRINCE GIGLIO AND PRINCE BULBO. A Fire-Side Pantomime for Great and Small Children. BY MR. M.A. TITMARSH (pseud). FOURTH EDITION. LONDON: SMITH, ELDER AND CO., 1866. IV, 128p.: front., vignette on title page, 5 plates, ill. Half bound in green leather. Originally published in 1855.
C 823.8 THA

228A **Another copy.**
By W.M. THACKERAY. RE-ILLUSTRATED BY J.R. MONSELL. LONDON: KEGAN PAUL, TRENCH TRUBNER AND COMPANY, 1911. XI, 128p.: col. front., vignette on title page, 11 col. plates, ill. Bound in red cloth with decorative cover.
C 823.8 THA

228B **Another copy.**
Edited by Dorothy Margaret Stuart. LONDON: MACMILLAN AND CO. LIMITED, 1926. VIII, 152p. + 2p. pub. cat.: vignette on title page, 2 plates, ill., by the author. Bound in maroon cloth, with decorative spine. English Literature Series.
YSC 398.4 THA

229 **THOMAS, W. JENKYN.**
The Welsh Fairy Book. By W. Jenkyn Thomas. With one hundred illustrations by Willy Pogany. LONDON: T. FISHER UNWIN, (191–?). XIV, 312p.: col. front., coloured pictorial title page, 9 plates, chapter and paragraph headings pictorially decorated in 2 colours, ill. Bound in blue cloth with coloured pictorial cover and grey pictorial endpapers.
C 398.2109429 THO

230 **TODD, E.**
IGNORAMUS, A FAIRY STORY. BY E. TODD. Illustrated by MAY CHATTERIS FISHER. MANCHESTER: SHERRATT AND HUGHES, 1901. 68p.: front., 5 plates, ill. Bound in green cloth with pictorial cover.
C 398.21 TOD

231 **TOWNSHEND, DOROTHEA.**
THE FAERY OF LISBAWN. BY DOROTHEA TOWNSHEND. LONDON: THOMAS NELSON AND SONS, 1900. 72p.: front., additional vignette title page. Bound in mustard cloth, with coloured pictorial cover. Also contains "Dennis Roe's Tower".
C 823.912 TOW

232 **THE TRUE ANNALS OF FAIRY LAND.**
In the Reign of KING HERLA. LONDON: J.M. DENT AND SONS LTD., (190–?). XVI, 365p.: decorative front and title page, 20 plates, ill., by Charles Robinson. Bound in blue cloth, with decorative spine. EVERYMAN'S LIBRARY FOR YOUNG PEOPLE.
YSC 398.4 HER

232A **TUCKER, ARCHIBALD NORMAN.**
THE DISAPPOINTED LION and Other Stories from the Bari of Central Africa. Collected by A.N. Tucker with a preface by "ELIZABETH" of the Children's Hour, illustrated by John Farleigh. LONDON: COUNTRY LIFE, 1937. 97p.: front., ill. Bound in orange cloth with a black pictorial paper dust wrapper.
C 398.210967 TUC

232B **UNCLE CHARLIE'S BOOK OF FAIRY TALES.**
With over One Hundred Illustrations by Richard Doyle, A. Chasemore, John Proctor, Will Gibbons and others. LONDON: GRIFFITH FARRAN BROWNE AND CO. (189–?). Unpaginated: vignette on title page, ill. Bound in cream paper with coloured pictorial covers.
C 398.21 UNC

233 **VALENTINE, (LAURA BELINDA)** *(Editor).*
EASTERN TALES. BY MANY STORY TELLERS. COMPILED AND EDITED FROM ANCIENT AND MODERN AUTHORS BY MRS. VALENTINE. WITH NUMEROUS ILLUSTRATIONS. LONDON: FREDERICK WARNE AND CO., (190–?). 540p.: front., ill. Bound in blue cloth, with coloured decorative cover and spine.
YSC 398.4 VAL

234 **VALENTINE, (LAURA BELINDA)** *(Editor).*
THE OLD OLD FAIRY TALES. COLLECTED AND EDITED BY MRS. VALENTINE. LONDON: FREDERICK WARNE AND CO., (1890). VIII, 566p. + 2p. pub. cat. Bound in blue cloth.
C 398.21 VAL

235 **Another copy.**
1890. With col. front. and 9 plates engraved by Dalziel. Bound in blue cloth with embossed decorative cover and spine.

236 **Another copy.**
With 2 col. plates and 7 plates engraved by Dalziel. Bound in brown cloth with embossed decorative cover and spine.

237 **VILLAMARIA.**
Fairy Circles, TALES AND LEGENDS OF Giants, Dwarfs, Fairies, Water-Sprites, and Hobgoblins. FROM THE GERMAN OF VILLAMARIA. WITH NUMEROUS ILLUSTRATIONS. LONDON: MARCUS WARD AND CO., 1877. 282p.: col. front., 5 plates, ill. Bound in brown cloth, with embossed decorative cover and spine.
YSC 398.4 VIL

238 **VREDENBURG, EDRIC** *(Editor).*
FAVOURITE Fairy Tales. Edited by EDRIC VREDENBURG. Illustrated by M. BOWLEY, S. JACOBS, E.J. ANDREWS, etc. etc. LONDON: RAPHAEL TUCK AND SONS LTD., (192–?). Unpaginated: col. front., vignette title page, ill. some col. Bound in red cloth, with coloured paper pictorial cover. Father Tuck's GOLDEN GIFT Series.
YSCQ 398.21 VRE

239 **VREDENBURG, EDRIC** *(Editor).*
Sunny Stories. Stories by M.A. HOYER, MARGERY WILLIAMS, ETC. ETC. Illustrated by T. NOYES LEWIS, HILDA COWHAM, M.F. TAYLOR, ETC. ETC. EDITED BY EDRIC VREDENBURG. LONDON: RAPHAEL TUCK AND SONS LTD., (1905). 72p.: col. front., ill. some col. Bound in red cloth, with coloured pictorial paper cover. Father Tuck's "GOLDEN GIFT" Series.
YOSC 823.91208 HOY

240 **WADDELL, HELEN** *(Translator).*
BEASTS AND SAINTS. TRANSLATIONS BY HELEN WADDELL. WOODCUTS BY ROBERT GIBBINGS. LONDON: CONSTABLE AND COMPANY LTD., 1934. XX, 151p.: front., pictorial title page, 5 plates, ill. Bound in red cloth with pictorial cover.
CBD 398.245 WAD

241 **WEDGWOOD, HENRY ALLEN.**
THE BIRD TALISMAN, AN EASTERN TALE by HENRY ALLEN WEDGWOOD. Illustrated by GWEN RAVERAT. LONDON: FABER AND FABER, LIMITED, 1939. VII, 70p.: col. front., 7 col. plates, ill., headpieces to chapters, decorative endpapers. Bound in pink cloth, with coloured pictorial dust jacket.
CBD 823.912 WED

242 **WESTALL, W.**
TALES AND LEGENDS OF SAXONY AND LUSATIA. BY W. WESTALL WITH ILLUSTRATIONS BY H.W. PETHERICK. LONDON: GRIFFITH AND FARRAN, 1877. 311p. +32p. pub. cat.: 4 plates. Bound in blue cloth with embossed decorative covers and spine.
C 398.210943 WES

243 **WESTERMAN, J.M. ELMENHORST.**
FAIRY TALES FROM WONDERLAND. BY J.M. ELMENHORST WESTERMAN. Illustrated by John Hassall R.I. LONDON: BLACKIE AND SON LIMITED, (193–?). 160p.: col. front., vignette on title page, 2 col. plates, 14 plates, ill. Bound in orange cloth with decorative cover and spine.
C 827.912 WES

244 **WHITEHORN, ALAN LESLIE.**
WONDER TALES OF OLD JAPAN, by ALAN LESLIE WHITEHORN. Illustrated by SHOZAN OBATA. LONDON: T.C. AND E.C. JACK, 1911. XI, 173p.: col. front., decorated title page, 8 col. plates. Bound in beige cloth, with coloured pictorial label on cover and embossed decorative cover and spine. Contains 21 stories.
C 823.912 WHI

245 **WILDE, OSCAR.**
The Happy Prince And Other Tales BY OSCAR WILDE. ILLUSTRATED BY WALTER CRANE AND JACOMB HOOD. SIXTH IMPRESSION. LONDON: DAVID NUTT, 1908. 116p.: front., 2 col. title page, 2 plates, headpieces, tailpieces. Bound in cream paper with coloured decorative cover. Originally published in 1888.
CBD 823.8 WIL

246 **WILDE, OSCAR.**
A HOUSE OF POMEGRANATES. BY OSCAR WILDE. WITH SIXTEEN ILLUSTRATIONS BY JESSIE M. KING. LONDON: METHUEN AND COY, LTD., 6th edition, 1915. VI, 162p.: col. decorative title page, 15 col. plates, decorative initials. Bound in blue cloth with decorative covers and spine. Originally published 1891.
CBD 398.4 WIL

247 **WILDE, OSCAR.**
A HOUSE OF POMEGRANATES, BY OSCAR WILDE. LONDON: METHUEN AND CO. LTD., NINTH EDITION, 1920. 179p. Rebound in red cloth.
YSC 398.4 WIL

248 **WILSON, ROMER** *(Editor).*
GREEN MAGIC. A COLLECTION OF THE WORLD'S BEST FAIRY TALES FROM ALL COUNTRIES EDITED AND ARRANGED By ROMER WILSON. WITH ILLUSTRATIONS IN COLOUR AND LINE BY VIOLET BRUNTON. LONDON: JONATHAN CAPE, 1928. 448p., 7 col. plates, 16 plates, ill. Bound in green cloth.
C 398.21 GRE

249 **WOODS, MARGARET L.**
"COME UNTO THESE YELLOW SANDS." BY MARGARET L. WOODS. ILLUSTRATED BY J. HANCOCK. LONDON: JOHN LANE, THE BODLEY HEAD, 1915. XIII, 234p. + 2p. pub. cat.: col. front., decorative title page, 15 col. plates, decorative endpapers. Bound in blue cloth, with pictorial/decorative cover and spine.
C 823.912 WOO

250 **WORTLEY, MARY STUART, COUNTESS OF LOVELACE.**
THE STORY OF ZELINDA AND THE MONSTER OR BEAUTY AND THE BEAST. RE-TOLD AFTER THE OLD ITALIAN VERSION AND DONE INTO PICTURES BY MARY STUART WORTLEY, COUNTESS OF LOVELACE. LONDON: J.M. DENT AND CO., 1895. 26p.: sepia front., col. decorative title page, 9 sepia plates. Bound in green-grey cloth with decorative endpapers, with coloured decorative cover.
CBD 398.210945 WOR

251 **YEATS, WILLIAM BUTLER** *(Editor).*
FAIRY AND FOLK TALES OF THE IRISH PEASANTRY: EDITED AND SELECTED BY W.B. YEATS. LONDON: WALTER SCOTT, (189–?). XVIII, 326p. + 16p. pub. cat. Bound in green cloth with decorative cover. THE SCOTT LIBRARY.
C 398.209415 FAI

# 4 POETRY, VERSES, RHYMES AND DRAMA

251A **ADCOCK, MARION ST. JOHN.**
THE LITTLEST ONE, BY MARION ST. JOHN ADCOCK (MRS SIDNEY H. WEBB) ILLUSTRATED BY MARGARET W. TARRANT. LONDON: GEORGE G. HARRAP AND COMPANY, 1914. VI, 41p.: col. front., vignette on title page, 3 col. plates. Bound in grey cloth with coloured pictorial cover.
M 821.9 ADC CHILDREN'S COLLECTION

251B **AUNT LOUISA'S LONDON TOY BOOKS. JOHN GILPIN.**
LONDON: FREDERICK WARNE AND CO., (191–?). 6p. text, title on front cover. 6 col. plates printed by J.M. Kronheim. Bound in pink card with decorative cover.
M 821 COW CHILDREN'S COLLECTION

252 **BARTLETT, KATHLEEN.**
Round the Cherry Tree. By Kathleen Bartlett, N.F.U. LONDON: SIR ISAAC PITMAN AND SONS LTD., 1938. 62p. + 1p. pub. cat.: ill. Bound in blue cloth, with coloured decorative paper covers.
YSC 821 BAR

253 **BELL, JOHN JOY.**
The New Noah's Ark. (By) J.J. Bell. LONDON: JOHN LANE, THE BODLEY HEAD, 1899. 64p.: col. front., col. pictorial title page, 22 col. plates, col. ill. by the author. Bound in beige cloth, with coloured pictorial cover.
C 821.8 BEL

254 **BELLOC, JOSEPH HILAIRE PIERRE.**
THE BAD CHILD'S BOOK OF BEASTS. Verses by H. BELLOC. Pictures by B.T.B. LONDON: DUCKWORTH, 1923, reprinted 1966. 48p.: pictorial title page, ill. Bound in light blue cloth with pictorial cover.
YSC 821 BEL

255 **BELLOC, JOSEPH HILAIRE PIERRE.**
Cautionary Verses. THE COLLECTED HUMOROUS POEMS OF H. BELLOC. LONDON: DUCKWORTH, 1939, reprinted 1958. 190p.: pictorial title page. Bound in green with pictorial cover.
YSC 827 BEL

256 **(BELLOC, JOSEPH HILAIRE PIERRE).**
THE MODERN TRAVELLER. BY H.B. AND B.T.B. (Lord Ian Basil Gawaine Temple Blackwood). LONDON: EDWARD ARNOLD, 1898. 80p.: 2 plates, ill. Bound in cream cloth, with coloured pictorial paper cover.
YSC 821 BEL

256A **(BELLOC, JOSEPH HILAIRE PIERRE).**
MORE BEASTS FOR WORSE CHILDREN. VERSES BY H.B., PICTURES BY B.T.B. LONDON: EDWARD ARNOLD. 1897. 48p.: pictorial title page, ill. Bound in buff buckram with coloured pictorial paper cover.
M 823 EGI CHILDREN'S COLLECTION

257 **BLAKE, WILLIAM.**
SONGS OF INNOCENCE. (BY) WILLIAM BLAKE. ILLUSTRATED BY OLIVE ALLEN. LONDON: T.C. AND E.C. JACK, (190–?). 31p.: col. front., decorative title page, 3 col. plates. Bound in brown parchment covers, with coloured decorative cover, and coloured pictorial paper label on cover.
YSC 821 BLA

258 **BLATCHFORD, ROBERT.**
THE DOLLY BALLADS. by ROBERT BLATCHFORD. Illustrated by Frank Chesworth. LONDON: THE CLARION PRESS, 1911. 75p.: front., 1 plate, ill. Bound in green cloth, with pictorial/decorative cover.
C 821.9 BLA

259 **THE BOY'S BOOK OF BALLADS.**
ILLUSTRATED WITH SIXTEEN ENGRAVINGS ON WOOD FROM DRAWINGS BY JOHN GILBERT. LONDON: BELL AND DALDY, 1861. VII, 187p.: front., 16 plates. Bound in purple cloth with embossed decorative covers and spine, with gilt edges.
CBD 808.814 BOY

260 **BROWNING, ROBERT.**
The PIED PIPER of Hamelin. A CHILD'S STORY (WRITTEN FOR, AND INSCRIBED TO, W.M. THE YOUNGER), by ROBERT BROWNING. Illustrations by T.H. Robinson. LONDON: RAPHAEL TUCK AND SONS, LTD., (192–?). Unpaginated: pictorial title page, 11 col. plates, pictorial endpapers. Bound in buff card with coloured pictorial covers.
CBD 821.8 BRO

261 **Another copy.**
Illustrated by Margaret W. Tarrant. LONDON: J.M. DENT AND SONS, 1928, reprinted 1962. 41p.: col. front., 7 col. plates, ill. Bound in red cloth with pictorial cover.
YSC 821 BRO

262 **BROWNING, ROBERT.**
THE PIED PIPER OF HAMELIN BY ROBERT BROWNING. ILLUSTRATED BY KATE GREENAWAY. LONDON: FREDERICK WARNE AND CO., LTD. Facsimile reprint of 1888 ed. 48p.: col. front., col. vignette on title page, col. ill. Bound in green linson with coloured decorative covers.
CBD 821.8 BRO

263 **BROWNING, ROBERT.**
THE PIED PIPER OF HAMELIN (BY ROBERT BROWNING) AND THE JACKDAW OF RHEIMS (BY REV. R.H. BARHAM). Illustrated by BRINSLEY LE FANU. LONDON: STEAD'S PUBLISHING HOUSE, (191–?). 56p. + 8p. pub. cat.: 21 plates, ill. Bound in pink paper, with vignette on cover. BOOKS FOR THE BAIRNS, No. 87.
C 821.8 BRO

264 **BURKE, THOMAS** *(Editor)*.
CHILDREN IN VERSE. FIFTY SONGS OF PLAYFUL CHILDHOOD. COLLECTED AND EDITED BY THOMAS BURKE. WITH ILLUSTRATIONS IN COLOUR AND IN BLACK AND WHITE BY HONOR C. APPLETON. LONDON: DUCKWORTH AND COMPANY, 1913. XI, 135p.: col. front., 7 col. plates, ill., pictorial endpapers. Bound in blue cloth with embossed pictorial cover and spine.
CBD 808.81 CHI

265 **CALMOUR, ALFRED C.**
RUMBO RHYMES; OR THE GREAT COMBINE: A SATIRE; WRITTEN BY ALFRED C. CALMOUR. RENDERED INTO PICTURES BY WALTER CRANE. LONDON: HARPER AND BROTHERS, 1911. 99p.: col. pictorial title page, 21 col. plates, ill. Rebound in brown cloth.
CBD 821.912 CAL

266 **CARROLL, LEWIS.**
THE HUNTING OF THE SNARK, an Agony in Eight fits. BY LEWIS CARROLL. WITH NINE ILLUSTRATIONS BY HENRY HOLIDAY. LONDON: MACMILLAN AND CO. LIMITED, 1898. XI, 83p.: front., 8 plates. Bound in red cloth, with embossed pictorial/decorative covers and gilt edges. Originally published in 1876.
C 821.8 CAR
Another copy.
1910. XII, 83p. + 2p. pub. cat.: front., 8 plates. Bound in red cloth, with embossed vignette on cover.

267 **CARROLL, LEWIS.**
PHANTASMAGORIA AND OTHER POEMS. BY LEWIS CARROLL. WITH ILLUSTRATIONS BY ARTHUR B. FROST. LONDON: MACMILLAN AND CO. LIMITED, 1911. VIII, 166p. + 2p. pub. cat.: 30 plates, ill. Bound in red cloth. Originally published 1869.
YSC 821.8 CAR

268 **CHAUCER, GEOFFREY.**
CHAUCER: THE PROLOGUE TO THE CANTERBURY TALES. EDITED BY THE REV. WALTER W. SKEAT. LITT. D. THIRD AND REVISED EDITION. OXFORD: CLARENDON PRESS, 1924. 96p. Bound in brown paper. School edition. Originally published 1890.
YSC 821 CHA

269 **CHAUCER, GEOFFREY.**
Chaucer's Canterbury Tales: The Nun's Priest's Tale. EDITED WITH INTRODUCTION AND NOTES BY Alfred W. Pollard. LONDON: MACMILLAN AND CO. LIMITED, 1907. XXIX, 67p. + 4p. pub. cat. Bound in red cloth, with embossed decorative cover.
YSC 821 CHA

270 **THE CHILDREN'S POETRY BOOK.**
BEING A Selection of Narrative Poetry FOR THE YOUNG. WITH SEVENTY ILLUSTRATIONS BY THOMAS DALZIEL, ENGRAVED BY THE BROTHERS DALZIEL. LONDON: GEORGE ROUTLEDGE AND SONS, 1868. VIII, 432p. + 8p. pub. cat.: ill. Bound in red cloth, with embossed decorative covers and spine.
C 821.008 CHI

270A **CHISHOLM, LOUEY** *(Editor)*.
THE GOLDEN STAIRCASE.
(Vol. 1) POETRY FOR THE Four, Five and Six Year Old.
(Vol. 2) POETRY FOR THE Six, Seven and Eight Year Old.
(Vol. 3) POETRY FOR THE Nine, Ten and Eleven Year Old.
(Vol. 4) POETRY FOR THE Eleven and Twelve Year Old.
With PICTURES BY M. DIBDIN SPOONER. LONDON: T.C. AND E.C. JACK (1906), 73p. 88p., 104p., 92p.: col. fronts., col. plates. First 2 vols. rebound, Vol. 3 and 4 bound in brown paper with pictorial paper label on cover.
M 821.008 CHI CHILDREN'S COLLECTION

271 **COLLINS, V.H.** *(Editor).*
THE NARRATIVE MUSE. Compiled by V.H. COLLINS AND H.A. TREBLE. PART I. 143p. + 2p. pub. cat., PART II. 191p. + 2p. pub. cat. OXFORD: CLARENDON PRESS, 1938. Bound in green cloth.
YSC 821 COL

272 **(CORNWELL, JAMES).**
(POETRY FOR BEGINNERS). (BY DR. CORNWELL). (LONDON: SIMPKIN AND CO., Second edition, (188–?)). Title page missing. 144p. Bound in brown cloth, with decorative cover.
YSC 821 COR

273 **COUSINS, MARY** *(Editor).*
INVITATION to the PLAY – 1. An Introduction to the Drama for Young Children. COMPILED BY MARY COUSINS. LONDON: THOMAS NELSON AND SONS, LTD. 1934. 96p. Bound in cream card with decorative covers.
YSC 822 COU

273A **COWPER, WILLIAM.**
THE DIVERTING HISTORY OF JOHN GILPIN. BY WILLIAM COWPER. ILLUSTRATED BY CHAS. E. BROCK. LONDON: ALDINE HOUSE, 1898. 50p.: front., decorative title page in red and sepia, 11 plates, ill. Bound in blue cloth with decorative cover and spine.
CBD 821.6 COW

273B **THE DANDIES' BALL; OR, HIGH LIFE IN THE CITY.**
Embellished with Sixteen Coloured Engravings. MANCHESTER: SHERRATT AND HUGHES, 1902. Unpaginated: col. front., col. vignette on title page, col. ill. Rebound in red cloth over original green card binding.
C 821.07 DAN

274 **DE LA MARE, WALTER.**
COME HITHER. A Collection of Rhymes and Poems for the Young of all Ages. MADE BY WALTER DE LA MARE. LONDON: CONSTABLE AND CO. LTD., 1928. XXXVIII, 824p. Bound in maroon cloth with gilt top.
C 821.912 DEL
Another copy.
Rebound in red cloth, with white spotted covers and spine.
YSC 821 DEL

275 **DE LA MARE, WALTER**
DOWN-ADOWN-DERRY. A Book of Fairy Poems by WALTER DE LA MARE with illustrations by Dorothy P. Lathrop. LONDON: CONSTABLE AND CO., LTD., (1922). VIII, 193p.: col. front., decorative title page, 2 col. plates, 32 plates, ill. Bound in black cloth with decorative cover.
CBD 821.912 DEL

276 **DE LA MARE, WALTER.**
PEACOCK PIE. A Book of Rhymes by WALTER DE LA MARE with illustrations by W. HEATH ROBINSON. LONDON: CONSTABLE AND CO., LTD., (190–?). VIII, 179p.: col. front., pictorial title page, 25 plates, ill. Bound in green cloth with pictorial cover.
CBD 821.912 DEL

277 **Another copy.**
LONDON: CONSTABLE AND COMPANY LTD., 1913. VIII, 122p. Bound in blue cloth.
C 821.912 DEL

278 **Another copy.**
WITH EMBELLISHMENTS BY C. LOVAT FRASER. LONDON: CONSTABLE AND COMPANY LTD., 1924. IX, 128p.: col. front., 15 col. plates. Bound in blue cloth with decorative cover.
CBD 821.912 DEL

279 **DE LA MARE, WALTER.**
SONGS OF CHILDHOOD. By WALTER DE LA MARE. WITH ILLUSTRATIONS BY ESTELLA CANZIANI. NEW EDITION. LONDON: LONGMANS, GREEN AND CO., 1923. XIII, 173p.: col. front., 7 col. plates, 7 plates, ill. Bound in blue cloth, with vignette on cover and spine.
C 821.912 DEL

280 **DOUGLAS, LORD ALFRED BRUCE.**
TAILS WITH A TWIST. THE VERSES BY "BELGIAN HARE" (pseud. for Lord Alfred Bruce Douglas). THE PICTURES BY E.T. REED. LONDON: EDWARD ARNOLD, (189–?). 72p.: 20 col. plates. Bound in cream cloth, with coloured pictorial cover.
C 821.912 DOU

281 **DRINKWATER, JOHN.**
ALL ABOUT ME: Poems for a Child, by JOHN DRINKWATER. Decorated with Illustrations by H.M. BROCK. LONDON: W. COLLINS SONS AND CO. LTD., 1928. 103p.: vignette front., pictorial title page, 9 plates, ill., pictorial endpapers. Bound in orange cloth, with pictorial dust jacket.
C 821.912 DRI

282 **DRINKWATER, JOHN.**
Modern Short Plays, FIRST SERIES. By JOHN DRINKWATER, SIR WALTER RALEIGH, LADY GREGORY, LAURENCE BINYON, "SAKI" (H.H. MUNRO), EDEN PHILLPOTTS, LORD DUNSANY. NEW IMPRESSION. LONDON: UNIVERSITY OF LONDON PRESS, LTD., 1936. 160p. Bound in blue cloth.
YSC 822 DRI

283 **EDGAR, MARRIOTT**
ALBERT AND BALBUS AND SAMUEL SMALL WRITTEN AND PERFORMED BY MARRIOTT EDGAR ("SAM'S MEDAL" BY MABEL CONSTANDUROS AND MICHAEL HOGAN) WITH 42 CHARACTER ILLUSTRATIONS BY JOHN HASSALL. LONDON: FRANCIS, DAY AND HUNTER, LTD., (193–?). 32p.: col. pictorial title page on cover, 5 col. plates, col. ill. Bound in green paper.
CBD 821.912 EDG

284 **EDGAR, MARRIOTT.**
ALBERT, 'AROLD AND OTHERS. COMPILED AND WRITTEN BY MARRIOTT EDGAR. PERFORMED BY STANLEY HOLLOWAY AND MARRIOTT EDGAR. WITH 46 CHARACTER ILLUSTRATIONS BY JOHN HASSALL. LONDON: FRANCIS, DAY AND HUNTER LTD., (193–?). 32p.: 5 plates, ill. Bound in mustard paper, with coloured pictorial label on cover.
C 821.912 EDG

285 **EDGAR, MARRIOTT**
NORMANS AND SAXONS AND SUCH. SOME ANCIENT HISTORY BY MARRIOTT EDGAR. WITH 45 CHARACTER ILLUSTRATIONS BY JOHN HASSALL. LONDON: FRANCIS, DAY AND HUNTER, LTD., (193–?). 32p.: col. pictorial title page on cover, 4 col. plates, col. ill. Bound in buff card.
CBD 821.912 EDG

285A **EDWARDS, M. BETHAM.**
LITTLE BIRD RED AND LITTLE BIRD BLUE, A TALE OF THE WOODS. ILLUSTRATED BY T. R. MACQUOID. LONDON: GEORGE ROUTLEDGE AND SONS, (1883), 48p.: col. front., col. decorative title page, ill. some col. Bound in brown cloth with coloured decorative paper cover.
M 821 EDW CHILDREN'S COLLECTION

286 **(ENGLISH ASSOCIATION).**
Poems of To-Day: an Anthology. LONDON: SIDGWICK AND JACKSON FOR THE ENGLISH ASSOCIATION. XXXII, 174p. + 2p. pub. cat. Rebound in blue cloth.
YSC 821 ENG

287 **EWING, JULIANA HORATIA.**
VERSES FOR CHILDREN, AND SONGS FOR MUSIC. BY JULIANA HORATIA EWING. LONDON: SOCIETY FOR PROMOTING CHRISTIAN KNOWLEDGE, (189–?). 202p. + 2p. pub. cat.: front., 2 plates, ill. Bound in brown cloth, with coloured decorative cover and gilt top.
C 821.8 EWI

288 **FARJEON, ELEANOR.**
ALL THE YEAR ROUND. By ELEANOR FARJEON. LONDON: W. COLLINS SONS AND CO. LTD., 1923. 95p. Bound in green cloth.
C 821.914 FAR

289 **FARJEON, ELEANOR.**
COME CHRISTMAS. By ELEANOR FARJEON. Decorated with Wood-Cuts by MOLLY McARTHUR. LONDON: W. COLLINS SONS AND CO. LTD., 1927. 71p.: decorative title page, ill. Bound in cream cloth, with coloured decorative covers.
C 821.912 FAR

289A **FARJEON, ELEANOR.**
Over the Garden Wall. By Eleanor Farjeon; with drawings by Gwendolen Raverat. LONDON: FABER AND FABER, LIMITED, 1933. 153p.: vignette on title page, ill. Bound in grey cloth.
M 821 FAR CHILDREN'S COLLECTION

290 **FIELD, EUGENE.**
LULLABY LAND. Songs of Childhood by EUGENE FIELD. Selected by KENNETH GRAHAME . . . and illustrated by CHARLES ROBINSON. LONDON: JOHN LANE THE BODLEY HEAD, 1898. 229p. + 12p. ill. pub. cat.: front., decorative title page, ill. Bound in green cloth with decorative cover and spine, with gilt edges.
CBD 811.4 FIE

291 **FRENCH COMEDIES FOR GIRLS.**
WITH QUESTIONS AND EXERCISES. LONDON: THOMAS NELSON AND SONS, LTD., 1930. 171p. Bound in orange cloth. NELSON'S "MODERN STUDIES" SERIES.
YSC 842 PRA

292 **FYLEMAN, ROSE.**
THE FAIRY FLUTE. BY ROSE FYLEMAN. SECOND EDITION. LONDON: METHUEN AND CO. LTD., 1922. 61p. Bound in green cloth, with embossed decorative cover.
C 821.912 FYL

293 **FYLEMAN, ROSE.**
THE FAIRY GREEN. BY ROSE FYLEMAN. SIXTH EDITION. LONDON: METHUEN AND CO. LTD., 1921. 63p. Bound in pink cloth, with embossed decorative cover.
C 821.912 FYL

294 **FYLEMAN, ROSE.**
JOY STREET POEMS. By ROSE FYLEMAN, MARIAN ALLEN, EDITH SITWELL, ETC. Illustrated by various Artists. OXFORD: BASIL BLACKWELL, (192–?). 27p.: 4 plates by K.M. Gibbs, 3 plates, ill., by Alec Buckels. Bound in grey paper, with coloured pictorial paper label on cover.
YSC 821 FYL

294A **GALE, NORMAN.**
SONGS FOR LITTLE PEOPLE. BY NORMAN GALE. (ILLUSTRATED BY HELEN STRATTON). LONDON: ARCHIBALD CONSTABLE AND COMPANY, 1896. VIII, 110p. + 1p. pub. advert.: col. decorative title page, 8 plates, ill., decorative head and tail pieces. Bound in orange cloth with decorative cover and spine.
M 821.8 GAL

295 **GILBERT, WILLIAM SCHWENCK.**
THE "BAB" BALLADS. Much Sound and Little Sense. BY W.S. GILBERT. WITH ILLUSTRATIONS BY THE AUTHOR. LONDON: GEORGE ROUTLEDGE AND SONS, (187–?).222p. + 4p. pub. cat.: front., vignette on title page, ill. Bound in green cloth and decorative cover, with gilt edges.
CBD 821.07 GIL

296 **GILBERT, WILLIAM SCHWENCK.**
FIFTY "BAB" BALLADS. Much Sound and Little Sense. BY W.S. GILBERT. WITH ILLUSTRATIONS BY THE AUTHOR. LONDON: GEORGE ROUTLEDGE AND SONS, 1878. 255p.: front., vignette title page, ill. Bound in brown cloth, with embossed decorative cover and spine and gilt edges.
YSC 821.07 GIL
Another copy.
Bound in green.
CBD 821.07 GIL
Another copy.
Bound in blue.
CBD 821.8 GIL

297 **GOWANS, ADAM L.** *(Editor)*.
A TREASURY OF ENGLISH VERSE. SELECTED BY ADAM L. GOWANS. ILLUSTRATED BY STEPHEN REID. LONDON: GOWANS AND GRAY LTD., 1907. XIV, 303p.: front., decorative title page, 49 plates, ill., decorative endpapers. Bound in green cloth, with pictorial cover and decorative spine.
C 821.008 TRE

298 **HAITE, GEORGE C.** *(Editor)*.
SEVEN OF US. ILLUSTRATED BY FANNIE MOODY, CHRISTINE AND GERTRUDE DEMAIN HAMMOND. EXPLANATORY VERSES BY ROWE LINGSTON. EDITED BY GEO. C. HAITE, F.L.S. LONDON: GRIFFITH, FARRAN AND CO., 1888. 32p.: vignette front., decorative title page, 10 plates, ill. Bound in yellow. With coloured pictorial covers. ST. PAULS SERIES.
CP 821.8 SEV

299 **HARRISON, ADA.**
LUCY'S VILLAGE, A Story for a little Girl. By Ada Harrison and Robert Austin. LONDON: OXFORD UNIVERSITY PRESS, (193–?). Unpaginated: col. front., vignette title page, 8 col. plates by Robert Austin. Bound in cream paper, with coloured pictorial dust jacket.
C 821.912 HAR

299A **HASSALL, JOHN** *(Illustrator)*.
JOHN GILPIN AND OTHER NURSERY RHYMES. Illustrated by JOHN HASSALL. LONDON: BLACKIE AND SON LIMITED (191–?). Unpaginated: col. front., vignette on title page, 1 double col. plate, 1 col. plate, ill. Bound in grey card with coloured pictorial cover. Book in fact only includes John Gilpin.
M 821 HAS CHILDREN'S COLLECTION

299B **HASSALL, JOHN** *(Illustrator)*.
LITTLE BOY BLUE AND OTHER NURSERY RHYMES. Illustrated by JOHN HASSALL. LONDON: BLACKIE AND SON LIMITED, (191–?). Unpaginated. Col. front., vignette on title page, 1 double col. plate, 1 col. plate, ill. Bound in grey card with coloured pictorial cover.
M 398.8 HAS CHILDREN'S COLLECTION

300 **HAWEIS, MARY ELIZA JOY.**
CHAUCER FOR CHILDREN, A Golden Key. BY MRS. H.R. HAWEIS. ILLUSTRATED WITH EIGHT COLOURED PICTURES AND NUMEROUS WOODCUTS BY THE AUTHOR. Third Edition, Revised. LONDON: CHATTO AND WINDUS, 1895. XVI, 112p.: col. front., pictorial title page, 7 col. plates, map, ill. Bound in blue cloth with embossed pictorial cover and spine.
C 821.1 HAW

300A **HENDRY, HAMISH.**
RED APPLE AND SILVER BELLS. A BOOK OF VERSE FOR CHILDREN OF ALL AGES BY HAMISH HENDRY. ILLUSTRATED BY ALICE B. WOODWARD. LONDON: BLACKIE AND SON LIMITED, (1897). 152p.: col. front., col. decorative title page, 20 plates, ill. Bound in green cloth with coloured pictorial cover and spine, with gilt edges.
M 821.8 HEN CHILDREN'S COLLECTION.

301 **HYETT, FLORENCE B.** *(Editor)*.
FIFTY LONDON RHYMES FOR CHILDREN. CHOSEN BY FLORENCE B. HYETT. OXFORD: BASIL BLACKWELL, (192–?). 64p. Bound in orange cloth, with pictorial paper label by C.T. Nightingale, on cover.
YSC 821 HYE

302 **JERROLD, WALTER.**
Nonsense, Nonsense! Written by Walter Jerrold and Pictured by Chas. Robinson. LONDON: BLACKIE AND SON LTD., 1902. Unpaginated: col. front., decorative title page, 30 col. plates, col. ill. Bound in brown cloth, with coloured pictorial covers.
C 821.07 JER

303 **KING, E.L.M.**
Fifty Country Rhymes for Children. (By) E.L.M. King. OXFORD: BASIL BLACKWELL, (192–?). 54p. Bound in green cloth, with pictorial paper label by C.T. Nightingale on cover.
YSC 821 KIN

303A **KONSTAM, GERTRUDE A.**
Dreams, dances and disappointments, by G.A. KONSTAM, E. CASELLA AND N. CASELLA. LONDON: THOS DE LA RUE AND CO., (1881). 32p.: ill. pictorial/decorative title page on cover, col. front., 11 col. plates, 4 plates, ill. Bound in cream paper.
CP 821.808 CON

304 **LACKOWITZ, WILHELM.**
Die Sommerreise. Ein komisches Heldengedicht für artige Kinder. Von W. Lackowitz. Mit zwanzig in Farben schön gemalten Bildern von Fedor Flinzer. GERMANY, LEIPZIG: VERLAG VON GUSTAV GERMANN. Unpaginated: col. front., col. ill. Bound in red cloth, with coloured pictorial cover.
C 831.8 LAC

305 **LAMB, CHARLES**
Beauty and The Beast BY CHARLES LAMB, WITH AN INTRODUCTION BY ANDREW LANG. LONDON: FIELD AND TUER, (1887). XXIV, 42p. + 2p. pub. cat.: front., 7 plates, musical score. Bound in black paper.
CBD 398.21 LAM

306 **LANG, ANDREW** *(Editor)*.
THE BLUE POETRY BOOK. EDITED BY ANDREW LANG. WITH NUMEROUS ILLUSTRATIONS BY H.J. FORD AND LANCELOT SPEED. LONDON: LONGMANS, GREEN, AND CO., 1891. XX, 351p.: front., vignette title page, 11 plates, ill. Bound in blue cloth, with embossed pictorial cover and spine and gilt edges.
C 821.008 BLU

307 **LEAR, EDWARD.**
A BOOK OF NONSENSE. BY EDWARD LEAR. LONDON: FREDERICK WARNE AND CO., (187–?). Unpaginated: col. pictorial title page, col. ill. by the author. Bound in brown cloth, with embossed pictorial/decorative cover. Originally published in 1846.
C 821.07 LEA

308 **LEAR, EDWARD.**
EDWARD LEAR'S Miniature Books, Containing 5 well-known Rhymes. LONDON: FREDERICK WARNE AND CO. LTD., (191–?). Box with coloured pictorial paper covered lid contains 5 booklets: CALICO PIE, THE DUCK AND THE KANGAROO, and THE OWL AND THE PUSSY CAT, with the original illustrations by the Author; and The Jumblies and The Pelican Chorus, with Illustrations by L. LESLIE BROOKE.
C 821.8 LEA

308A **LEAR, EDWARD.**
MORE NONSENSE. BY EDWARD LEAR. LONDON: FREDERICK WARNE AND CO, 1900. 109p. + 3p. pub. cat.: vignette on title page, ill. Bound in brown cloth with embossed decorative cover.
M 821.8 LEA CHILDREN'S COLLECTION

309 **LUCAS, EDWARD VERRALL.**
Another Book of Verses for Children. Edited by E.V. Lucas. Illustrations by F.D. Bedford. London: Wells, Gardner Darton and Co. Ltd. (1907). XIX, 431, 24p. ill. pub. cat.: col. front., col. pictorial title page, 18 plates, ill. Bound in cream buckram with gilded and coloured pictorial cover and gilt top. Decorative endpapers and bookjacket by F.D. Bedford.
C 821.008 LUC

310 **LUCAS, EDWARD VERRALL.**
A BOOK OF VERSES FOR CHILDREN, COMPILED BY EDWARD VERRALL LUCAS. LONDON: CHATTO AND WINDUS, 1926. XII, 348p.: col. pictorial title page, 7 col. plates, some by George Edward Collins 1909 and 1910. Bound in red cloth with pictorial cover.
CBD 821.008 LUC

311 **LUCAS, EDWARD VERRALL.**
PLAYTIME AND COMPANY, A BOOK FOR CHILDREN. VERSES BY E.V. LUCAS. PICTURES BY E.H. SHEPARD. SECOND EDITION. LONDON: METHUEN AND CO. LTD., 1925. 95p.: front., ill., decorative endpapers. Bound in pink cloth, with coloured pictorial cover.
C 821.912 LUC

312 **MACK, LIZZIE (LAWSON).**
Christmas Roses. By Lizzie Lawson and Robert Ellice Mack. LONDON: GRIFFITH FARRAN AND COMPANY, (188–?). 31p.: col. front., pictorial title page, 9 col. plates, ill. Bound in blue cloth, with coloured pictorial covers.
C 821.8 MAC

313 **MACKINSTRY, ELIZABETH.**
PUCK IN PASTURE. VERSE AND DECORATIONS BY ELIZABETH MACKINSTRY. LONDON: WILLIAM HEINEMANN LTD., 1926. VIII, 79p.: decorative title page, 10 plates, ill., decorative endpapers. Bound in black cloth, with coloured decorative covers.
C 821.912 MAC

314 **MAETERLINCK, MAURICE.**
THE BLUE BIRD. A FAIRY PLAY IN SIX ACTS. BY ALEXANDER TEIXEIRA DE MATTOS. FIFTY-NINTH EDITION. LONDON: METHUEN AND CO. LTD., 1934. 285p. Bound in blue cloth.
YSC 842 MAE

315 **Another copy.**
1928. WITH SIXTEEN ILLUSTRATIONS IN COLOUR BY F. CALEY ROBINSON.

316 **MASON, J.E.**
THE FIRST BOOK OF SENIOR PLAYS. Selected by J.E. MASON, M.A. With introduction and notes. Glasgow: Collins Clear-Type Press, 1935. 224p. Bound in green cloth. The Laurel and Gold Series.
YSC 822 MAS

317 **MILNE, ALAN ALEXANDER.**
THE CHRISTOPHER ROBIN VERSES, BEING "WHEN WE WERE VERY YOUNG" AND "NOW WE ARE SIX". WITH A PREFACE FOR PARENTS. BY A.A. MILNE. WITH TWELVE PLATES IN COLOUR AND TEXT DECORATIONS BY ERNEST H. SHEPARD. LONDON: METHUEN AND CO. LTD., 1949. XI, 210p.: col. front., 11 col. plates, ill. Bound in orange cloth, with vignette and decorative border on cover. Reprint of original 1932 edition.
C 821.912 MIL

318 **MILNE, ALAN ALEXANDER.**
NOW WE ARE SIX. BY A.A. MILNE. WITH DECORATIONS BY ERNEST H. SHEPARD. LONDON: METHUEN AND CO. LTD., 1927. Second Edition. X, 103p.: vignette title page, 7 plates, ill., pictorial endpapers. Bound in maroon cloth, with embossed vignette on covers, and gilt top.
C 821.912 MIL
Another copy.
1934. X, 103p.: vignette title page, 7 plates, ill. Bound in blue cloth, with blue pictorial dust jacket.

319 **MILNE, ALAN ALEXANDER.**
VERY YOUNG VERSES. BY A.A. MILNE. WITH 73 ILLUSTRATIONS BY E.H. SHEPARD. LONDON:

METHUEN AND CO. LTD., 1929. VIII, 88p.: 6 plates, ill. Bound in blue cloth, with embossed decorative cover.
C 821.912 MIL

320 **MILNE, ALAN ALEXANDER.**
When we were very young, with decorations by E.H. Shepard. METHUEN AND CO. LTD., 1924. X, 99p.: vignette front., vignette title page, ill. Bound in blue cloth, with embossed vignettes on covers and gilt top.
C 821.912 MIL

321 **Another copy.**
LONDON: METHUEN CHILDREN'S BOOKS, 1924, reprinted 1972. XII, 100p.: ill. Bound in blue linson with pictorial endpapers, and coloured pictorial paper jacket.
YSC 821 MIL

321A **MONSELL, JOHN ROBERT.**
THE HOODED CROW. Written and illustrated by J.R. MONSELL. OXFORD: BASIL BLACKWELL, (1926). Unpaginated: col. pictorial title page, col. ill. Bound in yellow cloth with coloured pictorial cover.
M 821 MON CHILDREN'S COLLECTION

322 **MOORHOUSE, REED** *(Editor).*
THE IVORY GATE: A BOOK OF VERSES FOR CHILDREN ARRANGED FOR SCHOOL USE BY REED MOORHOUSE. IN FOUR PARTS. FIRST PART. LONDON: J.M. DENT AND SONS LTD., (190–?). VI, 121p. front., ill. Bound in red cloth, with decorative cover.
YSC 821 MOO

322A **NEWBOLT, SIR HENRY JOHN.**
DRAKE'S DRUM AND OTHER SONGS OF THE SEA. By HENRY NEWBOLT. With illustrations in Colour by A.D. McCormick, R.I. LONDON: HODDER AND STOUGHTON, (1914). 144p. col. front., 11 col. plates. Bound in green cloth with coloured decorative cover, with decorative endpapers.
M 821.89 NEW CHILDREN'S COLLECTION

322B **'NORMAN'. A BOOK OF ELFIN RHYMES.**
BY 'NORMAN'. WITH 40 DRAWINGS IN COLOUR BY CARTON MOORE PARK. LONDON: GAY AND BIRD, 1900. Unpaginated: col. vignette on title page, 40 col. plates. Bound in red cloth.
M 821.8 NOR CHILDREN'S COLLECTION

322C **NORTON, MRS.**
AUNT CARRY'S BALLADS FOR CHILDREN. BY THE HONOURABLE MRS NORTON. ADVENTURES OF A WOOD SPRITE. THE STORY OF BLANCHE AND BRUTHIN WITH ILLUSTRATIONS BY JOHN ABSOLON. LONDON: JOSEPH CUNDALL, 1847. 53p.: col. front., 7 hand coloured lithographs printed in two colours. Bound in green cloth with embossed decorative covers.
C 821.8 NOR

322D **MURRAY, THOMAS BOYLES.**
AN ALPHABET OF EMBLEMS. BY THE REV. THOMAS BOYLES MURRAY, MA. LONDON: FRANCIS AND JOHN RIVINGTON, 1847. 72p.: ill. Bound in red cloth with vignette on cover.
M 821 MUR CHILDREN'S COLLECTION

323 **PALGRAVE, FRANCIS TURNER** *(Editor).*
THE GOLDEN TREASURY OF THE BEST SONGS AND LYRICAL POEMS IN THE ENGLISH LANGUAGE. SELECTED AND ARRANGED WITH NOTES BY FRANCIS TURNER PALGRAVE. LONDON: MACMILLAN AND CO., 1877. 332p. + 4p. pub. cat.: vignette title page. Bound in green cloth. Originally published 1861.
YSC 821 PAL

324 **PAYNE, JOSEPH.**
SELECT POETRY FOR CHILDREN: WITH BRIEF EXPLANATORY NOTES. ARRANGED FOR THE USE OF SCHOOLS AND FAMILIES BY JOSEPH PAYNE. NINTH EDITION. LONDON: ARTHUR HALL, VIRTUE AND CO., 1851. XII, 310p. + 2p. pub. cat.: front. by R. Westall, engraved by W. Findon. Half-bound in black leather.
C 821.708 SEL

325 **PAYNE, JOSEPH** *(Editor).*
STUDIES IN ENGLISH POETRY. WITH SHORT BIOGRAPHICAL SKETCHES AND NOTES. Intended as a Text-Book for the Higher Classes in Schools. BY JOSEPH PAYNE. SIXTH EDITION, REVISED AND CORRECTED. LONDON: LOCKWOOD AND CO., 1872. XII, 192p. Bound in maroon cloth. Originally published 1845.
YSC 821 PAY

326 **POCOCK, GUY N.** *(Editor).*
MODERN POETRY. EDITED BY GUY N. POCOCK, M.A. (LONDON: J.M. DENT AND SONS LTD., 1920). 160p.: front. (portrait), decorative title page. Bound in green cloth.
YSC 821 POC

327 **POPE, JESSIE.**
THE CAT SCOUTS, A PICTURE-BOOK FOR LITTLE FOLK. CATS BY LOUIS WAIN, VERSES AND TALES BY JESSIE POPE. LONDON: BLACKIE AND SON LIMITED, (191–?). Unpaginated: col. front., col. vignette title page, 5 col. plates, col. ill. Bound in blue cloth, with coloured pictorial label on cover.
C 821.912 POP

327A **RANDS, WILLIAM BRIGHTY.**
LILLIPUT LYRICS BY W.B. RANDS. ILLUSTRATED BY CHAS. ROBINSON. EDITED BY R. BRIMLEY JOHNSON. LONDON: JOHN LANE THE BODLEY HEAD, 1899. 330p.: col. front., col. pictorial title page, ill. Bound in buff cloth with coloured pictorial cover, with pictorial endpapers.
M 821.8 RAN CHILDREN'S COLLECTION

327B **RATCLIFFE, DOROTHY UNA.**
THE SHOEING OF JERRY-GO-NIMBLE AND OTHER DIALECT POEMS. BY DOROTHY UNA RATCLIFFE, F.R.G.S. WITH TWENTY PEN AND INK DRAWINGS. By FRED LAWSON. LONDON: JOHN LANE THE BODLEY HEAD LIMITED, 1926. (V), 67p.: front. 19 plates: Bound in green cloth.
M 821.08 RAT CHILDREN'S COLLECTION

327C **RHYS, GRACE** *(Editor).*
The CHILDREN'S GARLAND OF VERSE. GATHERED BY GRACE RHYS. With Eight Coloured Illustrations by CHARLES ROBINSON. LONDON: J.M. DENT AND SONS LTD., 1921. XXIII, 296p.: col. front., 7 col. plates. Bound in grey cloth with coloured decorative cover and spine.
C 821.008 RHY

328 **RILEY, JAMES WHITCOMB.**
RILEY CHILD-RHYMES. (BY) JAMES WHITCOMB RILEY. WITH HOOSIER PICTURES BY WILL VAWTER. U.S.A., INDIANAPOLIS: THE BOBBS-MERRILL COMPANY, 1905. 188p.: front., 35 plates, ill. Bound in green cloth, with embossed vignette on cover and spine.
C 811.4 RIL

329 **ROXBURGH, J.F.**
THE POETIC PROCESSION, A BEGINNER'S INTRODUCTION TO ENGLISH POETRY. BY J.F. ROXBURGH. OXFORD: BASIL BLACKWELL, Third Edition, 1930. VI, 90p. Bound in cream cloth. Originally published 1921.
YSC 821 ROX

329A **THE ROYAL PUNCH AND JUDY.**
AS PLAYED BEFORE THE QUEEN AT WINDSOR CASTLE AND THE CRYSTAL PALACE. LONDON: DEAN AND SON, (189–?). Unpaginated, col. pictorial pages with characters on a stage moved by tabs. Bound in blue cloth with coloured pictorial covers.
C 822.8 PUN

330 **SCOTT, SIR WALTER.**
THE LAY OF THE LAST MINSTREL. BY SIR WALTER SCOTT. WITH A SHORT BIOGRAPHY BY ANDREW LANG AND INTRODUCTION AND NOTES BY FRED. W. TICKNER, M.A. LONDON: LONGMANS, GREEN AND CO., 1905. XXII, 121p. Bound in orange cloth, with decorative cover. Longmans' Class-Books of English Literature.
YSC 821 SCO

331 **SHAIRP, A. MORDAUNT** *(Editor).*
MODERN PLAYS IN ONE ACT. FIRST SERIES. EDITED BY A. MORDAUNT SHAIRP, B.A. LONDON: J.M. DENT AND SONS LTD., 1929. 256p., front. Bound in blue cloth. The KINGS TREASURIES OF LITERATURE.
YSC 822 SHA

332 **SHAKESPEARE, WILLIAM.**
ANTONY AND CLEOPATRA. EDITED BY F. ALLEN, M.A. Third Symposium. LONDON: W.B. CLIVE, UNIVERSITY TUTORIAL PRESS LTD., 1926. XLIII, 214p. + 4p. pub. cat. Bound in blue cloth.
YSC 822.33 SHA

333 **SHAKESPEARE, WILLIAM.**
AS YOU LIKE IT WITH NOTES, INTRODUCTION AND GLOSSARY. EDITED BY FLORA MASSON. WITH SEVEN ILLUSTRATIONS AND COLOURED FRONTISPIECE BY DORA CURTIS. Also many illustrations in the introduction and glossary from contemporary prints. LONDON: J.M. DENT AND COMPANY, 1903. Text unpaginated, notes and glossary, XLV + 2p. pub. cat. Bound in green cloth with decorative cover.
YSC 822.33 SHA

334 **SHAKESPEARE, WILLIAM.**
A COMMENTARY AND QUESTIONNAIRE ON JULIUS CAESAR (SHAKESPEARE). BY J. MOODY, B.LITT., B.A. LONDON: SIR ISAAC PITMAN AND SONS, LTD., 1932. 32p. Bound in grey card.
YSC 822.33 MOO

335 **SHAKESPEARE, WILLIAM.**
JULIUS CAESAR. WITH AN INTRODUCTION AND NOTES. EDITED BY M.J.C. MEIKLEJOHN, B.A. LONDON: ALFRED M. HOLDEN, 1902. XIX, 136p. Bound in green cloth with decorative cover.
YSC 822.33 SHA

335A **SHAKESPEARE, WILLIAM.**
SHAKESPEARE'S HEROINES. CHARACTERISTICS OF WOMEN, MORAL, POETICAL AND HISTORICAL BY ANNA JAMESON WITH SIX COLOUR PLATES AND SEVENTY HALF TONE ILLUSTRATIONS BY W. PAGET. LONDON: ERNEST NISTER, (1904), 308p., col. front., 5 col. plates, ill. Bound in green cloth with coloured pictorial cover.
C822.33 SHA/JAM

335B **SHAKESPEARE, WILLIAM.**
SHAKESPEARE'S SONGS AND SONNETS. Illustrated by Sir John Gilbert. LONDON: SAMPSON, LOW, MARSTON, SEARLE AND RIVINGTON, LIMITED, (189–?). Unpaginated: vignette title page, ill., some col. Bound in green cloth with coloured pictorial paper covers. Miniature edition of work.
CBD 821.3 SHA and YSC 822.33H GIL

336 **SLATER, W.E.** *(Editor).*
HUMOUR IN VERSE; AN ANTHOLOGY. Compiled by W.E. SLATER. CAMBRIDGE: UNIVERSITY PRESS, 1937. XIII, 124p. Bound in green cloth.
YSC 821 SLA

336A **STEVENSON, BURTON EGBERT.**
THE HOME BOOK OF VERSE FOR YOUNG FOLKS. Selected and arranged by BURTON EGBERT STEVENSON. Decorations by WILLY POGANY. U.S.A. NEW YORK: HENRY HOLT AND COMPANY, 1915. XVIII, 538p.: col. decorative title page, each section preceded by pictorial title page, tailpiece. Bound in blue cloth with decorative cover and spine.
CBD 808.81 STE

337 **STEVENSON, ROBERT LOUIS.**
A CHILD'S GARDEN OF VERSES (BY) ROBERT LOUIS STEVENSON WITH ILLUSTRATIONS BY JESSIE WILLCOX SMITH. U.S.A., NEW YORK: CHARLES SCRIBNER'S SONS, 1905. XII, 125p.: col. pictorial title page, 12 col. plates, ill. Bound in black cloth with coloured pictorial paper cover. Originally published in 1885.
CBD 821.8 STE

338 **Another copy.**
ILLUSTRATED BY CHARLES ROBINSON. LONDON: JOHN LANE THE BODLEY HEAD, 1906. 137p. + 6p. pub. cat.: decorative title page, headpieces, tailpieces, ill. Bound in green cloth with decorative covers and spine.
CBD 821.8 STE
Another copy.
1909 with coloured pictorial end papers. Bound in green leather with pictorial cover.
Another copy.
1920. Bound in red cloth with pictorial cover and spine.

339 **STRANG, HERBERT** *(Pseud.) (Editor).*
TWO HUNDRED POEMS FOR BOYS AND GIRLS. SELECTED AND ARRANGED BY HERBERT STRANG (pseud. for GEORGE HERBERT ELY AND JAMES L'ESTRANGE). LONDON: OXFORD UNIVERSITY PRESS, 1929 reprint. XVI, 191p. Bound in cream cloth, with coloured pictorial cover.
YSC 821 STR

340 **SWINBURNE, ALGERNON CHARLES.**
THE SPRINGTIDE OF LIFE. POEMS OF CHILDHOOD, BY ALGERNON CHARLES SWINBURNE. WITH A PREFACE BY EDMUND GOSSE. ILLUSTRATED BY ARTHUR RACKHAM. LONDON: WILLIAM HEINEMANN, 1918. IX, 133p.: col. front., decorative title page, 7 col. plates, ill. Bound in green cloth with decorative cover.
CBD 821.8 SWI

341 **TAYLOR, ANN.**
THE "ORIGINAL POEMS" AND OTHERS. BY ANN AND JANE TAYLOR AND ADELAIDE O'KEEFFE. EDITED BY E.V. LUCAS. WITH ILLUSTRATIONS BY F.D. BEDFORD. LONDON: WELLS GARDNER, DARTON AND CO., 1905. XL, 414p.: col. front., col. pictorial title page, 39 plates. Bound in cream cloth, with coloured pictorial/decorative cover and spine, and gilt top. Originally published in 1804.
C 821.7 TAY

342 **TAYLOR, ANN.**
POEMS FOR CHILDREN. BY ANN AND JANE TAYLOR, AND ISAAC WATTS. LONDON: WARD, LOCK AND CO., (187–?). 64p. + 64p.: front., vignette title page, 6 plates, ill. Bound in blue cloth, with embossed decorative covers and spine.
YSC 821.7 TAY

342A **TAYLOR, JANE.**
LITTLE ANN AND OTHER POEMS. BY JANE AND ANN TAYLOR. Printed in colours by Edmund Evans. LONDON, FREDERICK WARNE AND CO., 64p.; vignette and front, decorative title page, col. ill. Bound in green cloth with coloured pictorial paper covers.
CBD 821.7 TAY

343 **TAYLOR, JANE.**
MEDDLESOME MATTY AND OTHER POEMS FOR INFANT MINDS BY JANE AND ANN(E) (sic) TAYLOR. With an introduction by Edith Sitwell. Illustrated by Wyndham Payne. LONDON: JOHN LANE AND THE BODLEY HEAD LIMITED, 1925. 54p.: col. vignette on title page, col. ill. Bound in buff buckram with coloured decorative paper covers. Printed by Cloister Press, Manchester.
C 821.7 TAY

POEMS FOR CHILDREN

BY

ANN AND JANE TAYLOR,

AND

ISAAC WATTS.

WARD, LOCK, AND CO.

LONDON: WARWICK HOUSE, SALISBURY SQUARE, E.C.

NEW YORK: BOND STREET.

342

344 **TENNYSON, ALFRED, LORD.**
The Marriage of Geraint, Geraint and Enid. By Alfred Lord Tennyson. WITH INTRODUCTION AND NOTES BY G.C. MACAULAY, M.A. LONDON: MACMILLAN AND CO. LTD., 1892. XLV, 125p. + 2p. pub. cat. Bound in red cloth, with embossed decorative cover.
YSC 821 TEN

345 **TENNYSON, ALFRED, LORD.**
TENNYSON FOR THE YOUNG. WITH INTRODUCTION AND NOTES BY ALFRED AINGER. LONDON: MACMILLAN AND CO. LIMITED, 1891. XIII, 120p. Bound in green cloth.
YSC 821 TEN

346 **THOMPSON, DARCY WENTWORTH.**
FUN AND EARNEST; OR, RHYMES WITH REASON. BY DARCY W. THOMPSON. ILLUSTRATED BY CHARLES H. BENNETT. LONDON: GRIFFITH AND FARRAN, 1865. 80p. + 32p. pub. cat.: col. front., vignette title page, 6 hand-coloured plates. Bound in green cloth, with embossed decorative cover and spine and gilt edge.
C 821.8 THO

347 **WAIN, LOUIS.**
Fun and frolic. By Louis Wain and Clifton Bingham. LONDON: ERNEST NISTER, (192–?). 144p.: col. front., pictorial title page, ill., many by Louis Wain. Bound in green cloth with coloured pictorial cover.
CBD 821.912 WAI

347A **WAUGH, IDA** *(Illustrator)*.
Holly Berries, with original illustrations by IDA WAUGH. LONDON: GRIFFITH AND FARRAN, (1881). Unpaginated, col. pictorial title page, col. ill. Bound in green cloth with coloured pictorial paper covers.
M 821 WAU CHILDREN'S COLLECTION

348 **WEATHERLY, FREDERIC EDWARD.**
The Maypole Dance. By Fred. E. Weatherly. Illustrated by Harriett M. Bennett. LONDON: C.W. FAULKNER, (189–?). Unpaginated: col. decorative title page, 6 col. plates. Bound in cream paper, with coloured pictorial cover.
YSC 821 WEA

349 **WEATHERLY, FREDERIC EDWARD.**
NURSERY LAND by FREDERIC E. WEATHERLY, ILLUSTRATED by HELENA J. MAGUIRE. LONDON: HILDESHEIM AND FAULKNER, (187–?). Unpaginated: col. front., col. pictorial title page. 7 col. plates, col. ill. Bound in brown cloth with coloured pictorial covers.
CBD 398.8 WEA

350 **WEATHERLY, FREDERIC EDWARD.**
SIXES AND SEVENS. Written by F.E. WEATHERLY. Illustrated by JANE M. DEALY. LONDON: HILDESHEIM AND FAULKNER, (188–?). 64p.: 2 col. fronts., decorative title page, 8 col. plates, col. ill. Bound in blue cloth with coloured pictorial paper covers.
CBD 811.4 WEA

350A **WEATHERLY, FREDERIC EDWARD.**
TENS AND ELEVENS. Written by F.E. WEATHERLY. Illustrated by JANE M. DEALY. USA, NEW YORK: E.P. DUTTON AND CO. (189–?). Unpaginated: col. front., pictorial title page, 6 col. plates, ill. Bound in green cloth and cream paper with coloured pictorial covers.
C 811.4 WEA

350B **WEBB, MARION ST. JOHN.**
THE HEATH FAIRIES. Verses by MARION ST. JOHN WEBB. Illustrations by MARGARET W. TARRANT. LONDON: MODERN ART SOCIETY LTD., 1927. 44p.: col. front., 5 col. plates, ill. Bound in beige paper with coloured pictorial paper label on cover.
C 821.912 WEB

351 **WILSON, RICHARD** *(Editor)*.
PATTERN POETRY. PART II. A Book of English Poems, Standard and Modern, with Helps to Contemplation and Mild Incitements to Emulation. Compiled by RICHARD WILSON. LONDON: THOMAS NELSON AND SONS LTD., 1926. 253p. + 3p. pub. cat.: front. portrait. Bound in blue cloth. The "Teaching of English" Series.
YSC 821 WIL

352 **WINGRAVE, MARION M.**
QUACKS, THE STORY OF THE UGLY DUCKLING. AFTER H.C. ANDERSEN. BY MARION M. WINGRAVE. LONDON: WARD, LOCK AND CO., (188–?). Unpaginated: col. decorative title page, 1 col. plate, col. ill. by the author, decorative endpapers. Bound in mustard cloth, with coloured pictorial/decorative label on cover.
C 821.8 WIN

353 **WOOD, ROBERT S.** *(Editor)*.
ILLUSTRATED RECITATIONS FROM THE SCHOOL AND THE HOME. With an Introduction for Teachers and Suggestions on Method. PART 1. Edited by ROBERT S. WOOD. LONDON: "BOOKS FOR THE BAIRNS" OFFICE, (189–?) 59p.: 8 plates, ill. by B. Le Fanu. Rebound in brown cloth. BOOKS FOR THE BAIRNS – No. 84.
YSC 821 WOO

## 5 NURSERY RHYMES AND ALPHABETS

353A **AFTERNOON TEA.**
RHYMES FOR CHILDREN WITH ORIGINAL ILLUSTRATIONS BY J.G. SOWERBY AND H.H. EMMERSON. LONDON: FREDERICK WARNE AND CO., (1880). 64p.: 19 col. plates, col. ill., decorative borders on title and other pages. Bound in green cloth with coloured pictorial cover.
C 398.8 AFT

353B **BIG BOOK OF NURSERY RHYMES.**
EDITED BY WALTER JERROLD. ILLUSTRATED BY CHARLES ROBINSON. LONDON: BLACKIE AND SON LTD., (193–?). 308p.: title page missing, col. front., 19 plates, some col., ill. Bound in red cloth with decorative spine.
C 398.9 BIG

354 **BLACKIE'S POPULAR NURSERY RHYMES.**
Illustrated by JOHN HASSALL. LONDON: BLACKIE AND SON LIMITED, (192–?). Unpaginated: vignette title page, 24 col. plates, 18 plates, ill. Bound in red cloth, with coloured pictorial paper cover.
C 398.8 BLA

354A **THE BOOK OF NURSERY RHYMES.**
Illustrated by Charles Robinson. LONDON: MINERVA PRESS LIMITED, facsimile of 1903 ed, 1975. 80p.: title page decorated in red, ill. Bound in brown buckram.
C 398.8 BOO

355 **A BOOK OF NURSERY RHYMES.**
Illustrated by ENID MARX. LONDON: CHATTO AND WINDUS, 1939. 64p.: ill. Bound in white paper with coloured pictorial covers and coloured pictorial paper dust jacket.
CBD 398.8 BOO

356 **A BOOK OF NURSERY RHYMES.**
ILLUSTRATED BY FRANCIS D. BEDFORD. LONDON: METHUEN AND CO., 1897. 91p.: col. front., col. decorative title page, 20 col. plates. Bound in green cloth, with coloured pictorial cover.
C 398.8 NUR

356A **A BOOK OF NURSERY SONGS AND RHYMES.**
EDITED BY B.S. BARING-GOULD: WITH ILLUSTRATIONS BY MEMBERS OF THE BIRMINGHAM ART SCHOOL UNDER THE DIRECTION OF A.J. GASKIN. LONDON: METHUEN AND COMPANY, 1895. XVI, 160p. front., vignette on decorative title page, ill., decorative borders to pages. Bound in black cloth with pictorial cover.
C 398.8 BOO

357 **CLODD, EDWARD.**
THE STORY OF THE ALPHABET. BY EDWARD CLODD. WITH NINETY ILLUSTRATIONS. LONDON: GEORGE NEWNES LTD., (191–?). 234p. + 2p. pub. cat.: front., ill. Bound in blue cloth.
YSC 411 CLO

358 **DARLOW, BIDDY** *(Illustrator).*
FIFTEEN Old Nursery Rhymes WITH NEW LINOCUTS By BIDDY DARLOW. BRISTOL: THE PERPETUA PRESS, edition limited to 150 copies, 1935. Unpaginated: coloured pictorial title page, 15 col. plates. Bound in grey and red buckram.
CBD 398.8 FIF

359 **FARJEON, ELEANOR.**
NURSERY RHYMES of LONDON TOWN. By Eleanor Farjeon. Illustrated by Macdonald Gill. LONDON: DUCKWORTH AND CO., 1916. 63p.: col. front., ill. Bound in blue cloth.
C 398.8 FAR

360 **FAVOURITE NURSERY RHYMES.**
LONDON: ERNEST NISTER, (188–?). Unpaginated: col. front., vignette title page, 3 plates, ill. Bound in brown cloth, with coloured pictorial paper cover.
C 398.8 FAV

361 **FRASER, CLAUD LOVAT** *(Illustrator).*
NURSERY RHYMES with pictures by C. LOVAT FRASER. LONDON: J.C. and E.C. JACK, (192–?). 46p.: coloured pictorial title page, col. ill., ill. Bound in grey cloth with coloured pictorial covers and grey dust jacket.
CBD 398.8 NUR

361A **FYLEMAN, ROSE.**
FIFTY-ONE NEW NURSERY RHYMES. BY ROSE FYLEMAN. ILLUSTRATED BY DOROTHY BURROUGHES. LONDON: METHUEN AND CO. LTD., 1931. IX, 100p.: 25 col. plates. Bound in purple cloth with cream paper coloured pictorial cover.
C 398.8 FYL

362 **GRANNIE'S LITTLE RHYME BOOK.**
No. 1 of OLD NURSERY RHYMES. Illustrated by H. Willebeek Le Mair. LONDON: AUGENER LTD., (192–?). Unpaginated: 12 col. plates. Bound in coloured decorative paper with circular coloured pictorial insert.
CBD 398.8 LEM

363 **GREENAWAY, KATE.**
A Apple Pie BY KATE GREENAWAY. ENGRAVED AND PRINTED BY EDMUND EVANS. LONDON: GEORGE ROUTLEDGE AND SONS, (1886). Unpaginated: 20 col. plates. Bound in grey cloth with coloured pictorial paper cover. An alphabet book.
CBD 421.1 GRE

363A **Another copy.**
LONDON: FREDERICK WARNE AND CO., LTD., n.d., printed by Edmund Evans Ltd. from original woodblocks engraved in 1886. Unpaginated: pictorial title page, coloured pictures on every page. Bound in cream cloth with coloured pictorial cover and matching jacket.
C 421.1 GRE

364 **GREENAWAY, KATE** *(Illustrator).*
MOTHER GOOSE or the OLD NURSERY RHYMES. Illustrated by KATE GREENAWAY. Engraved and printed by Edmund Evans. LONDON: FREDERICK WARNE AND CO., (1881). 48p.: col. front., col. decorative title page, col. ill. Bound in brown and grey cloth with decorative pattern on covers.
CBD 398.8 GRE

365 **HALLIWELL-PHILLIPPS, JAMES ORCHARD.**
THE NURSERY RHYMES OF ENGLAND. BY JAMES ORCHARD HALLIWELL. WITH ILLUSTRATIONS BY W.B. SCOTT. NEW EDITION. LONDON: FREDERICK WARNE AND CO., (1853). VIII, 333p. + 2p. pub. cat.: front., additional decorative title page, ill. Bound in brown cloth, with embossed decorative cover and spine. Originally published 1842.
C 398.8 HAL

365A **HAWTREY, MRS.**
THE ALPHABET OF FRUITS: For Good Children. By MRS HAWTREY. WITH ILLUSTRATIONS ENGRAVED BY EDMUND EVANS. LONDON: FREDERICK WARNE AND CO. (1865). (24p. + 4p. pub. cat.): ill. Bound in white card with coloured decorative cover.
CP 421.1 HAW

365B **HORTON, ALICE M.**
AN ALPHABET. WITH RHYMES AND PICTURES BY ALICE M. HORTON. LONDON: ELKIN MATHEWS, (190–?). Unpaginated: pictorial title page, ill. Bound in buff cloth with coloured pictorial paper cover.
M 428 HOR CHILDREN'S COLLECTION.

366 **MOFFAT, ALFRED.**
Our Old Nursery Rhymes. The original tunes harmonized by Alfred Moffat. Illustrated by H. Willebeek Le Mair. LONDON: AUGENER LTD., (1911). 63p.: decorative title page, 30 col. plates. Bound in blue cloth, with coloured pictorial paper label on cover.
C 398.8 MOF

366A **MONSELL, JOAN ROBERT.**
POLICHINELLE. OLD NURSERY SONGS OF FRANCE. TRANSLATED, SET AND ILLUSTRATED BY J.R. MONSELL. LONDON: HUMPHREY MILFORD, OXFORD UNIVERSITY PRESS, (192–?). Unpaginated: col. decorative title page, col. decorative pages with music, French and English words on one side of paper only. Bound in blue cloth with coloured pictorial cover.
C 398.80944 POL

367 **MOTHER GOOSE BOOK.**
*(Compiled)* BY E.M. BOLENIUS AND M.G. KELLOGG.

PROFUSELY ILLUSTRATED IN COLOUR BY GUSTAF TENGGREN. LONDON: GEORGE PHILIP AND SON LTD., 1929. 128p.: 13 col. plates, ill., decorative endpapers. Bound in green cloth, with coloured pictorial cover.
C 398.8 MOT

368 **NURSERY RHYMES, TALES AND JINGLES.**
WITH DRAWINGS BY L. LESLIE BROOKE. LONDON: FREDERICK WARNE AND CO., (191–?). Unpaginated: col. front., vignette title page, 7 col. plates, 2 plates, ill., decorative endpapers. Bound in grey cloth, with coloured, pictorial label on cover.
C 398.8 NUR

369 **OLD DUTCH NURSERY RHYMES.**
Illustrated by H. Willebeek Le Mair. English version by R.H. Elkin. The original tunes harmonised by J. Röntgen. LONDON: AUGENER LTD., (1917). 31p. + 1p. pub. cat.: col. vignette on title page, 15 col. plates. Bound in blue cloth, with coloured pictorial label on cover.
C 398.809492 OLD

370 **THE OLD MOTHER GOOSE NURSERY RHYME BOOK.**
LONDON: T.C. AND E.C. JACK LTD., (191–?). 143p.: col. front., vignette title page, 17 col. plates, ill. some col., decorative endpapers by Anne Anderson. Bound in cream cloth, with coloured pictorial cover and spine. Large format.
C 398.8 OLD

371 **THE OLD WOMAN AND HER PIG.**
Illustrated by A. CHASEMORE. LONDON: GRIFFITH, FARRAN AND CO., (189–?). Unpaginated: front., vignette on title page, 6 plates, ill. Bound in red cloth, with coloured pictorial paper cover. The Old Corner Series.
C 398.8 OLD

372 **PETER PIPER'S PRACTICAL PRINCIPLES OF PLAIN AND PERFECT PRONUNCIATION.**
Illustrated by A. Chasemore. LONDON: GRIFFITH, FARRAN AND CO., (189–?). Unpaginated: front., vignette title page, ill. Bound in red cloth, with coloured pictorial cover. The Old Corner Series.
C 398.8 PET

373 **POTTER, BEATRIX.**
APPLEY DAPPLY'S NURSERY RHYMES. BY BEATRIX POTTER. LONDON: FREDERICK WARNE AND CO., LTD., (1917). 49p.: col. front., 13 col. plates, by the author. Coloured pictorial endpapers. Bound in grey paper with inserted coloured illustrations, with pictorial paper jacket.
YSC 821.912 POT

374 **POTTER, BEATRIX.**
CECILY PARSLEY'S NURSERY RHYMES. BY BEATRIX POTTER. LONDON: FREDERICK WARNE AND CO., LTD., (1922). 53p., col. front., 14 col. plates by the author. Coloured pictorial endpapers. Bound in cream papers with inserted coloured illustration with pictorial paper jacket.
YSC 821.912 POT and C 821.912 POT

374A **ROBINSON, CHARLES** *(Illustrator).*
The book of Nursery Rhymes. Illustrated by Charles Robinson. LONDON: MINERVA, 1975, facsimile of 1903 edition. 80p.: decorative title page in red and black, 6 plates, ill. Bound in brown cloth with yellow decorative dust jacket.
C 398.8 ROB

375 **ROSSETTI, CHRISTINA GEORGINA.**
SING-SONG. A NURSERY RHYME. BY CHRISTINA G. ROSSETTI. WITH ONE HUNDRED AND TWENTY ILLUSTRATIONS BY ARTHUR HUGHES. ENGRAVED BY THE BROTHERS DALZIEL. LONDON: GEORGE ROUTLEDGE AND SONS, 1872. X, 130p. + 2p. pub. cat.: front., vignette title page, ill. Bound in blue cloth, with embossed decorative cover and spine, and gilt edges.
C 398.8 ROS

376 **Another copy.**
MACMILLAN AND CO., new and enlarged edition, 1893. XIV, 135p.: front., vignette on title page, ill. Bound in green cloth, with gilt edges.

377 **VALENTINE, MRS LAURA.**
NURSERY RHYMES, TALES AND JINGLES. THE CAMDEN EDITION. COMPILED BY MRS VALENTINE WITH FOUR HUNDRED ILLUSTRATIONS. LONDON: FREDERICK WARNE AND CO., (1874) VIII, 568p. front., ill. Bound in brown cloth.
YSC 398.8 VAL

377A **WALTER, L. EDNA** *(Editor).*
Mother Goose's Nursery Rhymes. COMPLETE EDITION CONTAINING EIGHT FULL-PAGE ILLUSTRATIONS IN COLOUR AND NUMEROUS ILLUSTRATIONS IN THE TEXT. LONDON: A. AND C. BLACK LTD., 1928. VIII, 216p. + 4p. pub. cat.: col. front., 7 col. plates, ill. by Charles Folkard. Bound in blue cloth with pictorial cover and spine.
C 398.8 MOT

378 **WEATHERLY, FREDERIC EDWARD.**
TWILIGHT TALES by F.E. WEATHERLY. Illustrated by M. ELLEN EDWARDS and JOHN C. STAPLES. NEW YORK: E.P. DUTTON AND CO., (188–?). Unpaginated: col. front., pictorial title page, 7 col. plates, ill. Bound in green cloth, with coloured pictorial/decorative paper covers.
C 398.8 WEA

379 **WOODWARD, ALICE B.** *(Illustrator).*
BANBURY CROSS AND OTHER NURSERY RHYMES. ILLUSTRATED BY ALICE B. WOODWARD. LONDON: J.M. DENT AND CO., 1893. Unpaginated: front., decorative title page, 28 plates, ill. Bound in red cloth with decorative cover. Banbury Cross Series.
C 398.8 BAN

# 6 GENERAL ADVICE AND INSTRUCTION

380 **AIKIN, JOHN.**
EVENINGS AT HOME; OR, THE JUVENILE BUDGET OPENED: A BOOK FOR The Instruction and Amusement of Young Persons. BY DR. AIKIN AND MRS. BARBAULD. LONDON: T. NELSON AND SONS., 1857. 383p.: front., additional vignette title page. Bound in blue cloth with embossed decorative cover and spine. Originally published 1792–6.
C 170.20222 AIK

380A **CHILDREN'S TREASURE HOUSE.**
A Companion to the Children's Encyclopaedia. Edited by Arthur Mee.
Vol 1. IMMORTAL HEROES OF THE WORLD
Vol 2. NATURE IN ALL HER GLORY
Vol 3. THE MOTHERLAND AND THE EMPIRE
Vol 4. THE REALMS OF GOLD
Vol 5. HOW AND WHY
Vol 6. THE PANORAMA OF THE WORLD
Vol 7. THE STORYTELLER
Vol 8. OUR WORLD AND THE OTHERS
Vol 9. THE BEDTIME BOOK
Vol 10. THE AMAZING ANIMAL KINGDOM
Vol 11. THE GREAT POETRY BOOK
Vol 12. THE FIRESIDE LESSON BOOK
LONDON: EDUCATIONAL BOOK COMPANY LTD. n.d. 351p., 356p., 360p., 352p., 352p., 367p., 368p., 351p., 352p., 351p., 367p., 344p.: col. front., plates, ill. Each volume separately indexed.
C 032 CHI

380B **COOK, H. CALDWELL.**
Littleman's Book of Courtesy. By H. Caldwell Cook. LONDON: J.M. DENT and SONS, 1920. 59p.: ill. by C.E. Brock. Bound in buff cloth with decorative cover.
C 821.912 CAL

381 **(FARRAR, ELIZA WARE).**
THE YOUNG LADY'S FRIEND; A MANUAL OF PRACTICAL ADVICE AND INSTRUCTION TO YOUNG FEMALES, ON THEIR ENTERING UPON THE DUTIES OF LIFE AFTER QUITTING SCHOOL. BY A LADY. THE FIFTH EDITION. LONDON: JOHN W. PARKER, 1845. VIII, 255p. Bound in green cloth, with embossed decorative cover. A modified reprint from an American original first published in 1836.
C 395.1233 YOU

382 **GOODRICH, S.G.** *(Editor).*
PARLEY'S NEW KEEPSAKE; Or, Sunshine for all Weathers. EDITED BY S.G. GOODRICH. LONDON: DARTON AND CO., 1858. VIII, 247p.: front., vignette title page, ill. Bound in red cloth with embossed decorative covers and spine.
C 823.8 PAR

383 **GURNEY, JOSEPH JOHN.**
THOUGHTS ON HABIT AND DISCIPLINE. BY JOSEPH JOHN GURNEY. NORWICH: JOSIAH FLETCHER, 1848. 240p. Bound in maroon cloth, with embossed decorative covers and spine.
YSC 241 GUR

384 **HAMMERTON, J.A.** *(Editor).*
OUR WONDERFUL WORLD; A Pictorial Account of the Marvels of Nature and the Triumphs of Man. Edited by J.A. HAMMERTON. Nearly Three Thousand Photographic Illustrations and Numerous Colour Plates. LONDON: AMALGAMATED PRESS LTD., (193–?). Vols 1 to 4. Plates, some col., ill. Bound in blue cloth.
YOSC 030 HAM

385 **THE ILLUSTRATED LONDON INSTRUCTOR.**
LONDON: ILLUSTRATED LONDON NEWS, THIRD EDITION, 1850. VIII, 264p.: front, decorative title page, ill. Bound in grey cloth with embossed decorative covers and spine.
C 828.008 ILL

386 **JOHNSON, JOSEPH.**
LIVING IN EARNEST; WITH LESSONS AND INCIDENTS FROM THE LIVES OF THE GREAT AND GOOD. A Book for Young Men. BY JOSEPH JOHNSON. LONDON: T. NELSON AND SONS, 1880. 266p. + 6p. pub. cat.: additional vignette title page. Bound in red cloth, with embossed decorative covers and spine.
YSC 170 JOH

387 **(MOGRIDGE, GEORGE).**
LEARNING TO CONVERSE. LONDON: THE RELIGIOUS TRACT SOCIETY, (185–?). 162p. + 14p. pub. cat.: front., ill. Bound in purple cloth with embossed decorative cover and spine.
C 177.2 MOG

388 **NEIL, SAMUEL** *(Editor).*
THE HOME TEACHER; A CYCLOPAEDIA OF SELF-INSTRUCTION. EDITED BY SAMUEL NEIL. ILLUSTRATED WITH NUMEROUS ENGRAVINGS. LONDON: WILLIAM MACKENZIE. (189–?). 3 volumes: Divisions II, III and V. p. 289–576, 577–864; 1153–1440, vol. V is last and includes index. Plates, some col. Bound in red cloth, with decorative cover and spine.
YOSC 030 NEI

389 **THE PARENTS' CABINET OF AMUSEMENT AND INSTRUCTION.**
A NEW EDITION. LONDON: SMITH, ELDER AND CO., 1859. 256p.: col. front., pictorial/decorative title page, 1 col. plate, ill. Bound in red cloth with embossed decorative covers and spine. One of a series of volumes appearing in 1858/9. Originally published 1833–5.
C 828.808 PAR

389A **(PARIS, J.A.).**
PHILOSOPHY IN SPORT MADE SCIENCE IN EARNEST: BEING AN ATTEMPT TO IMPLANT IN THE YOUNG MIND THE FIRST PRINCIPLES OF NATURAL PHILOSOPHY BY THE AID OF THE POPULAR TOYS AND SPORTS OF YOUTH. EIGHTH EDITION. LONDON: JOHN MURRAY, 1857. XXVII, 532p. + 32p. pub. cat.: front., vignette on title page, ill. Bound in brown cloth with embossed decorative cover and spine. Originally published in 1827.
C 823.8 PHI

390 **SOUTHGATE, HENRY.**
THINGS A LADY WOULD LIKE TO KNOW, CONCERNING DOMESTIC MANAGEMENT AND EXPENDITURE. ARRANGED FOR DAILY REFERENCE WITH Hints regarding the Intellectual as well as the Physical Life. BY HENRY SOUTHGATE. SIXTH EDITION. EDINBURGH: WILLIAM P. NIMMO AND CO., 1879. 543p. + 14p. pub. cat.: front., additional decorative title page. Bound in brown cloth, with decorative cover and spine, and gilt edges.
YSC 640 SOU

391 **TAIT, S.B.**
JARROLD'S EMPIRE HOME LESSON BOOKS. BY S.B. TAIT. LONDON: JARROLD AND SONS, eighth edition, (188–?). 5 vols.: 2nd, 4th, 5th, 6th and 7th standards. Bound in blue cloth, with decorative cover. THE EMPIRE EDUCATIONAL SERIES.
YSC 371.32 TAI

392 **TEGG, THOMAS.**
A PRESENT FOR AN APPRENTICE TO WHICH IS ADDED, FRANKLIN'S WAY TO WEALTH. BY THE LATE THOMAS TEGG, ESQ. SECOND EDITION. LONDON: WILLIAM TEGG AND CO., 1848. XVI, 381p.: front., additional vignette title page. Bound in blue cloth with embossed decorative cover and spine.
C 395 TEG

392A **TUTHILL, MRS. LOUISA C.**
HOME: A BOOK FOR YOUNG LADIES. LONDON: T. NELSON AND SONS, 1855. IV, 264p. Bound in blue cloth with embossed decorative cover and spine.
M 395 TUT CHILDREN'S COLLECTION

392B **(WARD, MRS. R.)**
THE CHILD'S GUIDE TO KNOWLEDGE; BEING A COLLECTION OF USEFUL AND FAMILIAR QUESTIONS AND ANSWERS ON EVERY-DAY SUBJECTS. Adapted for Young Persons. BY A LADY. (pseudonym for Mrs R. Ward). LONDON: SIMPKIN MARSHALL AND CO., 58TH ED. 1892. 314p. Bound in blue cloth with marbled paper covers.
M 001 CHI CHILDREN'S COLLECTION

393 **WATTS, ISAAC.**
THE IMPROVEMENT OF THE MIND, TO WHICH IS ADDED A DISCOURSE ON THE EDUCATION OF CHILDREN AND YOUTH. BY ISAAC WATTS, D.D. LONDON: MILNER AND COMPANY, (184–?). 380p. + 32p. pub. cat.: front., additional vignette title page. Bound in black cloth with decorative spine. Originally published in 1741. Spine title: WATTS ON THE MIND.
C 001 WAT

## 7 BIBLE AND RELIGIOUS INSTRUCTION

394 **ADAMS, WILLIAM.**
THE SHADOW OF THE CROSS. BY THE REV. WILLIAM ADAMS, M.A. New Edition, with Illustrations. LONDON: RIVINGTONS., 1880. 79p.: front., 3 plates. Bound in green cloth with embossed decorative cover.
YSC 800 ADA

395 **BLEBY, HENRY.**
THE STOLEN CHILDREN. A NARRATIVE Compiled from Authentic Sources BY HENRY BLEBY. LONDON: T.

WOOLMER, (189–?). 220p.: front., 1 plate, ill. Bound in brown cloth, with embossed pictorial/decorative cover and spine.
C 261.833154 BLE

396 **BRIGGS, G.W.** *(Editor)*.
THE DAILY SERVICE. PRAYERS AND HYMNS FOR SCHOOLS (MELODY EDITION). Editors: PRAYERS, G.W. BRIGGS; HYMNS, PERCY DEARMER, RALPH VAUGHAN WILLIAMS, MARTIN SHAW, G.W. BRIGGS. LONDON: OXFORD UNIVERSITY PRESS, 1936. 256p., musical score. Bound in blue cloth.
YSC 240 BRI

397 **BRIGHTWELL, CECILIA LUCY.**
SO GREAT LOVE! SKETCHES OF MISSIONARY LIFE AND LABOUR. BY MISS BRIGHTWELL. LONDON: JOHN SNOW AND CO., 1874. 318p. + 2p. pub. cat.: front., 19 plates, ill. Bound in green cloth, with embossed pictorial/decorative cover and spine.
C 266.00922 BRI

398 **BURNS, JABEZ.**
YOUTHFUL PIETY, EXEMPLIFIED IN THE HAPPY DEATHS OF YOUNG PERSONS . . . BY J. BURNS, MINISTER OF THE GOSPEL. LONDON: JOSEPH SMITH, 1840. XII, 180p.: front. Bound in brown cloth, with embossed decorative covers.
C 236.1 BUR

399 **BURNSIDE, W.F.**
OLD TESTAMENT HISTORY FOR SCHOOLS. BY W.F. BURNSIDE, M.A. WITH THREE MAPS. ELEVENTH EDITION. LONDON: METHUEN AND CO. LTD., 1924. XII, 330p.: front. (a map), 2 maps. Bound in dark blue cloth.
YSC 221 BUR

400 **THE CHILDREN OF THE BIBLE.**
LONDON: THE RELIGIOUS TRACT SOCIETY, (186–?). 75p.: col. front., vignette title page, 5 col. plates. Bound in purple cloth, with embossed decorative cover and spine, and gilt edges.
C 220.9505 CHI

401 **(CROSSE, J.H.)**
HISTORICAL TALES FOR YOUNG PROTESTANTS. LONDON: THE RELIGIOUS TRACT SOCIETY, (187–?). VIII, 180p. + 8p. pub. cat.: front., ill. Bound in green cloth, with embossed decorative covers and spine.
C 823.808 HIS

401A **DERRICK, FREDA.**
THE ARK BOOK. LONDON: BLACKIE AND SON LIMITED, (1920). (24p.): col. front., col. vignette on title page, col. ill. Bound in blue cloth with coloured pictorial paper cover.
C 221.9505 DER

402 **EARLY DUTIES AND EARLY DANGERS.**
LONDON: GALL AND INGLIS, (187–?). 112p.: col. front. by W. Dickes. Bound in maroon cloth, with embossed decorative cover and spine.
C 242.62 EAR

403 **EVANS, EDMUND.**
THE Illuminated Scripture Text Book, WITH Interleaved Diary for Memoranda, AND A Coloured Illustration for Every Day, BY EDMUND EVANS. LONDON: FREDERICK WARNE AND CO., (1880). 108p.: col. front., col. ill. Bound in red cloth, with embossed decorative covers and spine, and gilt edges.
C 242.2 EVA

403A **GREEN, SAMUEL, G.**
BIBLE SKETCHES AND THEIR TEACHINGS. For Young People. BY SAMUEL G. GREEN, B.A. FIRST SERIES: FROM THE CREATION TO THE ISRAELITES' ENTRANCE INTO CANAAN. LONDON: THE RELIGIOUS TRACT SOCIETY, (186–?). VIII, 234p. + 14p. pub. cat.: front. Bound in green cloth with embossed decorative cover and spine.
C 221.9505 GRE

403A

404 **GREGORY, ALFRED.**
ROBERT RAIKES: Journalist and Philanthropist. A HISTORY OF THE ORIGIN OF SUNDAY SCHOOLS. BY ALFRED GREGORY. FIFTH THOUSAND. LONDON: HODDER AND STOUGHTON, 1880. 189p.: front., vignette title page. Bound in blue cloth, with pictorial cover.
C 268.0924 RAI/GRE

405 **HALF HOURS IN THE HOLY LAND.**
Travels in Egypt, Palestine, Syria. WITH NUMEROUS ILLUSTRATIONS. LONDON: JAMES NISBET AND CO. LIMITED, (189–?). X, 341p. + 32p. pub. cat.: front., 28 plates, ill. Bound in blue cloth, with embossed pictorial/decorative cover and spine. THE HALF HOUR LIBRARY OF TRAVEL, NATURE AND SCIENCE FOR YOUNG READERS.
C 915.694 HAL

406 **HAWEIS, H.R.**
THE CHILD'S LIFE OF CHRIST BY THE REV. H.R. HAWEIS, M.A. Illustrated with colour pictures by John Lawson and full page Black and White Drawings by ARTHUR A. DIXON. LONDON: RAPHAEL TUCK AND SONS, LTD. (192–?). 144p. inc. 10p. ill. pub. cat.: col. front., 15 col. plates, 20 plates, ill. Bound in orange cloth with coloured pictorial covers.
YSC 232 HAW

407 **HAYES, ERNEST H.**
Wiliamu. MARINER – MISSIONARY. THE STORY OF JOHN WILLIAMS BY ERNEST H. HAYES. LONDON: RELIGIOUS EDUCATION PRESS, 1922. 111p.: ill. Bound in buff cloth with pictorial cover.
YSC 920 WIL

408 **HODGKIN, L.V.**
A BOOK OF QUAKER SAINTS BY L.V. HODGKIN. (Mrs. JOHN HOLDSWORTH). ILLUSTRATED BY F. CAYLEY-ROBINSON, A.R.A. LONDON: MACMILLAN AND CO. LTD., 1922. XIII, 548p.: col. front., 6 col. plates. Bound in black cloth with grey covers.
YSC 289 HOD

409 **HOUSE, ALBERT** *(Editor)*.
THE LIFE OF OUR LORD IN THE WORDS OF THE GOSPELS. ARRANGED BY ALBERT HOUSE, M.A. LONDON: OXFORD UNIVERSITY PRESS, 1938. 128p.: col. front., 15 plates, 3 maps.
YSC 226 HOU

410 **IBBOTSON, R.M.A.**
ADVENTURES OF MISSIONARY EXPLORERS. TRUE STORIES OF THE HEROISM, FORTITUDE, AND INDOMITABLE COURAGE OF . . . WELL-KNOWN MISSIONARIES IN ALL PARTS OF THE WORLD. BY R.M.A. IBBOTSON. WITH SIXTEEN ILLUSTRATIONS. LONDON: SEELEY, SERVICE AND CO. LIMITED, 1915. 316p. + 20p. pub. cat.: front., 15 plates. Bound in blue cloth, with coloured pictorial/decorative cover and spine.
C 266.09 IBB

411 **INGRAHAM, J.H.**
THE PRINCE OF THE HOUSE OF DAVID; OR, Three Years in the Holy City. BY THE REV. J.H. INGRAHAM, L.L.D. ILLUSTRATED. LONDON: GEORGE ROUTLEDGE AND SONS, (188–?). XVI, 410p. + 6p. pub. cat.: col. front., 3 col. plates engraved by Dalziel Brothers, 16 plates. Bound in brown cloth, with embossed decorative cover and spine, and gilt edges.
YSC 823.8 ING

412 **JONES, MARY.**
THE STORY OF MARY JONES AND HER BIBLE. COLLECTED FROM THE BEST MATERIALS AND RETOLD BY M.E.R. NEW EDITION. LONDON: BRITISH AND FOREIGN BIBLE SOCIETY, 1894. 166p.: 8 plates, ill. Bound in green cloth.
C 823.8 JON

413 **LANG, LEONORA BLANCHE (ALLEYNE).**
THE BOOK OF SAINTS AND HEROES. BY MRS. LANG. EDITED BY ANDREW LANG. WITH 12 COLOURED PLATES AND NUMEROUS OTHER ILLUSTRATIONS BY H.J. FORD. NEW IMPRESSION. LONDON: LONGMANS, GREEN AND CO., 1921. XII, 351p.: col. front., 11 col. plates, 18 plates. Bound in blue cloth, with embossed decorative cover and spine.
C 235.2 LAN

414 **(MACKARNESS, MATILDA ANNE).**
THE GOLDEN RULE: OR, STORIES ILLUSTRATIVE OF THE TEN COMMANDMENTS. BY THE AUTHOR OF "A TRAP TO CATCH A SUNBEAM", "INFLUENCE", ETC. ETC. NEW EDITION. LONDON: GEORGE ROUTLEDGE AND SONS, (186–?). 316p.: front., 7 plates, engraved by Dalziel Brothers. Bound in orange cloth, with coloured decorative cover and spine. Contains ten stories.
C 823.8 MAC

415 **MACY, MRS. S.B.**
THE BOOK OF THE KINGDOM, BEING THE BIBLE STORY FROM THE BIRTH OF SAMUEL TO THE DEATH OF DAVID. BY S.B. MACY. WITH COLOURED FRONTISPIECE AND 50 BLACK AND WHITE ILLUSTRATIONS BY T.H. ROBINSON. LONDON: LONGMANS, GREEN AND CO., 1912. XII, 388p. + 4p. pub. cat.: col. front., 17 plates, ill., decorative endpapers. Bound in green cloth, with embossed pictorial/decorative cover and spine.
C 222 MAC

416 **MEYER, FREDERICK BROTHERTON.**
Elijah: And the Secret of his Power. BY F.B. MEYER, B.A. LONDON: MORGAN AND SCOTT, (190–?). 187p. + 4p. ill. pub. cat.: front., 8 plates by W.L.J., engraved by C. Butterworth. Bound in blue cloth, with coloured decorative cover with inserted pictorial label and decorative spine.
C 221.924 ELI/MEY

417 **MOHN, PAUL.**
THE HOLY CHILD. Sixteen Coloured Illustrations by Paul Mohn. LONDON: SOCIETY FOR PROMOTING CHRISTIAN KNOWLEDGE, (191–?). Unpaginated: additional col. vignette title page. col. decorative title page, 14 col. plates. Bound in blue cloth, with coloured pictorial/decorative paper cover.
C 741.88 MOH

418 **MYERS, JOHN BROWN.**
THOMAS J. COMBER, Missionary Pioneer to the Congo. BY JOHN BROWN MYERS. THIRD EDITION. THIRTEENTH THOUSAND. LONDON: S.W. PARTRIDGE AND CO., (189–?). 160p. + 16p. pub. cat.: front., 15 plates, map, ill. Bound in red cloth, with embossed pictorial/decorative cover and spine.
C 266.0230924 COM/MYE

419 **NEWTON, RICHARD.**
RILLS FROM THE FOUNTAIN. BY THE REV. RICHARD NEWTON, D.D. LONDON: GEORGE ROUTLEDGE AND SONS, (187–?). VII, 150p.: col. front. Bound in brown cloth, with embossed decorative cover and spine, and gilt edges.
C 248.82 NEW

420 **OWEN, WILLIAM.**
PICTORIAL SUNDAY READINGS: COMPRISING A Series of Scripture Subjects, TREATED WITH SPECIAL REFERENCE TO THE TASTES AND REQUIREMENTS OF FAMILIES AND FORMING A COMPREHENSIVE REPERTORY OF BIBLICAL KNOWLEDGE. BY THE REV. WILLIAM OWEN. VOLUME I. LONDON: JAMES SANGSTER AND CO., (186–?). VI, 324pp. + 4p. index: double col. front., additional col. vignette title page, 36 col. plates. Bound in red cloth, with embossed decorative covers and spine, and gilt edges. VOLUME II. LONDON: JAMES SANGSTER AND CO., (186–?). 304p. + 4p. index: col. front., additional col. vignette title page, 38 col. plates. Bound in red cloth, with embossed decorative covers and spine, and gilt edges.
C 220.9505 OWE

421 **PATON, JAMES.**
THE STORY OF JOHN G. PATON, TOLD FOR YOUNG FOLKS; OR, Thirty Years among South Sea Cannibals. REARRANGED AND EDITED BY THE REV. JAMES PATON, B.A. EIGHTH EDITION COMPLETING FORTY-EIGHT THOUSAND. LONDON: HODDER AND STOUGHTON, 1899. 304p. + 16p. ill. pub. cat.: front, 6 plates, map, ill. Bound in green cloth, with coloured pictorial cover and spine.
C 266.50924 PAT/PAT

422 **THE PEEP OF DAY.**
OR, A SERIES OF THE EARLIEST RELIGIOUS INSTRUCTION THE INFANT MIND IS CAPABLE OF RECEIVING. WITH VERSES ILLUSTRATIVE OF THE SUBJECTS. Four hundred and second Thousand. LONDON: HATCHARDS, 1873. XIV, 208p.: col. front., 10 plates. Bound in red cloth, with embossed pictorial/decorative cover and spine.
C 220.9505 PEE

423 **PENNELL, ALICE M.**
A HERO OF THE AFGHAN FRONTIER; THE SPLENDID LIFE STORY OF T.L. PENNELL, M.D.,B.Sc.,F.R.C.S. RETOLD FOR BOYS AND GIRLS BY ALICE M. PENNELL. WITH MANY ILLUSTRATIONS. SECOND EDITION. LONDON: SEELEY, SERVICE AND CO. LIMITED, 1917. 208p. + 15p. pub. cat.: col. front., 8 plates. Bound in olive cloth, with coloured pictorial label on cover and coloured pictorial spine.
C 266.00924 PEN

424 **PETERSHAM, MAUD.**
THE CHRIST CHILD AS TOLD BY MATTHEW AND LUKE, MADE BY MAUD AND MISKA PETERSHAM. U.S.A., NEW YORK: DOUBLEDAY AND COMPANY, INC., 1931. 63p.: col. pictorial title page, col. ill., col. pictorial endpapers. Bound in blue cloth with coloured pictorial cover.
YSCO 232 PET

425 **PROCTER, FRANCIS.**
AN ELEMENTARY INTRODUCTION TO THE Book of Common Prayer. BY THE REV. FRANCIS PROCTER, M.A. AND THE REV. G.F. MACLEAR, D.D. LONDON: MACMILLAN AND CO. LIMITED, 1926. X, 196p. Bound in blue cloth. Originally published in 1868. ELEMENTARY THEOLOGICAL CLASS BOOKS.
YSC 242 PRO

427 **(ROPES, MARY EMILY).**
THE STORY OF MARY JONES AND HER BIBLE. COLLECTED FROM THE BEST MATERIALS AND RETOLD BY M.E.R. NEW EDITION. LONDON: BRITISH AND FOREIGN BIBLE SOCIETY, 1894. 166p.: col. front., 9 plates, ill. Bound in green cloth, with vignette on cover. Originally published 1882.
C 823.8 ROP

428 **SANDERS, E.M.**
THE HOLY LAND.
PART I THE LAND (SECOND EDITION)
PART II THE PEOPLE AND THEIR WORK (SECOND EDITION)
BOOK II BACKGROUND AND CUSTOMS
BY E.M. SANDERS B.A. LONDON: GEORGE PHILIP AND SON LTD., 1938. 32p., 36p., 64p. plates, ill. maps on inside covers. Parts 1 and 2 bound in manilla card, Book II in purple cloth.
YOSC 220 SAN

429 **SUNDAY HALF-HOURS IN FIFTY-TWO CHAPTERS.**
WITH ILLUSTRATIONS ON EVERY PAGE AND SIXTEEN TINTED ENGRAVINGS. LONDON: JAMES SANGSTER AND CO. (187–?) 184p. sepia front., additional pictorial title page and 14 plates, ill. Bound in blue cloth with embossed decorative cover and spine.
YSC 263.4 SUN

430 **TWEEDIE, WILLIAM KING.**
SEED-TIME AND HARVEST; OR, SOW WELL AND REAP WELL. A Book for the Young. By THE LATE REV. W.K. TWEEDIE, D.D. LONDON: T. NELSON AND SONS, 1872. 256p.: col. front., additional col. pictorial title page. Bound in green cloth, with embossed decorative cover and spine.
C 252.53 TWE

430A **WATTS, ISAAC.**
DIVINE AND MORAL SONGS FOR CHILDREN BY THE REVEREND ISAAC WATTS, D.D. LONDON: ELKIN MATTHEWS, (1896). 62p.: col. front., 12 col. plates by G.E.C. Gaskin. Bound in buff cloth with green pictorial cover.
M 821.6 WAT

431 **WEEKS, JOHN H.**
A Congo Pathfinder: W. HOLMAN BENTLEY AMONG AFRICAN SAVAGES. By JOHN H. WEEKS. SECOND IMPRESSION. LONDON: THE RELIGIOUS TRACT SOCIETY, (192–?). 251p.: col. front., 2 col. plates by Arch. Webb, 14 plates. Bound in green cloth, with coloured pictorial cover and spine.
C 266.60924 BEN/WEE

432 **WHITE, FRANK H.**
TYPES AND SHADOWS: OR, The Tabernacle in the Wilderness. A BOOK FOR THE YOUNG. BY FRANK H. WHITE. THIRD EDITION, ENLARGED. TWENTIETH THOUSAND. LONDON: S.W. PARTRIDGE AND CO., (1878). 46p. + 2p. pub. cat.: front., 5 plates, engraved by W. Dickes. Bound in brown cloth, with embossed decorative covers and gilt edges.
C 220.9505 WHI

433 **WILLIAMS, CHARLES.**
A BI-CENTENARY MEMORIAL OF JOHN BUNYAN, WHO DIED A.D. 1688. BY CHARLES WILLIAMS OF ACCRINGTON. LONDON: THE BAPTIST TRACT AND BOOK SOCIETY, (1888). VIII, 103p. + 4p. pub. cat.: front., 6 plates, ill. Bound in blue cloth with embossed pictorial/decorative cover and spine.
YSC 920 BUN

434 **THE WONDERFUL BOY.**
WITH COLOURED PICTURES BY HAROLD COPPING. LONDON: (RELIGIOUS TRACT SOCIETY, 191–?). 16p.: decorative title page, 4 col. plates. Bound in yellow paper-covered board, with coloured pictorial cover.
C 232.901 JES/WON

435 **YEAMES, JAMES.**
GILBERT GUESTLING; OR, The Story of a Hymn-Book. BY JAMES YEAMES. LONDON: WESLEYAN CONFERENCE OFFICE, (188–?). 123p. + 16p. pub. cat.: front., 2 plates. Bound in blue cloth with embossed decorative cover and inserted coloured pictorial label.
C 264.20924 GUE/YEA

436 **YONGE, CHARLOTTE MARY.**
AUNT CHARLOTTE'S STORIES OF BIBLE HISTORY FOR THE LITTLE ONES, BY CHARLOTTE M. YONGE. Twentieth Thousand. LONDON: MARCUS WARD'S HISTORIES PRINTED AND PUBLISHED BY MICAWI STEVENSON AND ORR, LIMITED, (189–?). 290p. ill. Bound in blue cloth.
YSC 220 YON

## 8 BIOGRAPHY AND HISTORY

437 **ALGER, HORATIO.**
ABRAHAM LINCOLN, THE BACKWOODS BOY; OR, HOW A YOUNG RAIL-SPLITTER BECAME PRESIDENT. BY HORATIO ALGER, JR. U.S.A., NEW YORK: JOHN R. ANDERSON AND HENRY S. ALLEN, 1883. 307p. + 4p. pub. cat.: double front., 3 plates. Bound in red cloth, with embossed pictorial/decorative cover and spine, and gilt edges. ILLUSTRIOUS AMERICAN SERIES.
C 813.4 ALG

438 **ALISON, A.**
EPITOME OF ALISON'S HISTORY OF EUROPE FROM THE COMMENCEMENT OF THE FRENCH REVOLUTION IN 1789 TO THE RESTORATION FOR THE USE OF SCHOOLS AND YOUNG PERSONS. SECOND EDITION. EDINBURGH: WILLIAM BLACKWOOD, 1848. Bound in grey and brown cloth with embossed decorative cover.
YSC 940.27 ALI

439 **ANDERSON, ROBERT E.**
THE STORY OF EXTINCT CIVILIZATIONS OF THE EAST. BY ROBERT E. ANDERSON, M.A., F.A.S. WITH MAPS ETC. LONDON: GEORGE NEWNES, LTD., 1898. 229p. + 2p., pub. cat.: front., ill. maps. Bound in blue cloth with decorative cover. (Library of Useful Stories).
YSC 930 AND

440 **BARING-GOULD, SABINE.**
CURIOSITIES OF OLDEN TIMES. BY S. BARING-GOULD, M.A. REVISED AND ENLARGED EDITION. EDINBURGH: JOHN GRANT, 1895. 301p. Bound in red cloth.
YSC 398.2 BAR

440A **BEGBIE, HAROLD.**
THE STORY OF BADEN-POWELL, 'The Wolf that never Sleeps'. LONDON: GRANT RICHARDS, 1900. IX, 213p.: front, 9 photographic plates. Bound in blue cloth with pictorial cover.
M 369.43092 BEG CHILDREN'S COLLECTION

441 **BELLOC, JOSEPH HILAIRE PIERRE.**
OLIVER CROMWELL. LONDON: ERNEST BENN LTD., NEW EDITION, 1931. 155p. + 4p. pub. cat. Bound in brown cloth. BENN'S ESSEX LIBRARY.
YSC 920 BEL

442 **BESANT, WALTER.**
THE STORY OF KING ALFRED. BY WALTER BESANT. WITH ILLUSTRATIONS. LONDON: GEORGE NEWNES, LIMITED, 1901. 207p.: front., ill. Bound in blue cloth with decorative cover. THE LIBRARY OF USEFUL STORIES.
YSC 920 ALF

443 **BROWNING, OSCAR.**
MODERN ENGLAND 1815–1885. BY OSCAR BROWNING, M.A. TWELFTH EDITION. LONDON, LONGMANS, GREEN AND CO., 1897. 80p. Bound in brown cloth. EPOCHS OF ENGLISH HISTORY SERIES.
YSC 942.07 BRO

444 **BULLOCK, CHARLES.**
THE QUEEN'S RESOLVE: "I WILL BE GOOD" AND Her "Doubly Royal" Reign. A GIFT FOR "THE QUEEN'S YEAR". BY CHARLES BULLOCK, B.D. TWO HUNDRED AND TWENTY-SEVENTH THOUSAND. LONDON: "HOME WORDS" PUBLISHING OFFICE, (189–?). 200p. + 8p. pub. cat.: front. portrait, 38 plates, ill.
YSC 941.0810924 VIC/BUL

445 **BULLOCK, CHARLES.**
1887. THE ROYAL YEAR: A CHRONICLE OF "Our Good Queen's Jubilee". A SEQUEL TO "THE QUEEN'S RESOLVE". COMPILED BY THE REV. CHARLES BULLOCK, B.D. FIFTH THOUSAND. LONDON: "HOME WORDS" PUBLISHING OFFICE, (1887). 202p. + 6p. pub. cat.: front., 25 plates, ill. Bound in blue cloth, with embossed pictorial/decorative cover and decorative spine.
C 941.081 BUL

446 **BURKE, EDMUND.**
CONCILIATION WITH AMERICA by EDMUND BURKE. LONDON: THOMAS NELSON AND SONS, LTD., 1937. 115p.: front. Bound in green cloth.
YSC 973.2 BUR

447 **CALLCOTT, LADY.**
LITTLE ARTHUR'S HISTORY OF ENGLAND. BY LADY CALLCOTT. NEW EDITION WITH THIRTY-SIX ILLUSTRATIONS. LONDON: JOHN MURRAY, 1883. 271p. + 16p. pub. cat.: front., 8 plates, ill. Bound in red cloth with embossed decorative cover and spine.
YSC 942 CAL

449 **CARTER, GEORGE.**
OUTLINES OF ENGLISH HISTORY FROM BC 55–AD 1901; WITH GENEALOGICAL TABLES AND SHORT BIOGRAPHICAL SKETCHES, FOR THE USE OF CANDIDATES PREPARING FOR THE OXFORD AND CAMBRIDGE LOCAL AND OTHER EXAMINATIONS: COMPILED AND ARRANGED BY GEORGE CARTER, M.A. TWELFTH EDITION. LONDON: RELFE BROTHERS, LTD. (1901). 227p. + 1p. pub. cat. Bound in red cloth.
YSC 942.00202 CAR

450 **THE CHILDREN'S PICTURE-BOOK OF GOOD AND GREAT MEN.**
Illustrated with fifty engravings. LONDON: BELL AND DALDY, 1860. VII, 278p. Vignette on title page, 50 plates. Bound in purple cloth with embossed decorative cover and spine, with gilt edges.
C 920.71 CHI

451 **COLLIER, WILLIAM FRANCIS.**
HISTORY OF THE BRITISH EMPIRE. BY WILLIAM FRANCIS COLLIER, LL.D. LONDON: NELSON AND SONS, 1875. 346p. + 6p. pub. cat. Bound in maroon cloth, with embossed decorative covers. Spine title: BRITISH HISTORY.
YSC 941 COL

452 **THE COMPLETE HISTORY READERS NO. V.**
(HISTORY OF ENGLAND). Title page missing. LONDON: BLACKIE AND SON, LIMITED, (190–?). 230p. (incomplete): 11 col. plates, 11 plates, ill. Bound in green cloth with decorative cover.
YSC 941 COM

453 **CORDERY, BERTHA MERITON.**
THE STRUGGLE AGAINST ABSOLUTE MONARCHY 1603–1688. BY BERTHA MERITON CORDERY. WITH TWO MAPS. THIRD EDITION. LONDON: LONGMANS, GREEN AND CO., 1878. 84p. + 4p. pub. cat. Bound in brown cloth. EPOCHS OF ENGLISH HISTORY SERIES.
YSC 942.06 GAR

454 **Another copy.**
By BERTHA MERITON GARDINER. FOURTEENTH EDITION, 1894.

455 **CREIGHTON, MANDELL.**
THE AGE OF ELIZABETH. BY THE RIGHT REV. MANDELL CREIGHTON, D.D., L.L.D. WITH MAPS AND TABLES. SIXTEENTH IMPRESSION. LONDON: LONGMANS, GREEN AND CO., 1904. XVIII, 236p.: col. front., maps, tables. Bound in brown cloth. Epochs of Modern History.
YSC 940.232 CRE

456 **CREIGHTON, MANDELL.**
THE TUDORS AND THE REFORMATION 1485–1603. BY MANDELL CREIGHTON, D.D., L.L.D. WITH THREE MAPS. FIFTEENTH EDITION. LONDON: LONGMANS, GREEN AND CO., 1896. VI, 91p.: maps. Bound in brown cloth. EPOCHS OF ENGLISH HISTORY.
YSC 942.05 CRE

457 **DANBY, PAUL.**
The British Army Book. BY PAUL DANBY AND Lieut.-Col. and Brevet Col. CYRIL FIELD, R.M.L.I. With 2 Coloured Plates and 32 Reproductions from Drawings and Photographs. LONDON: BLACKIE AND SON LIMITED, (191–?). 284p.: double col. front., 1 col. plate, 32 plates. Bound in olive cloth, with coloured pictorial cover and spine.
C 355.00941 DAN

459 **DAWE, C.S.**
THE HIGHER SCHOOL HISTORY. JUNIOR COURSE. EDITED BY REV. C.S. DAWE, B.A. LONDON: THE EDUCATIONAL SUPPLY ASSOCIATION, LIMITED, (190–?). 192p.: maps. Bound in green cloth with decorative cover. THE HIGHER SCHOOL SERIES.
YSC 942 HIG

460 **DERRY, KINGSTON.**
BRITISH HISTORY FROM 1782–1933. BY KINGSTON DERRY, D.Phil. LONDON: G. BELL AND SONS, LTD., 1934. 354p.: maps. Bound in red cloth.
YSC 941 DER

461 **DOORLY, ELEANOR.**
THE RADIUM WOMAN. A Youth Edition of the Life of Madame Curie, by ELEANOR DOORLY, and Woodcuts by ROBERT GIBBINGS. LONDON: HEINEMANN, 1939. 181p.: front., ill. Bound in cream paper with pictorial cover.
YSC 920 CUR

462 **DYER, OLIVER.**
THE BOY PATRIOT; OR, From Poverty to the Presidency, BEING THE STORY OF THE LIFE OF GENERAL JACKSON. BY OLIVER DYER. WITH ILLUSTRATIONS BY H.M. EATON. LONDON: HUTCHINSON AND CO., (190–?). 378p. + 6p. pub. cat.: front., 7 plates, decorative endpapers. Bound in brown cloth, with coloured pictorial cover and spine, and gilt edges.
C 973.560924 JAC/DYE

463 **EVERETT GREEN, EVELYN.**
CALLED OF HER COUNTRY, THE STORY OF JOAN OF ARC. BY EVELYN EVERETT GREEN. With Illustrations by E.F. SHERIE. LONDON: S.H. BOUSFIELD

AND CO. LIMITED, (190–?). VIII, 310p. + 2p. pub. cat.: front., 6 plates. Bound in blue cloth, with pictorial cover and spine, and gilt edges.
C 823.912 JOA/EVE

463A **FIELD, CYRIL.**
The British Navy Book. BY Lieut.-Col. and Brevet Col. CYRIL FIELD, R.M.L.I. With Full-page Illustrations in Colour and in Black-and-White and Numerous Illustrations in the Text. LONDON: BLACKIE AND SON LIMITED, (191–?). 312p.: front., 3 col. plates, 32 plates, ill. Bound in blue cloth, with coloured pictorial cover and spine.
C 359.00941 FIE

464 **FREEMAN, EDWARD AUGUSTUS.**
OLD ENGLISH HISTORY FOR CHILDREN. LONDON: J.M. DENT AND SONS, LTD., (191–?). IX, 337p.: 4 maps. Rebound in blue patterned cloth.
YSC 942 FRE

465 **GAMMON, FREDERIC T.**
THE CANAL BOY WHO BECAME PRESIDENT. BY FREDERIC T. GAMMON. LONDON: S.W. PARTRIDGE AND CO., (1894?). 152p. + 16p. pub. cat.: front., 4 plates. A biography of James Abram Garfield, President of U.S.A. (1880 & 1881).
C 823.8 GAM

466 **GARDINER, SAMUEL RAWSON.**
ILLUSTRATED ENGLISH HISTORY, PART III 1689–1886. BY S.R. GARDINER. NEW EDITION. LONDON: LONGMANS, GREEN AND CO., 1891. 260p., ill., maps. Bound in brown cloth with embossed decorative cover. English History Reading Books.
YSC 942 GAR

467 **GARDINER, SAMUEL RAWSON.**
A SCHOOL ATLAS OF ENGLISH HISTORY. EDITED BY SAMUEL RAWSON GARDINER, D.C.L., L.L.D. A COMPANION ATLAS TO THE STUDENT'S HISTORY OF ENGLAND BY SAMUEL RAWSON GARDINER. NEW IMPRESSION. LONDON: LONGMANS, GREEN AND CO., 1914. 8p., 88p. col. maps, 23p. index.
YSC 911.42 SCH

468 **GARDINER, SAMUEL RAWSON.**
A STUDENT'S HISTORY OF ENGLAND FROM THE EARLIEST TIMES TO 1885. BY SAMUEL R. GARDINER, D.C.L., L.L.D. VOL. 1. BC55–AD1509. NEW EDITION. LONDON: LONGMANS, GREEN AND CO., 1896. XXXII, 378p. 4p.: 12 plates, ill. Bound in brown cloth.
YSC 942 GAR

468A **GILLIAT, EDWARD.**
HEROES OF MODERN CRUSADES: TRUE STORIES OF THE UNDAUNTED CHIVALRY OF CHAMPIONS OF THE DOWNTRODDEN IN MANY LANDS. BY EDWARD GILLIAT. WITH SIXTEEN ILLUSTRATIONS. LONDON: SEELEY AND CO. LIMITED, 1909. 351p. + 8p. ill. pub. cat.: front., 15 plates. Bound in red cloth, with embossed pictorial/decorative cover and spine.
C 362.922 GIL

469 **GILL'S SCHOOL SERIES, MIDDLE ENGLAND FROM 1154–1689.**
DESCRIPTIVE AND PICTORIAL. HISTORICAL READER NO. III. ILLUSTRATED. LONDON: GEORGE GILL AND SONS, (1882). 248p.: front., 4 plates, ill., maps. Bound in turquoise cloth with embossed decorative cover.
YSC 942 MID

470 **(GRANDFATHER GREGORY).**
IN THE BRAVE DAYS OF OLD: OR, The Story of the Spanish Armada, IN THE YEAR OF GRACE, 1588. FOR BOYS AND GIRLS. EDINBURGH: WILLIAM P. NIMMO, 1871. 108p.: col. front. Bound in purple cloth, with coloured decorative cover and spine.
C 942.055 GRA

472 **HADDEN, JAMES CUTHBERT.**
THE BOY'S BOOK OF THE NAVY: ITS SHIPS AND SERVICES. REVISED BY J. CUTHBERT HADDEN. LONDON: S.W. PARTRIDGE AND CO. LTD., (191–?). 315p.: col. front., 3 col. plates, 12 plates, ill. Bound in green cloth, with coloured pictorial cover and spine.
C 359.00941 BOY

473 **HALF HOURS IN EARLY NAVAL ADVENTURE.**
WITH NUMEROUS ILLUSTRATIONS. LONDON: JAMES NISBET AND CO. LIMITED, 1904. XV, 360p. + 8p. pub. cat.: front., 36 plates, ill. Bound in red cloth, with embossed pictorial/decorative cover and spine. THE HALF HOUR LIBRARY OF TRAVEL, NATURE AND SCIENCE FOR YOUNG READERS.
C 823.912 HAL

474 **HALL, H.R.**
DAYS BEFORE HISTORY. BY H.R. HALL. WITH A PREFACE BY J.J. FINDLAY, M.A. Ph.D. LONDON: GEORGE G. HARRAP AND COMPANY, 1907. XVI, 144p.: front., 6 plates, ill. Bound in cream cloth, with coloured pictorial cover and spine, and gilt top.
YSC 823.912 HAL

475 **HANCOCK, MARY S.**
A SOCIAL HISTORY OF ENGLAND FOR GIRLS. BY MARY S. HANCOCK. LONDON: SIR ISAAC PITMAN AND SONS, LTD. (190–?). VI, 288p. 23 plates, ill. Bound in red cloth.
YSC 942 HAN

476 **HANSON, J.E.**
THE SPOTLIGHT GEOGRAPHICAL HISTORY OF ENGLAND. By J.E. HANSON, F.C.P., M.R.S.T. and P. ROUSE.
BOOK III. (Black Death to Age of Science).
BOOK IV. (Modern Industries to Great War).
LONDON: COLLINS CLEAR TYPE PRESS, 1939. 52 and 49 plates and maps; pockets with loose maps. Bound in yellow and purple card with decorative covers.
YSC 911 HAN

477 **HARTLEY, DOROTHY.**
LIFE AND WORK OF THE PEOPLE OF ENGLAND. A PICTORIAL RECORD from Contemporary Sources. THE FIFTEENTH CENTURY. BY DOROTHY HARTLEY AND MARGARET M. ELLIOT. LONDON: B.T. BATSFORD, LTD., 1925. 37p.: front., 48 plates. Rebound in quarter green leather and cloth. THE PEOPLE'S LIFE AND WORK SERIES.
YSC 942.04 HAR

478 **HENSON, JOSIAH.**
AN AUTOBIOGRAPHY OF THE REV. JOSIAH HENSON (MRS HARRIET BEECHER STOWE'S "UNCLE TOM"). From 1789–1877 WITH A PREFACE BY MRS HARRIET BEECHER STOWE. . . . EDITED BY JOHN LOBB, F.R.G.S. HUNDREDTH THOUSAND REVISED AND ENLARGED. LONDON: "CHRISTIAN AGE" OFFICE, 1878. 244p. inc. 3p. pub. cat.: front., 1 plate. Bound in blue cloth with embossed pictorial/decorative cover and spine.
YSC 920 HEN

478A **HIGHROADS OF HISTORY.**
Illustrated by the great Historical Paintings of John Petty etc. BOOK 4. Other days and Other Ways (from the Earliest times to 1485). LONDON: THOMAS NELSON AND SONS, 1913. 256p.: col. front., 12 col. plates, 8 plates. ill. maps. Bound in green cloth with decorative covers. ROYAL SCHOOL SERIES.
M 942 HIG CHILDREN'S COLLECTION

479 **HISTORICAL TALES.**
Illustrated. LONDON: GROOMBRIDGE AND SONS, 1879. Unpaginated + 16p. pub. cat.: col. front. by A.F. Lydon, 3 plates, ill. Bound in blue cloth, with embossed decorative cover and spine, and gilt edges.
C 909 HIS

480 **HOPE, EVA.**
GRACE DARLING, THE HEROINE OF THE FARNE ISLANDS: HER LIFE, AND ITS LESSONS. LONDON: ADAM AND CO., 1875. 312p.: front., additional vignette title page, 4 plates. Bound in red cloth, with embossed pictorial/decorative cover and spine.
C 910.4530294 DAR/HOP

481 **(HOPE, EVA).**
LIFE OF GENERAL GORDON. BY THE AUTHORS OF "OUR QUEEN", "NEW WORLD HEROES", ETC. LONDON: WALTER SCOTT LIMITED, (188–?). VIII, 369p. + 16p. pub cat.: col. front. Bound in brown cloth, with embossed decorative cover and spine.
C 355.00924 GOR/HOP

481A **THE HOUSE OF HISTORY.**
(VOL 1.) THE BASEMENT. FROM THE EARLIEST MEN TO FALL OF ROME BY DESIREE EDWARDS-REES. (VOL 2) THE FIRST STOREY. THE MIDDLE AGES. BY ELIZABETH ISAACSON. (VOL 3) THE SECOND STOREY. EARLY MODERN HISTORY. BY MURIEL MASEFIELD. (VOL 4) THE THIRD STOREY. LATER MODERN HISTORY. BY MURIEL MASEFIELD. (VOL 5) THE FOURTH STOREY. MODERN SOCIAL AND INDUSTRIAL HISTORY. BY DOROTHY GORDON. LONDON: THOMAS NELSON AND SONS, LTD. 1930–34. 288p., 274p., 330p., 334p., col. fronts., col. plates, plates, ill., maps. Bound in green cloth.
M 942 HOU CHILDREN'S COLLECTION

482 **HUME, DAVID.**
A HISTORY OF ENGLAND FROM THE EARLIEST TIMES TO THE REVOLUTION IN 1688 BASED ON THE HISTORY OF DAVID HUME. INCORPORATING THE CORRECTIONS AND RESEARCHES OF RECENT HISTORIANS: CONTINUED TO THE TREATY OF BERLIN IN 1878. NEW EDITION, REVISED AND CORRECTED BY J.S. BREWER, M.A. ILLUSTRATED BY MAPS AND ENGRAVINGS ON WOOD. LONDON: JOHN MURRAY, 1880. XXXVI, 793p. + 16p. pub. cat.: front., ill. maps. Bound in black cloth.
YSC 942 HUM

483 **JERROLD, WALTER.**
W.E. GLADSTONE: England's Great Commoner. BY WALTER JERROLD. SECOND EDITION, REVISED. LONDON: S.W. PARTRIDGE AND CO., (189–?). 160p. + 16p. pub. cat.: front. portrait, 7 plates, ill. Bound in blue cloth, with coloured pictorial cover.
YSC 941.0810924 GLA/JER

484 **JOHNSON, JOSEPH.**
CLEVER GIRLS OF OUR TIME Who Became Famous Women. BY JOSEPH JOHNSON. LONDON: GALL AND INGLIS, (188–?). IX, 276p.: front., 7 plates. Bound in red cloth with coloured pictorial/decorative cover.
YSC 920.72 JOH

485 **JOHNSON, SAMUEL.**
LIFE OF DRYDEN. LONDON: THOMAS NELSON AND SONS, LTD., 1937. 159p.: front. Bound in green cloth. A school edition with notes.
YSC 920 DRY

486 **KENDRICK, M.**
THE GIFT BOOK OF BIOGRAPHY FOR Young Ladies. BY MISS M. KENDRICK AND MRS L. MARIA CHILD. LONDON: THOMAS NELSON, 1848. 270p.: additional col. decorative title page. Bound in red cloth, with embossed decorative covers and spine, and gilt edges.
YSC 920.72 KEN

487 **KEY, C.E.**
A HISTORY OF THE BRITISH EMPIRE. LONDON: GEORGE G. HARRAP AND CO., LTD., 1936. 363p.: front., ill., maps. Bound in red cloth.
YSC 942 KEY

487A **KINGSTON, WILLIAM HENRY GILES.**
HOW BRITANNIA CAME TO RULE THE WAVES. The Story of the British Navy from the earliest times, by W.H.G. KINGSTON. LONDON: GALL AND INGLIS, (1908). 486p.: front. photograph, 12 plates, ill. Bound in green cloth with coloured pictorial cover and spine.
C 359.00941 KIN

488 **KINGSTON, WILLIAM HENRY GILES.**
OUR SAILORS: GALLANT DEEDS OF THE BRITISH NAVY DURING THE REIGN OF QUEEN VICTORIA. BY WILLIAM H.G. KINGSTON. A NEW EDITION, REVISED AND BROUGHT DOWN TO THE END OF 1900. ILLUSTRATED. LONDON: GRIFFITH FARRAN BROWNE AND CO. LIMITED, (190–?). 334p.: front., 4 plates. Bound in brown cloth, with coloured pictorial cover and spine. Originally published 1862.
C 359.00941081

489 **KINGSTON, WILLIAM HENRY GILES.**
OUR SOLDIERS: ANECDOTES OF THE CAMPAIGNS AND GALLANT DEEDS OF THE BRITISH ARMY DURING THE REIGN OF HER MAJESTY QUEEN VICTORIA. BY THE LATE WILLIAM H.G. KINGSTON. EDITED AND BROUGHT DOWN TO DATE BY G.A. HENTY. LONDON: GRIFFITH FARRAN OKEDEN AND WELSH, (188–?). VIII, 384p. + 4p. pub. cat.: front. Bound in green cloth, with coloured decorative cover, and gilt edges.
C 355.00941081 KIN

490 **LANG, ANDREW** *(Editor).*
THE RED TRUE STORY BOOK. EDITED BY ANDREW LANG. WITH NUMEROUS ILLUSTRATIONS BY HENRY J. FORD. LONDON: LONGMANS, GREEN, AND CO., 1895. XII, 419p.: front., vignette title page, 18 plates, ill. Bound in red cloth, with decorative cover and spine, and gilt edges.
C 398.21 RED

491 **LANG, ANDREW.** *(Editor).*
THE TRUE STORY BOOK. EDITED BY ANDREW LANG. With NUMEROUS ILLUSTRATIONS by L. BOGLE, LUCIEN DAVIS, H.J. FORD, C.H.M. KERR, and LANCELOT SPEED. LONDON: LONGMANS, GREEN AND CO., 1893. XIV, 337p. + 1p. pub. cat.: front., vignette title page, 8 plates, ill. Bound in blue cloth, with embossed pictorial cover and spine, and gilt edges.
C 909 TRU and YSC 920 LAN

493 **LAY, E.J.S.**
THE MODERN CLASS BOOK OF ENGLISH HISTORY. SENIOR BOOK V. VICTORIA AND MODERN TIMES. LONDON: MACMILLAN AND CO., LIMITED, 1939. 183p. + 4p. pub. cat.: vignette on title page, ill., maps.
YSC 942 LAY

494 **LIDDELL, HENRY G.**
A HISTORY OF ROME FROM THE EARLIEST TIMES TO THE ESTABLISHMENT OF THE EMPIRE. WITH CHAPTERS ON THE HISTORY OF LITERATURE AND ART. BY HENRY G. LIDDELL, D.D. ILLUSTRATED BY NUMEROUS ENGRAVINGS IN WOOD. LONDON: JOHN MURRAY, 1862. X, 676p.: front., ill., vignette on title page. The Student's Rome.
YSC 937.02 LID

495 **LIVES OF EMINENT WOMEN AND TALES FOR GIRLS FROM CHAMBERS'S MISCELLANY.**
LONDON: W. AND R. CHAMBERS, LIMITED, (190–?). 32p., 32p., 28p., 32p., 32p., 32p., 32p., 32p., 32p., 32p., 32p., 32p., 32p.: front., ill. Bound in red cloth, with pictorial/decorative cover and spine. Cover title: EMINENT WOMEN.
C 920.72 LIV

496 **LUDLOW, JOHN MALCOLM.**
THE WAR OF AMERICAN INDEPENDENCE. 1775–1783. BY JOHN MALCOLM LUDLOW. WITH FOUR MAPS. SECOND EDITION. LONDON: LONGMANS, GREEN AND CO., 1877. XVIII, 247p. + 4p. pub. cat.: maps. Bound in brown cloth. Epochs of Modern History.
YSC 973.3 LUD

497 **MACAULAY, THOMAS BABINGTON.**
ENGLAND IN 1685. By LORD MACAULAY. THOMAS NELSON AND SONS LTD., 1937. 175p.: front. Bound in green cloth.
YSC 942.06 MAC

498 **MACGREGOR, MARY.**
THE STORY OF GREECE. Told to Boys and Girls by MARY MACGREGOR. With nineteen plates in colour by Walter Crane. LONDON: THOMAS NELSON AND SONS, LTD., (192–?). XV, 356p.: col. front., vignette on title page, 18 plates, map. Bound in black cloth with coloured decorative cover.
CBD 398.220938 MAC

499 **MACMILLAN'S NEW HISTORY READERS. INTERMEDIATE.**
LONDON: MACMILLAN AND CO., LIMITED, 1906. 244p.: ill., maps. Bound in orange cloth.
YSC 941 MAC

500 **MANGNALL, RICHMAL.**
HISTORICAL AND MISCELLANEOUS QUESTIONS FOR THE USE OF YOUNG PEOPLE WITH A SELECTION OF BRITISH AND GENERAL BIOGRAPHY, ETC., ETC. BY RICHMAL MANGNALL. A NEW EDITION. CORRECTED AND ADAPTED FOR THE USE OF ENGLISH SCHOOLS. Illustrated with Forty Engravings. LONDON: WILLIAM TEGG AND CO., 1851. VIII, 494p. 40 plates. Bound in black cloth.
YSC 902.02 MAN

500A **MARSHALL, HENRIETTA ELIZABETH.**
A History of Germany. By H.E. Marshall. With illustrations in colour by A.C. Michael. LONDON: HENRY FROWDE AND HODDER AND STOUGHTON, 1913. (VIII), 449p.: col. front., vignette on title page, 9 col. plates, 2 maps. Bound in brown cloth with pictorial cover and pictorial endpapers.
C 943 MAR

501 **MARVIN, F.S.**
THE LIVING PAST. A SKETCH OF WESTERN PROGRESS. BY F.S. MARVIN. FOURTH EDITION. OXFORD: CLARENDON PRESS, 1920. XVI, 296p. + 2p. pub. cat. Bound in green cloth with decorative cover. Originally published in 1913.
YSC 940 MAR

502 **MAWER, ALLEN.**
THE VIKINGS. BY ALLEN MAWER, M.A. CAMBRIDGE UNIVERSITY PRESS, 1913. 150p.: front., 3 plates. Bound in red cloth with decorative cover.
YSC 948.02 MAW

503 **MEADOWS, P.**
Europe and England, 1789–1914. BY P. MEADOWS, M.A. LONDON: THOMAS NELSON AND SONS, LTD., 1929. 299p.: col. double front., map, 7 col. double maps, 2 col. maps, 1 plate, ill. Bound in red cloth. The Parallel Histories-Book IV B.
YSC 940.27 MEA

504 **MEARS, R.A.F.**
BRITAIN AND EUROPE; AN INTRODUCTION TO HISTORY. BY R.A.F. MEARS. M.A., B. Litt., F.R. Hist. S. BOOK I: FROM THE BEGINNINGS TO THE END OF THE MIDDLE AGES. LONDON: EDWARD ARNOLD AND CO., 1929. 255p. + 1p. pub. cat.: 16 plates, ill., maps. Bound in brown cloth, with vignette on cover.
YSC 940 MEA

505 **MILES, ALFRED HENRY** *(Editor)*.
With Fife and Drum: TRUE STORIES OF MILITARY LIFE AND ADVENTURE IN CAMP AND FIELD. TOLD AT FIRST HAND BY OFFICERS, PRIVATES AND OTHER EYEWITNESSES. EDITED BY ALFRED H. MILES. ILLUSTRATED. LONDON: HUTCHINSON AND CO., (189–?). VIII, 396p. + 4p. pub. cat.: front., 2 plates. Bound in blue cloth, with coloured pictorial cover and spine.
C 823.8 WIT

506 **MILNES, ALFRED.**
FROM GILD TO FACTORY. A FIRST SHORT COURSE OF ECONOMIC HISTORY. BY ALFRED MILNES, M.A. SECOND EDITION, REVISED. LONDON: MACDONALD AND EVANS, 1910. 84p. + 3p. pub. cat. Bound in red cloth.
YSC 330.9 MIL

507 **MOLESWORTH, WILLIAM NASSAU.**
THE HISTORY OF ENGLAND FROM THE YEAR 1830–1874. BY WILLIAM NASSAU MOLESWORTH, M.A. ABRIDGED EDITION. LONDON: GEORGE ROUTLEDGE AND SONS, 1887. 608p. Bound in maroon cloth.
YSC 942.081 MOL

508 **MONGAN, ROSCOE.**
THE OXFORD AND CAMBRIDGE HISTORY OF ENGLAND. FOR SCHOOL USE. FROM BC 55 TO AD 1905. BY ROSCOE MONGAN, B.A. LONDON: GEORGE GILL AND SONS, LTD., 1905. 205p. + 3p. pub. cat.: ill., col. maps, charts. Bound in yellow cloth.
YSC 941 MON

509 **MORRIS, EDWARD E.**
THE EARLY HANOVERIANS, BY EDWARD E. MORRIS. WITH MAPS AND PLANS. SIXTH IMPRESSION. LONDON: LONGMANS, GREEN AND CO., 1899. XXIII, 229p. + 2p. pub. cat.: col. front., maps, tables. Bound in brown cloth. Epochs of Modern History.
SC 941.07 MOR

510 **MOWAT, R.B.**
MAKERS OF BRITISH HISTORY. BY R.B. MOWAT, M.A.
BOOK I. 1066–1603.
BOOK II. 1603–1793.
BOOK III. 1793–1814.
ILLUSTRATED. LONDON: EDWARD ARNOLD AND CO., (1926). 192p., 192p., 224p. ill. Bound in red cloth.
YSC 942 MOW

511 **MUNDELL, FRANK.**
INTO THE UNKNOWN WEST; OR, THE STORY OF COLUMBUS. BY Frank Mundell. LONDON: GALL AND INGLIS, (191–?). IV, 253p.: front., 4 plates, 2 maps. Bound in brown cloth, with coloured pictorial cover and spine.
C 970.0150924 COL/MUN

512 **MUNRO, JOHN.**
THE STORY OF THE BRITISH RACE. NEW EDITION REVISED AND BROUGHT UP TO DATE. LONDON: GEORGE NEWNES, LIMITED, 1901. 250p.: maps. Bound in blue cloth with decorative cover. The Library of Useful Stories.
YSC 942 MON

513 **MYRES, J.L.**
A HISTORY OF ROME FOR MIDDLE AND UPPER FORMS OF SCHOOLS. WITH MAPS AND PLANS. BY J.L. MYRES, O.B.E., M.A., HON. D.Sc., F.B.A., F.S.A. NINTH IMPRESSION. LONDON: RIVINGTONS, 1937. 627p. Bound in green cloth. Originally published in 1902.
YSC 937 MYR

514 **OWEN, EMILY.**
THE Heroines of History. BY MRS. OCTAVIUS FREIRE OWEN. A NEW EDITION. With Eight Illustrations by Gilbert. LONDON: ROUTLEDGE, WARNE, AND ROUTLEDGE, 1862. VIII, 423p.: front., 7 plates, engraved by Dalziel Brothers. Bound in red cloth, with embossed decorative cover and spine.
C 823.009352 OWE

515 **PARROTT, J. EDWARD.**
THE PAGEANT OF BRITISH HISTORY, DESCRIBED BY J. EDWARD PARROTT AND DEPICTED BY THE FOLLOWING GREAT ARTISTS: J.M.W. Turner, G.F. Watts, Benjamin West, Lord Leighton, Sir John Gilbert, Daniel Maclise, C.W. Cope, John Opie, William Dyce, Sir L. Alma-Tadema, Sir John Millais, Paul Delaroche, W.Q. Orchardson, E.M. Ward, Stanhope Forbes, F. Goodall, Seymour Lucas, Ford Madox Brown, W.F. Yeames, Clarkson Stanfield, etc. etc. LONDON: THOMAS NELSON AND SONS, 1908. 384p.: col. front., 31 col. plates, 32 plates, decorative endpapers. Bound in cream buckram, with coloured pictorial and gilt cover, and gilt top.
C 941 PAR

516 **PARRY, DAVID HENRY.**
THE V.C. Its Heroes and Their Valour. From Personal Accounts, Official Records and Regimental Tradition. By D.H. PARRY, WITH EIGHT ILLUSTRATIONS BY STANLEY L. WOOD. NEW AND ENLARGED EDITION. LONDON: CASSELL AND COMPANY, LTD., 1913. XV, 520p.: front., 7 plates, ill. Bound in blue cloth with coloured decorative cover.
C 355.134 PAR

517 **THE PATRIOTIC HISTORICAL READER.**
BOOK V. Thirty Stories and Biographies from 1688 to 1901. NEW EDITION. LONDON: WILLIAM COLLINS, SONS, AND CO. LTD., (190–?). 264p.: 2 col. double plates, 14 col. plates, 3 plates, ill. Bound in red cloth, with coloured pictorial cover. COLLINS' SCHOOL SERIES.
YSC 941 PAT

518 **PEACH, L. DU GARDE.**
PLAYS OF THE FAMILY GOODMAN. 1485–1666, 1720–1914. Illustrated by Evelyn Simpson. LONDON: SIR ISAAC PITMAN AND SONS, LTD., 1939. 104p., 100p.: ill.
YSC 942 PEA

519 **PIKE, GODFREY HOLDEN.**
Shaftesbury: HIS LIFE AND WORK. BY G. HOLDEN PIKE. Second Edition. LONDON: S.W. PARTRIDGE AND CO., (1884). 97p. + 16p. pub. cat.: front., vignette title page, 5 plates. Bound in red cloth, with embossed pictorial cover and decorative spine.
C 941.0810924 SHA/PIK

520 **POLLARD, ELIZA F.**
FLORENCE NIGHTINGALE: The Wounded Soldier's Friend. BY ELIZA F. POLLARD. LONDON: S.W. PARTRIDGE AND CO., 1899. 160p. + 24p. ill. pub. cat.: front., 13 plates, ill. Bound in blue cloth, with coloured pictorial cover and spine.
C 610.730924 NIG/POL

521 **QUEEN VICTORIA AND HER PEOPLE.**
LONDON: THE EDUCATIONAL SUPPLY ASSOCIATION, LTD., (189–?). 256p.: front. portrait, 14 plates, ill. Bound in red paper, with blue paper covers. The Holborn Series.
YSC 941.081 QUE

522 **QUENNELL, MARJORIE.**
EVERYDAY LIFE IN ROMAN BRITAIN. WRITTEN AND ILLUSTRATED BY MARJORIE AND C.H.B. QUENNELL. Second Edition, revised and enlarged. LONDON: B.T. BATSFORD LTD., 1937. XI, 124p., col. front., vignette on title page. 2 col. plates, 33 plates, ill. Bound in purple cloth with decorative cover. THE EVERY DAY LIFE SERIES.
YSC 942.01 QUE

523 **QUENNELL, MARJORIE.**
EVERYDAY LIFE IN THE OLD STONE AGE. WRITTEN AND ILLUSTRATED BY MARJORIE AND C.H.B. QUENNELL. SECOND EDITION, REVISED. LONDON: B.T. BATSFORD LTD., 1926. XI, 113p. + 2p. pub. cat., col. front., vignette on title page, 11 plates, folding chart., ill. Bound in green cloth with pictorial cover.
YSC 930 QUE

523

524 **QUENNELL, MARJORIE.**
EVERYDAY THINGS IN ARCHAIC GREECE, BY MARJORIE AND C.H.B. QUENNELL. LONDON: B.T. BATSFORD, 1931. 146p.: Col. front., vignette on title page, 35 plates, ill., map and chart. Bound in orange cloth with pictorial cover.
YSC 938.03 QUE

525 **QUILLER-COUCH, Sir ARTHUR THOMAS.**
THE ROLL CALL OF HONOUR. By A.T. QUILLER-COUCH ("Q"). LONDON: THOMAS NELSON AND SONS, LTD., 1926. 261p. + 2p. pub. cat.: front., 6 plates by E. Heber Thompson. Bound in blue cloth.
YSC 920 QUI

526 **RANSOME, CYRIL.**
HISTORY OF ENGLAND. FOR THE ELEMENTARY USE OF LOWER FORMS OF SCHOOLS. BY CYRIL RANSOME, M.A. FIFTH EDITION. LONDON: RIVINGTON, PERCIVAL AND CO., 1897. VII, 250p. ill., maps. Bound in dark maroon cloth.
YSC 942 RAW

527 **RAYNER, ROBERT M.**
A MIDDLE SCHOOL HISTORY OF ENGLAND.
VOLUME I TO 1483.
VOLUME II 1485–1714.
With illustrations by Norman Hall, A.R.C.A. WITH SUPPLEMENT THE HISTORY OF LANCASHIRE AND CHESHIRE BY G.H. TUPLING, M.A., B.Sc., Ph.D. LONDON: JOHN MURRAY, 1933. 208, 207p., plates, ill., maps, charts. Pictorial/map endpapers. Bound in orange cloth with pictorial cover.
YSC 942 RAY

528 **REEVE, J.R.**
HISTORY THROUGH FAMILIAR THINGS. BY J.R. REEVE, B.A., B.Sc. PARTS I AND II. WITH 118 ILLUSTRATIONS AND EIGHT COLOURED PLATES. LONDON: UNIVERSITY OF LONDON PRESS, LTD., 1935. XVI, 270p.: front. Bound in buff cloth with coloured pictorial cover.
YSC 909 REE

529 **RENDER, WILLIAM H.**
THROUGH PRISON BARS: THE LIVES AND LABOURS OF JOHN HOWARD AND ELIZABETH FRY, The Prisoner's Friends. BY WILLIAM H. RENDER. LONDON: S.W. PARTRIDGE AND CO., (189–?). 160p. + 16p. pub. cat.: front., 10 plates, ill. Bound in brown cloth, with coloured pictorial cover and spine.
C 365.70922 REN

529A **RHODES, WALTER EUSTACE.**
A SCHOOL HISTORY OF LANCASHIRE. LONDON: METHUEN AND CO., 1907. XII, 215p. + 32p. pub. cat., front, 15 plates, 4 maps, ill. Bound in green cloth.

CLC 942.76 RHO and M 942.7 RHO CHILDREN'S COLLECTION

530 **ROWLEY, JAMES.**
RISE OF THE PEOPLE AND GROWTH OF PARLIAMENT. From the GREAT CHARTER to the ACCESSION OF HENRY VII. 1215–1485. BY JAMES ROWLEY. WITH FOUR MAPS. TWELFTH EDITION. LONDON: LONGMANS, GREEN AND CO., 1893. 111p. + 8p. pub. cat. Bound in brown cloth. EPOCHS OF ENGLISH HISTORY SERIES.
Y 942.03 ROW

531 **ROWLEY, JAMES.**
THE SETTLEMENT OF THE CONSTITUTION, 1689–1784 BY JAMES ROWLEY, M.A. WITH FOUR MAPS. NEW IMPRESSION. LONDON: LONGMANS, GREEN AND CO., 1900. 109p. + 2p. Pub. cat. Bound in brown cloth. EPOCHS OF ENGLISH HISTORY SERIES.
YSC 942.06 ROW

532 **RULE BRITANNIA.**
LONDON: HUMPHREY MILFORD, (193–?). Unpaginated: pictorial title page, 8 col. plates, ill. Bound in red cloth, with coloured pictorial paper cover with cut-out.
C 359.00941 RUL

532A **THE ST. GEORGE HISTORY READERS.**
BOOK III. STORIES FROM BRITISH HISTORY BC 55–AD 1485. LONDON: THOMAS NELSON AND SONS, 1901. 206p. + 2p. pub. cat.: front., 5 plates, ill., maps. Bound in red cloth with decorative cover. ROYAL SCHOOL SERIES.
M 942 SAI CHILDREN'S COLLECTION

533 **SALMON, EDWARD.**
THE STORY OF THE EMPIRE. BY EDWARD SALMON. LONDON: GEORGE NEWNES, LTD., 1902. 177p.: front., ill. Bound in blue cloth with decorative cover. LIBRARY OF USEFUL STORIES.
YSC 942 SAL

534 **SANDERSON, EDGAR.**
THE BRITISH EMPIRE IN THE NINETEENTH CENTURY.... BY EDGAR SANDERSON, M.A. ILLUSTRATED BY ENGRAVINGS AND MAPS. 6 VOLS. LONDON: BLACKIE AND SON, LTD., 1897. VIII, 356; VIII, 343; VIII, 344; VIII, 344; VIII, 362; VIII, 369p.: plates, maps.
YSC 942.08 SAN

535 **SEEBOHM, FREDERIC.**
THE ERA OF THE PROTESTANT REVOLUTION. BY FREDERIC SEEBOHM. WITH NUMEROUS MAPS. NEW EDITION. LONDON: LONGMANS, GREEN, AND CO., 1877. XV, 236p. + 4p. pub. cat.: maps. Coloured maps on endpapers. Bound in brown cloth. Epochs of Modern History.
YSC 940.23 SEE

536 **SPALDING, E.H.**
THE PIERS PLOWMAN SOCIAL AND ECONOMIC HISTORIES.
BOOK VI. 1760–1830. BY E.H. SPALDING, M.A.
BOOK VII. 1830 to the present Day. BY N. NIEMEYER AND E.H. SPALDING. FOURTH EDITION.
LONDON: GEORGE PHILIP AND SON, LTD. 1932. X, 232, XI, 291p.: ill. 2 vols rebound together in green cloth. Vol. 6 originally published in 1921.
YSC 942 SPA

537 **STIRLING, JOHN** *(Editor)*.
THE GATE OF KNOWLEDGE. THE STORY ATLAS through picture maps to the highways of learning. A new approach to the study of the Earth, the Race, the Ages, and the World of To-day. Edited by JOHN STIRLING.
Volume I. The Atlas Story of the Earth
The Atlas Story of the Race
Volume II. The Atlas Story of the Ages
The Atlas Story of To-Day
Volume III. The Atlas Story of the Modern World
LONDON: THE WAVERLEY BOOK COMPANY LIMITED, (192–?). 544p.: col. plates, plates, ill., maps. Bound in blue cloth with embossed decorative cover.
YOSC 030 STI

538 **THE STORIED PAST.**
A Book of Selections from English Literature Illustrative of English History. LONDON: EDWARD ARNOLD, (192–?). VII, 248 + 8p. pub. cat. : front., 7 plates. Bound in buff cloth with decorative cover.
YSC 820.8 STO

539 **STRONG, C.F.**
TODAY THROUGH YESTERDAY. BOOK TWO. KING AND PARLIAMENT 1603–1837. FOURTH EDITION. 1945. 180p.
BOOK THREE. PARLIAMENT AND PEOPLE 1837–Present Day. FOURTH EDITION (REVISED) 1944. 207p.
BOOK FOUR. THE YOUNG CITIZEN AND THE WORLD OF TODAY. NEW AND REVISED EDITION, 1944. 216p.
LONDON: UNIVERSITY OF LONDON PRESS, 1936–9. fronts., ill., maps, maps and charts on end paper. Bound in green, red and orange cloth with decorative cover.
YSC 909 STR

540 **TAYLOR, ISAAC.**
WORDS AND PLACES BY CANON ISAAC TAYLOR. Abridged and Edited by BEATRICE SAXON SNELL, M.A. LONDON: THOMAS NELSON AND SONS, LTD., 1925. 192p.: front. Bound in blue cloth. A Study of British and American place names.
YSC 929.4 TAY

541 **THAYER, WILLIAM M.**
FROM LOG-CABIN TO WHITE HOUSE: The Story of President Garfield's Life. BY WILLIAM M. THAYER. SIXTEENTH EDITION. COMPLETING EIGHTY-FOURTH THOUSAND. LONDON: HODDER AND STOUGHTON, 1883. XVI, 348p. + 4p. pub. cat.: front. Bound in blue cloth, with coloured pictorial cover and spine.
C 973.840924 GAR/THA

542 **THAYER, WILLIAM M.**
GEORGE WASHINGTON: His Boyhood and Manhood. BY WILLIAM M. THAYER. LONDON: HODDER AND STOUGHTON, 1883. XX, 422p. + 6p. pub. cat.: front. Bound in blue cloth, with coloured pictorial cover and spine.
C 973.410924 WAS/THA

543 **TICKNER, F.W.**
LONDON THROUGH THE AGES. BY F.W. TICKNER, D.LIT., B.Sc. LONDON: THOMAS NELSON AND SONS, LTD., 1935. 299p.: col. front., 13 col. plates, 52 plates, ill., maps, pictorial endpapers. Bound in red cloth.
YSC 942.1 TIC

544 **TILLOTSON, JOHN.**
THE YOUTHS' HISTORY OF CHINA: FROM THE EARLIEST PERIODS TO THE PRESENT TIME, INCLUDING A GEOGRAPHICAL SKETCH OF THE MANNERS AND CUSTOMS OF THE PEOPLE TOGETHER WITH AN ESSAY ON CHRISTIANITY IN CHINA. BY JOHN TILLOTSON. LONDON: THOMAS HOLMES, (1857). VIII, 248p.: front. Bound in red cloth, with embossed decorative covers and spine.
C 952 TIL

545 **TOUT, T.F.**
AN ADVANCED HISTORY OF GREAT BRITAIN.
PART II. FROM 1485 TO 1714 WITH 19 MAPS AND PLANS.
PART III. FROM 1714 TO 1934 WITH 14 MAPS AND PLANS.
LONDON: LONGMANS, GREEN AND CO. (1923), (1935). XV, 308–544; XVI, 536–805. Bound in red linson, and cloth. Originally published in 1902, 3.
YSC 942 TOU

546 **TUER, ANDREW W.**
Old London Street Cries AND THE CRIES OF TODAY. WITH Heaps of Quaint Cuts, including Hand coloured Frontispiece. LONDON: FIELD AND TUER, THE LEADEN HALL PRESS, 1885. 137p. + 6p. pub. cat.: col. front., 33 plates, ill. Bound in buff cloth with decorative paper covers.
YSC 398.2 TUE

547 **VALENTINE, LAURA.**
SEA FIGHTS AND LAND BATTLES: FROM SLUYS TO THE BOMBARDMENT OF ALEXANDRIA AND FROM HASTINGS TO THE WAR IN THE SOUDAN. BY MRS. VALENTINE. LONDON: FREDERICK WARNE AND CO., (189–?). X, 295p.: front., engraved by Dalziel Brothers. Bound in green cloth, with coloured decorative cover and spine. THE PRIZE LIBRARY.
C 823.8 VAL

548 **VAN LOON, HENDRIK.**
THE STORY OF MANKIND. LONDON: GEORGE C. HARRAP AND CO. LTD., 1922. XXVIII, 492p.: col. front., 8 col. plates, 8 plates, animated maps. Bound in blue cloth with inserted colour label of map of world.
YSC 960 VAN

549 **WARNER, GEORGE TOWNSEND.**
THE GROUNDWORK OF BRITISH HISTORY BY GEORGE TOWNSEND WARNER, M.A. AND C.H.K. MARTEN, M.A. LONDON: BLACKIE AND SON LIMITED, 1912. XIV, 749p. + 42p. pub. cat.: maps, charts. Bound in black cloth.
YSC 942 WAR

550 **WATNEY, CHARLES.**
THE WORKERS' DAILY ROUND. BY CHARLES WATNEY AND JAMES A. LITTLE. WITH EIGHT FULL-PAGE PLATES BY H.L. SHINDLER. LONDON: GEORGE ROUTLEDGE AND SONS LIMITED, (191–?). XII, 354p.: front., 7 plates. Bound in red cloth, with pictorial/decorative cover and pictorial spine.
C 301.55 WAT

551 **WELLS, HERBERT GEORGE.**
A SHORT HISTORY OF MANKIND. BY H.G. WELLS. ADAPTED AND EDITED FOR SCHOOL USE FROM THE AUTHOR'S "SHORT HISTORY OF THE WORLD". BY E.H. CARTER, O.B.E., M.A. OXFORD: BASIL BLACKWELL, 1925. VIII, 183p.: 13 plates, ill., maps. Bound in blue cloth, with decorative covers and spine.
YSC 900 WEL

552 **WESTELL, W. PERCIVAL.**
"LOOK AND FIND OUT". BOOK VIII. UNWRITTEN HISTORY AND HOW TO READ IT BY W. PERCIVAL WESTELL, F.L.S., F.R.S.A., F.S.A. SCOT. AND KATE HARVEY, M.Sc. Fully illustrated from photos and sketches, with Picture Tables by Doris Meyer. LONDON: MACMILLAN AND CO., LIMITED, 1939. 205p.: front., vignette on title page, ill., maps, picture tables. Bound in green cloth.
YSC 913 WES

553 **WHITE, H.**
ELEMENTS OF UNIVERSAL HISTORY, ON A NEW AND SYSTEMATIC PLAN; FROM THE EARLIEST TIMES TO THE TREATY OF VIENNA. TO WHICH IS ADDED, A SUMMARY OF THE LEADING EVENTS SINCE THAT PERIOD. For the Use of Schools and of Private Students. EDINBURGH: OLIVER AND BOYD, 1843. XII, 660p. + 24p. pub. cat. Bound in brown cloth with embossed decorative cover and spine.
YSC 909 WHI

554 **WIGGIN, KATE DOUGLAS.**
A CHILD'S JOURNEY WITH DICKENS. BY KATE DOUGLAS WIGGIN. LONDON: HODDER AND STOUGHTON, (191–?). 34p.: front. Bound in brown cloth, with pictorial cover.
C 818.54 WIG

555 **WILLSON, WINGROVE.**
BUFFALO BILL, CHIEF OF SCOUTS. THE STORY OF HIS LIFE AND ADVENTURES. BY WINGROVE WILLSON. LONDON: THE SHOE LANE PUBLISHING CO., (193–?). 126p.: col. front. by R. Prowse, 8 plates by Charles Gladwin. Bound in red cloth, with coloured pictorial paper cover.
C 973.80924 WIL

556 **WILMOT-BUXTON, ETHEL M.**
BRITAIN LONG AGO: STORIES FROM OLD ENGLISH AND CELTIC SOURCES. RETOLD BY E.M. WILMOT-BUXTON. LONDON: GEORGE G. HARRAP AND COMPANY, 1914. XV, 240p.: col. front., 15 plates, by Evelyn Paul, Chas. Sheldon, H.M. Brock, Gertrude Demain Hammond, R.I., and Herbert A. Bone, R.A. Bound in brown cloth, with coloured pictorial cover and spine, and gilt top.
C 398.22 WIL

557 **YONGE, CHARLOTTE MARY.**
AUNT CHARLOTTE'S STORIES OF AMERICAN HISTORY. BY CHARLOTTE M. YONGE AND H. HASTINGS WELD, D.D. LONDON: MARCUS WARD AND CO., LIMITED, 1883. 400p.: front., 15 plates. Bound in turquoise cloth with decorative cover and spine.
YSC 970 YON

558 **(YONGE, CHARLOTTE MARY).**
CAMEOS FROM ENGLISH HISTORY FROM ROLLO TO EDWARD II, BY THE AUTHOR OF THE HEIR OF REDCLYFFE. FIRST SERIES. THIRD EDITION. LONDON: MACMILLAN AND CO., 1874. XI, 385p. Bound in brown cloth.
YSC 942 YON

559 **(YONGE, CHARLOTTE MARY).**
LANDMARKS OF HISTORY. ANCIENT HISTORY: FROM THE EARLIEST TIMES TO THE MAHOMETAN CONQUEST. BY THE AUTHOR OF "THE HEIR OF REDCLYFFE". Twenty-fourth Edition. LONDON: WALTER SMITH, 1881. XX, 244p. + 4p. pub. cat. Bound in black cloth with embossed decoration. Originally published in 1852.
YSC 930 YON

560 **(YONGE, CHARLOTTE MARY).**
LANDMARKS OF HISTORY. MIDDLE AGES: FROM THE REIGN OF CHARLEMAGNE TO THAT OF CHARLES V. Eighth Edition. LONDON: WALTER SMITH, 1879. 310p. + 2p. pub. cat. Bound in green cloth with embossed decorative cover and spine.
YSC 909.07 YON

560A **YONGE, CHARLOTTE MARY.**
TWENTY STORIES AND BIOGRAPHIES FROM 1066 to 1485. adapted to the Requirements of the New Code. BY CHARLOTTE M. YONGE. LONDON: NATIONAL SOCIETY'S DEPOSITORY, (189–?). 219p. + 4p. pub. cat. front., a double page map of England and Wales, ill. Bound in blue cloth with pictorial cover. THE WESTMINSTER HISTORICAL READING BOOKS.
M 942 YON CHILDREN'S COLLECTION

## 9 TRAVEL AND GEOGRAPHY

561 **ALEXANDER, PHILIP F.** *(Editor).*
THE EARLIEST VOYAGES ROUND THE WORLD 1519–1617. EDITED BY PHILIP F. ALEXANDER, M.A. CAMBRIDGE: UNIVERSITY PRESS, 1925. XXIII, 216p.: front., 9 plates, 10 maps. Bound in green cloth. CAMBRIDGE TRAVEL BOOKS. Originally published in 1916.
YSC 910.4 ALE

562 **BAKER, W.G.**
GEOGRAPHICAL READER. NO. III. ENGLAND AND WALES. BY W.G. BAKER. LONDON: BLACKIE AND SON, (188–?). 128p.: ill., maps. Bound in grey cloth with

decorative cover. BLACKIE'S COMPREHENSIVE SCHOOL SERIES.
YSC 914.2 BAK

563 **BARTHOLOMEW, JOHN.**
PHILIPS' HANDY ATLAS OF THE COUNTIES OF ENGLAND. BY JOHN BARTHOLOMEW, F.R.G.S. NEW AND ENLARGED EDITION, WITH CONSULTING INDEX. LONDON: GEORGE PHILIP AND SON, 1882. 45p. index + 4p. pub. cat.: 43 col. maps. Bound in maroon cloth, with embossed decorative cover.
C 912.42 BAR

564 **BATES, HENRY WALTER.**
CENTRAL AMERICA, THE WEST INDIES AND SOUTH AMERICA. EDITED AND EXTENDED BY H.W. BATES. WITH ETHNOLOGICAL APPENDIX BY A.H. KEANE, M.A.I. MAPS AND ILLUSTRATIONS. THIRD EDITION. LONDON: EDWARD STANFORD, 1885. XVIII, 571p.: front., 20 plates, 13 col. maps, ill. Bound in green cloth, with embossed pictorial/decorative cover and spine. STANFORD'S COMPENDIUM OF GEOGRAPHY AND TRAVEL.
C 918 BAT

565 **BRASSEY, ANNIE, Baroness.**
SUNSHINE AND STORM IN THE EAST; OR, CRUISES TO CONSTANTINOPLE. BY LADY BRASSEY. WITH UPWARDS OF 100 ILLUSTRATIONS CHIEFLY FROM DRAWINGS BY THE HON. A.Y. BINGHAM. LONDON: LONGMANS, GREEN, AND CO., 1888. XXI, 488p.: front., vignette title page, 8 plates, 2 maps, ill. Bound in grey cloth, with pictorial cover and spine, and gilt edges.
C 910.091822 BRA

566 **BRASSEY, ANNIE,** *Baroness.*
A VOYAGE IN THE "SUNBEAM", OUR HOME ON THE OCEAN FOR ELEVEN MONTHS. BY LADY BRASSEY. WITH 66 ILLUSTRATIONS ENGRAVED ON WOOD BY G. PEARSON, CHIEFLY AFTER DRAWINGS BY THE HON. A.Y. BINGHAM. LONDON: LONGMANS, GREEN AND CO., 1886. XIX, 492p.: front., vignette title page, map, ill. Bound in olive cloth, with pictorial/decorative cover and spine, and gilt edges.
C 910.41 BRA

567 **BROOKS, LEONARD.**
COLUMBUS REGIONAL GEOGRAPHIES BY LEONARD BROOKS, MA AND ROBERT FINCH. SENIOR SERIES
BOOK II PART I. NORTH AMERICA
PART II. ASIA
BOOK III THE BRITISH ISLES AND EUROPE.
LONDON: UNIVERSITY OF LONDON PRESS, LTD. 1938, 1939, 1931. 256p. (Part 1 & 11), 320p.: fronts., 2,2,5 col. plates, ill. maps. Bound in orange (vol. 2, part 11 and Vol. 3) and green (vol. 2, part 1)
YSC 917, 916, 914 BRO

568 **BRUCE, HON. MRS. FINETTA MADELINA JULIA.**
PEEPS AT MANY LANDS: KASHMIR. BY HON. MRS. C.G. BRUCE. WITH TWELVE FULL-PAGE ILLUSTRATIONS IN COLOUR BY MAJOR E. MOLYNEUX, D.S.O. LONDON: ADAM AND CHARLES BLACK, 1911.
95p. + 4p. pub. cat.: col. front., 10 col. plates, map, decorative front endpapers. Bound in blue cloth, with coloured pictorial paper label on cover.
C 915.4604 BRU

569 **CARTER, C.C.**
THE WORLD OF MAN. BY C.C. CARTER AND E.C. MARCHANT.
BOOK III CONTINENTS NEW AND OLD EXCEPT EUROPE.
BOOK IV EUROPE, THE BRITISH ISLES AND THE WORLD.
LONDON: CHRISTOPHERS, 1937, 1939. 472, 300p.: ill., maps. Bound in green cloth.
YSC 910 CAR

570 **CHAMBERS'S ALTERNATIVE GEOGRAPHY READERS.**
STANDARD VII. LONDON: W. AND R. CHAMBERS, 1899. 224p., 4 plates, ill., maps, some col. Bound in green cloth with decorative cover.
YSC 910.0971241 CHA

571 **CHAMBERS'S GEOGRAPHICAL READER OF THE CONTINENTS.**
ASIA AND AFRICA. LONDON: W. AND R. CHAMBERS, 1907. 264p.: col. front., 6 col. plates, 4 plates, ill., maps, some col. Bound in yellow cloth with decorative cover.
YSC 910 CHA

572 **CLYDE, JAMES.**
ELEMENTARY GEOGRAPHY. BY JAMES CLYDE, LL.D. NINTH EDITION REVISED AND CORRECTED THROUGHOUT. EDINBURGH: OLIVER AND BOYD, 1865; VII, 156p. + 12p. pub. cat. Bound in red cloth with embossed decorative cover and spine.
YSC 910 CLY

573 **CLYDE, JAMES.**
SCHOOL GEOGRAPHY. BY JAMES CLYDE, M.A., LL.D. Twenty-second Edition. LONDON: SIMPKIN, MARSHALL, AND CO., 1884. 551p. + 24p. pub. cat.: 9 col. maps. Bound in brown cloth. Spine title: CLYDE'S GEOGRAPHY.
C 910 CLY

574 **COMPENDIUM OF GEOGRAPHY.**
BEING AN ABRIDGEMENT OF THE LARGER WORK ENTITLED AN EPITOME OF GEOGRAPHICAL KNOWLEDGE ANCIENT AND MODERN, COMPILED FOR THE USE OF THE TEACHERS AND ADVANCED CLASSES OF THE NATIONAL SCHOOLS IN IRELAND. NEW EDITION. REVISED. DUBLIN: ALEXANDER THOM, 1873. 192p.: col. decorative endpapers. Rebound in blue quarter leather, with coloured decorative covers.
C 910 COM

575 **CORNWELL, JAMES.**
GEOGRAPHY FOR BEGINNERS. BY JAMES CORNWELL, PH.D., F.R.G.S. TWENTY-SEVENTH EDITION. LONDON: SIMPKIN, MARSHALL AND CO., (186–?). 96p.: map, col. decorative endpapers. Rebound in red quarter leather, with coloured decorative covers.
C 910 COR

576 **DAUGHTRY, E.I.**
THE BRITISH EMPIRE. LONDON: WILLIAM HEINEMANN LTD., 1935. VIII, 270p.: 12 plates, ill., maps, diagrs. Bound in green cloth. Studies in Geography.
YSC 914.2 DAU

577 **DOUGLAS, MARY.**
BREAKING THE RECORD. The Story of THREE ARCTIC EXPEDITIONS. BY M. DOUGLAS. LONDON: THOMAS NELSON AND SONS, 1902. 229p. + 2p. pub. cat.: front., 16 plates. Bound in blue cloth, with decorative/pictorial cover and spine.
C 823.912 DOU

578 **DOUGLAS, MARY.**
IN LIONLAND: The Story of Livingstone and Stanley. BY M. DOUGLAS. WITH ILLUSTRATIONS. LONDON: THOMAS NELSON AND SONS, 1900. 275p. + 4p. pub. cat.: front., 14 plates. Bound in blue cloth, with coloured pictorial cover and spine.
C 916.704 LIV/DOU

579 **ELLIOT, GEORGE FRANCIS SCOTT.**
THE WONDERS OF SAVAGE LIFE. BY G.F. SCOTT ELLIOT. WITH FOURTEEN ILLUSTRATIONS. LONDON: SEELEY, SERVICE AND CO. LIMITED, 1914. 161p. + 18p. pub. cat.: front., 7 plates, ill. Bound in green cloth, with coloured pictorial cover and spine.
C 910 ELL

579A **FAIRFORD, FORD.**
CUBA. BY FORD FAIRFORD. WITH TWELVE FULL-PAGE ILLUSTRATIONS IN COLOUR BY CLAUDE PRATT. LONDON: ADAM AND CHARLES BLACK, 1913. VI, 88p. + 8p. pub. cat.: col. front., map, 11 col. plates. Bound in red cloth with coloured pictorial paper label on covers. PEEPS AT MANY LANDS.
C 917.291 FAI

579B **FAIRFORD, FORD.**
NEWFOUNDLAND. BY FORD FAIRFORD. CONTAINING TWELVE FULL-PAGE ILLUSTRATIONS IN COLOUR BY C.G. LOWTHER. LONDON: ADAM AND CHARLES BLACK, 1912. VIII, 88p. + 8p. pub. cat.: col. front., map, 11 col. plates. Bound in green cloth with coloured pictorial paper label on cover. PEEPS AT MANY LANDS.
C 917.18 FAI

580 **FERRIDAY, A.**
A MAP BOOK OF EUROPE FOR SCHOOL CERTIFICATE FORMS. By A. FERRIDAY, M.Sc. LONDON: MACMILLAN AND CO., LIMITED. (1939). 64p.: maps. Limp bound in orange card.
YSC 914 FER

581 **FERRIDAY, A.**
A MAP BOOK OF THE BRITISH ISLES FOR SCHOOL CERTIFICATE FORMS. By A. FERRIDAY, M.Sc. LONDON: MACMILLAN AND CO., LIMITED. (1937). 48p.: maps. Limp bound in blue card.
YSC 914.2 FER

582 **FINCH, ROBERT.**
GOLDEN HIND GEOGRAPHIES. FIRST SERIES.
BOOK ONE. OURSELVES AND OTHER PEOPLE. BY ROBERT FINCH.
BOOK TWO. VILLAGE PEOPLES BY GEORGE CONS.
BOOK THREE. BRITAIN AND THE BRITISH. BY ROBERT FINCH.
BOOK FOUR. MAN'S WORK IN THE WORLD. BY GEORGE CONS.
LONDON: UNIVERSITY OF LONDON PRESS LTD., 1937. 96, 127, 160, 176p.: col. fronts., col. plates, ill., maps. Bound in green, red, orange and blue cloth with pictorial cover.
YSC 910 FIN, 910 CON, 914.2 FIN, 914.2 CON

582A **FINNEMORE, JOHN.**
ITALY. BY JOHN FINNEMORE. WITH TWELVE FULL-PAGE ILLUSTRATIONS IN COLOUR. LONDON: ADAM AND CHARLES BLACK, 1907. VIII, 87p.: map, 11 plates by Ella Du Cane. Bound in blue cloth with coloured pictorial paper label on covers. PEEPS AT MANY LANDS.
C 914.5 FIN

582B **FINNEMORE, JOHN.**
JAPAN. BY JOHN FINNEMORE. WITH TWELVE FULL-PAGE ILLUSTRATIONS IN COLOUR BY ELLA DU CANE. LONDON: ADAM AND CHARLES BLACK, 1907. VII, 88p. + 8p. pub. cat.: col. front., map, 11 col. plates. Bound in blue cloth with coloured pictorial paper label on cover. PEEPS AT MANY LANDS.
C 915.2 FIN

582C **FINNEMORE, JOHN.**
SWITZERLAND. BY JOHN FINNEMORE. WITH TWELVE FULL-PAGE ILLUSTRATIONS IN COLOUR BY A.D. McCORMICK R.I., J. HARDWICKE LEWIS AND OTHERS. LONDON: ADAM AND CHARLES BLACK, 1908. VIII, 86p. + 6p. pub. cat.: col. front., 11 col. plates. Bound in blue cloth with coloured pictorial paper label on cover. PEEPS AT MANY LANDS.
C 914.94 FIN

582D **FOX, FRANK.**
AUSTRALIA. BY FRANK FOX. WITH TWELVE FULL-PAGE ILLUSTRATIONS IN COLOUR BY PERCY F.S. SPENCE ETC. LONDON: ADAM AND CHARLES BLACK, 1911. VIII, 88p.: col. front., map, 11 col. plates. Bound in red cloth with coloured pictorial paper cover. PEEPS AT MANY LANDS
C 919.4 FOX

583 **GELDART, HANNAH RANSOME.**
GLIMPSES OF OUR ISLAND HOME. BY MRS. THOMAS GELDART. A NEW EDITION, WITH ILLUSTRATIONS. LONDON: ROUTLEDGE, WARNE, AND ROUTLEDGE, 1864. VII, 242p. + 6p. pub. cat.: front., 3 plates, ill. Bound in green cloth, with embossed decorative covers and spine.
C 823.8 GEL

584 **GEOGRAPHY FOR TODAY.**
BOOK 1 AT HOME AND ABROAD.
BOOK III NORTH AMERICA AND ASIA.
LONDON: LONGMANS, GREEN AND CO., 1937 and 1939. XII, 243; XII, 404p.: ill., maps, diagrs. Bound in green and buff cloth. Edited by a committee headed by S.H. Beaver, M.A.
YSC 910 GEO, 917 GEO

585 **GILL, GEORGE.**
GILL'S ATLAS GEOGRAPHY OF AFRICA. By George Gill, F.R.G.S. LONDON: GEORGE GILL AND SONS, (189–?). 80p.: 9 col. full-page maps. Bound in grey cloth, with coloured pictorial cover.
C 916 GIL

586 **GILL, GEORGE.**
GILL'S IMPERIAL GEOGRAPHY, FOR College and School use. ILLUSTRATED WITH SIXTY-SEVEN MAPS AND NUMEROUS WOODCUTS. BY GEORGE GILL. REVISED EDITION, 1886. LONDON: GEORGE GILL AND SONS, 1886. 326p.: front., 66 full-page maps. Bound in mustard cloth, with decorative cover.
C 914.007

587 **GILL, GEORGE.**
A THIRD STANDARD GEOGRAPHY. CONTAINING THE OUTLINES OF THE NOTES OF LESSONS OF WHAT IS REQUIRED FROM THIRD STANDARD CHILDREN BY THE CODE OF 1875. BY GEORGE GILL. LONDON: GEORGE GILL AND SONS, (187–?). 16p. Maps, one of Cumberland and Westmorland. Bound in blue cloth with pictorial cover. Some pages incomplete.
YSC 914.2 GIL

587A **GOLDSMITH, J.**
A GRAMMAR OF GEOGRAPHY FOR THE USE OF SCHOOLS WITH MAPS AND ILLUSTRATIONS BY THE REV. J. GOLDSMITH. IMPROVED AND ENLARGED BY THE REV. C.N. WRIGHT, MA. LONDON: THOMAS TEGG, (1853) IV, 242p. + 2p. pub. cat.: front. vignette on title page, 10 plates, 7 folded maps. Bound in black cloth.
M 910 GOL CHILDREN'S COLLECTION

587B **GUY, JOSEPH.**
GUY'S SCHOOL GEOGRAPHY ON A New and Easy Plan COMPRISING NOT ONLY A COMPLETE GENERAL DESCRIPTION BUT MUCH TOPOGRAPHIC INFORMATION . . . EXPRESSLY ADAPTED TO EVERY AGE AND CAPACITY, AND TO EVERY CLASS OF LEARNERS BOTH IN LADIES' AND GENTLEMEN'S SCHOOLS. BY JOSEPH GUY. ILLUSTRATED WITH SEVEN NEW MAPS Finely Engraved by Becker. LONDON: CRADOCK AND CO., TWENTIETH EDITION. 1849. VII, 204p. + 4p. pub. cat.: front. (a double folded world map), 6 maps. Bound in red calf.
C 910 GUY

588 **GYFORD, C. BARRINGTON.**
The Skipper Ashore. By C. Barrington Gyford, B.Sc. Being some more letters from the Skipper of a Tramp Steamer, about his experiences ashore in various parts of the World. With Photographs sent by the Writer. LONDON: SIR ISAAC PITMAN AND SONS, LTD., 1938. 144p.: 16 plates. Bound in orange linson.
YSC 910.4 GYF

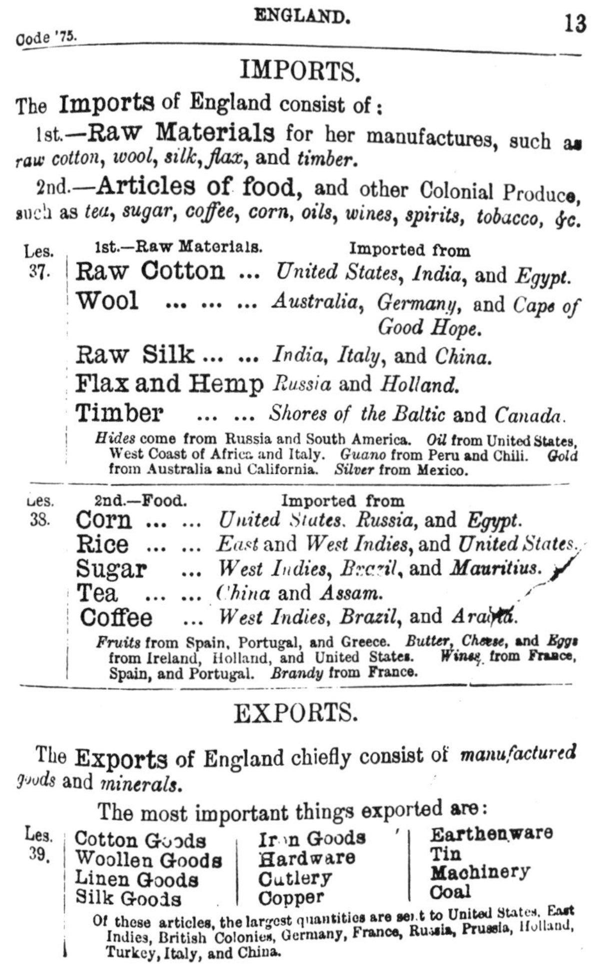
ENGLAND. 13

Code '75.

IMPORTS.

The **Imports** of England consist of:

1st.—**Raw Materials** for her manufactures, such as *raw cotton, wool, silk, flax,* and *timber.*

2nd.—**Articles of food,** and other Colonial Produce, such as *tea, sugar, coffee, corn, oils, wines, spirits, tobacco, &c.*

| Les. | 1st.—Raw Materials. | Imported from |
|---|---|---|
| 37. | Raw Cotton ... | *United States, India,* and *Egypt.* |
| | Wool ... ... ... | *Australia, Germany,* and *Cape of Good Hope.* |
| | Raw Silk ... ... | *India, Italy,* and *China.* |
| | Flax and Hemp | *Russia* and *Holland.* |
| | Timber ... ... | *Shores of the Baltic* and *Canada.* |

*Hides* come from Russia and South America. *Oil* from United States, West Coast of Africa and Italy. *Guano* from Peru and Chili. *Gold* from Australia and California. *Silver* from Mexico.

| Les. | 2nd.—Food. | Imported from |
|---|---|---|
| 38. | Corn ... ... | *United States. Russia,* and *Egypt.* |
| | Rice ... ... | *East* and *West Indies,* and *United States.* |
| | Sugar ... | *West Indies, Brazil,* and *Mauritius.* |
| | Tea ... ... | *China* and *Assam.* |
| | Coffee ... | *West Indies, Brazil,* and *Arabia.* |

*Fruits* from Spain, Portugal, and Greece. *Butter, Cheese,* and *Eggs* from Ireland, Holland, and United States. *Wines* from France, Spain, and Portugal. *Brandy* from France.

EXPORTS.

The **Exports** of England chiefly consist of *manufactured goods* and *minerals.*

The most important things exported are:

| Les. | | | |
|---|---|---|---|
| 39. | Cotton Goods | Iron Goods | Earthenware |
| | Woollen Goods | Hardware | Tin |
| | Linen Goods | Cutlery | Machinery |
| | Silk Goods | Copper | Coal |

Of these articles, the largest quantities are sent to United States, East Indies, British Colonies, Germany, France, Russia, Prussia, Holland, Turkey, Italy, and China.

587

589 **HARDY, E.J.**
JOHN CHINAMAN AT HOME. SKETCHES OF MEN, MANNERS AND THINGS IN CHINA. BY THE REV. E.J. HARDY, M.A. ILLUSTRATED. THIRD IMPRESSION. LONDON: T. FISHER UNWIN, 1907. 335p.: front., 35 plates. Bound in blue cloth with decorative cover and spine.
YSC 915.1 HAR

590 **HARDY, M.E.**
A JUNIOR PLANT GEOGRAPHY BY M.E. HARDY, D.Sc. OXFORD: THE CLARENDON PRESS, 1913. 192p.: 19 plates, ill., maps. Bound in green cloth with decorative cover.
YSC 910 HAR

591 **HATTERSLEY, CHARLES W.**
An English Boy's Life and Adventures in Uganda. By CHAS. W. HATTERSLEY. LONDON: THE RELIGIOUS TRACT SOCIETY, (191–?). 262p. + 10p. pub. cat.: col. front., 1 col. plate, 10 plates. Bound in brown cloth, with coloured pictorial cover and spine.
C 916.761 HAT

592 **HERDMAN, T.**
DISCOVERING GEOGRAPHY IN BRITAIN.
DISCOVERING GEOGRAPHY ABROAD.
DISCOVERING GEOGRAPHY, OUR FOOD.
DISCOVERING GEOGRAPHY, INDUSTRY.
LONGMANS 1938, 1940. 152, 154, 120, 122p.: ill., maps. Bound in grey cloth.
YSC 914.2 HER

593 **HUGHES, EDWARD.**
OUTLINES OF PHYSICAL GEOGRAPHY, DESCRIPTIVE OF THE INORGANIC MATTER OF THE GLOBE, AND THE DISTRIBUTION OF ORGANIZED BEINGS; DESIGNED FOR THE USE OF SCHOOLS AND PRIVATE READING. BY EDWARD HUGHES, F.R.G.S. FOURTH EDITION, GREATLY ENLARGED. LONDON: LONGMAN, BROWN, GREEN, AND LONGMANS, 1853. XII, 292p.: 8 col. double maps, diagrams, col. decorative endpapers. Rebound in red quarter leather, with coloured decorative covers.
C 910 HUG

594 **JACOBS, JOSEPH.**
The Story of Geographical Discovery. How the World Became Known. BY JOSEPH JACOBS. With Twenty-four maps etc. LONDON: GEORGE NEWNES, LIMITED, 1899. 224p., front., ill., maps. Bound in blue cloth with decorative cover and spine. Library of Useful Stories.
YSC 910.4 JAC

595 **JOHNSTON, KEITH.**
AFRICA. BY THE LATE KEITH JOHNSTON, F.R.G.S. REVISED AND CORRECTED BY E.G. RAVENSTEIN, F.R.G.S. WITH ETHNOLOGICAL APPENDIX BY A.H. KEANE, M.A.I. FOURTH EDITION. MAPS AND ILLUSTRATIONS. LONDON: EDWARD STANFORD, 1884. XVI, 616p.: front., 16 plates, 16 col. maps, ill. Bound in green cloth, with embossed pictorial/decorative cover and spine. STANFORD'S COMPENDIUM OF GEOGRAPHY AND TRAVEL.
C 916 JOH

596 **JONES, JOHN.**
COLLINS NEW SCHEME GEOGRAPHIES. VOLUME FIVE. AFRICA, ASIA AND THE OCEANS. LONDON: COLLINS CLEAR TYPE PRESS, 1933. 223p.: 4 sepia plates, ill., maps. Bound in green cloth.
YSC 910 JON

597 **JONES, M.**
DR. KANE, THE ARCTIC HERO. A Narrative of his Adventures and Explorations in the Polar Regions. By M. JONES. LONDON: T. NELSON AND SONS, 1896. 168p. + 8p. pub. cat.: front., 2 plates, ill. Bound in blue cloth, with pictorial/decorative cover and spine.
C 919.80924 KAN/JON

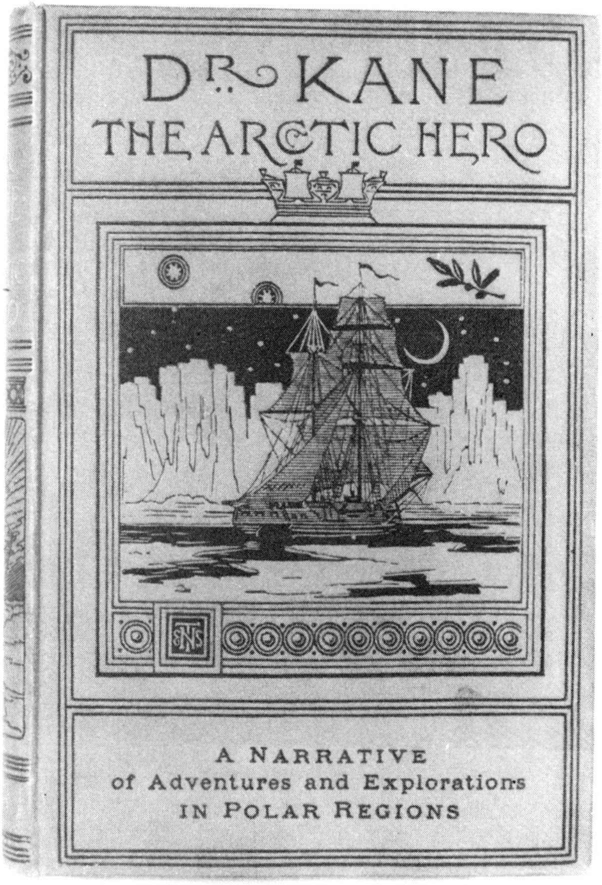


597

598 **KERMACK, W.R.**
OUR WORLD TODAY, A Modern Geography. BY W.R. KERMACK, B.A., F.R.G.S. Containing Eighty-Nine Maps and Diagrams and over Four Hundred Graded Exercises. LONDON: W. & A.K. JOHNSTON, LIMITED, 1938. 383p. Bound in red cloth.
YSC 910 KER

598A **KIDD, DUDLEY.**
SOUTH AFRICA. BY DUDLEY KIDD. WITH TWELVE FULL-PAGE ILLUSTRATIONS IN COLOUR BY A.M. GOODALL. LONDON: A. & C. BLACK, LTD., 1919. VIII, 87p.: col. front., decorative title page, map, 11 col. plates. Bound in grey paper with coloured pictorial label on cover. PEEPS AT MANY LANDS.
C 968.04 KID

599 **KINGSTON, WILLIAM HENRY GILES.**
SHIPWRECKS AND DISASTERS AT SEA. BY W.H.G. KINGSTON. WITH NUMEROUS ILLUSTRATIONS. LONDON: GEORGE ROUTLEDGE AND SONS, 1873. XII, 516p.: front., vignette title page, 51 plates, ill. Bound in brown cloth, with embossed pictorial/decorative cover and spine, and gilt edges.
C 910.453 KIN

600 **LEITH, MARY CHARLOTTE JULIA.**
ICELAND. BY MRS. DISNEY LEITH. WITH TWELVE WATER-COLOUR ILLUSTRATIONS BY M.A. WEMYSS AND THE AUTHOR. LONDON: ADAM AND CHARLES BLACK, 1908. VIII, 69p. + 2p. pub. cat.: col. front., 11 col. plates, map. Bound in blue cloth, with coloured pictorial paper label on cover. PEEPS AT MANY LANDS.
C 914.91204 LEI

601 **LONGMANS' NEW GEOGRAPHICAL READERS.**
THE FIFTH READER FOR STANDARD V. (EUROPE). NEW EDITION, REVISED. LONDON: LONGMANS, GREEN AND CO., 1900. 224p.: front., 15 plates, ill., 2 folding maps, maps. Bound in buff cloth with decorative cover.
YSC 910 LON

602 **LONGMANS' NEW GEOGRAPHICAL READERS.**
THE FIRST READER FOR STANDARD I. LONDON: LONGMANS, GREEN, AND CO., 1890. 128p.: front., 6 plates, ill. Bound in grey cloth, with pictorial cover.
C 910 LON

603 **MACKINDER, SIR HALFORD JOHN.**
LANDS BEYOND THE CHANNEL: An Elementary Study in Geography. BY H.J. MACKINDER, M.A. SIXTH EDITION. WITH ONE HUNDRED AND FIFTY-EIGHT ILLUSTRATIONS AND NINE COLOURED MAPS. LONDON: GEORGE PHILIP AND SON LIMITED, 1912. XVI, 276p.: front., 9 col. maps, 9 plates, 7 maps, ill. Bound in red cloth, with pictorial/decorative cover and spine.
C 910 MAC

604 **MACKINDER, SIR HALFORD JOHN.**
OUR OWN ISLANDS: An Elementary Study in Geography. BY SIR HALFORD MACKINDER, M.A. FIFTEENTH EDITION. WITH 167 ILLUSTRATIONS AND MAPS. LONDON: GEORGE PHILIP AND SON LIMITED, (1922). XV, 319p.: front., 19 plates, 2 double-page maps, 33 full-page maps, ill., maps. Bound in pink cloth, with pictorial/ decorative cover.
C 914.1 MAC

606 **MCLEOD, WALTER.**
THE GEOGRAPHY OF PALESTINE; OR The Holy Land, INCLUDING PHOENICIA AND PHILISTIA; WITH A DESCRIPTION OF THE TOWNS AND PLACES IN ASIA MINOR VISITED BY THE APOSTLES . . . BY WALTER MC LEOD, F.R.G.S. NEW EDITION. LONDON: LONGMANS, GREEN, AND CO., (187–?). XII, 105p. + 2p. pub. cat.: col. front. Bound in brown cloth, with decorative covers.
C 915.69 MAC

607 **MARVIN, CHARLES.**
THE REGION OF ETERNAL FIRE: AN ACCOUNT OF A JOURNEY TO THE PETROLEUM REGION OF THE CASPIAN IN 1883. BY CHARLES MARVIN. POPULAR EDITION. LONDON: W.H. ALLEN AND CO., 1888. XXII, 406p. + 2p. pub. cat.: front., 7 plates, 5 maps, ill. Bound in red cloth, with pictorial cover and spine.
C 914.77048 MAR

608 **MIDGLEY, CYRIL.**
INDIVIDUAL EXERCISES IN SCHOOL GEOGRAPHY. BOOK XII Intermediate Map Making and Map Reading. With special reference to 1" O.S. Maps.
(BY) CYRIL MIDGLEY, M.Sc. EXETER, A. WHEATON AND COMPANY, Ltd., 1931. 39p. + 1p. pub. cat.: maps. Limp bound in buff card.
YSC 526 MID

608A **THE MODERN ATLAS OF THE WORLD.**
LONDON: AMALGAMATED PRESS LTD., (192–?). 32p.: col. maps. Shows the British Empire at its height.
M 912 MOD CHILDREN'S COLLECTION

609 **MOSS, F.G.**
THE PEOPLES OF THE WORLD. VOLUME I PEOPLE AND HOMES IN MANY LANDS. BY F.G. MOSS, B.A.
VOLUME IV THE LANDS OF EASTERN PEOPLES. BY E.J.G. BRADFORD, M.Sc. AND F.G. MOSS, B.A.
VOLUME VI THE LANDS OF THE AMERICAN PEOPLES BY E.J.G. BRADFORD, M.Sc. AND F.G. MOSS, B.A.
LONDON: GEORGE G. HARRAP AND COMPANY LTD., 1930, 1932, 1934. 218p., 145p., 216p.: fronts., ill., maps. Bound in brown cloth. HARRAP'S NEW GEOGRAPHICAL SERIES.
YSC 910 MOS, 915 BRA

610 **MURRAY, ALLAN.**
REGIONAL GEOGRAPHY OF THE BRITISH ISLES. By ALLAN MURRAY, B.A. LONDON: COLLINS CLEAR-TYPE PRESS, 1936. 190p. maps. Limp bound in blue cloth. COLLINS NEW SCHEME GEOGRAPHIES, VOLUME VIIIA.
YSC 914.2 MUR

611 **NEWBIGIN, MARION I.**
THE BRITISH EMPIRE BEYOND THE SEAS. AN INTRODUCTION TO WORLD GEOGRAPHY. BY MARION I. NEWBIGIN, D.Sc. WITH MAPS AND DIAGRAMS. LONDON: G. BELL AND SONS, LTD., 1936. XII, 349p.: front., maps, diagrams. Rebound in green cloth.
YSC 910 NEW

612 **NEWBIGIN, MARION I.**
AN INTRODUCTION TO PHYSICAL GEOGRAPHY. BY MARION I. NEWBIGIN, D.Sc. WITH NUMEROUS ILLUSTRATIONS AND MAPS, 1919. XI, 336p.: maps, diagrams. Rebound in black cloth.
YSC 910 NEW

613 **NEWBIGIN, MARION I.**
THE MEDITERRANEAN LANDS. AN INTRODUCTORY STUDY IN HUMAN AND HISTORICAL GEOGRAPHY. BY MARION I. NEWBIGIN, D.Sc., F.R.G.S. WITH ILLUSTRATIONS AND SKETCH MAPS. LONDON: CHRISTOPHERS, 1938. New edition. 222p.: front., 7 plates, maps, maps on endpapers. Bound in brown cloth.
YSC 914 NEW

613A **OMOND, GEORGE, W.T.**
BELGIUM. BY GEORGE W.T. OMOND. ILLUSTRATED BY AMÉDÉE FORESTIER. LONDON: ADAM AND CHARLES BLACK, 1912. VII, 87p.: col. front., 10 col. plates, map. Bound in blue cloth with coloured pictorial label on cover. PEEPS AT MANY LANDS.
C 914.93 OMO

614 **ORFORD, E.J.**
SENIOR PRACTICAL GEOGRAPHY. TEACHER'S

BOOK. PUPIL'S BOOK. WITH DRAWINGS BY T.R. JEREMIAH AND OTHER ILLUSTRATIONS. LONDON: UNIVERSITY OF LONDON PRESS LTD., 1935, 6. 131, 200p.: ill., maps, diagrs. Bound in red and green cloth with pictorial covers.
YSC 910 ORF

615 **PARK, MUNGO.**
TRAVELS IN THE INTERIOR OF AFRICA. By MUNGO PARK. With Eight Illustrations in Colour by JOHN WILLIAMSON. LONDON: ADAM AND CHARLES BLACK, 1903. XVI, 392p. + 8p. pub. cat.: col. front., 7 col. plates. Bound in red cloth, with coloured pictorial cover and spine. Spine title: PARK'S TRAVELS IN AFRICA.
C 916.04 PAR

616 **PEATTIE, RODERICK.**
COLLEGE GEOGRAPHY. BY RODERICK PEATTIE. U.S.A. BOSTON: GINN AND COMPANY, 1926. XII, 495p.: front., 21 plates, ill., maps, diagrams. Bound in brown cloth.
YSC 910 PEA

617 **PERKINS, LUCY FITCH.**
THE NORWEGIAN TWINS by Lucy Fitch Perkins, illustrated by the author with an introduction by Rhoda Power. LONDON: JONATHAN CAPE, 1936. 190p.: pictorial title page, 25 plates, pictorial endpapers. Bound in grey linson.
YSC 914.8 PER

618 **PHILIPS' VISUAL CONTOUR ATLAS.**
SALFORD AND MANCHESTER EDITION. 40 COLOURED PLATES CONTAINING 58 MAPS AND DIAGRAMS WITH INDEX. LONDON: GEORGE PHILIP AND SON LIMITED, (193–?). 40p. maps, 16p. index. Bound in green cloth with green paper covers.
YSC 912 PHI

619 **PICKLES, THOMAS.**
THE BRITISH ISLES. BY THOMAS PICKLES, B.Sc. ILLUSTRATED WITH 80 MAPS AND DIAGRAMS AND 8 PAGES OF PHOTOGRAPHS. LONDON: J.M. DENT AND SONS, LTD., 1935. XIII, 240p.: front. Bound in blue cloth.
YSC 914.2 PIC

620 **PICKLES, THOMAS.**
EUROPE AND ASIA. BY THOMAS PICKLES, B.Sc. LONDON: J.M. DENT AND SONS, LTD., 1932. Col. front., ill., maps, decorative endpapers. Bound in blue cloth with decorative cover and spine. DENT'S MODERN SCHOOL GEOGRAPHIES.
YSC 914 PIC

621 **PICKLES, THOMAS.**
THE SOUTHERN CONTINENTS. BOOK I. South and Central AMERICA. BY THOMAS PICKLES, B.Sc. With Twelve Photographs and Forty-Six Maps and Diagrams. LONDON: J.M. DENT AND SONS, LTD., 1934. 132p.: front. Bound in red cloth.
YSC 918 PIC

622 **RIDER, S.W.**
SOUTH WALES, A PHYSICAL AND ECONOMIC GEOGRAPHY BY S.W. RIDER, B.A. M.Sc. AND A.E. TRUEMAN, D.Sc., F.G.S. WITH THIRTY FOUR MAPS AND DIAGRAMS. LONDON: METHUEN AND CO. LTD., 1929. VIII, 190p. Bound in orange cloth.
YSC 914.2 RID

623 **RITTER, CARL.**
COMPARATIVE GEOGRAPHY IN THE UNIVERSITY OF BERLIN. Translated for the Use of Schools and Colleges. BY WILLIAM L. GAGE. U.S.A., PHILADELPHIA: J.B. LIPPINCOTT AND CO., 1865. Facsimile reprint by AMS PRESS, NEW YORK, 1973. 220p. Bound in brown cloth.
YSC 910 RIT

623A **THE ROYAL ATLAS READERS.**
ENGLAND AND WALES. A Reader and Text Book in One. No. 111. LONDON: T. NELSON AND SONS, 1900. 224p.: ill. maps. Bound in red cloth.
M 914.2 ROY CHILDREN'S COLLECTION

624 **ROYAL GEOGRAPHICAL READERS.**
FIRST BOOK. For STANDARD II. LONDON: T. NELSON AND SONS, 1881. 64p.: front., vignette title page, 1 plate, maps, ill. Bound in brown cloth, with embossed pictorial/decorative cover. The Royal School Series.
C 910 ROY

625 **ROYAL GEOGRAPHICAL READERS.**
No. 3: THE BRITISH EMPIRE. WITH NUMEROUS ILLUSTRATIONS. LONDON: T. NELSON AND SONS, 1891. 96p. + 1p. pub. cat.: front., 9 plates, maps, ill. Bound in brown cloth, with embossed decorative cover. The Royal School Series.
C 910.09171241 ROY

626 **SCOTT, G. FIRTH.**
DARING DEEDS OF POLAR EXPLORERS: TRUE STORIES OF THE BRAVERY, RESOURCE, ENDURANCE AND ADVENTURES OF EXPLORERS AT THE POLES. BY G. FIRTH SCOTT. WITH MANY ILLUSTRATIONS. LONDON: SEELEY, SERVICE AND CO. LIMITED, 1922. 263p.: col. front., 8 plates. Bound in grey cloth, with coloured pictorial cover and spine.
C 919.8 SCO

627 **SEWELL, WILLIAM G.**
THE LAND AND LIFE OF CHINA. BY WILLIAM G. SEWELL OF THE WEST CHINA UNION UNIVERSITY AND THE LAND AND LIFE OF INDIA BY MARGARET READ AND THE LAND AND LIFE OF AFRICA BY MARGARET WRONG. LONDON: EDINBURGH HOUSE PRESS, 1933, 1934, 1935. 144p. each: plates, maps, charts. Rebound in brown cloth.
YSC 910 SEW

628 **SHACKLETON, SIR ERNEST.**
SOUTH. THE STORY OF SHACKLETON'S 1914–1917 EXPEDITION. BY SIR ERNEST SHACKLETON, C.V.O. Edited and abridged by W.T. HUTCHINS, M.A. With pen and ink drawings by N.A.D. Wallis. LONDON: LONGMANS, GREEN AND CO., 1938. 171p.: front., ill. Bound in green cloth.
YSC 919.9 SHA

629 **SMILES, SAMUEL** *(Editor)*.
A BOY'S VOYAGE ROUND THE WORLD; INCLUDING A RESIDENCE IN VICTORIA, AND A JOURNEY BY RAIL ACROSS NORTH AMERICA. EDITED BY SAMUEL SMILES. SEVENTH THOUSAND. WITH ILLUSTRATIONS. LONDON: JOHN MURRAY, 1872. XV, 304p.: front., maps, ill. Bound in green cloth, with embossed decorative covers and spine. Spine title: ROUND THE WORLD.
C 910.41

630 **STEMBRIDGE, JASPER H.**
THE OXFORD GEOGRAPHICAL NOTE-BOOKS FOR SECONDARY SCHOOLS.
No. III SOUTH AMERICA
No. VI ASIA
No. VII EUROPE
OXFORD: CLARENDON PRESS, 1936. 32p., 32p., 48p.: ill., maps. Limp bound in blue paper.
YSC 910 STE

631 **STEMBRIDGE, JASPER H.**
WORLD-WIDE GEOGRAPHY PRACTICAL NOTE-BOOKS FOR SENIOR SCHOOLS. By JASPER H. STEMBRIDGE AND S. EWART WILLIAMS, B.Sc.
BOOK 4. THE BRITISH ISLES.
LONDON: OXFORD UNIVERSITY PRESS, (193–?). 28p.: maps, diagrs.
YSC 914.2 STE

632 **STURT, MARY.**
GREAT VENTURERS. BY MARY STURT AND E.C. OAKDEN. LONDON: G. BELL AND SONS, LTD. 1928. XI, 211p.: 8 plates, ill., maps. Bound in red cloth with coloured decorative cover.
YSC 910.4 STU

633 **SULLIVAN, ROBERT.**
AN INTRODUCTION TO GEOGRAPHY AND HISTORY, ANCIENT AND MODERN. BY ROBERT SULLIVAN, LL.D., T.C.D. NEW EDITION. REVISED AND RE-ARRANGED. LONDON: LONGMANS AND CO., 1880. 209p. + 3p. pub. cat.: col. double front., 11 col. double maps. Bound in brown cloth, with embossed decorative covers. SULLIVAN'S SERIES OF SCHOOL BOOKS. Spine title: GEOGRAPHY AND HISTORY, WITH MAPS.
C 910 SUL

634 **TAYLOR, E.G.R.**
A SKETCH MAP GEOGRAPHY. A TEXT-BOOK OF WORLD AND REGIONAL GEOGRAPHY FOR THE MIDDLE AND UPPER SCHOOL. BY E.G.R. TAYLOR, D.Sc. LONDON: METHUEN AND CO. LTD., Eleventh Edition, 1935. 147p.: maps. Bound in blue cloth.
YSC 914.2 TAY

635 **TAYLOR, J.**
LEDSHAM'S Geographical Examination Questions. By J. TAYLOR. THIRD STANDARD. (MANCHESTER: J.B. LEDSHAM, Corporation Street, 1880) 12p. Covered with green card.
YSC 914.2 TAY

636 **TURLEY, CHARLES.**
THE VOYAGES OF CAPTAIN SCOTT. Retold from "The Voyage of the 'Discovery'" and "Scott's Last Expedition". BY CHARLES TURLEY. WITH AN INTRODUCTION BY SIR J.M. BARRIE, BART. WITH A PORTRAIT FRONTISPIECE IN PHOTOGRAVURE, 4 COLOURED PLATES, 28 PAGES OF HALF-TONE ILLUSTRATIONS (MOSTLY FROM PHOTOGRAPHS TAKEN BY MEMBERS OF THE "TERRA NOVA" EXPEDITION), FACSIMILE AND MAP. LONDON: SMITH, ELDER AND CO., 1914. VIII, 440p.: front., 4 col. plates, 28 plates, facsim., map. Bound in blue cloth, with coloured pictorial cover and spine, and gilt top.
C 910.924 SCO/TUR

637 **WALFORD, EDWARD.**
PLEASANT DAYS IN PLEASANT PLACES. BY EDWARD WALFORD, M.A. FOURTH EDITION. LONDON: W.H. ALLEN AND CO. LTD., (189–?). X, 293p. + 47p. pub. cat.: front., vignette title page, 14 plates, ill. Bound in brown cloth, with embossed pictorial/decorative cover and spine, and gilt top.
C 914.2 WAL

638 **WALTON, J.**
THE GEOGRAPHY OF CUMBERLAND AND WESTMORELAND FOR USE IN SCHOOLS. BY J. WALTON. LONDON: GEORGE PHILIP AND SON, 1872. 31p. Bound in blue paper.
YSC 914.28 WAL

639 **WHYBROW, S.J.B.**
GREAT BRITAIN AND IRELAND. A GEOGRAPHY NOTE-BOOK, by S.J.B. WHYBROW, B.Sc. LONDON: J.M. DENT AND SONS LTD., 1932. 47p.: maps. Limp bound in grey card.
YSC 914.2 WHY

640 **WILLIAMS, ARCHIBALD.**
THE ROMANCE OF MODERN EXPLORATION, WITH DESCRIPTIONS OF CURIOUS CUSTOMS, THRILLING ADVENTURES AND INTERESTING DISCOVERIES OF EXPLORERS IN ALL PARTS OF THE WORLD. BY ARCHIBALD WILLIAMS, F.R.G.S. WITH TWENTY-SIX ILLUSTRATIONS. LONDON: SEELEY AND CO. LIMITED, 1905. 383p. + 16p. pub. cat.: front., 23 plates. Bound in blue cloth, with coloured pictorial/decorative cover and spine.
C 910.4 WIL

641 **WILLSON, BECKLES.**
LOST ENGLAND: THE STORY OF OUR SUBMERGED COASTS. BY BECKLES WILLSON. WITH TWENTY FOUR ILLUSTRATIONS. LONDON: GEORGE NEWNES, LIMITED, 1902. 192p., front., 5 plates, ill., maps. The Library of Useful Stories. Bound in blue cloth with embossed decorative cover.
YSC 914.2 WIL

642 **WILMORE, ALBERT.**
GREAT BRITAIN AND IRELAND. BY ALBERT WHITMORE, D.Sc. (LOND.), F.G.S., F.R.G.S. LONDON: G. BELL AND SONS, LTD., Fourth Edition, 1935. VIII, 262p.: maps. Bound in blue cloth.
YSC 914.2 WIL

643 **YOUNG, EGERTON RYERSON.**
THE BATTLE OF THE BEARS AND Reminiscences of Life in the Indian Country. BY EGERTON R. YOUNG. LONDON: ROBERT CULLEY, (190–?). 318p. + 2p. pub. cat.: front., 7 plates. Bound in red cloth, with coloured pictorial cover and spine, and gilt top.
C 917.127 YOU

644 **YOUNG, EGERTON RYERSON.**
BY CANOE AND DOG-TRAIN AMONG THE CREE AND SALTEAUX INDIANS. BY EGERTON RYERSON YOUNG (MISSIONARY). WITH AN INTRODUCTION BY MARK GUY PEARSE. LONDON: CHARLES H. KELLY, 1890 267p.: front., 23 plates, ill. Bound in green cloth, with pictorial cover and spine.
C 917.1 YOU

## 10 SCIENCE AND NATURE

645 **AIKMAN, JAMES.**
A NATURAL HISTORY OF BEASTS, BIRDS AND FISHES: OR, STORIES OF ANIMATED NATURE. BY JAMES AIKMAN, ESQ. One Hundred Engravings. LONDON: T. NELSON AND SONS, 1854. XII, 372p. + 16p. pub. cat.: front., 36 plates. Bound in blue cloth, with embossed decorative covers and spine, and gilt edges.
C 591 AIK

646 **THE ALBANY SERIES OF ELEMENTARY SCIENCE READERS.**
No. II (Second Course) PHYSICS
No. IV (Second Course) PHYSICS
LONDON: GEORGE GILL AND SONS, (188–?), 1884. 160, 176p.: diagrs. Bound in brown cloth with decorative covers.
YSC 530 ELE

647 **ALLEN, GRANT.**
THE STORY OF PLANTS. BY GRANT ALLEN. WITH 49 ILLUSTRATIONS. SECOND EDITION. LONDON: GEORGE NEWNES LTD., 1896. 232p. Bound in blue cloth with decorative cover. Library of Useful Stories.
YSC 581 ALL

648 **ANDRADE, E.N. DA C.**
An Introduction to Science. By E.N. Da C. ANDRADE, D.Sc., PH.D. and JULIAN HUXLEY, M.A.
Book I. Things around us. With Drawings by L.R. Brightwell.
Book III. Forces at work. With Drawings by Comerford Watson.
OXFORD: BASIL BLACKWELL, 1932, 1934. 184p., 270p.: ill., diagrs. Bound in green, pink cloth.
YSC 500 AND

649 **ARCHIBALD, DOUGLAS.**
THE STORY OF THE EARTH'S ATMOSPHERE. BY DOUGLAS ARCHIBALD, M.A. WITH FORTY-FOUR ILLUSTRATIONS. LONDON: GEORGE NEWNES,

LIMITED, 1897. Bound in blue cloth with pictorial/decorative cover. Library of Useful Stories.
YSC 551.5 ARC

650 **BARKER, CICELY MARY.**
The Book of the FLOWER FAIRIES. POEMS AND PICTURES BY CICELY MARY BARKER. LONDON: BLACKIE AND SON LIMITED, (1927). 91p.: 74 col. plates, ill. Bound in green cloth with decorative cover.
CBD 821.912 BAR

651 **BIRD, CHARLES.**
ELEMENTARY GEOLOGY. BY CHARLES BIRD, B.A., F.G.S. THIRD EDITION. LONDON: LONGMANS, GREEN AND CO., 1895. VI, 252p.: vignette on title page, ill., diagrs. Bound in red cloth. ELEMENTARY SCIENCE MANUALS.
YSC 550 BIR

652 **BORRADAILE, L.A.**
ELEMENTARY ZOOLOGY FOR MEDICAL STUDENTS. LONDON: HUMPHREY MILFORD, OXFORD UNIVERSITY PRESS, THIRD EDITION, 1935. 429p.: diagrs. Bound in blue cloth.
YSC 590 BOR

653 **BOWEN, OLWEN.**
BEETLES AND THINGS. By OLWEN BOWEN. Illustrated by HARRY ROUNTREE. LONDON: ELKIN MATTHEWS AND MARROT, 1931. VII, 134p. + 2p. pub. cat.: ill. Bound in yellow cloth, with pictorial cover and spine.
C 595.76 BOW

654 **BREND, WILLIAM A.**
THE STORY OF ICE IN THE PRESENT AND PAST. BY WILLIAM A. BREND, B.A., B.SC., F.G.S. WITH THIRTY SEVEN ILLUSTRATIONS. LONDON: GEORGE NEWNES, LIMITED, 1899. 228p.: front. Bound in blue cloth with pictorial/decorative cover. Library of Useful Stories.
YSC 551.3 BRE

655 **BRIGGS, WILLIAM.**
ADVANCED MECHANICS. VOL. 1. – DYNAMICS. BEING "THE TUTORIAL DYNAMICS" TOGETHER WITH THE QUESTIONS IN DYNAMICS OF THE LAST FOURTEEN YEARS SET AT THE ADVANCED EXAMINATION OF THE SCIENCE AND ART DEPARTMENT, BY WILLIAM BRIGGS, M.A., F.C.S., F.R.A.S. AND G.H. BRYAN, Sc.D., F.R.S. Second Edition. LONDON: W.B. CLIVE, UNIVERSITY CORRESPONDENCE COLLEGE PRESS, (1899). VIII, 328p. + 16p. pub. cat.: diagrs. Bound in maroon cloth. The Organised Science Series.
YSC 531 BRI

656 **BRIGGS, WILLIAM.**
MATRICULATION MECHANICS AND HYDROSTATICS. BY WILLIAM BRIGGS LL.D., M.A., B.Sc. AND G.H. BRYAN, Sc.D., F.R.S. LONDON: UNIVERSITY TUTORIAL PRESS, LTD., 1933. VIII, 349, 208p.: diagrs. Bound in green cloth.
YSC 531 BRI

657 **BROWN, ROBERT** *(Editor)*.
SCIENCE FOR ALL. EDITED BY ROBERT BROWN, M.A., PH.D., F.L.S., F.R.G.S. ILLUSTRATED. LONDON: CASSELL AND COMPANY, LIMITED. (191–?).
Parts I + II. VIII, 384p.; VIII, 384p.
Parts III + IV. VIII, 384p.; VIII, 384p.
Part V. VIII, 384p.
ill., diagrs. Bound in black cloth.
YOSC 500 BRO

658 **BUCKLEY, ARABELLA B.**
THE FAIRY-LAND OF SCIENCE. BY ARABELLA B. BUCKLEY. ILLUSTRATED. THIRTY-FOURTH THOUSAND. LONDON: MACMILLAN AND CO. LIMITED, 1906. VIII, 274p.: front., 2 plates, ill. Bound in green cloth, with embossed pictorial/decorative cover and spine, and gilt edges.
C 500 BUC

659 **BUCKMASTER, J.C.**
THE ELEMENTS OF MAGNETISM AND ELECTRICITY. BY J.C. BUCKMASTER: REVISED BY CHARLES LEES. SIXTH EDITION. LONDON: LONGMANS AND CO., SIMPKIN, MARSHALL AND CO., 1872. XXIV, 212p., ill., diagrs. Bound in blue cloth.
C 537 BUC

660 **BURKE, MRS. L.**
THE COLOURED LANGUAGE OF FLOWERS COMPILED AND EDITED BY MRS L. BURKE. LONDON: GEORGE ROUTLEDGE AND SONS, (188–?). 128p.: col. front., col. vignette on title page, col. ill., ill. Half bound in green cloth with mottled buff-brown paper.
CBD 398.368213 BUR

661 **CAVEN, R.M.**
SYSTEMATIC QUALITATIVE ANALYSIS FOR STUDENTS OF INORGANIC CHEMISTRY. BY R.M. CAVEN, D.Sc., F.I.C. NEW EDITION. LONDON: BLACKIE AND SON LIMITED, 1929. XII, 243p.: tables. Bound in green cloth.
YSC 544 CAV

662 **CHAMBERS, GEORGE F.**
THE STORY OF ECLIPSES, SIMPLY TOLD FOR GENERAL READERS. WITH ESPECIAL REFERENCE TO THE TOTAL ECLIPSE OF THE SUN OF MAY 28, 1900. BY GEORGE F. CHAMBERS, F.R.A.S. LONDON: GEORGE NEWNES, LTD., 1899. front., ill., diagrs. Bound in blue cloth with decorative covers. Library of Useful Stories.
YSC 523 CHA

663 **CHAMBERS, GEORGE F.**
THE STORY OF THE SOLAR SYSTEM BY GEORGE F. CHAMBERS, F.R.A.S. LONDON: GEORGE NEWNES, LTD., 1895. 202p.: ill., diagrs. Bound in blue cloth with decorative cover. Library of Useful Stories.
YSC 523 CHA

664 **CHAMBERS, GEORGE F.**
THE STORY OF THE STARS, SIMPLY TOLD FOR GENERAL READERS. BY GEORGE F. CHAMBERS F.R.S. SECOND EDITION. LONDON: GEORGE NEWNES, LTD., 1896. 192p.: ill. tables. Bound in blue cloth with decorative cover. Library of Useful Stories.
YSC 523 CHA

665 **CHAMBERS, GEORGE F.**
THE STORY OF THE WEATHER, SIMPLY TOLD FOR GENERAL READERS. BY GEORGE F. CHAMBERS, F.R.A.S. LONDON: GEORGE NEWNES, LIMITED, 1897. 232p.: ill., tables. Bound in blue cloth with decorative/pictorial cover. Library of Useful Stories.
YSC 551.5 CHA

666 **THE CHILDREN'S PICTURE BOOK OF BIRDS.**
Illustrated with Sixty-one engravings by W. Harvey. LONDON: SAMPSON LOW, SON, AND CO., 1860. XII, 276p.; front., vignette on title page, 62 plates. Bound in red cloth with embossed decorative cover and spine.
C 598.2 CHI

667 **CLODD, EDWARD.**
THE STORY OF "PRIMITIVE" MAN. BY EDWARD CLODD. WITH ILLUSTRATIONS. LONDON: GEORGE NEWNES, LTD., 1895. 206p.: front. Bound in blue cloth with decorative/pictorial cover.
YSC 571 CLO

668 **COHEN, JULIUS B.**
THEORETICAL ORGANIC CHEMISTRY. BY JULIUS B. COHEN, Ph.D., B.Sc., D.Sc., F.R.S. LONDON: MACMILLAN AND CO., LTD., THIRD EDITION 1928. XV, 606p.: diagrs. Bound in purple cloth.
YSC 547 COH

669 **CONN, H.W.**
THE STORY OF GERM LIFE: BACTERIA. BY H.W. CONN. WITH THIRTY-FOUR ILLUSTRATIONS. LONDON: GEORGE NEWNES, LIMITED, 1898. 212p. Bound in blue cloth with decorative cover. Library of Useful Stories.
YSC 589 CON

670 **CONN, H.W.**
THE STORY OF LIFE'S MECHANISM. A REVIEW OF THE CONCLUSIONS OF MODERN BIOLOGY IN REGARD TO THE MECHANISM WHICH CONTROLS THE PHENOMENA OF LIVING ACTIVITY. BY H.W. CONN. WITH FIFTY ILLUSTRATIONS. LONDON: GEORGE NEWNES, LIMITED, 1899. 219p.: Bound in blue cloth. Library of Useful Stories.
YSC 576 CON

671 **COOKE, ARTHUR O.**
British Insects SHOWN TO THE CHILDREN BY ARTHUR O. COOKE. LONDON: T.C. AND E.C. JACK, LTD., (193–?). 138p.: front., col. plates, 32 plates. Bound in buff cloth with coloured pictorial cover.
YSC 595.7 COO

672 **DAGLISH, ERIC FITCH.**
ANIMALS IN BLACK AND WHITE No. 1. THE LARGER BEASTS, THE SMALLER BEASTS AND FISHES, AND SEA ANIMALS. LONDON: J.M. DENT AND SONS, LIMITED, 1936. 48p, 48p, 48p.: front., 57 plates, ill. Bound in cream paper with decorative cover, with pictorial cream dust jacket.
CBD 591 DAG

673 **DAGLISH, ERIC FITCH.**
THE LIFE STORY OF BEASTS. By ERIC FITCH DAGLISH. LONDON: J.M. DENT AND SONS LIMITED, 1931. X, 223p.: front., 20 plates, woodcuts by the author, ill. Bound in cream cloth, with pictorial cover.
C 599 DAG

674 **DOORLY, ELEANOR.**
THE INSECT MAN. . . . Jean Henri Fabre. By ELEANOR DOORLY. Introduction by WALTER DE LA MARE and Woodcuts by ROBERT GIBBINGS. LONDON: WILLIAM HEINEMANN LTD., 1936. XII, 174p.: ill. Bound in cream linson with pictorial cover.
YSC 920 FAB

675 **DOORLY, ELEANOR.**
THE MICROBE MAN. A Life of Pasteur for Children, by ELEANOR DOORLY . . . and Woodcuts by ROBERT GIBBINGS. LONDON: WILLIAM HEINEMANN LTD., 1938. 152p. + 2p. pub. cat.: front., vignette on title page, ill. Bound in cream linson with pictorial cover.
YSC 920 PAS

676 **DURELL, C.V.**
A SCHOOL MECHANICS PART II, BY C.V. DURELL, M.A. LONDON: G. BELL AND SONS, LTD., 1924. XV, p. 187–322, XVIIp. of answers: diagrs. Bound in blue cloth.
YSC 531 DUR

677 **EMANUEL, WALTER.**
THE ZOO, A SCAMPER. BY WALTER EMANUEL. With 50 Illustrations by John Hassall, and one by the Author. LONDON: ALSTON RIVERS, (190–?). 50p.: 12 plates, ill. Bound in paper-covered boards, with pictorial cover.
C 823.912 EMA

678 **EVENS, GEORGE BRAMWELL.**
OUT WITH ROMANY: ADVENTURES WITH BIRDS AND ANIMALS. By G. BRAMWELL EVENS, Romany of the B.B.C. Illustrations by Reg Gammon and Photographs by the Author. LONDON: UNIVERSITY OF LONDON PRESS LTD., 1937. VII, 184p.: front., 7 plates, ill. Bound in green cloth, with vignette on cover.
C 574.941 EVE

679 **EVENS, GEORGE BRAMWELL.**
OUT WITH ROMANY AGAIN. By G. BRAMWELL EVENS, Romany of the B.B.C. Illustrations by Reg Gammon and Photographs by the Author. LONDON: UNIVERSITY OF LONDON PRESS LTD., 1938. VII, 182p.: front., 7 plates, ill. Bound in orange cloth, with coloured pictorial dust jacket.
C 574.914 EVE

675

679A **EVENS, GEORGE BRAMWELL.**
A ROMANY IN THE FIELDS. BY G. BRAMWELL EVENS (THE ROMANY OF THE BBC). WITH ILLUSTRATIONS BY THE AUTHOR. WRAPPER BY P. DRAKE BROOKSHAW. LONDON: THE EPWORTH PRESS, 1929. 223p.: front., 3 plates (photographs), ill. Bound in green cloth with coloured pictorial paper dust cover.
C 574.941 EVE

680 **EVENS, GEORGE BRAMWELL.**
A ROMANY ON THE TRAIL. By the ROMANY OF THE B.B.C. (G. BRAMWELL EVENS). WITH ILLUSTRATIONS BY G.K. EVENS, WRAPPER BY P. DRAKE BROOKSHAW. LONDON: THE EPWORTH PRESS (EDGAR C. BARTON), 1934. 172p.: front., vignette title page, 3 plates, ill. Bound in green cloth, with coloured pictorial dust jacket.
C 630.1142 EVE

681 **THE FROZEN STREAM.**
OR, An Account OF THE NATURE, PROPERTIES, DANGERS AND USES OF ICE, IN VARIOUS PARTS OF THE WORLD. LONDON: SOCIETY FOR PROMOTING CHRISTIAN KNOWLEDGE, 1846. 150p.: front., 10 plates, engraved by Whimper, ill. Bound in green cloth, with embossed decorative covers.
C 551.31 SOC

682 **GATTY, MARGARET.**
PARABLES FROM NATURE. BY MARGARET GATTY. WITH A MEMOIR BY HER DAUGHTER JULIANA HORATIA EWING. ILLUSTRATED BY P.H. CALDERON, W. HOLMAN HUNT, OTTO SPECKTER, G.H. THOMAS, JOHN TENNIEL ETC. FIRST SERIES. LONDON: GEORGE BELL AND SONS, 1891. XXI, 106p.: front., 11 plates. Rebound retaining original illustrated paper covers.
C 823.8 GAT

682A **Another copy.**
ILLUSTRATED BY ALICE B. WOODWARD. LONDON: G. BELL AND SONS, LTD., 1910. X, 350p. + 2p. pub. cat.: col. front., 7 col. plates, 8 plates. Bound in green cloth with decorative cover and spine.
YSC 823.8 GAT

682B **Another copy.**
BY Mrs. ALFRED GATTY. The first four Series, illustrated by Allan Barraud and Others. LONDON: THE RELIGIOUS TRACT SOCIETY, (193–?). 384p.: front., 15 plates. Bound in blue cloth.
YSC 823.8 GAT

683 **GIRAUD, S. LOUIS** *(Editor).*
ANIMAL LIFE, in Fact, Fancy and Fun. Bookano "Living" Models Series. EDITED AND PRODUCED BY S. LOUIS GIRAUD, M.R.S.L. LONDON: DAILY SKETCH AND SUNDAY GRAPHIC, (193–?). Unpaginated: front., 6 col. pop-up sections, ill., pictorial endpapers. Bound in coloured pictorial paper covers.
CBD 591 ANI

684 **GOLDING, HARRY** *(Editor).*
THE WONDER Book of Nature FOR BOYS AND GIRLS. WITH ELEVEN COLOUR PLATES AND NEARLY 350 ILLUSTRATIONS. EDITED BY HARRY GOLDING, F.R.G.S. FOURTH EDITION. LONDON: WARD LOCK AND CO., LIMITED. (193–?). 256p.: col. front. Bound in red cloth with coloured pictorial paper cover.
YOSC 574 GOL

685 **GOSSE, P.H.**
THE OCEAN. BY THE LATE P.H. GOSSE, F.R.S. LONDON: SOCIETY FOR PROMOTING CHRISTIAN KNOWLEDGE, (188–?). XII, 360p. + 4p. pub. cat.: front., 3 plates, ill. Bound in red cloth with coloured pictorial cover and spine. Originally published in 1845.
YSC 574 GOS

686 **GREENAWAY, KATE.**
Language of Flowers. ILLUSTRATED BY KATE GREENAWAY. PRINTED IN COLOURS BY EDMUND EVANS. LONDON: GEORGE ROUTLEDGE AND SONS, (1884). 80p.: col. front., col. decorative title page, col. ill. Bound in green cloth with coloured decorative paper covers.
CBD 398.368213 GRE

687 **HALF HOURS UNDERGROUND.**
Volcanoes, mines and caves. WITH NUMEROUS ILLUSTRATIONS. LONDON: CHARLES BURNET AND CO., 1888. XII, 369p. + 3p. pub. cat.: front., 23 plates, ill. Bound in green cloth with embossed decorative cover and spine, and gilt edges.
YSC 551 HAL

688 **HALL, FRED.**
THE STORY OF COMMERCE. BY FRED HALL, M.A., B.Com., F.C.I.S. AND GEORGE COLLAR, B.A., B.Sc. (Lond.). LONDON: SIR ISAAC PITMAN AND SONS, LTD., 1922. IX, 214p.: front., 20 plates, map, ill. Bound in green cloth, with pictorial cover.
C 380 HAL

689 **HARTWIG, G.**
VOLCANOES AND EARTHQUAKES. A POPULAR DESCRIPTION OF THE MOVEMENTS IN THE EARTH'S CRUST. FROM "THE SUBTERRANEAN WORLD". BY DR. G. HARTWIG. With 30 Illustrations. LONDON: LONGMANS, GREEN AND CO., 1887. 158p. + 2p. pub. cat.: front., 3 plates, ill. Bound in blue cloth with coloured pictorial cover and spine.
YSC 551 HAR

690 **HARTWIG, G.**
WONDERS OF THE TROPICAL FORESTS FROM "THE TROPICAL WORLD". BY DR. G. HARTWIG. With 40 illustrations. LONDON: LONGMANS, GREEN AND CO., 1891. IX, 128p.: 5 plates, ill. Bound in green cloth with coloured pictorial cover and gilt edges.
YSC 581 HAR

691 **HAWKS, ELLISON.**
The Microscope. SHOWN TO THE CHILDREN BY CAPTAIN ELLISON HAWKS. LONDON: T.C. AND E.C. JACK, LTD. 154p.: col. front., 5 col. plates. 34 plates, ill., diagrs. Bound in green cloth with coloured pictorial cover.
YSC 578 HAW

692 **HENSLOW, G.**
THE STORY OF WILD FLOWERS BY REV. PROFESSOR G. HENSLOW M.A., F.L.S., F.G.S. WITH FIFTY-SIX FIGURES IN TEXT. LONDON: GEORGE NEWNES, LIMITED, 1901. 249p. + 2p. pub. cat. Bound in blue cloth with decorative cover. Library of Useful Stories.
YSC 582 HEN

693 **HILL, F.J.**
A "PROJECT" IN SCIENCE AND MECHANICS. ELECTRICITY. By F.J. Hill, M.Sc. LONDON: COLLINS CLEAR-TYPE PRESS, 1937. V, 89p.: map, diagrs. Limp bound in green cloth.
YSC 537 HIL

694 **HILL, MATTHEW DAVENPORT.**
ETON NATURE-STUDY AND OBSERVATION LESSONS. BY MATTHEW DAVENPORT HILL, M.A., F.L.S. AND WILFRED MARK WEBB, F.L.S. LONDON: DUCKWORTH AND CO., 1903. XVIII, 154; XVI, 174p.: front., ill., diagrs. 2 parts bound in 1 vol., in green cloth.
YSC 574 HIL

695 **HOLMES, ERNEST J.**
A MODERN BIOLOGY by ERNEST J. HOLMES, M.A., B.Sc. AND R. DARNLEY GIBBS, M.Sc., Ph.D., F.R.S.C. CAMBRIDGE: UNIVERSITY PRESS, SECOND EDITION, 1939. XV, 272p.: front., ill., diagrs. Bound in blue cloth.
YSC 570 HOC

696 **HOLMYARD, ERIC JOHN.**
AN ELEMENTARY CHEMISTRY BY ERIC JOHN HOLMYARD M.A., M.Sc., D.Litt., F.I.C. LONDON: EDWARD ARNOLD AND CO., THIRD EDITION, 1934. VIII, 468p.: front., 10 plates, diagrs. Bound in red cloth. Originally published in 1925.
YSC 540 HOL

697 **HOLMYARD, ERIC JOHN.**
A REVISION COURSE IN CHEMISTRY FOR THE SCHOOL CERTIFICATE AND MATRICULATION EXAMINATIONS. BY E.J. HOLMYARD, M.A., M.Sc., D.Litt., F.I.C. LONDON: J.M. DENT AND SONS, LTD., 1932. XVI, 252p.: diagrs. Bound in green cloth.
YSC 540 HOL

698 **HOUGHTON, WILLIAM.**
SEA-SIDE WALKS OF A NATURALIST WITH HIS CHILDREN. BY REV. W. HOUGHTON, M.A., F.L.S. ILLUSTRATED WITH EIGHT COLOURED PLATES AND NUMEROUS WOOD ENGRAVINGS. LONDON: GROOMBRIDGE AND SONS, 1870. VI, 154p. + 4p. pub. cat.: col. front., 7 col. plates, by A.F. Lydon, ill. Bound in blue cloth, with embossed pictorial/decorative cover and decorative spine, and gilt edges.
C 591.52636 HOU

699 **Another copy.**
THIRD EDITION. ILLUSTRATED. LONDON: GROOMBRIDGE AND SONS, 1878. VI, 154p.: col. front., 6. col. plates, ill. Bound in green cloth with embossed decorative cover and spine.
CBD 591.52636 HOU

700 **HOWITT, MARY.**
BIRDS AND THEIR NESTS, BY MARY HOWITT. With Twenty-Three Full-page illustrations by Harrison Weir. U.S.A., NEW YORK: GEORGE ROUTLEDGE AND SONS (1871). VI, 124p. + 8p. pub. cat.: front., 22 plates, ill. Bound in green cloth with embossed decorative cover and spine with inserted paper pictorial label.
CBD 598.2 HOW

701 **HUGHES, A.G.**
ELEMENTARY GENERAL SCIENCE, A Course for Boys and Girls. BY A.G. HUGHES, B.Sc., Ph.D., M.Ed. and J.H. PANTON, B.A. Book I. LONDON: BLACKIE AND SON, LIMITED, SECOND EDITION, 1933. 120p.: front., 3 plates, diagrs. Bound in brown cloth.
YSC 500 HUG

702 **HUTCHINSON, ROBERT W.**
HEAT (MATRICULATION STANDARD) BY ROBERT W. HUTCHINSON, M.Sc. LONDON: UNIVERSITY TUTORIAL PRESS, LTD., 1933. 266p.: diagrs. Bound in red cloth.
YSC 536 HUT

703 **HUXLEY, T.H.**
PHYSIOGRAPHY. AN INTRODUCTION TO THE STUDY OF NATURE. WITH ILLUSTRATIONS AND COLOURED PLATES. LONDON: MACMILLAN AND CO., LIMITED, 1900. XIX, 384p. 1 col. plate, ill., diagrs., and 3 col. maps, maps. Bound in red cloth. Reprint of third edition. Originally published in 1877.
YSC 500 HUX

703A **JACKSON, IDA H.**
Botanical Experiments for Schools. BY IDA H. JACKSON, M.A. (T.C.D.) ILLUSTRATIONS BY DOROTHEA COWIE. LONDON: BLACKIE AND SON LIMITED, 1912. VIII, 88p.: 24 plates. Bound in black cloth.
M 581 JAC CHILDREN'S COLLECTION

704 **JACKSON, THOMAS.**
OUR Feathered Companions; OR, CONVERSATIONS OF A FATHER WITH HIS CHILDREN ABOUT SEA-BIRDS, SONG-BIRDS AND OTHER FEATHERED TRIBES THAT LIVE IN OR VISIT THE BRITISH ISLES, THEIR HABITS, ETC. BY THE REV THOMAS JACKSON, M.A. LONDON: S.W. PARTRIDGE AND CO., (188–?). VIII, 148p. + 8p. pub. cat.: front., vignette on title page, 15 plates by Harrison Weir and R. Kretschmer, ill. Bound in blue cloth with embossed decorative cover and inserted paper pictorial label.
CBD 598.2941 JAC

705 **JONES, FRANCIS.**
A SCHOOL BOTANY (MATRICULATION STANDARD). BY FRANCIS JONES. LONDON: SIR ISAAC PITMAN AND SONS, LTD., 1932. VIII, 361p.: ill., diagrs. Bound in green cloth.
YSC 580 JON

706 **JOYCE, J.**
SCIENTIFIC DIALOGUES INTENDED FOR THE INSTRUCTION AND ENTERTAINMENT OF YOUNG PEOPLE . . . BY THE REV. J. JOYCE. NEW EDITION. COMPLETE IN ONE VOLUME, WITH 185 ENGRAVINGS ON WOOD. LONDON: THOMAS TEGG, 1844. VI, 362p. + 2p. pub. cat.: diagrs. Quarter bound in red leather and cream buckram.
YSC 500 JOY

707 **JUDD, JOHN W.**
THE COMING OF EVOLUTION. THE STORY OF A GREAT REVOLUTION IN SCIENCE, by JOHN W. JUDD, C.B., L.L.D., F.R.S. CAMBRIDGE: UNIVERSITY PRESS, 1910. 171p.: front., 3 plates. Bound in red cloth with decorative cover.
YSC 575 JUD

708 **KINGSLEY, CHARLES.**
MADAM HOW AND LADY WHY, OR FIRST LESSONS IN EARTH LORE FOR CHILDREN. BY CHARLES KINGSLEY. ILLUSTRATED. LONDON: MACMILLAN AND CO., 1889. XIII, 270p. + 2p. pub. cat.: 3 plates engraved by Dalziel Brothers, ill. Bound in maroon cloth.
YSC 823.8 KIN

709 **KNIGHT, ELSIE V.M.**
THE GOLDEN NATURE READERS BY ELSIE V.M. KNIGHT, B.Sc. Book Four. With Four Coloured Plates and other illustrations. LONDON: UNIVERSITY OF LONDON PRESS, LTD., 1932. 176p.: col. front. Limp bound in yellow cloth with decorative cover.
YSC 570 KNI

710 **LAMBERT, H.G.**
ELECTRICITY AND MAGNETISM. BY H.G. LAMBERT, B.Sc., A.I.C. AND P.E. ANDREWS, B.A., B.Sc. LONDON: UNIVERSITY TUTORIAL PRESS LTD., 1938. VII, 204p.: ill., diagrs. Bound in yellow cloth.
YSC 537 LAM

711 **LAUWERYS, J.A.**
CHEMISTRY (with some Geology) by J.A. LAUWERYS, B.Sc., F.R.I.C. and J. ELLISON, M.Sc. With numerous illustrations in Line and Half-Tone. LONDON: UNIVERSITY OF LONDON PRESS, LTD., 1938. XII, 356p.: ill., diagrs. Bound in red cloth. NEW GENERAL SCIENCE SERIES.
YSC 540 LAU

712 **LODGE, REGINALD B.**
THE BIRDS AND THEIR STORY: A BOOK FOR YOUNG FOLK. BY R.B. LODGE. LONDON: CHARLES H. KELLY, (190–?). 288p.: col. front., 7 col. plates, 42 plates, ill., decorative endpapers. Bound in green cloth, with embossed decorative cover and gilt edges.
C 598.2 LOD

713 **LONG, WILLIAM J.**
SCHOOL OF THE WOODS: Some Life Studies of Animal Instincts and Animal Training. By WILLIAM J. LONG. ILLUSTRATED BY CHARLES COPELAND. LONDON: GINN AND COMPANY, THE ATHENAEUM PRESS, 1902. XIII, 364p.: front., 11 plates, ill. Bound in green cloth, with embossed decorative cover and spine, and gilt top.
C 591.5 LON

714 **LYELL, SIR CHARLES.**
THE STUDENT'S ELEMENTS OF GEOLOGY. BY SIR CHARLES LYELL, BART, F.R.S. SECOND EDITION REVISED AND CORRECTED. LONDON: JOHN MURRAY, 1874. XIX, 672p.: front., ill., diagrs., tables. Bound in green cloth.
YSC 550 LYE

715 **MAETERLINCK, MAURICE.**
THE CHILDREN'S LIFE OF THE BEE, BY MAURICE MAETERLINCK. SELECTED AND ARRANGED BY ALFRED SUTRO AND HERSCHEL WILLIAMS. ILLUSTRATED BY EDWARD J. DETMOLD. LONDON: GEORGE ALLEN AND UNWIN, LTD., 1920. 192p.: col. front., 4 col. plates. Bound in brown cloth with coloured paper label on cover.
CBD 595.799 MAE

716 **MASON, JOHN.**
PRACTICAL BIOLOGY BY JOHN MASON, M.A., Ph.D. PARTS I AND II. LONDON: MCDOUGALL'S EDUCATIONAL CO., LTD., (193–?). 224p.: ill., diagrs. Bound in green cloth.
YSC 570 MAS

717 **MATT, UNCLE.**
AROUND A CORNFIELD IN A RAMBLE AFTER WILD FLOWERS. BY Uncle Matt. LONDON: T. NELSON AND SONS, 1895. 98p. + 16p. ill. pub. cat.: col. front., ill. Bound in green and yellow paper covers with coloured pictorial decoration.
YSC 582 MAT

718 **MATT, UNCLE.**
DOWN THE LANE AND BACK IN SEARCH OF WILD FLOWERS. BY Uncle Matt. LONDON: T. NELSON AND SONS, 1895. 114p.: col. front., 2 plates, ill. Bound in green and yellow paper covers with coloured pictorial decoration.
YSC 582 MAT

721 **MIVART, ST. GEORGE.**
THE COMMON FROG. BY ST. GEORGE MIVART, F.R.S. ETC. WITH NUMEROUS ILLUSTRATIONS.

LONDON: MACMILLAN AND CO., 1874. VII, 158p.: front., ill., diagrs. Bound in brown cloth.
YSC 597 MIV

722 **MOIR, JOHN A.**
ELECTRICITY AND MAGNETISM. LONDON: EDWARD ARNOLD AND CO., 1929. VI, 208p.: ill., diagrs. Bound in green cloth.
YSC 537 MOI

722A **NATURAL PHENOMENA.**
LONDON: THE SOCIETY FOR PROMOTING CHRISTIAN KNOWLEDGE, 1852. IV, 128p.: pictorial title page, ill. Bound in green cloth with embossed decoration.
C 500.9 NAT

723 **NATURE'S WONDERS.**
OR, GOD'S CARE OVER ALL HIS WORKS. BY THE AUTHOR OF "PEEPS AT NATURE". LONDON: THE RELIGIOUS TRACT SOCIETY, (186–?). VI, 226p. + 6p. pub. cat.: front., ill. Bound in green cloth with embossed decorative covers and spine.
YSC 574 NAT

724 **NICHOLSON, H. ALLEYNE.**
AN INTRODUCTORY TEXT-BOOK OF ZOOLOGY FOR THE USE OF JUNIOR CLASSES. BY H. ALLEYNE NICHOLSON. FIFTH EDITION, REVISED AND ENLARGED. EDINBURGH: WILLIAM BLACKWOOD AND SONS, 1881. 232p. + 18p. pub. cat.: ill. Bound in black cloth with embossed decorative covers.
YSC 590 NIC

725 **OLCOTT, FRANCES JENKINS.**
THE BOOK OF NATURE'S MARVELS. By FRANCES JENKINS OLCOTT. WITH THIRTY ILLUSTRATIONS. LONDON: GEORGE G. HARRAP AND CO. LTD., 1936. 287p.: col. front., vignette title page, 29 plates. Bound in green cloth, with coloured pictorial cover and matching dust jacket.
C 500.9 OLC

726 **OLIVER, DANIEL.**
LESSONS IN ELEMENTARY BOTANY. THE PART OF SYSTEMATIC BOTANY BASED UPON MATERIAL LEFT IN MANUSCRIPT BY THE LATE PROFESSOR HENSLOW. WITH NUMEROUS ILLUSTRATIONS. BY DANIEL OLIVER, F.R.S., F.L.S. NEW EDITION. LONDON: MACMILLAN AND CO., 1882. VIII, 300p. + 12p. pub. cat. Bound in green cloth.
YSC 580 OLI

726A **ORPEN, T.H.**
THE RAIN-CHILDREN. A FAIRY TALE IN PHYSICS. BY T.H. ORPEN MA, WITH SEVEN ILLUSTRATIONS BY C.E. BROCK, RI. LONDON: SOCIETY FOR PROMOTING CHRISTIAN KNOWLEDGE, (1916). VIII 112p.: col. front., 5 col. plates, 5 plates. Bound in green cloth with coloured pictorial cover.
C 823.912 ORP

727 **OSCROFT, P.W.**
A MANUAL OF ELEMENTARY PRACTICAL CHEMISTRY FOR USE IN THE LABORATORY. BY P.W. OSCROFT, M.A. AND R.P. SHEA, M.A. LONDON: RIVINGTONS, 1910. VIII, 134p. + 2p. pub. cat.: diagrs. Bound in blue cloth.
YSC 540 OSC

728 **PARLEY, PETER** *(Pseud.).*
TALES ABOUT ANIMALS. BY PETER PARLEY. Tenth Edition, Greatly Enlarged. WITH UPWARDS OF FIVE HUNDRED ENGRAVINGS ON WOOD. LONDON: WILLIAM TEGG AND CO., 1847. XVI, 640p. + 1p. pub. cat.: front., vignette title page, ill. Bound in red cloth, with embossed decorative covers and spine, and gilt edges. Originally published in 1832 by Thomas Tegg under Samuel Goodrich's pseudonym of Peter Parley.
C 591 PAR

729 **PATTERSON, ROBERT.**
FIRST STEPS TO ZOOLOGY. BY ROBERT PATTERSON. WITH 244 ILLUSTRATIONS. LONDON: SIMMS AND McINTYRE, 1849. 252p.: ill. Bound in grey cloth with embossed decorative cover.
YSC 590 PAT

730 **PEPPER, JOHN HENRY.**
THE BOY'S PLAYBOOK OF SCIENCE. INCLUDING THE Various Manipulations and Arrangements OF CHEMICAL AND PHYSICAL APPARATUS. . . . BY JOHN HENRY PEPPER. THE SECOND EDITION. ILLUSTRATED WITH 470 ENGRAVINGS, CHIEFLY EXECUTED FROM THE AUTHOR'S SKETCHES, by H.G. HINE. LONDON: ROUTLEDGE, WARNE, AND ROUTLEDGE, 1860. VII, 440p.: front., ill. Bound in blue cloth with embossed decorative cover.
C 500 PEP

731 **PLANTS.**
LONDON: RELIGIOUS TRACT SOCIETY, (186–?). IV, 160p.: decorative title page, 5 plates, ill. Bound in green cloth, with embossed decorative covers and gilt edges.
C 582 REL

732 **PROCTOR, MARY.**
THE CHILDREN'S BOOK OF THE HEAVENS. BY MARY PROCTOR, F.R.A.S., F.R.Met.S. WITH ONE HUNDRED AND TWENTY ILLUSTRATIONS. LONDON: GEORGE G. HARRAP AND COMPANY LTD., 1924. 267p.: col. front., vignette title page, 3 col. plates, 33 plates, ill., diagrammatic endpapers. Bound in blue cloth, with coloured pictorial cover and matching dust jacket.
C 523.2 PRO

733 **PYCRAFT, W.P.**
THE STORY OF REPTILE LIFE BY W.P. PYCRAFT F.Z.S., A.L.S. LONDON: GEORGE NEWNES, LTD., 1905. 212p. + 4p. pub. cat.: front., ill. Bound in blue cloth with decorative/pictorial cover. Library of useful stories.
YSC 598.1 PYC

734 **REID, THOMAS MAYNE.**
QUADRUPEDS, WHAT THEY ARE AND WHERE FOUND, A Book of Zoology for Boys. By CAPTAIN MAYNE REID. Illustrated by William Harvey. LONDON: T. NELSON AND SONS, 1867. 168p.: front., 23 plates. Bound in purple cloth, with decorative cover and pictorial spine.
C 599 REI

735 **REMARKABLE INSECTS.**
LONDON, RELIGIOUS TRACT SOCIETY, 1842. 160p.: illustrated title page, ill. Bound in green cloth with embossed decorative cover.
C 595.7 REM

736 **RODWAY JAMES.**
THE STORY OF FOREST AND STREAM BY JAMES RODWAY, F.L.S. WITH TWENTY-SEVEN ILLUSTRATIONS. LONDON: GEORGE NEWNES, LIMITED, 1897. 202p.: front., 14 plates, ill. Bound in blue cloth with decorative/pictorial cover. Library of Useful Stories.
YSC 634 ROD

737 **SEELEY, H.G.**
THE STORY OF THE EARTH IN PAST AGES. BY H.G. SEELEY, F.R.S. WITH FORTY ILLUSTRATIONS. LONDON: GEORGE NEWNES, LTD., 1901. 196p. + 2p. pub. cat.: front. Bound in blue cloth with pictorial/decorative cover. Library of Useful Stories.
YSC 551.1 SEE

738 **STENHOUSE, ERNEST.**
AN INTRODUCTION TO NATURE-STUDY BY ERNEST STENHOUSE, B.Sc. LONDON: MACMILLAN AND CO., LIMITED, 1905. X, 432p.: ill., diagrs.
YSC 570 STE

739 **SUTCLIFFE, A.**
GENERAL SCIENCE. BY A. SUTCLIFFE, M.A., B.Sc., J.W. CANHAM, M.A., (and) P.C. CHAPMAN, M.A., B.Sc. LONDON: JOHN MURRAY, 1939. VIII, 472p.: 6 plates, ill., diagrs. Rebound in green cloth.
YSC 500 SUT

740 **TAYLOR, J.E.**
NOTES ON COLLECTING AND PRESERVING NATURAL OBJECTS. . . . EDITED BY J.E. TAYLOR, PH.D., F.L.S., F.G.S. LONDON: HARDWICKE AND BOGUE, 1876. VIII, 215p. + 20p. pub. cat.: diagrs. Bound in green cloth with embossed decorative cover.
YSC 507 TAY

741 **THOMPSON, SILVANUS P.**
ELEMENTARY LESSONS IN ELECTRICITY AND MAGNETISM. BY SILVANUS P. THOMPSON, D.Sc., B.A., F.R.S., F.R.A.S. LONDON: MACMILLAN AND CO., LIMITED, 1901. XV, 626p. + 2p. pub. cat.: front., ill., diagrs. Bound in maroon cloth.
YSC 621.3 THO

742 **THORNTON, JOHN.**
ELEMENTARY PHYSIOGRAPHY: AN INTRODUCTION OF THE STUDY OF NATURE. BY JOHN THORNTON, M.A. WITH 10 MAPS AND 156 ILLUSTRATIONS. LONDON: LONGMANS, GREEN, AND CO., 1888. VIII, 248p.: front., ill., maps, diagrs. Bound in red cloth.
YSC 500 THO

743 **TURNER, D.M.**
MAKERS OF SCIENCE. Electricity and Magnetism. By D.M. TURNER, M.A., B.Sc. LONDON: OXFORD UNIVERSITY PRESS, 1927. XV, 184p.: 5 plates, ill., diagrs. Bound in blue cloth.
YSC 509 TUR

743A **UNWIN, ERNEST E.**
POND PROBLEMS. CAMBRIDGE: UNIVERSITY PRESS, 1914. 119 p.: front, 3 plates, ill., some photographs. Bound in green cloth with pictorial cover.
M 574 UNW

744 **VERNE, JULES.**
THE GREAT NAVIGATORS OF THE EIGHTEENTH CENTURY. BY JULES VERNE. WITH 96 ILLUSTRATIONS BY PHILIPPOTEAUX, BENETT, AND MATTHIS, AND 20 MAPS BY MATTHIS AND MORIEU. TRANSLATED FROM THE FRENCH. LONDON: SAMPSON LOW, MARSTON, SEARLE, AND RIVINGTON, 1880. XVI, 409p. + 1p. pub. cat.: front., vignette title page, 95 plates, 20 maps. Bound in brown cloth, with embossed decorative cover and pictorial spine. CELEBRATED TRAVELS AND TRAVELLERS.
C 508.322 VER

745 **WATTS, W. MARSHALL.**
A SCHOOL FLORA FOR THE USE OF ELEMENTARY BOTANICAL CLASSES. BY W. MARSHALL WATTS D.Sc., B.Sc. NEW IMPRESSION WITH 205 ILLUSTRATIONS. LONDON: LONGMANS GREEN AND CO., 1921. VII, 208p. Bound in green cloth. Originally published in 1905.
YSC 580 WAT

746 **WELLS, DAVID A.**
SCIENCE POPULARLY EXPLAINED . . . BY DAVID A. WELLS A.M. With additions by the Editor. LONDON: W. KENT AND CO., (1856). VIII, 568p., ill., diagrs. Half bound in purple leather.
C 500 WEL

747 **WESTELL, W. PERCIVAL** *(Editor).*
THE STREAM I KNOW. EDITED BY W. PERCIVAL WESTELL, F.L.S. AND HENRY E. TURNER. WITH 13 COLOURED AND MANY BLACK AND WHITE ILLUSTRATIONS. LONDON: J.M. DENT AND COMPANY, (193–?). 77p.: col. front., 6 col. plates, plates, ill. Bound in yellow cloth with decorative cover.
YSC 581 WES

747A **WESTON, JAMES.**
STORIES AND PICTURES OF BIRDS, BEASTS, FISHES AND OTHER CREATURES . . . BY JAMES WESTON. ILLUSTRATED BY J. GIACOMELLI, W. RAINEY, HARRISON WEIR, R. KRETCHMER and others. LONDON: S.W. PARTRIDGE AND CO., (1889) 96p.: front, pictorial title page, 26 plates, ill. Bound in brown cloth with coloured pictorial covers.
M 574 WES CHILDREN'S COLLECTION.

748 **WHITEHEAD, E.E.**
HEAT, LIGHT AND SOUND. BOOK 1. BY E.E. WHITEHEAD. LONDON: GEORGE G. HARRAP AND CO., LTD., 1934. 256p.: front., diagrs. Bound in blue cloth. MODERN SCHOOL PHYSICS SERIES.
YSC 530 WHI

749 **WHITEHOUSE, R.H.**
THE DISSECTION OF THE FROG. BY R.H. WHITEHOUSE, D.Sc. AND A.J. GROVE, D.Sc. M.A. LONDON: UNIVERSITY TUTORIAL PRESS LTD., SECOND EDITION, 1937. X. 101p.: diagrs. Bound in blue cloth.
YSC 597 WHI

750 **WHO WAS THE FIRST PAPER-MAKER?**
LONDON: T. NELSON AND SONS, 1876. 72p.: col. front., decorative title page, 2 plates, ill. Bound in brown cloth, with coloured decorative label on cover. An account of the nests built by wasps and other hymenoptera. Includes a presentation plate of the City of Manchester School Board, 1877.
C 595.798 WHO

751 **WILLIAMS, ARCHIBALD.**
How It Works; Dealing in Simple language with Steam, Electricity, Light, Heat, Sound, Hydraulics, Optics, etc. and with their applications to Apparatus in Common Use. By ARCHIBALD WILLIAMS. LONDON: THOMAS NELSON AND SONS, (190–?). 461p.: front., 20 plates, ill. Bound in grey cloth, with coloured pictorial cover and spine.
C 530 WIL

752 **WOOD, J.G.**
THE BOY'S OWN BOOK OF NATURAL HISTORY. BY THE REV. J.G. WOOD, M.A., F.L.S. WITH EIGHT FULL-PAGE ILLUSTRATIONS IN COLOUR AND NUMEROUS ILLUSTRATIONS IN THE TEXT. LONDON: GEORGE ROUTLEDGE AND SONS, LIMITED. (191–?). VI, 378p.: col. front., 7 col. plates, ill. Bound in green cloth with coloured pictorial cover and spine. Originally published in 1861.
C 500.9 WOO

## 11 GAMES, SPORTS AND PASTIMES

753 **ADAMS, MORLEY** *(Editor).*
THE COMPLETE SCOUT. EDITED BY MORLEY ADAMS. WITH MANY ILLUSTRATIONS FROM PHOTOGRAPHS AND DIAGRAMS. LONDON: HENRY FROWDE HODDER AND STOUGHTON, 1915. VIII, 288p.: col. front., 15 plates, ill. Bound in red cloth with coloured pictorial paper cover.
C 369.43 COM

754 **ALEXANDER, V.C.**
THE EVERYDAY GAMES BOOK FOR EVERY OCCASION. GIRL GUIDES, PARTIES, THE FIRESIDE, SOCIALS, OUTINGS, SCHOOLS. By V.C. ALEXANDER. LONDON: EVANS BROTHERS LIMITED. (193–?) 144p. Bound in orange cloth.
YSC 790 ALE

755 **BADEN-POWELL, SIR ROBERT.**
ROVERING TO SUCCESS. A BOOK OF LIFE-SPORT FOR YOUNG MEN. BY SIR R. BADEN-POWELL WITH

60 ILLUSTRATIONS BY THE AUTHOR. LONDON: HERBERT JENKINS, LTD., 1922. 253p. + 2p. pub. cat.: front., ill. Bound in green cloth.
C 301.411 BAD

755A **ELSTON, FRANK.**
ORGANISED GAMES FOR THE SCHOOL, THE HALL OR THE PLAYGROUND. BY FRANK ELSTON. LONDON: E.J. ARNOLD AND SON LTD., THIRD EDITION REVISED. (1912). 192p. + 2p. pub. cat.: ill., diagrs, music. Bound in green cloth.
C 796.1 ELS

755B **(FRANCIS, LYDIA MARY, afterwards CHILD).**
(THE GIRL'S OWN BOOK). Title page missing. LONDON: TEGG (186?). p. 65–362: ill. Bound in brown cloth with embossed covers.
M 793 GAM CHILDREN'S COLLECTION

755C **GALLOWAY, R.W.**
ANATOMY AND PHYSIOLOGY OF PHYSICAL TRAINING. BY COLONEL R.W. GALLOWAY. D.S.O., M.B. CH.B., R.A.M.C. WITH AN INTRODUCTION BY E.P. CATHCART, LL.D., M.D., D.Sc. LONDON: EDWARD ARNOLD AND CO., 1937. VII, 182p.: ill. Bound in grey cloth.
YSC 612 GAL

756 **GEORGE, UNCLE.**
PARLOUR PASTIME FOR THE YOUNG. CONSISTING OF PANTOMIME AND DIALOGUE. CHARADES, FIRESIDE GAMES, Riddles, Enigmas, Charades, Conundrums, ARITHMETICAL AND MECHANICAL PUZZLES, PARLOUR MAGIC, ETC. ETC. EDITED BY UNCLE GEORGE. LONDON: JAMES BLACKWOOD, 1857. 208p.; front., 1 plate, ill. Bound in blue cloth with embossed pictorial/decorative cover and gilt edges.
YSC 790 GEO

757 **HUTCHISON, G.A.** *(Editor).*
INDOOR GAMES AND RECREATIONS, A Popular Encyclopaedia for boys by DR GORDON STABLES, R.N. . . . AND MANY OTHERS. EDITED BY G.A. HUTCHISON. WITH OVER SEVEN HUNDRED ILLUSTRATIONS. LONDON: THE RELIGIOUS TRACT SOCIETY, (189–?) 528p.: front., 9 plates, ill. Bound in brown cloth with pictorial/decorative covers and spine, with gilt edges.
YSC 794 HUT

758 **KIDSON, FRANK** *(Editor).*
100 SINGING GAMES, OLD, NEW AND ADAPTED. Edited by Frank Kidson and arranged with Piano Forte accompaniments by Alfred Moffat. LONDON: BAYLEY AND FERGUSON, 1916. 115p. Originally with decorative covers retained when rebound.
YOSC 790 KID

758A **THE LITTLE BOY'S OWN BOOK**
CONSISTING OF GAMES AND PASTIMES WITH DIRECTIONS FOR THE BREEDING AND MANAGEMENT OF RABBITS, BIRDS AND PIGEONS ETC. FOR THE Recreation and Amusement of Good Boys. BY UNCLE CHARLES WITH ILLUSTRATIONS BY HENRY SEARS. LONDON: HENRY ALLMAN, 1850. VII, 200p.: col. front., 7 col. plates, hand painted. Bound in blue cloth with embossed cover and spine.
M 790 LIT CHILDREN'S COLLECTION

758B **LUCAS, EDWARD VERRALL**
THREE HUNDRED GAMES AND PASTIMES. OR What shall we do now? A BOOK OF SUGGESTIONS FOR CHILDREN'S GAMES AND EMPLOYMENTS BY EDWARD VERRALL LUCAS AND ELIZABETH LUCAS. LONDON: CHATTO AND WINDUS, 1925. VII, 354p.: ill., diagrs. Bound in red cloth with decorative cover.
C 793.01922 LUC

759 **WILMAN, STANLEY V.**
GAMES FOR PLAYTIME AND PARTIES WITH AND WITHOUT MUSIC FOR CHILDREN OF ALL AGES. BY STANLEY V. WILMAN, PICTURED BY MARGARET W. TARRANT. LONDON: T.C. AND E.C. JACK, (192–?). 83p. ill., some col., musical score. Bound in cream cloth with coloured pictorial/decorative cover.
YOSC 793 WIL

759

759A **WOOD, ERIC.**
THE BOY SCOUTS' BOOK OF HONOUR. By Eric Wood. Foreword by Lieut-Gen. Sir Robert Baden-Powell K.C.B. K.C.V.O. With a Colour Frontispiece and 8 other illustrations. LONDON: CASSELL AND COMPANY, LTD., 1914. 308p.: Bound in red buckram with coloured pictorial cover and spine.
C 369.430922 WOO

## 12 POPULAR SONGS AND RHYMES SET TO MUSIC

760 **CRAMPTON, THOMAS.**
AUNT EFFIE'S RHYMES FOR LITTLE CHILDREN. SET TO MUSIC BY T. CRAMPTON. WITH THIRTY-SIX ILLUSTRATIONS BY HABLOT K. BROWNE. LONDON: GEORGE ROUTLEDGE AND SONS, (187–?). 91p. + 4p. pub. cat.: col. front., ill., musical score. Bound in blue cloth, with coloured pictorial paper cover.
C 784.624 CRA

761 **CRANE, WALTER** *(Illustrator).*
THE BABY'S OPERA. A BOOK OF OLD RHYMES WITH NEW DRESSES BY WALTER CRANE. THE MUSIC BY THE EARLIEST MASTERS. ENGRAVED AND PRINTED IN COLOURS BY EDMUND EVANS. LONDON: FREDERICK WARNE AND CO., LTD., (189–?). 56p.: col. front., col. decorative title page, 10 col. plates, col. ill., musical score.
CBD 398.8 CRA

761A **CRANE, WALTER** *(Illustrator).*
PAN-PIPES. A BOOK OF OLD SONGS NEWLY ARRANGED AND WITH ACCOMPANIMENTS BY THEO MARZIALS: SET TO PICTURES BY WALTER CRANE. ENGRAVED AND PRINTED IN COLOURS BY EDMUND EVANS. LONDON: GEORGE ROUTLEDGE AND SONS. 1883. 52p.: 4 col. fronts., decorative col. title page, col. ill. and decorative borders. Bound in brown cloth with brown pictorial paper covers.
CBD 784.4942 CRA

761B **Another copy.**
Second edition. LONDON: NOVELLO AND CO., GEORGE ROUTLEDGE AND SONS, (1884?) 52p.: 2 front., col. decorative title page, text as before. Bound in brown cloth with green pictorial paper covers.

762 **ELLIOTT, JAMES WILLIAM.**
NATIONAL NURSERY RHYMES AND NURSERY SONGS. Set to Original Music BY J.W. ELLIOTT. WITH ILLUSTRATIONS, ENGRAVED BY THE BROTHERS DALZIEL. LONDON: NOVELLO AND COMPANY, LIMITED, (187–?). 111p.: front., vignette title page, 3 plates, ill., musical score. Bound in brown cloth, with pictorial/decorative covers and spine, and gilt edges.
C 784.624 NAT

763 **FROEBEL, FRIEDRICH.**
MOTHER'S SONGS, GAMES AND STORIES. Fröbel's "Mutter-und Rose-Lieder". RENDERED IN ENGLISH BY FRANCES AND EMILY LORD. CONTAINING THE WHOLE OF THE ORIGINAL ILLUSTRATIONS AND THE MUSIC, RE-ARRANGED FOR CHILDREN'S VOICES, WITH PIANOFORTE ACCOMPANIMENT. STUDENTS' EDITION. LONDON: WILLIAM RICE, 1907. XXXVI, 238p. + 75p.: ill., musical score. Bound in grey cloth. Originally published 1843.
YSC 372.21 FRO

764 **GOMME, ALICE B.**
CHILDREN'S SINGING GAMES. Edited by ALICE B. GOMME and CECIL J. SHARP.
SET 1. LONDON: NOVELLO AND COMPANY LIMITED, n.d. (reprinted 1951). 23p.: musical score. Bound in blue paper, with pink paper protective cover.
YSC 790 GOM

764A **HALLWORD, REGINALD FRANCIS.**
FLOWERS OF PARADISE. MUSIC, VERSE, DESIGN AND ILLUSTRATION BY REGINALD FRANCIS HALLWORD. (Printed by EDMUND EVANS). LONDON: MACMILLAN AND CO., 39p.: decorative title page in red, ill., some col., music, text in script. Bound in black cloth, with coloured decorative paper covers.
M 784 HAL CHILDREN'S COLLECTION

765 **HUTCHISON, WILLIAM M.**
SEE-SAW; A BOOK OF SONGS AND PICTURES FROM "ST. NICHOLAS". WITH ORIGINAL MUSIC BY WILLIAM H. HUTCHISON. LONDON: FREDERICK WARNE AND CO., (188–?). 93p.: front., vignette title page, 4 plates, ill., musical score. Bound in grey cloth, with coloured pictorial paper cover.
YSC 784 HUT

766 **LESLIE, HENRY.**
LITTLE SONGS FOR ME TO SING. The Illustrations by J.E. MILLAIS, R.A. (Engraved by Joseph Swain) WITH MUSIC COMPOSED BY HENRY LESLIE. LONDON: CASSELL, PETTER AND GALPIN, (1865). (36)p.: front., 6 plates, ill., musical score. Bound in purple cloth, with embossed decorative covers.
C 784.624 LES

767 **MACMAHON, DESMOND.**
NELSON'S New National and Folk SONG BOOK. PART 1. BY DESMOND MACMAHON, D.Mus. VOCAL PARTS IN BOTH NOTATIONS. LONDON: THOMAS NELSON AND SONS LIMITED, 1938. VIII, 148p.: musical score. Bound in grey cloth.
YSC 784 MAC

768 **MOORE, H. KEATLEY.**
THE NURSERY SONG BOOK: TRADITIONAL NURSERY SONGS. COLLECTED, EDITED AND HARMONIZED BY H. KEATLEY MOORE, MUS. BAC., B.A. AND ILLUSTRATED BY MAY SANDHEIM. LONDON: GEORGE ROUTLEDGE AND SONS LTD., (192–?). 63p.: col. front., col. pictorial title page, 2 col. plates, 3 plates, ill., decorative endpapers, musical score. Bound in blue cloth, with coloured pictorial cover and spine.
C 398.8 NUR

768A **ROUTLEDGE, WILLIAM.**
THE CHILDREN'S MUSICAL CINDERELLA. TOLD IN FAMILIAR WORDS TO FAMILIAR TUNES BY WILLIAM ROUTLEDGE AND LOUIS N. PARKER. WITH PICTURES BY WALTER CRANE. LONDON: GEORGE ROUTLEDGE AND SONS, 1879. 29p.: col. front. col. ill., music. Bound in yellow card, with coloured pictorial cover.
M 398.2 CRA CHILDREN'S COLLECTION

769 **STEPHAN, EMILE M. A BOOK OF FRENCH SONGS.**
SELECTED BY EMILE M. STEPHAN. LONDON: HUMPHREY MILFORD, OXFORD UNIVERSITY PRESS, 1939. 90p.: musical score. Bound in grey cloth, with decorative cover.
YSC 841 STE

## 13 ENGLISH LANGUAGE AND READING

770 **BARING-GOULD, SABINE.**
THE BARING-GOULD CONTINUOUS READER, ARRANGED BY G.H. ROSE. WITH FIVE ILLUSTRATIONS AND A MAP. LONDON: METHUEN AND CO., 1908. VI, 204 + 20p. pub. cat.: front., 4 plates, map. Bound in blue cloth with pictorial cover.
YSC 428 ROS

771 **BUTTER, HENRY.**
THE ETYMOLOGICAL SPELLING BOOK AND

EXPOSITOR. AN INTRODUCTION TO THE SPELLING, PRONUNCIATION, AND DERIVATION OF THE ENGLISH LANGUAGE. BY HENRY BUTTER. THREE HUNDRED AND NINETEENTH EDITION. LONDON: SIMKIN AND CO., 1870. 158p. + 2p. pub. cat. Bound in black cloth with embossed decorative covers.
YSC 422 BUT

774 **THE CHILD'S NEW LESSON BOOK.**
OR, Stories for little readers. LONDON: JOSEPH MASTERS. (186–?). 132p.: front., 12 plates. Incomplete words divided by hyphens according to the sound rather than strict orthography. The Little Christian's Story Book.
C 428.6 CHI

775 **COLES, MARGARET J.**
THE HAPPY TRAVELLER READERS: GIRLS. BY MARGARET J. COLES, L.L.A. AND A.P. NIELD.
II. WAYSIDE JOYS. 192p. Bound in blue cloth.
III. THE RIGHT ROAD. 208p. Bound in buff cloth.
LONDON: BLACKIE AND SON LIMITED, 1936/7, 192p.: col. front., ill.
YSC 372.4 COL

776 **THE COMPANION LETTER WRITER.**
A complete Guide to Correspondence on ALL SUBJECTS RELATING TO FRIENDSHIP, LOVE, AND BUSINESS, WITH NUMEROUS COMMERCIAL FORMS. BY ONE OF THE COMPILERS OF THE ENQUIRE WITHIN SERIES. LONDON: FREDERICK WARNE AND CO., (188–?). XI, 187p. + 3p. pub. cat. Bound in black cloth.
YSC 808 COM

777 **CROSSLAND, JOHN R.**
PLAIN ENGLISH, A Course in Four Books by JOHN R. CROSSLAND.
INTRODUCTORY BOOK A 64p. 1939. Limp bound in yellow cloth.
BOOK I. 1935. Limp bound in red cloth.
BOOK III. 1935. Limp bound in green cloth.
LONDON: COLLINS CLEAR-TYPE PRESS. Ill.
YSC 426 CRO

778 **D, S.N.**
The Songs The Letters Sing, By S.N.D. Pictured by MARGARET W. TARRANT. BOOK 1A. 40p., 6 col. plates, ill. BOOK III. 92p., 5 col. plates, col. ill. LONDON: GRANT EDUCATIONAL CO., LTD., (193–?). Bound in blue cloth with coloured pictorial paper covers.
YSC 372.4 SND

779 **DALE, N.**
THE WALTER CRANE INFANT READER. WRITTEN BY N. DALE OF THE HIGH SCHOOL FOR GIRLS, WIMBLEDON AND ILLUSTRATED BY WALTER CRANE. BOOKS I & II. LONDON: J.M. DENT AND CO., 1899. Unpaginated, numbered in Sections 48–86.: 4 col. plates + col. plates marking start of Books II and II(1), pictorial title page in two colours, col. ill. Rebound in green cloth.
CBD 428.6 DAL

780 **DIXON, JAMES MAIN**
ENGLISH IDIOMS. By JAMES MAIN DIXON, M.A. F.R.S.E. LONDON: THOMAS NELSON AND SONS, LTD., 1927. VI, 288p. Bound in dark green cloth.
YSC 423 DIX

781 **ENFIELD, WILLIAM.**
THE SPEAKER; OR, MISCELLANEOUS PIECES SELECTED FROM THE BEST ENGLISH WRITERS, AND DISPOSED UNDER PROPER HEADS WITH A VIEW TO FACILITATE THE IMPROVEMENT OF YOUTH IN READING AND SPEAKING. TO WHICH IS PREFIXED AN ESSAY ON ELOCUTION. BY W.M. ENFIELD, L.L.D., LECTURER OF THE BELLES LETTRES IN THE ACADEMY AT WARRINGTON. A NEW EDITION. MANCHESTER: THOMAS JOHNSON, 1849. VIII, 376p.: front. Bound in black cloth with embossed decorative covers and spine.
C 808.545 ENF

782 **EVESON, T.E.** *(Editor).*
THE REALM OF READING. General Editor T.E. EVESON, M.A.
BOOK ONE. STORYLAND 160p.
BOOK TWO. HAPPY HOURS 176p.
BOOK THREE. GOLDEN TALES 191p.
BOOK FOUR. HIGH ADVENTURE 239p.
BOOK FIVE. TALES AND VENTURES 239p.
LONDON: BLACKIE AND SON LIMITED, 1938. Col. fronts., col. plates, ill. Bound in buff cloth with decorative covers.
YSC 372.4 EVE

783 **GILL, GEORGE.**
THIRD STANDARD ENGLISH GRAMMAR. CODE 1880. BY GEORGE GILL. LONDON: GEO. GILL AND SONS, (188–?). 16p. Limp bound in blue paper. Gills School Series.
YSC 425 GIL

784 **GRATTAN, J.H.G.**
OUR LIVING LANGUAGE. A NEW GUIDE TO ENGLISH GRAMMAR. By J.H.G. GRATTAN AND P. GURREY. LONDON: THOMAS NELSON AND SONS LTD., 1925. 323p. Bound in dark blue cloth.
YSC 425 GRA

785 **HAMMOND, C.E.L.**
PROGRESSIVE EXERCISES IN ENGLISH COMPOSITION. (BY) C.E.L. HAMMOND. OXFORD: CLARENDON PRESS, 1921. 64p. Bound in blue cloth.
YSC 808.042076 HAM

786 **HEYWOOD, JOHN.**
JOHN HEYWOOD'S MANCHESTER READERS: FOR ELEMENTARY SCHOOLS OF ALL GRADES. THE THIRD BOOK, COMPILED TO SUIT THE REQUIREMENTS OF STANDARD III OF NEW CODE. NEW EDITION. MANCHESTER: JOHN HEYWOOD, (188–?). 160p. + 5p. pub. cat.: front., decorative title page, ill. Bound in buff cloth.
YSC 428 HEY

787 **HIGHAM, J.**
IVANHOE ("SIR WALTER SCOTT" CONTINUOUS READERS) BY J. HIGHAM, M.A. LONDON: ADAM AND CHARLES BLACK, 1899. XXIV, 216p.: front., 5 plates, ill. Bound in brown cloth.
YSC 823 SCO

788 **JAGGER, J.H.** *(Editor).*
THE WESTMINSTER READERS.
JOYOUS HOURS. SECOND SERIES. BOOK ONE.
WITH THIRTY SIX ILLUSTRATIONS IN BLACK AND WHITE AND FOUR PLATES IN COLOUR BY FRANK ROGERS. 1934. Bound in blue cloth with decorative cover.
THE CHARM OF BOOKS. SECOND SERIES. BOOK TWO.
WITH THIRTY THREE ILLUSTRATIONS IN BLACK AND WHITE AND FOUR PLATES IN COLOUR BY LORNA R. STEELE. 1933. Bound in orange cloth with decorative cover. COMPILED BY J.H. JAGGER, M.A., D.LITT. LONDON: UNIVERSITY OF LONDON PRESS, LTD.
YSC 428 JAG

789 **JEPSON, R.W.**
ENGLISH EXERCISES FOR SCHOOL CERTIFICATE. BY R.W. JEPSON, M.A. LONDON: EDWARD ARNOLD AND CO., 1935. 192p. Bound in green cloth.
YSC 425 JEP

790 **JOHNSON, DR.**
AN ILLUSTRATED DICTIONARY OF THE ENGLISH LANGUAGE, FOR THE USE OF SCHOOLS AND GENERAL STUDENTS. BY DR. JOHNSON. LONDON: GEORGE ROUTLEDGE AND SONS, (187–?). XXVIII, 251p. + 6p. pub. cat.: 1 plate. Bound in black cloth with embossed decorative covers.
YSC 423 JOH

791 **LAY, E.J.S.** *(Editor).*
TALK, TALE AND SONG FOR SECONDARY SCHOOLS.
EASY STUDY SERIES, GENERAL EDITOR, E.J.S. LAY.
PREPARATORY BOOK, 80p.
BOOK ONE. 96p.
BOOK TWO. 128p.
BOOK THREE. 128p.
LONDON: MACMILLAN AND CO., LIMITED, (193–?): col. ill., limp bound with coloured paper covers.
YSC 372.4 LAY

792 **MANUAL OF ENGLISH SPELLING.**
CONTAINING ALL THE DIFFICULTIES OF SPELLING, IN A SERIES OF SYSTEMATICALLY GRADUATED LESSONS, WITH NUMEROUS PRACTICAL EXERCISES. LONDON: JOHN MARSHALL AND CO., (188–?) 192p. Bound in red cloth with embossed decorative cover.
YSC 421 MAN

793 **MAVOR, WILLIAM.**
The English Spelling-Book. ACCOMPANIED BY A PROGRESSIVE SERIES OF EASY AND FAMILIAR LESSONS, BY WILLIAM MAVOR, LL.D. ILLUSTRATED BY KATE GREENAWAY. ENGRAVED AND PRINTED BY EDMUND EVANS. LONDON: GEORGE ROUTLEDGE AND SONS, 1885. 108p.: front., vignette on title page, ill. Bound in grey paper with coloured pictorial cover.
CBD 428.1 MAV

793

794 **MORELL, J.D.**
A COMPLETE MANUAL OF SPELLING ON THE PRINCIPLES OF CONTRAST AND COMPARISON WITH Numerous Exercises. BY J.D. MORELL, LL.D. NINETY-EIGHT THOUSAND. LONDON: CASSELL AND COMPANY, LIMITED, (189–?). IV, 128p. + 4p. pub. cat. on end papers. Bound in pink cloth with embossed decorative cover.
YSC 421 MOR

795 **MOWAT, GEORGE.**
TRAINING IN READING AND STUDY. A COURSE FOR CENTRAL AND SECONDARY SCHOOLS AND ADVANCED DIVISIONS. BY GEORGE MOWAT, M.A., B.Ed.
INTRODUCTORY BOOK. AGE 10-11-12 YEARS. 119p. Bound in buff cloth.
BOOK 1. AGE 11-12-13 YEARS. 216p. Bound in buff cloth with blue decorative cover.
BOOK II. AGE 12-13-14 YEARS. 271p. Bound in buff cloth with green decorative cover.
EDINBURGH: OLIVER AND BOYD, (1934). Ill.
YSC 428 MOW

795A **MURRAY, LINDLEY.**
ENGLISH GRAMMAR ADAPTED TO THE DIFFERENT CLASSES OF LEARNERS. WITH AN APPENDIX CONTAINING RULES AND OBSERVATIONS, FOR ASSISTING THE MORE ADVANCED STUDENTS TO WRITE WITH PERSPICUITY AND ACCURACY. BY LINDLEY MURRAY. DERBY: HENRY MOZLEY AND SONS, 1846. 328p. + 4p. pub. cat. Bound in green calf.
YSC 425 MUR

796 **THE NEW ROYAL READERS.**
ADAPTED TO THE LATEST REQUIREMENTS OF THE EDUCATION DEPARTMENT. STANDARD II. LONDON: T. NELSON AND SONS, 1884. 127p.: ill. Bound in maroon cloth with embossed decorative cover.
YSC 372.4 NEW

797 **NIELD, A.P.**
THE HAPPY TRAVELLER READERS: BOYS.
I. THE BROAD HIGHWAY. 176p. Bound in red cloth.
III. PATHFINDERS. 208p. Bound in green cloth.
BY A.P. NIELD AND J.G. FYFE, M.A. LONDON: BLACKIE AND SON LIMITED, 1935. Col. front., ill.
YSC 372.4 NIE

798 **OLIPHANT, LANCELOT.**
A MATRICULATION AND GENERAL ENGLISH COURSE. By LANCELOT OLIPHANT, B.A. Hons. FOURTH EDITION. LONDON: THE GREGG PUBLISHING COMPANY, LTD., 1933. VIII, 467p. Bound in blue cloth.
YSC 428 OLI

799 **POCOCK, GUY N.**
A FIRST PRÉCIS BOOK (PASSAGES FROM LITERATURE). BY GUY N. POCOCK, M.A. LONDON: J.M. DENT AND SONS LTD., 1925. VII, 184p. Bound in green cloth with decorative cover.
YSC 426 POC

800 **POCOCK, GUY N.**
JUNIOR EXERCISES IN ENGLISH. Or the adventures of two brothers and a sister. By GUY N. POCOCK, M.A. Illustrated by Tom Peddie. LONDON: J.M. DENT AND SONS, LTD., 1927. X, 117p. 10 plates. Bound in green cloth with decorative cover.
YSC 428 POC

801 **POLKINGHORNE, R.K.**
THE LAND OF WORDS BY R.K. AND M.I.R. POLKINGHORNE
BOOK 1. 64p. Limp bound in green cloth.
BOOK 2. 80p. Limp bound in orange cloth.
BOOK 3. 95p. Limp bound in blue cloth.
BOOK 4. 112p. Limp bound in buff cloth.
LONDON: G. BELL AND SONS LTD., 1935. ill.
YSC 425 POL

802 **POLKINGHORNE, R.K.**
LANGUAGE AND SPEECH TRAINING STORIES BY R.K. AND M.I.R. POLKINGHORNE. LONDON: UNIVERSITY OF LONDON PRESS, LTD., 1932. 238p. ill. Bound in blue cloth. Intended to be told to children of five to eight.
YSC /F POL

803 **POLKINGHORNE, R.K.** *(Editor).*
THE ROMANCE OF READING FIRST SERIES. EDITED BY R.K. AND M.I.R. POLKINGHORNE. BOOK 1. MERRY MOMENTS, 168p. Bound in blue cloth.
BOOK II. HAPPY HOURS. 200p. Bound in buff cloth.
BOOK III. PLEASANT PATHS. 192p. Bound in blue cloth.
BOOK IV. COSY COMPANY. 224p. Bound in buff cloth.
LONDON: OXFORD UNIVERSITY PRESS, 1936. Col. fronts., ill., decorative covers.
YSC 372.4 POC

804 **POTTER, F.F.**
PITMAN'S COMMON-SENSE ENGLISH COURSE. SENIOR SERIES BOOK 1. (FOR PUPILS 11-12 YEARS) BY F.F. POTTER, M.A., B.Sc. LONDON: SIR ISAAC PITMAN AND SONS, LTD., 1929. 80p. Bound in blue cloth.
YSC 425 POT

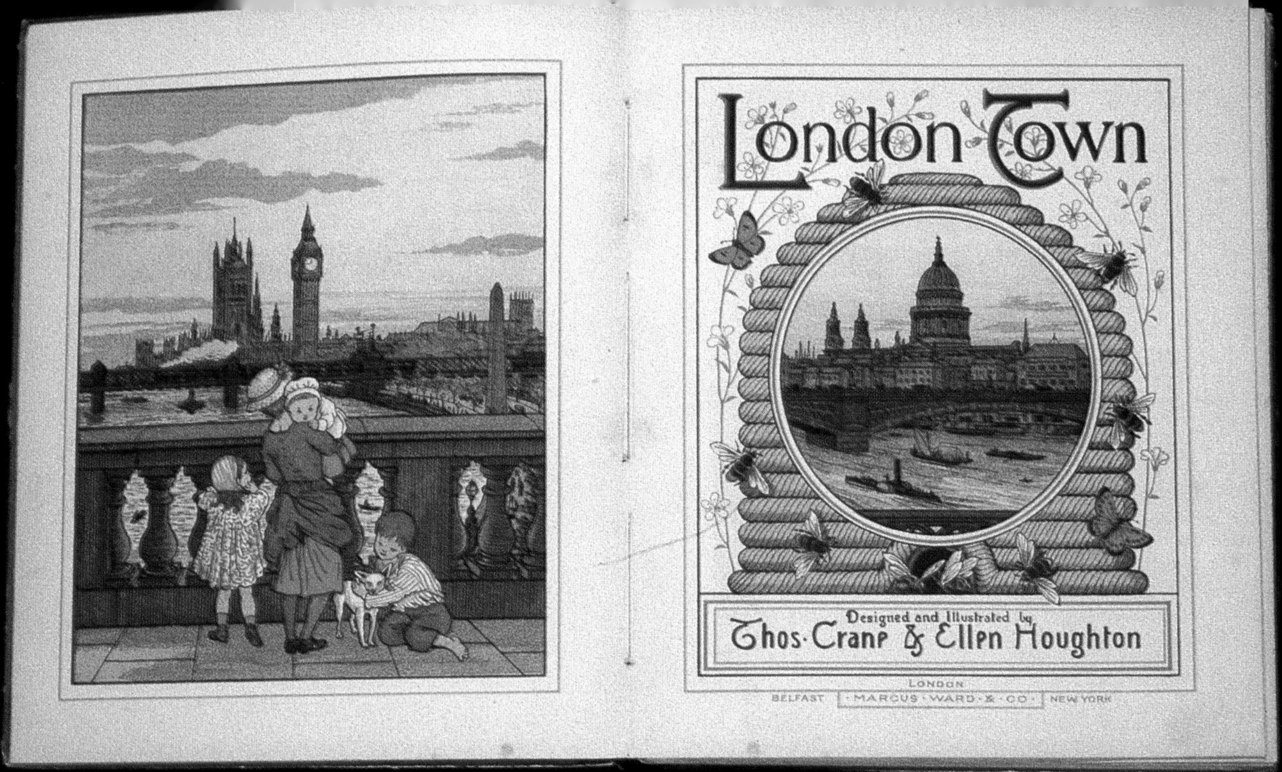
London Town
Designed and Illustrated by
Thos. Crane & Ellen Houghton
LONDON
BELFAST
· MARCUS · WARD · & · CO ·
NEW YORK

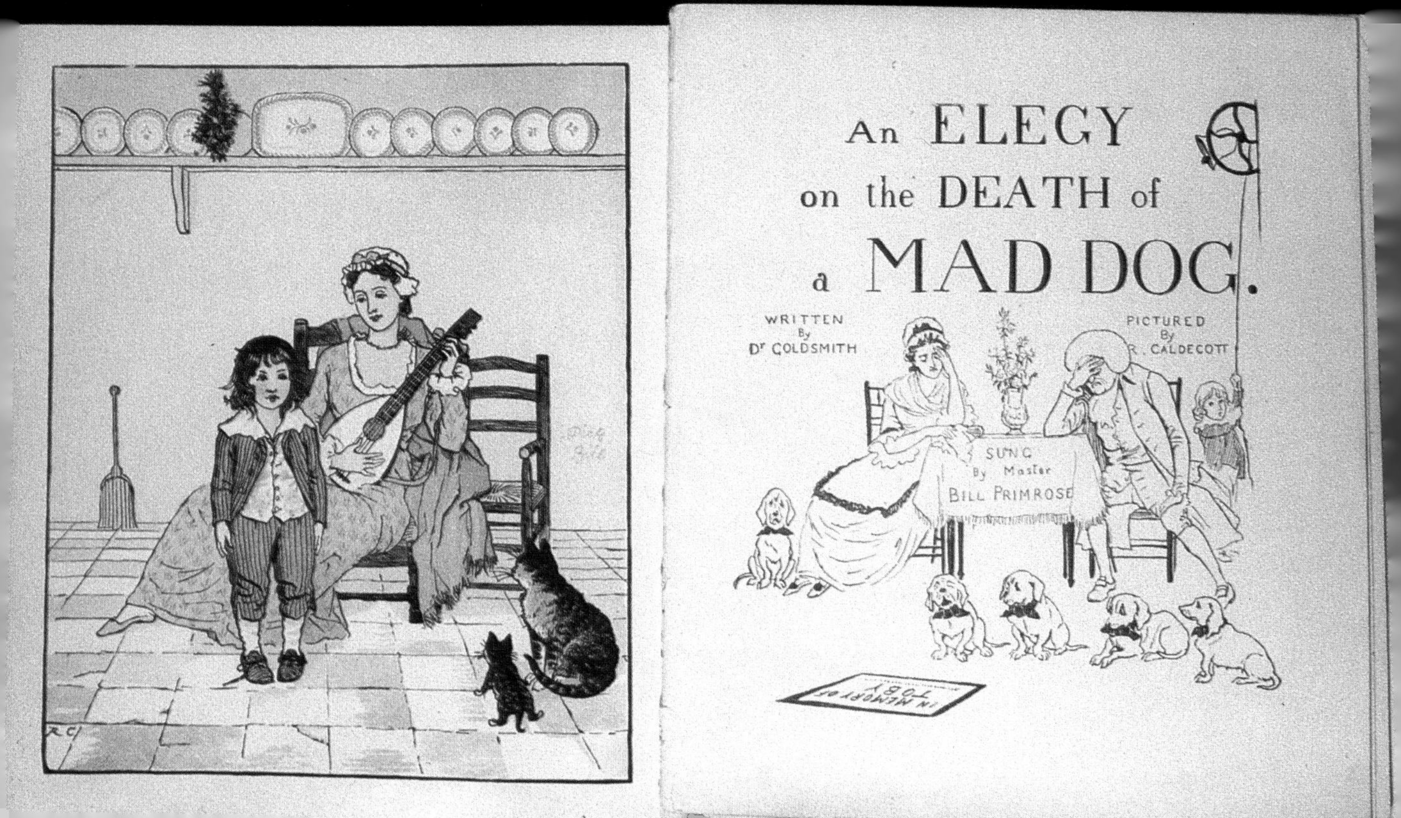
An ELEGY
on the DEATH of
a MAD DOG.
WRITTEN
By
Dr GOLDSMITH
PICTURED
By
R. CALDECOTT
SUNG
By Master
BILL PRIMROSE
IN MEMORY of
TOBY

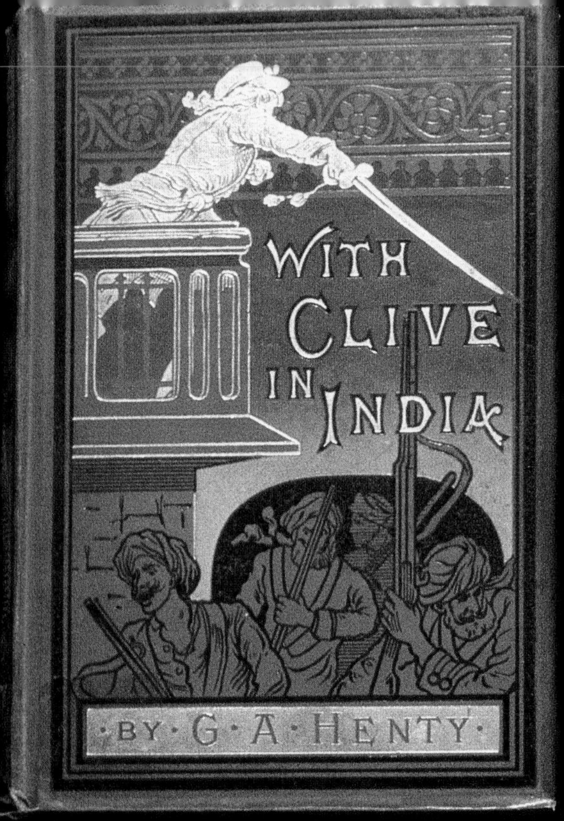
WITH
CLIVE
IN INDIA
BY · G · A · HENTY ·

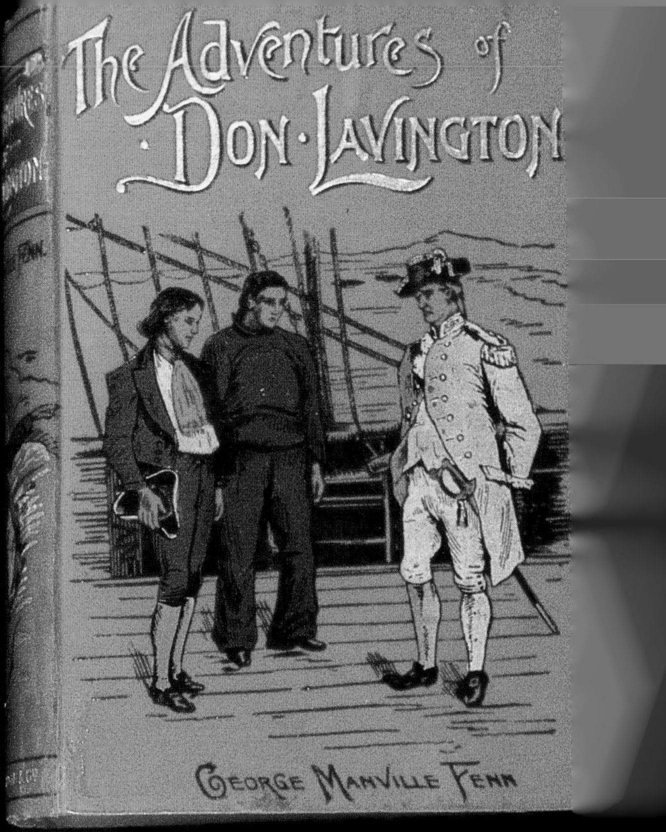
The Adventures of
· DON · LAVINGTON
GEORGE MANVILLE FENN

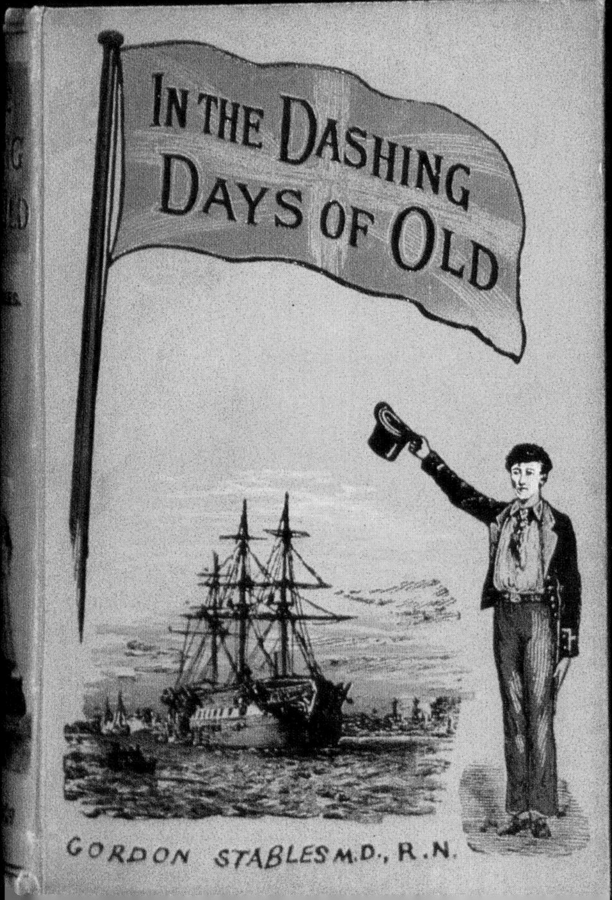
IN THE DASHING
DAYS OF OLD
GORDON STABLES M.D., R.N.

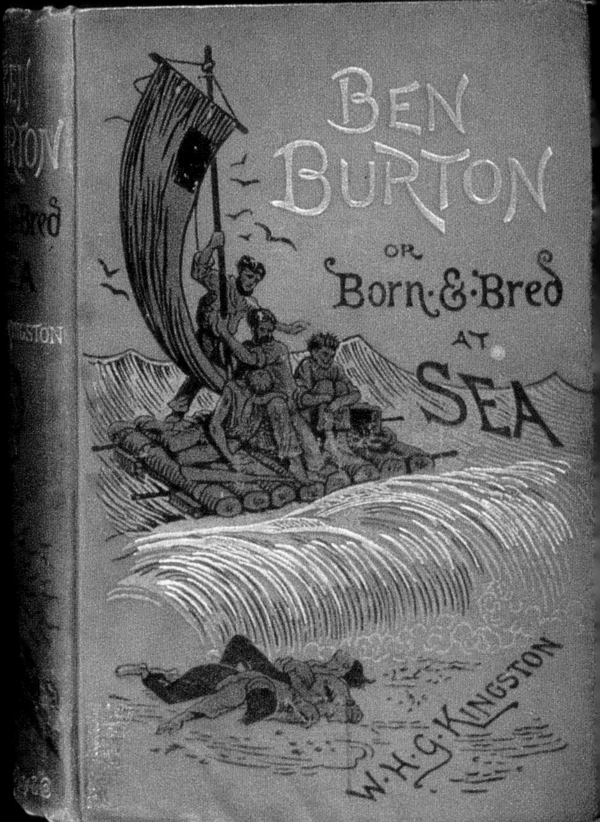
BEN
BURTON
OR
Born · & · Bred
AT
SEA
W. H. G. KINGSTON

805 **RIDGWAY, JAMES.**
THE ACADEMIC PROGRESSIVE READER. SIXTH BOOK FOR BOYS. WITH HOME EXERCISES ON THE LESSONS. Illustrated. Collins School Series. LONDON: WILLIAM COLLINS, SONS AND COMPANY, 1874. 405p. + 2p. pub. cat. Diagrs.
C 428.6 ACA

806 **THE ROYAL READERS.**
NO IV. ILLUSTRATED, NO V. and NO VI ILLUSTRATED. LONDON: THOMAS NELSON AND SONS LTD., 1946 reprint of (189–?) edition. 288p.: ill. Bound in buff cloth with decorative cover.
YSC 372.4 ROY and C 428.6 ROY

807 **THE ROYAL STAR READERS.**
SIXTH BOOK. LONDON: T. NELSON AND SONS, 1892. 256p. front. ill. Bound in red cloth. Royal School Series.
YSC 372.4 ROY

808 **SOPWITH, S.S.** *(Editor).*
ENGLISH SAMPLER. SOME ESSENTIAL PASSAGES OF PROSE AND POETRY IN ENGLISH LITERATURE. CHOSEN AND EDITED BY S.S. SOPWITH, M.A. LONDON: G. BELL AND SONS, LTD., 1938. XXX, 183p. Bound in blue cloth.
YSC 828 SOP

809 **SOUTER, J.**
SOUTER'S SCHOOL SPELLING BOOK. Title page missing. LONDON: J. SOUTER, (187–?). 140p. Bound in grey cloth.
YSC 421 SOU

810 **SPENCER, JANE.**
SIXTY LETTER AND READING GAMES. BY JANE SPENCER. LONDON: MACMILLAN AND CO., LIMITED., 1939. 64p. Bound in green cloth.
YSC 372.4 SPE

811 **STEPHENSON, JOHN D.**
THINK IT OUT. A Course in Criticism and Composition, by JOHN D. STEPHENSON, M.A. LONDON: METHUEN AND CO., LTD., 1938. IX, 163p. Bound in buff cloth.
YSC 100 STE

812 **STEVENS, E.T.**
THE NEW CODE. THE GRADE LESSON BOOKS IN SIX STANDARDS. BY REV. E.T. STEVENS, M.A. AND REV. CHARLES HOLE. LONDON: LONGMANS GREEN AND CO., (188–?). 156p. Bound in buff cloth.
YSC 372 STE

813 **TURNBULL, E. LUCIA** *(Editor).*
THE TEACHER'S OMNIBUS OF STORIES TO TELL. COMPILED AND EDITED BY E. LUCIA TURNBULL WITH A STORY PREFACE BY ELEANOR FARJEON. LONDON: OXFORD UNIVERSITY PRESS, 1936. 317p. Bound in blue cloth.
YSC 372.4 TUR

814 **TURNER, J.W.**
APPLIED GRAMMAR. By J.W. TURNER, B.A. LONDON: ELKIN MATHEWS AND MARROT, LTD., 1934. 88p. Bound in green cloth with decorative cover.
YSC 425 TUR

815 **WILSON, MARK.**
THE FIRST READING BOOK. BY MARK WILSON. WITH ONE HUNDRED AND TWENTY ILLUSTRATIONS. LONDON: SAMPSON LOW, SON, AND CO., (186–?). 128p.: front., vignette title page, ill. Bound in red cloth, with coloured decorative paper cover. Cover title: WILSON'S FIRST READER.
C 428.6 WIL

816 **WINDROSS, RONALD.**
EXERCISES IN THE USE AND UNDERSTANDING OF ENGLISH, BY RONALD WINDROSS, M.A. LONDON: EDWARD ARNOLD AND CO., 1934. 127p. Bound in orange cloth.
YSC 420.76 WIN

# 14 PICTURE BOOKS

817 **ADAMS, FRANK** *(Illustrator).*
THE STORY OF TOM THE PIPER'S SON. ILLUSTRATED BY FRANK ADAMS. LONDON: BLACKIE AND SON, LIMITED (193–?). Unpaginated: 11 col. plates, ill., col. pictorial endpapers. Bound in red cloth and paper with coloured pictorial label.
CBD 823.912 ADA

818 **ATTWELL, MABEL LUCIE.**
THE BOO-BOOS AT THE SEA-SIDE. BY MABEL LUCIE ATTWELL. DUNDEE: VALENTINE AND SONS, (192–?). Unpaginated: col. front., vignette title page, 12 col. plates by the author, ill., pictorial endpapers. Bound in brown paper, with inserted pictorial paper label.
C 823.912 ATW

819 **(AUSTIN, HILDA).**
(LITTLE BLUE RABBIT AND HIS ADVENTURES.) Title page missing. n.d. Unpaginated: 23 col. plates, col. ill. Rebound in red cloth.
YSC 823.912 AUS

820 **BANNERMAN, HELEN.**
The Story of Little Black Sambo, BY HELEN BANNERMAN. LONDON: CHATTO AND WINDUS, 1899, reprinted 1971. 61p.: 28 col. plates. Bound in blue cloth with pictorial cover.
YSC 823.912 BAN

821 **BINGHAM, CLIFTON.**
THE ANIMALS' PICNIC. Described By CLIFTON BINGHAM. Pictured by G.H. THOMPSON. LONDON: ERNEST NISTER, (190–?). Pictorial title page, 8 col. plates, 12 plates, ill., pictorial endpapers. Bound in blue cloth with coloured pictorial paper cover.
C 821.912 BIN

822 **THE BOOK OF BOSH.**
WITH WHICH ARE INCORPORATED SOME AMUSING AND INSTRUCTIVE NURSERY STORIES IN RHYME. SECOND EDITION. LONDON: SIMPKIN, MARSHALL, HAMILTON, KENT AND CO., (190–?). Compiled and printed in colours by GEORGE FALKNER & SONS, The Deansgate Press, Manchester. 26p.: col. ill. Bound in green cloth with coloured pictorial paper cover.
C 821.912 BOO

823 **BROOKE, LEONARD LESLIE.**
THE GOLDEN GOOSE AND THE THREE BEARS. With numerous Drawings in Colour and Black-and-White by L. LESLIE BROOKE. LONDON: FREDERICK WARNE AND CO. LTD., (192–?). Unpaginated: front., vignette on title page, 16 col. plates, ill. Bound in cream cloth with red cloth cover containing coloured pictorial paper insert. Originally published in 1905.
CBD 398.245 GOL

824 **BROOKE, LEONARD LESLIE.**
JOHNNY CROW'S GARDEN. A PICTURE BOOK. DRAWN BY L. LESLIE BROOKE. LONDON: FREDERICK WARNE AND COMPANY, LTD., 1903. (1968 facsimile reprint). Unpaginated: 7 col. plates, ill., col. pictorial endpapers. Bound in cream and red linson with coloured pictorial cover and matching dust jacket.
C 823.912 BRO

825 **BROOKE, LEONARD LESLIE.**
LITTLE BO-PEEP. A NURSERY RHYME PICTURE BOOK. With Drawings by L. LESLIE BROOKE. LONDON: FREDERICK WARNE AND CO., LTD. (190–?). Unpaginated: pictorial title page, 8 col. plates, ill. Bound in cream paper with coloured pictorial cover and matching paper jacket. Leslie Brooke's Little Books.
C 398.8 BRO

826 **BROOKE, LEONARD LESLIE.**
THIS LITTLE PIG WENT TO MARKET. A NURSERY RHYME PICTURE BOOK With Drawings by L. LESLIE BROOKE. LONDON: FREDERICK WARNE AND CO., LTD. (190–?). Unpaginated: pictorial title page, 8 col. plates, ill. Bound in cream cloth with coloured pictorial cover and matching paper jacket. Leslie Brooke's Little Books.
C 398.8 BRO

827 **CALDECOTT, RANDOLPH.**
The BABES in the WOOD. ONE OF R. CALDECOTT'S PICTURE BOOKS. LONDON: FREDERICK WARNE AND CO. LTD. n.d. 30p. Title page on cover: 8 col. plates, ill. Bound in cream paper with coloured pictorial covers. Originally published 1879.
C 398.8 CAL

828 **CALDECOTT, RANDOLPH.**
COME LASSES AND LADS. R. CALDECOTT'S PICTURE BOOKS. LONDON: FREDERICK WARNE AND CO. LTD., n.d. 22p.: title page on cover: 6 col. plates, ill. Bound in cream paper with coloured pictorial covers. Originally published 1884.
C 398.8 CAL

829 **(CALDECOTT, RANDOLPH).**
(THE DIVERTING HISTORY OF JOHN GILPIN.) Title page missing. LONDON: FREDERICK WARNE AND CO. n.d. Reprint. 31p.: 2 double col. plates, 2 col. plates, col. ill., col. endpapers. Limp bound in white paper, with coloured pictorial cover. Originally published 1878.
YSC 821 COW

829A **Another copy.**
Title page on cover.
C 398.8 CAL

830 **CALDECOTT, RANDOLPH.**
An ELEGY on the DEATH of a MAD DOG. WRITTEN By Dr. GOLDSMITH, PICTURED By R. CALDECOTT, SUNG By Master BILL PRIMROSE. LONDON: FREDERICK WARNE AND CO. LTD. n.d. Reprint. 30p.: title page on cover, 6 col. plates, ill., coloured pictorial endpapers. Limp bound in yellow paper, with coloured pictorial cover. Originally published 1880.
YSC 821 CAL and C 398.8 CAL

831 **CALDECOTT, RANDOLPH.**
An Elegy to the Glory of her Sex. MRS. MARY BLAIZE. R. CALDECOTT'S PICTURE BOOKS. LONDON: FREDERICK WARNE AND CO. LTD., n.d. 22p.: title page on cover, col. front., 5 col. plates, ill. Bound in cream paper, with coloured pictorial cover. Originally published 1885.
C 398.8 CAL

832 **CALDECOTT, RANDOLPH.**
THE FARMER'S BOY. ONE OF R. CALDECOTT'S PICTURE BOOKS. LONDON: FREDERICK WARNE AND CO. LTD., n.d. 30p.: title page on cover, 8 col. plates, ill. Bound in cream paper with coloured pictorial covers. Originally published 1881.
C 398.8 CAL and CBDP 398.8 CAL

833 **CALDECOTT, RANDOLPH.**
The FOX jumps over the Parson's Gate. LONDON: FREDERICK WARNE AND CO., n.d. 24p.: title page on cover, 6 col. plates. ill. Limp bound in buff paper with coloured pictorial cover. Originally published 1883.
C 398.8 CAL

834 **CALDECOTT, RANDOLPH.**
A FROG he would a – Wooing go. R. CALDECOTT'S PICTURE BOOKS. LONDON: FREDERICK WARNE AND CO. LTD., n.d. 22p.: title page on cover: 6 col. plates, ill. Bound in cream paper with coloured pictorial covers. Originally published 1883.
C 398.8 CAL

835 **CALDECOTT, RANDOLPH.**
THE GREAT PANJANDRUM HIMSELF. R. CALDECOTT'S PICTURE BOOKS. LONDON: FREDERICK WARNE AND CO. LTD., n.d. 28p.: title page on cover: 6 col. plates, ill. Bound in cream paper with coloured and pictorial covers. Originally published 1885.
C 398.8 CAL

834

836 **CALDECOTT, RANDOLPH.**
HEY DIDDLE DIDDLE and BABY BUNTING. R. CALDECOTT'S PICTURE BOOKS. LONDON: FREDERICK WARNE AND CO. LTD., n.d. 23p.: title page on cover: 6 col. plates, ill. Bound in cream paper, with coloured pictorial cover. Originally published 1882.
C 398.8 CAL

837 **CALDECOTT, RANDOLPH.**
THE HOUSE THAT JACK BUILT. ONE OF R. CALDECOTT'S PICTURE BOOKS. LONDON: FREDERICK WARNE AND CO., LTD., n.d. 30p.: title page on cover: 8 col. plates, ill. Bound in cream paper with coloured pictorial cover. Originally published 1878.
C 398.8 CAL

838 **CALDECOTT, RANDOLPH.**
THE MILKMAID. An Old Song exhibited and explained in many designs by R. Caldecott. R. CALDECOTT'S PICTURE BOOKS. LONDON: FREDERICK WARNE AND CO. LTD., n.d. 22p. title page on cover: col. front., 5 col. plates, ill. Limp bound in cream paper, with coloured pictorial cover. Originally published 1882.
C 398.8 CAL + CBD 398.8 CAL

839 **CALDECOTT, RANDOLPH.**
The Queen of Hearts. ONE OF R. CALDECOTT'S PICTURE BOOKS. LONDON: FREDERICK WARNE AND CO., LTD., n.d. 30p.: title page on cover: 8 col. plates, ill. Bound in cream paper with coloured pictorial covers. Originally published 1881.
C 398.8 CAL

840 **CALDECOTT, RANDOLPH.**
R. CALDECOTT'S collection of PICTURES AND SONGS containing The Diverting History of John Gilpin, The House that Jack Built, An Elegy on the Death of a Mad Dog, The Babes in the Wood, The Three Jovial Huntsmen, Sing a Song for Sixpence, The Queen of Hearts, The Farmer's Boy. All exhibited in beautiful Engravings, many of which are Printed in Colours. DRAWN BY R.C. ENGRAVED AND PRINTED BY E. EVANS. LONDON: GEORGE ROUTLEDGE AND SONS, (1881). 31p., 30p., 31p., 31p., 31p., 31p., 31p., 31p.: 40 col. plates, ill. Rebound in black cloth.
CBD 398.8 CAL

841 **CALDECOTT, RANDOLPH.**
R. CALDECOTT'S PICTURE BOOK Containing The Diverting History of John Gilpin, The House that Jack Built, The Babes in the Wood, and An Elegy on the Death of a Mad Dog. All exhibited in beautiful engravings, many of which are Printed in Colours. DRAWN BY R.C., ENGRAVED AND PRINTED BY E. EVANS. LONDON: GEORGE ROUTLEDGE AND SONS. Reprint, n.d. 31p., 30p., 30p.,

31p.: col. fronts. (1 missing), col. plates, ill. Bound in buff cloth, with coloured pictorial covers. Incomplete.
C 398.8 CAL

842 **Another copy.**
(Includes) THE DIVERTING HISTORY OF JOHN GILPIN, THE HOUSE THAT JACK BUILT, THE BABES IN THE WOOD, AN ELEGY ON THE DEATH OF A MAD DOG, SING A SONG FOR SIXPENCE. LONDON: GEORGE ROUTLEDGE AND SON, (189–?). 31p., 30p., 31p., 31p., 30p.: 25 col. plates, ill. Bound in buff cloth with coloured pictorial cover.
CBD 398.8 CAL

843 **CALDECOTT, RANDOLPH.**
R. CALDECOTT'S PICTURE BOOK (NO. 1) CONTAINING THE DIVERTING HISTORY OF JOHN GILPIN, THE THREE JOVIAL HUNTSMEN, AN ELEGY ON THE DEATH OF A MAD DOG. ALL ILLUSTRATED IN COLOUR AND BLACK AND WHITE BY RANDOLPH CALDECOTT. LONDON: FREDERICK WARNE AND CO. LTD., n.d. 88p.: col. front., 2 double plates, 18 col. plates, ill., decorative endpapers. Bound in buff paper, with coloured pictorial covers. Miniature edition.
C 398.8 CAL

844 **CALDECOTT, RANDOLPH.**
R. CALDECOTT'S PICTURE BOOK (NO. 2) CONTAINING THE HOUSE THAT JACK BUILT, SING A SONG FOR SIXPENCE, THE QUEEN OF HEARTS. ALL ILLUSTRATED IN COLOUR AND BLACK AND WHITE BY RANDOLPH CALDECOTT. LONDON: FREDERICK WARNE AND CO., n.d. 88p.: col. front., 23 col. plates, ill., decorative endpapers. Bound in buff paper, with coloured pictorial covers. Miniature edition.
C 398.8 CAL

845 **CALDECOTT, RANDOLPH.**
R. CALDECOTT'S SECOND COLLECTION OF PICTURES AND SONGS. Containing THE MILKMAID, HEY DIDDLE DIDDLE AND BABY BUNTING, THE FOX JUMPS OVER THE PARSON'S GATE, A FROG HE WOULD A-WOOING GO, COME LASSES AND LADS, RIDE A COCK HORSE TO BANBURY CROSS, AND A FARMER WENT TROTTING UPON HIS GREY MARE, MRS. MARY BLAIZE, THE GREAT PANJANDRUM HIMSELF. All exhibited in beautiful Engravings, many of which are printed in Colour. DRAWN BY R.C. ENGRAVED AND PRINTED BY E. EVANS. LONDON: GEORGE ROUTLEDGE AND SONS, [1885]. 23p., 24p., 24p., 23p., 23p., 23p., 23p.: 40 col. plates, ill. Rebound in grey cloth.
CBD 398.8 CAL

846 **CALDECOTT, RANDOLPH.**
RIDE A-COCK HORSE TO BANBURY+ AND A FARMER WENT TROTTING UPON HIS GREY MARE. R. CALDECOTT'S PICTURE BOOKS. LONDON: FREDERICK WARNE AND CO., n.d. 23p. title page on cover: 6 col. plates, ill., bound in cream paper, with coloured pictorial cover. Originally published 1884.
C 398.8 CAL

847 **CALDECOTT, RANDOLPH.**
SING A SONG FOR SIXPENCE. ONE OF R. CALDECOTT'S PICTURE BOOKS. LONDON: FREDERICK WARNE AND COMPANY, LTD., n.d. 30p.: title page on cover: 8 col. plates, ill. Bound in cream paper with coloured pictorial covers. Originally published 1880.
C 398.8 CAL

848 **CALDECOTT, RANDOLPH.**
The Three Jovial Huntsmen. ONE OF R. CALDECOTT'S PICTURE BOOKS. LONDON: FREDERICK WARNE AND CO., LTD., n.d. 30p.: title page on cover: 8 col. plates, ill. Bound in cream paper with coloured pictorial covers. Originally published 1880.
C 398.8 CAL

849 **CHRISTMAS PICTURES BY CHILDREN.**
WITH AN INTRODUCTION BY EDMUND DULAC. LONDON: J.M. DENT AND SONS, LTD., 1922. Unpaginated: 14 col. plates. Bound in grey cloth with coloured decorative paper cover. Pictures are by children attending Prof. Cižek's class in Vienna.
C 750.2 CHR

850 **CLIBBORN, ROLAND** *(Illustrator)*.
CURLEY WEE. (Author MAUD BUDDEN, Artist ROLAND CLIBBORN). LIVERPOOL: LIVERPOOL ECHO, (193–?). 108p.: col. pictorial title page, col. ill. Bound in blue paper, with coloured pictorial covers.
YSC 823.912 CLI

851 **COME TO LIFE STORIES.**
No. 4. LONDON, SANDLE BROTHERS, LTD. n.d. 8p. including endpapers: col. ill., 2 col. pop up sections. Bound in red paper with coloured pictorial covers. Includes the stories of Hansel and Gretel and Snowwhite.
CBD 823.914 COM

851A **CRANE, THOMAS.**
Abroad. (BY) THOS. CRANE AND ELLEN E. HOUGHTON. LONDON: MARCUS WARD AND CO. (1882). 56p.: col. front., col. pictorial title page, col. ill. and col. decorative borders. Bound in blue cloth with coloured pictorial paper covers and decorative endpapers.
C 823.8 CRA

851B **CRANE, THOMAS.**
London Town. Designed and Illustrated by Thos. Crane and Ellen Houghton. LONDON: MARCUS WARD AND CO., (1883). 56p.: 3 col. front., col. pictorial title page, 8 col. plates, col. ill. Bound in brown cloth with coloured pictorial paper covers with decorative endpapers.
CBD 821.8 LEI

852 **CRANE, WALTER.**
ALADDIN'S PICTURE BOOK CONTAINING ALADDIN, THE YELLOW DWARF, PRINCESS BELLE-ETOILE, THE HIND IN THE WOOD, WITH TWENTY-FOUR PAGES OF ILLUSTRATIONS BY WALTER CRANE. PRINTED IN COLOURS BY EDMUND EVANS. LONDON: GEORGE ROUTLEDGE AND SONS, (1876). 6p.: 1 double col. plate, 2 col. plates each. Rebound in black cloth.
CBD 398.210953 CRA

852A **CRANE, WALTER.**
BEAUTY AND THE BEAST PICTURE BOOK: CONTAINING BEAUTY AND THE BEAST, THE FROG PRINCE, AND THE HIND IN THE WOOD: WITH EIGHTEEN COLOURED PICTURES BY WALTER CRANE: ENGRAVED AND PRINTED BY EDMUND EVANS. LONDON: JOHN LANE, THE BODLEY HEAD, (1900). 3 × 6p. + plates; col. front., 18 col. plates. Bound in green cloth with pictorial covers and pictorial decorative end papers.
M 398.2 CRA CHILDREN'S COLLECTION

853 **CRANE, WALTER.**
BLUEBEARD'S PICTURE BOOK. CONTAINING BLUEBEARD, THE SLEEPING BEAUTY AND BABY'S OWN ALPHABET WITH THE ORIGINAL COLOURED DESIGNS BY WALTER CRANE. ENGRAVED AND PRINTED BY EDMUND EVANS. LONDON: JOHN LANE THE BODLEY HEAD, 1899. 3 × 8p.: coloured pictorial title page, col. ill., pictorial endpapers to each. Rebound in blue cloth. Originally published in 1875.
CBD 398.21 CRA

854 **CRANE, WALTER.**
FLORA'S FEAST. A MASQUE OF FLOWERS PENNED AND PICTURED BY WALTER CRANE. LONDON: CASSELL AND COMPANY LIMITED, 1889. 40 double pages + 8p. pub. cat.: col. pictorial title page, col. ill. Bound in green cloth with coloured decorative covers.
CBD 821.8 CRA

855 **CRANE, WALTER.**
THE FORTY THIEVES. LONDON: JOHN LANE, THE BODLEY HEAD, n.d. 8p.: col. ill. Bound in buff paper, col. title page on cover. WALTER CRANE'S PICTURE BOOKS REISSUE (of 1898 edition).
CBD 398.210953 CRA

856 **CRANE, WALTER.**
GOODY TWO SHOES' PICTURE BOOK CONTAINING GOODY TWO SHOES, BEAUTY AND THE BEAST, THE FROG PRINCE, AN ALPHABET OF OLD FRIENDS WITH TWENTYFOUR PAGES OF ILLUSTRATIONS BY WALTER CRANE, PRINTED IN COLOURS BY EDMUND EVANS. LONDON: GEORGE ROUTLEDGE AND SONS, (1875). 6p.: 1 double col. plate, 4 col. plates each. Bound in brown cloth with embossed decorative cover and spine.
CBD 398.21 CRA

857 **CRANE, WALTER.**
KING LUCKIE BOY'S PARTY. LONDON: JOHN LANE, (1895). 8p.; title page on cover, col. ill.: decorative endpapers. Bound in cream paper with coloured pictorial cover. WALTER CRANE'S PICTURE BOOKS. RE-ISSUE.
C 821.8 CRA

858 **CRANE, WALTER.**
Legends for Lionel: in pen and pencil BY WALTER CRANE. LONDON: CASSELL AND COMPY. LIMITED, 1884. 40 double p. + 8p. pub. cat.: col. pictorial title page, col. ill., decorative endpapers. Bound in grey paper with coloured pictorial covers.
CBD 823.8 CRA

858A **CRANE, WALTER.**
LITTLE QUEEN ANNE and Her Majesty's Letters. (Patent). Penned and pictured by WALTER CRANE. LONDON: MARCUS WARD AND CO. LIMITED, 1886. Unpaginated (23p.): col. pictorial title page, col. ill. Bound in brown cloth with brown pictorial paper cover with pink pictorial end papers.
CBD 823.8 CRA

858B **CRANE, WALTER.**
PUSS IN BOOTS AND THE FORTY THIEVES. BY WALTER CRANE. LONDON: JOHN LANE THE BODLEY HEAD, 1914. Unpaginated: col. front., 11 col. plates, 2 double page col. plates. Bound in grey card with coloured pictorial cover, with decorative endpapers.
M 398.2 CRA CHILDREN'S COLLECTION

858C **CRANE, WALTER.**
SING A SONG FOR SIXPENCE. LONDON: GEORGE ROUTLEDGE AND SONS, (189–?). Unpaginated: printed on 1 side only: col. decorative title page on cover, col. ill. Bound in yellow paper.
CBDP 398.8 SIN

858D **CRANE, WALTER.**
THE SLEEPING BEAUTY AND BLUE BEARD. BY WALTER CRANE. LONDON: JOHN LANE THE BODLEY HEAD, 1914. Unpaginated: col. front., 11 col. plates, 2 double page col. plates. Bound in grey card with coloured pictorial cover with pictorial endpapers.
M 398.2 CHILDREN'S COLLECTION

858E **CRANE, WALTER.**
THE THREE BEARS AND MOTHER HUBBARD. BY WALTER CRANE. LONDON: JOHN LANE THE BODLEY HEAD, 1914. Unpaginated: col. front., 11 col. plates, 2 double page col. plates. Bound in grey card with coloured pictorial cover, with decorative endpapers.
M 398.2 CRA CHILDREN'S BOOKS

858F **CRANE, WALTER.**
VALENTINE AND ORSON. LONDON: ROUTLEDGE AND SONS, (187–?). 8p.: col. decorative title page on cover, col. ill. Bound in yellow cloth. WALTER CRANE'S TOY BOOKS. NEW SERIES.
CBDP 398.220944 VAL

858G **Another copy.**
In larger format. WALTER CRANE'S PICTURE BOOKS, RE-ISSUE. LONDON: JOHN LANE. n.d. 8p. Bound in blue card with coloured pictorial cover.

858H **DARWIN, BERNARD.**
THE TALE OF MR. TOOTLEOO BY BERNARD DARWIN AND ELEANOR DARWIN. LONDON: THE NONESUCH PRESS, c1920. Unpaginated: pictorial title page, 20 col. plates. Bound in red and brown paper with embossed decorative cover.
CBD 821.9 DAR

859 **DICK WHITTINGTON AND HIS CAT.**
LONDON: FREDERICK WARNE AND CO., n.d. Unpaginated: col. pictorial title page on cover: 4 col. plates, col. ill. Bound in brown paper covers. WARNE'S EXCELSIOR LONDON TOY BOOKS, NEW SERIES.
C 821.8 DIC

860 **DOYLE, RICHARD.**
JACK THE GIANT KILLER. By RICHARD DOYLE LONDON: EYRE AND SPOTTISWOODE, (1888). 48p.: coloured decorative title page, text and col. ill. reproduced from MS of 1842. Bound in brown cloth. Publisher's introduction and letter from Ruari McLean tipped in.
CBD 398.21 DOY

860A **DULAC, EDMUND.**
Lyrics pathetic and humorous from A to Z by EDMUND DULAC. LONDON: FREDERICK WARNE AND CO., 1908. Unpaginated: decorative title page in red and black, col. ill. Bound in buff buckram with coloured pictorial paper cover.
M 823 DUL CHILDREN'S COLLECTION.

861 **DULAC, EDMUND.**
PICTURE-BOOK FOR THE FRENCH RED CROSS. LONDON: HODDER AND STOUGHTON FOR THE DAILY TELEGRAPH, (1915). 136p.: col. front. 18 col. plates, 1 plate. Bound in buff cloth with decorative cover and buff dust jacket with coloured pictorial label.
CBD 398.21 DUL

862 **EGAN, CONSTANCE.**
EPAMINONDAS HELPS IN THE GARDEN. By CONSTANCE EGAN. ILLUSTRATED BY A.E. KENNEDY. LONDON: COLLINS, Reprint (192–?). 63p.: col. pictorial title page, 30 col. plates, pictorial endpapers. Bound in blue paper, with coloured pictorial label.
YSC 823.912 EGA

863 **THE FARMYARD SCRAP BOOK.**
LONDON: ERNEST NISTER, (190–?) Unpaginated. Consists entirely of coloured plates with captions, mounted on mull.
C 741.642 FAR

863A **FINLAY, H.C.**
AUNT NELLY'S BOOK OF NONSUCH. By H.C. FINLAY. GLASGOW: DAVID BRYCE AND SON, 1891. 32p.: col. front., pictorial title page, ill., some col. Bound in buff card with coloured pictorial cover.
C 821.8 FIN

864 **FLACK, MARJORIE.**
ANGUS AND THE CAT. Told and pictured by MARJORIE FLACK. LONDON: THE BODLEY HEAD, 1933. (32p.): pictorial title page, ill., some col. Bound in coloured pictorial paper with coloured pictorial endpapers.
YSC 823.912 FLA

865 **FLACK, MARJORIE.**
ANGUS AND TOPSY. Told and pictured by MARJORIE FLACK. LONDON: THE BODLEY HEAD, 1935. (32p.): pictorial title page, ill., some col. Bound in coloured pictorial paper with coloured pictorial endpapers.
YSC 823.912 FLA

866 **FLACK, MARJORIE.**
ANGUS AND WAG-TAIL-BESS. Told and pictured by MARJORIE FLACK. LONDON: THE BODLEY HEAD,

(193–?), (32p.): ill. some col. Bound in coloured pictorial paper with coloured pictorial endpapers.
YSC 823.912 FLA

867 **FLACK, MARJORIE.**
ANGUS LOST. Told and pictured by MARJORIE FLACK. LONDON: THE BODLEY HEAD, 1933. (32p.): pictorial title page, ill., some col. Bound in coloured pictorial paper with coloured pictorial endpapers.
YSC 823.912 FLA

868 **GÁG, WANDA.**
MILLIONS OF CATS BY WANDA GÁG. LONDON: FABER AND FABER LIMITED, 1929. Unpaginated: 4 plates, ill. Bound in yellow paper with coloured pictorial covers, with matching paper dust jacket.
YSC 813.52 GAG

869 **GIFT, THEO.**
CAPE TOWN DICKY or COLONEL JACKS' BOY, by THEO GIFT. Illustrated by ALICE HAVERS. MONOTINTS BY ERNEST WILSON. LONDON: HILDESHEIMER AND FAULKNER, (189–?). 64p.: col. front., pictorial title page, 15 col. plates., ill., Bound in brown cloth with coloured pictorial covers.
C 823.8 GIF

871 **GREENAWAY, KATE.**
A DAY IN A CHILD'S LIFE, ILLUSTRATED BY KATE GREENAWAY. MUSIC BY MYLES B. FOSTER. ENGRAVED AND PRINTED BY EDMUND EVANS. LONDON: GEORGE ROUTLEDGE AND SONS, (1881). 29p.: col. front., col. pictorial title page, col. ill., music score. Bound in green cloth with coloured pictorial paper covers.
CBD 821.8 GRE

872 **GREENAWAY, KATE.**
KATE GREENAWAY PICTURES FROM ORIGINALS PRESENTED BY HER TO JOHN RUSKIN AND OTHER PERSONAL FRIENDS. (Hitherto unpublished) With AN APPRECIATION By H.M. CUNDALL, I.S.O. F.S.A. LONDON: FREDERICK WARNE AND CO. LTD., 1921. 11p.: front., 19 col. plates. Bound in buff and green buckram.
CBDQ 741.0924 GRE

873 **GREENAWAY, KATE.**
KATE GREENAWAY'S BIRTHDAY BOOK for CHILDREN. WITH 382 ILLUSTRATIONS DRAWN BY KATE GREENAWAY, PRINTED BY EDMUND EVANS. VERSES BY MRS SALE BARKER. LONDON: GEORGE ROUTLEDGE AND SONS., 1880. 130p.: col. front., 11 col. plates, ill. Bound in buff cloth with coloured decorative covers.
CBD 821.8 GRE

874 **GREENAWAY, KATE.**
MARIGOLD GARDEN. Pictures and Rhymes. By KATE GREENAWAY. PRINTED IN COLOURS By EDMUND EVANS. LONDON: GEORGE ROUTLEDGE AND SONS, (1885). 60p.: col. front., col. pictorial title page, 3 col. plates, col. ill. Bound in brown cloth with coloured pictorial covers.
CBD 821.8 GRE

875 **GREENAWAY, KATE.**
UNDER THE WINDOW. PICTURES AND RHYMES for Children by KATE GREENAWAY. LONDON: FREDERICK WARNE AND CO. LTD. Reprint. 56p.: col. pictorial title page, col. ill., col. pictorial endpapers. Bound in green and buff paper, with coloured pictorial covers. Originally published 1878.
YSC 821 GRE

876 **HARTMAN, ROBERT.**
FITZROY AND MOLEY. Written and illustrated by ROBERT HARTMAN. LONDON: ARTHUR BARKER LTD., 1936. 79p.: 12 col. plates, col. ill., coloured decorative endpapers. Bound in green cloth with coloured decorative paper dust jacket. THE BUFFIN BOOKS.
C 823.912 HAR

877 **HEWARD, CONSTANCE.**
AMELIARANNE AND THE GREEN UMBRELLA. Told by Constance Heward, and pictured by Susan Beatrice Pearse. LONDON: GEORGE G. HARRAP AND CO. LTD., 1920. Unpaginated: col. pictorial title page, 30 col. plates, ill., col. pictorial endpapers. Bound in paper-covered boards, with coloured pictorial label on cover.
C 823.912 HEW
Another copy.
(192–?). Unpaginated: col. pictorial title page, 28 col. plates, ill., col. pictorial endpapers. Bound in paper-covered boards with coloured pictorial cover.

878 **(HOFFMANN, HEINRICH).**
(THE ENGLISH STRUWWELPETER OR PRETTY STORIES AND FUNNY PICTURES.) Title page missing. LONDON: GEORGE ROUTLEDGE AND SONS, LIMITED, (189–?). 24p.: col. ill. Bound in red cloth, with buff coloured pictorial paper cover.
YSC 837 HOF

879 **HORRABIN, J.F.**
THE NOAHS ON HOLIDAY . . . with JAPHET. By J.F. HORRABIN. From the Children's Corner of the Daily News. LONDON: CASSELL AND COMPANY, LTD., (192–?). 100p.: ill. Bound in cream paper with coloured decorative cover.
C 823.912 HOR

880 **JOAN, NATALIE.**
AMELIARANNE AND THE BIG TREASURE. Told by Natalie Joan. Pictured by S.B. Pearse. LONDON: GEORGE G. HARRAP AND CO. LTD., 1932. Unpaginated: col. pictorial title page, 29 col. plates, col. pictorial endpapers. Bound in paper-covered boards, with coloured pictorial label on cover.
C 823.912 JOA

881 **KONSTAM, G.A.**
THE MAYPOLE, ILLUSTRATED BY G.A. KONSTAM, E. CASELLA AND N. CASELLA. LONDON: THOS. DE LA RUE AND CO., 1882. 26p., pictorial title page, 8 col. plates, 5 plates, ill., music score. Bound in white paper with coloured pictorial cover.
C 821.8 MAY

882 **LAUGHTER LAND.**
Comical Pictures and Rhymes for Children. LONDON: ERNEST NISTER, (189–?). Unpaginated: col. front., pictorial title page, 5 plates, ill. Bound in green cloth with coloured pictorial paper cover.
C 821.8 LAU

883 **LAWSON, LIZZIE.**
Christmas Roses by Lizzie Lawson and Robert Ellice Mack. LONDON: GRIFFITH FARRAN AND COMPANY, (188–?). 32p.: col. front., 9 col. plates, col. ill., lithographed by Ernest Nister of Nuremberg. Bound in green cloth with pictorial paper covers.
C 821.8 MAC

884 **LE MAIR, H. WILLEBEEK.**
LITTLE PEOPLE. Rhymes by R.H. Elkin. Illustrations by H. Willebeek Le Mair. LONDON: AUGENER LTD., (191–?). Unpaginated: col. vignette title page, 15 col. plates. Bound in purple cloth, with inserted coloured paper label.
YSC 821 ELK

885 **LEAR, EDWARD.**
NONSENSE SONGS BY EDWARD LEAR. WITH DRAWINGS BY L. LESLIE BROOKE. LONDON: FREDERICK WARNE AND CO., LTD. (1923). Unpaginated: col. front., 11 plates, ill. Bound in brown cloth, with pictorial cover, with buff coloured paper dust jacket.
CBD 821.8 LEA

886 **LEFÈVRE, FÉLICITÉ.**
THE COCK, THE MOUSE AND THE LITTLE RED HEN. AN OLD TALE RETOLD BY FÉLICITÉ LEFÈVRE. WITH 24 ILLUSTRATIONS BY TONY

SARG. NINETEENTH PRINTING. LONDON: THE RICHARDS PRESS. Reprint of 1907 edition. 104p.: front., 25 col. plates, ill. Bound in buff cloth, with coloured pictorial cover and coloured pictorial dust jacket.
YSC 813.52 LEF

887 **LITTLE BO PEEP.**
LONDON: GEORGE ROUTLEDGE AND SONS, (188–?). 10p.: col. front., 5 col. plates (by Kronheim and Co.). Bound in yellow card with coloured decorative cover. ROUTLEDGE'S THREEPENNY TOY BOOKS.
CBDP 823.8 LIT

888 **LITTLE PICTURE MAKERS**
THE FARMYARD. LONDON: ERNEST NISTER, (189–?). Unpaginated: 6 col. plates into which are to be cut out and inserted coloured pictures on 2 further plates. Bound in buff paper with coloured pictorial cover.
CBD 741.642 FAR

889 **The MARRIAGE of ALLAN-A-DALE.**
LONDON: FREDERICK WARNE AND CO., n.d. Unpaginated: col. pictorial title page on cover: 4 col. plates, col. ill. Bound in brown paper covers. WARNE'S EXCELSIOR LONDON TOY BOOKS. NEW SERIES.
C 821.8 MAR

890 **MOORE, CLEMENT C.**
DENSLOW'S NIGHT BEFORE CHRISTMAS, by CLEMENT C. MOORE, L.L.D. Made into a book and illustrated by W.W. Denslow. LONDON: WILLIAM HEINEMANN, 1903. Unpaginated: col. pictorial title page: 17 col. plates, col. ill., coloured pictorial endpapers. Bound in red cloth with coloured pictorial paper covers.
C 811.2 MOO

890A **THE NURSERY FRIEND.**
CONTAINING MAMMA'S PICTURE ALPHABET. MASTER MOUSE'S SUPPER PARTY. THE DEATH AND BURIAL OF COCK ROBIN. LITTLE RED RIDING HOOD. LONDON: WARD, LOCK AND CO., (1878) Unpaginated: 24 col. plates. Bound in brown cloth with embossed decorative cover. THE PLAY-HOUR PICTURE BOOKS.
M 823 NUR CHILDREN'S COLLECTION

891 **OFF WE GO!**
A PICTURE STORY BOOK FOR LITTLE PEOPLE. LONDON: S.W. PARTRIDGE AND CO., LTD. (192–?). Unpaginated: 5 col. plates, 16 plates, ill. 6p. advertisements. Bound in brown cloth with coloured pictorial paper covers.
C 823.912 OFF

892 **POTTER, BEATRIX.**
THE TAILOR OF GLOUCESTER. BY BEATRIX POTTER. LONDON: FREDERICK WARNE AND CO., LTD. (1902). 59p.: col. front., 25 col. plates by the author; coloured pictorial endpapers. Bound in brown paper with inserted coloured illustration.
YSC 823.912 POT

893 **POTTER, BEATRIX.**
THE TALE OF BENJAMIN BUNNY. BY BEATRIX POTTER. LONDON: FREDERICK WARNE AND CO., LTD., (1904). 59p.: col. front., 25 col. plates by the author, coloured pictorial endpapers. Bound in cream paper with inserted coloured label, white pictorial paper dust jacket.
YSC 823.912 POT
Another copy.
Rebound in dark brown cloth with buff paper cover with inserted coloured label.
C 823.912 POT

894 **POTTER, BEATRIX.**
THE TALE OF GINGER AND PICKLES. BY BEATRIX POTTER. LONDON: FREDERICK WARNE AND CO. LTD., (1909). 75p.: col. front., 8 col. plates, 14 plates, ill. by the author, coloured pictorial endpapers. Bound in cream paper with inserted coloured illustration, with pictorial paper jacket.
YSC 823.912 POT

895 **POTTER, BEATRIX.**
THE TALE OF JEMIMA PUDDLEDUCK. BY BEATRIX POTTER. LONDON: FREDERICK WARNE AND CO., LTD., (1908). 59p.: col. front., 26 col. plates, coloured pictorial endpapers. Bound in grey paper, with inserted coloured pictorial label, and matching paper dust jacket.
C 823.912 POT

896 **POTTER, BEATRIX.**
THE TALE OF LITTLE PIG ROBINSON. By BEATRIX POTTER. LONDON: FREDERICK WARNE AND CO. LTD., (1930). 112p.: col. front., 5 col. plates, 21 plates, ill., by the author, coloured pictorial endpapers. Bound in cream paper with inserted coloured illustration, with white pictorial paper dust jacket.
YSC 823.912 POT

897 **POTTER, BEATRIX.**
THE TALE OF MR. JEREMY FISHER BY BEATRIX POTTER. LONDON: FREDERICK WARNE AND CO. LTD., (1906). 59p.: col. front., 26 plates by the author, coloured pictorial endpapers. Bound in brown paper with inserted coloured illustration.
YSC 823.912 POT

898 **POTTER, BEATRIX.**
THE TALE OF MRS. TIGGY-WINKLE. BY BEATRIX POTTER. LONDON: FREDERICK WARNE AND CO., LTD., (1905). 85p.: col. front., 26 plates by the author, coloured pictorial endpapers. Bound in cream paper with inserted coloured label with pictorial paper dust jacket.
YSC 823.912 POT
Another copy.
Rebound in green cloth with green paper cover with inserted coloured label.

899 **POTTER, BEATRIX.**
THE TALE OF MRS. TITTLEMOUSE. BY BEATRIX POTTER. LONDON: FREDERICK WARNE AND CO., LTD., (1910). 59p.: col. front., 26 col. plates by the author. Coloured pictorial endpapers. Bound in cream paper with inserted coloured illustration.
YSC 823.912 POT

900 **POTTER, BEATRIX.**
The Tale of Mrs. Tittlemouse. LONDON: FREDERICK WARNE AND CO. LTD., 1979 (facsimile of original MS of 1910). Unpaginated: 9 col. plates, decorative blue endpapers. Includes essays by Margaret Lane and Joyce Irene Whalley. Bound with coloured deckled edges in black calf to look like the original notebook, in slip case.
CBD 823.912 POT

901 **POTTER, BEATRIX.**
THE TALE OF PETER RABBIT. BY BEATRIX POTTER. LONDON: FREDERICK WARNE AND CO., LTD. (1901). 59p.: front., 26 col. plates by the author, coloured pictorial endpapers. Bound in cream paper, with inserted coloured label with white pictorial paper dust jacket.
YSC 823.912 POT

902 **POTTER, BEATRIX.**
THE TALE OF PIGLING BLAND. BY BEATRIX POTTER. LONDON: FREDERICK WARNE AND CO. LTD., 1913. 93p.: col. front., vignette title page, 14 col. plates, ill., col. pictorial/decorative endpapers. Bound in grey, with coloured pictorial label on cover.
C 823.912 POT

903 **POTTER, BEATRIX.**
THE TALE OF SAMUEL WHISKERS, OR THE ROLY-POLY PUDDING, BY BEATRIX POTTER. LONDON: FREDERICK WARNE AND CO. LTD., (193–?). 75p.: col. front., 17 col. plates, ill. by the author, coloured pictorial endpapers. Bound in red paper, with inserted coloured illustration.
YSC 823.912 POT and C 823.912 POT

904 **Another copy.**
In larger format, entitled The Roly Poly Pudding. LONDON:

FREDERICK WARNE AND CO., (1908). 70p.: col. front., 17 col. plates, ill. by the author, col. pictorial endpapers. Bound in red cloth, with inserted coloured pictorial label.
C 823.912 POT

905 **POTTER, BEATRIX.**
THE TALE OF THE PIE AND THE PATTY-PAN. BY BEATRIX POTTER. LONDON: FREDERICK WARNE AND CO., LTD., (1905). 76p.: col. front., 9 col. plates, ill. by the author. Bound in cream paper with inserted coloured illustrations, with white pictorial paper dust jacket.
YSC 823.912 POT

906 **POTTER, BEATRIX.**
THE TALE OF TOM KITTEN. BY BEATRIX POTTER. LONDON: FREDERICK WARNE AND CO., LTD., (1907). 59p.: col. front., 26 col. plates by the author. Coloured pictorial endpapers. Bound in cream paper with inserted coloured illustration.
YSC 823.912 POT

907 **ROBINSON, WILLIAM HEATH.**
THE ADVENTURES OF UNCLE LUBIN. TOLD AND ILLUSTRATED BY W. HEATH ROBINSON. LONDON: THE MINERVA PRESS, facsimile edition 1927 of 1902 first edition. 117p.: front., decorative title page, 48 plates, ill. Bound in yellow cloth with yellow pictorial paper jacket.
CBD 823.912 ROB

908 **ROUTLEDGE'S COLOURED PICTURE BOOK.**
CONTAINING HOW JESSIE WAS LOST. GRAMMAR IN RHYME. THE BABES IN THE WOOD. LITTLE DOG TRUSTY. WITH THIRTY-TWO PAGES OF ILLUSTRATIONS. LONDON: GEORGE ROUTLEDGE AND SONS, (187–?). 8p., 8p., 8p., 8p. + 2p. pub. cat.: col. ill. Bound in brown cloth embossed with decoration and inserted coloured paper label.
CBD 823.8 ROU

910 **ROUTLEDGE'S NURSERY PICTURE BOOK.**
WITH NINETY-SIX PAGES OF ILLUSTRATIONS. LONDON: GEORGE ROUTLEDGE AND SONS, 1880. 96p.: vignette title page, ill. Bound in brown cloth, with embossed coloured pictorial cover.
YOSC 372.4 ROU

911 **SCHOFIELD, LILY.**
TOM CATAPUS AND POTIPHAR. A TALE OF ANCIENT EGYPT, BY LILY SCHOFIELD. LONDON: FREDERICK WARNE AND CO., 1903. 7 pages of text: front., 1 double col. plate, 7 plates, pictorial endpapers. Printed on one side of paper only. Bound in grey buckram with coloured pictorial cover.
C 821.912 SCH

912 **SIR FRANCIS DRAKE AND HIS GOBLINS.**
LONDON: FREDERICK WARNE AND CO., n.d. Unpaginated: col. pictorial title page on cover: 4 col. plates, col. ill. Bound in brown paper covers. WARNE'S EXCELSIOR LONDON TOY BOOKS, NEW SERIES.
C 821.8 SIR

912A **SOWERBY, J.G.**
AT HOME. ILLUSTRATED BY J.G. SOWERBY. DECORATED BY THOMAS CRANE. LONDON: MARCUS WARD AND CO., (1881?) 56p.: col. front., col. decorative/pictorial title page, 7 col. plates. col. ill. Bound in brown cloth with coloured pictorial paper covers, with decorative endpapers.
CBD 821.8 ATH and CBD 821.912 SOW

912B **SOWERBY, JOHN G.**
AT HOME AGAIN (BY) J.G. SOWERBY AND THOS. CRANE. THE VERSES BY ELIZA KEARY. LONDON: MARCUS WARD AND CO. LIMITED, (1888). 59p.: 4 col. fronts., col. decorative title page, 5 plates, col. ill. Bound in brown cloth with coloured pictorial paper covers.
CBD 821.8 ATH

913 **TEMPLAR, J.S.**
JANE: A TALE OF HAIR. DEPICTED BY J.S. TEMPLAR. (LONDON): JAMES NISBET AND CO., 1904.

AT HOME WITH HIS PETS.

910

95p.: col. decorative title page, 23 col. plates. Bound in green cloth, with coloured pictorial cover.
C 823.8 JAN

914 **TOM THUMB.**
LONDON: FREDERICK WARNE AND CO., n.d. Unpaginated: col. pictorial title page on cover: 4 col. plates, col. ill. Bound in brown paper covers. WARNE'S EXCELSIOR LONDON TOY BOOKS, NEW SERIES.
C 821.8 TOM

915 **UPTON, BERTHA.**
THE GOLLIWOGG'S FOX-HUNT. PICTURES BY Florence Upton, Verses by Bertha Upton. LONDON: LONGMANS, GREEN AND CO., (190–?). 66p. col. pictorial title page, 28 col. plates ill. Bound in brown cloth with coloured pictorial paper cover. Uses particularly vivid colours for illustrations.
C 821.912 UPT

915A **WEBB, CLIFFORD.**
A JUNGLE PICNIC BY CLIFFORD WEBB. LONDON: FREDERICK WARNE AND CO. LTD. n.d. 53p.: col. front., decorative title page, 26 col. plates, pictorial endpapers. Originally published in 1934.
Y 823.912 WEB

916 **WEEDON, L.L.**
LITTLE PEOPLE'S BOOK OF FUN. A Volume of Pictures and Verses by L.L. Weedon and Clifton Bingham. LONDON: ERNEST NISTER, (190–?). Pictorial title page, 4 col. plates, 1 plate, ill., some col., partly by G.H. Thompson. Bound in red cloth with coloured pictorial cover. Large format.
C 821.8 WEE

917 **WHITTEMORE, W. MEYNELL** *(Editor).*
MY VERY OWN PICTURE STORY BOOK. EDITED BY W.M. WHITTEMORE, D.D. LONDON: GEORGE STONEMAN, (189–?). Unpaginated: front., vignette title page, 46 plates, ill., some engraved by Butterworth and Heath. Bound in green cloth, with coloured pictorial/decorative cover and spine.
C 823.8 WHI

## 15 MATHEMATICS

919 **ATKINSON, C.B.**
THE COMMERCIAL SCHOOL CERTIFICATE ARITHMETIC. BY C.B. ATKINSON AND W.G. BATE, B.Sc. LONDON: SIR ISAAC PITMAN AND SONS, LTD., 1935. VIII, 110p. + 64p. answers. Bound in green cloth.
YSC 511 ATK

920 **BALLARD, P.B.**
THE LONDON ARITHMETICS, FIRST SERIES. By P.B. BALLARD, M.A., D.LIT. and JOHN BROWN, M.A., B.Sc.
PUPILS BOOKS 2, 3, 4. 64p., 64p., 80p. Limp bound in buff cloth.
Title page on cover. Ill.
TEACHER'S BOOK 1, 3, 4. 79p., 76p., 90p.
Limp bound in brown cloth.
TEST CARDS FOR USE WITH THE LONDON ARITHMETICS, FIRST SERIES, BOOK 4 SECOND QUARTERS. Cards held in pink box. ANSWERS ONLY BOOKS 1–4 20p., 23p., 19p., 23p. Limp bound in red cloth.
LONDON: UNIVERSITY OF LONDON PRESS, LTD., 1934.
YSC 511 BAL

SHOPPING.—1

PRICE LIST

| | |
|---|---|
| Sugar . . . $2\frac{3}{4}$d. per lb. | Loaves . . . $3\frac{1}{2}$d. each. |
| Tea . . . 2s. 10d. per lb. | Milk . . . 3d. per pint. |
| Potatoes . . . $1\frac{1}{2}$d. per lb. | Eggs . . . 1s. 6d. per dozen. |
| Coal . . . £2 10s. per ton. | Cream . . . 3s. per pint. |
| Oranges . . . $1\frac{3}{4}$d. each. | Rolls . . . 8 for 6d. |
| Apples . . . 7d. per lb. | Buns . . . $\frac{1}{2}$d. each. |
| Coffee . . . 2s. 9d. per lb. | Bacon . . . 1s. 4d. per lb. |
| Lemon squash . . . 1s. 11d. per bottle. | Pepper . . . $3\frac{1}{4}$d. per oz. |

| A | B |
|---|---|
| How much should you pay for the following : | How much change from half-a-crown should you get if you bought the following : |
| (1) 3 lb. tea ? | (1) 6 lb. sugar ? |
| (2) 4 lb. sugar ? | (2) 1 stone potatoes ? |
| (3) 3 loaves ? | (3) $\frac{1}{2}$ dozen oranges ? |
| (4) 2 bottles of lemon squash ? | (4) $\frac{1}{2}$ lb. coffee ? |
| (5) 1 dozen rolls ? | (5) 3 loaves ? |
| (6) $\frac{1}{4}$ lb. pepper ? | (6) $1\frac{1}{2}$ dozen eggs ? |
| (7) 1 dozen oranges ? | (7) $\frac{1}{4}$ pt. cream ? |
| (8) 8 oz. bacon ? | |

920

921 **BALLARD, P.B.**
THE LONDON ARITHMETICS. SECOND SERIES by B.P. BALLARD, M.A., D. LIT., and JOHN BROWN, M.A., B.Sc.
PUPILS BOOKS 2 and 4.
LONDON: UNIVERSITY OF LONDON PRESS, LTD. (193–?). 80p. each. Title page on cover, ill., diagrs. Limp bound in buff cloth.
YSC 511 BAL

922 **BENNY, L.B.**
MATHEMATICS FOR STUDENTS OF TECHNOLOGY. BY L.B. BENNY, M.A., B.A.
SENIOR COURSE. PARTS ONE AND TWO.
LONDON: OXFORD UNIVERSITY PRESS, SECOND EDITION, 1929. VII, 451p. + XXVIIp. answers and VIIp. index: diagrs. Bound in red cloth.
YSC 510 BEN

923 **BLACKIE'S ADAPTABLE ARITHMETICS.**
Teacher's Handbook TO THE Adaptable Arithmetics. BOOK IV MENSURATION. LONDON: BLACKIE AND SON, LIMITED. 1908. 93p. + 8p. pub. cat.: diagrs. Bound in blue cloth.
YSC 511 BLA

924 **BORCHARDT, W.G.**
A FIRST COURSE IN ALGEBRA. BY W.G. BORCHARDT, M.A., B.Sc. THIRD EDITION. LONDON: RIVINGTONS, 1934. VIII, 259p. + XLVIIp. answers: diagrs. Bound in grey cloth.
YSC 512 BOR

925 **BORCHARDT, W.G.**
A NEW TRIGONOMETRY FOR SCHOOLS BY W.G. BORCHARDT, M.A. B.Sc. AND THE REV. A.D. PERROTT, M.A. (Parts I and II). LONDON: G. BELL AND SONS, LTD. (new edition, 1926). VIII, 400p. + XIIIp. tables, XXII, XIIp. answers: diagrs. Bound in brown cloth.
YSC 516.24 BOR

926 **BREWSTER, G.W.**
COMMONSENSE of the CALCULUS. By G.W. BREWSTER, M.A. OXFORD: CLARENDON PRESS, 1923. 80p.: diagrs. Bound in yellow cloth with decorative cover.
YSC 512 BRE

927 **BROWN, J.T.**
THE ELEMENTS OF ANALYTICAL GEOMETRY BY J.T. BROWN, M.A., B.Sc. AND C.W.M. MANSON, M.A. LONDON: MACMILLAN AND CO., LIMITED, 1938. 325p. + XVIIp. answers: diagrs. Bound in orange cloth.
YSC 513 BRO

928 **BROWN, J.T.**
THREE-GRADE ARITHMETIC BY J.T. BROWN, M.A., B.Sc.
Books One, Two, Three With Answers 80p.
Book Four With Answers 96p.
LONDON: THOMAS NELSON AND SONS, LTD., (193–?). Ill. Limp bound in blue cloth.
YSC 511 BRO

929 **CASTLE, FRANK.**
WORKSHOP MATHEMATICS. PART 1. BY FRANK CASTLE, M.I.M.E. LONDON: MACMILLAN AND CO., LTD., 1900. 154p.: diagrs. Bound in red cloth.
YSC 510.2468 CAS

930 **CHIGNELL, N.J.**
NUMERICAL TRIGONOMETRY. BY N.J. CHIGNELL, B.A. OXFORD: CLARENDON PRESS, 1925. 126p. + XIIp. answers: diagrs. Bound in green cloth with decorative cover.
YSC 516.24 CHI

931 **CHOPE, R.H.**
KEY TO THE TUTORIAL ARITHMETIC. BY R.H. CHOPE, B.A. LONDON: W.B. CLIVE, UNIVERSITY TUTORIAL PRESS LTD., 1909. VIII, 582p. + 16p. pub. cat. Bound in green cloth.
YSC 511 CHO

931A **CLOTHIER, ETHEL M.**
HOUSEHOLD COSTING, AN ARITHMETIC FOR GIRLS. BY ETHEL M. CLOTHIER. EDITED BY CATHERINE R. GORDON. LONDON: SIR ISAAC PITMAN AND SONS LTD. 1929. VI, 146p.: diagrs. Bound in green cloth.
M 640.42 CLO CHILDREN'S COLLECTION

932 **COCKSHOTT, ARTHUR.**
A TREATISE ON GEOMETRICAL CONICS IN ACCORDANCE WITH THE SYLLABUS OF THE ASSOCIATION FOR THE IMPROVEMENT OF GEOMETRICAL TEACHING. BY ARTHUR COCKSHOTT, M.A. AND REV. F.B. WALTERS, M.A. LONDON: MACMILLAN AND CO., LIMITED, SECOND EDITION, 1907. VII, 208p. Bound in maroon cloth.
YSC 513 COC

933 **COLEMAN, PERCY.**
CO-ORDINATE GEOMETRY, AN ELEMENTARY

COURSE. BY PERCY COLEMAN, M.A. OXFORD: CLARENDON PRESS, 1914. 240p. Bound in red cloth.
YSC 513 COL

934 **CURZON, H.E.J.**
THE CITIZEN ARITHMETICS. BY H.E.J. CURZON, M.A. D.Sc. and F.A.W. GREENGRASS.
PUPILS BOOKS 1–111 80p. each. Limp bound in green cloth with decorative covers.
TEACHERS BOOKS 1–111. 104p., 99p., 96p. Limp bound in orange cloth.
LONDON: THOMAS NELSON AND SONS, LTD., (193–?). Diagrs.
YSC 511 CUR

935 **CURZON, H.E.J.**
THE FOUNDATIONS OF ARITHMETIC. BY H.E.J. CURZON, M.A., D.Sc. AND T.O.Y. DAVIES.
BOOK 1 40p. Limp bound in green cloth.
BOOK 2 48p. Limp bound in blue cloth.
BOOK 3 64p. Limp bound in blue cloth.
BOOK 4 80p. Limp bound in red cloth.
LONDON: THOMAS NELSON AND SONS, LTD., (193–?). Diagrs.
YSC 511 CUR

936 **DAKIN, A.**
ELEMENTARY ANALYSIS BY A. DAKIN, O.B.E., M.A., B.Sc. AND R.I. PORTER, M.B.E., M.A. LONDON: G. BELI AND SONS LTD., 1938. X, 315p. + XLp. answers: diagrs. Bound in brown cloth.
YSC 512 DAK

937 **DURELL, C.V.**
ELEMENTARY ALGEBRA. BY C.V. DURELL, M.A. AND G.W. PALMER, M.A. LONDON: G. BELL AND SONS LTD., 1920. VI, 256p. + VIIIp. answers: diagrs. Bound in red cloth.
YSC 512.9042 DUR

938 **DURELL, C.V.**
ELEMENTARY CALCULUS. VOLUME 1. WITH APPENDIX BY C.V. DURELL, M.A. AND A. ROBSON, M.A. LONDON, G. BELL AND SONS LTD., 1933. VIII, 240p.: diagrs. Bound in yellow cloth.
YSC 517 DUR

939 **ENGLAND, WILLIAM C.**
The Foundations of Arithmetic. Homely Problems. Pupils Books X, Y, Z. LONDON: THOMAS NELSON AND SONS, LTD. (193–?). 32p. each. Limp bound in green paper.
YSC 511 ENG

940 **FIRST BOOK OF ARITHMETIC.**
FOR THE USE OF SCHOOLS REVISED AND CORRECTED. IRISH NATIONAL SCHOOLBOOKS. LONDON: WILLIAM COLLINS, SONS, AND COMPANY, (188–?). 143p. Bound in blue cloth with embossed decorative cover.
YSC 511 COL

941 **FLAVELL, ALFRED.**
THE MODERN "GUIDE" ARITHMETICS. Based on the New Psychology of Teaching Practice and on Proved Educational Methods.
By ALFRED FLAVELL, M.A.

| | | |
|---|---|---|
| BOOK 1. | THE SIMPLE RULES BOOK. | 48p. |
| BOOK 2. | THE NUMBER BOOK. | 56p. |
| BOOK 3. | THE MONEY BOOK. | 64p. |
| BOOK 5. | THE FRACTION BOOK. | 80p. |
| BOOK 6. | THE DECIMAL BOOK. | 88p. |
| BOOK 7. | THE PERCENTAGE BOOK. | 96p. |

BIRMINGHAM: DAVIS AND MOUGHTON, LTD. (193–?). Diagrs. Bound in grey cloth with decorative cover.
YSC 511 FLA

942 **FOUNDATIONS OF ARITHMETIC.**
My Little Sum Book. LONDON: THOMAS NELSON AND SONS, LTD. (193–?). 48p. Limp bound in brown cloth with pictorial cover.
YSC 511 FOU

40

COMPOUND DIVISION.

Case I.—*When the Divisor does not exceed* 12.

Divide £8 12*s*. $7\frac{1}{2}$*d*. by 6.

RULE WITH EXAMPLE.—Proceed thus, 6 in 8 once and 2 over, set down the 1 under the 8, and carry 40*s*. for the 2*l*. to the 12; then 6 in 52, 8 times and 4 over, set down the 8 and carry 48*d*. for the 4*s*. to the 7; then 6 in 55, 9 times and 1 over, set down the 9 and carry 4 farthings to the farthing, 4 and 2 are 6, 6 in 6 once; set down ¼.

| £ | s. | d |
|---|---|---|
| 6)8 | 12 | $7\frac{1}{2}$ |
| 1 | 8 | $9\frac{1}{4}$ |

EXERCISES.

2) 74 16 $8\frac{1}{2}$
£37 8 $4\frac{1}{4}$

3) 76 12 $2\frac{3}{4}$
£25 10 $8\frac{3}{4}$

| | | £ | s. | d. | | | | | £ | s. | d. | | |
|---|---|---|---|---|---|---|---|---|---|---|---|---|---|
| 1. | Divide | 68 | 17 | $9\frac{1}{2}$ | by | 2 | 12. | Divide | 98 | 14 | $7\frac{1}{4}$ | by | 7 |
| 2. | | 42 | 12 | $3\frac{1}{4}$ | | 3 | 13. | | 47 | 13 | $6\frac{1}{2}$ | | 8 |
| 3. | | 69 | 18 | $7\frac{3}{4}$ | | 4 | 14. | | 67 | 19 | $1\frac{1}{4}$ | | 9 |
| 4. | | 748 | 15 | $0\frac{1}{2}$ | | 5 | 15. | | 864 | 1 | $7\frac{3}{4}$ | | 12 |
| 5. | | 176 | 19 | $10\frac{3}{4}$ | | 6 | 16. | | 587 | 14 | $10\frac{1}{2}$ | | 6 |
| 6. | | 407 | 14 | $2\frac{1}{2}$ | | 7 | 17. | | 311 | 7 | $11\frac{1}{4}$ | | 5 |
| 7. | | 8647 | 17 | $11\frac{3}{4}$ | | 8 | 18. | | 4000 | 18 | $0\frac{1}{2}$ | | 10 |
| 8. | | 7508 | 13 | $6\frac{1}{2}$ | | 9 | 19. | | 8681 | 11 | $3\frac{1}{2}$ | | 12 |
| 9. | | 5060 | 0 | $7\frac{1}{4}$ | | 10 | 20. | | 7010 | 18 | $0\frac{1}{4}$ | | 9 |
| 10. | | 8687 | 18 | $11\frac{3}{4}$ | | 11 | 21. | | 3671 | 2 | $11\frac{1}{2}$ | | 8 |
| 11. | | 4711 | 11 | $7\frac{1}{2}$ | | 12 | 22. | | 8762 | 17 | $0\frac{3}{4}$ | | 12 |

23. A tradesman had in the savings bank 96*l*. 16*s* 6*d*.; this sum he had saved in 5 years; how much did he save on an average each year?

24. Ten men rented a house at 46*l*. 14*s*. 8*d*.; how much had each to pay.

25 A father left 426*l*. 16*s*. 6*d*. to be divided equally among his eight children; how much did each get?

26. Twelve persons subscribed 28*l*. 15*s*. 6*d*. per annum, for the support of a school; how much did each subscribe?

27. A piece of cloth containing nine yards was bought for 4*l*. 16*s*. 8*d*.; how much was that per yard?

940

943 **GARDINER, ALFONZO.**
HOW TO TEACH THE METHOD OF UNITY. (CODE 1883: SCHEDULE 1, ARITHMETIC) . . . BY ALFONZO GARDINER, THIRD EDITION, REVISED AND ENLARGED. MANCHESTER: JOHN HEYWOOD, 1883. 142p. + 2p. pub. cat. Bound in brown cloth with embossed decorative cover.
YSC 511 GAR

944 **GIBSON'S MANY EXAMPLES ARITHMETIC.**
BOOKS I–V. 64p., 72p., 80p., 96p., 128p. GLASGOW: ROBERT GIBSON AND SONS, LTD., 1932. Limp bound in green cloth.
YSC 511 GIB

945 **HALL, H.S.**
EXAMPLES IN ARITHMETIC TAKEN FROM SCHOOL ARITHMETIC BY H.S. HALL, M.A. AND F.H. STEVENS, M.A. LONDON: MACMILLAN AND CO., LIMITED, 1912. X, 281p. + 2p. pub. cat.: diagrs. Bound in green cloth.
YSC 513 HAL

946 **HALL, H.S.**
A SCHOOL ALGEBRA. PART II. BY H.S. HALL, M.A. LONDON: MACMILLAN AND CO., LIMITED, 1911. p. 308–456: tables. Bound in red cloth.
YSC 513 HAL

947 **HALL, H.S.**
A SCHOOL GEOMETRY. PARTS I–VI. (Containing Plane and Solid Geometry, treated both theoretically and graphically). BY H.S. HALL, M.A. AND F.H. STEVENS, M.A. LONDON: MACMILLAN AND CO., LIMITED. SECOND EDITION. 1904. XXIV, 442p. + XIIp. answers + 2p. pub. cat.: diagrs. Bound in red cloth.
YSC 513 HAL

948 **HOWARD, B.A.**
FIRST IDEAS OF TRIGONOMETRY. BY B.A. HOWARD, M.A. BEING PART ONE OF THE AUTHOR'S SCHOOL TRIGONOMETRY. LONDON: GINN AND COMPANY LTD., 1924. 95p.: diagrs., tables. Bound in brown cloth.
YSC 516.24 HOW

949 **HUNTER, WILLIAM.**
GROUNDWORK OF CALCULUS. BY WILLIAM HUNTER. LONDON: UNIVERSITY TUTORIAL PRESS, LTD. 1929. 220p.: diagrs. Bound in yellow cloth.
YSC 517 HUN

950 **LATIMER, J.L.**
A COURSE IN GEOMETRY BY J.L. LATIMER, M.A. AND T. SMITH, B.Sc. LONDON: GEORGE G. HARROP AND COMPANY LTD., 1937. 375p.: diagrs. Bound in dark brown cloth.
YSC 516 LAT

951 **LONEY, S.L.**
ARITHMETIC WITH ANSWERS. BY S.L. LONEY, M.A. AND L.W. GRENVILLE, M.A. LONDON: MACMILLAN AND CO., LIMITED, 1930. 186p. + XXIVp. answers. Bound in blue cloth.
YSC 511 LON

952 **MACKAY, JOHN S.**
ARITHMETICAL EXERCISES FOR ALL CLASSES OF SCHOOLS. BY JOHN S. MACKAY, M.A. PART I. EXERCISES IN THE SIMPLE RULES. ENGLISH CODE, STANDARDS I, II AND PART OF III.
PART II EXERCISES IN THE COMPOUND RULES (MONEY) ENGLISH CODE, STANDARD III AND PART OF IV.
LONDON: W. & R. CHAMBERS, 1878. 2 vols. 64p. Limp bound in green paper.
YSC 511 MAC

953 **MCKENZIE, ELIZABETH.**
NISBET'S GIRLS REALISTIC ARITHMETIC TOGETHER WITH SUPPLEMENTARY EXERCISES. By Mrs. ELIZABETH McKENZIE and H.G. WOOD. BOOK V. LONDON: JAMES NISBET AND CO., LTD., (193–?). 64p.: title page on cover, diagrs. Limp bound in blue cloth.
YSC 511 MAC

954 **MANSFORD, CHARLES.**
A SCHOOL ALGEBRA TO QUADRATIC EQUATIONS, WITH NUMEROUS EXAMPLES BY CHARLES MANSFORD B.A., MATHEMATICAL TUTOR IN THE WESTMINSTER TRAINING COLLEGE CENTRAL AGENCY, SCHOOL BOOK DEPOT TRAINING COLLEGE, WESTMINSTER, (187–?). 104p. Bound in brown cloth, with embossed decorative cover. Includes explanation, exercises and answers. Flyleaf signed by Walter Radcliffe April 9th 1878, Cowhill School, Oldham.
C 512.9042 MAN

955 **MAYNE, A.B.**
THE ESSENTIALS OF SCHOOL ALGEBRA. BY A.B. MAYNE, M.A. LONDON: MACMILLAN AND CO., LIMITED, 1938. XII, 499p.: diagrs., tables. Bound in orange cloth.
YSC 512.9 MAY

956 **THE MODERN "GUIDE" MENTAL ARITHMETICS.**
BOOKS 1 & 2 24p.
BOOKS 3, 4, 5 32p.
BIRMINGHAM: DAVIS AND MOUGHTON, LTD., (193–?). Limp bound in grey cloth with decorative cover.
YSC 511 MOD

957 **PENDLEBURY, CHARLES.**
A PREPARATORY ARITHMETIC. LONDON: G. BELL AND SONS, LTD., 5th edition, 1924. X, 290p.: diagrs. Bound in red cloth.
YSC 511 PEN

958 **POTTER, F.F.**
COMMON-SENSE ARITHMETIC FOR JUNIORS BY F.F. POTTER, M.A., B.Sc. PUPIL'S BOOK I. LONDON: SIR ISAAC PITMAN AND SONS, LTD., 1934. 48p. Limp bound in red cloth.
YSC 513 POT

958A **RILEY, E.**
AN ARITHMETIC FOR CITIZENSHIP BY E. RILEY, BSc (ECON), FSS and J. RILEY, BSc. LONDON: SIDGWICK AND JACKSON, LTD, 1922. IV, 124p. Bound in green cloth.
M 640.42 RIL CHILDREN'S COLLECTION

959 **ROBERTSON, JOHN W.**
A SHILLING ARITHMETIC BY JOHN W. ROBERTSON, M.A. B.Sc. LONDON: G. BELL AND SONS, LTD., 1916. VIII, 191p. + XXVIIp. answers + 4p. pub. cat. Limp bound in blue cloth.
YSC 510 ROB

960 **ROSS, P.**
ELEMENTARY ALGEBRA FOR THE USE OF SCHOOLS. BY P. ROSS, M.A., B.Sc. LONDON: LONGMANS, GREEN AND CO., 1911. XII, 484p. + 64p. answers: diagrs. Bound in black cloth.
YSC 512 ROS

961 **SANKEY, E.**
EXAMPLES IN EASY PRACTICAL MATHEMATICS FOR THE FIRST YEAR PRELIMINARY TECHNICAL COURSE. BY E. SANKEY. BOOK ONE. SPECIALLY DRAWN UP FOR USE IN THE UPPER STANDARDS OF PRIMARY SCHOOLS AND FOR FIRST YEAR STUDENTS IN EVENING SCHOOLS AND BRANCH TECHNICAL SCHOOLS. LONDON: EDWARD ARNOLD, (193–?). 64p.: diagrs. Limp bound in brown cloth.
YSC 510.76 SAN

962 **SARGENT, W.**
LEDSHAM'S Arithmetical Examination Questions, by W. SARGENT. THIRD STANDARD. MANCHESTER. J.B. LEDSHAM, (188–?). 28p. Lacks original paper cover.
YSC 511 SAR

963 **SAXELBY, F.M.**
A COURSE IN PRACTICAL MATHEMATICS. BY F.M. SAXELBY, M.Sc., B.A. LONDON: LONGMANS, GREEN AND CO., FIFTH EDITION, 1913. XI, 472p.: diagrs. Bound in green cloth.
YSC 510 SAX

964 **SYMON, ALEXANDER.**
THE NEW GEOMETRY. THE AGREED SCHEME drawn up by the Incorporated Association of Assistant Masters in Cooperation with the Educational Institute of Scotland. (by) ALEXANDER SYMON, M.A., B.Sc. PARTS I, II and III. GLASGOW: ROBERT GIBSON AND SONS, 1931. XV, 272, XVII–XXIIIp.: front., diagrs. Bound in grey cloth.
YSC 513 SYM

965 **TATE, THOMAS.**
A TREATISE ON THE FIRST PRINCIPLES OF ARITHMETIC AFTER THE METHOD OF PESTALOZZI. . . . Designed for the use of Teachers and Monitors in Elementary Schools. BY THOMAS TATE, F.R.A.S. NEW EDITION. LONDON: LONGMANS, GREEN AND CO., (1882). XII, 108p. + 16p. pub. cat. Bound in purple cloth with embossed decorative covers. Originally published 1847.
YSC 511 TAT

966 **TAYLOR, RICHARD V.**
Golden Mean Arithmetics.
Books 1 and 2. 64p. each
Book 3. 72p.
EXETER: A. WHEATON AND CO., LTD., 1936. Diagrs. Limp bound in orange cloth with decorative covers.
YSC 511 TAY

967 **TAYLOR, RICHARD V.**
Golden Mean Arithmetics. By RICHARD V. TAYLOR and JAMES BURLEY.
JUNIOR BOOKS I–IV.
EXETER: A. WHEATON AND CO., LTD. (193–?). Ill., diagrs. Limp bound in orange cloth.
YSC 511 TAY

968 **WARRELL, CHARLES.**
SANE ARITHMETIC FOR SENIORS BY CHARLES WARRELL.
BOOKS 1–111. 64p. each
BOOK IV. 80p.
LONDON: GEORGE HARROP AND CO. LTD., (193–?). Title page on cover: ill., diagrs. Limp bound in card, green, grey, pink and blue, with pictorial covers.
YSC 511 WAR

969 **WILLIAMS, J.M.**
THE ELEMENTS OF EUCLID: CONTAINING THE FIRST SIX BOOKS, AND THE FIRST TWENTY-ONE PROPOSITIONS OF THE ELEVENTH BOOK. (WITH THE PLANES SHADED.) CHIEFLY From the Text of Dr. Simson. ADAPTED TO THE USE OF STUDENTS BY MEANS OF SYMBOLS. BY THE REV. J.M. WILLIAMS, B.A. NINTH EDITION, WITH AN APPENDIX. LONDON: DAVID BOGUE, 1854. XII, 287p.: diagrams. Bound in black cloth, with embossed decorative covers and spine. Spine title: WILLIAMS'S SYMBOLICAL EUCLID.
C 516.2 EUC

970 **WISDOM, ALFRED.**
CENTURY SUM BOOKS. BY ALFRED WISDOM, B.A., B.Sc.
BOOK ONE 700 SUMS FOR CHILDREN OF 7. SERIES B. Limp bound in blue cloth.
BOOK TWO 800 SUMS FOR CHILDREN OF 8. SERIES A. Limp bound in yellow cloth.
SERIES B. Limp bound in orange cloth.
BOOK THREE 900 SUMS FOR CHILDREN OF 9. SERIES A. Limp bound in dark grey cloth
SERIES B. Limp bound in brown cloth.
BOOK FOUR 1000 SUMS FOR CHILDREN OF 10. SERIES A. Limp bound in green cloth
SERIES B. Limp bound in buff cloth.
BOOK FIVE 1100 SUMS FOR CHILDREN OF 11. SERIES A. Limp bound in light grey cloth.
SERIES B. Limp bound in light blue cloth.
LONDON: UNIVERSITY OF LONDON PRESS, 1933–5. Books 1–3, 48p. each; 4, 5, 64p. each. Decorative covers.
YSC 511 WIS

971 **YOUNG, THOMAS M.**
MANY EXAMPLES ARITHMETIC. BOOK VI. POST-PRIMARY BY THOMAS M. YOUNG, M.A. AND JAMES G. LOCKHART, M.A. B.Sc. FOR FIRST YEAR in MODERN, SENIOR, CENTRAL ADVANCED DIVISION AND SECONDARY SCHOOLS. GLASGOW: ROBERT GIBSON AND SONS (GLASGOW) LTD. 1931. 192p. Diagrs. Limp bound in decorative blue cloth.
YSC 511 GIB

## 16 INVENTION, HEALTH AND PRACTICAL ARTS

972 **BINNS, CHARLES F.**
THE STORY OF THE POTTER. . . . BY CHARLES F. BINNS. WITH FIFTY-SEVEN ILLUSTRATIONS. LONDON: GEORGE NEWNES, LIMITED, 1898. 248p.: front., 3 plates. Bound in blue cloth with decorative/pictorial cover.
YSC 738 BIN

973 **BOOK OF TRADES.**
Title page missing. (SOCIETY FOR PROMOTING CHRISTIAN KNOWLEDGE), (187–?). 238p. + 4p. pub. cat. ill. Bound in brown cloth with embossed decorative cover and spine.
YSC 600 BOO

973A **BOWEN, FRANK C.**
SHIPS FOR ALL. BY FRANK C. BOWEN. THIRD EDITION, WITH NEARLY A HUNDRED ILLUSTRATIONS. LONDON: WARD LOCK AND CO. LIMITED, (193–?). 384p.: front., 50 plates. Bound in green cloth with pictorial paper dust jacket.
C 623.82 BOW

973B **BROWNE, EDITH A.**
PEEPS AT INDUSTRIES. SUGAR. BY EDITH A. BROWNE. LONDON: ADAM AND CHARLES BLACK, 1911. VII, 88p. + 5p. pub. cat.: 24 photographic plates. Bound in blue cloth with photographic pictorial label on cover.
C 338.17361 BRO

973C **BUCKTON, CATHERINE M.**
FOOD AND HOME COOKERY. A COURSE OF INSTRUCTION IN PRACTICAL COOKERY AND CLEANING FOR CHILDREN IN ELEMENTARY SCHOOLS, AS FOLLOWED IN THE SCHOOLS OF THE LEEDS SCHOOL BOARD. BY CATHERINE M. BUCKTON, MEMBER OF THE LEEDS SCHOOLBOARD. LONDON: LONGMANS, GREEN AND CO., 1879. XI, 108p. front., 3 plates, ill. Bound in black cloth.
M 641.5 CHILDREN'S COLLECTION

974 **BURNLEY, JAMES.**
THE STORY OF BRITISH TRADE AND INDUSTRY. BY JAMES BURNLEY. LONDON: GEORGE NEWNES, LTD., 1904. 224p. Bound in blue cloth with decorative/pictorial covers. Library of Useful Stories.
YSC 380 BUR

975 **CLAXTON, WILLIAM J.**
OUR COUNTRY'S INDUSTRIAL HISTORY. BY WILLIAM J. CLAXTON. WITH OVER ONE HUNDRED ILLUSTRATIONS. LONDON: GEORGE G. HARRAP AND COMPANY, 1915. 246p.: front., ill. Bound in grey cloth with pictorial cover.
YSC 942 CLA

976 **CORBIN, THOMAS W.**
MARVELS OF SCIENTIFIC INVENTION, AN INTERESTING ACCOUNT IN NON-TECHNICAL LANGUAGE OF THE INVENTION OF GUNS, TORPEDOES, SUBMARINES, MINES, UP-TO-DATE SMELTING, FREEZING, COLOUR PHOTOGRAPHY, AND MANY OTHER RECENT DISCOVERIES OF SCIENCE. BY THOMAS W. CORBIN. WITH 32 ILLUSTRATIONS AND DIAGRAMS. LONDON: SEELEY, SERVICE AND CO. LIMITED, 1917. 251p.: front., 14 plates, ill. Bound in grey cloth, with coloured pictorial cover and spine.
C 609 COR

977 **CORFIELD, W.H.**
THE LAWS OF HEALTH BY W.H. CORFIELD. M.A. M.D. F.R.C.P. FIFTH EDITION, REVISED AND CORRECTED. LONDON: LONGMANS, GREEN AND CO., 1887. XII, 153p. + 2p. pub. cat.: diagrs. Bound in cream cloth. THE LONDON SCIENCE CLASS-BOOKS.
YSC 613 COR

978 **CRESSWELL, ERNEST J.J.**
SPONGES: THEIR NATURE, HISTORY, MODES OF FISHING, VARIETIES, CULTIVATION, ETC. BY ERNEST J. CRESSWELL. LONDON: SIR ISAAC PITMAN AND SONS, LTD., (192–?). VII, 126p. + 16p. pub. cat.: front., 13 plates, ill. Bound in green cloth. PITMAN'S COMMON COMMODITIES AND INDUSTRIES SERIES.
YSC 593 CRE

979 **DODD, GEORGE.**
NATURE'S GIFTS AND HOW WE USE THEM. A FAMILIAR ACCOUNT OF OUR EVERY-DAY WANTS, COMFORTS AND LUXURIES. BY GEORGE DODD. ILLUSTRATED BY W. HARVEY. LONDON: WARD, LOCK AND CO., (188–?). 283p.: vignette on title page: 6 plates. Bound in blue cloth with embossed decorative cover.
YSC 600 DOD

980 **EDGAR, WILLIAM C.**
THE STORY OF A GRAIN OF WHEAT. BY WILLIAM C. EDGAR. WITH FORTY ILLUSTRATIONS. LONDON: GEORGE NEWNES, LTD., (190–?). 195p.: front., 8 plates, ill., tables. Bound in blue cloth with decorative/pictorial cover. Library of Useful Stories.
YSC 633 EDG

981 **FAVELL, A.J.**
COMMERCE FOR COMMERCIAL AND SECONDARY SCHOOLS COVERING STAGE I. (ELEMENTARY) AND STAGE II. (INTERMEDIATE) SYLLABUS OF THE ROYAL SOCIETY OF ARTS AND SIMILAR EXAMINING BODIES. BY A.J. FAVELL, B.Sc (ECON) A.C.I.S. LONDON: SIR ISAAC PITMAN AND SONS, LTD., 1937. XI, 226p. + 32p. pub. cat.: diagrs. Bound in brown cloth.
YSC 380 FAV

982 **FRITH, HENRY.**
COIL AND CURRENT; OR, The Triumphs of Electricity. BY HENRY FRITH, AND W. STEPNEY RAWSON, M.I.E.E. WITH NUMEROUS ILLUSTRATIONS. LONDON: WARD, LOCK AND CO. LIMITED, (1896). VIII, 294p. + 10p. pub. cat.: front., 15 plates, ill. Bound in blue cloth, with coloured pictorial cover and spine.
C 621.3 FRI

983 **FRITH, HENRY.**
THE FLYING HORSE. THE STORY OF THE LOCOMOTIVE AND THE RAILWAY. BY HENRY FRITH. WITH NUMEROUS ILLUSTRATIONS. LONDON: GRIFFITH, FARRAN, BROWNE AND CO., LIMITED, 1893. XII, 290p.: front., 23 plates, ill. Bound in orange cloth with decorative cover and spine.
C 385.36 FRI

984 **GIBSON, CHARLES R.**
GREAT INVENTIONS AND HOW THEY WERE INVENTED. . . . BY CHARLES R. GIBSON, LL.D., F.R.S.E. WITH ILLUSTRATIONS. LONDON: SEELEY, SERVICE AND CO., LIMITED, 1932. 240p. + 16p. pub. cat.: front., 8 plates, diagrs. Bound in green cloth with coloured decorative cover.
YSC 608 GIB

985 **GIBSON, CHARLES R.**
THE ROMANCE OF MODERN ELECTRICITY, DESCRIBING IN NON-TECHNICAL LANGUAGE WHAT IS KNOWN ABOUT ELECTRICITY AND MANY OF ITS INTERESTING APPLICATIONS. BY CHARLES R. GIBSON, F.R.S.E. NEW AND REVISED EDITION. WITH MANY ILLUSTRATIONS. LONDON: SEELEY, SERVICE AND CO. LIMITED, 1930. 344p. + 6p. pub. cat.: front., 9 plates, ill. Bound in blue cloth, with coloured pictorial cover and spine.
C 621.3 GIB

986 **GIFFORD, M.K.**
NEEDLEWORK. BY M.K. GIFFORD. WITH 19 PLATES AND 273 DIAGRAMS AND SKETCHES. LONDON: THOMAS NELSON AND SONS. (192–?). VIII, 294p. Bound in red cloth. THE HOBBY BOOKS EDITED BY ARCHIBALD WILLIAMS.
YSC 646 GIF

986A **GOLDING, HARRY** *(Editor).*
THE WONDER BOOK OF AIRCRAFT. LONDON: WARD, LOCK AND CO., 6th ed. (1928), 256 p.: col. front., 11 col. plates, 54 plates, ill., pictorial endpapers by Thomas Maybank. Bound in orange cloth with coloured pictorial cover.
C 629.13 GOL

987 **GOLDING, HARRY** *(Editor).*
THE WONDER BOOK OF RAILWAYS WITH EIGHT COLOUR PLATES AND NEARLY 300 ILLUSTRATIONS. FIFTEENTH EDITION. EDITED BY HARRY GOLDING, F.R.G.S. LONDON: WARD LOCK AND CO., LIMITED (193–?). 256p.: front., vignette on title page, 3 col. plates, ill., comic pictorial endpapers. Bound in green cloth with coloured pictorial paper cover.
C 625.26 WON

988 **GOLDING, HARRY** *(Editor).*
THE WONDER BOOK OF SHIPS. WITH TWELVE COLOUR PLATES AND NEARLY 300 ILLUSTRATIONS. EDITED BY HARRY GOLDING, F.R.G.S. FOURTEENTH EDITION. LONDON: WARD LOCK AND CO., LIMITED, (193–?). 256p.: col. front., vignette on title page, 10 col. plates, ill., comic pictorial endpapers. Bound in blue cloth with coloured pictorial cover.
C 623.82 WON

989 **GREAT INVENTORS.**
THE SOURCES OF THEIR USEFULNESS, AND THE RESULTS OF THEIR EFFORTS. PROFUSELY ILLUSTRATED. LONDON: WARD, LOCK, AND TYLER, (187–?). XII, 308p. + 32p. pub. cat.: front., vignette title page, ill. Bound in green cloth, with embossed decorative cover and spine.
C 609 GRE

990 **HALL, C.J.**
A SHORT HISTORY OF ENGLISH AGRICULTURE AND RURAL LIFE. BY C.J. HALL. LONDON: A. AND C. BLACK, LTD., 1924. VIII, 152p.: front., 7 plates, ill. Limp bound in turquoise cloth with decorative cover.
YSC 630 HAL

991 **HALL, CYRIL.**
Wood and What We Make of It. BY CYRIL HALL. ILLUSTRATED BY THIRTY-TWO REPRODUCTIONS FROM PHOTOGRAPHS AND NUMEROUS TEXT CUTS. LONDON: BLACKIE AND SON LIMITED, (191–?). VIII, 287p.: front., 31 plates, ill. Bound in green cloth, with coloured pictorial cover and spine. TRIUMPHS OF ENTERPRISE.
C 674 HAL

991A **HALL, FRED.**
SUNNYSIDE: A STORY OF INDUSTRIAL HISTORY AND COOPERATION FOR YOUNG PEOPLE. BY FRED HALL, MA, BCom. MANCHESTER: COOPERATIVE UNION LTD. 1922. 212p. 11 plates, ill. Bound in red cloth. Partially fictional.
M 335.1 HAL CHILDREN'S COLLECTION.

992 **HILL, LEONARD.**
MANUAL OF HUMAN PHYSIOLOGY BY SIR LEONARD HILL, M.B., LL.D., F.R.S., HON. A.R.I.A. FOURTH EDITION. LONDON: EDWARD ARNOLD AND CO., 1935. XII, 470p.: diagrs.
YSC 612 HIL

993 **HOLMES, FREDERIC MORELL.**
CELEBRATED MECHANICS AND THEIR ACHIEVEMENTS: STORIES OF LIGHTHOUSES AND THEIR BUILDERS – HARBOURS AND BREAKWATERS – DIVING AND DIVERS – CANALS – THE STEAM-HAMMER – WONDERS OF WATER POWER. BY F.M. HOLMES. LONDON: S.W. PARTRIDGE AND CO., (189–?). 160p. + 16p. pub. cat.: front., vignette title page, 6 plates, ill. Bound in blue cloth, with coloured pictorial/decorative cover and spine.
C 620.00922 HOL

994 **HOLMES, FREDERIC MORELL.**
THE MARVELS OF METALS: STORIES OF METAL-WORKERS AND THEIR VICTORIES. BY F.M. HOLMES. LONDON: S.W. PARTRIDGE AND CO., (189–?). 160p. + 24p. ill. pub. cat.: front., vignette title page, 7 plates, ill. Bound in brown cloth, with coloured pictorial cover and spine.
C 620.16 HOL

994A **KIRBY, MARY.**
AUNT MARTHA'S CORNER CUPBOARD. A Story for Little Boys and Girls. BY MARY AND ELIZABETH KIRBY. LONDON: T. NELSON AND SONS, 1875. 175p.: col. front., 12 plates, ill. Bound in green cloth with embossed decorative cover and spine. Information on tea, coffee, sugar, rice etc. in story form.
M 641.3 CHILDREN'S COLLECTION

994A

994B **Another copy.**
With sub-title stories about Tea, Coffee, Sugar, Rice etc. WITH THIRTY-SIX ENGRAVINGS, 1889. Bound in purple cloth with coloured pictorial cover and spine.

995 **KNOX, GORDON D.**
ALL ABOUT ELECTRICITY, A BOOK FOR BOYS. BY GORDON D. KNOX. With a Frontispiece in Colour and a large number of Photographs and Diagrams. LONDON: CASSELL AND COMPANY LTD., 1914. XX, 356p.: col. front., 32 plates, ill. Bound in blue cloth, with coloured pictorial cover and spine.
C 621.3 KNO

996 **LYSTER, ROBERT A.**
A FIRST COURSE IN HYGIENE. BY ROBERT A LYSTER, M.D., Ch.B., B.Sc., D.P.H. LONDON: UNIVERSITY TUTORIAL PRESS, NINTH EDITION, 1937. VIII, 376p.: diagrs. Bound in green cloth.
YSC 613 LYS

997 **MANCHESTER SCHOOL OF DOMESTIC ECONOMY AND COOKERY.**
MIDDLE CLASS COOKERY BOOK. COMPILED AND EDITED FOR THE MANCHESTER SCHOOL OF DOMESTIC ECONOMY AND COOKERY, SOUTH PARADE, DEANSGATE, MANCHESTER. LONDON: MACMILLAN AND CO., 1890. VIII, 211p. + 6p. pub. cat.: diagrs. Bound in red cloth.
YSC 641 MAN

998 **MARTIN, EDWARD A.**
THE STORY OF A PIECE OF COAL, WHAT IT IS, WHENCE IT COMES, AND WHITHER IT GOES. BY EDWARD A. MARTIN, F.G.S. WITH THIRTY-EIGHT ILLUSTRATIONS. LONDON: GEORGE NEWNES, LTD., 1898. 179p.: front. Bound in blue cloth with decorative/pictorial cover.
YSC 622 MAR

999 **OUR FARM OF FOUR ACRES.**
HOW WE MANAGED IT, THE MONEY WE MADE BY IT, AND HOW IT GREW INTO ONE OF SIX ACRES. TWELFTH EDITION, WITH A MONTHLY CALENDAR OF RURAL OPERATIONS. ILLUSTRATED, CAREFULLY REVISED, AND GREATLY ENLARGED. LONDON: CHAPMAN AND HALL, 1871. VIII, 224p.: front., ill. Bound in green cloth with embossed decorative cover.
YSC 630 OUR

1000 **PETERSHAM, MAUD.**
THE STORY BOOK OF SILK BY MAUD AND MISKA PETERSHAM. REDHILL: WELLS GARDNER, DARTON AND CO., LTD. (192–?). Unpaginated: col. pictorial title page, col. ill. Bound in blue paper with coloured pictorial cover.
YSC 677 PET

1001 **PHYTHIAN, J. ERNEST.**
THE STORY OF ART IN THE BRITISH ISLES. BY J. ERNEST PHYTHIAN WITH TWENTY-EIGHT ILLUSTRATIONS. LONDON: GEORGE NEWNES, LIMITED, 1901. 216p.: front., 3 plates, ill. Bound in blue cloth with decorative/pictorial cover. Library of Useful Stories.
YSC 709 PHY

1002 **THE PICTURE BOOK OF SHIPS.**
WITH TWENTY-FOUR COLOUR PLATES AND NUMEROUS ILLUSTRATIONS. LONDON: WARD, LOCK AND CO. LIMITED, Unpaginated: col. front., col. pictorial title page, 22 col. plates, 23 plates, ill. Bound in grey cloth, with coloured pictorial paper cover.
C 623.8 PIC

1003 **POOLE, N.A.**
THE ROMANCE OF CRAFT SERIES, BOOKS II, III AND IV. BY N.A. POOLE (MRS. T. REED). LONDON: THOMAS NELSON AND SONS, LTD., 1929. 71, 86, 84p.: ill., diagrs. Limp bound in blue cloth.
YSC 745 POO

1004 **RAWLINGS, GERTRUDE BURFORD.**
THE STORY OF BOOKS. BY GERTRUDE BURFORD RAWLINGS. LONDON: GEORGE NEWNES, LIMITED, 1901. 171p.: front., 2 plates, ill. Bound in blue cloth with decorative/pictorial cover. Library of Useful Stories.
YSC 655 RAW

1005 **ROUTLEDGE, ROBERT.**
DISCOVERIES AND INVENTIONS OF THE NINETEENTH CENTURY. BY ROBERT ROUTLEDGE, B.Sc., F.C.S. NINTH EDITION REVISED AND PARTLY RE-WRITTEN, WITH ADDITIONS. LONDON: GEORGE ROUTLEDGE AND SONS LTD., 1891. XIV, 681p. + 6p. pub. cat.: front., 9 plates, ill., maps, diagrams. Bound in blue cloth, with pictorial cover and spine, and gilt edges.
C 609.034 ROU

1005A **SHEPHERD, MRS E.R.**
FOR GIRLS: A SPECIAL PHYSIOLOGY; BEING A SUPPLEMENT TO THE STUDY OF GENERAL PHYSIOLOGY. USA: NEW YORK: FOWLER AND WELLS CO., 1892. 225p. + 14p. pub. cat.: ill. Bound in yellow cloth.
M 612.6 SHE CHILDREN'S COLLECTION

1006 **STORY, ALFRED T.**
THE STORY OF PHOTOGRAPHY. BY ALFRED T. STORY. WITH THIRTY-EIGHT ILLUSTRATIONS LONDON: GEORGE NEWNES, LIMITED, 1898. 181p. Bound in blue cloth with decorative/pictorial cover. Library of Useful Stories.
YSC 770 STO

1006A **TATE, LOUISA S.**
THE CHILD'S COOKERY BOOK BY LOUISA S. TATE. LONDON: ALEXANDER MORING LTD. (192–?). 141p. Bound in blue cloth. Originally published in 1887.
M 641.5 TAT CHILDREN'S COLLECTION.

1007 **THE TRIUMPHS OF STEAM.**
OR, Stories from the Lives of WATT, ARKWRIGHT, AND STEPHENSON. BY THE AUTHOR OF "MIGHT NOT RIGHT", "OUR EASTERN EMPIRE", "THE MARTYR LAND", ETC. WITH ILLUSTRATIONS BY JOHN GILBERT. Second Edition. LONDON: GRIFFITH AND FARRAN, 1860. VIII, 264p. + 32p. pub. cat.: front., 4 plates, engraved by Dalziel Brothers, ill. Bound in green cloth, with embossed decorative covers and spine.
C 621.10922 TRI

1008 **WAY, R. BARNARD.**
FROM LOG TO LINER. LONDON: SIR ISAAC PITMAN AND SONS, LTD., (193–?). 116p.: ill. Bound in green cloth with pictorial cover.
YSC 387 WAY

1008A **WEATHERS, JOHN.**
A PRACTICAL GUIDE TO SCHOOL, COTTAGE AND ALLOTMENT GARDENING. BY JOHN WEATHERS. WITH SIXTY-SIX ILLUSTRATIONS AND EXAMINATION QUESTIONS ON COTTAGE GARDENING. LONDON: LONGMANS, GREEN AND CO., 1908. XIII, 248p.: ill., plans, tables. Bound in blue cloth with decorative cover.
M 635 WEA CHILDREN'S COLLECTION

1009 **WILKINSON, FRED.**
THE STORY OF THE COTTON PLANT. BY F. WILKINSON, F.G.S. WITH TWENTY-EIGHT ILLUSTRATIONS. LONDON: GEORGE NEWNES LIMITED, 1898. 199p.: front. Bound in blue cloth with decorative cover. Library of Useful Stories.
YSC 677 WIL

1010 **WILLIAMS, ARCHIBALD.**
LET ME EXPLAIN. BY ARCHIBALD WILLIAMS. WITH OVER 150 SKETCHES, DIAGRAMS AND PHOTOGRAPHS. LONDON: WELLS GARDNER, DARTON AND CO. LTD., (1920). XI, 370p.: col. front., 26 plates, ill. Bound in green cloth, with coloured pictorial cover and spine.
C 620 WIL

1011 **WILLIAMS, ARCHIBALD.**
Victories of the Engineer. By ARCHIBALD WILLIAMS. SECOND EDITION. LONDON: THOMAS NELSON AND SONS, (191–?). 487p.: col. front., 59 plates, ill. Bound in blue cloth, with coloured pictorial cover and spine.
C 620 WIL

1012 **WILLSON, BECKLES.**
THE STORY OF RAPID TRANSIT. BY BECKLES WILLSON. LONDON: GEORGE NEWNES, LTD., 1903. 197p.: front., 15 plates, ill. Bound in blue cloth with decorative/pictorial cover.
YSC 385 WIL

1013 **WILSON, RICHARD.**
A BOOK OF SHIPS AND SEAMEN EDITED BY RICHARD WILSON D. LITT. WITH AN INTRODUCTION BY Q. LONDON: J.M. DENT AND SONS, LTD., 1936. 272p. Bound in red cloth.
YSC 387 WIL

1014 **WYATT, CHARLES HENRY.**
GARDENING FOR CHILDREN AND OTHERS. BY CHARLES HENRY WYATT, M.A. ILLUSTRATED. MANCHESTER: THOMAS WYATT, 1910. 92p.: front., vignette title page, ill. Bound in green cloth, with pictorial paper cover.
C 635 WYA

## 17 STORIES 1840–1899

1015 **ADAMS, HENRY CADWALLADER.**
TALES OF WALTER'S SCHOOL-DAYS: A SEQUEL TO TALES OF CHARLTON SCHOOL. 1. THE DOCTOR'S BIRTHDAY 2. WALTER'S FRIEND, BY THE REV. H.C. ADAMS, VICAR OF DRY SANDFORD. WITH ILLUSTRATION. LONDON: GEORGE ROUTLEDGE AND SONS, 1873. 156p., 156p. + 16p. pub. cat.: front., 3 plates by Dalziel. Bound in blue cloth with decorative cover.
C 823.8 ADA

1016 **ADAMS, WILLIAM.**
THE CHERRY-STONES; OR, CHARLTON SCHOOL: A Tale for Youth. PARTLY FROM THE MSS. OF THE REV. WILLIAM ADAMS. EDITED BY THE REV. H.C. ADAMS. Third Edition. LONDON: FRANCIS AND JOHN RIVINGTON, 1853. 143p.: front. Bound in blue cloth.
C 823.8 ADA

1017 **ADAMS, WILLIAM.**
TALES OF CHARLTON SCHOOL; 1. THE CHERRY STONES, PARTLY FROM THE MSS. OF THE REV. W. ADAMS. TENTH EDITION. 2. THE FIRST OF JUNE, BY THE REV. H.C. ADAMS. EIGHTH EDITION WITH ILLUSTRATIONS BY ABSOLON. LONDON: ROUTLEDGE, WARNE AND ROUTLEDGE, 1864. VIII, 143p., VI, 158p. + 26p. pub. cat.: front., 5 plates. Bound in red cloth with embossed decorative cover and spine.
C 823.8 ADA

1018 **Another copy.**
1892. Illustrated by F.A. Fraser.

1019 **AFTER FIVE YEARS.**
LONDON: SOCIETY FOR PROMOTING CHRISTIAN KNOWLEDGE, (188–?). 159p. + 4p. pub. cat.: front., 2 plates. Bound in grey cloth with decorative cover and spine and gilt edges.
C 823.8 AFT

1020 **AGUILAR, GRACE.**
THE DAYS OF BRUCE, A Story of Scottish History, BY GRACE AGUILAR . . . MANCHESTER: JOHN HEYWOOD, (189–?). 506p. Bound in purple cloth with pictorial cover and spine. THE BEACON LIBRARY on cover.
C 823.8 AGU

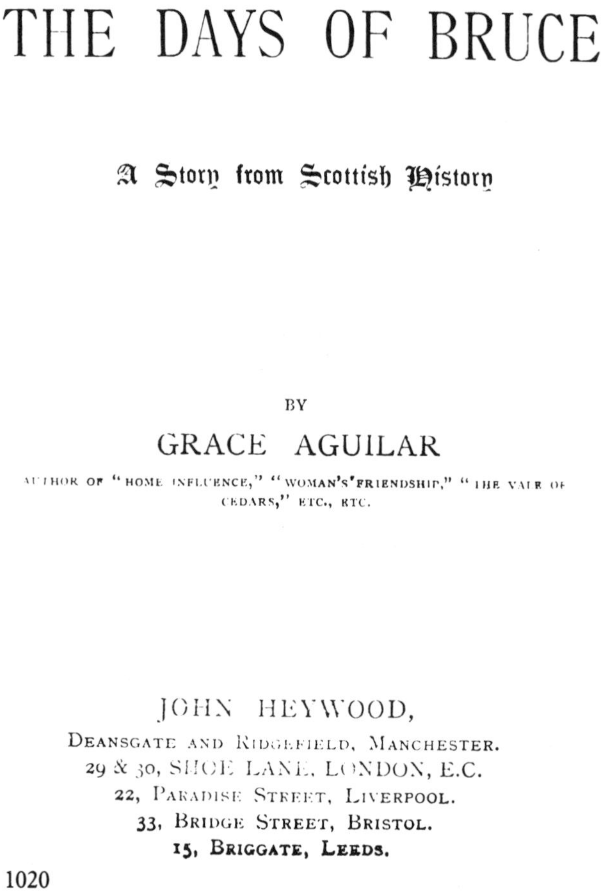
THE DAYS OF BRUCE

A Story from Scottish History

BY

GRACE AGUILAR

AUTHOR OF "HOME INFLUENCE," "WOMAN'S FRIENDSHIP," "THE VALE OF CEDARS," ETC., ETC.

JOHN HEYWOOD,
DEANSGATE AND RIDGEFIELD, MANCHESTER.
29 & 30, SHOE LANE, LONDON, E.C.
22, PARADISE STREET, LIVERPOOL.
33, BRIDGE STREET, BRISTOL.
15, BRIGGATE, LEEDS.

1020

1021 **AIMARD, GUSTAVE.**
LOYAL HEART, A Tale of the prairies, CONTAINING "THE WHITE SCALPER", AND "THE TRAPPERS OF ARKANSAS", BY GUSTAVE AIMARD. LONDON: WARD, LOCK, AND CO., (189–?). VIII, 352, IV, 337p.: front., 6 plates. Bound in green cloth embossed in gilt.
C 823.8 AIM

1022 **AINSWORTH, WILLIAM HARRISON.**
BOSCOBEL OR THE ROYAL OAK, A TALE OF THE YEAR 1651. BY WILLIAM HARRISON AINSWORTH. AUTHOR'S COPYRIGHT EDITION. LONDON: GEORGE ROUTLEDGE AND SONS, LIMITED, (189–?). 436p. Bound in red cloth with embossed decorative cover.
YSC 823.8 AIN

1023 **ALCOCK, DEBORAH.**
THE SPANISH BROTHERS. A TALE OF THE SIXTEENTH CENTURY. By the author of "THE CZAR: A TALE OF THE FIRST NAPOLEON". LONDON: T. NELSON AND SONS, 1888. 412p. + 4p. pub. cat.: additional vignette title page. Bound in green cloth with decorative cover and spine.
YSC 823.8 ALC

1024 **ALCOTT, LOUISA MAY.**
LITTLE WOMEN AND GOOD WIVES. By LOUISA M. ALCOTT. With Illustrations by H.M. BROCK, R.I. LONDON: SEELEY, SERVICE AND CO. LIMITED, (191–?). 199p. + 216p.: col. front., 8 plates. Bound in buff cloth, with decorative cover and spine. Originally published in 1868 and 1869.
C 813.4 ALC

1025 **Another copy.**
WITH SIX ILLUSTRATIONS. LONDON: S.W. PARTRIDGE AND CO. LTD., (191–?). VIII, 415p. + 32p. pub. cat.: front., 5 plates, by Charles Horrell. Bound in brown cloth, with coloured decorative cover and spine.
YSC 813.4 ALC

1026 **ALCOTT, LOUISA MAY.**
LITTLE WOMEN AND LITTLE WOMEN MARRIED. BY LOUISA M. ALCOTT. LONDON: GEORGE ROUTLEDGE AND SONS LIMITED, (191–?). VIII, 198p., IV, 219p.: front., 3 plates, by J.S. Eland. Bound in blue cloth, with embossed decorative cover and spine.
YSC 813.4 ALC

1026A **ALDEN, ISABELLA** *(Pseud).*
ESTER RIED YET SPEAKING. BY PANSY. LONDON: S.W. PARTRIDGE & CO. (189–?). 320p. + 16p. pub. cat., 4p. ill. pub. cat. inside cover: front., 4 plates, ill. Bound in red cloth with coloured decorative cover and spine.
C 823.8 PAN

1027 **ALDEN, ISABELLA** *(Pseud).*
THREE PEOPLE. BY PANSY, AUTHOR OF "JESSIE WELLS", "ESTHER RIED", ETC. LONDON: S.W. PARTRIDGE AND CO., (189–?). 308p. + 16p. pub. cat.: front., 10 plates. Bound in blue cloth with coloured decorative cover and spine.
YSC 813.4 ALD

1028 **ALFRED IN INDIA.**
OR SCENES IN HINDOOSTAN. LONDON: W. & R. CHAMBERS, (188–?). 152p.: col. front., col. title page. Bound in green cloth with embossed cover, with inserted coloured vignette, and spine.
YSC 823.8 ALF

1029 **ALICE ERROLL AND OTHER TALES.**
LONDON: W. & R. CHAMBERS LTD., (188–?). 125p. + 1p. pub. cat.: front. Bound in red cloth with pictorial and decorative cover and decorative spine.
YSC 823.8 ALI

1030 **ALLEN, PHOEBE.**
THE BLACK WITCH OF HONEYCRITCH, BY PHOEBE ALLEN. . . . ILLUSTRATED, BY F. DADD. LONDON: SOCIETY FOR PROMOTING CHRISTIAN KNOWLEDGE, (188–?). 256p.: front., 2 plates. Bound in brown cloth with pictorial cover and spine, with gilt edges.
C 823.8 ALL

1031 **A.L.O.E.** *(Pseud).*
BATTLING WITH THE WORLD; OR, THE STORY OF THE ROBY FAMILY. A SEQUEL TO "THE GIANT KILLER; OR, THE BATTLE WHICH ALL MUST FIGHT." BY A.L.O.E. (A LADY OF ENGLAND, pseudonym for Charlotte Maria Tucker). LONDON: T. NELSON AND SONS, 1883. 167p.: front., 6 plates by Dalziel. Bound in green cloth with gilt edges.
C 823.8 ALO

1032 **A.L.O.E.** *(Pseud).*
CLAUDIA. A TALE. BY A.L.O.E. LONDON: THOMAS NELSON AND SONS, 1881. 301p.: front. by Dalziel. Bound in brown cloth with decorative cover and spine.
C 823.8 ALO

1033 **A.L.O.E.** *(Pseud).*
THE CORD OF LIFE. A Tale. BY A.L.O.E. LONDON: GALL AND INGLIS, (187–?). 60p.: front. Bound in orange cloth with embossed decorative design.
C 823.8 ALO

1034 **A.L.O.E.** *(Pseud).*
DRIVEN INTO EXILE, A Story of the Huguenots, BY A.L.O.E. LONDON: T. NELSON AND SONS, 1892. 212p.: front., additional vignette title page. Bound in blue cloth with pictorial cover.
C 823.8 ALO

1034A **A.L.O.E.** *(Pseud).*
FAIRY KNOW-A-BIT, OR, A NUTSHELL OF KNOWLEDGE. BY A.L.O.E. LONDON: T. NELSON AND SONS, 1868. 196p.: front., decorative title page, ill., index. Bound in green with embossed decorative cover and spine with gilt edges. Information given in fictional form on many topics listed in index from abolition of slavery to Worcester, Marquis of.
M 823 ALO CHILDREN'S COLLECTION

1035 **A.L.O.E.** *(Pseud).*
FLORA; OR, SELF-DECEPTION. BY A.L.O.E. LONDON: T. NELSON AND SONS, 1871. 182p. + 9p. pub. cat.: front., 5 plates, engraved by Dalziel Brothers. Bound in green cloth, with embossed decorative cover and spine, and gilt edges.
YSC 823.8 FLO

1036 **A.L.O.E.** *(Pseud).*
THE GIANT KILLER OR, THE BATTLE WHICH ALL MUST FIGHT. By A.L.O.E. LONDON: T. NELSON AND SONS, 1864. 165p. + 10p. pub. cat.: col. front. Bound in blue cloth with embossed decorative cover.
YSC 823.8 ALO

1037 **Another copy.**
WITH 40 ENGRAVINGS. LONDON: T. NELSON AND SONS, 1894. 201p.: front., 39 ill. by Dalziel. Bound in blue cloth, embossed with decorative pattern on cover and spine.
C 823.8 ALO

1038 **A.L.O.E.** *(Pseud).*
HAROLD HARTLEY, OR PICTURES OF ST. PAUL IN AN ENGLISH HOME, BY A.L.O.E. LONDON: GALL AND INGLIS, (188–?). 352p.: front., ill., 13 plates. Bound in blue cloth with pictorial cover and spine, gilt edges.
C 823.8 ALO

1039 **A.L.O.E.** *(Pseud).*
HOUSE BEAUTIFUL, OR, The Bible Museum, BY A.L.O.E. LONDON: T. NELSON AND SONS, 1868. 243p.: front., additional vignette title page. Bound in blue cloth with pictorial cover and spine.
C 823.8 ALO

1040 **A.L.O.E.** *(Pseud).*
Idols in the Hearth, A TALE (title page missing, title from cover) BY A.L.O.E. (LONDON: T. NELSON AND SONS), (188–?) 270p.: 6 plates by Dalziel. Bound in brown cloth with pictorial cover, decorative spine and gilt edges.
C 823.8 ALO

1041 **A.L.O.E.** *(Pseud).*
The Lost Jewel, A Tale. BY A.L.O.E. NEW EDITION, WITH ILLUSTRATIONS. LONDON: JOHN F. SHAW AND CO., (188–?). 206p.: front., 5 plates. The plates are engraved by W. Cheshire after A.H.C. Bound in olive cloth with coloured pictorial cover and spine.
C 823.8 ALO

1042 **A.L.O.E.** *(Pseud).*
THE MINE OR, DARKNESS AND LIGHT, BY A.L.O.E. LONDON: T. NELSON AND SONS, 1865. 192p.: front., additional vignette title page. Bound in green cloth with decorative cover and spine.
C 823.8 ALO

1043 **Another copy.**
1895. 175p. + 2p. pub. cat.: front., 4 plates by Dalziel. Bound in blue cloth with embossed decorative cover and spine.
YSC 823.8 ALO

1044 **A.L.O.E.** *(Pseud).*
MIRACLES OF HEAVENLY LOVE IN DAILY LIFE. BY A.L.O.E. WITH ILLUSTRATIONS. LONDON: T. NELSON AND SONS, 1888. VI, 176p.: front., 6 plates. Plates are engraved by various engravers after William Small. Bound in green cloth with pictorial cover and spine and gilt edges.
C 823.8 ALO

1045 **A.L.O.E.** *(Pseud).*
PICTURES OF ST. PETER IN AN ENGLISH HOME. BY A.L.O.E. LONDON: T. NELSON AND SONS, 1887. 429p.: front., 5 plates by S. Dore. Bound in blue cloth with pictorial cover and spine, and gilt edges.
C 823.8 ALO

1046 **A.L.O.E.** *(Pseud).*
THE RAMBLES OF A RAT. BY A.L.O.E. LONDON: T. NELSON AND SONS, 1885. 160p.: front., 5 plates by Dalziel. Bound in blue cloth with pictorial cover and spine, and gilt edges.
C 823.8 ALO

1047 **A.L.O.E.** *(Pseud).*
RESCUED FROM EGYPT, BY A.L.O.E. WITH TWENTY-SEVEN ENGRAVINGS. LONDON: T. NELSON AND SONS, 1883. VIII, 412p.: front., 26 ill., engraved by Dalziel. Bound in blue cloth with decorative cover and spine.
C 823.8 ALO

1048 **A.L.O.E.** *(Pseud).*
THE ROBBER'S CAVE. A TALE OF ITALY. BY A.L.O.E. LONDON: T. NELSON AND SONS, 1883. 200p.: front. Bound in brown cloth with pictorial cover and spine.
C 823.8 ALO

1049 **A.L.O.E.** *(Pseud).*
THE TINY RED NIGHT-CAP AND OTHER STORIES BY A.L.O.E. LONDON: T. NELSON AND SONS, 1833. 64p.: front. Bound in green cloth with embossed decorative cover including inserted coloured vignette.
YSC 823.8 ALO

1050 **A.L.O.E.** *(Pseud).*
THE TRIUMPH OVER MIDIAN. BY A.L.O.E. LONDON: T. NELSON AND SONS, 1871. 302p.: front., ill. by Dalziel. Bound in red cloth with decorative cover and spine.
C 823.8 ALO

1051 **Another copy.**
(189–?) 280p., front. by Dalziel, additional vignette title page. Bound in blue cloth embossed with decorative pattern on cover and spine.

1052 **A.L.O.E.** *(Pseud).*
WHISPERING UNSEEN; OR, "BE YE DOERS OF THE WORD, AND NOT HEARERS ONLY", BY A.L.O.E. LONDON: T. NELSON, 1881. 254p.: front., 3 plates. Bound in green cloth with decorative initials to title.
C 823.8 ALO

1052A **(ALSOP, ALFRED).**
DRIVEN FROM HOME AND OTHER LIFE STORIES, BY A DELVER. MANCHESTER: JOHN HEYWOOD, 1885. 124p.: front., 1 plate, ill. Bound in brown cloth with embossed pictorial cover and spine. Stories based on experiences in Wood St. Children's Mission, Manchester.
M 823.08 DEL CHILDREN'S COLLECTION

1052B **(ALSOP, ALFRED).**
FROM DARK TO LIGHT; OR, VOICES FROM THE SLUMS. BY A DELVER. MANCHESTER: JOHN HEYWOOD, 1882. 107p.: front., 3 plates. Bound in brown cloth with pictorial cover and spine. Stories based on experiences in Wood Street Children's Mission, Manchester.
M 823.08 DEL CHILDREN'S COLLECTION

1052C **(ALSOP, ALFRED).**
STREET CHILDREN SOUGHT AND FOUND; AND OTHER STORIES. BY A DELVER. MANCHESTER: JOHN HEYWOOD, 1884. 124p.: front., 1 plate, ill. Bound in green cloth with embossed pictorial cover. Based on experiences in Wood Street Children's Mission, Manchester.
M 823.08 DEL CHILDREN'S COLLECTION

1053 **ANDRÉ, R.**
EBB AND FLO: A Story of Home and Abroad. BY R. ANDRÉ. LONDON: FREDERICK WARNE AND CO., 1887. 124p.: front., vignette title page, 2 plates, ill. Bound in blue and brown cloth with pictorial cover and spine.
C 823.8 AND

1054 **ARCHIE'S CHANCES.**
AND The Child's Victory. LONDON: T. NELSON AND SONS, 1886. 141p. + 2p. pub. cat.: front., additional vignette title page. Bound in blue cloth with decorative cover and spine.
C 823.8 ARC

1055 **ARMSTRONG, JESSIE.**
DAN'S LITTLE GIRL. A Story by JESSIE ARMSTRONG. LONDON: THE RELIGIOUS TRACT SOCIETY, (189–?). 256p.: front., 3 plates, ill. by C.W. Bound in brown cloth with pictorial cover and spine.
C 823.8 ARM

1056 **ARTHUR, T.S.**
CEDARDALE; OR, THE PEACEMAKERS. A STORY OF VILLAGE LIFE. BY T.S. ARTHUR. U.S.A., PHILADELPHIA, 1869. 208p.: front., additional vignette title page, Arthur's Juvenile Library, 4 plates. Bound in red cloth.
C 813.4 ART

1057 **ARTHUR, T.S.**
HAVEN'T-TIME AND DON'T-BE-IN-A-HURRY, AND OTHER STORIES BY T.S. ARTHUR. WITH ILLUSTRATIONS FROM ORIGINAL DESIGNS BY CROOME. U.S.A., PHILADELPHIA: J.B. LIPPINCOTT AND CO., 1869. 153p.: front., additional vignette title page, Arthur's JUVENILE LIBRARY, 4 plates. Bound in red cloth.
C 813.4 ART

1058 **ARTHUR, T.S.**
THE LAST PENNY, AND OTHER STORIES. BY T.S. ARTHUR. WITH ILLUSTRATIONS FROM ORIGINAL DESIGNS BY CROOME. U.S.A., PHILADELPHIA: J.B. LIPPINCOTT AND CO., 1869. 153p.: front., additional vignette title page, Arthur's Juvenile Library, 4 plates. Bound in red cloth.
C 813.4 ART

1059 **ARTHUR, T.S.**
MAGGY'S BABY, AND OTHER STORIES. BY T.S. ARTHUR. WITH ILLUSTRATIONS FROM ORIGINAL DESIGNS BY CROOME. U.S.A., PHILADELPHIA: J.B. LIPPINCOTT AND CO., 1869. 153p.: front., additional vignette title page, Arthur's JUVENILE LIBRARY, 4 plates. Bound in red cloth.
C 813.4 ART

1060 **ARTHUR, T.S.**
OUR LITTLE HARRY, AND OTHER POEMS AND

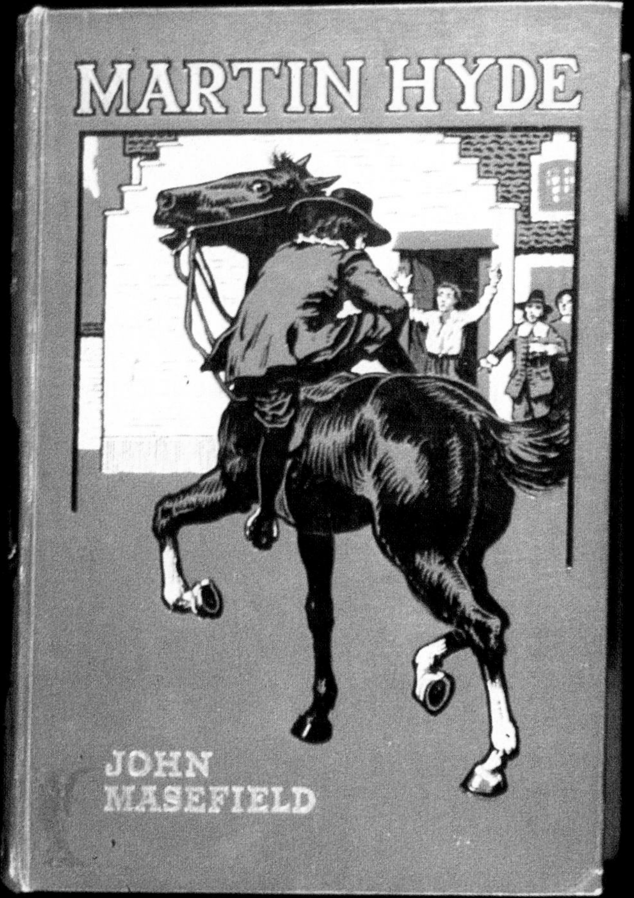
MARTIN HYDE
JOHN
MASEFIELD

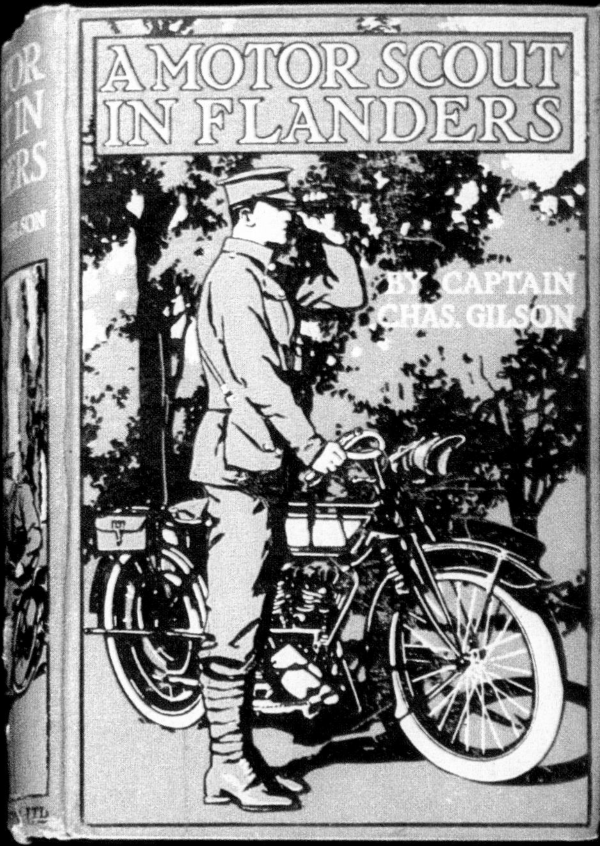
A MOTOR SCOUT
IN FLANDERS
BY CAPTAIN
CHAS. GILSON

ROSALY'S
NEW
SCHOOL
ELSIE
OXENHAM

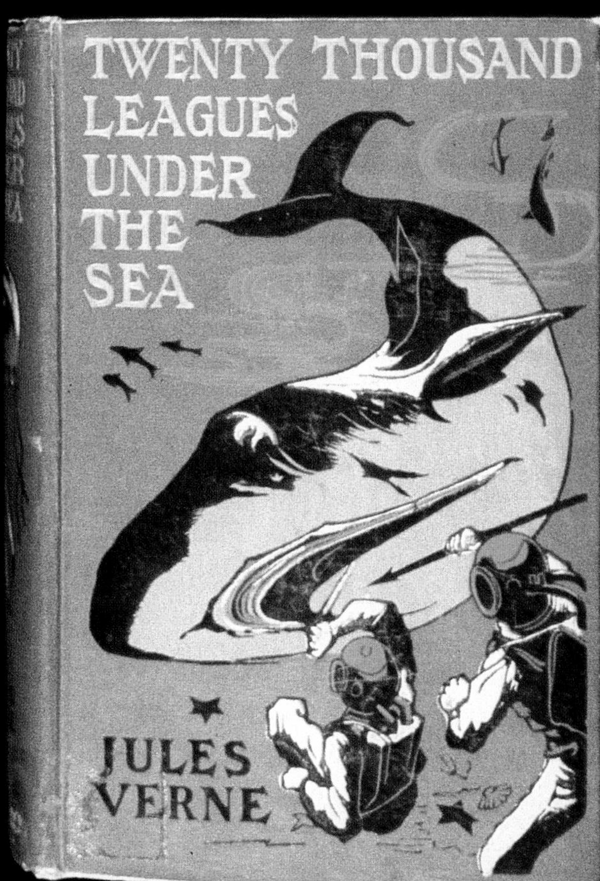
TWENTY THOUSAND
LEAGUES
UNDER
THE
SEA
JULES
VERNE

OUR DOG CARLO

THE

# CHILD'S COMPANION,

AND

JUVENILE INSTRUCTOR.

1861.

LONDON:
THE RELIGIOUS TRACT SOCIETY;
Instituted 1799.
SOLD AT THE DEPOSITORIES, 56, PATERNOSTER ROW; 65,
ST. PAUL'S CHURCHYARD; AND 164, PICCADILLY;
AND BY THE BOOKSELLERS.

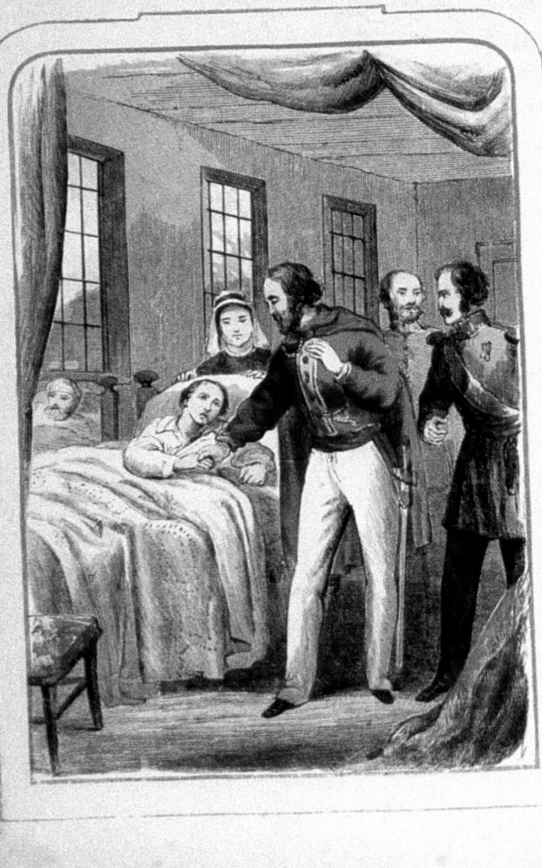

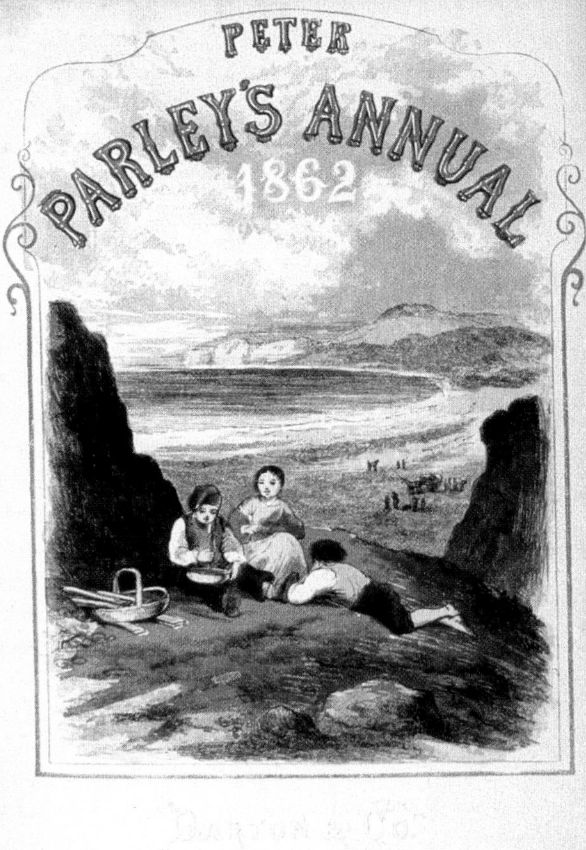


DARTON & CO.
HOLBORN HILL, LONDON.

STORIES. BY T.S. ARTHUR. WITH ILLUSTRATIONS FROM ORIGINAL DESIGNS BY CROOME. U.S.A., PHILADELPHIA: J.B. LIPPINCOTT AND CO., 1869. 152p.: front., additional vignette title page, Arthur's JUVENILE LIBRARY, 4 plates. Bound in red cloth.
C 813.4 ART

1061 **ARTHUR, T.S.**
PIERRE, THE ORGAN BOY, AND OTHER STORIES. BY T.S. ARTHUR, WITH ILLUSTRATIONS FROM ORIGINAL DESIGNS BY CROOME. U.S.A., PHILADELPHIA: J.B. LIPPINCOTT AND CO., 1869. 150p.: front., additional vignette title page, Arthur's JUVENILE LIBRARY, 4 plates. Bound in red cloth.
C 813.4 ART

1062 **ARTHUR, T.S.**
THE POOR WOODCUTTER, AND OTHER STORIES. BY T.S. ARTHUR. WITH ILLUSTRATIONS, FROM ORIGINAL DESIGNS, BY CROOME. HALIFAX: MILNER AND SOWERBY, 1859. 151p.: front., additional vignette title page, Arthur's JUVENILE LIBRARY, 4 plates. Bound in red cloth with pictorial cover and gilt edges.
C 813.4 ART

1063 **Another copy.**
U.S.A., PHILADELPHIA: J.B. LIPPINCOTT AND CO., 1869. 151p.: front., additional vignette title page, Arthur's JUVENILE LIBRARY, 4 plates. Bound in red cloth.

1064 **ARTHUR, T.S.**
TWENTY YEARS AGO AND NOW. A Book for Young Men and Women. BY T.S. ARTHUR. WAKEFIELD: WILLIAM NICHOLSON AND SONS, (187–?). 318p.: col. front. Bound in blue cloth with decorative cover and spine including pictorial insert.
C 813.4 ART

1065 **ARTHUR, T.S.**
UNCLE BEN'S NEW-YEAR'S GIFT, AND OTHER STORIES. BY T.S. ARTHUR. WITH ILLUSTRATIONS FROM ORIGINAL DESIGNS BY CROOME. U.S.A., PHILADELPHIA: J.B. LIPPINCOTT AND CO., 1869. 154p.: front., additional vignette title page, Arthur's JUVENILE LIBRARY, 4 plates. Bound in red cloth.
C 813.4 ART

1066 **ARTHUR, T.S.**
WHO IS GREATEST? AND OTHER STORIES. BY T.S. ARTHUR. WITH ILLUSTRATIONS, FROM ORIGINAL DESIGNS, BY CROOME. LONDON: MILNER AND COMPANY, (186–?). 151p.: front., additional pictorial title page, ARTHUR'S JUVENILE LIBRARY. HALIFAX, MILNER AND COMPANY, 4 plates. Bound in blue cloth with pictorial cover and gilt edges.
C 813.4 ART

1067 **ARTHUR, T.S.**
THE WOUNDED BOY, AND OTHER STORIES. BY T.S. ARTHUR. WITH ILLUSTRATIONS FROM ORIGINAL DESIGNS BY CROOME. U.S.A., PHILADELPHIA: J.B. LIPPINCOTT AND CO., 1869. 154p.: front., additional vignette title page, Arthur's JUVENILE LIBRARY, 4 plates. Bound in red cloth.
C 813.4 ART

1068 **ATKINSON, J.C.**
THE LAST OF THE GIANT KILLERS OR THE EXPLOITS OF SIR JACK OF DANBY DALE, BY REV. J.C. ATKINSON D.C.L. ILLUSTRATED EDITION. LONDON: MACMILLAN AND CO., 1893. VIII, 244p.: front., additional vignette title page, illustrated by Nelly Ericksen, 6 plates. Bound in light blue cloth with pictorial cover and spine.
C 823.8 ATK

1069 **ATKINSON, WILLIAM.**
WESTERN STORIES BY WILLIAM ATKINSON. LONDON: W. & R. CHAMBERS, 1893. 293p. + 36p. ill. pub. cat.: front., ill. by W.S. Stacey. Bound in brown cloth with decorative cover and spine.
C 813.4 ATK

1070 **ATTERIDGE, HELEN.**
"FOREMOST IF I CAN". BY HELEN ATTERIDGE. WITH ORIGINAL ILLUSTRATIONS BY GORDON BROWNE. LONDON: CASSELL AND COMPANY LIMITED, 1891. 208p. + 16p. pub. cat.: front., 3 plates. Bound in green cloth with decorative cover and spine. The "Golden Mottoes" series.
C 823.8 ATT

1071 **AVERY, CHARLES HAROLD.**
SOLDIERS OF THE QUEEN OR JACK FENLEIGH'S LUCK. A Story of the dash to Khartoum. LONDON: THOMAS NELSON AND SONS., 1898. 284p.: front., additional vignette title page, ill. by J. Williamson. Bound in blue cloth with pictorial cover and spine.
C 823.8 AVE

1072 **AVERY, CHARLES HAROLD.**
STOLEN OR STRAYED. BY HAROLD AVERY. LONDON: THOMAS NELSON AND SONS, 1899. 126p.: front., additional vignette title page, ill. by Arch. Webb. Bound in light blue cloth with pictorial cover and spine.
C 823.8 AVE

1073 **AVERY, CHARLES HAROLD.**
THE TRIPLE ALLIANCE. (BY) HAROLD AVERY. LONDON: THOMAS NELSON AND SONS LTD., 1899. 326p. + 4p. pub. cat.: col. front., 3 col. plates. Bound in brown cloth, with coloured, pictorial cover and spine. New Era Series.
C 823.8 AVE

1074 **B., M.C.**
JESSIE'S VISIT TO THE SUNNY BANK. A True Story. BY M.C.B. LONDON: THE RELIGIOUS TRACT SOCIETY, (188–?). 59p.: col. front., ill. Bound in brown cloth with coloured decorative cover. LITTLE DOT SERIES.
C 823.8 MCB

1075 **BAKER, SAMUEL W.**
CAST UP by the SEA. A Boy's Story, BY SIR SAMUEL W. BAKER, M.A., F.R.S., F.R.G.S. WITH ILLUSTRATIONS BY HUARD. NEW EDITION. LONDON: MACMILLAN AND CO., 1890. XIII, 456p. + 8p. pub. cat.: front., illustrated title page, 9 plates. Bound in green cloth with pictorial cover and spine. Originally published in 1868.
C 823.8 BAK

1076 **Another copy.**
LONDON: J.M. DENT AND SONS LTD., n.d. XXIII, 336p.: Everyman's Library edited by Ernest Rhys, for young people. Rebound.

1077 **BALFOUR, CLARA LUCAS.**
JOB TUFTON. A Story of Life Struggles. BY MRS. CLARA LUCAS BALFOUR. LONDON: NATIONAL TEMPERANCE PUBLICATION DEPOT. (189–?). 152p.: front. Bound in brown cloth with decorative cover.
C 823.8 BAL

1078 **BALFOUR, CLARA LUCAS.**
TWO CHRISTMAS DAYS; AND THE CHRISTMAS BOX. WITH ILLUSTRATIONS BY SIR J. GILBERT, HENRY ANELAY, ETC. BY MRS. C.L. BALFOUR. LONDON: S.W. PARTRIDGE AND CO., (188–?). 80p. + 8p. pub. cat.: front., 3 plates, ill. Bound in green cloth with embossed decorative cover with small inserted coloured pictorial paper label.
C 823.8 BAL

1079 **BALLANTYNE, ROBERT MICHAEL.**
AWAY IN THE WILDERNESS OR LIFE AMONG THE RED INDIANS AND FUR-TRADERS OF NORTH AMERICA. BY R.M. BALLANTYNE. LONDON: JAMES NISBET AND CO. LIMITED, (189–?). 127p.: front., additional vignette title page, 2 plates. Bound in green cloth with pictorial coloured cover and spine. Vol. 2 of Ballantyne's miscellany.
C 823.8 BAL

1080 **BALLANTYNE, ROBERT MICHAEL.**
THE BATTLE AND THE BREEZE OR THE FIGHTS AND FANCIES OF A BRITISH TAR. BY R.M. BALLANTYNE. LONDON: JAMES NISBET AND CO., (189–?). 124p. + 6p. pub. cat.: front., 2 plates. Bound in brown cloth with coloured pictorial cover and spine.
C 823.8 BAL

1080A **BALLANTYNE, ROBERT MICHAEL.**
BLOWN TO BITS, OR LONELY MAN OF RAKATA. A Tale of the Malay Archipelago. By R.M. Ballantyne. LONDON: JAMES NISBET AND CO., 1894. VII, 438p. + 72p. pub. cat.: front. and additional vignette title page, 3 plates. Bound in blue cloth with coloured pictorial cover and spine.
C 823.8 BAL

1081 **BALLANTYNE, ROBERT MICHAEL.**
BLUE LIGHT OR HOT WORK IN THE SOUDAN, A Tale of Soldier Life in several of its phases. BY R.M. BALLANTYNE. With Illustrations. LONDON: JAMES NISBET AND CO., (1888). VIII, 425p.: front., additional vignette title page, 4 plates by E. Giberne, engraved by Pearson. Bound in green cloth with coloured pictorial cover and spine.
C 823.8 BAL

1081A **BALLANTYNE, ROBERT MICHAEL.**
THE BUFFALO RUNNERS. A TALE OF THE RED RIVER PLAINS. BY R.M. BALLANTYNE. With Illustrations by the Author. LONDON: JAMES NISBET AND CO., (189–?). VIII, 416p. + 8p. pub. cat.: front., 2 plates. Bound in blue cloth with coloured pictorial cover and spine.
C 823.8 BAL

1082 **BALLANTYNE, ROBERT MICHAEL.**
THE CORAL ISLAND: A Tale of the Pacific Ocean. BY ROBERT MICHAEL BALLANTYNE. WITH ILLUSTRATIONS BY DALZIEL. LONDON: THOMAS NELSON AND SONS, 1884. 438p.: front., additional coloured vignette title page, 6 plates. Bound in green cloth with pictorial cover and spine in gold and red.
C 823.8 BAL

1083 **Another copy.**
1898. 336p. without text illustrations, bound in red cloth with decorative cover and spine, bearing series title R.M. BALLANTYNE'S BOOKS FOR BOYS.

1084 **Another copy.**
LONDON: J.M. DENT AND SONS, 1907. ix, 280p.: decorative title page. Rebound in brown leather and cloth (quarter leather). EVERYMAN'S LIBRARY FOR YOUNG PEOPLE No. 245.

1085 **BALLANTYNE, ROBERT MICHAEL.**
THE CREW OF THE WATER WAGTAIL, A STORY OF NEWFOUNDLAND. BY R.M. BALLANTYNE. LONDON: JAMES NISBET AND CO., (189–?). IV, 243p.: front., 3 plates by W. and J.R. Cheshire. Bound in brown cloth with coloured pictorial cover and spine.
C 823.8 BAL

1085A **BALLANTYNE, ROBERT MICHAEL.**
DEEP DOWN. A TALE OF THE CORNISH MINES. TWENTY SIXTH EDITION. LONDON: JAMES NISBET AND CO., LIMITED, (188–?). 420p. + 32p. pub. cat.: front., 3 plates by Arthur Twidle. Bound in blue cloth with coloured pictorial cover and spine. Originally published in 1868.
C 823.8 BAL

1085B **BALLANTYNE, ROBERT MICHAEL.**
DIGGING FOR GOLD, OR ADVENTURES IN CALIFORNIA. BY R.M. BALLANTYNE. LONDON: JAMES NISBET AND CO., LIMITED, (188–?). 124p. + 6p. pub. cat.: front., 2 plates. Incomplete. Bound in brown cloth with coloured pictorial cover and spine.
C 823.8 BAL

1086 **BALLANTYNE, ROBERT MICHAEL.**
THE DOG CRUSOE AND HIS MASTER. A Story of Adventure in the Western Prairies. By Robert Michael Ballantyne. WITH ILLUSTRATIONS. LONDON: NELSON AND SONS, 1890. 356p.: front., 4 plates in sepia, additional vignette title page. Bound in blue cloth, with pictorial cover and spine.
C 823.8 BAL

1087 **Another copy.**
New Edition, 1897, 336p.: without col. front. and partly different additional col. title page. Bound in brown cloth with pictorial cover and spine, including series title R.M. BALLANTYNE'S BOOKS FOR BOYS.

1088 **Another copy.**
BLACKIE AND SON LIMITED, (1910). 237p.: front., and 3 plates by R.B.M. Paxton.

1088A **BALLANTYNE, ROBERT MICHAEL.**
DUSTY DIAMONDS, CUT AND POLISHED, A TALE OF CITY-ARAB LIFE AND ADVENTURE. BY R.M. BALLANTYNE. LONDON: JAMES NISBET AND CO., 1884. VII, 430p. + 2p. pub. cat.: front., additional title page, 4 plates. Bound in red cloth with coloured pictorial cover and spine.
C 823.8 BAL

1088B **BALLANTYNE, ROBERT MICHAEL.**
THE EAGLE CLIFF. A Tale of the Western Isles. BY R.M. BALLANTYNE. LONDON: S.W. PARTRIDGE AND CO., (189–?). 320p. + 16p. pub. cat.: front., vignette on title page, 8 plates, ill. headpieces and tail pieces to chapters, by W.H.C. Groome. Bound in grey cloth with coloured pictorial cover and spine and decorative endpapers.
C 823.8 BAL

1088C **BALLANTYNE, ROBERT MICHAEL.**
FIGHTING THE FLAMES. A TALE OF THE LONDON FIRE BRIGADE. BY R.M. BALLANTYNE. LONDON: JAMES NISBET AND CO., (189–?). VII, 420p. + 10p. pub. cat.: col. front., 3 col. plates. Bound in red with coloured pictorial cover and spine.
C 823.8 BAL

1089 **BALLANTYNE, ROBERT MICHAEL.**
FIGHTING THE WHALES OR DOINGS AND DANGERS ON A FISHING CRUISE. BY R.M. BALLANTYNE. LONDON: JAMES NISBET AND CO., (189–?). 126p. + 32p. pub. cat.: front., additional vignette title page, BALLANTYNE'S MISCELLANY, 2 plates. Bound in blue cloth with coloured pictorial cover and spine.
C 823.8 BAL

1090 **Another copy.**
In a smaller format, 124p., bound in red cloth with decorative cover and spine.

1090A **BALLANTYNE, ROBERT MICHAEL.**
THE FLOATING LIGHT OF THE GOODWIN SANDS. BY R.M. BALLANTYNE. With illustrations by the author. LONDON: JAMES NISBET AND CO., LIMITED, (189–?). 403p. + 32p. pub. cat.: front, 3 plates. Bound in blue cloth with coloured decorative cover and spine. Originally published in 1870.
M 823 BAL CHILDREN'S COLLECTION

1091 **BALLANTYNE, ROBERT MICHAEL.**
THE FUGITIVES OR THE TYRANT QUEEN OF MADAGASCAR. BY R.M. BALLANTYNE. With Illustrations. LONDON: JAMES NISBET AND CO., (189–?). VII, 431p. + 32p. pub. cat.: front., vignette title page. 4 plates. Bound in olive cloth with coloured pictorial cover and spine.
C 823.8 BAL

1092 **BALLANTYNE, ROBERT MICHAEL.**
THE GARRET AND THE GARDEN, or, Low Life High Up AND JEFF BENSON, or, The Young Coastguardsman. BY R.M. BALLANTYNE. WITH ILLUSTRATIONS. LONDON: JAMES NISBET AND CO., (189–?). IV, 260p.

+ 32p. pub. cat.: front. 3 plates by Frederic W. Burton. Bound in brown cloth with pictorial cover and spine.
C 823.8 BAL

1093 **BALLANTYNE, ROBERT MICHAEL.**
THE HOT SWAMP, A ROMANCE OF OLD ALBION. BY R.M. BALLANTYNE. With Illustrations. LONDON: JAMES NISBET AND CO., 1892. VI, 408p. + 7p. pub. cat.: front., vignette title page by Frederic W. Burton. Bound in yellow cloth with pictorial coloured cover and spine.
C 823.8 BAL

1094 **BALLANTYNE, ROBERT MICHAEL.**
LIFE IN THE RED BRIGADE. A Fairy Tale. AND FORT DESOLATION OR Solitude in the Wilderness. BY R.M. BALLANTYNE WITH ILLUSTRATIONS. LONDON: JAMES NISBET AND CO., (189–?). 241p.: front., 3 plates by Lawton. Bound in red cloth with coloured pictorial cover and spine.
C 823.8 BAL

1095 **BALLANTYNE, ROBERT MICHAEL.**
THE LIVELY POLL: A TALE OF THE NORTH SEA. BY R.M. BALLANTYNE. LONDON: JAMES NISBET AND CO., 1886. 164p.: front., vignette title page, BALLANTYNE'S MISCELLANY, ill. Bound in blue cloth with decorative cover and spine.
C 823.8 BAL

1096 **BALLANTYNE, ROBERT MICHAEL.**
LOST IN THE FOREST OR WANDERING WILL'S ADVENTURES IN SOUTH AMERICA. BY R.M. BALLANTYNE. LONDON: JAMES NISBET AND CO., 1880. 126p.: front., vignette title page, BALLANTYNE'S MISCELLANY, 2 plates. Bound in red cloth with coloured vignette inserted.
C 823.8 BAL

1096A **BALLANTYNE, ROBERT MICHAEL.**
THE MADMAN AND THE PIRATE. BY R.M. BALLANTYNE. LONDON: JAMES NISBET AND CO. LIMITED, (189–?). 256p. + 2p. pub. cat.: front., 6 plates. Bound in red cloth with coloured pictorial cover and spine.
C 823.8 BAL

1097 **BALLANTYNE, ROBERT MICHAEL.**
THE MIDDY AND THE MOORS. AN ALGERINE STORY, BY R.M. BALLANTYNE, With Illustrations. LONDON: JAMES NISBET AND CO., (1888). VIII, 242p.: front., by Henry Austin, ill. by W.S. Stacey. Bound in red cloth with pictorial cover and spine.
C 823.8 BAL

1098 **BALLANTYNE, ROBERT MICHAEL.**
THE NORSEMEN IN THE WEST OF AMERICA BEFORE COLUMBUS, A Tale. BY R.M. BALLANTYNE. With Illustrations. LONDON: JAMES NISBET AND CO., (188–?). VI, 406p.: front., additional vignette title page, 4 plates by Pearson. Bound in blue cloth with pictorial coloured cover and spine. Reprint of original 1873 edition.
C 823.8 BAL

1098A **BALLANTYNE, ROBERT MICHAEL.**
POST HASTE, A TALE OF HER MAJESTY'S MAILS, BY R.M. BALLANTYNE. LONDON: JAMES NISBET & CO., 1880. VII, 424p. + 16p. pub. cat.: additional vignette title page, engraved by Pearson, 4 plates. Bound in blue cloth with embossed title and vignette on cover.
C 823.8 BAL

1098B **BALLANTYNE, ROBERT MICHAEL.**
THE RED ERIC, OR THE WHALER'S LAST CRUISE. BY R.M. BALLANTYNE. LONDON: JAMES NISBET AND CO. LIMITED, (189–?). VII, 400p. + 1p. pub. cat.: front., 7 plates by Dalziel. Bound in red cloth with decorative cover and spine.
C 823.8 BAL

1099 **BALLANTYNE, ROBERT MICHAEL.**
THE RED MAN'S REVENGE. A Tale of THE RED RIVER FLOOD. BY R.M. BALLANTYNE. With Illustrations. LONDON: JAMES NISBET AND CO., (189–?). VIII, 264p. + 16p. pub. cat.: front., 3 plates, ill. Bound in red cloth with coloured pictorial cover and spine. First published 1880.
C 823.8 BAL

1100 **BALLANTYNE, ROBERT MICHAEL.**
Saved by the lifeboat. A TALE OF WRECK AND RESCUE ON THE COAST. VOL. VIII OF BALLANTYNE'S MISCELLANY. WITH ILLUSTRATIONS. JAMES NISBET AND CO., 1873. 124p.: front., vignette title page, 3 plates. Bound in purple cloth with decorative cover and spine.
C 823.8 BAL

1101 **BALLANTYNE, ROBERT MICHAEL.**
THE THOROGOOD FAMILY. BY R.M. BALLANTYNE LONDON: JAMES NISBET AND CO., LIMITED, (189–?). 112p. + 16p. pub. cat.: front., 3 plates. Bound in red cloth with pictorial cover and spine.
C 823.8 BAL

1102 **Another copy.**
(189–?) 112p. + 16p. pub. cat.: front., vignette title page, BALLANTYNE'S MISCELLANY, 2 plates. Bound in blue cloth with coloured pictorial cover and spine.

1104 **BALLANTYNE, ROBERT MICHAEL.**
UNGANA: A TALE OF ESQUIMAUX-LAND. BY ROBERT MICHAEL BALLANTYNE. With Illustrations by the Author. LONDON: T. NELSON AND SONS, 1868. 509p. + 2p. pub. cat.: front. engraved by Dalziel, additional vignette title page, 6 plates. Bound in green cloth with pictorial spine.
C 823.8 BAL

1104A **Another copy.**
NEW EDITION. T. NELSON AND SONS, 1899. 393p.: col. front. additional coloured vignette title page. 4 plates by Dalziel. Bound in blue cloth with pictorial cover and spine in gold and red.

1105 **BALLANTYNE, ROBERT MICHAEL.**
THE WALRUS HUNTERS, A ROMANCE OF THE REALMS OF ICE. BY R.M. BALLANTYNE. WITH ILLUSTRATIONS. FOURTH EDITION. LONDON: JAMES NISBET AND CO., (1893). VIII, 410p. + 12p. pub. cat.: front., plates by TWB.
C 823.8 BAL

1106 **BALLANTYNE, ROBERT MICHAEL.**
THE WORLD OF ICE OR The Whaling Cruise of "The Dolphin" AND The Adventures of Her Crew in the Polar Regions. By Robert Michael Ballantyne. NEW EDITION. LONDON: T. NELSON AND SONS, 1897. VIII, 327p.: col. front., additional col. vignette title page. Bound in grey/green cloth with pictorial cover and spine, including series title R.M. BALLANTYNE'S BOOKS FOR BOYS.
C 823.8 BAL

1107 **Another copy.**
1909. VIII, 327p. + 9p. pub. cat.: col. front., 7 col. plates by W.H.C. Groome. Bound in blue cloth, with coloured pictorial cover and spine.

1108 **BALLANTYNE, ROBERT MICHAEL.**
THE YOUNG FUR-TRADERS OR Snowflakes and Sunbeams from the Far North. By Robert Michael Ballantyne. NEW EDITION. LONDON: T. NELSON AND SONS, 1897. 402p.: col. front., additional col. vignette title page. Bound in red cloth with pictorial cover and spine, including series title R.M. BALLANTYNE'S BOOKS FOR BOYS. Originally published 1856.
C 823.9 BAL

1109 **Another copy.**
(191–?). 296p. with col. front. and 6 col. plates by W.H.C. Groome bound in blue cloth with decorative cover and spine.

1110 **Another copy.**
LONDON: JOHN F. SHAW AND CO. (191–?). 318p.: col. front. Bound in blue cloth with embossed decorative cover and spine.
YSC 823.8 BAL

1111 **BAMFORD, JOHN M.**
ELIAS POWER, OR EASE-IN-ZION. BY JOHN M. BAMFORD. LONDON: CHARLES H. KELLY, 1891. 220p.: front., pictorial chapter headings. Bound in blue cloth with pictorial cover and spine in gold and black, gilt edges.
C 823.8 BAM

1112 **BANKS, MRS. G. LINNAEUS.**
MORE THAN CORONETS. BY MRS. G. LINNAEUS BANKS. ILLUSTRATED BY J. COPLESTON AND G.G. BANKS. MANCHESTER: ABEL HEYWOOD AND SON, 1882. VI, 270p. + 16p. pub. cat.: front., vignette on title page. Bound in red cloth with decorative cover and spine.
YSC 823.8 BAN

1113 **BARKER, LUCY D. SALE.**
THOSE BOYS. BY MRS. SALE BARKER. WITH ILLUSTRATIONS. LONDON: GEORGE ROUTLEDGE AND SONS, LIMITED. (189–?). 80p.: front., vignette on title page, 40 plates. Bound with cloth spine with coloured pictorial paper covers.
C 823.8 BAR

1114 **BARSTOW, CHARLES H.**
OLD RANSOM; OR Light after Darkness. A STORY OF STREET LIFE. BY CHARLES H. BARSTOW. WITH ORIGINAL ILLUSTRATIONS. LONDON: FREDERICK WARNE AND CO., (188–?). 86p.: front., 2 plates, ill. Bound in olive cloth with decorative cover.
C 823.8 BAR

1115 **BATTERSBY, T. PRESTON.**
THE GARDEN OF CYMODOCE. BY T. PRESTON BATTERSBY. LONDON: GEORGE CAUDWELL, (189–?). 121p. + 22p. ill. pub. cat.: front., decorative chapter headings, 2 plates. Bound in blue cloth with coloured pictorial cover and spine.
C 823.8 BAT

1117 **BELL, CATHERINE DOUGLAS.**
MARY ELLIOT: OR, KINDNESS OF HEART. BY CATHERINE D. BELL. WITH ILLUSTRATIONS. New Edition. LONDON: FREDERICK WARNE AND CO., (187–?). 242p. + 6p. pub. cat.: col. front., additional col. title page. Bound in green cloth with embossed decorative cover and spine. Home Circle Library.
C 823.8 BEL

1118 **BESANT, WALTER.**
THE GOLDEN BUTTERFLY. A NOVEL BY WALTER BESANT AND JAMES RICE. A NEW EDITION. LONDON: CHATTO & WINDUS, 1895. 170p. + 1p. pub. cat.: vignette on title page. Printed in 2 columns. Bound in brown cloth.
YSC 823.8 BES

1119 **BETHAM-EDWARDS, M.**
CHARLIE AND ERNEST; OR, PLAY AND WORK. A STORY OF HAZLEHURST SCHOOL. BY M. BETHAM-EDWARDS. WITH ORIGINAL ILLUSTRATIONS BY W. GUNSTON. LONDON: FREDERICK WARNE AND CO., (188–?). 188p.: front., 3 plates. Bound in brown cloth with decorative cover and spine, with gilt edges. Originally published in 1859.
C 823.8 BET

1120 **BEVAN, TOM.**
WHITE IVORY AND BLACK. A Tale of the Zambesi Basin AND OTHER STORIES BY TOM BEVAN, E. HARCOURT BURRAGE, AND JOHN A. HIGGINSON. LONDON: S.W. PARTRIDGE AND CO., (189–?). 320p. + 24p. ill. pub. cat.: front. Bound in blue with coloured pictorial cover and spine. Includes also the Man who found Klondyke, by E. Harcourt Burrage, and the Adventures of Norman Pawle, by John A. Higginson.
C 823.8 BEV

1121 **BIRLEY, CAROLINE.**
WE ARE SEVEN. BY CAROLINE BIRLEY. ILLUSTRATED BY T. PYM. LONDON: WELLS GARDNER, DARTON & CO., SECOND EDITION (1870). 136p.: front., vignette on title page, 2 plates. Bound in red cloth with coloured pictorial cover.
M 823 BIR CHILDRENS COLLECTION

1121A **Another copy.**
THIRD EDITION, 1880. 136p.: 2 plates.
YSC 823.8 BIR

1122 **THE BLIND BOY OF DRESDEN AND HIS SISTER.**
A STORY FOR THE YOUNG. LONDON: BLACKIE AND SON., (188–?). 128p.: col. front., vignette on title page. Bound in green cloth with decorative cover and spine.
C 823.8 BLI

1123 **BLACK, M.M.**
A WOMAN AND PITIFUL, A Deeside Story. BY M.M. BLACK. EDINBURGH: OLIPHANT, ANDERSON AND FERRIER, 1893. 190p.: front., by Cheshire. Bound in blue cloth with pictorial cover and spine.
C 823.8 BLA

1124 **BOB THE SHOEBLACK AND AMONG THE WOLVES.**
ILLUSTRATED. LONDON: SUNDAY SCHOOL UNION, (188–?). 64p.: front., 4 plates. Bound in olive cloth with decorative cover.
C 823.8 BOB

1125 **A BOOK OF THE HOUSEHOLD.**
A True Briton, and other Tales. LONDON: JARROLD AND SONS, (187–?). 32p., 32p., 32p., 32p., 32p., + 6p. pub. cat.: col. front. Bound in brown cloth with decorative cover and spine.
C 823.8 TRU

1126 **BOULTWOOD, HARRIETT.**
CECIL ARLINGTON'S QUEST. A Story. THIRD EDITION. LONDON: JARROLD AND SONS, 1898. 142p. + 20p. ill. pub. cat.: front. Bound in blue cloth with decorative cover and spine.
C 823.8 BOU

1127 **BOWEN, C.E.**
CHRISTIAN HATHERLEY'S CHILDHOOD. A Tale. BY C.E.B., AUTHOR OF "WORK FOR ALL", "RICH AND POOR", ETC. WITH FOUR ILLUSTRATIONS. SEELEY, JACKSON, AND HALLIDAY, 1872. 165p. + 6p. pub. cat.: front., 3 plates by F. Gilbert, engraved by J.S. Dalziel. Bound in blue cloth with embossed decoration and label on cover and decorative spine.
YSC 823.8 BOW

1128 **BOY AND MAN.**
A Story for Young and Old. LONDON: THE RELIGIOUS TRACT SOCIETY, (1880). 339p. + 4p. pub. cat.: front., vignette on title page, 12 plates. Bound in green cloth with pictorial cover and spine.
C 823.8 BOY

1129 **BRAMSTON, MARY.**
EVERINGHAM GIRLS. BY M. BRAMSTON. ILLUSTRATED BY J. NASH. LONDON: SOCIETY FOR PROMOTING CHRISTIAN KNOWLEDGE, (189–?). 220p. + 4p. pub. cat.: front., 2 plates. Bound in green cloth with pictorial cover.
C 823.8 BRA

1130 **BRAMSTON, MARY.**
HOME AND SCHOOL: A Story for School Girls. SEQUEL TO "THE SNOWBALL SOCIETY"., BY M. BRAMSTON. ILLUSTRATED BY ALFRED PEARSE. LONDON: SOCIETY FOR PROMOTING CHRISTIAN KNOWLEDGE, (189–?). 255p. + 8p. pub. cat.: front., 3 plates. Bound in blue with coloured pictorial cover and spine.
C 823.8 BRA

1131 **BRAMSTON, MARY.**
ROSAMOND'S GIRLS: A SCHOOL STORY. BY M. BRAMSTON. ILLUSTRATED BY HAROLD PIFFARD.

LONDON: SOCIETY FOR PROMOTING CHRISTIAN KNOWLEDGE, (189–?). 224p. + 16p. pub. cat.: front. Bound in brown cloth with coloured pictorial cover and decorative spine.
YSC 823.8 BRA

1132 **BRAMSTON, MARY.**
THE SNOWBALL SOCIETY: A story for children BY M. BRAMSTON. LONDON: SOCIETY FOR PROMOTING CHRISTIAN KNOWLEDGE, (187–?). 251p. + 4p. pub. cat.: front., 1 plate, 1 ill. Bound in blue cloth with decorative cover and spine.
YSC 823.8 BRA

1133 **BRAVE BASTIA.**
OR, THE THREAD OF GOLD BY THE AUTHOR OF "MY GRANDMOTHER'S MONKEYS," ETC. LONDON: S.W. PARTRIDGE AND CO., (187–?). 104p.: front., by Dalziel. Bound in brown cloth.
C 823.8 BRA

1134 **BRETT, EDWIN J.**
EDWIN J. BRETT'S HARKAWAY SERIES OF STORIES VOLUME I CONTAINING JACK HARKAWAY'S SCHOOLDAYS, COMPLETE, WITH NUMEROUS ILLUSTRATIONS AND COLOURED PLATES. LONDON: EDWIN J. BRETT, 1877. 192p., 3 col. plates, 14 plates. Rebound in same volume. JACK HARKAWAY. After Schooldays: HIS ADVENTURES AFLOAT AND ASHORE., 1878. 313p., plates, some col., and JACK HARKAWAY AT OXFORD. 1878. 319p., plates, and JACK HARKAWAY AMONG THE BRIGANDS. Rebound in Vol 2. JACK HARKAWAY AND HIS SON'S ADVENTURES ROUND THE WORLD. BEAUTIFULLY ILLUSTRATED. VOLUME II. LONDON: BOYS OF ENGLAND OFFICE, 1879. 277p., plates, and JACK HARKAWAY AND HIS SON'S ADVENTURES. 596p., plates, and YOUNG JACK HARKAWAY AND HIS BOY TINKER. 276p. plates.
C 823.8 BRE

1135 **BROAD, C.E.**
MARY LORN: THE STORY OF AN OCEAN WAIF. A Tale for the Young. BY C.E. BROAD. GLASGOW: JOHN S. MARR AND SONS, (187–?). 128p. front., 2 plates. Bound in blue cloth with pictorial cover and spine.
C 823.8 BRO

1136 **BRODERIP, FRANCES FREELING.**
TALES OF THE TOYS, TOLD BY THEMSELVES. BY FRANCES FREELING BRODERIP. With Illustrations by Tom Hood. LONDON: GRIFFITH AND FARRAN, 1869. 220p. + 32p. pub. cat.: col. front., 3 col. plates engraved by Ferrier. Bound in blue cloth with decorative cover and spine and gilt edges.
C 823.8 BRO

1137 **BROWNE, FRANCES.**
THE ORPHANS OF ELFHOLM, AND OTHER STORIES BY FRANCES BROWNE. CONTAINING . . . THE POOR COUSIN. THE YOUNG FORESTERS. LONDON: GROOMBRIDGE AND SONS, (186–?). 6 plates, ill. Bound in purple cloth.
C 823.8 BRO

1138 **BUNYAN, JOHN.**
THE PILGRIM'S PROGRESS AND THE HOLY WAR. BY JOHN BUNYAN. A LARGE TYPE EDITION WITH ILLUSTRATIONS. LONDON: FREDERICK WARNE AND CO., (189–?). XVIII, 678p.: front., 11 plates by Dalziel, ill. Bound in brown cloth with pictorial cover and spine.
C 823.8 BUN

1139 **BUNYAN, JOHN.**
THE PILGRIM'S PROGRESS, FROM THIS WORLD TO THAT WHICH IS TO COME. BY JOHN BUNYAN. WITH NOTES BY THE REV. ROBERT MAGUIRE, M.A. Illustrated by H.C. SELOUS, Esq., and M. PAOLO PRIOLO. LONDON: CASSELL, PETTER, AND GALPIN, (189–?). XVI, 399p.: front., 48 plates, ill. Half bound in black leather, with embossed decorative spine. Originally published 1678.
YOSC 244 BUN

1140 **BUNYAN, JOHN.**
THE PILGRIM'S PROGRESS FROM THIS WORLD TO THAT WHICH IS TO COME DELIVERED UNDER THE SIMILITUDE OF A DREAM BY JOHN BUNYAN. WITH EIGHT COLOURED ILLUSTRATIONS BY HAROLD COPPING. LONDON: THE RELIGIOUS TRACT SOCIETY, (190–?). 320p.: col. front., 7 col. plates. Bound in brown cloth with coloured pictorial cover and spine.
C 823.4 BUN

1141 **Another copy.**
With 16 additional plates, bound in blue cloth with decorative cover and spine, including inserted coloured vignette, with gilt edges.

1142 **BUNYAN, JOHN.**
THE Pilgrim's Progress. By John Bunyan. with an Introduction by the Right Rev. Handley C.O. Moule, D.D., Lord Bishop of Durham. Illustrated by Walter Paget. LONDON: ERNEST NISTER, (190–?). 348p.: col. front., 4 col. plates, 12 plates, ill. Bound in green cloth with coloured pictorial cover and spine.
C 823.4 BUN

1143 **Another copy.**
ILLUSTRATED WITH 25 DRAWINGS ON WOOD BY GEORGE CRUIKSHANK FROM THE COLLECTION OF EDWIN TRUMAN. HENRY FROWDE OXFORD UNIVERSITY PRESS, 1904. 338p. front., plates, ill. Bound in blue cloth with pictorial cover and spine.
C 823.4 BUN

1144 **BUNYAN, JOHN.**
A TRUE RELATION OF THE HOLY WAR MADE BY King Shaddai upon Diabolus, FOR THE REGAINING OF THE METROPOLIS OF THE WORLD; OR, THE LOSING AND TAKING AGAIN OF THE TOWN OF MANSOUL. BY JOHN BUNYAN. ILLUSTRATED WITH THE AUTHOR'S OWN REFERENCES, AND EXPLANATORY NOTES BY W. MASON. LONDON: MILNER AND COMPANY, LIMITED, (188–?). 416p. + pub. cat.: front., engraved by Banks and Co., vignette title page. Bound in red cloth. Miniature edition.
C 823.4 BUN

1145 **Another copy.**
With Illustrations Printed in Colours. LONDON: FREDERICK WARNE AND CO. (188–?). 223p. + 27p. pub. cat.: col. front., 12 col plates. Bound in green cloth with decorative cover and spine. Warne's National Books on spine.
C 823.4 BUN

1146 **BURCH, FLORENCE E.**
TWO LITTLE FORTUNE-HUNTERS OR WHERE DUTY CALLS. BY FLORENCE E. BURCH. LONDON: THE RELIGIOUS TRACT SOCIETY, (189–?). 127p. + 16p. pub. cat.: front., 2 plates, ill., by J.F.W. and Ferrier. Bound in blue cloth with coloured pictorial cover and spine.
C 823.8 BUR

1147 **BURCH, HARRIETTE E.**
LALLY THE HOP-PITCHER OR GATHERED IN. BY HARRIETTE E. BURCH. THE RELIGIOUS TRACT SOCIETY, (189–?). 80p.: col. front. Bound in brown cloth with coloured decorative cover and spine.
C 823.8 BUR

1148 **BURNETT, FRANCES HODGSON.**
THE CAPTAIN'S YOUNGEST, PICCINO AND OTHER CHILD STORIES. BY FRANCES HODGSON BURNETT. LONDON: FREDERICK WARNE AND CO., 1894. VIII, 183p.: front., 14 plates by Reginald B. Birch. Bound in brown cloth with decorative cover and spine. Includes How Fauntleroy occurred and Little Betty Kitten tells her story.
C 813.4 BUR and YSC 813.4 BUR

1149 **BURNETT, FRANCES HODGSON.**
DOLLY. A LOVE STORY. BY FRANCES HODGSON BURNETT. WITH ILLUSTRATIONS BY HAL LUDLOW. LONDON: FREDERICK WARNE AND CO., 1892. IX, 324p.: front., 7 plates, ill. Bound in brown cloth with coloured pictorial cover and spine.
C 813.4 BUR

1150 **BURNETT, FRANCES HODGSON.**
LITTLE LORD FAUNTLEROY. BY FRANCES HODGSON BURNETT. LONDON: FREDERICK WARNE AND CO., 1893. XI, 267p. + 6p. ill. pub. cat.: front., 9 plates, ill. Bound in green cloth with black pictorial cover and spine. Illustrated from drawings by Reginald B. Birch. Originally published 1885.
YSC 813.4 BUR and C 813.4 BUR
Another copy.
1902 XI, 269p. + 6p. ill. pub. cat.: front., 12 plates, ill. Bound in brown cloth with black pictorial cover and spine. Some plates coloured by previous owners of book.

1151 **BURNETT, FRANCES HODGSON.**
LITTLE SAINT ELIZABETH AND OTHER STORIES. BY FRANCES HODGSON BURNETT. ILLUSTRATED BY R.B. BIRCH, ALFRED BRENNAN AND O.A. LONDON: FREDERICK WARNE AND CO. 1890. 189p.: front., 15 plates, ill. Bound in brown cloth, with coloured pictorial cover and spine. Includes the story of Prince Fairy-foot. The proud little Grain of Wheat, Behind the white brick.
C 813.4 BUR

1152 **BURNETT, FRANCES HODGSON.**
THE ONE I KNEW THE BEST OF ALL. BY MRS. F.H. BURNETT. WITH ILLUSTRATIONS BY REGINALD BIRCH. LONDON: FREDERICK WARNE AND CO., (1893). XV, 292p. + 12p. pub. cat.: front., ill. Bound in grey cloth with pictorial cover and spine.
C 813 4 BUR
Another copy.
Facsimile edition 1974 of 1893 edition. XV, 292p.: front., vignette title page, ill. Bound in pink cloth.
YSC 813.4 BUR

1153 **BURNETT, FRANCES HODGSON.**
SARA CREWE OR WHAT HAPPENED AT MISS MIN-CHIN'S AND EDITHA'S BURGLAR. BY FRANCES HODGSON BURNETT. LONDON: FREDERICK WARNE AND CO., (1888). 159p.: front., 14 plates by Reginald B. Birch. Bound in blue cloth with pictorial cover and spine.
C 813.4 BUR

1154 **CALLWELL, J.M.**
THE SQUIRE'S GRANDSON: A DEVONSHIRE STORY. BY J.M. CALLWELL. ILLUSTRATED. LONDON: BLACKIE AND SON, 1888. 192p. + 32p. pub. cat.: front., 2 plates. Bound in blue cloth with pictorial cover and spine.
C 823.8 CAL

1155 **CAMERON, VERNEY LOVETT.**
IN SAVAGE AFRICA OR, The Adventures of Frank Baldwin From the Gold Coast to Zanzibar. BY VERNEY LOVETT CAMERON C.B., D.C.L. WITH THIRTY TWO ILLUS-TRATIONS. LONDON: T. NELSON AND SONS, 1887. 359p.: front., additional vignette title page, 30 plates. Bound in brown cloth with coloured pictorial cover and spine.
C 823.8 CAM

1156 **CAMERON, VERNEY LOVETT.**
JACK HOOPER. His Adventure at Sea and in South Africa. BY VERNEY LOVETT CAMERON C.B., D.C.L. WITH 23 FULL-PAGE ILLUSTRATIONS. LONDON: T. NELSON AND SONS, 1887. 348p. + 2p. pub. cat.: front., additional vignette title page, 21 plates. Bound in red cloth with pictorial cover and spine, inscribed THE LIBRARY OF TRAVEL AND ADVENTURE.
C 823.8 CAM

1157 **CAMPBELL, C.C.**
HOME FOR THE HOLIDAYS. BY MRS. C.C. CAMPBELL. WITH TWENTY ILLUSTRATIONS. LONDON: T. NELSON AND SONS, 1888. 216p. + 8p. pub. cat.: front., additional vignette title page, 17 plates.
C 823.8 CAM

1157A **CAMPBELL, WALTER DOUGLAS.**
BEYOND THE BORDER. BY WALTER DOUGLAS CAMPBELL. WITH 167 ILLUSTRATIONS BY HELEN STRATTON. LONDON: ARCHIBALD CONSTABLE AND CO., 1898. 455p. + 16p. pub. cat.: vignette on title page, 38 plates, ill. Bound in blue cloth with embossed pictorial/decorative cover and spine, with gilt edges.
C 823.8 CAM

1158 **A CANDLE LIGHTED BY THE LORD.**
A Life Story for the Old and the Young, and the Rich and the Poor. WITH TWENTY FOUR ILLUSTRATIONS. BELFAST: WILLIAM MULLAN AND SON, 1877. 228p. + 6p. ill. pub. cat.: ill. by Dalziel Brothers. Bound in brown cloth, with pictorial cover and spine.
YSC 823.8 CAN

1159 **Another copy.**
1887. 228p.: front., 7 plates, ill. by Dalziel Brothers. Bound in brown cloth, with pictorial cover and spine.
C 823.8 CAN

1160 **CAPES, HARRIET M.**
A CHANGE FOR THE WORSE: OR, THE LESSON OF A DAY. BY HARRIET M. CAPES. LONDON: BLACKIE AND SON, LIMITED, (189–?). 127p. + 8p. pub. cat.: sepia front. Bound in brown cloth with decorative cover and spine.
C 823.8 CAP

1161 **CAREW, MAUD.**
LITTLE KING RICHARD, BY MAUD CAREW. ILLUS-TRATED BY W.S. STACEY. LONDON: SOCIETY FOR PROMOTING CHRISTIAN KNOWLEDGE, (189–?). 256p. + 32p. pub. cat.: front., 2 plates. Bound in olive cloth with pictorial cover.
C 823.8 CAR

1162 **CARRINGTON, EDITH.**
COUSIN CATHERINE'S SERVANTS. BY EDITH CAR-RINGTON. WITH ILLUSTRATIONS BY W. WEEKES. LONDON: GRIFFITH, FARRAN, BROWNE AND CO., LTD. (188–?). 62p.: front., ill. Bound in blue cloth with coloured pictorial cover.
C 823.8 CAR

1163 **CARROLL, LEWIS.**
THE LEWIS CARROLL PICTURE BOOK. A SELEC-TION FROM THE UNPUBLISHED WRITINGS AND DRAWINGS OF LEWIS CARROLL, TOGETHER WITH REPRINTS FROM SCARCE AND UNACKNOWL-EDGED WORK. EDITED BY STUART DODGSON COL-LINGWOOD, B.A. CHRIST CHURCH, OXFORD. ILLUSTRATED. LONDON: T. FISHER UNWIN, 1899. XV, 375p.: front., (portrait of Carroll), 9 plates, ill. Bound in red cloth with pictorial cover and decorative spine.
YSC 823.8 CAR

1164 **Another copy.**
LONDON: COLLINS' CLEAR-TYPE PRESS, (1899). 271p. + 1p. pub. cat.: front. (portrait of Carroll), ill., pictorial endpapers. Bound in red cloth, with embossed decorative cover and spine. COLLINS' WIDE WORLD LIBRARY.
C 823.8 CAR

1165 **CARROLL, LEWIS.**
SYLVIE AND BRUNO BY LEWIS CARROLL. WITH FORTY-SIX ILLUSTRATIONS BY HARRY FURNISS. LONDON: MACMILLAN AND CO., LIMITED, 1898. XXIII, 400p.: front., 3 plates, ill. Bound in green cloth with coloured pictorial cover. First published 1889.
YSC 823.8 CAR

1166 **CARROLL, LEWIS.**
SYLVIE AND BRUNO CONCLUDED. BY LEWIS CARROLL. WITH FORTY-SIX ILLUSTRATIONS BY HARRY FURNISS. LONDON: MACMILLAN AND CO.,

LIMITED, 1898. XXXI, 421p. + 5p. pub. cat.: front., 3 plates, ill. Bound in green cloth with coloured pictorial cover. First published 1893.
YSC 823.8 BUR

1167 **CARROLL, LEWIS.**
THROUGH THE LOOKING GLASS And What Alice Found There. BY LEWIS CARROLL. WITH FIFTY ILLUSTRATIONS BY JOHN TENNIEL. LONDON: MACMILLAN AND CO. LTD., reprinted 1955. 208p.: front., ill. Bound in green cloth with coloured pictorial cover. Originally published 1871.
YSC 823.8 CAR

1168 **CERVANTES, SAAVEDRA MIGUEL DE.**
THE ADVENTURES OF DON QUIXOTE DE LA MANCHA. ADAPTED FOR THE YOUNG BY M. JONES. WITH 206 ILLUSTRATIONS BY SIR JOHN GILBERT, R.A. AND OTHER ARTISTS. LONDON: GEORGE ROUTLEDGE AND SONS, LIMITED, (189–?). X, 503p.: col. front., vignette on title page, 29 plates, ill. Bound in red cloth, with coloured pictorial/decorative cover and spine.
C 823.912 JON

1169 **CERVANTES, SAAVEDRA MIGUEL DE.**
THE ADVENTURES OF DON QUIXOTE OF LA MANCHA BY MIGUEL DE CERVANTES. ILLUSTRATED BY W. HEATH ROBINSON. LONDON: J.M. DENT AND CO., 1902. XXI, 531p.: front., title page and front decorated with red border, 43 plates, with decorative endpapers. Bound in green cloth with coloured pictorial cover and spine.
CBD 863.3 CER

1170 **CERVANTES, SAAVEDRA MIGUEL DE.**
DON QUIXOTE OF THE MANCHA. RETOLD BY JUDGE PARRY. ILLUSTRATED BY WALTER CRANE. ALTRINCHAM: JOHN SHERRATT AND SON (191–?). 245p.: col. front., col. pictorial title page. 10 col. plates, headpieces to chapters. Bound in red cloth with coloured pictorial cover. Originally published in 1900.
CBD 863.3 CER

1171 **CERVANTES, SAAVEDRA MIGUEL DE.**
THE STORY OF DON QUIXOTE AND HIS SQUIRE SANCHO PANZA. BY M. JONES. LONDON: GEORGE ROUTLEDGE AND SONS, 1875. 377p. + 32p. pub. cat.: col. front., 5 col. plates. Bound in blue cloth with embossed decorative cover and spine.
Y 823.912 JON

1172 **CHALLACOMBE, MRS.**
THE BROTHER'S PROMISE. BY MRS. CHALLACOMBE. LONDON: THE RELIGIOUS TRACT SOCIETY, (189–?). 80p. + 16p. ill. pub. cat.: front., ill. Bound in blue cloth with coloured decorative cover and spine.
C 823.8 CHA

1173 **CHARLESWORTH, MARIA LOUISA.**
MINISTERING CHILDREN. A TALE DEDICATED TO CHILDHOOD. BY MARIA LOUISA CHARLESWORTH. LONDON: WARD LOCK AND CO., LIMITED, 1899. 318p. + 2p. pub. cat.: front. by M. Barstow. Bound in blue cloth with embossed decorative cover and spine.
YSC 823.8 CHA

1174 **CHARLESWORTH, MARIE LOUISA.**
(MINISTERING CHILDREN. A SEQUEL). LONDON: SEELEY AND CO., (187–?). VI, 434p. + 2p. pub. cat.: 6 plates. Rebound in blue cloth. Title page missing. Originally published 1866.
YSC 823.8 CHA

1175 **CHARLIE BURTON.**
A TALE. PUBLISHED UNDER THE DIRECTION OF THE COMMITTEE OF GENERAL LITERATURE AND EDUCATION. . . . (S.P.C.K.) LONDON: SOCIETY FOR PROMOTING CHRISTIAN KNOWLEDGE, 1842. 108p.: front., ill. by WHIMPEY. Bound in dark brown cloth.
C 823.8 CHA

1176 **CHESTER, A.S.M.**
Up the Chimney To Ninny Land. A STORY FOR CHILDREN. By A.S.M. CHESTER. WITH NUMEROUS ILLUSTRATIONS. LONDON: T. NELSON AND SONS, 1894. 86p.: 4 plates, ill. Bound in blue cloth with coloured pictorial cover and spine.
YSC 823.8 CHE

1177 **CHEYNE, A.E.**
DICK LAYARD; OR, A SCHOOLBOY'S TRIAL. BY A.E. CHEYNE. ILLUSTRATED BY E.J. WHEELER. LONDON: THE SOCIETY FOR PROMOTING CHRISTIAN KNOWLEDGE, (189–?). 156p. + 4p. pub. cat.: front, 2 plates. Bound in green cloth with coloured pictorial cover.
C 823.8 CHE

1178 **THE CHILDREN'S ISLAND.**
OR, THE PLEASURES OF LABOUR. WITH COLOURED FRONTISPIECE. LONDON: FREDERICK WARNE., (189–?). Col. front., 2 plates by Dalziel. Bound in green cloth with coloured pictorial cover.
C 823.8 CHI

1179 **CLARA WOODWARD AND HER DAY-DREAMS.**
A NEW EDITION. LONDON: FREDERICK WARNE AND CO., (187–?). 186p.: col. front. Bound in blue cloth with embossed decorative cover and spine, gilt edge.
C 823.8 CLA

1180 **CLARE, AUSTIN.**
THE CARVED CARTOON: A Picture of the Past. BY AUSTIN CLARE. THIRTIETH THOUSAND. LONDON: SOCIETY FOR PROMOTING CHRISTIAN KNOWLEDGE, (189–?). XVI, 304p. + 16p. pub. cat.: front., 3 plates. Bound in beige cloth, with coloured pictorial cover and spine.
YSC 823.8 CLA

1181 **CLARE, AUSTIN.**
A GUIDING STAR. BY AUSTIN CLARE. LONDON: SOCIETY FOR PROMOTING CHRISTIAN KNOWLEDGE, (188–?). 127p. + 4p. pub. cat.: front., ill. Bound in beige cloth, with coloured decorative cover and spine.
YSC 823.8 CLA

1182 **CLEMENTS, M.E.**
CORDS OF LOVE; OR WHO IS MY NEIGHBOUR. BY M.E. CLEMENTS. LONDON: THOMAS NELSON AND SONS, 1888. 144p.: front., additional vignette title page by Dalziel. Bound in blue cloth with coloured decorative cover and spine.
C 823.8 CLE

1183 **CLEVER BOYS AND OTHER STORIES.**
LONDON: W. AND R. CHAMBERS, (188–?). 143p.: col. front., col. pictorial title page. Bound in red cloth with decorative cover and spine, inserted coloured vignette on cover. CHAMBER'S JUVENILE LIBRARY.
C 823.8 CLE

1184 **COBB, JAMES FRANCIS.**
A FEAST OF STORIES FROM FOREIGN LANDS, BY JAMES F. COBB F.R.G.S. LONDON: WELLS, GARDNER, DARTON AND CO., 1894. 341p. + 12p. pub. cat.: front., 6 plates. Bound in blue cloth with coloured pictorial cover and spine.
C 823.8 COB

1185 **COLBECK, ALFRED.**
THE FALL OF THE STAINCLIFFES. BY ALFRED COLBECK. WITH FIVE ILLUSTRATIONS. £100 PRIZE TALE ON GAMBLING. LONDON: THE SUNDAY SCHOOL UNION, (1891). 160p. front., 1 plate, ill. Bound in green cloth with pictorial cover.
C 823.8 COL

1186 **COLERIDGE, CHRISTABEL R.**
MAUD FLORENCE NELLIE OR DON'T CARE! BY C.R. COLERIDGE. WITH FOUR FULL PAGE ILLUSTRATIONS. LONDON: NATIONAL SOCIETY'S DEPOSITORY, (188–?). VII, 237p. + 16p. pub. cat.: 3 plates by C.J. Staniland. Bound in blue cloth with coloured pictorial cover and spine.
C 823.8 COL

1187 **COLERIDGE, CHRISTABEL R.**
Minstrel – Dick. A tale of the XIVth Cent. By Christabel R. Coleridge. LONDON: GARDNER, DARTON AND CO., 1896. VII, 288p. + 10p. pub. cat.: front., 1 plate, decorative chapter headings. Bound in cream buckram with decorative cover and spine.
C 823.8 COL

1187A **COLLINGWOOD, HARRY.**
The Pirate Island. A Story of the South Pacific. BY HARRY COLLINGWOOD. WITH SIX PAGE ILLUSTRATIONS BY C.J. STANILAND AND J.R. WELLS. LONDON: BLACKIE AND SON LIMITED, 1885. 339p. + 32p. pub. cat.: front., 5 plates. Bound in green cloth with coloured pictorial cover and spine.
C 823.912 COL

1188 **COOLIDGE, SUSAN.**
WHAT KATY DID, A Story. BY SUSAN COOLIDGE (pseud. for Sarah Woolsey). LONDON: FREDERICK WARNE AND CO., (188–?) 219p. + 4p. pub. cat. Bound in green cloth, with embossed decorative cover and spine. Warne's Star Series. Originally published 1872.
YSC 813.4 COO

1189 **COOLIDGE, SUSAN.**
WHAT KATY DID NEXT. BY SUSAN COOLIDGE, (pseud. for Sarah Woolsey). LONDON: FREDERICK WARNE AND CO., (188–?). 323p. + 8p. pub. cat. Bound in brown cloth, with embossed decorative cover and spine. Warne's Star Series. Originally published 1886.
YSC 813.4 COO

1190 **COOPER, JAMES FENIMORE.**
COOPER'S LEATHER-STOCKING TALES FOR BOYS AND GIRLS. WITH ILLUSTRATIONS. LONDON: GEORGE ROUTLEDGE AND SONS, LIMITED, 1892. 192p., 192p., 192p., 192p., 192p.: col. front., vignette title page, 5 col. plates, ill. by Fritz Bergen. Bound in brown cloth, with embossed pictorial/decorative cover and spine. Contains the Deerslayer, the Last of the Mohicans, the Pathfinder, the Pioneers and the Prairie.
C 813.2 COO

1191 **COOPER, JAMES FENIMORE.**
THE DEERSLAYER, OR THE FIRST WAR-PATH. A TALE BY J. FENIMORE COOPER. LONDON: GEORGE ROUTLEDGE AND SONS, (187–?). XL, 591p.: front. Bound in green cloth with embossed decorative cover and spine. Originally published 1841.
C 813.2 COO

1192 **COOPER, J. FENIMORE.**
THE PRAIRIE, A TALE. BY J. FENIMORE COOPER. LONDON: GEORGE ROUTLEDGE AND SONS, (187–?). XXXII, 468p.: front., 1 plate. Bound in green cloth with embossed decorative cover and spine. Originally published 1827.
C 813.2 COO

1193 **COOPER, MRS.**
TOM, BY MRS. COOPER. LONDON: THE RELIGIOUS TRACT SOCIETY, (189–?). 64p.: col. front. Bound in red cloth with coloured decorative cover. Little Dot Series.
C 823.8 COO

1194 **THE CORNISH FISHERMEN'S WATCH-NIGHT, AND OTHER STORIES.**
LONDON: THE RELIGIOUS TRACT SOCIETY, (188–?). 96p. + 16p. ill. pub. cat.: front., 3 plates, ill. Bound in red cloth with decorative cover and spine.
C 823.8 COR

1192

1195 **COUSIN JACK'S ADVENTURES.**
LONDON: THE RELIGIOUS TRACT SOCIETY, (189–?). 79p. + 16p. ill. pub. cat.: col. front., vignette title page, ill. Bound in pink cloth with decorative cover and spine.
C 823.8 COU

1196 **CROCKETT, SAMUEL RUTHERFORD.**
THE SURPRISING ADVENTURES OF SIR TOADY LION WITH THOSE OF GENERAL NAPOLEON SMITH, AN IMPROVING HISTORY FOR OLD BOYS, YOUNG BOYS, GOOD BOYS, BAD BOYS, BIG BOYS, LITTLE BOYS, COWBOYS AND TOM-BOYS. BY S.R. CROCKETT. ILLUSTRATED BY GORDON BROWNE. LONDON: GARDNER, DARTON AND CO., 1897. 379p. + 10p. pub. cat.: front., 16 plates, col. folded map, ill. Bound in grey-green cloth with pictorial cover and spine.
C 823.8 CRO

1197 **CROCKETT, SAMUEL RUTHERFORD.**
SWEETHEART TRAVELLERS. A CHILD'S BOOK FOR CHILDREN, FOR WOMEN, AND FOR MEN. BY S.R. CROCKETT. ILLUSTRATED BY GORDON BROWNE AND W.H.C. GROOME. LONDON: WELLS, GARDNER, DARTON AND CO., 1895. XV, 310p. + 26p. pub. cat.: front., vignette title page, 10 plates, ill. Bound in grey cloth with pictorial cover and spine.
C 823.8 CRO

1198 **CULE, W.E.**
SIR CONSTANT, Knight of the Great King. BY W.E. CULE. WITH ILLUSTRATIONS BY A. BAUERLE. LONDON: ANDREW MELROSE, (189–?). 192p. + 16p. ill. pub. cat.: front., 5 plates. Bound in blue cloth with pictorial cover and gilt edges.
C 823.8 CUL

1199 **CUMING, CONSTANCE.**
ILTID'S FRIEND. BY CONSTANCE CUMING. LONDON: THE RELIGIOUS TRACT SOCIETY, 1892. 160p. + 16p. ill. pub. cat.: front., 2 plates, ill. by Paul Hardy.

Bound in beige cloth with coloured decorative cover and spine.
C 823.8 CUM

1200 **CUMMINS, MARIA SUSANNA.**
The Lamplighter, BY MISS CUMMINS. LONDON: BLACKIE AND SON LIMITED, (189–?). 256p. + 12p. pub. cat.: front. Bound in blue cloth with coloured decorative cover and spine. First published 1854.
C 823.8 CUM

1201 **Another copy.**
LONDON: GEORGE ROUTLEDGE AND SONS, LIMITED. (190–?). 587p. + 4p. pub. cat., col. front., 3 col. plates by Dorothy Foulger.

1202 **CUPPLES, ANNE JANE BERTHA.**
BLUFF CRAG; OR, A GOOD WORD COSTS NOTHING. A Tale for the Young. BY MRS. GEORGE CUPPLES. LONDON: T. NELSON AND SONS, 1883. 72p.: ill. Bound in blue cloth with embossed decorative cover and spine, with inserted coloured pictorial paper label.
C 823.8 CUP

1203 **CUPPLES, ANNE JANE BERTHA.**
MARCHMONT; OR, ALL IS NOT GOLD THAT GLITTERS. A Tale for the Young. BY MRS. GEORGE CUPPLES. LONDON: T. NELSON AND SONS, 1881. 72p.: col. front., ill. Bound in red cloth, with decorative cover and inserted coloured vignette.
C 823.8 CUP

1204 **CUTTS, EDWARD L.**
THE FIRST RECTOR OF BURGSTEAD. A Tale of the Saxon Church. BY THE REV. EDWARD L. CUTTS, B.A. LONDON: SOCIETY FOR PROMOTING CHRISTIAN KNOWLEDGE, (187–?). 175p., 2 plates. Bound in brown cloth, with embossed decorative cover and spine, and gilt edges.
YSC 823.8 CUT

1205 **DARNTON, P.W.**
THE ADVENTURES OF JACK POMEROY, A Book for Boys. BY P.W. DARNTON. LONDON: THE RELIGIOUS TRACT SOCIETY, (189–?). 64p.: col. front., vignette title page, ill. Bound in green cloth with decorative cover and inserted coloured vignette. Little Dot Series.
C 823.8 DAR

1206 **DAUNT, ACHILLES.**
CRAG, GLACIER, AND AVALANCHE. Narratives of Daring and Disaster. By Achilles Daunt. WITH 13 ILLUSTRATIONS. LONDON: T. NELSON AND SONS, 1894. 212p. + 4p. pub. cat.: front., additional vignette title page, 11 plates. Bound in blue cloth with pictorial cover and spine.
C 823.8 DAU

1207 **DAVIES, G. CHRISTOPHER.**
THE SWAN AND HER CREW, OR THE ADVENTURES OF THREE YOUNG NATURALISTS AND SPORTSMEN ON THE BROADS AND RIVERS OF NORFOLK. BY G. CHRISTOPHER DAVIES. THIRD EDITION WITH POSTSCRIPT AND NUMEROUS ILLUSTRATIONS. LONDON: FREDERICK WARNE AND CO., (188–?) XX, 294p.: front., 5 plates, ill. by Dalziel. Bound in brown cloth with embossed decorative cover and spine.
C 823.8 DAV

1207A **DAY, THOMAS.**
THE HISTORY OF SANDFORD AND MERTON: A BOOK FOR THE YOUNG BY THOMAS DAY. LONDON: T. NELSON AND SONS, 1855. 468p.: front., additional vignette title page. Bound in red cloth with embossed decorative cover and spine. Originally published 1783–9.
M 823 DAY CHILDREN'S COLLECTION

1208 **DEBENHAM, MARY H.**
ONE RED ROSE. BY MARY H. DEBENHAM. WITH FIVE FULL-PAGE ILLUSTRATIONS BY GERTRUDE D. HAMMOND. LONDON: NATIONAL SOCIETY'S DEPOSITORY, (189–?). 292p. + 16p. pub. cat.: front., 4 plates. Bound in beige cloth with coloured decorative cover and spine.
C 823.8 DEB

1209 **DEFOE, DANIEL.**
THE ADVENTURES OF ROBINSON CRUSOE. BY DANIEL DEFOE. Newly edited after the Original Editions. WITH TWENTY ILLUSTRATIONS BY KAUFFMAN. LONDON: T. FISHER UNWIN, 1889. IX, 289p. + 24p. pub. cat.: front., 18 plates. Bound in grey cloth with coloured pictorial cover and spine, and gilt edges. Originally published 1719.
C 823.5 DEF

1210 **DEFOE, DANIEL.**
ADVENTURES OF ROBINSON CRUSOE, BY DANIEL DEFOE. LONDON: STEAD'S PUBLISHING HOUSE, (189–?). 62p. + 2p. pub. cat.: title page on cover, ill. Paper covers. Books for the Bairns Series.
C 823.8 ADV

1211 **DEFOE, DANIEL.**
COMPLETE EDITION. THE LIFE AND ADVENTURES OF ROBINSON CRUSOE OF YORK, MARINER. Six Coloured Engravings on Steel. EDINBURGH: GALL and INGLIS, (186–?). VIII, 560p.: col. front. 5 plates. Bound in green cloth with embossed pictorial cover and spine and gilt edges.
C 823.5 DEF

1212 **(DEFOE, DANIEL).**
THE LIFE AND ADVENTURES OF Robinson Crusoe. EDINBURGH: OLIVER AND BOYD, n.d. 247p. + 2p. pub. cat.: vignette on title page. Soft cloth binding with pictorial/decorative covers. Gordon's Schools and Home Series.
YSC 823.5 DEF

1213 **(DEFOE, DANIEL).**
LIFE AND ADVENTURES OF ROBINSON CRUSOE. WRITTEN BY HIMSELF. LONDON: T. NELSON AND SONS, 1874. 593p.: additional col. pictorial title page, 5 col. plates. Bound in orange cloth, with coloured pictorial paper label on cover, embossed decorative cover and spine, and gilt edges.
YSC 823.5 DEF

1214 **DEFOE, DANIEL.**
The Life And Strange Surprising Adventures of Robinson Crusoe of York, Mariner. BY DANIEL DEFOE. LONDON: W. AND R. CHAMBERS, LIMITED, (189–?). 272p. + 48p. ill. pub. cat.: front., ill. Bound in blue cloth with pictorial cover and spine.
C 823.5 DEF

1215 **DEFOE, DANIEL.**
The LIFE and strange surprising ADVENTURES of ROBINSON CRUSOE of York, Mariner. Written by Daniel Defoe. LONDON: FREDERICK ETCHELLS AND HUGH MACDONALD, 1929. 332p. + 4p. editorial notes: col. front., col. vignette on title page, 5 col. plates by E. McKnight Kauffer. Bound in faded blue buckram with decorative cover. Edited by Kathleen Campbell.
CBD 823.5 DEF

1216 **DEFOE, DANIEL.**
The Life and Strange Surprising Adventures of Robinson Crusoe of York, Mariner, by DANIEL DEFOE. With illustrations by J. Ayton Symington. LONDON: J.M. DENT AND CO., 1905. VII, 472p.; col. front., col. decorative title page, 15 col. plates, ill. Bound in blue cloth with coloured pictorial covers and spine.
C 823.5 DEF

1217 **DEFOE, DANIEL.**
The Life and Strange Surprising Adventures of Robinson Crusoe of York, Mariner as Related by Himself. BY DANIEL DEFOE. ILLUSTRATED. LONDON: ERNEST NISTER, (191–?). 328p.: col. front., 5 col. plates, ill, by J. Finnemore, G.H. Thompson and Archibald Webb. Bound in blue cloth with coloured pictorial cover and spine.
C 823.5 DEF

1218 **DEFOE, DANIEL.**
THE LIFE AND STRANGE SURPRISING ADVENTURES OF ROBINSON CRUSOE of York, Mariner. AS RELATED BY HIMSELF. BY DANIEL DEFOE. With upwards of One Hundred Illustrations. LONDON: CASSELL, PETTER, AND GALPIN, (188–?). XIV, 394p.: front. port., 49 plates, ill., decorative coloured endpapers. Half bound in maroon leather, with embossed decorative spine.
YOSC 823.5 DEF

1219 **(DEFOE, DANIEL).**
The Life and Strange Surprising Adventures of ROBINSON CRUSOE, of York, Mariner, as Related by Himself. Embellished with Plates after designs by NOEL POCOCK. LONDON: HENRY FROWDE AND HODDER AND STOUGHTON, 1910. 352p.: col. front., 23 col. plates mounted on grey paper. Bound in blue cloth with coloured pictorial cover and spine, and coloured endpapers representing the sea.
C 823.8 DEF

1220 **DEFOE, DANIEL.**
ROBINSON CRUSOE. BY DANIEL DEFOE. LONDON: J.M. DENT AND SONS LTD., 1906. XII, 453p. + 8p. pub. cat.: decorative front. and title page, 3 plates, ill., decorative endpapers. Bound in blue cloth, with embossed decorative spine. EVERYMAN'S LIBRARY FOR YOUNG PEOPLE, NO. 59.
YSC 823.5 DEF

1220A **DICKENS, CHARLES.**
A CHILD'S DREAM OF A STAR. BY CHARLES DICKENS. WITH ILLUSTRATIONS BY HAMMATT BILLINGS. USA. NEW YORK: JOHN R. ANDERSON AND CO., 1881. 15p.: printed on one side only, front., 10 plates, decorative initial and tailpiece. Bound in blue cloth with pictorial cover.
M 823 DIC CHILDREN'S COLLECTION

1221 **DODGE, MARY MAPES.**
HANS BRINKER; OR, THE SILVER SKATES. A Story of Life in Holland. BY MRS. M.E. DODGE. NEW EDITION. LONDON: SAMPSON LOW, MARSTON, SEARLE AND RIVINGTON, (189–?). X, 303p. + 32p. pub. cat.: front., 6 plates by T.H. Schuler. Bound in blue cloth with pictorial cover and spine. First published 1865.
C 813.4 DOD

1222 **Another copy.**
LONDON: J.M. DENT AND SONS LTD., (191–?). 246p. Edited by Ernest Rhys. Rebound in brown buckram and quarter leather. EVERYMAN'S LIBRARY FOR YOUNG PEOPLE.

1223 **DOUDNEY, SARAH.**
FAITH HARROWBY OR The Smugglers' Cave. BY SARAH DOUDNEY. LONDON: THE SUNDAY SCHOOL UNION, (189–?). 128p.: front., 3 plates, ill. Bound in green cloth with coloured pictorial cover and spine.
C 823.912 DOU

1224 **EDGAR, JOHN GEORGE.**
THE BOY CRUSADERS. A Story of the days of Louis IX. BY J.G. EDGAR. Eight Full Page Illustrations. EDINBURGH: GALL AND INGLIS, (1870). 283p.: col. front., 6 plates by R. Dudley. Bound in red cloth with embossed decorative cover and spine.
C 823.8 EDG

1225 **EDGAR, JOHN GEORGE.**
BOY'S ADVENTURES IN THE BARON'S WARS; OR, HOW I WON MY SPURS. BY J.G. EDGAR. Illustrated by Numerous Woodcuts, from designs principally by R. Huttula and J.C. Danby. LONDON: WARD, LOCK AND TYLER, (187–?). XVIII, 413p.: col. front., ill. Bound in green cloth with embossed pictorial cover and spine. The Boys' Own Library.
C 823.8 EDG

1226 **EDGEWORTH, MARIA.**
THE BIRTH-DAY PRESENT, AND OTHER STORIES. BY MARIA EDGEWORTH. LONDON: MILNER AND COMPANY, (186–?). 160p.: front., additional vignette title page, engraved by W. Banks and Son. Rebound in cream cloth. Contains also: The Little Merchants; The Orange Man, or the Honest Boy and the Thief.
YSC 823.7 EDG

1227 **EDGEWORTH, MARIA.**
EARLY LESSONS BY MARIA EDGEWORTH. A New Edition, ILLUSTRATED BY BIRKET FOSTER. LONDON: ROUTLEDGE, WARNE AND ROUTLEDGE. 1864. 427p.: front., 6 plates. Bound in red cloth with embossed decorative cover and spine. Includes Rosamond, Little Dog Trusty, The Orange-man, Cherry-orchard, Frank, and Harry and Lucy.
C 823.7 EDG

1228 **EDGEWORTH, MARIA.**
THE GRATEFUL NEGRO AND THE BIRTHDAY PRESENT. BY MARIA EDGEWORTH. LONDON: WILLIAM P. NIMMO, 1874. 72p.: col. front. Bound in green with decorative cover.
C 823.8 EDG

1229 **EDGEWORTH, MARIA.**
ROSAMOND: A Series of Tales. BY MARIA EDGEWORTH. NEW EDITION. LONDON: ROUTLEDGE, WARNE, AND ROUTLEDGE, 1864. 190p. + 2p. pub. cat.: front., additional vignette title page, engraved by Dalziel Brothers. Bound in blue cloth, with embossed decorative covers and spine. Contains seventeen stories. Derived from Early Lessons, originally published 1801.
YSC 823.7 EDG

1229A **Another copy.**
LONDON: GEORGE ROUTLEDGE AND SONS, (1872). 190p. + 32p. pub. cat.: col front., col. vignette on title page. Bound in blue cloth with embossed decorative cover and spine and coloured paper vignette on cover.
M 823 EDG CHILDREN'S COLLECTION

1230 **EDITH VERNON'S LIFE-WORK.**
BY THE AUTHOR OF "LOST PIECE OF SILVER", "HARRY'S BATTLES", ETC. Sixteenth Edition. LONDON: WELLS GARDNER, DARTON AND CO., (189–?). VIII, 364p. + 12p. pub. cat.: front., additional vignette title page. Bound in green cloth with pictorial cover and spine.
C 823.8 EDI

1231 **EFFIE MAURICE.**
OR, WHAT DO I LOVE BEST? LONDON: GALL AND INGLIS, (187–?). 112p.: col. front. by W. Dickes. Bound in red cloth with decorative cover and spine.
C 823.8 EFF

1232 **EILOART, ELIZABETH.**
BOYS OF BEECHWOOD, BY MRS. EILOART. WITH ILLUSTRATIONS. LONDON: GEORGE ROUTLEDGE AND SONS, (188–?). VII, 395p. + 14p. pub. cat.: front., 5 plates engraved by Dalziel after A.B. Houghton. Bound in blue cloth with coloured pictorial cover and spine. First published 1868.
C 823.8 EIL

1233 **(ELLIOTT, EMILY STEELE).**
MATTY'S HUNGRY MISSIONARY-BOX, AND THE MESSAGE IT BROUGHT. A Tale for the Young. BY THE AUTHOR OF "COPSLEY ANNALS", "VILLAGE MISSIONARIES", etc. LONDON: T. NELSON AND SONS, 1875. 120p.: col. front., additional col. vignette title page, engraved by Dalziel. Bound in green cloth, with embossed decorative cover and spine.
C 823.8 ELL

1233A **ELLIS, EDWARD SYLVESTER.**
CAPTURED BY INDIANS, A TALE OF THE AMERICAN FRONTIER. BY EDWARD S. ELLIS. WITH

ILLUSTRATIONS BY GORDON BROWNE, R.I.B.A. FIFTH THOUSAND. LONDON: CASSELL AND COMPANY, LIMITED, 1898. 152p. + 16p. pub. cat.: front., 5 plates. Bound in green cloth, with coloured, pictorial cover and spine.
C 823.8 ELL

1233B **ELLIS, EDWARD SYLVESTER.**
THE GREAT CATTLE TRAIL. BY EDWARD S. ELLIS. LONDON: CASSELL AND COMPANY LIMITED, 1894. IV, 313p. + 16p. pub. cat.: front., 3 plates by White. Bound in brown cloth with pictorial cover and spine.
C 813.4 ELL

1234 **ELLIS, EDWARD SYLVESTER.**
NED IN THE WOODS, A Tale of the Early Days in the West. BY EDWARDS S. ELLIS. SIXTH EDITION. LONDON: CASSELL AND COMPANY LIMITED, 1894. IV, 290p. + 16p. pub. cat.: front., 2 plates. Bound in red with pictorial cover and spine.
C 823.8 ELL

1235 **ELLIS, EDWARD SYLVESTER.**
PONTIAC CHIEF OF THE OTTAWAS. A Tale of the Siege of Detroit. BY EDWARD S. ELLIS WITH EIGHT FULL PAGE ILLUSTRATIONS. LONDON: CASSELL AND COMPANY, LIMITED., 1897. VIII, 300p. + 16p. pub. cat.: front., 6 plates by W. de la M. Cary. Bound in olive cloth with coloured pictorial cover and spine.
C 813.4 ELL

1235A **ELLIS, EDWARD SYLVESTER.**
SHOD WITH SILENCE. A TALE OF THE FRONTIER. BY EDWARD S. ELLIS. LONDON: CASSELL AND COMPANY LIMITED, 1896. 363p. + 16p. pub. cat.: front., 3 plates by White. Bound in green cloth with coloured pictorial cover and spine.
C813.4 ELL

1235B **ELMSLIE, THEODORA C.**
THE LITTLE LADY OF LAVENDER. BY THEODORA C. ELMSLIE (BAYNTON FOSTER). ILLUSTRATED BY EDITH SCANNELL AND H.L.E. LONDON: GRIFFITH FARRAN BROWNE AND CO., LIMITED, (189–?). XIII, 312p.: front., and 3 plates by Edith Scannell, headpieces and tailpieces. Bound in blue cloth with vignette on cover.
M 823 ELM CHILDREN'S COLLECTION

1236 **EMMETT, GEORGE.**
YOUNG TOM'S SCHOOLDAYS. BY GEORGE EMMETT, PROFUSELY ILLUSTRATED BY PHIZ. AND YOUNG TOM WILDRAKE'S ADVENTURES In Europe, Asia, Africa and America, PROFUSELY ILLUSTRATED BY EMINENT ARTISTS. LONDON: WILLIAM CATE, HOGARTH HOUSE, 1871, 2 and 3. 211p., 199p.: ill. 2 parts bound together in red cloth.
C 823.8 EMM

1238 **EVERETT-GREEN, EVELYN.**
THE HEIRESS OF WYLMINGTON. By EVELYN EVERETT-GREEN. LONDON: T. NELSON AND SONS, 1888. 480p.: front., vignette title page by F.A.F., engraved by Dalziel Brothers. Bound in blue cloth, with embossed decorative cover and spine, and gilt edges.
YSC 823.8 EVE

1239 **EWING, JULIANA HORATIA.**
DADDY DARWIN'S DOVECOT. A Country Tale by JULIANA HORATIA EWING. . . . ILLUSTRATED BY RANDOLPH CALDECOTT. LONDON: SOCIETY FOR PROMOTING CHRISTIAN KNOWLEDGE, (1884). 52p.: col. front., pictorial title page, 3 plates, ill., text and plates in sepia. Bound in buff paper with col. pictorial cover.
CBD 823.8 EWI

1240 **EWING, JULIANA HORATIA.**
DANDELION CLOCKS AND OTHER TALES. BY JULIANA HORATIA EWING. ILLUSTRATED BY GORDON BROWNE & OTHER ARTISTS. ENGRAVED AND PRINTED BY EDMUND EVANS. LONDON: SOCIETY FOR PROMOTING CHRISTIAN KNOWLEDGE, (1887) 48p. + 1p. pub. cat.: front., vignette on title page, 3 plates, ill. + 4 woodcuts. Bound in yellow paper with pictorial engraved cover and pub. cat. on back.
YSC 823.8 EWI

1241 **EWING, JULIANA HORATIA.**
A FLAT IRON FOR A FARTHING; OR, SOME PASSAGES IN THE LIFE OF AN ONLY SON. BY J.H. EWING. WITH TWELVE ILLUSTRATIONS BY MRS ALLINGHAM (H. PATERSON). THIRTEENTH EDITION. LONDON: GEORGE BELL AND SONS, 1883. XI, 290p. + 24p. cat.: front., 11 plates. Bound in brown cloth with gold pictorial cover and spine. Originally published 1873.

YSC 832.8 EWI

1241A **Another copy.**
LONDON: SOCIETY FOR PROMOTING CHRISTIAN KNOWLEDGE, (189–?) XI, 282p. Quarter bound in brown cloth with decorative paper covers.
M 823 EW1 CHILDREN'S COLLECTION

1242 **EWING, JULIANA HORATIA.**
A GREAT EMERGENCY, AND OTHER TALES. BY JULIANA HORATIA EWING. WITH ILLUSTRATIONS. LONDON: GEORGE BELL AND SONS, 1886. 128p.: front., ill. by H. Paterson. Rebound retaining original pictorial grey covers. Originally published 1877.
C 832.8 EWI

1243 **EWING, JULIANA HORATIA.**
JACKANAPES. BY JULIANA HORATIA EWING. WITH ILLUSTRATIONS BY RANDOLPH CALDECOTT. LONDON: SOCIETY FOR PROMOTING CHRISTIAN KNOWLEDGE, (188–?). 45p., sepia print: col. front., vignette, 1 plate, ill. Rebound in green cloth. Engraved by Edmund Evans. Includes also DADDY DARWIN'S DOVECOT: A Country Tale by JULIANA HORATIA EWING. ILLUSTRATED BY RANDOLPH CALDECOTT. 47p., sepia print.: col. front., vignette, 3 plates, ill. Includes also LOB LIE-BY-THE-FIRE; OR, THE LUCK OF LINGBOROUGH. 73p. in sepia print (173 in all): 2 plates, ill.
YSC 823.8 EWI

1244 **EWING, JULIANA HORATIA.**
JACKANAPES, BY JULIANA HORATIA EWING, WITH ILLUSTRATIONS BY RANDOLPH CALDECOTT. LONDON: SOCIETY FOR PROMOTING CHRISTIAN KNOWLEDGE, (1883). 47p.: front., pictorial title page, ill. Bound in blue cloth with coloured pictorial paper covers.
CBD 823.8 EWI

1245 **EWING, JULIANA HORATIA.**
JAN OF THE WINDMILL. A STORY OF THE PLAINS, BY JULIANA HORATIA EWING. LONDON: GEORGE BELL AND SONS, (1885). VIII, 151p.: front., ill. by H. Paterson. Rebound retaining original illustrated blue covers. Originally published 1876.
C 823.8 EWI

1246 **Another copy.**
Illustrated by M.V. Wheelhouse. LONDON: G. BELL AND SONS LTD., 1914. X, 307p.: col. front., vignette, 7 col. plates. Bound in blue cloth, with yellow pictorial cover and decorative spine. QUEEN'S TREASURE SERIES.
YSC 823.8 EWI

1247 **EWING, JULIANA HORATIA.**
LOB LIE-BY-THE-FIRE; OR, THE LUCK OF LINGBOROUGH. BY JULIANA HORATIA EWING, ILLUSTRATED BY RANDOLPH CALDECOTT. ENGRAVED AND PRINTED BY EDMUND EVANS. LONDON: SOCIETY FOR PROMOTING CHRISTIAN KNOWLEDGE, (1885). 72p.: front., ill., text and ill. printed in sepia. Bound in buff paper with coloured pictorial front cover and booklist on back cover. Originally published 1874.
CBD 823.8 EWI

1247A **EWING, JULIANA HORATIA.**
MARY'S MEADOW AND Letters from a Little Garden. BY JULIANA HORATIA EWING. ILLUSTRATED BY GORDON BROWNE. LONDON: SOCIETY FOR PROMOTING CHRISTIAN KNOWLEDGE, (1886). 96p.: front., vignette on title page, 4 plates, pictorial initials to chapters. Bound in blue paper, with coloured pictorial cover.
M 823 EWI CHILDREN'S COLLECTION

1248 **EWING, JULIANA HORATIA.**
MELCHIOR'S DREAM AND OTHER TALES. BY JULIANA HORATIA EWING (J.H.G.) EDITED BY MRS. ALFRED GATTY, AUTHOR OF "PARABLES FROM NATURE", ETC. ILLUSTRATED BY GORDON BROWNE. NEW EDITION. LONDON: GEORGE BELL AND SONS, 1886. 112p.: front., 7 plates. Bound in buff card with pictorial cover. Originally published 1862.
C 823.8 EWI

1248A **EWING, JULIANA HORATIA.**
THE PEACE EGG AND OTHER TALES. BY JULIANA HORATIA EWING. LONDON: SOCIETY FOR PROMOTING CHRISTIAN KNOWLEDGE, (189–?). 176p.: Quarter bound in brown cloth with coloured decorative paper covers. Originally published 1887.
M 823 EWI CHILDREN'S COLLECTION

1249 **EWING, JULIANA HORATIA.**
SIX TO SIXTEEN. A STORY FOR GIRLS. BY JULIANA HORATIA EWING. WITH TEN ILLUSTRATIONS BY MRS. W. ALLINGHAM. NEW EDITION. LONDON: GEORGE BELL AND SONS, 1885. VIII, 120p.: front., ill. Rebound retaining original blue illustrated paper covers. Originally published 1876.
C 823.8 EWI

1250 **EWING, JULIANA HORATIA.**
SNAP-DRAGONS. A Tale of Christmas Eve and Old Father Christmas, An Old-fashioned Tale of the Young Days of a Grumpy Old Godfather. BY JULIANA HORATIA EWING. ILLUSTRATED BY GORDON BROWNE. ENGRAVED AND PRINTED BY EDMUND EVANS. LONDON: SOCIETY FOR PROMOTING CHRISTIAN KNOWLEDGE, 1888. 68p.: front., 2 plates, ill. Bound in grey paper with pictorial front cover and booklist on back.
CBD 823.8 EWI

1251 **EWING, JULIANA HORATIA.**
THE STORY OF A SHORT LIFE. BY JULIANA HORATIA EWING. ILLUSTRATED BY GORDON BROWNE LONDON: SOCIETY FOR PROMOTING CHRISTIAN KNOWLEDGE, (1885). 77p.: front., 4 plates, ill. Bound in brown paper with pictorial cover containing bibliographic details on front and pub. cat. on back. Engraved by Edmund Evans.
YSC 823.8 EWI

1252 **EWING, JULIANA HORATIA.**
WE AND THE WORLD: A BOOK FOR BOYS, BY JULIANA HORATIA EWING. WITH SEVEN ILLUSTRATIONS BY W.L. JONES. NEW EDITION. LONDON: GEORGE BELL AND SONS, 1886. 117p.: front., ill. Rebound retaining original illustrated grey paper covers. Originally published 1880.
C 823.8 EWI

1253 **EXPELLED: BEING THE STORY OF A YOUNG GENTLEMAN.**
ILLUSTRATED BY GORDON BROWNE. LONDON: JAMES NISBET AND CO., (189–?). 347p. + 2p. pub. cat. Bound in brown cloth with pictorial cover.
C 823.8 EXP

1254 **EXPERIENCE TEACHES.**
AND OTHER stories for the Young ILLUSTRATIVE OF FAMILY PROVERBS. WITH THIRTY NINE ILLUSTRATIONS. EDINBURGH: WILLIAM P. NIMMO AND CO., 1881. 128p. + 4p. pub. cat.: col. front., 3 plates, ill. Bound in red cloth with decorative cover and spine with inserted coloured vignette.
C 823.8 EXP

1255 **FANNY RAYMOND.**
Or, THE COMMANDMENT WITH PROMISE. EDINBURGH: GALL AND INGLIS, (186–?). 112p.: col. front. Bound in maroon cloth with embossed decorative covers and spine.
CBD 823.7 FAN

1256 **FARRAR, FREDERIC WILLIAM.**
ERIC; OR, LITTLE BY LITTLE, A TALE OF ROSLYN SCHOOL. BY FREDERIC W. FARRAR. ILLUSTRATED BY GORDON BROWNE. EDINBURGH: ADAM AND CHARLES BLACK, 1890. XIV, 368p.: front., vignette title page, ill. Bound in green cloth, with gilt pictorial cover and spine, and gilt edges. Originally published 1858.
YSC 823.8 FAR

1256A **Another copy.**
LONDON: ADAM AND CHARLES BLACK, 1905. XIV, 368p. + 8p. pub. cat.: front., vignette title page, ill. Bound in brown cloth, with coloured pictorial cover and spine.
C 823.8 FAR

1257 **Another copy.**
LONDON: A. AND C. BLACK LTD., 1914. 314p.: col. front. by G.D. Rowlandson, decorative title page. Bound in red cloth, with decorative cover.
YSC 823.8 FAR

1258 **FENN, GEORGE MANVILLE.**
THE ADVENTURES OF DON LAVINGTON. BY GEORGE MANVILLE FENN. LONDON: S.W. PARTRIDGE AND CO., 1899. VIII, 416p. + 28p. pub. cat.: front., 8 plates, ill. Bound in red cloth with coloured pictorial cover and spine.
C 823.8 FEN

1259 **Another copy.**
7 plates, ill. by W. Rainey. Bound in blue cloth with coloured pictorial cover and spine.

1260 **FENN, GEORGE MANVILLE.**
BEGUMBAGH, A TALE OF THE INDIAN MUTINY, AND OTHER STORIES BY GEORGE MANVILLE FENN. LONDON: W. & R. CHAMBERS, LIMITED, (1893). 192p. + 32p. ill. pub. cat.: front. Bound in brown cloth with coloured decorative cover and spine.
C 823.8 FEN

1260A **FENN, GEORGE MANVILLE.**
THE BLACK TOR. A TALE OF THE REIGN OF JAMES I. BY GEORGE MANVILLE FENN. WITH EIGHT ILLUSTRATIONS BY W.S. STACEY. LONDON: W. AND R. CHAMBERS, LIMITED, (1896). 342p.: front., 7 plates. Bound in green cloth and coloured pictorial cover and spine.
C 823.8 FEN

1261 **FENN, GEORGE MANVILLE.**
BROWNSMITH'S BOY, A ROMANCE IN A GARDEN. BY G. MANVILLE FENN. WITH ILLUSTRATIONS. LONDON: BLACKIE & SON, LIMITED, 1892. 383p. + 32p. pub. cat.: front., 5 plates. Bound in brown cloth with coloured pictorial cover and spine.
C 823.8 FEN

1261A **FENN, GEORGE MANVILLE.**
BUNYIP LAND. OR, AMONG THE BLACKFELLOWS IN NEW GUINEA, BY G. MANVILLE FENN WITH SIX PAGE ILLUSTRATIONS BY GORDON BROWNE. LONDON: BLACKIE AND SON LIMITED, (1894). 384p. + 32p., pub. cat.: front., 5 plates. Bound in yellow cloth with coloured pictorial cover and spine and tinted edges.
C 823.8 FEN

1261B **FENN, GEORGE MANVILLE.**
CROWN AND SCEPTRE. A WEST COUNTRY STORY, BY GEORGE MANVILLE FENN. ILLUSTRATED BY J. NASH. LONDON: SOCIETY FOR PROMOTING CHRISTIAN KNOWLEDGE, (189–?), 531p. + 8p. pub. cat.: front, 4 plates, decorative headpieces and tailpieces to

chapters. Bound in grey cloth with coloured pictorial cover and spine.
C 823.8 FEN

1262 **FENN, GEORGE MANVILLE.**
THE CRYSTAL HUNTERS, A Boy's Adventures in the Higher Alps BY GEO. MANVILLE FENN. LONDON: S.W. PARTRIDGE AND CO., (1892). 415p. + 32p. pub. cat.: front., 4 plates, ill. by Fredric W. Burton. Bound in red cloth with coloured pictorial cover and spine.
C 823.8 FEN

1263 **FENN, GEORGE MANVILLE.**
THE DINGO BOYS OR THE SQUATTERS OF WALLABY RANGE. BY GEORGE MANVILLE FENN. WITH SIX ILLUSTRATIONS BY W.S. STACEY. LONDON: W. AND R. CHAMBERS, LIMITED, 1892. 312p. + 32p. ill. pub. cat.: front., 5 plates. Bound in red cloth with coloured pictorial cover and spine.
C 823.8 FEN

1263A **FENN, GEORGE MANVILLE.**
FIRE ISLAND, BEING THE ADVENTURES OF UNCERTAIN NATURALISTS IN AN UNKNOWN TRACK. BY GEORGE MANVILLE FENN. WITH ILLUSTRATIONS. NEW AND CHEAPER EDITION. LONDON: SAMPSON LOW, MARSTON AND COMPANY LIMITED, (188–?). VII, 334p. + 1p. pub. cat.: front., 7 plates, by F.W. Burley. Bound in green cloth, with coloured pictorial cover and spine.
YSC 823.8 FEN

1264 **FENN, GEORGE MANVILLE.**
FIRST IN THE FIELD, A Story of New South Wales. BY GEO. MANVILLE FENN. ILLUSTRATED BY W. RAINEY R.I. THIRD EDITION. LONDON: S.W. PARTRIDGE, (189–?). 416p. + 24p. ill. pub. cat.: front., 5 plates. Bound in brown cloth with coloured pictorial cover and spine.
C 823.8 FEN

1265 **FENN, GEORGE MANVILLE.**
FIX BAY'NETS!, OR REGIMENT IN THE HILLS. BY G. MANVILLE FENN. WITH EIGHT ILLUSTRATIONS BY W.H.C. GROOME. LONDON: W. & R. CHAMBERS, LIMITED, 1899. 400p. + 32p. ill. pub. cat.: front., 7 plates. Bound in blue cloth with coloured pictorial cover and spine.
C 823.8 FEN

1266 **FENN, GEORGE MANVILLE.**
GIL THE GUNNER; OR, THE YOUNGEST OFFICER IN THE EAST. BY GEORGE MANVILLE FENN. ILLUSTRATED BY W.H. OVEREND. LONDON: SOCIETY FOR PROMOTING CHRISTIAN KNOWLEDGE, (189–?). 542p. + 8p. pub. cat.: front., 4 plates. Bound in grey cloth with coloured pictorial cover and spine.
C 823.8 FEN

1267 **FENN, GEORGE MANVILLE.**
IN THE KING'S NAME: OR, THE CRUISE OF THE "KESTREL". BY G. MANVILLE FENN. ILLUSTRATED BY GORDON BROWNE. LONDON: BLACKIE & SON. (189–?). 374p. + 32p. pub. cat.: front., 11 plates (tinted). Bound in brown cloth with pictorial cover and spine.
C 823.8 FEN

1268 **FENN, GEORGE MANVILLE.**
IN THE MAHDI'S GRASP. BY GEO. MANVILLE FENN. SIX ILLUSTRATIONS BY LANCELOT SPEED. LONDON: S.W. PARTRIDGE & CO., (1899). 428p. + 24p. ill. pub. cat.: front., 5 plates. Bound in blue cloth with coloured pictorial cover and spine.
C 823.8 FEN

1269 **Another copy.**
BY GEO. MANVILLE FENN. LONDON: DEAN AND SON LTD., (190–?). 248p.: col. front. Bound in green cloth, with decorative spine.
C 823.8 FEN

1270 **FENN, GEORGE MANVILLE.**
JUNGLE AND STREAM, OR THE ADVENTURES OF TWO BOYS IN SIAM. BY GEO. MANVILLE FENN. LONDON: S.W. PARTRIDGE & CO., 1898. 427p. + 20p. pub. cat.: front., 5 plates. Bound in red cloth with coloured pictorial cover and spine.
C 823.8 FEN

1271 **FENN, GEORGE MANVILLE.**
THE LOST MIDDY. BEING THE SECRET OF THE SMUGGLERS' GAP. BY G. MANVILLE FENN. ILLUSTRATED BY STANLEY L. WOOD. LONDON: ERNEST NISTER, (189–?). 408p. + 8p. pub. cat.: front., 7 plates. Bound in brown cloth with coloured pictorial cover and spine.
C 823.8 FEN

1272 **FENN, GEORGE MANVILLE.**
MENHARDOC: A STORY OF CORNISH NETS AND MINES. BY G. MANVILLE FENN. WITH EIGHT FULL-PAGE ILLUSTRATIONS BY C.J. STANILAND, R.I. LONDON: BLACKIE & SON, (1885). 352p. + 32p. pub. cat.: front., 7 plates. Bound in green cloth with coloured pictorial cover and spine.
C 823.8 FEN

1272A **FENN, GEORGE MANVILLE.**
MOTHER CAREY'S CHICKEN: HER VOYAGE TO THE UNKNOWN ISLE. BY G. MANVILLE FENN. WITH EIGHT FULL PAGE ILLUSTRATIONS BY A. FORESTIER. LONDON: BLACKIE AND SON, 1888. 351p. + 32p. pub. cat.: 7 plates. Bound in red cloth with pictorial cover and spine.
C 823.8 FEN

1272B **FENN, GEORGE MANVILLE.**
OFF TO THE WILDS: BEING THE ADVENTURES OF TWO BROTHERS. BY GEO. MANVILLE FENN. NEW AND CHEAPER EDITION. LONDON: SAMPSON LOW, MARSTON AND COMPANY, (189–?). VII, 331p. + 33p. pub. cat.: front., vignette on title page, ill. Bound in brown cloth with pictorial cover and spine.
C 823.8 FEN

1273 **FENN, GEORGE MANVILLE.**
PATIENCE WINS: OR WAR IN THE WORKS. BY G. MANVILLE FENN. WITH EIGHT FULL-PAGE ILLUSTRATIONS BY GORDON BROWNE. LONDON: BLACKIE & SON, 1886. 352p. + 40p. ill. pub. cat.: front., 7 plates. Bound in green cloth with pictorial cover and spine.
C 823.8 FEN

1274 **Another copy.**
WITH SIX PAGE ILLUSTRATIONS. LONDON: BLACKIE AND SON LIMITED, (190–?). 352p.: col. front., 6 plates. Bound in blue cloth, with coloured, pictorial cover and spine.
C 823.8 FEN

1275 **FENN, GEORGE MANVILLE.**
PLANTER JACK, OR THE CINNAMON GARDEN. BY G. MANVILLE FENN. Illustrated by Gordon Browne. LONDON: SOCIETY FOR PROMOTING CHRISTIAN KNOWLEDGE, (189–?). 574p. + 8p. pub. cat.: front., 4 plates. Bound in blue cloth with coloured pictorial cover and coloured decorative spine.
C 823.8 FEN

1276 **FENN, GEORGE MANVILLE.**
QUICKSILVER: OR, THE BOY WITH NO SKID TO HIS WHEEL. BY G. MANVILLE FENN. WITH TEN FULL PAGE ILLUSTRATIONS BY FRANK DADD. LONDON: BLACKIE & SON, (1889). VI, 382p. + 32p. pub. cat.: front., 9 plates. Bound in green cloth with pictorial cover and spine.
C 823.8 FEN

1277 **FENN, GEORGE MANVILLE.**
REAL GOLD, A STORY OF ADVENTURE BY GEORGE MANVILLE FENN. WITH EIGHT ILLUSTRATIONS BY W.S. STACEY. LONDON: W. & R. CHAMBERS, LIMITED, 1894. 384p. + 40p. ill. pub. cat.: front., 7 plates. Bound in green cloth with coloured cover and spine.
C 823.8 FEN

1277A **FENN, GEORGE MANVILLE.**
A TERRIBLE COWARD AND SON PHILIP. BY G. MANVILLE FENN. LONDON: BLACKIE AND SON LIMITED (1885). 159p. + 32p. pub. cat.: front., 1 plate. Bound in green cloth with decorative cover and spine.
C 823.8 FEN

1278 **FENN, GEORGE MANVILLE.**
TO WIN OR TO DIE. A TALE OF THE KLONDIKE GOLD CRAZE. BY G. MANVILLE FENN. ILLUSTRATED BY PAUL HARDY. LONDON: S.W. PARTRIDGE & CO., (189–?). 408p. + 32p. pub. cat.: front., 11 plates. Bound in red cloth with coloured pictorial cover and spine.
C 823.8 FEN

1279 **FENN, GEORGE MANVILLE.**
VINCE THE REBEL OR THE SANCTUARY IN THE BOG. BY G. MANVILLE FENN. WITH EIGHT ILLUSTRATIONS BY W.H.C. GROOME. LONDON: W. AND R. CHAMBERS, LIMITED. (1897). 384p. + 32p. ill. pub. cat.: front., 7 plates. Bound in green cloth with coloured pictorial cover and spine.
C 823.8 FEN

1280 **FERRY, JEANIE.**
MAGGIE'S LIFE WORK. BY JEANIE FERRY. LONDON: ROBERT CULLEY, (189–?). 180p. + 8p. pub. cat.: front., 2 plates, ill. by H. Prater. Bound in red cloth with pictorial cover and decorative spine.
C 823.8 FER

1281 **FLETCHER, JOSEPH SMITH.**
THE MAKING OF MATTHIAS (by) J.S. FLETCHER. ILLUSTRATED BY LUCY KEMP WELCH. LONDON: JOHN LANE: THE BODLEY HEAD, 1898. 141p. + 12p. pub. cat.: front., pictorial/decorative title page, 13 plates, headpieces, tailpieces, decorative initials. Bound in blue cloth with pictorial cover and decorative spine.
CBD 823.912 FLE

1282 **FLETCHER, JOSEPH SMITH.**
THE REMARKABLE ADVENTURE OF WALTER TRELAWNEY, PARISH 'PRENTICE OF PLYMOUTH IN THE YEAR OF THE GREAT ARMADA. RE-TOLD BY J. S. FLETCHER. WITH FRONTISPIECE BY W.S. STACEY. LONDON: W. AND R. CHAMBERS LIMITED, 1894. 216p. + 36p. ill. pub. cat.: front., ill. Bound in green cloth, with coloured pictorial cover and spine.
C 823.912 FLE

1283 **FLORA SELWYN.**
OR, HOW TO BEHAVE. A BOOK FOR LITTLE GIRLS. WITH COLOURED ILLUSTRATIONS. LONDON: CASSELL, PETTER, AND GALPIN, (187–?). 126p. + 4p. pub. cat.: col. front., 1 col. plate. Bound in maroon cloth, with embossed decorative covers and spine.
YSC 823.8 FLO

1283A **FORTESCUE, J. W.**
THE DRUMMER'S COAT. BY THE HON. J. W. FORTESCUE. WITH ILLUSTRATIONS BY H.M. BROCK. LONDON: MACMILLAN AND CO., LIMITED, 1899. 184p.: front. 3 plates. Bound in red cloth, with pictorial cover.
C 823.8 FOR

1284 **FOSTER, A. J.**
THE ROBBER BARON OF BEDFORD CASTLE. A Story of the 13th Century. By A.J. FOSTER AND E.E. CUTHELL. LONDON: T. NELSON AND SONS, 1896. 219p. + 4p. pub. cat.: front., vignette title page. Bound in red cloth with embossed pictorial cover and spine.
C 823.8 FOS

1285 **FRISWELL, J. HAIN.**
OUT AND ABOUT, A BOY'S ADVENTURES. WRITTEN FOR ADVENTUROUS BOYS. BY J. HAIN FRISWELL. ILLUSTRATED. LONDON: GROOMBRIDGE AND SONS, 1875. XII, 240p. + 4p. pub. cat.: col. front. by A.F. Lydon, 10 plates, ill. Bound in brown cloth, with embossed decorative cover and spine, and gilt edges.
YSC 823.8 FRI

1286 **FRITH, HENRY.**
THE LOST TRADER. OR, THE MYSTERY OF THE 'LOMBARDY'. BY HENRY FRITH WITH FOUR ILLUSTRATIONS BY W. BOUCHER. LONDON: W. AND R. CHAMBERS LIMITED (1893). 320p. + 32p. pub. cat.: col. front., 3 plates, decorative headpieces to chapters. Bound in red cloth with coloured pictorial cover and spine.
C 823.912 FRI

1288 **(GAYE, SELINA).**
ALL'S WELL THAT ENDS WELL. A Story of Brittany. By S.G., AUTHOR OF DICKIE WINTON. LONDON: THOMAS NELSON AND SONS, 1896. 240p.: front., additional vignette title page, by Rhind. Bound in beige cloth with coloured pictorial cover and spine.
C 823.8 GAY

1289 **GIBERNE, AGNES.**
NEXT-DOOR NEIGHBOURS. BY AGNES GIBERNE. LONDON: THE RELIGIOUS TRACT SOCIETY. (188–?). 128p. + 16p. ill. pub. cat.: front., 2 plates, ill. Bound in brown cloth with decorative cover and spine.
C 823.8 GIB

1290 **(GIBERNE, AGNES).**
A VISIT TO AUNT AGNES, FOR VERY LITTLE CHILDREN. LONDON: THE RELIGIOUS TRACT SOCIETY, (186–?). 80p.: col. front., 3 col. plates engraved by J. M. Kronheim and Co. Bound in purple cloth with decorative cover, with gilt edges.
CBD 823.8 GIB

1291 **GIBERNE, AGNES.**
WILL FOSTER OF THE FERRY. BY AGNES GIBERNE. NEW EDITION WITH ILLUSTRATIONS. LONDON: JOHN F. SHAW AND CO., (189–?). 224p.: front., 3 plates by M. Irwin. Bound in red cloth with decorative cover and spine. First published 1885.
C 823.8 GIB

1292 **GILBERT GRESHAM.**
AN AUTOBIOGRAPHY. LONDON: THE RELIGIOUS TRACT SOCIETY, (186–?). 184p. + 8p. pub. cat.: front., 4 plates by Geo. Meason. Bound in blue cloth with embossed decorative cover and spine.
C 823.8 GIL

1293 **GLANVILLE, ERNEST.**
THE GOLDEN ROCK. BY ERNEST GLANVILLE. WITH A FRONTISPIECE BY STANLEY WOOD. LONDON: CHATTO AND WINDUS, 1895. 278p. + 32p. pub. cat.: front., map. Bound in green cloth with coloured pictorial cover and spine.
C 823.8 GLA

1294 **THE GOLDEN RULE.**
OR, "DO TO OTHERS AS YOU WOULD HAVE OTHERS DO TO YOU". LONDON: T. NELSON AND SONS, 1880. 155p. + 8p. pub. cat.: front. Bound in blue cloth with decorative cover and spine.
C 823.8 GOL

1294A **GOMME, GEORGE LAURENCE** *(Editor)*.
THE QUEEN'S STORY BOOK, BEING HISTORICAL STORIES COLLECTED OUT OF ENGLISH ROMANTIC LITERATURE IN ILLUSTRATIONS OF THE REIGNS OF ENGLISH MONARCHS FROM THE CONQUEST TO QUEEN VICTORIA, AND EDITED WITH AN INTRODUCTION BY GEORGE LAURENCE GOMME. ILLUSTRATED BY W. H. ROBINSON. LONDON: ARCHIBALD CONSTABLE AND CO., 1898. XV, 446p. + 16p. pub. cat.: front., 19 plates. Bound in blue cloth with decorative cover and spine.
M 823 GOM CHILDREN'S COLLECTION

1295 **GORDON, W.J.**
THE PURSUED: A Tale of the Yellowstone. BY W.J. GOR-

DON. LONDON: FREDERICK WARNE AND CO., 1887. 124p.: front., 1 plate, ill. Bound in red cloth with coloured pictorial cover and spine.
C 823.8 GOR

1296 **GOURAUD, MADAME.**
THE TWO CHILDREN OF ST. DOMINGO. FROM THE FRENCH OF MADAME FOUAUD. WITH NUMEROUS ILLUSTRATIONS. LONDON: SAMPSON LOW, MARSTON, LOW AND SEARLE, 1875. 178p. + 4p. pub. cat.: front., 17 plates by Emile Bayard engraved by Hildibrand, ill. Bound in red cloth with decorative cover and spine.
C 843.8 GOU

1296A **GRAHAME, KENNETH.**
DREAM DAYS BY KENNETH GRAHAME. ILLUSTRATED BY MAXFIELD PARRISH. LONDON: JOHN LANE THE BODLEY HEAD, 1898. 228p. + 5p. pub. cat.: front., pictorial title page, 8 plates. Bound in green cloth, with coloured pictorial cover, with gilt top edge.
CBD 823.8 GRA

1296B **GRAHAME, KENNETH.**
DREAM DAYS, BY KENNETH GRAHAME. LONDON: JOHN LANE THE BODLEY HEAD LTD., fifth ed. 1922. 243p. + 12p. pub. cat. Bound in yellow cloth with decorative cover and spine.
CBD 823.912 GRA

1296C **GRAHAME, KENNETH.**
Dream Days by KENNETH GRAHAME. With Illustrations and Decorations by ERNEST H. SHEPARD. LONDON: THE BODLEY HEAD, fourth edition, 1930. VIII, 163p.: front., 10 plates, ill. Bound in grey linson with green and black pictorial jacket.
YSC 823.912 GRA

1297 **GRATITUDE AND PROBITY.**
AND OTHER Stories for the Young. WITH TWENTY-ONE ILLUSTRATIONS. LONDON: WILLIAM P. NIMMO, 1878. 128p.: col. front. 4 plates, ill. by Foulquier. Bound in green cloth with decorative cover and spine, inserted coloured vignette on cover.
C 823.8 GRA

1298 **GRAY-JONES, A.G.G.**
MAY CARSTAIRS, A SUCCOURER OF MANY. BY A.G.G. GRAY-JONES. LONDON: THE RELIGIOUS TRACT SOCIETY, (188–?). 192p. + 16p. pub. cat.: front., 2 plates. Bound in blue cloth with pictorial cover and spine.
C 823.8 GRA

1299 **GRAYDON, WILLIAM MURRAY.**
Lost in the Slave Land OR THE MYSTERY OF THE SACRED LAMP ROCK. BY WM. MURRAY GRAYDON. ILLUSTRATIONS BY A.J. JOHNSON. LONDON: S.W. PARTRIDGE AND CO., (189–?). 332p. + 32p. pub. cat.: front., 3 plates. Bound in red cloth with coloured pictorial cover and spine.
C 823.8 GRA

1300 **GRAYDON, WILLIAM MURRAY.**
ON WINDING WATERS, A TALE OF ADVENTURE AND PERIL, BY WILLIAM MURRAY GRAYDON. SIX ILLUSTRATIONS BY J. R. BURROW. LONDON: S. W. PARTRIDGE AND CO., (189–?). 330p. + 32p. pub. cat.: front., 5 plates. Bound in green cloth with pictorial cover and spine.
C 823.8 GRA

1301 **GREENE, MRS.**
THE GREEN HOUSE ON THE HILL; OR "Trust in God and Do the Right". BY THE HONBLE MRS. GREENE. LONDON: T. NELSON AND SONS, 1889. 205p.: front. Bound in blue cloth with coloured decorative cover and spine.
YSC 823.8 GRE

1302 **GREENE, MRS.**
THE STAR IN THE DUSTHEAP. BY THE HON. MRS. GREENE. WITH ILLUSTRATIONS. LONDON: FREDERICK WARNE AND CO., (189–?). 316p. + 28p. pub. cat.: front., 3 plates by Gunston engraved by Dalziel. Bound in blue cloth with coloured pictorial cover.
C 823.8 GRE

1303 **GREENWOOD, JAMES.**
THE HATCHET THROWERS. BY JAMES GREENWOOD. WITH THIRTY-SIX ILLUSTRATIONS, DRAWN ON WOOD, BY ERNEST GRISET, FROM HIS ORIGINAL DESIGNS. LONDON: JOHN CAMDEN HOTTEN, 1866. 164p. + 16p. ill. pub. cat.: 23 col. plates, col. ill. Bound in blue cloth with gilt pictorial cover. Colour is added by hand to the wood engravings.
C 823.8 GRE

1304 **GREENWOOD, JAMES.**
THE TRUE HISTORY OF A LITTLE RAGAMUFFIN. BY JAMES GREENWOOD. With Illustrations by Phiz and J. Gordon Thomson. LONDON: WARD, LOCK AND CO., (1870). VIII, 359p. + 16p. pub. cat.: front., additional vignette title page, 9 plates. First published 1866.
C 823.8 GRE

1305 **GROVES, JOHN PERCY.**
THE DUKE'S OWN; OR, THE ADVENTURES OF PETER DALY. BY J. PERCY GROVES. ILLUSTRATED BY LIEUT.-COLONEL MARSHMAN. LONDON: GRIFFITH, FARRAN, OKEDEN AND WELSH, 1887. 320p. + 16p. pub. cat.: front., 11 plates. Bound in blue cloth, with coloured pictorial/decorative cover and spine, and gilt edges.
YSC 823.8 GRO

1305A **Another copy.**
HENRY FROWDE, HODDER AND STOUGHTON, 1911. 320p.: col. front., vignette on title page. Bound in red cloth with coloured pictorial cover and spine.
C 823.912 GRO

1306 **(HABBERTON, JOHN).**
HELEN'S BABIES, WITH SOME ACCOUNT OF THEIR WAYS: INNOCENT, DROLL, FASCINATING, ROGUISH, MISCHIEVOUS AND NAUGHTY. ALSO, A PARTIAL RECORD OF THEIR ACTIONS, DURING TEN DAYS OF THEIR EXISTENCE. BY THEIR LATEST VICTIM, UNCLE HARRY. GLASGOW: DAVID BRYCE & SON, 1877. 183p.: pictorial title page. Bound in pictorial paper cover. Originally published 1876.
C 823.8 BUR

1307 **Another copy.**
HELEN'S BABIES; WITH SOME ACCOUNT OF THEIR WAYS, INNOCENT, CRAFTY, ANGELIC, IMPISH, WITCHING, AND REPULSIVE. ALSO A PARTIAL RECORD OF THEIR ACTIONS DURING TEN DAYS OF THEIR EXISTENCE. BY THEIR LATEST VICTIM. WITH FORTY-TWO ILLUSTRATIONS. LONDON: FREDERICK WARNE AND CO., (187–?). 185p. + 3p. pub. cat.: 6 plates, ill., engraved by the Dalziel Brothers. Rebound in green cloth.
YSC 823.8 HEL

1308 **HAGGARD, HENRY RIDER.**
ALLAN QUARTERMAIN, BEING AN ACCOUNT OF HIS FURTHER ADVENTURES AND DISCOVERIES IN COMPANY WITH SIR HENRY CURTIS, BART., COMMANDER JOHN GOOD, R.N. AND ONE UMSLOPOGAAS. BY H. RIDER HAGGARD. WITH TWENTY ILLUSTRATIONS BY CHARLES H.M. KERR. NEW EDITION. LONDON: LONGMANS, GREEN AND CO., 1888. X, 278p. + 16p. pub. cat.: front., 19 plates. Rebound in maroon cloth. Originally published 1887.
YSC 823.8 HAG

1309 **HAGGARD, HENRY RIDER.**
CLEOPATRA, BEING AN ACCOUNT OF THE FALL AND VENGEANCE OF HARMACHIS, THE ROYAL EGYPTIAN, AS SET FORTH BY HIS OWN HAND. BY H. RIDER HAGGARD. NEW EDITION. LONDON: LONGMANS, GREEN AND CO., 1891. XVI, 336p. + 16p. pub. cat.: front., 28 plates by M. Greiffenhagen and R. Caton Woodville. Rebound in maroon cloth. Originally published 1889. YSC 823.8 HAG

1310 **HAGGARD, HENRY RIDER.**
ERIC BRIGHTEYES. BY H. RIDER HAGGARD. IN TWO VOLUMES. GERMANY LEIPSIG: HEINEMANN AND BALESTIER, 1891. XVI, 238p. + 16p. pub. cat., VI, 239–487p. + 16p. pub. cat. Bound in buff paper. The English Library.
YSC 823.8 HAG

1311 **HAGGARD, HENRY RIDER.**
KING SOLOMON'S MINES. BY H. RIDER HAGGARD. One Hundredth Thousand. WITH ILLUSTRATIONS BY WALTER PAGET. LONDON: CASSELL AND COMPANY LIMITED, 1895. 320p.: front., 8 plates, map. Rebound in red cloth. Originally published 1885.
YSC 823.8 HAG

1312 **HARDING, EMILY GRACE.**
A BRAVE SURRENDER; OR, HONOUR'S REWARD. BY EMILY GRACE HARDING. With Six Illustrations by T. Eyre Macklin. LONDON: WALTER SCOTT LIMITED, (189–?). 448p. + 16p. pub. cat.: front., 4 plates. Bound in purple cloth, with coloured cover and spine, and gilt edges.
C 823.8

1313 **HARDING, EMILY GRACE.**
HAZEL: OR, PERILPOINT LIGHTHOUSE. BY E.G. Harding. With Six Full-page illustrations by Thos. Eyre Macklin. LONDON: WALTER SCOTT, LTD. (1889). VIII, 452p. + 16p. pub. cat.: front., 5 plates. Bound in blue cloth with embossed decorative cover and spine.
C 823.8 HAR

Another copy.
Bound in green cloth, with embossed decorative cover and spine.
YSC 823.8 HAR

1314 **HARRISON, F.**
AS GOOD AS GOLD. A Tale. BY F. HARRISON. LONDON: SOCIETY FOR PROMOTING CHRISTIAN KNOWLEDGE, (1885). 128p.: front., 2 plates. Bound in blue cloth with decorative cover and spine.
YSC 823.8 HAR

1315 **HARTE, FRANCIS BRET.**
THE QUEEN OF THE PIRATE ISLE BY BRET HARTE. ILLUSTRATED BY KATE GREENAWAY. ENGRAVED AND PRINTED BY EDMUND EVANS. LONDON: FREDERICK WARNE AND CO., (1886). 58p.: col. front., col. vignette on title page, col. ill. Bound in green and grey cloth with coloured pictorial cover.
CBD 823.8 HAR

1316 **HARTLEY, EMILY.**
ODD MOMENTS OF THE WILLOUGHBY BOYS. By EMILY HARTLEY. LONDON: T. NELSON AND SONS, 1883. 211p. + 10p. pub. cat.: front., additional vignette title page. Bound in brown cloth with decorative cover and spine.
YSC 823.8 HAR

1317 **HAYCRAFT, MARGARET SCOTT.**
RUNNELBROOK VALLEY. A Temperance Story. BY MRS. HAYCRAFT. LONDON: ROBERT CULLEY, (189–?). 160p. + 8p. pub. cat.: front., 1 plate, ill., by H. Prater. Bound in grey cloth with coloured pictorial cover and decorative spine.
C 823.8 HAY

1318 **HAYENS, HERBERT.**
CLEVELY SAHIB. A Tale of the Khyber Pass. BY HERBERT HAYENS. LONDON: THOMAS NELSON AND SONS, 1897. 413p. + 2p. pub. cat.: front., 7 plates. Bound in blue cloth with coloured pictorial cover and spine.
C 823.912 HAY

1318A **HAYENS, HERBERT.**
An Emperor's Doom; or, The Patriots of Mexico. By HERBERT HAYENS. LONDON: T. NELSON AND SONS, 1898. 432p.: front., 5 plates. Bound in blue cloth, with coloured pictorial cover and spine.
C 823.912 HAY

1318B **HAYENS, HERBERT.**
A Fighter in Green. A TALE OF ALGERIA. By HERBERT HAYENS. LONDON: T. NELSON AND SONS, 1899. 426p. + 6p. pub. cat.: front., 7 plates by R. Talbot Kelly. Bound in blue cloth with coloured pictorial cover and spine.
C 823.912 HAY

1318C **HAYENS, HERBERT.**
PARIS AT BAY. A STORY OF THE SIEGE AND THE COMMUNE. BY HERBERT HAYENS. WITH EIGHT ILLUSTRATIONS BY STANLEY L. WOOD. LONDON: BLACKIE AND SON LIMITED, 1898. 352p. + 32p. pub. cat.: front., 7 plates. Bound in green cloth with coloured pictorial cover and spine and tinted edges.
C 823.912 HAY

1319 **HAYENS, HERBERT.**
Under the Lone Star, A STORY OF REVOLUTION IN NICARAGUA. By HERBERT HAYENS. WITH SIX FULL-PAGE ILLUSTRATIONS BY W.S. STACEY. LONDON: T. NELSON AND SONS, 1896. 390p. + 2p. pub. cat. front., 5 plates. Bound in blue cloth with embossed decorative cover and spine.
C 823.8 HAY

1319A **HELEN'S STEWARDSHIP.**
A Story for Boys and Girls. LONDON: THE RELIGIOUS TRACT SOCIETY, (1877). 63p.: col. front. Decorative head-pieces and tailpieces to chapters. Bound in blue cloth with embossed decorative covers.
C 823.8 HEL

1320 **HELLIS, NELLIE.**
LITTLE KING DAVIE OR "Kings and Priests unto God". BY NELLIE HELLIS. LONDON: JARROLD AND SONS, 1896. 118p.: front. by Miller Smith. Bound in green cloth with decorative cover and spine.
C 823.8 HEL

1320A **HENTY, GEORGE ALFRED.**
AT ABOUKIR AND ACRE. A STORY OF NAPOLEON'S INVASION OF EGYPT. BY G.A. HENTY. WITH EIGHT FULL-PAGE ILLUSTRATIONS BY WILLIAM RAINEY, R.I. AND THREE PLANS. LONDON: BLACKIE AND SON LIMITED, 1899. 352p. + 32p. pub. cat.: front., 7 plates, 3 plans. Bound in red cloth with coloured pictorial cover and spine and tinted edges.
C 823.8 HEN

1320B **HENTY, GEORGE ALFRED.**
AT AGINCOURT. A TALE OF THE WHITE HOODS OF PARIS. WITH TWELVE ILLUSTRATIONS BY WAL PAGET. LONDON: BLACKIE AND SON, LIMITED, 1897. 384p. + 32p. pub. cat.: front., 11 plates. Bound in green cloth with coloured pictorial cover and spine and tinted edges.
C 823.8 HEN

1321 **HENTY, GEORGE ALFRED.**
BY ENGLAND'S AID: OR, THE FREEING OF THE NETHERLANDS. (1385–1604). BY G.A. HENTY. WITH TEN PAGE ILLUSTRATIONS BY ALFRED PEARSE AND FOUR MAPS. LONDON: BLACKIE AND SON LIMITED, (1891). 384p. + 32p. pub. cat.: front., 9 plates, 4 plans. Bound in blue cloth with coloured pictorial cover and spine.
C 823.8 HEN

1321A **HENTY, GEORGE ALFRED.**
BY PIKE AND DIKE. A TALE OF THE DUTCH REPUBLIC. BY G.A. HENTY. WITH TEN FULL-PAGE ILLUSTRATIONS BY MAYNARD BROWN AND FOUR MAPS. LONDON: BLACKIE AND SON, LIMITED (189–?). 384p. + 32p. pub. cat.: front., 9 plates, double page map, 2 plans. Bound in brown cloth with coloured pictorial cover and spine with tinted edges. Another copy in blue cloth.
C 823.8 HEN and YSC 823.8 HEN

1322 **HENTY, GEORGE ALFRED.**
CAPTAIN BAYLEY'S HEIR. A Tale of the Gold Fields of California. BY G.A. HENTY. ILLUSTRATED BY H.M.

PAGET. LONDON: BLACKIE AND SON LIMITED, (189–?). 386p. + 16p. pub. cat.: front., 7 plates. Bound in green cloth with coloured pictorial cover and spine.
C 823.8 HEN

1323 **Another copy.**
386p. + 32p. ill. pub. cat.: front., 5 plates. Bound in red cloth, with coloured pictorial cover and spine.
YSC 823.8 HEN

1324 **HENTY, GEORGE ALFRED.**
CONDEMNED AS A NIHILIST: A STORY OF ESCAPE FROM SIBERIA. BY G.A. HENTY. ILLUSTRATED BY WALTER PAGET. LONDON: BLACKIE AND SON LIMITED, 1893. 352p. + 32p. pub. cat.: 6 plates, col. map. Bound in olive cloth with pictorial cover and spine.
C 823.8 HEN

1325 **HENTY, GEORGE ALFRED.**
THE CORNET OF HORSE. A Tale of Marlborough's Wars. BY G.A. HENTY. WITH EIGHT FULL PAGE ILLUSTRATIONS BY H. PETHERICK AND FIVE PLANS OF BATTLE-FIELDS. LONDON: SAMPSON LOW, MARSTON AND COMPANY, 1893. VIII, 278p. + 1p. pub. cat.: front., 7 plates, 5 plans. Bound in red cloth with pictorial/decorative cover and spine.
YSC 823.8 HEN

1326 **HENTY, GEORGE ALFRED.**
For the Temple. A Tale of the Fall of Jerusalem. BY G.A. HENTY. ILLUSTRATED BY SOLOMON J. SOLOMON. LONDON: BLACKIE AND SON LIMITED, (189–?). 384p. + 16p. pub. cat.: front., 8 plates. Bound in blue cloth with coloured pictorial cover and spine.
C 823.8 HEN

1327 **HENTY, GEORGE ALFRED.**
IN THE HEART OF THE ROCKIES. A STORY OF ADVENTURE IN COLORADO. BY G.A. HENTY. WITH EIGHT FULL-PAGE ILLUSTRATIONS BY G.C. HINDLEY. LONDON: BLACKIE AND SON, LIMITED, 1895. 352p. + 32p. ill. pub. cat.: front., 7 plates. Bound in grey cloth with coloured pictorial cover and spine.
YSC 823.8 HEN

Another copy.
(190–?). 352p.: 4 plates by G.C. Hindley. Bound in green cloth, with coloured pictorial cover and spine.
C 823.8 HEN

Another copy.
(193–?). 352p.: front., 3 plates, by G.C. Hindley. Bound in blue cloth.
YSC 823.8 HEN

1328 **HENTY, GEORGE ALFRED.**
IN THE REIGN OF TERROR: THE ADVENTURES OF A WESTMINSTER BOY. BY G.A. HENTY. WITH EIGHT FULL-PAGE ILLUSTRATIONS BY J. SCHÖNBERG. LONDON: BLACKIE AND SON, LIMITED, (189–?). 351p. + 32p. pub. cat.: front., 6 plates. Bound in olive cloth with pictorial cover and spine.
C 823.8 HEN

1329 **HENTY, GEORGE ALFRED.**
JACK ARCHER, A Tale of the Crimea. BY G.A. HENTY. LONDON: SAMPSON LOW, MARSTON & COMPANY, NEW AND CHEAPER EDITION, (1888). 302p.: front., 7 plates, 5 plans. Bound in blue cloth with pictorial cover and spine.
C 823.8 HEN

1330 **HENTY, GEORGE ALFRED.**
The Lion of St. Mark. A Story of Venice in the Fourteenth Century. BY G.A. HENTY. ILLUSTRATED. LONDON: BLACKIE AND SON LIMITED, (189–?). 384p. + 16p. ill. pub. cat.: front., 7 plates. Bound in dark blue cloth with coloured pictorial cover and spine.
C 823.8 HEN

1331 **HENTY, GEORGE ALFRED.**
ST. BARTHOLOMEW'S EVE: A TALE OF THE HUGUENOT WARS. BY G.A. HENTY. WITH TWELVE ILLUSTRATIONS BY H.J. DRAPER, AND MAP OF FRANCE. LONDON: BLACKIE & SON, LIMITED, 1894. 384p. + 32p. ill. pub. cat.: front., 10 plates, ill., map. Bound in green cloth with pictorial design on cover and spine.
C 823.8 HEN

1332 **HENTY, GEORGE ALFRED.**
ST. GEORGE FOR ENGLAND, A TALE OF CRESSY AND POITIERS. BY G.A. HENTY, WITH EIGHT FULL-PAGE ILLUSTRATIONS BY GORDON BROWNE. LONDON: BLACKIE & SON, LIMITED, (188–?). 352p. + 16p. ill. pub. cat.: front., 7 plates. Bound in blue cloth with pictorial design on cover and spine.
C 823.8 HEN

1333 **HENTY, GEORGE ALFRED.**
STURDY AND STRONG: OR, HOW GEORGE ANDREWS MADE HIS WAY. BY G.A. HENTY. WITH FOUR FULL-PAGE ILLUSTRATIONS BY ROBERT FOWLER. LONDON: BLACKIE AND SON, 1888. VI, 224p.: front., 3 plates. Bound in blue cloth with pictorial cover and decorative spine.
YSC 823.8 HEN

1333A **HENTY, GEORGE ALFRED.**
THROUGH THE FRAY: A TALE OF THE LUDDITE RIOTS. BY G.A. HENTY. WITH TWELVE FULL-PAGE ILLUSTRATIONS BY H.M. PAGET. LONDON: BLACKIE AND SON, 1886. 384p. + 40p. pub. cat., headpieces and tailpieces to chapters. Bound in brown cloth with coloured pictorial cover and spine.
M 823 HEN CHILDREN'S COLLECTION

1333B **Another copy.**
(190–?) Title page missing. 384p. + 32p. pub. cat.: (front. missing), 4 plates, 1 missing. Bound in green cloth, with coloured pictorial cover and spine.
YSC 823.8 HEN

1334 **HENTY, GEORGE ALFRED.**
UNDER DRAKE'S FLAG. A TALE OF THE SPANISH MAIN. BY G.A. HENTY. WITH TWELVE FULL-PAGE ILLUSTRATIONS BY GORDON BROWNE. LONDON: BLACKIE AND SON, LIMITED, (189–?). 368p. + 32p. ill. pub. cat.: front., 11 plates. Rebound in green cloth.
YSC 823.8 HEN

1335 **HENTY, GEORGE ALFRED.**
WITH FREDERICK THE GREAT, A STORY OF THE SEVEN YEARS' WAR. BY G.A. HENTY. WITH TWELVE ILLUSTRATIONS BY WAL. PAGET. LONDON: BLACKIE & SON, LIMITED, 1898. 384p. + 32p. ill. pub. cat.: front., 11 plates, ill., map, 7 plans. Bound in red cloth with coloured pictorial cover and spine.

1336 **Another copy.**
ILLUSTRATED BY WAL. PAGET. NEW EDITION. LONDON: BLACKIE AND SON LIMITED, 1909. 384p. + 16p. pub. cat.: front., 7 plates, map, 7 plans. Bound in red cloth with coloured pictorial cover and spine.

1337 **HENTY, GEORGE ALFRED.**
WITH MOORE AT CORUNNA. BY G.A. HENTY. WITH TWELVE ILLUSTRATIONS BY WAL. PAGET. LONDON: BLACKIE AND SON, LIMITED, 1898. 384p. + 32p. ill. pub. cat.: front., 11 plates, plan. Bound in dark green cloth with coloured pictorial cover and spine.
C 823.8 HEN

1338 **HENTY, GEORGE ALFRED.**
THE YOUNG BUGLERS. A TALE OF THE PENINSULAR WAR. BY G.A. HENTY. WITH EIGHT ILLUSTRATIONS BY J. SCHÖNBERG AND TEN PLANS OF BATTLES. LONDON: GRIFFITH FARRAN BROWNE AND CO. LIMITED., (189–?). 346p.: front., 7 plates, 10 plans. Bound in blue cloth, front cover missing.
C 823.8 HEN

1339 **HILLYARD, W. HEARD.**
THE CAPTIVE'S DAUGHTER, AND OTHER STORIES, BY W. HEARD HILLYARD. CONTAINING . . . THE LITTLE TRAPPER, THE PLANTER'S SON. Illustrated. LONDON: GROOMBRIDGE AND SONS, (187–?). Front., 5 plates, ill., engraved by E. Whymper. Bound in blue cloth with embossed decorative cover and spine.
YSC 823.8 HIL

1340 **HINDERED AND HELPED.**
A story for Boys. LONDON: THE RELIGIOUS TRACT SOCIETY, (188–?). 191p. + 16p. ill. pub. cat.: front., ill. Bound in green cloth with pictorial cover and spine.
C 823.8 HIN

1341 **HIS OWN ENEMY.**
BY THE AUTHOR OF "BARBARA'S REVENGE", "SHRIMP", ETC. LONDON: THE RELIGIOUS TRACT SOCIETY, (188–?). 64p., col. front. Bound in brown cloth with decorative cover and inserted coloured vignette. Little Dot Series.
C 823.8 HIS

1342 **THE HISTORY OF ANN AND HER ELEVEN SISTERS.**
DISPLAYING THE VARIOUS ADVENTURES THEY ENCOUNTERED IN THEIR TRAVELS. LONDON: YORKSHIRE JOINT STOCK PUBLISHING AND STATIONERY COMPANY LIMITED, (186–?). 93p. + 2p. pub. cat.: front. Bound in blue cloth with embossed design.
C 823.8 HIS

1343 **THE HISTORY OF FINETTE.**
OR, A DOLL'S FORTUNES. WITH COLOURED FRONTISPIECE. LONDON: FREDERICK WARNE AND CO., (187–?). Col. front. Bound in green cloth with decorative cover and inserted coloured vignette (damaged).
C 823.8 FIN

1344 **HOARE, EDWARD NEWENHAM.**
BETWEEN TWO OCEANS; OR, GEORGE EARLEY AT PANAMA. BY EDWARD N. HOARE. ILLUSTRATED BY J. NASH. LONDON: SOCIETY FOR PROMOTING CHRISTIAN KNOWLEDGE, (188–?). 222p. + 2p. pub. cat.: front., 3 plates. Bound in red cloth with pictorial cover and spine.
C 822.8 HOA

1345 **HOARE, EDWARD NEWENHAM.**
A BRAVE FIGHT. BEING A NARRATIVE OF THE MANY TRIALS OF MASTER WILLIAM LEE, INVENTOR. BY EDWARD NEWENHAM HOARE, M.A. LONDON: SOCIETY FOR PROMOTING CHRISTIAN KNOWLEDGE, (189–?). 224p. + 16p. pub. cat.: front., 2 plates. Bound in brown cloth with pictorial cover and decorative spine.
C 823.8 HOA

1346 **HOCKING, SILAS KITTO.**
THE BLINDNESS OF MADGE TYNDALL ETC. BY SILAS K. HOCKING, F.R.H.S. LONDON: FREDERICK WARNE AND CO., 1899. VI, 247p.: front., 3 plates by Lancelot Speed, engraved by W.M.H. Ward and Co. Bound in brown cloth with embossed pictorial/decorative cover and spine.
YSC 823.8 HOC

1347 **HOCKING, SILAS KITTO.**
POOR MIKE: THE STORY OF A WAIF BY SILAS K. HOCKING, F.R.H.S. WITH ORIGINAL ILLUSTRATIONS. NEW EDITION. LONDON: FREDERICK WARNE AND CO., (1882). 83p. + 4p. ill. pub. cat.: front., ill. Bound in blue cloth with decorative cover. Story is concerned partly with life in Manchester.
C 823.8 HOC

1348 **HOCKING, SILAS KITTO.**
REAL GRIT. BY SILAS K. HOCKING, F.R.H.S. With Original Illustrations. LONDON: FREDERICK WARNE AND CO., (188–?). (X), 304p. + 8p. pub. cat.: front., 5 plates, engraved by Dalziel Brothers. Bound in brown cloth with embossed pictorial/decorative cover and spine.
YSC 823.8 HOC

1349 **HOFLAND, BARBARA HOOLE.**
INTEGRITY, A TALE BY MRS. HOFLAND. LONDON: T. NELSON AND SONS, (187–?). 200p.: col. front., col. vignette title page, 4 col. plates. Bound in blue cloth with decorative design on cover and spine. Originally published in 1823.
C 823.8 HOF

1349A **HOHLER, MRS. EDWIN.**
THE BRAVEST OF THEM ALL. A Story for Young People. BY MRS. EDWIN HOHLER. ILLUSTRATED BY CHARLES E. BROCK. LONDON: MACMILLAN AND CO., LIMITED, 1899. VIII, 214p.: front., 7 plates, Bound in blue cloth with decorative cover and spine.
C 823.8 HOH

1350 **HOHLER, MRS. EDWIN.**
THE PICTURE ON THE STAIRS. A Romance for Children. BY MRS. EDWIN HOHLER. LONDON: SOCIETY FOR PROMOTING CHRISTIAN KNOWLEDGE, (1897). 127p. + 16p. pub. cat.: front. Bound in turquoise cloth with pictorial cover and decorative spine.
YSC 823.8 HOH

1351 **HOLT, EMILY SARAH.**
For the Master's Sake. A STORY OF THE DAYS OF QUEEN MARY. BY EMILY SARAH HOLT. LONDON: JOHN F. SHAW AND CO., (187–?). VIII, 175p. + 24p. pub. cat.: front., 2 plates by H. Petherick.
C 823.8 HOL

1352 **THE HOLY WELL.**
An Irish Story, TO WHICH IS ADDED, AN IRISH CONVERT'S LETTER. LONDON: THE RELIGIOUS TRACT SOCIETY, (187–?). 64p.: col. front. Bound in purple cloth with decorative cover.
C 823.8 HOL

1353 **HOME, C.M.**
REDMINTON SCHOOL. BY C.M. HOME. LONDON: ART AND BOOK COMPANY, 1894. 406p. + 6p. pub. cat.: pictorial chapter headings. Rebound in green cloth.
YSC 823.8 HOM

1354 **HOOD, THOMAS.**
RAINBOW'S REST. BY THOMAS HOOD. AND OTHER STORIES CONTAINING (ALSO) . . . PETER DRAKE'S DREAM. BY MRS. BRODERIP. WEE MAGGIE. BY MRS. BRODERIP. Illustrated. LONDON: GROOMBRIDGE AND SONS, (187–?). Front., 3 plates, ill. Bound in green cloth with decorative cover and spine.
C 823.8 HOO

1355 **HOPE, ASCOTT ROBERT** *(Pseud).*
"DUMPS" AND OTHER STORIES BY ASCOTT R. HOPE. (pseudonym for ASCOTT ROBERT HOPE-MONCRIEFF). EDINBURGH: W.P. NIMMO, HAY, AND MITCHELL, (1898). 128p. + 16p. pub. cat.: front. Bound in olive cloth with coloured decorative cover and spine.
C 823.8 HOP

1356 **HOPE, ASCOTT ROBERT** *(Pseud).*
THE WIGWAM AND THE WARPATH: OR TALES OF THE RED INDIANS. BY ASCOTT R. HOPE. WITH ILLUSTRATIONS. LONDON: BLACKIE & SON LIMITED. (1884). 352p. + 32p. pub. cat.: front., 4 plates. Bound in green cloth with coloured pictorial cover and spine. Illustrations by Gordon Browne.
C 823.8 HOP

1357 **HORNIBROOK (EMMA E.?).**
ONE LINK IN A CHAIN BY MRS. HORNIBROOK. LONDON: GALL AND INGLIS, (188–?). 128p.: front., 1 plate. Bound in blue cloth with decorative cover and spine. Includes presentation plate of Manchester School Board, Vine St. Board School.
YSC 823.8 HOR

1358 **HOWE, HARRIET D'OYLEY.**
CLARA EVESHAM; OR, THE LIFE OF A SCHOOL GIRL. A Narrative founded upon Fact. ILLUSTRATED WITH FOUR ETCHINGS ON STEEL BY ALFRED ASHLEY. LONDON: WILLIAM MACKINTOSH, 1866. 124p. 3 plates (frontispiece missing). Bound in blue cloth with decorative cover and spine.
C 823.8 HOW

1359 **HOWITT, MARY.**
LITTLE COIN, MUCH CARE: OR, HOW POOR MEN LIVE. A Tale for Young Persons. BY MARY HOWITT. SIXTH EDITION. LONDON: WILLIAM TEGG AND CO., 1857. 171p. + 38p. pub. cat.: front., additional vignette title page. Bound in blue cloth with embossed cover and spine, and gilt edges. First published 1842.
C 823.8 HOW

1360 **HOWITT, MARY.**
Our Cousins in Ohio. BY MARY HOWITT WITH Four Illustrations on Steel, FROM ORIGINAL DESIGNS BY ANNA MARY HOWITT. SECOND EDITION. LONDON: A.W. BENNETT, 1866. VIII, 280p.: front., 3 plates. Bound in red cloth with embossed decorative cover.
C 823.8 HOW

1361 **HUGH NOLAN, THE LOBSTER-BOY.**
OR, A Foolish Son is a Heaviness to his Mother. EDINBURGH: GALL AND INGLIS, (187–?). 112p., col. front. Bound in blue cloth with embossed decorative cover and spine. Includes an award plate of the Manchester School Board, marked with Holy Trinity Board School, Hulme.
C 823.8 HUG

1362 **(HUGHES, THOMAS).**
TOM BROWN AT OXFORD. BY THE AUTHOR OF "TOM BROWN'S SCHOOL DAYS". NEW EDITION WITH ILLUSTRATIONS BY SIDNEY P. HALL. LONDON: MACMILLAN AND CO., 1875. XII, 546p. + 2p. pub. cat.: front., 6 plates. Bound in brown cloth with decorative cover and spine.
C 823.8 HUG

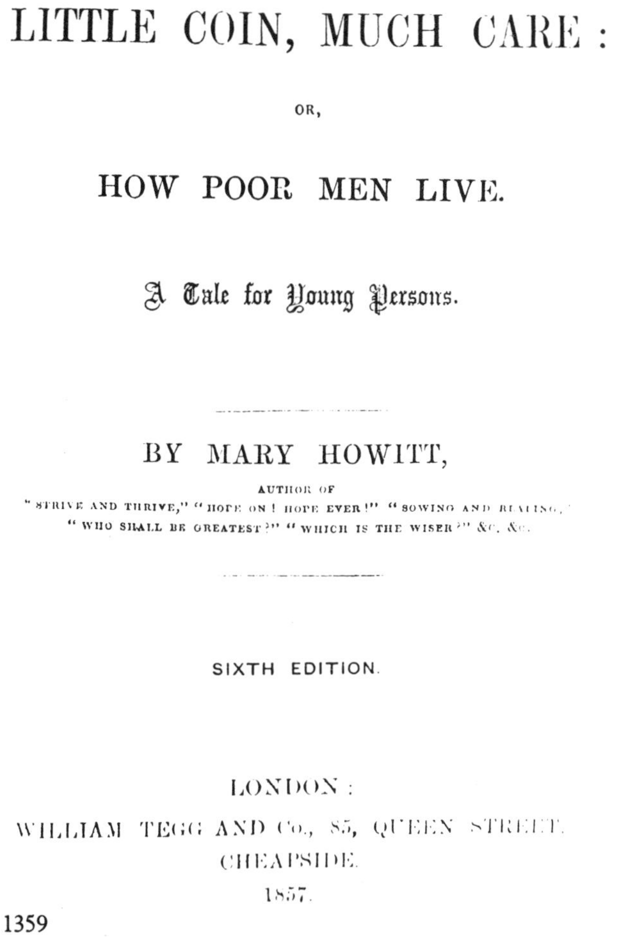
LITTLE COIN, MUCH CARE:

OR,

HOW POOR MEN LIVE.

A Tale for Young Persons.

BY MARY HOWITT,

AUTHOR OF
"STRIVE AND THRIVE," "HOPE ON! HOPE EVER!" "SOWING AND REAPING,"
"WHO SHALL BE GREATEST?" "WHICH IS THE WISER?" &c. &c.

SIXTH EDITION.

LONDON:
WILLIAM TEGG AND Co., 85, QUEEN STREET,
CHEAPSIDE.
1857.

1359

1363 **(HUGHES, THOMAS).**
TOM BROWN'S SCHOOL DAYS. BY AN OLD BOY. ELEVENTH THOUSAND. CAMBRIDGE: MACMILLAN AND CO., Fifth edition 1858. VIII, 420p. + 24p. pub. cat. Bound in blue cloth with embossed patterned cover and spine. Originally published 1857.
C 823.8 HUG

1364 **Another copy.**
WITH ILLUSTRATIONS BY EDMUND J. SULLIVAN. LONDON: MACMILLAN AND CO., LIMITED, 1897. XXII, 312p.: front., 19 plates, ill. map. Bound in black cloth with embossed gilt decorative cover and spine, with gilt edges. Cranford Series.

*... games of chariot-racing, cock-fighting, and bolstering went on in the vacant space.*

1364

1365 **Another copy.**
WITH NUMEROUS ILLUSTRATIONS MADE AT RUGBY SCHOOL BY LOUIS RHEAD WITH AN INTRODUCTION BY W.D. HOWELLS. NEW YORK: HARPER AND BROTHERS, 1911. XXIV, 376p.: col. front., 33 plates including map of Rugby School, ill. Bound in black cloth with coloured paper label on cover.

1366 **Another copy.**
LONDON: HENRY FROWDE HODDER AND STOUGHTON, (191–?). 263p.: col. front. by H.M. BROCK. Bound in purple decorative paper with coloured pictorial paper label on cover.

1367 **Another copy.**
With illustrations by ARTHUR HUGHES AND SYDNEY PRIOR HALL. LONDON: MACMILLAN AND CO., 6th edition, 1889. (Facsimile reprint by GODFREY CAVE ASSOCIATES LTD., 1979) XXII, 308p.: front., 16 plates, ill., pictorial initials. Bound in brown linson with pictorial paper jacket.

1368 **HUTCHESON, JOHN CONROY.**
CROWN AND ANCHOR OR Under the Pen'ant. BY JOHN C. HUTCHESON. LONDON: F.V. WHITE AND CO., 1898. VII, 306p. + 4p. pub. cat.: front., 5 plates by J.B. Greene. Bound in blue cloth with coloured pictorial cover and spine.
C 823.8 HUT

1369 **HUTCHINSON, JOHN ROBERT.**
THE QUEST OF THE GOLDEN PEARL. BY J.R. HUTCHINSON. WITH ILLUSTRATIONS BY HUME NISBET. LONDON: WARD AND DOWNEY LIMITED, 1897. VIII, 278p. + 2p. pub. cat.: front., 3 plates, ill. Bound in olive cloth with coloured pictorial cover and spine.
C 823.8 HUT

1370 **HUTTON, BARBARA.**
TALES OF THE WHITE COCKADE. BY BARBARA HUTTON. WITH ILLUSTRATIONS BY I. LAWSON. LONDON: GRIFFITH, FARRAN, OKEDEN AND WELSH, (1890). 383p.: front., 5 plates. Bound in red cloth with pictorial cover.
C 823.8 HUT

1371 **HYNE, CHARLES JOHN CUTCLIFFE WRIGHT.**
ADVENTURES OF CAPTAIN KETTLE. BY CUTCLIFFE HYNE. ILLUSTRATED BY STANLEY L. WOOD. LONDON: C. ARTHUR PEARSON LIMITED, 1898. VIII, 318p. + 16p. pub. cat.: 14 plates, ill., headpieces to chapters. Bound in red with pictorial cover.
CBD 823.8 HYN

1371A **HYNE, CHARLES JOHN CUTCLIFFE WRIGHT.**
THE CAPTURED CRUISER OR TWO YEARS FROM LAND. BY C.J. HYNE. ILLUSTRATED BY F. BRANGWYN. LONDON: BLACKIE, 1893. 288p. + 32p. ill. pub. cat.: front., 5 plates. Bound in brown cloth with coloured pictorial cover and spine.
C 823.8 HYN

1372 **HYNE, CHARLES JOHN CUTCLIFFE WRIGHT.**
THE WILD-CATTERS. A Tale of the Pennsylvanian Oil-Fields. BY C.J. CUTCLIFFE HYNE. ILLUSTRATIONS BY H.S. GREIG. LONDON: THE SUNDAY SCHOOL UNION, (189–?). 256p. + 16p. ill. pub. cat.: front., 9 plates. Bound in brown cloth with coloured pictorial cover and spine.
C 823.8 HYN

1373 **INGELOW, JEAN.**
A SISTER'S BYE HOURS. By JEAN INGELOW. LONDON: WELLS GARDNER, DARTON AND CO., 1889. 467p.: front., vignette on title page. Bound in blue cloth with coloured pictorial/decorative cover and spine. Originally published 1868. Includes a Manchester School Board presentation plate.
C 823.8 ING

1374 **INGOLDSBY, THOMAS** *(Pseud for BARHAM, RICHARD HARRIS).*
THE INGOLDSBY LEGENDS OR MIRTH AND MARVELS, BY THOMAS INGOLDSBY ESQUIRE FIRST SERIES, SECOND SERIES, THIRD SERIES FIFTH EDITION. (3 VOLS). LONDON: RICHARD BENTLEY, 1852. XII, 339; VII, 288; VI, 364: front. of author in third series vol., decorative title pages, 7, 5, 5 plates, ill. Bound in blue cloth with embossed decorative covers and spine. Originally published 1840.
CBD 823.8 ING

1375 **INGOLDSBY, THOMAS.**
INGOLDSBY LEGENDS OR MIRTH AND MARVELS BY THOMAS INGOLDSBY, ESQ. ILLUSTRATED BY ARTHUR RACKHAM, A.R.W.S. LONDON: J.M. DENT AND CO., 1905. XXIII, 638p.: col. front., 11 col. plates, ill., pictorial endpapers. Bound in dark green cloth with decorative covers and spine.
CBD 823.8 ING

1376 **Another copy.**
Illustrated by Arthur Rackham, A.R.W.S. LONDON: WILLIAM HEINEMANN, 1919. XIX, 549p.: col. decorative title page, 23 col. plates, 12 tinted plates, ill. Bound in grey cloth with decorative cover and spine.
CBD 823.8 ING

1378 **(INMAN, HERBERT ESCOTT).**
HARDY THE FOOLHARDY. BY THE AUTHOR OF "HONOR BRIGHT", "THE TWO BLACKBIRDS", etc. LONDON: WELLS, GARDNER, DARTON AND CO., 1895. 127p.: front., 2 plates. Bound in blue cloth with coloured pictorial cover and spine.
C 823.912 INM

1379 **IRVING, WASHINGTON.**
Rip Van Winkle, by Washington Irving. U.S.A. NEW YORK: G.P. PUTNAM'S SONS, 1899. V, 115p.: front., 6 plates, ill. by T.S. Coburn. Title page and text pages decorated with illustrations facing every page of text. Bound in cream buckram with coloured decorative cover, spine and end papers.
C 813.2 IRV

1380 **(JACSON, CATHERINE).**
THE STORM'S GIFT, A Lancashire Story. LONDON: THOMAS NELSON AND SONS, 1891, 128p.: front., additional vignette title page, 2 plates. Bound in light blue cloth with pictorial cover and spine.
C 823.8 JAC

1381 **JAMES, BROTHER.**
THE FALSE FRIEND. A Tale of the Times. BY BROTHER JAMES. DUBLIN: JAMES DUFFY AND CO., LIMITED. (187–?). 133p., front. Bound in brown cloth with embossed decorative cover and decorative spine.
C 823.8 BRO

1382 **JAMES, HARRY A.**
THE DOLL-MAN'S GIFT, by Harry A. James. Illustrated by K.M. Skeaping. LONDON: GEORGE NEWNES LTD., (189–?). 198p. + 2p. pub. cat.: pictorial title page, front., 16 plates, ill. Bound in blue cloth.
YSC 823.8 JAM

1383 **JAY, W.M.L.**
WITHOUT AND WITHIN: A New England Story. BY W.M.L. JAY. SPECIAL EDITION. LONDON: PRINTED FOR THE BOOKSELLERS, 1881. VIII, 434p. + 4p. cat. of James Nisbet and Co's publications.: col. front., 1 col. plate. Bound in blue cloth with embossed decorative cover and spine including inserted vignette.
C 823.8 JAY

1384 **JENKYNS, ANNIE.**
THE Wreckers of Lavernock. BY ANNIE JENKYNS. LONDON: T. FISHER UNWIN, 1885. 343p. + 32p. pub. cat. Bound in beige cloth with coloured pictorial cover.
C 823.8 JEN

1385 **JOE AND SALLY.**
OR A GOOD DEED AND ITS FRUITS. BY THE AUTHOR OF GRUMBLING TOMMY ETC. LONDON: S.W. PARTRIDGE AND CO., (189–?). 96p. + 16p. pub. cat.: front., 4 plates, ill. Bound in blue cloth with coloured pictorial cover and spine.
C 823.8 JOE

1386 **JOHNSTONE, DAVID LAWSON.**
THROUGH FIGHT TO FORTUNE or The Surprising Adventures of Richard Tregellas. By DAVID LAWSON JOHNSTONE. WITH SIXTEEN ORIGINAL ILLUSTRATIONS BY W. BOUCHER. NEW EDITION. EDINBURGH: OLIPHANT ANDERSON AND FERRIER, (189–?). 313p. + 6p. pub. cat.: front., 15 plates. Bound in blue cloth with coloured decorative cover and spine.
C 823.8 JOH

1387 **JONES, C.A.**
LITTLE SIR NICHOLAS. A STORY FOR CHILDREN. BY C.A. JONES. LONDON: FREDERICK WARNE AND

CO., (189–?). XII, 250p. + 10p. pub. cat.: front., vignette on title page, 5 plates, ill. by Caroline Paterson. Bound in grey cloth with coloured pictorial cover and spine.
C 823.8 JON

1388 **JONES, C.A.**
UNDER THE KING'S BANNER. Stories of the Soldiers of Christ in all Ages. BY C.A. JONES. WITH INTRODUCTORY PREFACE BY THE LORD BISHOP OF WAKEFIELD. LONDON: WELLS GARDNER, DARTON AND CO., 1891. XII, 259p. + 22p. pub. cat.: front., 12 plates. Bound in red cloth with pictorial/decorative cover and spine.
YSC 823.8 JON

1389 **JONES, S.R.**
STRUGGLING UPWARD. A Tale of Mining Life. BY S.R. JONES. With Illustrations. LONDON: GALL AND INGLIS, (188–?). 287p.: front., 5 plates. Bound in blue cloth with embossed decorative cover and spine, with gilt edges.
C 823.8 JON

1390 **KENNEDY, GRACE.**
JESSY ALLAN, THE LAME GIRL: A STORY FOUNDED ON FACTS. BY GRACE KENNEDY. NEW EDITION. EDINBURGH: WILLIAM OLIPHANT AND CO., (187–?). 72p.: front. Bound in brown cloth with inserted coloured pictorial picture on cover.
C 823.8 KEN

1391 **KER, DAVID.**
SWEPT OUT TO SEA. BY DAVID KER. WITH SIX ILLUSTRATIONS. By J. AYTON SYMINGTON. LONDON: W. AND R. CHAMBERS, 1897, 297p. + 52p. ill. pub. cat.: front., 5 plates, ill. Bound in red cloth with pictorial cover and spine.
C 823.8 KER

1392 **KEY, AMY.**
TREGARVON: A TALE OF THE CORNISH COAST. BY AMY KEY (pseud for AMY KEY CLARKE). LONDON: SUNDAY SCHOOL UNION, (189–?). 105p. + 2p. pub. cat.: front., 2 plates. Bound in brown cloth, with embossed decorative covers and spine.
C 823.8 KEY

1393 **KIMMINS, G.T.**
POLLY OF PARKER'S RENTS. BY G.T. KIMMINS ("SISTER GRACE") WITH FORTY FIVE ILLUSTRATIONS BY F. MABELLE PEARSE. LONDON: JAMES BOWDEN, 1899. VIII, 232p. + 24p. ill. pub. cat.: front., vignette on title page, 7 plates, ill. Bound in orange cloth with coloured pictorial cover.
C 823.8 KIM

1394 **KING JACK OF HAYLANDS.**
A Tale of School Life. By the Author of "HOPE ON", "SUSY'S FLOWERS" ETC. ETC. LONDON, T. NELSON AND SONS. 1888. 160p.: front., ill. Bound in red cloth with pictorial cover.
C 823.8 KIN

1395 **KINGSLEY, CHARLES.**
THE WATER-BABIES; A Fairy Tale for a Land-Baby. BY THE REV. CHARLES KINGSLEY. WITH TWO ILLUSTRATIONS BY J. NOEL PATON, R.S.A. LONDON AND CAMBRIDGE: MACMILLAN AND CO., (1st Edition) 1863. (VI), 350p.: front., 1 plate. Half bound in black leather with marbled paper covers.
M 823 KIN CHILDREN'S COLLECTION

1395A **Another copy.**
ILLUSTRATIONS BY SIR NOEL PATON, R.S.A. AND PERCIVAL SKELTON. NEW EDITION. LONDON: MACMILLAN AND CO., 1880. 388p. + 1p. pub. cat.: front., 3 plates. Bound in blue cloth.
YSC 823.8 KIN

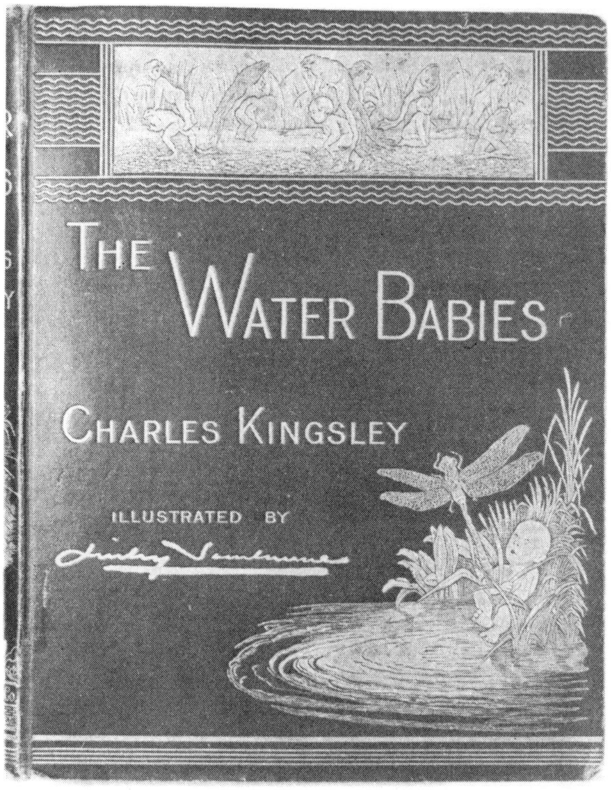


1396

1396 **Another copy.**
NEW EDITION WITH ONE HUNDRED ILLUSTRATIONS BY LINLEY SAMBOURNE. LONDON: MACMILLAN AND CO., 1885. 371p.: ill., headpieces to chapters. Bound in blue cloth with decorative cover and spine, with gilt edges.
CBD 823.8 KIN

1396A **Another copy.**
WITH COLOUR PLATES BY HARRY G. THEAKER. LONDON: WARD, LOCK AND CO., LIMITED, n.d. 224p.: col. front., 17 col. plates. Bound in coloured pictorial paper.
YSC 823.8 KIN

1396B **Another copy.**
With illustrations by W. HEATH ROBINSON. LONDON: CONSTABLE AND COMPANY LIMITED, 1915. X, 320p.: col. front., decorative title page, 7 col. plates, ill. Bound in green cloth, with light green coloured pictorial paper jacket.
CBD 823.8 KIN

1397 **KINGSLEY, CHARLES.**
WESTWARD HO! OR THE VOYAGES AND ADVENTURES OF Sir Amyas Leigh, Knight, OF BURROUGH, IN THE COUNTY OF DEVON, IN THE REIGN OF HER MOST GLORIOUS MAJESTY QUEEN ELIZABETH. RENDERED INTO MODERN ENGLISH BY CHARLES KINGSLEY. WITH ILLUSTRATIONS BY CHARLES E. BROCK. IN TWO VOLS. LONDON: MACMILLAN AND CO., LTD., 1896. X, 484p.; VIII, 476p.: fronts., 25 plates, 25 plates, headpieces to chapters. Bound in blue cloth with decorative cover and spine. Originally published 1855.
CBD 823.8 KIN

1398 **KINGSLEY, CHARLES.**
WESTWARD HO! By Charles Kingsley. Eight Coloured Illustrations. LONDON: COLLINS' CLEAR-TYPE PRESS, (190–?). 596p.: col. front., 7 col. plates by G.C. Hindley, decorative endpapers. Bound in blue cloth, with coloured decorative cover and spine.
YSC 823.8 KIN

1399 **KINGSLEY, CHARLES.**
WESTWARD HO! or, the Voyages and Adventures of Sir Amyas Leigh, Knight, of Burro in the County of Devon. In the reign of Her Most Glorious Majesty Queen Elizabeth. BY CHARLES KINGSLEY. Pictures by N.C. WYETH. LONDON: HODDER AND STOUGHTON, 1920. VIII, 413p.: col. front., col. pictorial title page, 13 col. plates, col. pictorial endpapers. Bound in blue cloth with decorative cover and spine.
CBD 823.8 KIN

1400 **KINGSLEY, HENRY.**
THE RECOLLECTIONS OF GEOFFREY HAMLYN. BY HENRY KINGSLEY. NEW EDITION. WITH A MEMOIR OF HENRY KINGSLEY BY CLEMENT SHORTER. ILLUSTRATED BY HERBERT RAILTON. LONDON: WARD, LOCK AND BOWDEN, LIMITED, 1894. XXIII, 468p.: 1 plate, ill. Bound in red cloth.
CBD 823.8 KIN

1401 **KINGSTON, WILLIAM HENRY GILES** *(Editor)*.
ADVENTURES IN AFRICA, BY AN AFRICAN TRADER. EDITED BY WILLIAM H.G. KINGSTON. WITH 42 ILLUSTRATIONS. LONDON: GEORGE ROUTLEDGE AND SONS, LIMITED, (189–?). IV, 188p.: vignette on title page, 34 plates. Bound in grey cloth with decorative cover and spine.
C 823.8 KIN

1402 **KINGSTON, WILLIAM HENRY GILES.**
ADVENTURES IN INDIA BY WILLIAM H.G. KINGSTON. WITH THIRTY SIX ILLUSTRATIONS. LONDON: GEORGE ROUTLEDGE AND SONS, LIMITED, VI, 186p.: vignette on title page, 26 plates. Bound in green cloth with coloured decorative cover, inscribed EVERY BOY'S LIBRARY.
C 823.8 KIN

1402A **KINGSTON, WILLIAM HENRY GILES.**
ADVENTURES IN THE FAR WEST. BY WILLIAM H.G. KINGSTON. LONDON: GEORGE ROUTLEDGE AND SONS, LIMITED, (189–?). 192p.: vignette on title page, 29 plates, ill., tailpieces to some chapters. Bound in green cloth with coloured pictorial covers.
C 823.8 KIN

1402B **KINGSTON, WILLIAM HENRY GILES.**
ADVENTURES OF DICK ONSLOW AMONG THE RED INDIANS. BY WILLIAM H.G. KINGSTON. WITH 8 ILLUSTRATIONS. LONDON: GALL AND INGLIS, (187–?). VIII, 319p.: front., 7 plates. Bound in red cloth with embossed decorative cover and spine, with gilt edges.
C 823.8 KIN

1403 **KINGSTON, WILLIAM HENRY GILES.**
AFAR IN THE FOREST. A Tale of Adventure in North America. BY THE LATE W.H.G. KINGSTON. WITH 41 FULL-PAGE ILLUSTRATIONS. LONDON: T. NELSON AND SONS, 1895. XII, 393p. + 6p. pub. cat.: front., 40 plates. Bound in purple cloth with pictorial cover and spine.
C 823.8 KIN

1404 **KINGSTON, WILLIAM HENRY GILES.**
THE AFRICAN TRADER OR, Harvey Bayford's Adventures. LONDON: GALL AND INGLIS, (188–?). 128p.: front. Bound in blue cloth with coloured decorative cover and spine.
C 823.8 KIN

1405 **KINGSTON, WILLIAM HENRY GILES.**
AMONG THE RED-SKINS; OR, Over the Rocky Mountains. BY W.H.G. KINGSTON. SECOND EDITION. LONDON: CASSELL, PETTER, GALPIN AND CO., (188–?). VIII, 128p. + 4p. pub. cat.: front., 8 plates, ill. Bound in green cloth with decorative cover and spine.
C 823.8 KIN

1406 **KINGSTON, WILLIAM HENRY GILES.**
ANTONY WAYMOUTH; OR, THE GENTLEMEN ADVENTURERS. A Chronicle of the Sea. BY WILLIAM H.G. KINGSTON. LONDON: FREDERICK WARNE, 1865. VIII, 271p. + 24p. ill. pub. cat.: front., 9 plates by A.P., engraved by W.L. Thomas. Bound in red cloth with embossed decorative cover.
C 823.8 KIN

1407 **KINGSTON, WILLIAM HENRY GILES.**
BEN BURTON OR, BORN AND BRED AT SEA. BY W.H.G. KINGSTON. NEW AND CHEAPER EDITION. LONDON: SAMPSON, LOW, MARSTON, AND COMPANY, 1892. 332p. + 32p. pub. cat.: front. by Sydney Hall. Bound in brown cloth with coloured pictorial cover and spine.
C 823.8 KIN

1407A **KINGSTON, WILLIAM HENRY GILES.**
BEN HADDEN; OR, Do Right, Whatever Comes of It. BY W.H.G. KINGSTON. LONDON: THE RELIGIOUS TRACT SOCIETY, (188–?). 160p. + 16p. pub. cat.: vignette title page, ill., decorations at chapter beginnings and ends. Bound in red cloth with pictorial cover and spine and decorative endpapers.
C 823.8 KIN

1407B **KINGSTON, WILLIAM HENRY GILES.**
THE BOY WHO SAILED WITH BLAKE. BY WILLIAM H.G. KINGSTON. LONDON: SUNDAY SCHOOL UNION, 7TH ED., (1880). (3), 182p. + 2p. pub. cat.: front., 9 plates, ill., decorative chapter headings and headpieces. Bound in green with coloured pictorial cover and spine with gilt top edge.
C 823.8 KIN

1408 **KINGSTON, WILLIAM HENRY GILES.**
CLARA MAYNARD; OR The true and the false. A TALE OF THE TIMES. BY W.H.G. KINGSTON. LONDON: HODDER AND STOUGHTON, 1879. 279p. + 4p. pub. cat. Bound in brown cloth with embossed decorative cover and spine with inserted coloured vignette.
C 823.8 KIN

1409 **KINGSTON, WILLIAM HENRY GILES.**
THE CRUISE OF THE "DAINTY", OR ROVINGS IN THE PACIFIC. BY THE LATE WILLIAM H.G. KINGSTON. LONDON: SOCIETY FOR PROMOTING CHRISTIAN KNOWLEDGE, (189–?). 192p. + 8p. pub. cat.: front., 2 plates. Bound in green cloth with pictorial cover.
C 823.8 KIN

1410 **KINGSTON, WILLIAM HENRY GILES.**
THE CRUISE OF THE FROLIC. A SEA STORY BY WILLIAM H.G. KINGSTON. U.S.A. BOSTON: J.E. TILTON AND COMPANY, 1866. XI, 396p., 4 plates. Bound in green cloth.
C 823.8 KIN

1411 **KINGSTON, WILLIAM HENRY GILES.**
THE DIARY OF MILICENT COURTENAY; OR, The Experiences of a Young Lady at Home and Abroad. BY W.H.G. KINGSTON. LONDON: GALL AND INGLIS, (189–?). 448p.: front., 3 plates. Bound in blue cloth with decorative cover and spine, with gilt edges.
C 823.8 KIN

1411A **KINGSTON, WILLIAM HENRY GILES.**
DICK CHEVELEY. HIS ADVENTURES AND MISADVENTURES. BY W.H.G. KINGSTON. NEW AND CHEAPER EDITION. LONDON: SAMPSON, LOW, MARSTON AND COMPANY (188–?). XII, 388p. + 32p. pub. cat.: front., vignette title page, 7 plates engraved by C.H. Barbant.
C 823.8 KIN

1412 **KINGSTON, WILLIAM HENRY GILES.**
FRED MARKHAM IN RUSSIA; OR, THE BOY TRAVELLERS IN THE LAND OF THE CZAR. BY W.H.G. KINGSTON. WITH ILLUSTRATIONS BY R.T. LANDELLS. LONDON: GRIFFITH, FARRAN, OKEDEN AND WELSH, (1888). 320p. + 16p. pub. cat.: front., 7 plates. Bound in red cloth with decorative cover.
C 823.8 KIN

1413 **KINGSTON, WILLIAM HENRY GILES.**
THE FRONTIER FORT; OR, STIRRING TIMES IN THE NORTH-WEST TERRITORY OF BRITISH AMERICA BY THE LATE W.H.G. KINGSTON. LONDON: SOCIETY FOR PROMOTING CHRISTIAN KNOWLEDGE, (189–?). 160p. + 8p. pub. cat.: front., 2 plates by D.H. Friston. Bound in green cloth, with coloured pictorial cover and decorative spine.
C 823.8 KIN

1414 **Another copy.**
ILLUSTRATED BY ARCHIE WEBB. LONDON: THE SHELDON PRESS, (190–?). 160p. + 16p. pub. cat.: col. front. Bound in brown cloth, with coloured pictorial cover and spine.

1415 **KINGSTON, WILLIAM HENRY GILES.**
THE GILPINS AND THEIR FORTUNES. An Australian tale. BY WILLIAM H.G. KINGSTON. LONDON: THE SOCIETY FOR PROMOTING CHRISTIAN KNOWLEDGE, (189–?). 159p. + 8p. pub. cat.: front., 3 plates. Bound in red cloth with coloured pictorial cover.
C 823.8 KIN

1415A **Another copy.**
THE GILPINS AND THEIR FORTUNES, A Story of Early Days in Australia. BY WILLIAM H.G. KINGSTON. ILLUSTRATED BY ARCHIE WEBB. LONDON: THE SHELDON PRESS, (193–?). 159p. + 1p. pub. cat.: col. front. Bound in green cloth, with pictorial cover and spine.

1416 **KINGSTON, WILLIAM HENRY GILES.**
THE GOLDEN GRASSHOPPER. A STORY OF THE DAYS OF SIR THOMAS GRESHAM, KNT. AS NARRATED IN THE DIARY OF ERNST VERNER, WHILOM HIS PAGE AND SECRETARY, DURING THE REIGNS OF QUEENS MARY AND ELIZABETH. BY WILLIAM H.G. KINGSTON. LONDON: THE RELIGIOUS TRACT SOCIETY, (188–?). 352p. + 18p. pub. cat.: vignette portrait of author, 2 plates, ill. Bound in green cloth with coloured decorative cover and spine, with gilt edges.
C 823.8 KIN

1416A **KINGSTON, WILLIAM HENRY GILES.**
HENDRICKS THE HUNTER; OR, The Border Farm. A TALE OF ZULULAND. BY W.H.G. KINGSTON. LONDON: HODDER AND STOUGHTON, 1893. IV, 313p. + 32p. ill. pub. cat.: front., 4 plates.
C 823.8 KIN

1416B **KINGSTON, WILLIAM HENRY GILES.**
HURRICANE HURRY; OR, THE ADVENTURES OF A NAVAL OFFICER AFLOAT AND ON SHORE. BY THE LATE W.H.G. KINGSTON. WITH ILLUSTRATIONS BY R. HUTTULA. LONDON: GRIFFITH, FARRAN, OKEDEN AND WELSH, (1891). VII, 472p. + 32p. ill. pub. cat.: front., 4 plates. Bound in blue cloth with coloured decorative cover, with gilt edges. Originally published 1873.
C 823.8 KIN

1416C **KINGSTON, WILLIAM HENRY GILES.**
IN NEW GRANADA; OR, HEROES AND PATRIOTS. A Tale for Boys. BY W.H.G. KINGSTON WITH THIRTY SIX ENGRAVINGS. LONDON: T. NELSON AND SONS, 1898. 368p.: front., 35 plates. Bound in brown cloth with embossed pictorial cover and spine with decorative endpapers.
C 823.8 KIN

1417 **KINGSTON, WILLIAM HENRY GILES.**
IN THE EASTERN SEAS: OR, THE REGION OF THE BIRD OF PARADISE. A TALE FOR BOYS. BY W.H.G. KINGSTON. LONDON: T. NELSON AND SONS, 1879, XII, 608p.: front., 17 plates, ill. Bound in brown cloth with decorative cover and spine, with gilt edges.
C 823.8 KIN

1417A **Another copy.**
LONDON: THOMAS NELSON AND SONS, (191–?). 510p.: with front. and 4 col. plates by John Hassall. Bound in green cloth with coloured pictorial cover and spine.

1418 **KINGSTON, WILLIAM HENRY GILES.**
IN THE WILDS OF AFRICA. A TALE FOR BOYS. BY W.H.G. KINGSTON. LONDON: T. NELSON AND SONS, 1871. XII, 560p.: front., 30 plates, ill. Bound in green cloth with embossed cover and spine, with gilt edges.
C 823.8 KIN

1419 **Another copy.**
With 65 illustrations, 1898. Bound in blue cloth with decorative cover and spine.

1420 **Another copy.**
THOMAS NELSON AND SONS, (191–?). 464p.: col. front., 4 col. plates by A. Pearse. Bound in blue cloth, with coloured pictorial cover and spine.

1421 **KINGSTON, WILLIAM HENRY GILES.**
JACK BUNTLINE OR LIFE ON THE OCEAN. BY WILLIAM H.G. KINGSTON. LONDON: SAMPSON LOW, SON, AND CO., 1861. VIII, 154p. + 16p. pub. cat. Bound in blue cloth with embossed decorative cover.
C 823.8 KIN

1422 **KINGSTON, WILLIAM HENRY GILES.**
JAMES BRAITHWAITE, THE SUPER CARGO. The Story of His Adventures, Ashore and Afloat. BY W.H.G. KINGSTON. LONDON: HODDER AND STOUGHTON, 1882. XII, 266p. + 26p. ill. pub. cat.: front., 5 plates. Bound in grey cloth with coloured pictorial cover and spine, with gilt edges.
C 823.8 KIN

1422A **KINGSTON, WILLIAM HENRY GILES.**
JANET MCLAREN, OR, The Faithful Nurse. BY WILLIAM H.G. KINGSTON. LONDON: GALL AND INGLIS, (188–?). 128p. + 32p. ill. pub. cat.: col. front. Bound in grey cloth with decorative covers and sping.
C 823.8 KIN

1423 **KINGSTON, WILLIAM HENRY GILES.**
JOHN DEANE: HISTORIC ADVENTURES BY LAND AND SEA. BY WILLIAM H.G. KINGSTON. Fully Illustrated. LONDON: GRIFFITH, FARRAN, BROWNE AND CO. LIMITED, (189–?). VIII, 416p.: 3 plates. Bound in green cloth with coloured pictorial cover and spine.
C 823.8 KIN

1424 **KINGSTON, WILLIAM HENRY GILES.**
THE LOG HOUSE BY THE LAKE. A Tale of Canada. BY THE LATE W.H.G. KINGSTON. LONDON: SOCIETY FOR PROMOTING CHRISTIAN KNOWLEDGE. (188–?). 128p. + 4p. pub. cat.: front., 3 plates. Bound in green cloth with coloured pictorial cover and spine.
C 823.8 KIN

1425 **KINGSTON, WILLIAM HENRY GILES.**
MARK SEAWORTH. A TALE OF THE INDIAN OCEAN. BY WILLIAM H.G. KINGSTON. WITH ILLUSTRATIONS BY C.J. DE LACY. LONDON: GRIFFITH FARRAN BROWNE AND CO. LIMITED. (189–?). 384p.: front., 2 plates. Bound in brown cloth with coloured pictorial cover.
C 823.8 KIN

1426 **KINGSTON, WILLIAM HENRY GILES.**
THE MATE OF THE "LILY"; OR, Notes from Harvey Musgrave's Log Book. BY W.H.G. KINGSTON. LONDON: SOCIETY FOR PROMOTING CHRISTIAN KNOWLEDGE, (1885). 160p. + 4p. pub. cat.: front., 2 plates. Bound in green cloth with pictorial cover and decorative spine.
C 823.8 KIN

1427 **Another copy.**
(189–?). 160p. + 8p. pub. cat.: front., 1 plate. Bound in blue cloth with coloured pictorial cover.

1428 **KINGSTON, WILLIAM HENRY GILES.**
MICHAEL PENGUYNE; OR, Fisher Life on the Cornish Coast. BY WILLIAM H.G. KINGSTON. LONDON, SOCIETY FOR PROMOTING CHRISTIAN KNOWLEDGE, (1873). 157p. + 3p. pub. cat.: front., 2 plates. Bound in green cloth with coloured pictorial cover.
C 823.8 KIN

1428A **KINGSTON, WILLIAM HENRY GILES.**
THE MISSING SHIP: OR, NOTES FROM THE LOG OF THE "OUZEL" GALLEY. BY THE LATE W.H.G. KINGSTON. WITH ILLUSTRATIONS BY C.O. MURRAY. NINTH THOUSAND. LONDON: GRIFFITH, FARRAN, OKEDEN AND WELSH, (1888). XII, 444p. + 16p. pub. cat.: front., 5 plates, headpieces to chapters. Bound in grey cloth with coloured decorative cover.
C 823.8 KIN

1428B **Another copy.**
THE MISSING SHIP, OR THE LOG OF THE "OUZEL" GALLEY. BY W.H.G. KINGSTON. LONDON: GRIFFITH, FARRÁN, BROWNE AND CO. LIMITED, (190–?). VI, 444p.: front., 1 plate. Bound in red cloth, with embossed decorative cover and spine, and gilt edges.
YSC 823.8 KIN

1429 **KINGSTON, WILLIAM HENRY GILES.**
MOUNTAIN MOGGY; OR, THE STONING OF THE WITCH. A Tale for the Young. BY THE LATE WILLIAM H.G. KINGSTON. LONDON: SOCIETY FOR PROMOTING CHRISTIAN KNOWLEDGE, (189–?). 125p.: front., 1 plate. Bound in green cloth with pictorial cover.
C 823.8 KIN

1430 **KINGSTON, WILLIAM HENRY GILES.**
THE RIVAL CRUSOES. BY W.H.G. KINGSTON. LONDON: GRIFFITH, FARRAN, BROWNE AND CO. LIMITED., (188–?). 378p.: front., 7 plates. Bound in maroon cloth with decorative cover and spine.
C 823.8 KIN

1431 **KINGSTON, WILLIAM HENRY GILES.**
RONALD MORTON; OR, THE FIRE SHIPS: A STORY OF THE LAST NAVAL WAR. BY W.H.G. KINGSTON. LONDON: GALL AND INGLIS, (188–?). 448p.: front., 3 plates. Bound in red cloth with pictorial cover and spine with gilt edges.
C 823.8 KIN

1432 **KINGSTON, WILLIAM HENRY GILES.**
SALT WATER. THE SEA LIFE AND ADVENTURES OF NEIL D'ARCY, THE MIDSHIPMAN. BY WILLIAM H.G. KINGSTON. ILLUSTRATED BY C.J. DE LACY. LONDON, RICHARD EDWARD KING, (187–?). 371p.: front., 6 plates. Bound in green cloth with embossed decoration.
C 823.8 KIN

1433 **KINGSTON, WILLIAM HENRY GILES.**
THE SCHOOL FRIENDS OR SOMETHING NEW. THE BROTHERS, A Tale of Three Lives. THE IVORY TRADER, A Tale of Africa. ALONE ON AN ISLAND. LONDON: GEORGE ROUTLEDGE AND SONS, (187–?). 48p., 48p., 48p., 47p. + 32p. pub. cat.: double coloured front. Bound in green cloth with embossed decorative cover and spine.
C 823.8 KIN

1434 **KINGSTON, WILLIAM HENRY GILES.**
THE SETTLERS: A TALE OF VIRGINIA. BY WILLIAM H.G. KINGSTON. LONDON, SOCIETY FOR PROMOTING CHRISTIAN KNOWLEDGE, (1880). 252p. + 4p. pub. cat.: front., 2 plates, ill. Bound in brown cloth with embossed decorative cover and spine.
C 823.8 KIN

1435 **KINGSTON, WILLIAM HENRY GILES.**
SNOW SHOES AND CANOES; OR, THE EARLY DAYS OF A FUR-TRADER IN THE HUDSON'S BAY TERRITORY. BY W.H.G. KINGSTON. NEW AND CHEAPER EDITION. LONDON: SAMPSON LOW, MARSTON, SEARLE AND RIVINGTON, 1887. VII, 336p. + 32p. pub. cat.: front., 7 plates by S. Davis. Bound in grey cloth with embossed pictorial cover and spine.
C 823.8 KIN

1436 **Another copy.**
LONDON: THOMAS NELSON AND SONS, (190–?). 394p. + 6p. pub. cat.: col. front., 3 col. plates by Norman Little. Bound in red cloth, with coloured pictorial cover and spine.

1437 **KINGSTON, WILLIAM HENRY GILES.**
STORIES OF THE SAGACITY OF ANIMALS. The Horse and Other Animals. BY W.H.G. KINGSTON. WITH 27 ILLUSTRATIONS BY HARRISON WEIR. LONDON: T. NELSON AND SONS, 1888. 166p.: front., 33 plates. Bound in blue cloth with pictorial cover and spine.
C 823.8 KIN

1438 **KINGSTON, WILLIAM HENRY GILES.**
THE THREE ADMIRALS, AND THE ADVENTURES OF THEIR YOUNG FOLLOWERS. BY W.H.G. KINGSTON. ILLUSTRATED BY J.R. WELLS AND C.J. STANILAND. LONDON: GRIFFITH, FARRAN, OKEDEN AND WELSH. (188–?). VIII, 440p.: front., 7 plates. Bound in red cloth with pictorial cover, with gilt edges.
C 823.8 KIN

1439 **Another copy.**
LONDON: HUMPHREY MILFORD, OXFORD UNIVERSITY PRESS, 1930. X, 410p. + 8p. pub. cat.: col. front., by Arch. Webb, decorative title page. Bound in red cloth, with coloured pictorial dust jacket.

1440 **KINGSTON, WILLIAM HENRY GILES.**
THE THREE COMMANDERS; OR ACTIVE SERVICE AFLOAT IN MODERN DAYS. BY WILLIAM H.G. KINGSTON. ILLUSTRATIONS BY D.H. FRISTON. LONDON: GRIFFITH, FARRAN, OKEDEN AND WELSH, (188–?). 464p.: front., 7 plates. Bound in blue cloth with embossed decorative cover, with gilt edges.
C 823.8 KIN

1441 **KINGSTON, WILLIAM HENRY GILES.**
THE THREE LIEUTENANTS; OR, NAVAL LIFE IN THE NINETEENTH CENTURY. BY THE LATE W.H.G. KINGSTON. WITH ILLUSTRATIONS BY D.H. FRISTON. LONDON: GRIFFITH, FARRAN, OKEDEN AND WELSH, (1892). 463p. + 32p. ill. pub. cat.: front., 5 plates. Bound in brown cloth with embossed decorative cover and spine, with gilt edges.
C 823.8 KIN

1442 **Another copy.**
NEW EDITION. ILLUSTRATED IN COLOUR BY ARCHIBALD WEBB. LONDON: HENRY FROWDE, (191–?). 463p. + 16p. pub. cat.: col. front., 5 col. plates. Bound in red cloth, with coloured pictorial cover and spine.

1443 **KINGSTON, WILLIAM HENRY GILES.**
THE THREE MIDSHIPMEN. BY THE LATE W.H.G. KINGSTON. WITH ILLUSTRATIONS BY GEORGE THOMAS, JULIAN PORTCH, ETC. LONDON: GRIFFITH, FARRAN AND CO., (188–?). 414p. + 48p. pub. cat.: front., 6 plates. Bound in green cloth with decorative cover and spine.
C 823.8 KIN

1444 **Another copy.**
Eight Coloured Illustrations. LONDON: COLLINS' CLEAR-TYPE PRESS, (190–?). 336p.: col. front., 7 col. plates by Richard Tod. Bound in blue cloth, with embossed decorative cover and spine.

1445 **KINGSTON, WILLIAM HENRY GILES.**
THE TWO SUPERCARGOES OR ADVENTURES IN SAVAGE AFRICA. BY W.H.G. KINGSTON, With Numerous Illustrations. LONDON: SAMPSON LOW, MARSTON AND COMPANY (LIMITED), (189–?). XV, 298p. + 32p. pub. cat.: front., 7 plates. Bound in blue cloth with pictorial cover.
C 823.8 KIN

1446 **Another copy.**
LONDON: THOMAS NELSON AND SONS LTD., (193–?). XV, 298p. + 6p. pub. cat.: col. front., 3 col. plates by E.F. Skinner. Bound in red cloth with vignette on cover and spine.

1447 **KINGSTON, WILLIAM HENRY GILES.**
THE TWO WHALERS; OR, Adventures in the Pacific. BY WILLIAM H.G. KINGSTON. LONDON, SOCIETY FOR PROMOTING CHRISTIAN KNOWLEDGE. (188–?). 128p. + 4p. pub. cat.: front. Bound in dark blue cloth with embossed decorative cover and spine, with gilt edges.
C 823.8 KIN

1448 **KINGSTON, WILLIAM HENRY GILES.**
VILLEGAGNON: A TALE OF The Huguenot Persecution BY W.H.G. KINGSTON. FIRST EDITION. LONDON: SUNDAY SCHOOL UNION, (188–?). 206p.: 8 plates. Bound in beige cloth with decorative cover and spine.
C 823.8 KIN

1448A **KINGSTON, WILLIAM HENRY GILES.**
A VOYAGE ROUND THE WORLD. A BOOK FOR BOYS. LONDON: T. NELSON AND SONS, 1869. 460p. + 4p. pub. cat.: front., vignette on title page, 9 plates, ill., head-pieces. Bound in purple cloth with embossed decorative cover and spine.
C 823.8 KIN

1448B **Another copy.**
LONDON: NELSON, (191–?). 416p.: col. front. 3 col. plates by George Soper. Bound in dark grey cloth with coloured pictorial cover and spine.

1448C **KINGSTON, WILLIAM HENRY GILES.**
THE VOYAGES OF THE "RANGER" AND "CRUSADER" AND WHAT BEFELL Their Passengers and Crews. By W.H.G. KINGSTON. LONDON: GALL AND INGLIS, (188–?). 352p.: front., 2 plates. Bound in olive cloth with coloured pictorial cover and spine with gilt edges.
C 823.8 KIN

1449 **KINGSTON, WILLIAM HENRY GILES.**
WAIHOURA; OR, The New Zealand Girl. BY WILLIAM H.G. KINGSTON. LONDON: GALL AND INGLIS, (1873). 127p.: col. front. Bound in blue cloth with decorative cover and spine.
C 823.8 KIN

1450 **KINGSTON, WILLIAM HENRY GILES.**
WASHED ASHORE; OR, THE TOWER OF STORMOUNT BAY. BY W.H.G. KINGSTON. With Illustrations. LONDON: FREDERICK WARNE AND CO., (189–?). IV, 213p. + 2p. pub. cat.: front., 3 plates. Bound in beige cloth with coloured pictorial cover and decorative spine.
C 823.8 KIN

1451 **KINGSTON, WILLIAM HENRY GILES.**
WITH AXE AND RIFLE, OR THE WESTERN PIONEERS. BY W.H.G. KINGSTON. NEW AND CHEAPER EDITION. LONDON: SAMPSON LOW, MARSTON, SEARLE AND RIVINGTON, (1887). VIII, 382p. + 32p. pub. cat.: vignette on title page, 22 plates by H. Meyer. Bound in red cloth with embossed pictorial cover and spine.
C 823.8 KIN

1451A **Another copy.**
LONDON: THOMAS NELSON AND SONS, (191–?). 410p. + 6p. pub. cat.: col. front., 3 col. plates by Norman Little. Bound in blue cloth with pictorial cover and spine.

1452 **KINGSTON, WILLIAM HENRY GILES.**
A YACHT VOYAGE ROUND ENGLAND. BY WILLIAM H.G. KINGSTON. NEW EDITION, REVISED AND ENLARGED. LONDON: THE RELIGIOUS TRACT SOCIETY, (189–?). 320p.: front., 22 plates, ill. Bound in beige cloth with coloured pictorial cover and spine, with gilt edges.
C 823.8 KIN

1453 **KINGSTON, WILLIAM HENRY GILES.**
THE YOUNG BERRINGTONS: OR, THE BOY EXPLORERS. BY W.H.G. KINGSTON. SECOND EDITION. LONDON: CASSELL AND COMPANY, LIMITED, (188–?). VII, 152p. + 4p. pub. cat.: front., vignette on title page, 6 plates, ill. Bound in red cloth with coloured decorative cover and spine.
C 823.8 KIN

"THE ATTACK OF THE BLACKS" (*see* p. 131).

1453

1454 **KIPLING, RUDYARD.**
"CAPTAINS COURAGEOUS", A STORY OF THE GRAND BANKS. BY RUDYARD KIPLING. WITH ILLUSTRATIONS BY I.W. TABER. LONDON: MACMILLAN AND CO. LIMITED, 1897. VIII, 245p. + 2p. pub. cat.: front., 21 plates. Bound in blue cloth, with embossed pictorial cover and spine.
YSC 823.8 KIP

1455 **KIPLING, RUDYARD.**
THE LIGHT THAT FAILED. BY RUDYARD KIPLING. LONDON: HEINEMANN AND BALESTIER LIMITED, 1891. 278p. + 16p. pub. cat. Rebound in blue cloth. THE ENGLISH LIBRARY, NO. 1. Originally published 1890.
YSC 823.8 KIP

1456 **KIPLING, RUDYARD.**
STALKY AND CO. BY RUDYARD KIPLING. LONDON: MACMILLAN AND CO. LIMITED, 1899. IX, 272p. + 4p. pub. cat. Bound in red cloth.
YSC 823.8 KIP

1456A **KIPLING, RUDYARD.**
WEE WILLIE WINKIE, UNDER THE DEODARS, THE PHANTOM RICKSHAW AND OTHER STORIES. BY RUDYARD KIPLING. LONDON: SAMPSON LOW, MARSTON, AND COMPANY LIMITED, 1892. 314p. Bound in blue cloth, with decorative cover and spine.
YSC 823.8 KIP

1457 **KIRBY, MARY.**
JULIA MAITLAND OR PRIDE GOES BEFORE A FALL. BY MARY AND ELIZABETH KIRBY. WITH ILLUSTRATIONS BY JOHN ABSOLON. LONDON: GRIFFITH AND FARRAN, (187–?). 160p. + 32p. pub. cat.: front., 3 plates. Bound in dark grey cloth with decorative cover and spine.
C 823.8 KIR

1458 **KIRTON, JOHN WILLIAM.**
"Buy your own Cherries!" AND OTHER TALES. BY JOHN W. KIRTON, LL.D. TWENTY-SECOND EDITION. LONDON: JARROLD AND SONS, (187–?). 106p. + 4p. pub. cat.: front. Bound in green cloth with decorative cover and spine. Originally published 1862.
C 823.8 KIR

1458A **KIRTON, JOHN WILLIAM.**
BUY YOUR OWN CHERRIES, A STORY BY DR. J.W. KIRTON. 700TH THOUSAND. LONDON: JARROLD AND SONS, (190–?) 62p. + 8p. pub. cat.: front., vignette on title page. Bound in red cloth, with pictorial cover and spine. Contains also "The Wonder-Working Bedstead" and "Romantic Search for a Wife."
C 823.912 KIR

1459 **KIRTON, JOHN WILLIAM.**
FRANK SPENCER'S RULE OF LIFE AND HOW IT LED TO HIS PROSPERITY. (FOUNDED ON FACT). BY JOHN W. KIRTON. LONDON: (187–?). S.W. PARTRIDGE AND CO., 92p. + 16p. pub. cat.: front., 2 plates, ill. Bound in green cloth with embossed pictorial cover.
C 823.8 KIR

1460 **KNATCHBULL-HUGESSEN, E.H.**
THE MOUNTAIN-SPRITE'S KINGDOM AND OTHER STORIES, BY THE RIGHT HON. E.H. KNATCHBULL-HUGESSEN (LORD BRABOURNE). WITH ILLUSTRATIONS BY ERNEST GRISET. LONDON, GEORGE ROUTLEDGE AND SONS, 1881. VIII, 372p. + 4p. pub. cat.: front., 11 plates, ill. Bound in blue cloth with pictorial cover and spine.
C 823.8 KNA

1461 **KNIGHT, ARTHUR LEE.**
THE CRUISE OF THE "CORMORANT" OR Treasure-Seekers of the Orient. BY ARTHUR LEE KNIGHT. WITH ILLUSTRATIONS BY W.S. STACEY. LONDON: WARD, LOCK AND CO. LIMITED, (189–?). IV, 252p.: front., 3 plates. Bound in brown cloth, with coloured pictorial cover and spine.
C 823.8 KNI

1461A **KNIGHT, ARTHUR LEE.**
RONALD HALLIFAX; OR, HE WOULD BE A SAILOR. WITH ORIGINAL ILLUSTRATIONS. LONDON: FREDERICK WARNE AND CO., (1887). 415p.: 4 plates by W.S. Stacey. Bound in red cloth with coloured pictorial cover and spine and decorative end papers.
C 823.8 KNI

1462 **KNOX, KATHLEEN.**
CAPTAIN EVA. THE STORY OF A NAUGHTY GIRL. BY KATHLEEN KNOX. LONDON: SOCIETY FOR PROMOTING CHRISTIAN KNOWLEDGE, (188–?). 160p. + 4p. pub. cat.: front., 2 plates. Bound in brown cloth with decorative cover and spine.
C 823.8 KNO

1462A **KUPPORD, SKELTON.**
THE UNCHARTED ISLAND. BY SKELTON KUPPORD. LONDON: THOMAS NELSON AND SONS, 1899. 350p. + 2p. pub. cat.: front., additional vignette title page, 4 plates by W. Rainey. Bound in blue cloth with coloured pictorial cover and spine.
C 823.8 KUP

1463 **L., C.**
THE ORPHAN BOY; OR, FROM PEASANT TO PRINCE. (From the German). BY C.L., M.A. LONDON: WARD, LOCK AND TYLER (187–?). 152p. + 4p. ill. pub. cat.: front., vignette. Bound in green cloth with black decorative cover and spine, and 2 coloured portraits inset on cover. Beaton's Good Aim Series.
C 823.8 ORP

1464 **LAMB, CHARLES.**
TALES FROM SHAKESPEARE. BY CHARLES AND MARY LAMB. Illustrated. SECOND EDITION. MANCHESTER: JOHN HEYWOOD, (189–?). 203p. XI, 203p.: front., vignette on title page, ill. Bound in blue cloth with pictorial cover and spine. Originally published 1807.
C 823.7 LAM

1465 **Another copy.**
With introductory preface by Andrew Lang, illustrations by Robert Anning Bell. LONDON: ARCHIBALD CONSTABLE AND CO. LTD., 1903. 372p.: front., 14 plates. Bound in green cloth with decorative cover and spine.
CBD 823.7 LAM

1466 **Another copy.**
WITH TWELVE ILLUSTRATIONS BY A. RACKHAM. LONDON: J.M. DENT AND COMPANY, 1905. VII, 362p.: col. front., col. decorative title page, 11 plates. Bound in blue cloth with decorative cover and spine.
CBD 823.7 LAM

1466A **Another copy.**
1906. XI, 338p. + 2p. pub. cat.: decorative front and title page, 11 plates by Arthur Rackham. Bound in maroon leather with embossed decorative spine and gilt top.
C 823.7 LAM

1467 **Another copy.**
WITH ILLUSTRATIONS BY BYAM SHAW. LONDON: GEORGE BELL AND SONS, 1907. XI, 363p.: front., 23 plates. Bound in red cloth with decorative cover.
CBD 823.7 LAM

1468 **Another copy.**
WITH SIXTEEN FULL PAGE ILLUSTRATIONS BY W.H. ROBINSON. LONDON: SANDS AND COMPANY, (1902) IV, 296p.: front., 15 plates. Bound in red cloth with pictorial cover and spine.
823.7 LAM

1470 **LAMB, RUTH.**
CAPTAIN CHRISTIE'S GRAND-DAUGHTER. BY MRS. LAMB (RUTH BUCK). WELLS, GARDNER, DARTON AND CO., (188–?). VIII, 243p. + 4p. pub. cat.: front., 2 plates. Bound in olive cloth with pictorial cover and spine.
C 823.8 LAM

1471 **LA MOTTE FOUQUÉ, FRIEDRICH HEINRICH KARL DE, FREIHERR.**
THE MAGIC RING, A KNIGHTLY ROMANCE. BY DE LA MOTTE FOUQUÉ. ILLUSTRATED. LONDON: GEORGE ROUTLEDGE AND SONS, (187–?). 326p.: front., 3 plates engraved by Dalziel Brothers. Bound in blue cloth, with coloured pictorial/decorative cover and spine.
C 833.6 LAM

1472 **LA MOTTE FOUQUÉ, FRIEDRICH HEINRICH KARL DE, FREIHERR.**
SINTRAM AND HIS COMPANIONS BY LA MOTTE FOUQUÉ. TRANSLATED BY A.C. FARQUHARSON WITH A FRONTISPIECE FROM AN ENGRAVING BY ALBRECHT DÜRER (1513) AND TWENTY ILLUSTRATIONS BY EDMUND J. SULLIVAN. LONDON: METHUEN AND CO., 1908. VIII, 193p.: front., decorative title page, 20 plates. Bound in olive cloth with decorative cover and spine.
CBD 833.6 LAM

1473 **LA MOTTE FOUQUÉ, FRIEDRICH HEINRICH KARL DE, FREIHERR.**
Sintram and his Companions and Undine. BY DE LA MOTTE FOUQUÉ. WITH INTRODUCTION BY CHARLOTTE M. YONGE. DRAWINGS BY GORDON BROWNE. LONDON: GARDNER, DARTON AND

CO., Second edition. 1901. XIX, 279p. + 16p. pub. cat.: front., pictorial/decorative covers and spine, and gilt top.
YSC 833.6 LAM

1474 **Another copy.**
3rd. edition 1910, 279p. + 20p. ill. pub. cat.: vignette title page, 13 plates, ill. Bound in turquoise cloth, with pictorial covers and spine.

1475 **LA MOTTE FOUQUÉ, FRIEDRICH HEINRICH KARL DE, FREIHERR.**
SINTRAM AND HIS COMPANIONS. ASLAUGA's KNIGHT. BY LA MOTTE FOUQUÉ. LONDON: CASSELL AND COMPANY, LIMITED, 1887. 192p. + 2p. pub. cat. Bound in brown cloth, with decorative cover. CASSELL'S NATIONAL LIBRARY.
YSC 833.6 LAM

1476 **LA MOTTE FOUQUÉ, FRIEDRICH HEINRICH KARL DE, FREIHERR.**
THIODOLF The Icelander. BY DE LA MOTTE FOUQUÉ. LONDON: GEORGE ROUTLEDGE AND SONS, 1877. 172p. + 32p. pub. cat.: front., 1 plate, ill. by Edward Corbould. Bound in green cloth, with embossed decorative cover and spine.
C 833.6 LAM

1477 **LA MOTTE FOUQUÉ, FRIEDRICH HEINRICH KARL DE, FREIHERR.**
Undine, A Romance. From the German of De La Motte Fouqué. A New Translation, With Eleven Illustrations. Designed by Tenniel, and Engraved by Bastin. LONDON: EDWARD LUMLEY, 1854. XXIV, 96p.: front., additional vignette title page, ill. Half bound in brown calf with coloured marble paper cover, with gilt edges.
CBD 833.6 LAM

1477A **Another copy.**
A TALE FROM THE GERMAN, BY THE HON. C.L. LYTTELTON. WITH ILLUSTRATIONS. LONDON: BELL AND DALDY, 1859. 122p. + 32p. pub. cat.: front., ill. Bound in blue cloth with embossed decorative cover and spine.
YSC 823.8 LYT

1479 **LANE, LAURA M.**
DR. MAYNARD'S DAUGHTER. BY LAURA M. LANE. ILLUSTRATED BY W.H. EVEREND. LONDON, SOCIETY FOR PROMOTING CHRISTIAN KNOWLEDGE, (188–?). 223p. + 4p. pub. cat.: front., 1 plate.
C 823.8 LAN

1480 **LANG, ANDREW.**
THE Gold of Fearnilee. BY ANDREW LANG. FRONTISPIECE BY T. SCOTT, DRAWINGS BY E.A. LEMANN. BRISTOL, J.W. ARROWSMITH, (1888). 86p. + 2p. pub. cat.: col. front., 12 col. plates. Bound in green cloth.
C 823.8 LAN

1482 **(LE FEUVRE, AMY.)**
ODD. BY THE AUTHOR OF "ERIC'S GOOD NEWS", "PROBABLE SONS", "TEDDY'S BUTTON", "DWELL DEEP". LONDON: THE RELIGIOUS TRACT SOCIETY, (189–?). 160p. + 16p. front., 1 plate. Bound in brown cloth with decorative cover.
C 823.8 LEF

1483 **LEIGHTON, ROBERT.**
Wreck of the Golden Fleece. The Story of a North Sea Fisher-Boy. BY ROBERT LEIGHTON. ILLUSTRATED BY FRANK BRANGWYN. LONDON: BLACKIE AND SON, LIMITED, (1894). 352p.: front., 5 plates. Bound in green cloth with coloured pictorial cover and spine.
C 823.8 LEI

1484 **LESLIE, EMMA.**
BEFORE THE DAWN. A tale of Wycliffe and Bohemia. BY EMMA LESLIE. With illustrations by J.D. Watson. LONDON: THE RELIGIOUS TRACT SOCIETY, (188–?). 240p. + 4p. pub. cat. front., 4 plates, ill. Bound in brown cloth with embossed pictorial and decorative cover and spine.
C 823.8 LES

1485 **LESLIE, EMMA.**
PETER THE APPRENTICE. A historical tale OF THE REFORMATION IN ENGLAND, BY THE AUTHOR OF "FAITHFUL, BUT NOT FAMOUS", "FANNY THE FLOWER GIRL", ETC. (EMMA LESLIE). LONDON: THE RELIGIOUS TRACT SOCIETY, (187–?). 187p.: front., 3 plates. Bound in brown cloth with decorative cover and spine.
C 823.8 LES

1485A **LESLIE'S SCHOLARSHIP.**
OR, THE SECRET OF SUCCESS. LONDON: THE RELIGIOUS TRACT SOCIETY, (187–?). 126p. + 2p. pub. cat.: front., 2 plates by J.E. Weedon, engraved by Butterworth and Heath. Bound in brown cloth with embossed decorative cover and spine.
YSC 823.8 LES

1486 **LESTER, MARY E.**
LOVE'S GOLDEN KEY OR The Witch of Berryton. BY MARY E. LESTER. LONDON: S.W. PARTRIDGE AND CO., (189–?) 96p. + 16p. pub. cat.: front., 2 plates. Bound in blue cloth with coloured pictorial cover and decorative spine.
YSC 823.8 LES

1487 **LISETTA AND THE BRIGANDS.**
OR, SAVED BY A MULE. LONDON: THE RELIGIOUS TRACT SOCIETY, (189–?). 63 p. + 16p. ill. pub. cat.: col. front., pictorial initial letters to chapters. Bound in green cloth with inserted coloured vignette and coloured decorative cover. Little Dot Series.
C 823.8 LIS

1488 **THE LITTLE FRENCH PROTÉGÉ.**
BY THE AUTHOR OF "Spring Flowers and Summer Blossoms." LONDON: DEAN AND SON, LIMITED, (189–?). 63p. Bound in green cloth with coloured decorative cover and spine.
YSC 823.8 LIT

1489 **LITTLE PETE.**
OR Tried and True. By the Author of "THE FISHERMAN'S BOY". LONDON: T. NELSON AND SONS, 1898. 96p.: front., additional vignette title page. Bound in blue cloth with decorative cover and spine.
YSC 823.8 LIT

1490 **THE LITTLE TIGER LILY AND HER COUSIN ALICE.**
OR, HOW A BAD TEMPER WAS CURED. LONDON: T. NELSON AND SONS, (187–?). 118p. + 6p. pub. cat.: front., vignette on title page. Bound in blue cloth with embossed decorative cover and spine.
C 823.8 LIT

1491 **THE LITTLE TRAVELLER AND OTHER TALES.**
FOR THE INSTRUCTION AND AMUSEMENT OF YOUTH. JUVENILE SERIES, HOME AND HAPPINESS, INSTRUCTION AND AMUSEMENT. LONDON: D. OMER SMITH, (186–?). 212p., front., vignette title page, 6 plates. Bound in dark blue cloth with embossed decorative cover and spine.
C 823.8 LIT

1492 **LOCKER, MRS. FREDERICK.**
SHAW'S FARM. BY MRS. FREDERICK LOCKER. LONDON: THE RELIGIOUS TRACT SOCIETY, (188–?). 96p. + 8p. pub. cat. front., pictorial title page, 1 plate, by W. Rainey, engraved by R. and E. Taylor. Bound in brown cloth with decorative cover and spine.
C 823.8 LOC

1493 **LOWNDES, CECILIA SELBY.**
A LUCKY MISTAKE. BY CECILIA SELBY LOWNDES. LONDON: SOCIETY FOR PROMOTING CHRISTIAN KNOWLEDGE, (188–?). 80p. + 4p. pub. cat.: front. Bound in blue cloth with decorative cover.
C 823.8 LOW

1494 **LUCY AND HER FRIENDS.**
OR All is not Gold that Glitters. EDINBURGH: GALL AND INGLIS, (187–?). 111p.: col. front. Bound in green cloth with embossed decorative cover and spine.
C 823.8 LUC

1495 **LYSTER, ANNETTE.**
THE BOY WHO NEVER LOST A CHANCE OR Roger Read's History. BY ANNETTE LYSTER. LONDON: THE RELIGIOUS TRACT SOCIETY, (189–?). 128p.: front., 2 plates, ill. by J.F.W. Bound in blue cloth with coloured pictorial cover and decorative spine.
C 823.8 LYS

1496 **LYSTER, ANNETTE.**
DOROTHY THE DICTATOR. BY ANNETTE LYSTER. ILLUSTRATED BY F. BARNARD. LONDON: SOCIETY FOR PROMOTING CHRISTIAN KNOWLEDGE, (189–?). 250p. + 6p. pub. cat.: front., 3 plates. Bound in beige cloth with coloured pictorial cover.
C 823.8 LYS

1497 **LYSTER, ANNETTE.**
HATHERLEY'S HOMESPUNS. BY ANNETTE LYSTER. Illustrated by Alfred J. Johnson. SOCIETY FOR PROMOTING CHRISTIAN KNOWLEDGE, 1891. 251p. + 5p. pub. cat.: front., 1 plate. Bound in grey cloth with coloured pictorial cover and spine.
C 823.8 LYS

1499 **LYTTON, EDWARD BULWER.**
THE DISOWNED. BY SIR EDWARD BULWER LYTTON, BART. LONDON: CHAPMAN AND HALL, 1852. VIII, 312p.: front., by J. Godwin, engraved by Dalziel, printed in 2 columns. Bound in grey cloth with embossed cover and spine.
YSC 823.8 LYT

1500 **MACAULAY, JAMES.**
FROM MIDDY TO ADMIRAL OF THE FLEET. THE STORY OF COMMODORE ANSON RE-TOLD TO BOYS. BY DR. MACAULAY. LONDON: HUTCHINSON & CO., (189–?). XV, 390p. + 2p. pub. cat.: front., vignette on title page, 4 plates. Bound in brown cloth with coloured pictorial cover.
C 823.8 MAC

1501 **MACDONALD, GEORGE.**
AT THE BACK OF THE NORTH WIND. BY GEORGE MACDONALD, L.L.D. WITH SEVENTY-FIVE ILLUSTRATIONS BY ARTHUR HUGHES. LONDON: BLACKIE & SON LIMITED, (188–?). VI, 378p. + 32p. pub. cat.: ill. Bound in blue cloth, cover and spine embossed with gold designs. Originally published 1871.
C 823.8 MAC

1502 **Another copy.**
FRONTISPIECE AND COVER-DESIGN BY LAURENCE HOUSMAN. NEW EDITION. LONDON: BLACKIE AND SON LIMITED, 1900. 378p. + 32p. pub. cat.: front., ill. Bound in blue cloth with gold embossed on spine and brown design embossed on cover.
C 823.8 MAC

1503 **MACDONALD, GEORGE.**
DEALINGS WITH THE FAIRIES. BY GEORGE MACDONALD. LONDON: ALEXANDER STRAHAN & CO., 1868. 308p. + 4p. pub. cat.: front., 10 plates by Arthur Hughes, engraved by Dalziel. Bound in green cloth with gold embossed on cover and spine and black decoration.
C 823.8 MAC

1504 **MACGREGOR, SIR DUNCAN.**
THE LOSS OF THE KENT EAST INDIAMAN IN THE BAY OF BISCAY. NARRATED IN A LETTER TO A FRIEND BY GENERAL SIR DUNCAN MACGREGOR, KCB. NEW EDITION, WITH ADDITIONS. LONDON: THE RELIGIOUS TRACT SOCIETY, (188–?). 90p.: front., 4 plates by R.V.E. TAYLOR. Bound in brown cloth with embossed pictorial/decorative cover.
C 826.7080356 MAC

1507 **(MACKARNESS, MATILDA ANNE.)**
WHEN WE WERE YOUNG; AND OTHER STORIES. BY THE AUTHOR OF "A TRAP TO CATCH A SUNBEAM", ETC., Illustrated. LONDON: GROOMBRIDGE AND SONS, (187–?). Unpaginated. Front., 2 plates by E.H.F. engraved by E. Whimper. Bound in blue cloth with embossed decorative cover and spine.
C 823.8 MAC

1508 **MACKENNA, STEPHEN, J.**
BRAVE MEN IN ACTION. THRILLING STORIES OF THE BRITISH FLAG. BY STEPHEN J. MACKENNA AND JOHN AUGUSTUS O'SHEA. A NEW EDITION WITH EIGHT ILLUSTRATIONS BY STANLEY L. WOOD. LONDON: CHATTO & WINDUS, 1899. 586p. + 32p. pub. cat.: front., vignette, ill. Bound in red cloth with coloured pictorial cover and spine.
C 823.8 MAC

1509 **MCKNIGHT, CHARLES.**
CAPTAIN JACK; OR, OLD FORT DUQUESNE. A STORY OF INDIAN ADVENTURE. BY CHARLES MCKNIGHT. WITH ORIGINAL ILLUSTRATIONS. LONDON: FREDERICK WARNE AND CO., (187–?). VII, 472p.: front., ill. Bound in red cloth with black and gold embossed on cover and spine.
C 823.8 MAC

1510 **MACSORLEY, CATHERINE MARY.**
A STEEP ROAD. BY CATHERINE MARY MACSORLEY. LONDON: SOCIETY FOR PROMOTING CHRISTIAN KNOWLEDGE (189–?). 123p. + 4p. pub. cat.: front. Bound in red cloth with pictorial cover and decorative spine.
C 823.8 MAC

1511 **MADDICK, MAUD.**
MOTHER'S EYES; OR, "Faithful in the least." BY MAUD MADDICK. LONDON: THE RELIGIOUS TRACT SOCIETY. (189–?). 80p. + 16p. pub. cat.: col. front., wood engravings. Bound in brown cloth with coloured decorative cover and spine. NINEPENNY SERIES.
C 823.8 MAD

1512 **MAGDALENE AND RAPHAEL.**
OR THE WONDER OF VISION. A Story for Children. TRANSLATED FROM THE GERMAN. With Illustrations. LONDON: ROUTLEDGE, WARNE AND ROUTLEDGE, 1862. 152p. + 8p. pub. cat. front. Bound in blue cloth with embossed decorative cover and spine.
YSC 823.8 MAG

1513 **MALET, H.P.**
JACKY NORY; OR, COURAGE AND PERSEVERANCE. BY H.P. MALET. WITH ILLUSTRATIONS. LONDON: FREDERICK WARNE AND CO. (189–?). 107p.: col. front. by Dalziel. Bound in red cloth with coloured decorative cover. Cover title – JACKY NORY OR THE SAILOR BOY.
C 823.8 MAL

1514 **MANSFORD, CHARLES J.**
UNDER THE NAGA BANNER. BY CHARLES J. MANSFORD. WITH ILLUSTRATIONS BY J. AYTON SYMINGTON. LONDON: JOHN HOGG, (189–?). 349p. + 2p. pub. cat.: front., 8 plates. Bound in grey cloth, with pictorial cover and spine.
C 823.8 MAN

1515 **MANWELL, M.B.**
GEORDIE STUART. A Story of Waterloo. T. NELSON AND SONS, 1896. 123p. + 4p. pub. cat.: front., additional vignette title page, by A. Rhind. Bound in blue cloth with decorative cover and spine.
C 823.8 MAN

1516 **MANWELL, M.B.**
GRANNY'S GIRLS. BY M.B. MANWELL. WITH FOUR ILLUSTRATIONS. LONDON: S.W. PARTRIDGE & CO. (189–?). 168p. + 32p. pub. cat.: front., 3 plates by F. Reason. Bound in red cloth with pictorial cover and decorative spine.
C 823.8 MAN

1517 **MANY WAYS OF BEING USEFUL.**
ILLUSTRATED IN A SERIES OF STORIES. LONDON: THE RELIGIOUS TRACT SOCIETY, (187–?). 64p.: col. front. Bound in red cloth with pictorial cover and inserted coloured paper vignette.
823.01 MAN

1518 **MARGY AND HER FEATHER.**
A STORY FOR GIRLS, BY THE AUTHOR OF "SHADOW AND SUNSHINE". SIXTH EDITION. LONDON: HOULSTON AND SONS, 1887. 106p. + 8p. Pub. cat.: front. Bound in green cloth with embossed decorative cover.
C 823.8 MAR

1519 **MARRYAT, FREDERICK.**
THE CHILDREN OF THE NEW FOREST. BY CAPTAIN MARRYAT. WITH FIFTY-FOUR ILLUSTRATIONS BY PAUL HARDY AND EIGHT FULL-PAGE PLATES BY SIR JOHN GILBERT, R.A. LONDON: GEORGE ROUTLEDGE AND SONS, LIMITED, 1895. 409p. + 2p. pub. cat.: front., vignette on title page, 8 plates, ill. Bound in red cloth with green decorative and pictorial cover and spine. Originally published 1847.
C 823.8 MAR

1520 **MARRYAT, FREDERICK.**
JAPHET IN SEARCH OF A FATHER. BY CAPTAIN MARRYAT. ILLUSTRATED BY HENRY M. BROCK. WITH AN INTRODUCTION BY DAVID HANNAY. LONDON: MACMILLAN AND CO., 1895. XXV, 401p.: front., 13 plates, ill., decorative endpapers. Bound in blue cloth with decorative cover and spine. Originally published 1836.
CBD 823.8 MAR

1521 **MARRYAT, FREDERICK.**
THE KING'S OWN. BY CAPTAIN MARRYAT. ILLUSTRATED BY F.H. TOWNSEND. WITH AN INTRODUCTION BY DAVID HANNAY. LONDON: MACMILLAN AND CO., LTD., 1896. XVI, 428p.: front., 39 plates, col. decorative endpapers. Bound in blue cloth with decorative cover and spine, with gilt edges. Originally published 1830.
CBD 823.8 MAR

1522 **MARRYAT, FREDERICK.**
MASTERMAN READY; OR, THE WRECK OF THE PACIFIC. BY CAPTAIN MARRYAT. WITH ORIGINAL ILLUSTRATIONS. LONDON: FREDERICK WARNE AND CO., (189–?). 334p. + 2p. pub. cat.: front., vignette on title page, 60 ill. by E.J.W., engraved by Dalziel. Bound in green cloth with pictorial cover and spine. Originally published 1841.
C 823.9 MAR

1523 **MARRYAT, FREDERICK.**
THE MISSION OR SCENES IN AFRICA. WRITTEN FOR YOUNG PEOPLE BY CAPTAIN MARRYAT. LONDON: GEORGE ROUTLEDGE AND SONS (1887). VIII, 292p. Bound in black cloth. Originally published 1845.
C 823.8 MAR

1524 **MARRYAT, FREDERICK.**
THE POACHER BY CAPTAIN MARRYAT. LONDON: CROOME AND CO., (187–?). VIII, 344p.: Bound in red cloth. Originally published as Joseph Rushbrook, the Poacher, in 1840.
C 823.8 MAR

1525 **MARRYAT, FREDERICK.**
TALES FROM THE WORKS OF CAPTAIN MARRYAT, R.N., INCLUDING "JAPHET IN SEARCH OF A FATHER", "THE PHANTOM SHIP", "PETER SIMPLE", "JACOB FAITHFUL", "FRANK MILDMAY", "MIDSHIPMAN EASY", "NEWTON FORSTER", "TOM BEAZELEY", "THE PASHA OF MANY TALES", "SIMPLE AT SEA", "THE DEMON DOG", "CAPTAIN CAIN THE PIRATE". Carefully collated with, Abridged and Edited from the Original Test. LONDON: J. AND R. MAXWELL, (189–?). 32p., 32p., 32p., 32p., 32p., 32p., 32p., 32p., 32p., 32p., 32p., 32p. Rebound in brown cloth. British Standard Library of Fiction.
YSC 823.7 MAR

1526 **MARSH, RICHARD.**
Curios; Some Strange Adventures of Two Bachelors. By Richard Marsh. Illustrated by J. Ayton Symington. THIRD EDITION. LONDON: JOHN LONG, 1898. 287p. + 8p. pub. cat.: front., 6 plates. Bound in red cloth with pictorial cover.
C 823.8 MAR

1527 **MARSHALL, EMMA.**
EASTWARD HO!, A STORY FOR GIRLS. BY EMMA MARSHALL. SECOND EDITION. LONDON: JAMES NISBET AND CO., (189–?). VIII, 398p. + 10p. pub. cat.: front., 5 plates engraved by Waterlowe. Bound in blue cloth with coloured pictorial cover and spine.
C 823.8 MAR

1528 **MARSHALL, EMMA.**
A LITTLE CURIOSITY. BY EMMA MARSHALL. New Edition. LONDON: JOHN F. SHAW AND CO. LTD., (190–?). 158p. + 18p. ill. pub. cat.: col. front. Bound in olive cloth with decorative cover and spine.
YSC 823.8 MAR

1529 **MARSHALL, EMMA.**
MARJORY; OR, THE GIFT OF PEACE. BY EMMA MARSHALL. LONDON: JAMES NISBET AND CO., 1878. 157p. + 2p. pub. cat.: front., 2 plates, ill. Bound in green cloth with embossed decorative cover and spine and inserted coloured pictorial label.
YSC 823.8 MAR

1530 **MARSHALL, EMMA.**
THEODORA'S CHILDHOOD; OR, THE OLD HOUSE AT WYNBOURN. (A STORY FOR CHILDREN). BY EMMA MARSHALL. LONDON, FREDERICK WARNE AND COMPANY, 1868. VI, 123p. + 1p. pub. cat.: col. front., additional col. vignette title page dated 1867. Bound in red cloth with embossed decorative cover and spine.
C 823.8 MAR

1531 **MARSHALL, EMMA.**
UNDER THE DOME OF ST. PAUL'S. A STORY OF ST. CHRISTOPHER WREN'S DAYS. BY EMMA MARSHALL. With Illustrations. BY T. HAMILTON CRAWFORD. R.S.W. LONDON: SEELEY AND CO. LIMITED, 1898. VII, 330p. + 4p. pub. cat.: front., 7 plates. Bound in brown cloth with decorative cover.
YSC 823.8 MAR

1532 **MARTEL, CHARLES.**
A BETTER PATRIMONY THAN GOLD. "IT IS ONLY A PIN." A TALE FOR YOUTH. BY CHARLES MARTEL. ILLUSTRATED WITH ENGRAVINGS. LONDON: DEAN AND SON, (186–?). 180p. + 18p. pub. cat.: front., additional vignette title page, 4 plates. Bound in brown cloth with embossed decorative cover and spine.
C 823.8 MAR

1533 **MARTINEAU, HARRIET.**
THE Crofton Boys. BY HARRIET MARTINEAU. WITH NUMEROUS ILLUSTRATIONS. EDITED BY ALFONSO GARDINER. MANCHESTER, JOHN HEYWOOD, (1895). VI, 168p.: front., vignette on title page, ill. Bound in blue cloth with coloured pictorial cover and spine. Originally published 1841.
C 823.8 MAR

1534 **MARTINEAU, HARRIET.**
THE SETTLERS AT HOME: LONDON: GEORGE ROUTLEDGE AND SONS, (188–?). 117p. + 4p. pub. cat. Bound in brown cloth with embossed coloured decorative cover and spine with gilt edges. Originally published 1841.
YSC 823.8 MAR

1535 **MARZETTI, ADA C.**
IN THE LAND OF NOD. BY ADA C. MARZETTI WITH ILLUSTRATIONS BY F. CARRUTHERS GOULD. LONDON: GRIFFITH, FARRAN, OKEDEN AND WELSH, 1889. 81p.: front., ill. Bound in dark green with decorative cover.
C 823.8 MAR

1535A **MEADE, L.T.**
THE ANGEL OF LOVE BY L.T. MEADE (Pseud. for ELIZABETH THOMASINA SMITH). WITH ILLUSTRATIONS BY T. PYM. LONDON: HODDER & STOUGHTON, THIRD EDITION, 1896. VIII, 207p.: ill., headpieces, tailpieces, and decorative initials. Bound in blue cloth with decorative cover and spine.
C 823.912 MEA

1536 **MEADE, L.T.**
A BAND OF THREE. BY L.T. MEADE. WITH ILLUSTRATIONS BY R. BARNES. LONDON: ISBISTER AND COMPANY, LIMITED (189–?). 271p. + 1p. pub. cat.: front., 5 plates. Bound in blue cloth with coloured decorative cover and spine. ISBISTER'S HOME LIBRARY.
C 823.912 MEA

1537 **MEADE, L.T.**
THE Children's Kingdom: The Story of a Great Endeavour. BY L.T. MEADE. NEW EDITION. LONDON: JOHN F. SHAW AND CO., (189–?). VIII, 338p. + 4p. pub. cat.: 2 plates. Bound in green cloth, with coloured decorative cover and spine.
YSC 823.912 MEA

1538 **MEADE, L.T.**
DICKORY DOCK. BY L.T. MEADE. LONDON: W. AND R. CHAMBERS, LIMITED, 1891. 64p.: front. Bound in green cloth, with pictorial cover.
C 823.912 MEA

1538A **MEADE, L.T.**
Jill the Irresistible. BY L.T. MEADE. WITH SIX ILLUSTRATIONS by William Rainey. LONDON: W. & R. CHAMBERS, LIMITED (189–?). 316p.: col. front., 5 col. plates. Bound in red cloth with coloured pictorial cover and spine.
C 823.912 MEA

1538B **MEADE, L.T.**
THE LADY OF THE FOREST BY L.T. MEADE. LONDON: S.W. PARTRIDGE AND CO., (189–?). 318p. + 16p. pub. cat.: front., 14 plates by J.B. Yeats, headpieces and tailpieces to chapters. Bound in brown with coloured pictorial cover and spine.
M 823 MEA CHILDREN'S COLLECTION

1539 **MEADE, L.T.**
A LITTLE MOTHER TO THE OTHERS. BY L.T. MEADE. With Illustrations by FRED BARNARD. LONDON: F.V. WHITE AND CO., 1896. IX, 294p.: front., 5 plates. Bound in green cloth, with coloured pictorial cover and spine and gilt edges.
C 823.912 MEA

1539A **MEADE, L.T.**
A SWEET GIRL GRADUATE. BY L.T. MEADE. WITH EIGHT ORIGINAL ILLUSTRATIONS BY HAL LUDLOW. LONDON: CASSELL AND COMPANY, LIMITED, 1893. 288p. + 16p. pub. cat.: front. 7 plates. Bound in buff and green cloth with decorative cover and spine. Inscribed "Edith Kimpton from her affectionate Father as a reward for progress in music, 1895."
M 823 MEA CHILDREN'S COLLECTION

1540 **MEADE, L.T.**
WILD KITTY. BY L.T. MEADE. WITH EIGHT ILLUSTRATIONS BY J. AYTON SYMINGTON. LONDON: W. AND R. CHAMBERS LIMITED, (189–?). 364p. + 36p. ill. pub. cat.: front., 7 plates. Bound in beige cloth, with coloured pictorial vignette on cover and spine.
C 823.912 MEA

1541 **MERCIER, MRS. JEROME.**
THE WREATH OF MALLOW, And other Stories, MORE OR LESS TRUE. BY MRS. JEROME MERCIER. LONDON: SOCIETY FOR PROMOTING CHRISTIAN KNOWLEDGE, (187–?). 184p. + 4p. pub. cat.: front., 1 plate. Bound in purple cloth with embossed decorative cover and spine.
YSC 823.8 MER

1542 **METCALFE, WILLIAM CHARLES.**
Steady Your Helm OR Stowed Away. BY WILLIAM CHAS. METCALFE. LONDON: JAMES NISBET & CO., Ltd. 1897. 413p. + 32p. pub. cat.: front., 6 plates by Frederic W. Burton. Bound in red cloth with coloured pictorial cover and spine, with gilt edges.
C 823.8 MET

1543 **THE MISSING BOAT.**
A true story. LONDON: THE RELIGIOUS TRACT SOCIETY (188–?). 90p.: front., vignette on title page, 2 plates. Bound in limp lilac cloth with embossed decorative cover.
C 823.8 MIS

1544 **MITCHELL, ELIZABETH HARCOURT.**
ENGEL THE FEARLESS. A Tale. BY ELIZABETH HARCOURT MITCHELL. ILLUSTRATED BY J. NASH. LONDON: SOCIETY FOR PROMOTING CHRISTIAN KNOWLEDGE, (189–?). 383p. + 4p. pub. cat.: front., 1 plate. Bound in grey cloth with decorative cover and spine.
YSC 823.8 MIT

1545 **MITCHELL, ELIZABETH HARCOURT.**
KATE, THE PRIDE OF THE PARISH. BY ELIZABETH HARCOURT MITCHELL, Illustrated by William Rainey. LONDON: SOCIETY FOR PROMOTING CHRISTIAN KNOWLEDGE (188–?). 253p. + 17p. pub. cat.: front., 2 plates. Bound in pink cloth with coloured pictorial spine and cover.
C 823.8 MIT

1545A **MOLESWORTH, MARY LOUISA.**
THE ADVENTURES OF HERR BABY. BY MRS MOLESWORTH. ILLUSTRATED BY WALTER CRANE. LONDON: MACMILLAN AND CO., 1881. VIII, 171p.: front. 12 plates. Bound in pink cloth with pictorial decorative cover.
M 823 MOL CHILDREN'S COLLECTION

1546 **MOLESWORTH, MARY LOUISA.**
THE BOYS AND I. A Child's Story for Children. BY MRS. MOLESWORTH. WITH ILLUSTRATIONS BY M.E. EDWARDS. LONDON: GEORGE ROUTLEDGE AND SONS, 1883. 234p.: front., 11 plates. Bound in mustard cloth with embossed decorative cover and spine, with gilt edges.
CBD 823.8 MOL

1547 **MOLESWORTH, MARY LOUISA.**
The Boys and I. A Child's Story for Children by Mrs. Molesworth. ILLUSTRATED BY LEWIS BAUMER. LONDON: W. & R. CHAMBERS LTD. (1899). 264p. + 48p. pub. cat.: front., 14 plates, ill. Bound in green cloth with pictorial cover and spine.
C 823.8 MOL

1548 **MOLESWORTH, MARY LOUISA.**
"CARROTS": JUST A LITTLE BOY. BY MRS MOLESWORTH ILLUSTRATED BY WALTER CRANE. LONDON: MACMILLAN & CO. LTD., 1876. (Republished 1957). 241p.: front., vignette on title page, 6 plates. Bound in cream cloth with decorative cover and red pictorial paper dust jacket.
YSC 823.8 MOL

1549 **MOLESWORTH, MARY LOUISA.**
CHRISTMAS-TREE LAND. BY MRS MOLESWORTH. ILLUSTRATED BY WALTER CRANE. LONDON: MACMILLAN AND CO., 1884. VII, 223p. + 32p. pub. cat.: front., vignette on title page, 7 plates. Bound in red cloth with decorative cover and spine.
CBD 823.8 MOL

1550 **MOLESWORTH, MARY LOUISA.**
FOUR WINDS FARM. BY MRS. MOLESWORTH. ILLUSTRATED BY WALTER CRANE. LONDON: MACMILLAN & CO. LTD., 1886. (REPRINTED IN 1920) 180p.: front., vignette on title page, 6 plates. Bound in blue cloth with black decorative cover and spine.
YSC 823.8 MOL
Another copy
1887. VI, 180p. + 4p. pub. cat.: decorative title page, 6 plates. Bound in red cloth with decorative cover and spine.
CBD 823.8 MOL

1551 **MOLESWORTH, MARY LOUISA.**
"GRANDMOTHER DEAR" A Book for Boys and Girls. BY MRS. MOLESWORTH. ILLUSTRATED BY WALTER CRANE. LONDON: MACMILLAN & CO., 1878. 262p. + 36p. pub. cat.: front., vignette on title page, 6 plates. Bound in red cloth with decorative cover and spine.
CBD 823.8 MOL

1552 **MOLESWORTH, MARY LOUISA.**
GREAT-UNCLE HOOT-TOOT BY MRS. MOLESWORTH. ILLUSTRATED BY GORDON BROWNE, E.J. WALKER, LIZZIE LAWSON, J. BLIGH AND MAYNARD BROWN. LONDON: SOCIETY FOR PROMOTING CHRISTIAN KNOWLEDGE, (1889). 96p.: front., 4 plates, ill. Bound in buff cloth with coloured pictorial cover.
C 823.8 MOL

1553 **MOLESWORTH, MARY LOUISA.**
HERMY, the story of a little girl, by Mrs. Molesworth. Illustrated by Lewis Baumer. LONDON: W. and R. CHAMBERS, (1898). 288p. + 48p. ill. pub. cat.: front., 10 plates, ill. Bound in pink cloth with pictorial cover and spine. Originally published 1881.
C 823.8 MOL

1554 **MOLESWORTH, MARY LOUISA.**
HOODIE. ILLUSTRATED. BY LEWIS BAUMER. LONDON: W. & R. CHAMBERS LTD., 1897. 266p. + 32p. ill. pub. cat.: front., 8 plates, ill. Bound in grey cloth with gold pictorial cover and spine. Originally published 1882.
Y 823.8 MOL

1555 **MOLESWORTH, MARY LOUISA.**
LEO'S POST-OFFICE AND BRAVE LITTLE DENIS. BY MRS. MOLESWORTH. LONDON: W. AND R. CHAMBERS LIMITED, (189–?). 73p.: front., 2 plates, ill. Bound in blue cloth, with coloured pictorial cover.
C 823.8 MOL

1556 **MOLESWORTH, MARY LOUISA.**
LETTICE. BY MRS MOLESWORTH. WITH ILLUSTRATIONS BY F. DADD. LONDON: SOCIETY FOR PROMOTING CHRISTIAN KNOWLEDGE, (1884). 224p. + 4p. pub. cat front., 2 plates. Bound in blue cloth with coloured decorative cover and spine.
CBD 823.8 MOL

1557 **MOLESWORTH, MARY LOUISA.**
THE NEXT-DOOR HOUSE. BY MRS. MOLESWORTH. LONDON: W. AND R. CHAMBERS, 1893. 226p. + 32p. ill. pub. cat.: front., 5 plates by W. Hatherell. Bound in grey cloth with coloured pictorial cover and spine.
C 823.8 MOL

1558 **MOLESWORTH, MARY LOUISA.**
ROBIN REDBREAST, A STORY FOR GIRLS. BY MRS. MOLESWORTH. WITH SIX ILLUSTRATIONS BY ROBERT BARNES. LONDON: W. AND R. CHAMBERS, (1892). 291p. + 32p. ill. pub. cat.: 5 plates. Bound in green cloth with pictorial cover and spine.
YSC 823.8 MOL

1559 **MOLESWORTH, MARY LOUISA.**
ROSY. BY MRS. MOLESWORTH. ILLUSTRATED BY WALTER CRANE. LONDON: MACMILLAN AND CO., 1882. VII, 204p. + 24p. pub. cat.: front., vignette on title page, 6 plates. Bound in red cloth with decorative cover and spine.
CBD 823.8 MOL

1560 **MOLESWORTH, MARY LOUISA.**
"US", AN OLD FASHIONED STORY BY MRS MOLESWORTH. WITH ILLUSTRATIONS BY WALTER CRANE. LONDON: MACMILLAN AND CO., 1886. VII, 240p.: front., vignette on title page, 6 plates. Bound in red cloth with decorative cover. Originally published 1885.
CBD 823.8 MOL

1561 **A MONTH AT ASHFIELD FARM.**
OR, ELLEN AND ROBERT'S FIRST JOURNEY FROM HOME. WITH ILLUSTRATIONS, PRINTED IN COLOURS BY KRONHEIM. LONDON: CASSELL, PETTER, AND GALPIN, (187–?). 128p. + 4p. pub. cat.: col. front., 2 col. plates. Bound in blue cloth with embossed decorative cover.
C 823.8 MON

1562 **MOORE, EMILY JANE.**
LITTLE BET; OR, THE RAILWAY FOUNDLING. BY EMILY JANE MOORE. LONDON: WILLIAM NICHOLSON AND SONS, (188–?). 252p. + 4p. pub. cat. Bound in red cloth with decorative cover and spine.
C 823.8 MOO

1563 **MOORE, F. FRANKFORT.**
THE ICE PRISON. BY F. FRANKFORT MOORE. Illustrated by W.H. Overend. LONDON: SOCIETY FOR PROMOTING CHRISTIAN KNOWLEDGE, (189–?). 319p. + 8p. pub. cat.: front., 3 plates. Bound in red cloth with coloured pictorial cover and spine.
C 823.8 MOO

1564 **THE MORE HASTE, THE WORSE SPEED.**
SUNDAY SCHOOL STORIES NO 11. (LONDON:) T. NELSON AND SONS, (188–?). 12p.: front. by Dalziel. Bound in paper with decorative title page on cover. Includes list of the series.
Cp 823.8 MOR

1565 **MOTHER'S BLESSING, And Other Stories.**
(LONDON:) THE RELIGIOUS TRACT SOCIETY, (188–?). 96p. + 16p. ill. pub. cat.: front., vignette on title page, ill. Bound in red cloth with embossed decorative cover and spine.
C 823.8 MOT

1566 **MUNROE, KIRK.**
AT WAR WITH PONTIAC OR, THE TOTEM OF THE BEAR, A TALE OF REDCOAT AND REDSKIN. BY KIRK MUNROE. WITH EIGHT ILLUSTRATIONS BY J. FINNEMORE. LONDON: BLACKIE AND SON, LIMITED, 1896. VI, 320p. + 32p. ill. pub. cat.: front., 7 plates. Bound in dark grey cloth with coloured pictorial cover and spine.
C 823.8 MUN

1567 **MUNROE, KIRK.**
THROUGH SWAMP AND GLADE. A TALE OF THE SEMINOLE WAR BY KIRK MUNROE. WITH EIGHT ILLUSTRATIONS BY VICTOR PERARD. LONDON: BLACKIE & SON, LIMITED. 1897. IX, 353p. + 32p. ill. pub. cat.: front., 8 plates. Bound in blue cloth with coloured pictorial cover and spine.
C 823.8 MUN

1568 **MUSSET, PAUL DE.**
MR. WIND AND MADAM RAIN. BY PAUL DE MUSSET. TRANSLATED, WITH PERMISSION OF THE AUTHOR, BY Emily Makepeace. WITH ILLUSTRATIONS BY CHARLES BENNETT. LONDON: SAMPSON LOW, SON, AND CO., 1864. 112p.: front., vignette title page, 3 plates, ill. Bound in green cloth, with embossed decorative covers, and gilt edges.
YSC 843.8 MUS

1569 **NAOMI.**
THE STORY OF THE BEACON-FIRE; OR, "Trust in God, and do the Right." A TALE OF THE CORNISH COAST. BY NAOMI. LONDON: T. NELSON AND SONS, 1887. 137p. + 6p. pub. cat.: front. Bound in lilac cloth with coloured decorative cover and spine.
C 823.8 NAO

1570 **NEALE, ERSKINE.**
THE BISHOP'S DAUGHTER. BY THE REV. ERSKINE NEALE, M.A. LONDON: GEORGE ROUTLEDGE AND CO., 1853. 256p.: front., additional vignette title page. Bound in black cloth with embossed decorative cover and spine.
Y 823.8 NEA

1571 **NED HEATHCOTE'S MODEL ENGINE.**
LONDON: THE RELIGIOUS TRACT SOCIETY, (187–?). 128p.: front., 2 plates by A Lady. Bound in blue cloth with decorative cover and spine.
C 823.8 CHA

1573 **NESBIT, EDITH.**
The Story of the Treasure Seekers, BEING THE ADVENTURES OF THE BASTABLE CHILDREN IN SEARCH OF A FORTUNE BY E. NESBIT (pseud. for EDITH NESBIT BLAND). WITH ILLUSTRATIONS BY GORDON BROWNE AND LEWIS BAUMER. LONDON: T. FISHER UNWIN, 1899. XII, 296p. + 10p. pub. cat.: front., 16 plates. Bound in green cloth.
Y 823.8 NES

1574 **NICHOLINA: A STORY ABOUT AN ICEBERG.**
AND OTHER TALES OF THE FAR NORTH. LONDON: BLACKIE AND SON, 1882. 59p.: col. front., vignette on title page. Bound in brown cloth with coloured decorative cover.
C 823.8 NIC

1575 **NIERITZ, GUSTAV.**
THE TOUCHSTONE OF LIFE. A True Story of the Russian Peerage. BY GUSTAV NIERITZ. TRANSLATED FROM THE GERMAN BY MRS. ALEXANDER KERR. LONDON: THE RELIGIOUS TRACT SOCIETY. 1897. 159p. + 32p. ill. pub. cat.: front., 15 plates, ill. Illustrated by C.W. Bound in blue cloth with coloured decorative cover and spine.
C 823.8 NIE

1576 **NORWAY, G.**
HUSSEIN THE HOSTAGE OR A BOY'S ADVENTURES IN PERSIA. BY G. NORWAY. WITH SIX ILLUSTRATIONS BY JOHN SCHÖNBERG. LONDON: BLACKIE AND SON, LIMITED, (189–?). 352p. + 32p. ill. pub. cat.: front., 5 plates. Bound in grey cloth with coloured pictorial cover and spine.
C 823.8 NOR

1577 **NORWAY, G.**
THE LOSS OF JOHN HUMBLE, WHAT LED TO IT AND WHAT CAME OF IT. BY G. NORWAY. WITH SIX FULL-PAGE ILLUSTRATIONS BY JOHN SCHÖNBERG. NEW EDITION. LONDON: BLACKIE AND SON LIMITED, 1897. 351p. + 32p. ill. pub. cat.: front., 5 plates. Bound in blue cloth with coloured pictorial cover and spine.
C 823.8 NOR

1578 **O'BRIEN, CHARLOTTE.**
Mother's Warm Shawl. A TALE. BY CHARLOTTE O'BRIEN. LONDON: WELLS GARDNER, DARTON AND CO., 1893. 107p. + 16p. pub. cat.: front., 1 plate. Bound in red cloth with coloured decorative cover and spine.
CBD 823.8 OBR

1579 **(OLIPHANT, MARGARET).**
THE LAND OF DARKNESS ALONG WITH SOME FURTHER CHAPTERS IN THE EXPERIENCES OF THE LITTLE PILGRIM. LONDON: MACMILLAN AND CO., 1888. 238p. Bound in grey cloth. Contains The Land of Darkness; The Little Pilgrim; On the Dark Mountain.
YSC 823.8 OLI

1580 **OPIE, AMELIA.**
TALES OF THE PEMBERTON FAMILY FOR THE USE OF CHILDREN. BY AMELIA OPIE. THIRD EDITION. LONDON: HARVEY AND DARTON, 1844. 74p. Bound in olive cloth with decorative cover.
YSC 823.7 OPI

1581 **THE ORPHANS OF GLENULUA.**
A Story of Scottish Life. BY THE AUTHOR OF "THE PIOUS BROTHERS", "THE EVERLASTING KINGDOM". FIFTH EDITION. EDINBURGH: WILLIAM OLIPHANT AND CO. (188–?). 192p. + 16p. ill. pub. cat.: front., 2 plates. Illustrated by L.M. Corner and W. Small. Engraved by Williamson. Bound in green cloth with black decorative cover and spine, with gilt edges.
C 823.8 ORP

1582 **ORR, A.S.**
LEAH: A Tale of Ancient Palestine. Illustrative of the STORY OF NAAMAN THE SYRIAN. BY MRS. A.S. ORR. EDINBURGH: W.P. NIMMO, HAY & MITCHELL (1893). 222p. + 16p. pub. cat.: front., 3 plates. Illustrated by J. McW. and Halswell. Engraved by R. Paterson and M. Corner. Bound in brown cloth with coloured decorative cover and spine. THE GIRL'S OWN LIBRARY.
C 823.8 ORR

1583 **OVEREND, MRS. CAMPBELL.**
THE MAGIC GLASS; OR, The Secret of Happiness. Translated, with additions, BY MRS. CAMPBELL OVEREND. EDINBURGH: WILLIAM P. NIMMO & CO. 1883. 110p.: col. front. Bound in red cloth with decorative cover and spine.
C 823.8 MAG

1584 **OXLEY, J. MACDONALD.**
FERGUS MACTAVISH OR A BOY'S WILL. A Story of the Far North-West. BY J. MACDONALD OXLEY, LL.B. WITH TWELVE ILLUSTRATIONS. LONDON: HODDER AND STOUGHTON 1893. 384p.: front., 11 plates. Illustrated by W.T. Smedley, F.B. Schell, H.A. Ogden, Hogan, J. Finnemore, and Marquis of Lome. Engraved by Andre and Sleigh. Bound in fawn cloth with coloured pictorial cover and spine with gilt edges.
C 823.8 OXL

1584A **OXLEY, J. MACDONALD.**
THE WRECKERS OF SABLE ISLAND. LONDON: T. NELSON AND SONS, 1894. 121p. + 6p. pub. cat.: front., additional vignette title page, by T.M. Paterson. Bound in green cloth with decorative cover and spine.
C 823.8 OXL

1585 **PAE, DAVID.**
JESSIE MELVILLE; OR, The Double Sacrifice. AN EDINBURGH TALE. BY DAVID PAE. EDINBURGH: W.P. NIMMO, HAY & MITCHELL 1888. 317p.: front., 7 plates. Bound in brown cloth.
C 823.8 PAE

1586 **PAGE, JESSE.**
HARRY THE HERO, OR FORGIVENESS WINS. BY JESSE PAGE. LONDON: RELIGIOUS TRACT SOCIETY (189–?). 64p.: col. front., vignette, ill. Bound in red cloth with coloured decorative cover. Little Dot Series.
C 823.8 PAG

1587 **PALGRAVE, MARY E.**
IN CHARGE. A STORY OF ROUGH TIMES BY MARY E. PALGRAVE. WITH FIVE FULL-PAGE ILLUSTRATIONS. LONDON: NATIONAL SOCIETY'S DEPOSITORY (1890). 266p. + 19p. pub. cat.: front., 4 plates, by W.S. Stacey. Bound in blue cloth with coloured pictorial cover and spine.
C 823.8 PAL

1588 **PALGRAVE, MARY E.**
UNDER THE BLUE FLAG. A STORY OF MONMOUTH'S REBELLION. BY MARY E. PALGRAVE. LONDON: SOCIETY FOR PROMOTING CHRISTIAN KNOWLEDGE, (1882). 224p. + 16p. pub. cat.: front., 1

plate. Bound in blue cloth with coloured decorative cover and spine.
YSC 823.8 PAL

1588A **PALMER, ELLEN.**
HELEN SIDDAL: A Story for children. BY ELLEN PALMER. EDINBURGH: W.P. NIMMO, HAY AND MITCHELL, (1871). 94p. Bound in beige cloth with coloured pictorial cover and spine.
C 823.8 PAL

1590 **PARLEY, PETER** *(Pseud).*
CHEERFUL CHERRY; OR, Make the Best of it. WITH OTHER TALES. BY PETER PARLEY. LONDON: CASSELL, PETTER AND GALPIN, (1863). IV, 170p.: front., additional vignette title page, ill. Bound in red cloth with embossed decorative cover and spine. Probably not the work of the original "Peter Parley" the American, Samuel Griswold Goodrich.
C 823.8 PAR

1591 **PARLEY, PETER** *(Pseud).*
PETER PARLEY'S TALES FOR YOUTH. LONDON: RICHARD T. BOWYER, (187–?). 188p.: front. Bound in blue cloth with embossed decorative cover. Probably produced by one of the authors who pirated Peter Parley (S.G. Goodrich)'s name.
YSC 823.8 PAR

1591A **PARRY, EDWARD ABBOTT.**
BUTTERSCOTIA, OR, A CHEAP TRIP TO FAIRY-LAND. BY HIS HONOUR JUDGE EDWARD ABBOTT PARRY. ILLUSTRATED BY ARCHIE MACGREGOR. LONDON: DAVID NUTT, 1896. 170p. + 12p. pub. cat.: front. pictorial title page, folded map, page of music, 1 plate, ill. Bound in grey cloth with pictorial cover and spine.
C 823.8 PAR

1592 **PARRY, EDWARD ABBOTT.**
The Scarlet Herring And Other Stories By His Honour Judge Edward Abbott Parry. With illustrations by Athelstan D. Rusden. LONDON: SMITH, ELDER, & CO., 1899. 253p.: front., 8 plates, ill. Bound in green cloth with red pictorial cover and spine.
C 823.8 PAR

1593 **PARSONS, CHARLES R.**
CALEB AND BECKLEY. BY CHARLES S.R. PARSONS. LONDON: CHARLES H. KELLY, 1896. 190p. + 2p. pub. cat.: front., ill. Illustrated by J.B.F. Bound in brown cloth with coloured decorative cover and spine., with gilt edges.
C 823.8 PAR

1594 **PARSONS, CHARLES R.**
THE MAN WITH THE WHITE HAT; OR, The Story of an Unknown Mission. BY C.R. PARSONS. LONDON: T. WOOLMER 1888. 211p. + 12p. pub. cat.: front., ill. Bound in blue cloth with pictorial cover and spine.
C 823.8 PAR

1595 **(PAUL, ADRIEN).**
(WILLIS THE PILOT: a sequel to "The Swiss Family Robinson") (LONDON:) F. WARNE AND CO., (187–?). Title page missing. 342p. + 10p. pub. cat.: col. front., 2 plates. Bound in red cloth, with embossed decorative cover and spine. WARNE'S Incident and Adventure LIBRARY.
YSC 843.8 PAU

1596 **PAULL, MRS. H.B.**
KNOWING AND DOING. EIGHT STORIES FOUNDED ON BIBLE PRECEPTS. BY MRS. HENRY H.B. PAULL. With Five Full-page Illustrations. LONDON: HODDER AND STOUGHTON, 1897. 502p.: front., 4 plates. Bound in blue cloth with embossed decorative cover and spine with gilt edges.
YSC 823.8 PAU

1597 **PAULL, MRS. H.B.**
MARY ELTON; OR, SELF-CONTROL. BY MRS. H.B. PAULL. LONDON: FREDERICK WARNE AND CO., 1869. 123p. + 4p. pub. cat.: col. front., additional col. vignette title page, by Dalziel. Bound in blue cloth with embossed decorative cover and spine, with gilt edges.
C 823.8 PAU

1598 **(PHELAN) CHARLOTTE ELIZABETH.**
GLIMPSES OF THE PAST. BY CHARLOTTE ELIZABETH. THIRD EDITION. LONDON: R.B. SEELEY AND W. BURNSIDE, 1842. 341p. + 4p. pub. cat.: additional vignette title page, ill. Bound in green cloth with embossed decorative cover and spine.
C 823.8 PHE

1599 **PHELPS, ELIZABETH STUART.**
THE GATES AJAR. BY ELIZABETH STUART PHELPS. LONDON: GEORGE ROUTLEDGE AND SONS. (1868). 188p. + 16p. pub. cat.: front., 1 plate. Bound in green cloth with embossed decorative cover and small inserted coloured pictorial label.
YSC 823.8 PHE

1600 **PICKERING, EDGAR.**
An Old-time Yarn, Wherein is set forth divers desperate mischances which befell Anthony Ingram of Plymouth and his shipmates who adventured to the West Indies and Mexico with John Hawkins and Francis Drake in the year of Our Lord one thousand five hundred and sixty-seven. By Edgar Pickering. Illustrated with Six Pictures drawn by Alfred Pearse. LONDON: BLACKIE AND SON LIMITED, 1893. 288p. + 32p. pub. cat.: front., 5 plates. Bound in beige cloth with pictorial cover and spine.
C 823.8 PIC

1601 **POLLARD, ELIZA F.**
NAN; OR, THE POWER OF LOVE. BY ELIZA F. POLLARD. SECOND EDITION. LONDON: S.W. PARTRIDGE AND CO., (189–?). 96p. + 16p. pub. cat.: front., 4 plates, ill. Bound in grey cloth, with coloured pictorial cover.
YSC 823.8 POL

1602 **POLLARD, ELIZA F.**
ROBERT ASKE, A STORY OF THE REFORMATION, BY ELIZA F. POLLARD. LONDON: S.W. PARTRIDGE AND CO. (189–?). 316p. + 16p. pub. cat.: front., 6 plates. Bound in red cloth with coloured pictorial cover and spine.
C 823.8 POL

1603 **POLLOCK, ROBERT.**
Tales of The Covenanters. BY ROBERT POLLOCK, M.A. WITH BIOGRAPHICAL SKETCH OF THE AUTHOR BY THE REV. ANDREW THOMSON, D.D. AND ILLUSTRATIONS BY H.M. BROCK. EDINBURGH: OLIPHANT, ANDERSON AND FERRIER, 1895. 317p.: front., 6 plates, ill. Bound in blue buckram.
C 823.083 POL

1604 **PORTER, JANE.**
THE SCOTTISH CHIEFS. By Miss Jane Porter. With Six Full-page Illustrations by Steward Orr. LONDON: WALTER SCOTT, LTD. IV, 350p. + 16p. pub. cat.: front., 5 plates. Bound in brown cloth with coloured pictorial cover and decorative spine, with gilt edges.
C 823.8 POR

1605 **PORTER, JANE.**
SIR EDWARD SEAWARD'S NARRATIVE OF HIS SHIPWRECK AND CONSEQUENT DISCOVERY OF CERTAIN ISLANDS IN THE CARIBBEAN SEAS WITH A DETAIL OF MANY EXTRAORDINARY AND HIGHLY INTERESTING EVENTS IN HIS LIFE, FROM THE YEAR 1733–1749. BY JANE PORTER. WITH A PREFACE BY W.H.G. KINGSTON. LONDON: GEORGE ROUTLEDGE AND SONS, (188–?). XXIV, 607p. + 8p. pub. cat.: front., 2 plates. Bound in blue cloth with coloured decorative cover and spine.
C 823.8 POR

1606 **POWER, HARRIET.**
CLIFFE THORPE; OR, THE PROGRESS OF CHARACTER. BY HARRIET POWER. LONDON: WARD, LOCK AND TYLER, (187–?). 281p. + 10p. pub. cat.: front., 5 plates, by Dalziel Brothers. Bound in blue cloth, with embossed decorative cover and spine, and gilt edges.
YSC 823.8 POW

1607 **POWER, P.B.**
THE ONE-TALENTED PEOPLE. BY THE REV. P.B. POWER, M.A. LONDON: THE RELIGIOUS TRACT SOCIETY, (189–?). 128p. + 16p. ill. pub. cat.: front., 1 plate. Bound in blue cloth with pictorial cover and spine.
YSC 823.8 POW

1608 **THE POWER OF TRUTH.**
A STORY OF A BORROWED BIBLE. LONDON: T. NELSON AND SONS, 1895. 64p.: col. front. Bound in blue cloth with embossed cover inlaid with coloured pictorial vignette.
C 823.8 POW

1609 **(PRENTISS, ELIZABETH.)**
LITTLE THREADS; OR, TANGLE THREAD, SILVER THREAD AND GOLDEN THREAD. BY THE AUTHOR OF "LITTLE SUSY". With Illustrations by Absolon. LONDON: JAMES NISBET AND CO., 1865. 148p.: front., 3 plates. Bound in red cloth with embossed cover and spine.
C 823.8 PRE

1610 **PRENTISS, ELIZABETH.**
STEPPING HEAVENWARD. BY E. PRENTISS. NEW EDITION. LONDON: JAMES NISBET AND CO., 1874. VII, 273p. + 6p. pub. cat.: col. front., 5 plates by J.D.W. Bound in red cloth with decorative cover and spine.
C 823.8 PRE

1611 **Another copy.**
LONDON: THOMAS NELSON AND SONS, 1897. 312p. + 8p. pub. cat.: front. Bound in blue cloth with decorative cover and spine.

1611A **Another copy.**
NEW EDITION. WITH FOUR ILLUSTRATIONS IN COLOUR. LONDON: HODDER AND STOUGHTON, 1909. XII, 426p. + 16p. pub. cat.: col. front., 3 col. plates. Bound in green cloth, with coloured pictorial label on cover and spine.

1612 **RAND, EDWARD A.**
TOO LATE FOR THE TIDE-MILL. BY REV. EDWARD A. RAND. LONDON: JAMES NISBET & CO., (189–?). 307p. + 32p. pub. cat.: front., 2 plates. Illustrated by E. Austen. Bound in blue cloth with embossed pictorial cover and spine.
C 823.8 RAN

1613 **(RASPE, RUDOLPH ERICH).**
THE ADVENTURES OF BARON MUNCHAUSEN. A New And Revised Edition. WITH AN INTRODUCTION BY T. TEIGNMOUTH SHORE, M.A. ILLUSTRATED BY GUSTAVE DORÉ. LONDON: CASSELL, PETTER AND GALPIN, 1866. XV, 216p. + 4p. pub. cat.: front., title page printed in red and black, 30 plates, ill., headpieces, tailpieces. Bound in red cloth with decorative cover. Originally published 1783.
CBDQ 823.6 ADV
Another copy.
A New and Revised Edition. THIRD EDITION, smaller format. Bound in blue with embossed decorative cover and spine with gilt edges.
CBDQ 823.6 ADV

1614 **(RASPE, RUDOLF ERICH).**
THE SURPRISING ADVENTURES OF BARON MUNCHAUSEN. REPRINTED FROM THE EARLIEST COMPLETE EDITION WITH THE ORIGINAL ILLUSTRATIONS. EDITED WITH AN INTRODUCTION AND APPENDIX BY F.J. HARVEY DARTON. LONDON: NAVARRE SOCIETY LIMITED, 1930. XXXI, 258p.: front., 38 plates. Bound in maroon cloth.
C 823.6 RAS

1615 **(RASPE, RUDOLPH ERICH).**
THE TRAVELS AND Surprising Adventures of BARON MUNCHAUSEN. WITH FIVE ILLUSTRATIONS BY G. CRUIKSHANK AND TWENTY-TWO FULL PAGE CURIOUS ENGRAVINGS. LONDON: WILLIAM TEGG, (1868). XXII, 268p.: hand col. front., 22 plates, ill. Rebound in blue cloth.
CBD 823.6 MUN/RAS

1616 **READE, F.E.**
AUNT EDNA. BY THE AUTHOR OF "CLARY'S CONFIRMATION", "BOB CURTMAN'S WIFE", "AFTER 5 YEARS", "CHIMNEY PARK". ILLUSTRATED BY J. NASH. LONDON: SOCIETY FOR PROMOTING CHRISTIAN KNOWLEDGE (189–?). 160p. + 4p. pub. cat.: front., 2 plates. Bound in grey cloth with decorative green cover and spine.
C 823.8 REA

1617 **READE, F.E.**
BLACK JACK AND OTHER TEMPERANCE TALES FOR BOYS AND GIRLS. BY F.E. READE. LONDON: SOCIETY FOR PROMOTING CHRISTIAN KNOWLEDGE, (189–?). 160p. + 16p. pub. cat.: front., 2 plates. Bound in cream cloth with pictorial cover.
YSC 823.8 REA

1618 **READE, F.E.**
SEVEN IDOLS. A Tale for Girls. BY F.E. READE. ILLUSTRATED BY PERCY MACQUOID. LONDON: SOCIETY FOR PROMOTING CHRISTIAN KNOWLEDGE (1890?). 160p. + 16p. pub. cat.: front., 2 plates. Bound in blue cloth with yellow decorative cover and spine.
C 823.8 REA

1619 **REED, TALBOT BAINES.**
ROGER INGLETON, MINOR. BY TALBOT BAINES REED. ILLUSTRATED. NEW AND CHEAPER EDITION. LONDON: SAMPSON LOW, MARSTON AND COMPANY Ltd., 1896. 307p. + 5p. pub. cat.: front., 5 plates. Illustrated by A. Hitchcock. Bound in red cloth with coloured pictorial cover and spine.
C 823.8 REE

1620 **(REEVES, MRS. HELEN BUCKINGHAM MATHERS).**
David Lyall's Love Story. By the Author of "The Land o' the Leal". LONDON: HODDER AND STOUGHTON, (189–?). VII, 302p. + 2p. pub. cat. Bound in blue cloth, with coloured pictorial cover and spine.
C 823.912 REE

1621 **REID, THOMAS MAYNE.**
THE CLIFF CLIMBERS. BY CAPTAIN MAYNE REID. LONDON: GEORGE ROUTLEDGE AND SONS, LTD. (189–?). VIII, 408p.: front., 5 plates. Engraved by Edmund Evans. Bound in red cloth with coloured decorative cover and spine.
C 823.8 REI

1622 **REID, THOMAS MAYNE.**
THE DEATH SHOT. A Story Retold. BY CAPTAIN MAYNE REID. STEREOTYPED EDITION. LONDON: SWAN SONNENSCHEIN AND CO., (188–?). 348p. Bound in red cloth with decorative cover and spine.
C 823.8 REI

1623 **Another copy.**
LONDON: GEORGE ROUTLEDGE AND SONS LIMITED, 1905. 348p.: front., 3 plates by F.C. Tilney. Bound in red cloth, with coloured pictorial cover and spine.
C 823.912 REI

1624 **REID, THOMAS MAYNE.**
THE FATAL CORD. BY CAPTAIN MAYNE REID. LONDON: GEORGE ROUTLEDGE AND SONS, LIMITED, (188–?). 307p. Bound in grey cloth with coloured pictorial cover.
C 823.8 REI

1624A **REID, THOMAS MAYNE.**
THE FINGER OF FATE. BY CAPTAIN MAYNE REID. ILLUSTRATED BY STANLEY L. WOOD. LONDON: JAMES BOWDEN, 1899. VIII, 319p + 8p. pub. cat. including biographical information about authors: front., 2 plates. Bound in blue cloth with coloured pictorial cover and spine.
C 823.8 REI

1625 **REID, THOMAS MAYNE.**
THE FLAG OF DISTRESS. A Story of the South Sea. BY CAPTAIN MAYNE REID. STEREOTYPED EDITION. LONDON: SWAN SONNENSCHEIN AND CO., (188–?). 392p.: front., by T.D. Collins. Bound in red cloth with decorative cover and spine.
C 823.8 REI

1626 **REID, THOMAS MAYNE.**
THE FREE LANCES, A ROMANCE OF THE MEXICAN VALLEY. BY THE LATE CAPTAIN MAYNE REID. STEREOTYPED EDITION. LONDON: SWAN, SONNENSCHEIN AND CO. LTD., 1888. 324p. Bound in red cloth with decorative cover and spine.
C 823.8 REI

1627 **REID, THOMAS MAYNE.**
GASPAR, THE GAUCHO, A TALE OF THE GRAN CHACO. WITH ILLUSTRATIONS. LONDON: GEORGE ROUTLEDGE AND SONS, 1880. IV, 347p.: front., 20 plates. Bound in blue cloth with embossed decorative cover and spine.
C 823.8 REI
Another copy.
(189–?). IV, 347p. (inc. adverts. for Maud Muller by Whittier with col. picture and Eno's Fruit Salts).

1628 **REID, THOMAS MAYNE.**
THE GIRAFFE HUNTERS. A SEQUEL TO THE "BUSH BOYS" AND "THE YOUNG YAGERS" BY CAPTAIN MAYNE REID. LONDON: GEORGE ROUTLEDGE AND SONS, LIMITED, (189–?). 392p.: front., 7 plates. Bound in red cloth with pictorial cover and spine.
C 823.8 REI

1629 **REID, THOMAS MAYNE.**
THE GUERILLA CHIEF AND OTHER TALES. BY CAPTAIN MAYNE REID. LONDON: GEORGE ROUTLEDGE AND SONS, LTD., (189–?). IV, 314p. Bound in grey cloth with coloured decorative and pictorial cover and spine.
C 823.8 REI

1630 **REID, THOMAS MAYNE.**
THE HALF-BLOOD. A TALE OF THE FLOWERY LAND. BY CAPTAIN MAYNE REID. LONDON: GEORGE ROUTLEDGE AND SONS LIMITED, (189–?). 438p. + 4p. pub. cat. Bound in maroon cloth, with embossed decorative spine and gilt top.
C 823.8 REI

1631 **REID, THOMAS MAYNE.**
THE HEADLESS HORSEMAN: A Strange Tale of Texas. BY CAPTAIN MAYNE REID. LONDON: CHARLES H. CLARKE, (1869). IV, 470p.: front., 20 plates. Bound in brown cloth, with embossed pictorial/decorative cover and spine. Originally published 1866.
C 823.8 REI

1632 **REID, THOMAS MAYNE.**
THE HUNTER'S FEAST; OR, CONVERSATIONS AROUND THE CAMP-FIRE. BY CAPT. MAYNE REID. LONDON: THOMAS HODGSON, (186–?). 336p. + pub. cat. on endpapers. Bound in green paper with decorative cover and spine. THE PARLOUR LIBRARY, CXX.
C 823.8 REI

1633 **Another copy.**
LONDON: GEORGE ROUTLEDGE & SONS, LTD. (189–?). VIII, 334p. + 2p. col. ill. adverts. (tribute to Maud Muller by Whittier, and "Eno's Fruit Salts"). Bound in blue cloth with coloured pictorial cover and decorative spine.

1634 **REID, THOMAS MAYNE.**
THE LONE RANCH. BY CAPTAIN MAYNE REID. LONDON: GEORGE ROUTLEDGE AND SONS, 1885. 408p.: vignette on title page, 10 plates. Bound in green cloth with coloured decorative cover and spine.
C 823.8 REI

1635 **REID, THOMAS MAYNE.**
THE MAROON. BY CAPTAIN MAYNE REID. LONDON: GEORGE ROUTLEDGE AND SONS, LIMITED (189–?). 491p.: 5 plates. Bound in brown cloth with coloured decorative cover and spine.
C 823.8 REI

1636 **REID, THOMAS MAYNE.**
THE PIERCED HEART, And Other Stories. BY CAPT. MAYNE REID. NEW EDITION. ILLUSTRATED. LONDON: GRIFFITH, FARRAN & CO. 1893. 312p. + 48p. ill. pub. cat.: front., 3 plates. Bound in green cloth with coloured pictorial cover and spine.
C 823.8 REI

1637 **REID, THOMAS MAYNE.**
THE QUADROON; OR, Adventures in the Far West. BY CAPTAIN MAYNE REID. WITH TWELVE ILLUSTRATIONS BY WM. HARVEY, ENGRAVED BY EVANS. LONDON: J. & C. BROWN AND CO., 1856. 447p.: front., 10 plates. Rebound in blue buckram.
C 823.8 REI

1638 **Another copy.**
GEORGE ROUTLEDGE AND SONS LIMITED, (189–?). 447p. Bound in grey with coloured pictorial and decorative cover and spine.

1639 **REID, THOMAS MAYNE.**
RAN AWAY TO SEA, An Autobiography for Boys. BY CAPTAIN MAYNE REID. LONDON: GEORGE ROUTLEDGE AND SONS, LIMITED, (189–?). 485p. + 6p. pub. cat. Bound in grey cloth with coloured decorative cover and spine.
C 823.8 REI

1640 **REID, THOMAS MAYNE.**
THE SCALP-HUNTERS, A ROMANCE OF NORTHERN MEXICO. BY CAPTAIN MAYNE REID. ILLUSTRATED BY W.B. HANDFORTH. LONDON: DOWNEY AND CO. LIMITED, (189–?). 371p.: front., 5 plates. Bound in blue cloth, with embossed decorative cover and spine. Originally published 1851.
C 823.8 REI

1642 **REID, THOMAS MAYNE.**
THE VEE-BOERS. A TALE OF ADVENTURE IN SOUTHERN AFRICA. BY CAPTAIN MAYNE REID. LONDON: GEORGE ROUTLEDGE AND SONS, (188–?). 216p. + 2p. pub. cat.: vignette on title page, 13 plates, ill. Bound in brown cloth with coloured decorative cover and spine.
C 823.8 REI

1643 **REID, THOMAS MAYNE.**
THE WAR TRAIL OR THE HUNT OF THE WILD HORSE. BY CAPTAIN MAYNE REID. LONDON: GEORGE ROUTLEDGE AND SONS, LIMITED, (188–?). 418p. + 12p. pub. cat. Bound in grey cloth with coloured pictorial cover.
C 823.8 REI

1644 **REID, THOMAS MAYNE.**
THE WHITE CHIEF, A LEGEND OF NORTHERN MEXICO. BY CAPTAIN MAYNE REID. LONDON: GEORGE ROUTLEDGE AND SONS, LIMITED, (188–?). 444p. Bound in grey cloth with coloured pictorial cover.
C 823.8 REI

1645 **REID, THOMAS MAYNE.**
THE WILD HUNTRESS. BY CAPTAIN MAYNE REID. LONDON: C.H. CLARKE. FIFTH EDITION (189–?). IV, 320p. + 4p. pub. cat. on inside covers. Bound in brown cloth with coloured pictorial cover and spine, with pub. cat. on back. THE MAYNE REID LIBRARY.
C 823.8 REI

1645A **Another copy.**
GEORGE ROUTLEDGE AND SONS (189–?), 320p.: 6 plates engraved by E. Evans. Bound in red cloth with coloured decorative cover and spine.

1646 **REID, THOMAS MAYNE.**
THE WOOD RANGERS. From the French of Bellamare. By CAPTAIN MAYNE REID. LONDON: DARTON & HODGE, (189–?). 340p. + 3p. pub. cat. Bound with coloured pictorial cover and pub. cat. on back. THE PARLOUR LIBRARY.
C 823.8 REI

1647 **REVOIL, M. BENEDICT.**
IN THE BUSH AND ON THE TRAIL. ADVENTURES IN THE FORESTS OF NORTH AMERICA. A BOOK FOR BOYS. BY M. BENEDICT REVOIL. WITH SEVENTY ILLUSTRATIONS. LONDON: T. NELSON AND SONS, 1895. XII, 393p. + 2p. pub. cat.: front., pictorial title page, ill. by VAN DARGENT. Bound in blue cloth with embossed pictorial cover and spine.
C 823.8 REV

1648 **REYNOLDS, GEORGE W.M.**
ALFRED; OR THE ADVENTURES OF A FRENCH GENTLEMAN. LONDON: HENRY LEA (184–?). 237p.: front. Bound in purple cloth with embossed decoration.
C 823.8 REY

1649 **REYNOLDS, GEORGE W.M.**
MASTER TIMOTHY'S BOOKCASE: OR THE MAGIC LANTHORN OF THE WORLD. BY GEORGE W.M. REYNOLDS. NEW EDITION WITH NUMEROUS ILLUSTRATIONS. LONDON: "REYNOLDS MISCELLANY", 1847. 373p. ill. by H. ANELAY engraved by Griffin and Duvergier. Rebound in maroon cloth.
C 823.8 REY

1650 **RICHARDSON, SAMUEL.**
PAMELA; OR, VIRTUE REWARDED: IN A SERIES OF FAMILIAR LETTERS FROM A BEAUTIFUL YOUNG DAMSEL TO HER PARENTS: PUBLISHED IN ORDER TO CULTIVATE THE PRINCIPLES OF VIRTUE AND RELIGION IN THE MINDS OF THE YOUTH OF BOTH SEXES. BY MR. SAMUEL RICHARDSON. LONDON: MILNER AND COMPANY, (187–?). 384p.: col. front. Bound in blue cloth: miniature edition. Originally published 1740.
C 823.6 RIC

1651 **RICHMOND, LEGH.**
ANNALS OF THE POOR, BY REV. LEGH RICHMOND. LONDON: T. NELSON AND SONS, 1861. XIX, 208p.: front., 7 plates. Bound in blue cloth with embossed decoration on cover and spine.
C 823.8 RIC

1652 **Another copy.**
(188–?). 188p. + 4p. pub. cat.: col. front. ill. Bound in green cloth with embossed decorative cover and spine.

1652A **Another copy.**
LONDON: T. NELSON AND SONS, 1882. 203p. + 8p. pub. cat.: front., additional vignette title page. Bound in grey with decorative cover and spine.

1652B **Another copy.**
LONDON: GEORGE ROUTLEDGE AND SONS, (189–?). 188p. + 4p. pub. cat.: col. front., ill. Bound in pink cloth, with coloured pictorial/decorative cover and spine.

1653 **RIDLEY, M.L.**
THE THREE CHUMS. BY M.L. RIDLEY. LONDON: JOHN F. SHAW AND CO., (1882). 224p. + 16p. pub. cat.: front., 3 plates by H. Petherick. Bound in green cloth with embossed pictorial cover and spine.
C 823.8 RID

1654 **RIGG, MRS.**
THE PEARLY GATES BY MRS. RIGG AND "ALMOST A SACRIFICE" BY MRS. ELLEN ROSS. LONDON: S.W. PARTRIDGE AND CO., (188–?). 64p. + 16p. pub. cat.: col. front., 4 plates. Bound in blue cloth with coloured pictorial cover.
C 823.8 RIG

1655 **THE RIVAL CLERKS AND OTHER TALES.**
LONDON: W. AND R. CHAMBERS, 1882. 192p.: front. Bound in blue cloth with embossed decoration on cover and spine.
C 823.8 RIV

1656 **ROBERTS, MARGARET.**
THE ATELIER DU LYS, OR AN ART STUDENT IN THE REIGN OF TERROR. BY THE AUTHOR OF "MADEMOISELLE MORI" (MARGARET ROBERTS). NEW EDITION. LONDON: LONGMANS, GREEN, AND CO., 1897. VIII, 358p. + 32p. pub. cat. Bound in grey cloth with pictorial cover.
C 823.8 ROB

1657 **ROBIN AND LINNET.**
BY THE AUTHOR OF "HONOR BRIGHT". With Illustrations by A. Forester. THIRD EDITION. LONDON: WELLS, GARDNER, DARTON AND CO., 147p.: front., 4 plates. Bound in blue cloth with coloured pictorial cover and spine.
C 823.8 ROB

1658 **RODING, MARY.**
PAUL'S PARTNER. BY MARY RODING. LONDON: SOCIETY FOR PROMOTING CHRISTIAN KNOWLEDGE, (189–?). 79p. + 8p. pub. cat.: front. Bound in grey cloth with coloured pictorial cover.
C 823.8 ROD

1658A **ROE, EDWARD PAYSON.**
BARRIERS BURNED AWAY. BY THE REV. EDWARD P. ROE. MANCHESTER: JOHN HEYWOOD, (189–?). 406p.: front., 1 plate. Bound in brown cloth, with coloured decorative cover and spine, and gilt edges.
YSC 813.4 ROE

1658B **Another copy.**
LONDON: WARD, LOCK AND CO. LIMITED, (190–?). 488p. + 18p. pub. cat.: front., 1 plate by St. Clair Simmons. Bound in olive cloth, with coloured pictorial/decorative cover and spine and gilt edges.
C 813.4 ROE

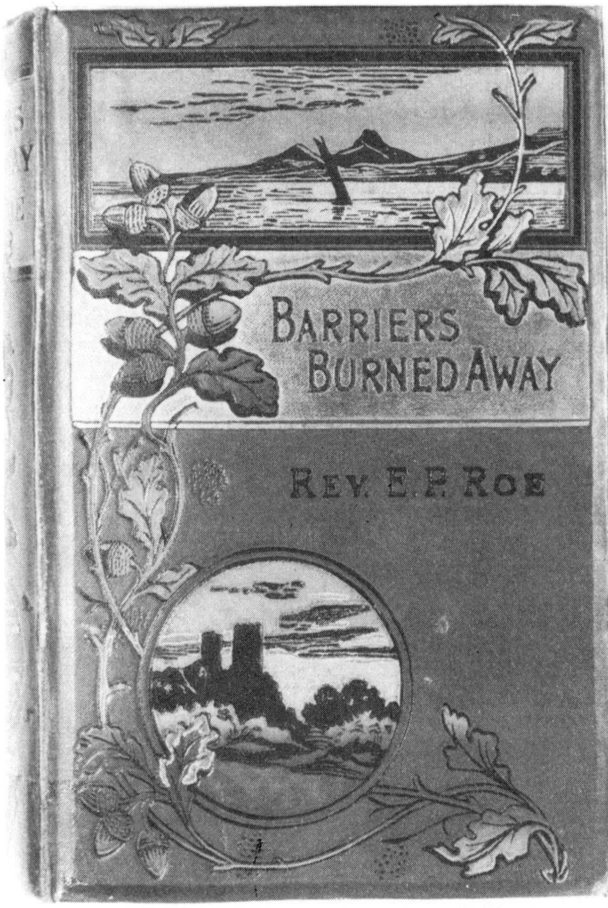


1658B

1659 **ROE, EDWARD PAYSON.**
FROM JEST TO EARNEST. BY REV. E.P. ROE. LONDON: WARD, LOCK AND CO. (188–?). XIV, 288p. + 18p. pub. cat. Bound in blue cloth with decorative cover.
C 813.4 ROE

1660 **Another copy.**
LONDON: W. NICHOLSON AND SONS, LIMITED, (189–?). 377p. + 5p. pub. cat.: front., additional vignette title page. Bound in red cloth with decorative cover and spine.

1661 **ROE, EDWARD PAYSON.**
A YOUNG GIRL'S WOOING: A LOVE STORY. BY THE REV. E.P. ROE. LONDON: FREDERICK WARNE AND CO., (1884). 330p.: Bound in blue cloth, with embossed decorative cover and spine.
YSC 813.4 ROE

1662 **Another copy.**
BY THE REV. EDWARD P. ROE. MANCHESTER: JOHN HEYWOOD, (189–?). 406p.: front., 1 plate. Bound in brown cloth, with coloured decorative cover and spine and gilt edges.
YSC 813.4 ROE

1663 **ROOPER, W.L.**
A JOKE FOR A PICNIC. BY W.L. ROOPER. LONDON: BLACKIE AND SON, LIMITED, (189–?). 96p. + 8p. pub. cat.: front. Bound in orange cloth with coloured pictorial cover.
C 823.8 ROO

1664 **ROOPER, W.L.**
Piecrust promises. By W.L. Rooper. LONDON: BLACKIE AND SON, LIMITED. (189–?). 128p. + 8p. pub. cat.: front. Bound in grey cloth with coloured decorative cover and spine.
C 823.8 ROO

1665 **ROPES, MARY EMILY.**
THE MYSTERY OF HOYLE'S MOUTH, OR The Adventures of Two Runaway Boys. BY M.E. ROPES. WITH ILLUSTRATIONS BY J. AYTON SYMINGTON. LONDON: THE SUNDAY SCHOOL UNION, (189–?). 160p.: front., 3 plates. Bound in blue cloth with coloured pictorial cover.
C 823.8 ROP

1666 **ROPES, MARY EMILY.**
TWO LITTLE FINNS. BY MARY E. ROPES. LONDON: RELIGIOUS TRACT SOCIETY, (189–?). 80p.: col. front. Bound in blue cloth with coloured decorative cover and spine.
C 823.8 ROP

1667 **ROTTENSTAKE ALLEY.**
A Tale of the Plaiting Districts (Founded on Fact). LONDON: SOCIETY FOR PROMOTING CHRISTIAN KNOWLEDGE, (1873). 128p. + 7p. pub. cat.: front., 2 plates. Bound in brown cloth with decorative cover and spine.
C 823.8 ROT

1668 **ROWSELL, MARY C.**
THE PEDLAR AND HIS DOG. BY MARY C. ROWSELL. WITH TWO FULL-PAGE ILLUSTRATIONS BY GEO. CRUICKSHANK. LONDON: BLACKIE AND SON, LIMITED, (188–?). 160p. + 32p. pub. cat.: front., 1 plate. Bound in red cloth, with pictorial/decorative cover and spine.
C 823.8 ROW
Another copy.
160p. + 16p. pub. cat.: front., 1 plate. Bound in green cloth, with coloured decorative cover and spine.
YSC 823.8 ROW

1669 **RUSSELL, FOX.**
The First Cruise of Three Middies. BY FOX RUSSELL. LONDON: WELLS, GARDNER, DARTON, AND CO., (189–?). 258p.: front., 19 plates by H.J. Rhodes. Bound in green cloth with coloured pictorial cover and decorative spine.
C 823.8 RUS

1670 **ST. LEGER, HUGH.**
"HALLOWE'EN" AHOY! OR, LOST ON THE CROZET ISLANDS. BY HUGH ST. LEGER. WITH SIX FULL-PAGE ILLUSTRATIONS BY HERBERT J. DRAPER. LONDON: BLACKIE AND SON, LIMITED, 1896. 320p. + 32p. ill. pub. cat.: front., 5 plates. Bound in green cloth with coloured pictorial cover and spine.
C 823.8 SAI

1671 **SADLER, S. WHITCHURCH.**
THE GOOD SHIP BARBARA. A STORY OF TWO BROTHERS. BY S. WHITCHURCH SADLER, R.N. WITH ILLUSTRATIONS BY W.H. OVEREND. LONDON: SOCIETY FOR PROMOTION OF CHRISTIAN KNOWLEDGE, (188–?). 370p. + 12p. pub. cat.: front., 3 plates. Bound in olive cloth with decorative cover and spine.
823.8 SAD

1672 **SARGENT, GEORGE ETELL.**
FRANK LAYTON, AN AUSTRALIAN STORY. BY GEORGE E. SARGENT. LONDON: THE RELIGIOUS TRACT SOCIETY, (189–?). 375p. + 12p. pub. cat.: front., 3 plates, by G.E. Robertson. Bound in blue cloth, with coloured pictorial cover and spine.
C 823.8 SAR

1673 **SARGENT, GEORGE ETELL.**
THE POOR CLERK AND HIS CROOKED SIXPENCE. BY GEORGE E. SARGENT. LONDON: THE RELIGIOUS TRACT SOCIETY. (187–?). 216p., front., 9 plates. Bound in green cloth with embossed decorative cover and spine.
C 823.8 SAR

1673A **SCHMID, JOHANN CHRISTOPHER VON.**
THE BASKET OF FLOWERS AND OTHER TALES. TRANSLATED FROM THE GERMAN OF CHRISTOPHER VON SCHMID. LONDON: MILNER AND COMPANY, LIMITED, (189–?). 318p.: front., vignette title page. Bound in red cloth.
C 823.8 BAS

1674 **SCHMID, JOHANN CHRISTOPHER VON.**
THE PET LAMB, AND OTHER TALES. TRANSLATED FROM THE GERMAN OF CHRISTOPHER VON SCHMID. LONDON: MILNER AND COMPANY, (187–?). 158p. + 2p. pub. cat.: front., additional vignette title page, engraved by W. Banks and Son. Bound in purple cloth, with embossed decorative cover and spine, and gilt edges.
C 833.6 SCH
Another copy.
(187–?). 158p.: col. front., engraved by W. Banks and Son. Bound in green cloth, with embossed decorative cover.
YSC 833.6 VON

1675 **SCOTT, MICHAEL.**
TOM CRINGLE'S LOG. BY MICHAEL SCOTT. WITH ILLUSTRATIONS BY FRANK BRANGWYN. TWO VOLUMES. LONDON: GIBBINGS AND CO. Ltd. 1894. 397, 387p.: decorative title pages, 2 plates, 2 plates. Bound in blue cloth with decorative cover and spine. Originally published 1836.
CBD 823.8 SCO

1676 **SEAMER, MARY.**
SHAKESPEARE'S STORIES SIMPLY TOLD. By MARY SEAMER. WITH 130 ILLUSTRATIONS. LONDON: THOMAS NELSON AND SONS, (187–?). 312p. + 4p. pub. cat.: front., additional vignette title page, ill. Bound in brown cloth, with embossed decorative cover and spine, and gilt edges. Contains twenty six stories.
C 823.8 SEA

1677 **SEARCHFIELD, EMILY.**
"AIM AT A SURE END" BY EMILY SEARCHFIELD. WITH ORIGINAL ILLUSTRATIONS BY W.S. STACEY. LONDON: CASSELL AND COMPANY, LIMITED, 1886. 208p. + 16p. pub. cat.: front., 3 plates. Bound in olive cloth with decorative cover and spine. The "Golden Mottoes" series.
C 823.8 SEA

1678 **SEDGWICK, A.K.**
TALES OF TEMPERANCE AND SOBRIETY, FOR THE MIDDLE AND LOWER RANKS OF SOCIETY. BY

A.K. SEDGWICK. LONDON: A.K. NEWMAN AND COMPANY, 1842. 416p.: front. Bound in brown cloth with embossed decorative cover and spine.
C 823.8 SED

1679 **SEDGWICK, CATHERINE MARIA.**
PRETTY LITTLE STORIES FOR PRETTY LITTLE PEOPLE. A SUITABLE CHRISTMAS OR NEW YEAR'S GIFT BY MISS SEDGWICK. HALIFAX, MILNER AND SOWERBY, 1855. 160p.: col. decorative front. including title, ill. Bound in red cloth with embossed decorative cover, with gilt edges.
C 823.8 SED

1680 **SEELEY, EMMA LOUISA.**
BORDER LANCES. A ROMANCE of the NORTHERN MARCHES in the Reign of EDWARD THE THIRD. By the AUTHOR OF "BELT AND SPUR". With many illustrations. LONDON: SEELEY AND CO., 1886. VII, 272p. + 4p. pub. cat.: col. front., 11 col. plates, ill. Bound in dark blue cloth with decorative cover and spine.
C 823.8 SEE

1681 **(SELOUS, HENRY COURTENEY).**
THE CHILDREN OF THE PARSONAGE. WITH ILLUSTRATIONS BY K. GREENAWAY. GRIFFITH, FARRAN, OKEDEN AND WELSH, (188–?). 159p. + 16p. pub. cat.: front., 2 plates. Bound in blue cloth with embossed pictorial/decorative cover.
C 823.8 SEL

1682 **(SELOUS, HENRY COURTENEY).**
HUMBLE LIFE: A TALE FOR HUMBLE HOMES BY THE AUTHOR OF "GERTY AND MAY", "CHILDREN OF THE PARSONAGE", "SUNNY DAYS", ETC. ILLUSTRATIONS BY T.C. COLLINS. LONDON: GRIFFITH, FARRAN, OKEDEN, AND WELSH. (188–?). 149p. + 32p. pub. cat.: front., 3 plates. Bound in green cloth with embossed decorative cover and spine and inserted coloured vignette.
C 823.8 SEL

1683 **SHADWELL, MRS. LUCAS.**
ARNOLD'S RESOLVE, BY MRS. LUCAS SHADWELL. GLASGOW: SCOTTISH TEMPERANCE LEAGUE, 1884. 133p. + 8p. pub. cat. Bound in blue cloth with embossed decorative cover and spine.
C 823.8 SHA

1684 **SHADWELL, MRS. LUCAS.**
MAGGIE'S MISTAKE; OR, Bright Light in the Clouds. BY MRS. LUCAS SHADWELL. LONDON: JOHN F. SHAW AND CO., (188–?). 192p. + 16p. pub. cat.: front., 2 plates by M. Irwin. Bound in olive cloth with coloured decorative cover and spine.
C 823.8 SHA

1685 **SHERWOOD, MARY MARTHA.**
BOYS WILL BE BOYS; OR, THE DIFFICULTIES OF A SCHOOLBOY'S LIFE. A SCHOOLBOY'S MISSION. BY MRS. SHERWOOD, AND HER DAUGHTER, MRS. KELLY. HALIFAX: MILNER AND SOWERBY, 1860. V–VIII, 149p. + 2p. pub. cat.: front., vignette on title page engraved by W. Banks and Son, Edinburgh. Bound in blue cloth. Preface by Sophia Kelly (1854). Originally published 1854.
C 823.8 SHE

1686 **SHERWOOD, MARY MARTHA.**
CHARLES LORRAINE OR THE YOUNG SOLDIER. DRAWN FROM SCENES OF REAL LIFE. BY MRS. SHERWOOD. COPYRIGHT EDITION, ILLUSTRATED. LONDON: HOULSTON AND SONS (1887). Illustrated by J.M. Kronheim & Co. 128p. + 8p. ill. pub. cat.: col. front., 4 plates. Bound in red cloth with decorative cover and spine. Originally published c1830. Includes poems. Reflections on the hours of the night.
C 823.8 SHE

1687 **SHERWOOD, MARY MARTHA.**
THE FLOWERS OF THE FOREST. BY THE AUTHOR OF "LITTLE HENRY AND HIS BEARER" (MARY MARTHA SHERWOOD) LONDON: WILLIAM NICHOLSON AND SONS, (188–?). 142p. + 2p. pub. cat.: front., additional title page with vignette, ill. Bound in blue cloth with decorative cover and spine. Originally published 1830.
C 823.8 SHE

1687A **SHERWOOD, MARY MARTHA.**
THE HISTORY OF THE FAIRCHILD FAMILY OR The Child's Manual. BEING A COLLECTION OF STORIES CALCULATED TO SHOW THE IMPORTANCE AND EFFECTS OF A RELIGIOUS EDUCATION. BY MRS SHERWOOD. LONDON: GEORGE ROUTLEDGE AND SONS (188–?). 572p. + 4p. pub. cat.: front., 5 plates. Bound in purple cloth with coloured decorative cover and spine. Originally published 1847.
M 823 SHE CHILDREN'S COLLECTION

1688 **SHERWOOD, MARY MARTHA.**
THE LITTLE WOODMAN AND HIS DOG CAESAR. BY MRS. SHERWOOD. WITH ILLUSTRATIONS. LONDON: GEORGE ROUTLEDGE AND SONS, (187–?). 117p. + 6p. pub. cat.: col. front., ill. Bound in brown cloth with decorative cover and spine. Originally published 1818.
C 823.8 SHE

1688A **SHERWOOD, MARY MARTHA.**
LUCY CLARE. BY MRS SHERWOOD. LONDON: MILNER AND SOWERBY, NEW ED., 1860. 123p.: front., additional vignette title page. Bound in brown paper with coloured decorative cover. JUVENILE SERIES.
M 823 SHE CHILDREN'S COLLECTION.

1689 **SHERWOOD, MARY MARTHA.**
THE MAY-BEE. BY MRS. SHERWOOD. Tenth Edition. And THE BERKSHIRE SHEPHERD By Mrs Cameron. SIXTH EDITION. LONDON: PRINTED FOR HOULSTON AND CO., (184–?). 29, 34p.: 2 fronts. Half bound in brown calf with marbled paper covers. Originally published c. 1820.
CBD 823.8 SHE

1690 **SHIPLEY, MARY E.**
LITTLE HELPERS; OR, What Children may do for Jesus. BY MARY E. SHIPLEY. LONDON: SOCIETY FOR PROMOTING CHRISTIAN KNOWLEDGE, (187–?). 128p. + 4p. pub. cat.: front. Bound in green cloth with embossed decorative cover and spine.
C 823.8 SHI

1691 **SHIPLEY, MARY E.**
LOFTY AIMS AND LOWLY EFFORTS: A Tale of Christian Ministry. BY MARY E. SHIPLEY. LONDON: SOCIETY FOR PROMOTING CHRISTIAN KNOWLEDGE, (188–?). 260p. + 4p. pub. cat.: 1 plate. Bound in brown cloth, with decorative cover and spine.
YSC 823.8 SHI

1692 **SHIPTON, HELEN.**
CROOKED. ILLUSTRATED BY R.C. WOODVILLE. LONDON: SOCIETY FOR PROMOTING CHRISTIAN KNOWLEDGE, (189–?). 223p. + 8p. pub. cat.: front., 2 plates. Bound in blue cloth with decorative cover and spine.
C 823.8 SHI

1693 **SILVERPEN** *(Pseud.)*.
THE DELFT JUG BY SILVERPEN, AND OTHER STORIES. CASSELL, PETTER, GALPIN AND CO., (188–?). 89p. + 2p. pub. cat.: front. Bound in black cloth with coloured pictorial cover. Attributed on endpaper to Eliza Meteyard.
C 823.8 SIL

1694 **SILVERPEN** *(Pseud.)*.
THE DELFT JUG BY SILVERPEN: FOLLOWED BY THE BOY AND THE MAN (from the German of Christopher Von Schmidt) AND THE WHITE VIOLET, by Susan Pindar. LONDON: CASSELL, PETTER AND GALPIN, (187–?). 104p. + 16p. pub. cat.: front., 1 plate. Bound in blue cloth with embossed decorative cover and spine.
C 823.8 SIL

1695 **SINCLAIR, CATHERINE.**
HOLIDAY HOUSE; A BOOK FOR THE YOUNG. BY CATHERINE SINCLAIR. LONDON: WARD, LOCK AND TYLER, (187–?). XII, 347p.: front., 6 plates. Bound in brown cloth with embossed decorative cover and spine, with gilt edges. Originally published 1839.
C 823.8 SIN

1696 **SKERTCHLY, J.A.**
SPORT IN ASHANTI OR MELINDA THE CABOCEER, A TALE OF THE GOLD COAST IN THE DAYS OF KING KOFFEE KALCALLI. BY J.A. SKETCHLEY. WITH ORIGINAL ILLUSTRATIONS. LONDON: FREDERICK WARNE AND CO., XI, 358p. + 8p. pub. cat.: front., 3 plates by J.B. Greene. Bound in blue cloth with pictorial/decorative cover and spine.
C 823.8 SKE

1697 **SMITH, ALBERT.**
THE ADVENTURES OF CHRISTOPHER TADPOLE. BY ALBERT SMITH. INVERNESS: GEORGE YOUNG, (189–?). 461p. + 1p. pub. cat. Bound in maroon cloth, with gilt top. THE NESS LIBRARY OF STANDARD AUTHORS.
YSC 823.8 SMI

1698 **THE SOLDIER AND THE SUBSTITUTE.**
And other Stories, BEING "BUDS OF PROMISE" FOR YOUNG PEOPLE. Narratives illustrative of Gospel Truth. FOURTH SERIES. LONDON: ALFRED HOLNESS, (187–?). 55p. + 8p. pub. cat.: front., ill. Bound in brown cloth with inserted coloured paper vignette.
C 823.8 SOL

1699 **SOMERTON, ALICE.**
THE TORN BIBLE; OR, HUBERT'S BEST FRIEND. BY ALICE SOMERTON. A NEW EDITION. With Illustrations. LONDON: FREDERICK WARNE AND CO., (188–?). 175p. + 8p. pub. cat.: front., 5 plates by Dalziel. Bound in red cloth with pictorial/decorative cover and spine, with gilt edges.
C 823.8 SOM

1700 **SONNENBURG, FERDINAND.**
THE HERO OF DANZIG; OR, KONRAD THE STANDARD-BEARER. BY FERD. SONNENBURG. Translated with the Author's Permission BY "LUIGI". LONDON: S.W. PARTRIDGE AND CO., (189–?). 253p.: front., 5 plates. Bound in brown cloth with embossed pictorial/decorative cover and decorative spine.
C 833.8 SON

1701 **SOUTHWORTH, EMMA D.E.N.**
THE FATAL MARRIAGE BY MRS. EMMA D.E.N. SOUTHWORTH. LONDON: MILNER AND COMPANY, (187–?). 320p. + 32p. pub. cat.: front., additional vignette title page. Bound in blue cloth with embossed decorative cover and spine.
C 813.4 SOU

1703 **SPYRI, JOHANNA.**
SWISS STORIES FOR CHILDREN, AND THOSE WHO LOVE CHILDREN. FROM THE GERMAN OF MADAM JOHANNA SPYRI. BY LUCY WHEELOCK. ILLUSTRATED BY HORACE PETHERICK. LONDON: BLACKIE AND SON, (188–?). 208p. + 32p. pub. cat.: front., 2 plates. Bound in blue cloth, with coloured pictorial cover and spine. Contains five stories.
YSC 833.8 SPY

1704 **STABLES, WILLIAM GORDON.**
AS WE SWEEP THROUGH THE DEEP. A Story of the Stirring Times of old. BY DR. GORDON STABLES, R.N. T. NELSON AND SONS, 1897. 214p., additional vignette title page, 4 plates by A. Rhind. Bound in green cloth with embossed pictorial/decorative cover and spine.
C 823.8 STA

1704A **STABLES, WILLIAM GORDON.**
BORN TO COMMAND. A Tale of the Sea and Sailors. BY GORDON STABLES. ILLUSTRATED BY W.H. OVEREND. LONDON: SOCIETY FOR PROMOTING CHRISTIAN KNOWLEDGE, (1892). 533p. + 9p. pub. cat.: front., 4 plates. Bound in blue cloth with coloured pictorial cover and spine.
C 823.8 STA

1705 **STABLES, WILLIAM GORDON.**
BY SEA AND LAND. A Tale of the Blue and the Scarlet. BY GORDON STABLES, M.D., R.N. WITH ORIGINAL ILLUSTRATIONS BY W.S. STACEY. LONDON: FREDERICK WARNE AND CO., 1890. 352p.: front., 5 plates. Bound in green cloth with pictorial cover and spine.
C 823.8 STA

1706 **STABLES, WILLIAM GORDON.**
THE CRUISE OF THE ROVER CARAVAN. BY GORDON STABLES, M.D., R.N. LONDON: JAMES NISBET AND CO., LIMITED, 1896. VIII, 311p. + 8p. pub. cat.: front., 3 plates by C. Whymper. Bound in green cloth with embossed decorative cover and spine.
C 823.8 STA

1707 **STABLES, WILLIAM GORDON.**
EVERY INCH A SAILOR. BY GORDON STABLES, M.D., C.M. SURGEON ROYAL NAVY. T. NELSON AND SONS, 1897. 440p. + 8p. pub. cat.: front., additional vignette title page, 12 plates. Bound in green cloth with pictorial/decorative cover and spine.
C 823.8 STA

1708 **STABLES, WILLIAM GORDON.**
EXILES OF FORTUNE. A Tale of a far North Land. BY GORDON STABLES, C.M., M.D., R.N. LONDON: JOHN F. SHAW AND CO., (188–?). 382p. + 24p. pub. cat.: front., 6 plates. Bound in brown cloth with coloured pictorial cover and spine.

Another copy.
NEW EDITION. LONDON: JOHN F. SHAW AND CO., (189–?). 382p. + 20p. pub. cat.: front., 6 plates. Bound in green cloth with coloured pictorial cover and spine, with gilt edges.
C 823.8 STA

1709 **STABLES, WILLIAM GORDON.**
Facing Fearful Odds. A Tale of Flood and Field. BY GORDON STABLES, M.D., C.M. NEW EDITION. LONDON: JOHN F. SHAW AND CO., (189–?). 374p.: front., 7 plates. Bound in blue cloth with coloured pictorial cover and spine, with gilt edges.
823.8 STA

1709A **STABLES, WILLIAM GORDON.**
For Honour Not Honours: BEING THE STORY OF GORDON OF KHARTOUM. BY GORDON STABLES, M.D., C.M. NEW EDITION. LONDON: JOHN F. SHAW AND CO. (189–?). 372p. + 16p. pub. cat.: front., 7 plates, headpieces, tailpieces. Bound in cream cloth with coloured pictorial cover and spine with gilt edges.
C 823.8 STA

1709B **STABLES, WILLIAM GORDON.**
FRANK HARDINGE. FROM TORRID ZONES TO REGIONS OF PERPETUAL SNOW. BY GORDON STABLES, M.D., C.M., R.N. WITH EIGHT ILLUSTRATIONS BY SYDNEY COWELL. LONDON: HODDER AND STOUGHTON, 1898. VII, 352p. + 8p. pub. cat.: front., 7 plates. Bound in green cloth with coloured pictorial cover and spine, with gilt edges.
C 823.8 STA

1710 **STABLES, WILLIAM GORDON.**
FROM SQUIRE TO SQUATTER. A Tale of the Old Land and the New. BY GORDON STABLES. LONDON: JOHN F. SHAW, NEW ED. (189–?) 384p.: front., 5 plates, decorative chapter headings. Bound in red cloth with pictorial cover and spine.
C 823.8 STA

1711 **STABLES, WILLIAM GORDON.**
Hearts of Oak. A STORY OF NELSON AND THE NAVY. BY GORDON STABLES, M.D., C.M. NEW EDITION. LONDON, JOHN F. SHAW AND CO., (189–?). 374p. + 16p. pub. cat.: 6 plates, map. Bound in grey cloth with coloured pictorial cover and spine, with gilt edges.
C 823.8 STA

1711A **STABLES, WILLIAM GORDON.**
The Hermit Hunter of the Wilds. BY GORDON STABLES. LONDON: BLACKIE AND SON LIMITED (189–?). 224p. + 16p. pub. cat.: front., 3 plates. Bound in brown cloth with coloured pictorial cover and spine.
C 823.8 STA

1712 **STABLES, WILLIAM GORDON.**
In Search of Fortune. A TALE OF THE OLD LAND AND THE NEW. BY GORDON STABLES, M.D., C.M. NEW EDITION. LONDON: JOHN F. SHAW AND CO., (189–?). 384p. +16p. ill. pub. cat.: front., 7 plates. Bound in blue cloth, with coloured pictorial cover and spine, and gilt edges.
YSC 823.8 STA

1713 **STABLES, WILLIAM GORDON.**
In the Dashing Days of Old or the WORLD-WIDE ADVENTURES OF WILLIE GRANT BY GORDON STABLES M.D., C.M. NEW EDITION. LONDON: JOHN F. SHAW AND CO., (189–?). 380p. + 6p. pub. cat.: front., 5 plates by M. Irwin. Bound in blue cloth with coloured pictorial cover and spine.
C 823.8 STA

1714 **STABLES, WILLIAM GORDON.**
A LIFE ON THE OCEAN WAVE OR The Cruise of The Good Ship 'Boreas'. BY GORDON STABLES, M.D., C.M., R.N., NEW EDITION. LONDON: JOHN F. SHAW AND CO., (189–?). 344p. + 8p. pub. cat.: front., 2 plates. Bound in red cloth with coloured decorative cover and spine.
C 823.8 STA

1714A **STABLES, WILLIAM GORDON.**
On to the Rescue. A TALE OF THE INDIAN MUTINY. BY GORDON STABLES. LONDON: JOHN F. SHAW AND CO., (1894). 374p. + 16p. pub. cat.: front., 3 plates, 1 plan, decorative head pieces to chapters. Bound in red cloth with coloured pictorial cover and spine; with decorative endpapers.
823.8 STA

1715 **STABLES, WILLIAM GORDON.**
REMEMBER THE MAINE. A Story of The Spanish-American War. By Gordon Stables, C.M., M.D. LONDON: JAMES NISBET AND CO. LIMITED, 1899. 329p. + 18p. pub. cat.: front., map, 4 plates by John H. Betts. Bound in blue cloth with pictorial cover and spine and gilt edges.
C 823.8 STA

1716 **STABLES, WILLIAM GORDON.**
Shoulder to shoulder: A STORY OF THE STIRRING TIMES OF OLD. BY GORDON STABLES, M.D., C.M. NEW EDITION. LONDON: JOHN F. SHAW AND CO., (189–?). 374p. + 6p. pub. cat.: front., 2 plates. Bound in blue cloth with coloured pictorial cover and spine, with gilt edges.
C 823.8 STA

1717 **STABLES, WILLIAM GORDON.**
STANLEY GRAHAME BOY AND MAN. A Tale of the Dark Continent. BY GORDON STABLES, M.D., R.N. WITH EIGHTEEN ILLUSTRATIONS. LONDON: HODDER AND STOUGHTON, 1897. VIII, 349p. + 8p. pub. cat.: front., 6 plates, ill. Bound in blue cloth with pictorial/decorative cover and spine, with gilt edges.
C 823.8 STA

1718 **STABLES, WILLIAM GORDON.**
Two Sailor Lads. A STORY OF STIRRING ADVENTURES ON SEA AND LAND. BY GORDON STABLES, M.D., C.M. NEW EDITION. LONDON: JOHN F. SHAW AND CO., (189–?). 378p. + 10p. pub. cat.: front., 3 plates. Bound in brown cloth, with coloured pictorial cover and spine.
C 823.8 STA

1719 **STABLES, WILLIAM GORDON.**
WESTWARD WITH COLUMBUS. BY GORDON STABLES, M.D., C.M. ILLUSTRATED BY ALFRED PEARSE. LONDON: BLACKIE AND SON, LIMITED, 1894. 352p. + 32p. pub. cat.: front., 7 plates. Bound in grey cloth with coloured pictorial cover and spine.
C 823.8 STA

1720 **Another copy.**
Illustrated. LONDON: BLACKIE AND SON LIMITED, (192–?). 352p.: col. front. by Arch. Webb, 3 plates by A.P. Bound in red cloth, with coloured pictorial cover and spine.

1720A **STABLES, WILLIAM GORDON.**
WILD ADVENTURES IN WILD PLACES. BY GORDON STABLES. LONDON: CASSELL AND COMPANY, LIMITED, (1881). 224p. + 16p. pub. cat. front., 5 plates, ill. Bound in red cloth with coloured decorative cover and spine.
C 823.8 STA

1721 **STEBBING, GRACE.**
Brave Geordie. THE STORY OF AN ENGLISH BOY. BY GRACE STEBBING. NEW EDITION. LONDON: JOHN F. SHAW AND CO., (189–?). VI, 208p. + 10p. pub. cat.: front., 3 plates by H. PETHERICK. Bound in blue cloth with coloured pictorial cover and spine. Originally published 1879.
C 823.8 STE

1722 **STEBBING, GRACE.**
Never Give In. A TALE OF THE LIFE AND TIMES OF GUSTAVUS ADOLPHUS. BY G. STEBBING. NEW EDITION. LONDON: JOHN F. SHAW, (189–?). 384p.: front., 2 plates, ill. Bound in red cloth with coloured pictorial cover and spine, with gilt edges. Originally published 1896.
C 823.8 STE

1723 **STEBBING, GRACE.**
A REAL HERO, OR GOLD AND GLORY. A STORY OF The Conquest of Mexico. BY GRACE STEBBING. New Edition. LONDON: JOHN F. SHAW AND CO., (1892). VIII, 359p.: front., 4 plates. Bound in red with pictorial cover and spine.
C 823.8 STE

1724 **STEBBING, GRACE.**
THAT AGGRAVATING SCHOOL-GIRL. BY GRACE STEBBING. LONDON: JAMES NISBET AND CO., (1885). VI, 295p. + 18p. pub. cat.: front., 1 plate, ill. Bound in green cloth with coloured decorative panels on cover and spine.
C 823.8 STE

1726 **STEVENSON, ROBERT LOUIS.**
CATRIONA, A SEQUEL TO "KIDNAPPED", BEING MEMOIRS OF THE FURTHER ADVENTURES OF DAVID BALFOUR AT HOME AND ABROAD . . . (BY) ROBERT LOUIS STEVENSON. With SIXTEEN ILLUSTRATIONS by W.B. HOLE, R.S.A. TWENTY-SEVENTH THOUSAND. LONDON: CASSELL AND COMPANY LIMITED, 1893. VI, 371p. + 28p. pub. cat.: front., 16 plates. Bound in blue cloth.
YSC 823.8 STE

1727 **STEVENSON, ROBERT LOUIS.**
TREASURE ISLAND. BY ROBERT LOUIS STEVENSON. Illustrated Edition. SIXTY-NINTH THOUSAND. LONDON: CASSELL AND COMPANY LIMITED, 1896. VIII, 292p. + 28p. pub. cat.: front., additional pictorial title page, vignette title page, 24 plates. Bound in blue cloth, with coloured pictorial cover and spine. Originally published 1883.
YSC 823.8 STE

1727A **Another copy.**
ILLUSTRATED BY MONRO S. ORR LONDON: COLLINS, 1934. VII, 248p.: col. front (map), 10 col. plates. Bound in red cloth with coloured pictorial paper jacket.
C 823.8 STE

1728 **STEWART, DOUGLAS.**
THE PIRATE QUEEN: OR, CAPTAIN KIDD AND THE

TREASURE. BY DOUGLAS STEWART. LONDON: RICHARDS AND CO., 1867. 257p.: front. Bound in blue cloth with embossed decorative cover and spine, with gilt edges.
C 823.8 STE

1729 **STODDART, ISABELLA.**
THE SCOTTISH ORPHANS, A Moral Tale, FOUNDED ON AN HISTORICAL FACT. BY LADY STODDART, (MRS. BLACKFORD). New Edition. LONDON: GRANT AND GRIFFITH, 1850. 128p.: front., vignette on title page. Bound in cream paper with green and red leaf and berry decoration. Originally published 1822.
C 823.8 STO

1730 **STOWE, HARRIET ELIZABETH BEECHER.**
A DOG'S MISSION; OR The Story of the Old Avery House, And Other Stories. BY HARRIET BEECHER STOWE. WITH ILLUSTRATIONS. LONDON: THOMAS NELSON AND SONS, 1887. 146p.: front., additional vignette title page, 6 plates. Bound in green cloth with embossed pictorial cover and spine.
C 813.3 STO

1731 **STOWE, HARRIET ELIZABETH BEECHER.**
DRED; A Tale of the Great Dismal Swamp. BY HARRIET BEECHER STOWE. LONDON: SAMPSON LOW, SON AND CO., 1856. VIII, 524p. + 12p. pub. cat. Bound in red cloth with embossed decorative cover. Includes a preface discussing the effect on the attitudes to slavery following the publication of Uncle Tom's Cabin. Originally published c. 1841.
C 813.3 STO

1732 **STOWE, HARRIET ELIZABETH BEECHER.**
UNCLE TOM'S CABIN OR, NEGRO LIFE IN THE SLAVE STATES OF AMERICA. BY HARRIET BEECHER STOWE. WAKEFIELD: WILLIAM NICHOLSON AND SONS, (187–?). 358p. + 2p. pub. cat.: col. front. Bound in red cloth with embossed decorative cover and spine.
C 813.3 STO

1733 **STOWE, HARRIET ELIZABETH BEECHER.**
UNCLE TOM'S CABIN. By Harriet Beecher Stowe. Illustrations by A.S. Forrest. LONDON: THOMAS NELSON AND SONS LTD., (190–?). V, 531p. + 7p. pub. cat.: col. front., 16 plates. Bound in green cloth, with pictorial spine. Originally published 1852.
YSC 813.3 STO

1734 **Another copy.**
UNCLE TOM'S CABIN, A Tale OF LIFE AMONG THE LOWLY . . . With a preface BY THE RIGHT HON. THE EARL OF CARLISLE. LONDON: GEORGE ROUTLEDGE AND SONS, LIMITED, (188–?). XVI, 480p. Bound in brown cloth with coloured pictorial cover and spine.

1735 **Another copy.**
WITH FIVE ILLUSTRATIONS. LONDON: HODDER AND STOUGHTON, (188–?). 426p.: front., 4 plates. Bound in grey cloth, with coloured decorative cover and spine.
YSC 813.3 STO

1736 **Another copy.**
LONDON: NICHOLSON AND SONS, (188–?). Lacking title page. 368p. Bound in blue cloth, with embossed decorative cover and spine.

1737 **Another copy.**
LONDON: WARD LOCK AND CO. LIMITED, (189–?). VIII, 424p. + 16p. pub. cat.: front. Bound in blue cloth with pictorial/decorative cover and spine.
C 813.3 STO

1738 **Another copy.**
LONDON: T. NELSON AND SONS, 1899. 516p.: front., additional vignette title page, 6 plates. Bound in blue cloth with pictorial/decorative cover and spine.

1739 **STRETTON, HESBA.**
BEDE'S CHARITY. BY HESBA STRETTON. LONDON: THE RELIGIOUS TRACT SOCIETY INCORPORATED, (188–?). 224p.: front., vignette title page, 6 plates. Bound in red cloth, with coloured pictorial/decorative cover and spine.
YSC 823.8 STR

1740 **STRETTON, HESBA.**
CASSY, BY HESBA STRETTON. NEW EDITION WITH SEVEN ILLUSTRATIONS. LONDON: THE RELIGIOUS TRACT SOCIETY, (188–?). 159p.: front., 5 plates by W.S. Stacey. Bound in blue cloth with coloured decorative cover and spine.
C 823.8 STR

1741 **(STRETTON, HESBA).**
THE CHILDREN OF CLOVERLEY. BY THE AUTHOR OF "JESSICA'S FIRST PRAYER", . . . LONDON: THE RELIGIOUS TRACT SOCIETY, (188–?). 157p. + 3p. pub. cat.: front., vignette on title page, 4 plates. Bound in brown cloth, with embossed pictorial/decorative cover and spine.
C 823.8 STR

1742 **(STRETTON, HESBA).**
ENOCH RODEN'S TRAINING. BY THE AUTHOR OF "JESSICA'S FIRST PRAYER", . . . LONDON: THE RELIGIOUS TRACT SOCIETY, (189–?). 159p.: front., 3 plates. Bound in brown cloth, with embossed pictorial/decorative cover and spine.
C 823.8 STR

1743 **(STRETTON, HESBA).**
FERN'S HOLLOW. By the Author of "Jessica's First Prayer" . . . LONDON: THE RELIGIOUS TRACT SOCIETY, (187–?) 194p. + 2p. pub. cat.: front., vignette on title page, 2 plates. Bound in blue cloth with embossed decorative cover and spine.
C 823.8 STR

1744 **(STRETTON, HESBA).**
JESSICA'S FIRST PRAYER. LONDON: THE RELIGIOUS TRACT SOCIETY, (188–?). 92p. + 4p. pub. cat.: front., 4 plates, ill. Bound in purple cloth.
C 823.8 STR

1745 **STRETTON, HESBA.**
LITTLE MEG'S CHILDREN. BY HESBA STRETTON. WITH ILLUSTRATIONS BY EDWARD WHYMPER. LONDON: THE RELIGIOUS TRACT SOCIETY, (188–?). 158p. + 18p. ill. pub. cat.: front., 1 plate, ill. Bound in olive cloth with coloured decorative cover and spine.
C 823.8 STR

1746 **STRETTON, HESBA.**
LOST GIP. BY HESBA STRETTON. WITH SEVEN ILLUSTRATIONS. LONDON: THE RELIGIOUS TRACT SOCIETY, (189–?). 160p.: front., 1 plate, ill. by Whymper. Bound in red cloth with coloured decorative cover and spine.
C 823.8 STR

1747 **STRETTON, HESBA.**
Max Krömer, A STORY OF THE SIEGE OF STRASBOURG. BY THE AUTHOR OF "Jessica's First Prayer' . . . (HESBA STRETTON). LONDON: THE RELIGIOUS TRACT SOCIETY, 1871. 143p.: front., 5 plates, ill. by A.A.B. engraved by Butterworth and Heath. Bound in brown cloth.
C 823.8 STR

1748 **(STRETTON, HESBA).**
PILGRIM STREET, A STORY OF MANCHESTER LIFE. BY THE AUTHOR OF "JESSICA'S FIRST PRAYER", . . . LONDON: THE RELIGIOUS TRACT SOCIETY, (188–?). 160p.: front., vignette on title page, 4 plates. Bound in brown cloth, with embossed pictorial/decorative cover and spine.
C 823.8 STR

FOUND AT LAST. [See page 153.

1749

1749 **STRETTON, HESBA.**
A THORNY PATH. BY HESBA STRETTON. LONDON: THE RELIGIOUS TRACT SOCIETY, (187–?). 160p.: front., 7 plates, decorations at beginning and end of chapters. Bound in brown cloth with embossed pictorial cover and decorative spine.
C 823.8 STR

1750 **STUART, ESMÈ.**
FOR HALF A CROWN. A STORY. BY ESMÈ STUART. WITH FOUR FULL-PAGE ILLUSTRATIONS. LONDON: NATIONAL SOCIETY'S DEPOSITORY. 257p. + 8p. pub. cat.: front., 3 plates by Francis Barraud. Bound in green with coloured pictorial cover and spine.
C 823.8 STU

1751 **STUART, ESMÈ.**
THE GOLDMAKERS BY ESMÈ STUART. ILLUSTRATED BY F. DADD. LONDON: SOCIETY FOR PROMOTING CHRISTIAN KNOWLEDGE, (189–?). 160p. + 4p. pub. cat.: front., 2 plates. Bound in blue cloth with coloured pictorial cover and spine.
C 823.8 STU

1752 **SURR, ELIZABETH.**
GOOD OUT OF EVIL. A TALE FOR CHILDREN. BY MRS. SURR WITH THIRTY TWO ILLUSTRATIONS BY GIACOMELLI. LONDON: THOMAS NELSON AND SONS, 1879. 119p. + 8p. pub. cat.: front., 6 plates, ill. Bound in green cloth with embossed decorative cover and spine with coloured pictorial paper vignette inserted, with gilt edges.
C 823.8 SUR

1753 **SUSAN AND MAGDALENE.**
BY THE AUTHOR OF "THE COUSINS RECONCILED". EDINBURGH: OLIPHANT, ANDERSON AND FERRIER, 1881. 96p.: col. front. Bound in blue cloth with embossed decorative cover and spine with coloured pictorial paper vignette inserted.
C 823.8 SUS

1754 **THE SWEDISH BROTHERS.**
A Tale. LONDON: JOSEPH MASTERS, 1847. 125p.: decorative title page, ill. Bound in red cloth, with embossed decorative covers. THE JUVENILE Englishman's Library, VIII.
YSC 823.8 SWE

1755 **SWIFT, JONATHAN.**
GULLIVER'S TRAVELS. By JONATHAN SWIFT. Illustrated by HERBERT COLE. LONDON: JOHN LANE, THE BODLEY HEAD, 1900. XX, 355p.: front., vignette on title page, 26 plates, ill. Bound in green cloth, with coloured pictorial cover and pictorial/decorative spine. Originally published 1726.
C 823.5 SWI

1756 **Another copy.**
LONDON: J.M. DENT AND CO., 1906. XX, 279p.: decorative front. and title page, 11 plates by A. Rackham, 6 maps, decorative endpapers. Bound in blue cloth with decorative spine. EVERYMAN'S LIBRARY (OF) CHILDREN'S BOOKS.
YSC 823.5 SWI

1757 **Another copy.**
EDITED BY PADRAIC COLUM. PRESENTED BY WILLY POGANY. LONDON: G. HARRAP AND COMPANY LTD., 1919. XIX, 296p.: col. front., 3 col. plates, headpieces, decorative initials. Bound in brown cloth with pictorial cover.
CBD 823.5 SWI

1758 **SWIFT, JONATHAN.**
GULLIVER'S TRAVELS AMONG THE LITTLE PEOPLE OF LILIPUT. BY DEAN SWIFT. ILLUSTRATED. LONDON: "REVIEW OF REVIEWS" OFFICE, (189–?). 58p. + 2p. pub. cat.: ill. Bound in paper covers. Books for the Bairns Series.
C 823.8 GUL

1759 **SWIFT, JONATHAN.**
GULLIVER'S TRAVELS INTO SEVERAL REMOTE NATIONS OF THE WORLD. BY JONATHAN SWIFT, D.D. WITH A MEMOIR OF THE AUTHOR. ILLUSTRATED WITH UPWARDS OF 300 WOOD-ENGRAVINGS, FROM DESIGNS BY J.G. THOMSON, ENGRAVED BY W.L. THOMAS. LONDON: S.O. BEETON, 1864. XXXVI, 364p.: col. front., additional col. pictorial title page, ill. Bound in purple cloth with embossed decorative cover and spine, with gilt edges.
C 823.5 SWI

1760 **Another copy.**
ILLUSTRATED BY ARTHUR RACKHAM. LONDON: THE TEMPLE PRESS, 1899. XV, 291p. + 10p. pub. cat.: col. front., 11 col. plates, 2 plates, ill. Bound in blue cloth.
CBD 823.5 SWI

1761 **Another copy.**
WITH TWELVE ILLUSTRATIONS BY ARTHUR RACKHAM. LONDON: J.M. DENT AND COMPANY, 1901. XIV, 363p.: col. front. and col. decorative title page, 11 plates. Bound in blue calf.
CBD 823.5 SWI

1762 **SWIFT, JONATHAN.**
GULLIVER'S TRAVELS RETOLD FOR LITTLE FOLK BY AGNES GROZIER HERBERTSON. Illustrated by John Hassall, R.I. LONDON: BLACKIE AND SON LIMITED, (193–?). 80p.: col. front., vignette on title page, 7 col. plates, 15 plates, ill. Bound in red cloth with coloured pictorial paper cover.
C 823.912 HER

1763 **SWIFT, JONATHAN.**
GULLIVER'S TRAVELS: THE FIRST THREE VOYAGES. BY JONATHAN SWIFT. Edited, with an Introduction and Notes, by F.E. BUDD. LONDON: MACMILLAN AND CO. LIMITED, 1939. XXXVIII, 310p.: front., 12 plates, ill. by C.E. Brock, 4 maps. Bound in green cloth. THE SCHOLAR'S LIBRARY.
YSC 823.5 SWI

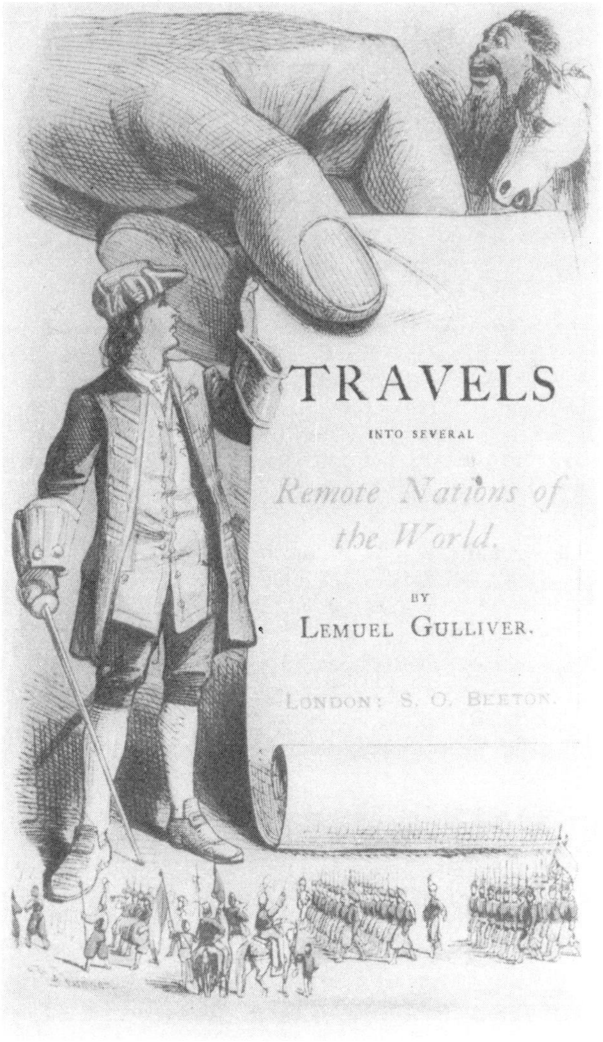


1759

1764 **SWIFT, JONATHAN.**
GULLIVER'S TRAVELS TO LILLIPUT AND BROBDINGNAG. BY JONATHAN SWIFT. ILLUSTRATED BY R.G. MOSSA. LONDON: HODDER AND STOUGHTON, (192–?). 301p.: col. front., decorative title page, 11 col. plates, 11 plates, ill. Bound in blue cloth.
CBD 823.5 SWI

1765 **(SWIFT, JONATHAN).**
TRAVELS INTO SEVERAL REMOTE NATIONS OF THE WORLD BY LÉMUEL GULLIVER. WITH A PREFACE BY HENRY CRAIK AND ONE HUNDRED ILLUSTRATIONS BY CHARLES E. BROCK. LONDON: MACMILLAN AND CO., 1894, XXXII, 381p. + 2p. pub. cat.: front., 14 plates, ill., maps. Bound in green cloth with pictorial cover and spine.
CBD 823.5 SWI

1766 **Another copy.**
WITH SIXTEEN FULL-PAGE ILLUSTRATIONS IN COLOUR BY STEPHEN BAGHOT DE LA BERE. LONDON: ADAM AND CHARLES BLACK, 1904. 307p. + 8p. pub. cat.: col. front., decorative title page, 14 col. plates (1 missing). Bound in green cloth, with coloured pictorial cover and spine.
C 823.5 SWI

1767 **SYBIL'S SACRIFICE.**
AND OTHER Choice Stories for the Young. With Twelve Illustrations. EDINBURGH: WILLIAM D. NIMMO, 1870. 120p. + 8p. pub. cat.: col. front., 12 plates. Bound in red cloth with embossed decorative cover and spine, with coloured pictorial paper vignette inserted.
C 823.8 SYB

1768 **TEMPLE, CRONA.**
PRINCESS LOUISE: A Tale of the Stuarts. BY CRONA TEMPLE. LONDON: T. NELSON AND SONS. 1897. 156p. + 4p. pub. cat.: front. additional vignette title page by A. Rhind. Bound in blue cloth with embossed decorative cover and spine.
C 823.8 TEM

1769 **THORN, ISMAY.**
GEOFF AND JIM. BY ISMAY THORN. LONDON: WELLS, GARDNER, DARTON AND CO., 1891. 188p. + 4p. pub. cat.: front., 5 plates. Bound in red cloth with coloured pictorial/decorative cover and spine.
C 823.8 THO

1770 **THORN, ISMAY.**
THE HARRINGTONS AT HOME. BY ISMAY THORN. LONDON: WELLS, GARDNER, DARTON AND CO., FOURTH EDITION, 1902. 112p. + 16p. pub. cat.: front., vignette on title page, 12 plates, ill. Bound in blue cloth with coloured pictorial cover and spine.
C 823.8 THO

1771 **THORN, ISMAY.**
QUITE UNEXPECTED. BY ISMAY THORN. ILLUSTRATED. LONDON: GARDNER, DARTON AND CO., (189–?). 161p. + 16p. ill. pub. cat.: front., 6 plates. Bound in yellow cloth with coloured pictorial/decorative cover and spine.
C 823.8 THO

1772 **TIDDEMAN, LIZZIE ELLEN.**
GRANNIE'S TREASURES And How They Helped Her. BY L.E. TIDDEMAN. LONDON: S.W. PARTRIDGE AND CO., (188–?). 96p. + 16p. pub. cat.: front., 4 plates, ill. Bound in blue cloth with coloured pictorial cover and decorative spine.
C 823.8 TID

1773 **TIM THE NEWSBOY.**
By the Author of "Buy an orange, Sir," "Don't say so," "Bible Pictures for Little People," etc. LONDON: THE SUNDAY SCHOOL UNION, (188–?). 64p.: front by W. Cheshire. Bound in beige cloth with embossed decorative cover and pictorial paper vignette inserted.
C 823.8 TIM

1774 **TIRED OF HOME.**
A Story for Girls. LONDON: THE RELIGIOUS TRACT SOCIETY, (187–?). 64p.: col. front. Bound in brown cloth with embossed decorative cover.
C 823.8 TIR

1775 **TODD, JOHN.**
THE ANGEL OF THE ICEBERG And Other Stories ILLUSTRATING GREAT TRUTHS. DESIGNED CHIEFLY FOR THE YOUNG. BY THE REV. JOHN TODD, D.D. LONDON: KNIGHT AND SON, (1859). 128p. + 36p. pub. cat.: col. front. Bound in red cloth with embossed decorative cover and spine.
C 823.8 TOD

1776 **TOM'S OPINION.**
BY THE AUTHOR OF "Honor Bright," "The Two Blackbirds," etc. etc. LONDON: WELLS, GARDNER, DARTON AND CO., 1895. 125p.: front. Bound in brown cloth with coloured pictorial/decorative cover and spine.
C 823.8 TOM

1777 **TRAILL, CATHERINE.**
IN THE FOREST; OR, PICTURES OF LIFE AND SCENERY IN THE WOODS OF CANADA. A Tale By MRS. TRAILL. WITH 19 ILLUSTRATIONS. LONDON: T. NELSON AND SONS., 1894. 188p.: front., additional vignette title page, 13 plates, ill. Bound in brown cloth with pictorial cover and spine.
C 823.8 TRA

1778 **TREANOR, THOMAS STANLEY.**
THE LOG OF A SKY PILOT OR WORK AND ADVENTURE AROUND THE GOODWIN SANDS. BY THE REV. THOMAS STANLEY TREANOR, M.A. SECOND EDITION. LONDON: THE RELIGIOUS TRACT SOCIETY, 1894. 256p.: front. 16 plates, ill. Bound in blue cloth with coloured pictorial cover and spine.
C 823.8 TRE

1779 **TRIMMER, SARAH.**
THE HISTORY OF THE ROBINS. BY MRS. TRIMMER. LONDON: GRIFFITH AND FARRAN, (188–?). 126p.: col. front. Bound in grey paper with brown cloth spine and coloured pictorial cover. THE FAVOURITE LIBRARY VOLUME III. Originally published as Fabulous Histories in 1786. Includes a presentation book plate of the Manchester School Board, 28 February, 1886.
C 823.8 TRI

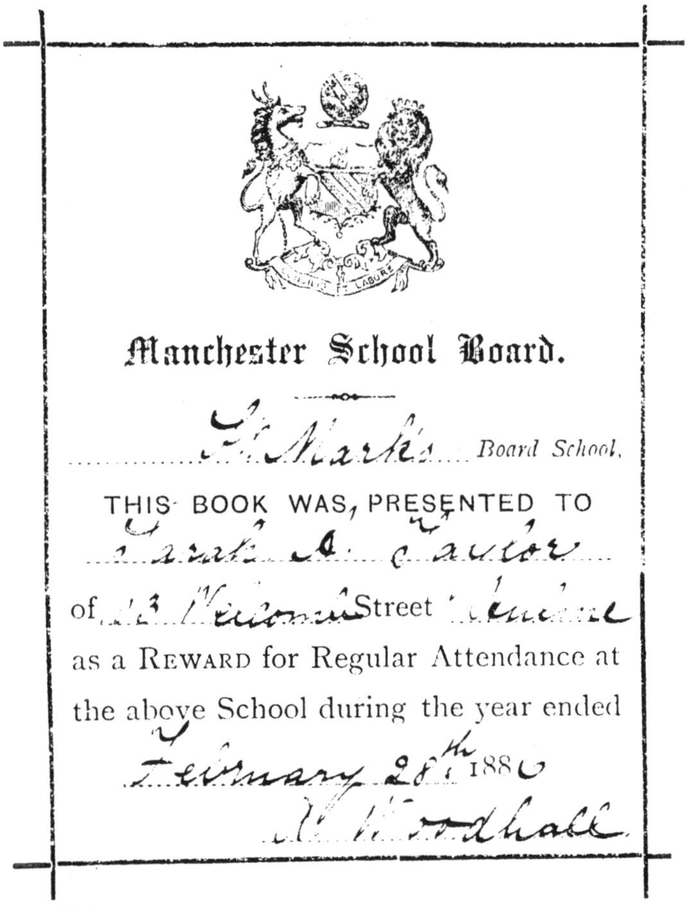
Manchester School Board.
Board School.
THIS BOOK WAS PRESENTED TO
of Street
as a REWARD for Regular Attendance at the above School during the year ended

1779

1780 **TRIMMER, SARAH.**
THE HISTORY OF THE ROBINS FOR THE INSTRUCTION OF CHILDREN ON THEIR TREATMENT OF ANIMALS BY MRS TRIMMER. WITH TWENTY-FOUR ILLUSTRATIONS BY HARRISON WEIR. LONDON: GRIFFITH AND FARRAN, 1869. 141p. + 10p. pub. cat.: front., vignette on title page, 23 plates engraved by J. Greenaway, decorative chapter initials.
CBD 823.8 TRI

1780A **TRIMMER, SARAH.**
THE STORY OF THE ROBINS DESIGNED TO TEACH CHILDREN THE PROPER TREATMENT OF ANIMALS. BY MRS TRIMMER. With Illustrations printed in colours by Edmund Evans, FROM ORIGINAL DESIGNS. LONDON: FREDERICK WARNE AND CO., 1870. 160p. 16 col. ill. at the beginning of each chapter. Bound in purple cloth with decorative cover and spine. THE LANSDOWNE GIFT BOOKS.
M 823 TRI CHILDREN'S COLLECTION

1781 **TRUTH AND TRUST.**
LONDON: W. & R. CHAMBERS, (188–?). 128p.: col. front., col. title page with vignette. Bound in green cloth with decorative cover and spine. Chamber's Juvenile Library. Includes Jervis Ryland and Victor and Lisette.
823.8 TRU

1781A **TWAIN, MARK.**
TOM SAWYER ABROAD. BY MARK TWAIN (SAMUEL L. CLEMENS) WITH 26 ILLUSTRATIONS BY DAN BEARD. LONDON: CHATTO AND WINDUS, 1894. 208p. + 32p. pub. cat.: front., vignette on title page, 17 plates, ill. Bound in red cloth with pictorial cover and spine.
M 813 TWA CHILDREN'S COLLECTION

1782 **TWAIN, MARK.**
A YANKEE AT THE COURT OF KING ARTHUR. BY MARK TWAIN, (SAMUEL L. CLEMENS). A NEW EDITION. WITH 220 ILLUSTRATIONS BY DAN. BEARD. LONDON: CHATTO AND WINDUS, 1897. XVI, 525p. + 32p. pub. cat.: front., 56 plates, ill. Bound in blue cloth. Originally published 1889.
YSC 813.4 TWA

1783 **Another copy.**
A NEW IMPRESSION. LONDON: CHATTO AND WINDUS, 1915. 298p.: front. Bound in pink cloth, with embossed decorative cover.

1784 **UNCLE NED'S STORIES OF THE TROPICS.**
LONDON: THE RELIGIOUS TRACT SOCIETY, (188–?). 190p. + 2p. pub. cat.: front., 9 plates, ill. Bound in brown cloth with embossed pictorial cover and spine.
C 398.23913 UNC

1785 **UPS AND DOWNS.**
The Story of a Newspaper Boy. LONDON: THE RELIGIOUS TRACT SOCIETY, (188–?). 128p. + 16p. ill. pub. cat.: front., 2 plates, headpieces and tailpieces. Bound in red cloth with embossed decorative cover and spine.
C 823.8 UPS

1786 **VAN SOMMER, E.**
MARTIN'S INHERITANCE OR, The Story of a Life's Chances. A TEMPERANCE TALE. BY E. VAN SOMMER. LONDON: T. NELSON AND SONS, 1892. 233p. + 6p. pub. cat.: front., additional vignette title page. Bound in blue cloth with coloured decorative cover and spine.
C 823.8 VAN

1787 **VERNE, JULES.**
THE ADVENTURES OF CAPTAIN HATTERAS. CONTAINING "THE ENGLISH AT THE NORTH POLE", AND "THE ICE DESERT." BY JULES VERNE. ILLUSTRATED BY HENRY AUSTIN. 248p., 223p.: front., 1 plate. Bound in blue cloth with coloured pictorial cover and spine. Originally published 1866.
C 843.8 VER

1787A **VERNE, JULES.**
THE CHILD OF THE CAVERN; OR, STRANGE DOINGS UNDERGROUND. BY JULES VERNE. TRANSLATED BY W.H.G. KINGSTON. THIRD EDITION. LONDON: SAMPSON LOW, MARSTON, SEARLE AND RIVINGTON, 1883. XI, 246p.: front., 43 plates, by P. Ferat, engraved by Ch. Barbant. Bound in green cloth, with embossed pictorial/decorative cover and spine, and gilt edges. Originally published 1877.
YSC 843.8 VER

1788 **VERNE, JULES.**
THE ENGLISH AT THE NORTH POLE. BY JULES VERNE. LONDON: WARD, LOCK, AND TYLER, (187–?). 218p.: col. front., 2 col. plates. Bound in green cloth. Originally published 1866.
YSC 843.8 VER

1789 **Another copy.**
LONDON: GEORGE ROUTLEDGE AND SONS LIMITED, (188–?). 254p. Bound in beige cloth, with coloured decorative cover and spine. EVERY BOY'S LIBRARY.

1790 **VERNE, JULES.**
A FAMILY WITHOUT A NAME. BY JULES VERNE.

NEW AND CHEAPER EDITION. ILLUSTRATED. LONDON: SAMPSON LOW, MARSTON AND COMPANY, (1895). 134p. + 32p. pub. cat.: front., 15 plates. Bound in red cloth with coloured pictorial cover and spine. Originally published 1891.
C 843.8 VER

1792 **VERNE, JULES.**
A FLOATING CITY, AND THE BLOCKADE RUNNERS. BY JULES VERNE. TRANSLATED FROM THE FRENCH. THIRD EDITION. LONDON: SAMPSON LOW, MARSTON, SEARLE, AND RIVINGTON, 1882. IV, 286p.: front., vignette title page, 41 plates by P. Ferat. Bound in green cloth, with pictorial/decorative cover and spine. Originally published 1871.
Y 843.8 VER

1792A **VERNE, JULES.**
A FLOATING CITY. BY JULES VERNE. WITH COLOURED FRONTISPIECE. (AUTHOR'S COPYRIGHT EDITION). LONDON: SAMPSON LOW, MARSTON AND COMPANY LIMITED, (191–?). 200p.: col. front. Bound in blue cloth, with decorative cover and spine.
YSC 843.8 VER

1793 **VERNE, JULES.**
FLOATING ISLAND; OR, THE PEARL OF THE PACIFIC. BY JULES VERNE. NEW AND CHEAPER EDITION. LONDON: SAMPSON LOW, MARSTON AND COMPANY, LIMITED, (1896). VII, 382p.: front., vignette title page, 78 plates. Bound in green cloth, with coloured pictorial cover and spine.
YSC 843.8 VER

1794 **VERNE, JULES.**
FROM THE EARTH TO THE MOON DIRECT IN 97 HOURS 20 MINUTES. BY JULES VERNE. TRANSLATED FROM THE FRENCH BY LOUIS MERCIER, AND ELEANOR E. KING. AUTHOR'S ILLUSTRATED EDITION. LONDON: SAMPSON LOW, MARSTON AND COMPANY, LIMITED, 1892. 160p.: 7 plates. Bound in red cloth with pictorial cover. Originally published 1865.
C 843.8 VER

1795 **VERNE, JULES.**
A JOURNEY INTO THE INTERIOR OF THE EARTH. BY JULES VERNE. LONDON: WARD LOCK AND CO., (187–?). IV. 267p. + 14p. pub. cat. Bound in red cloth with embossed decorative cover and spine. Originally published in French 1864.
C 843.8 VER

1796 **VERNE, JULES.**
MARTIN PAZ. TRANSLATED FROM THE FRENCH OF JULES VERNE BY ELLEN E. FREWER. AUTHOR'S ILLUSTRATED EDITION. LONDON: SAMPSON LOW, MARSTON, SEARLE, AND RIVINGTON, 1876. 126p. + 16p. pub. cat.: front., 12 plates. Bound in red cloth, with embossed pictorial/decorative cover and spine, and gilt edges.
YSC 843.8 VER

1797 **VERNE, JULES.**
MICHAEL STROGOFF, THE COURIER OF THE CZAR. By JULES VERNE . . . TRANSLATED BY W.H.G. KINGSTON, WITH NUMEROUS ILLUSTRATIONS. IN TWO PARTS. NEW EDITION (1890). LONDON: SAMPSON LOW, MARSTON AND COMPANY. 341p.: 7 plates, by P. Ferat engraved by C.H. Barbant. 2 parts bound together in green cloth with pictorial cover, with gilt edges. Originally published 1876.
C 843.8 VER

1798 **VERNE, JULES.**
THE MYSTERIOUS ISLAND (PART II). ABANDONED. BY JULES VERNE. TRANSLATED FROM THE FRENCH BY W.H.G. KINGSTON. THIRD EDITION. LONDON: SAMPSON LOW, MARSTON, SEARLE AND RIVINGTON, 1879. VIII, 304p.: front., 50 plates by P. Ferat, engraved by Barbant. Bound in green cloth with pictorial/decorative cover and spine. Originally published 1875.
C 843.8 VER

1799 **VERNE, JULES.**
THE MYSTERIOUS ISLAND (PART III). THE SECRET OF THE ISLAND. BY JULES VERNE. TRANSLATED FROM THE FRENCH BY W.H.G. KINGSTON. THIRD EDITION. LONDON: SAMPSON LOW, MARSTON, SEARLE AND RIVINGTON, 1879. VIII, 299p. + 3p. pub. cat.: front., 51 plates by P. Ferat, engraved by C.H. Barbant. Bound in green cloth with embossed pictorial/decorative cover and spine. Originally published 1875.
C 843.8 VER

1800 **VERNE, JULES.**
ON THE TRACK. BY JULES VERNE. LONDON: WARD, LOCK, AND TYLER, (187–?). 179p. + 12p. pub. cat.: col. front., 2 col. plates. Bound in green cloth, with pictorial/decorative cover and spine. THE YOUTH'S LIBRARY OF WONDER AND ADVENTURE. Originally published 1868.
YSC 843.8 VER

1801 **VERNE, JULES.**
THE SECRET of the ISLAND. BY JULES VERNE. Translated from the French By W.H.G. KINGSTON. LONDON: J.M. DENT AND SONS LTD., 1909. XIV, 230p.: decorative front. and title page, 49 plates by P. Ferat, engraved by C.H. Barbant, decorative endpapers. Bound in blue cloth, with decorative spine. EVERYMAN'S LIBRARY FOR YOUNG PEOPLE, NO. 369. Originally published 1875.
YSC 843.8 VER

1802 **VERNE, JULES.**
TWENTY THOUSAND LEAGUES UNDER THE SEA. BY JULES VERNE. ILLUSTRATED BY HENRY AUSTIN. LONDON: WARD, LOCK AND CO. (189–?). 185p. + 6p. pub. cat.: front., 1 plate. Bound in green cloth with coloured pictorial cover and spine. Originally published 1870.
C 843.8 VER

1803 **VERNE, JULES.**
VOYAGES AND ADVENTURES OF CAPTAIN HATTERAS. THE ENGLISH AT THE NORTH POLE. TRANSLATED FROM THE FRENCH OF "JULES VERNE". LONDON: WARD, LOCK AND TYLER, (188–?). 248p. + 8p. pub. cat. Bound in green cloth with decorative cover and spine. Originally published 1866.
C 843.8 VER

1804 **Another copy.**
LONDON: CROOME AND CO., (188–?). 248p. Bound in blue cloth with decorative cover and spine.

1805 **VERNE, JULES.**
VOYAGES AND ADVENTURES OF CAPTAIN HATTERAS. THE ICE DESERT. TRANSLATED FROM THE FRENCH OF "JULES VERNE". LONDON: WARD, LOCK, AND TYLER, (188–?). 223p. + 16p. pub. cat. Bound in green cloth with embossed decorative cover and spine. Originally published 1866.
C 843.8 VER

1806 **VERNE, JULES.**
THE WONDERFUL TRAVELLERS. BY JULES VERNE. CONTAINING "A Journey to the Interior of the Earth", AND "Five Weeks in a Balloon". LONDON: WARD, LOCK, AND TYLER, (187–?). IV, 267p., 268p. + 26p. pub. cat.: col. front., 3 col. plates. Rebound including original pictorial paper cover and spine.
YSC 843.8 VER

1807 **VIDAL, MRS.**
RACHEL CHARLECOTE: A VILLAGE STORY. BY MRS. VIDAL. LONDON: WELLS GARDNER, DARTON AND CO., 1893. 109p. + 12p. pub. cat.: front., 2 plates. Bound in blue cloth with coloured pictorial/decorative cover and spine.
C 823.8 VID

1808 **(VILES, E.).**
BLACK BESS OR, THE KNIGHT OF THE ROAD, A ROMANCE. Originally published in weekly parts. 2 vols. LONDON: E. HARRISON, (1868). 2028p.: ill. Rebound in black cloth. Describes the adventures of Dick Turpin.
C 823.8 VIL

1809 **WALFORD, L.B.**
THE FIRST CRUISE OF THE GOOD SHIP "BETHLEHEM"; AND A WOODLAND CHOIR. BY L.B. WALFORD. LONDON: SOCIETY FOR PROMOTING CHRISTIAN KNOWLEDGE, (189–?). 107p.: front. Bound in red cloth with pictorial cover.
C 823.8 WAL

1809A **WALKER, MRS E.A.**
(ETHEL LINTON.) (By E.A.W.) (LONDON: WALTER SCOTT, (189–?)). Title page missing. VII, 248p.: front., engraved by Williamson. Bound in red cloth, with coloured decorative cover and spine.
YSC 823.8 ETH

1810 **WALLACE, LEW.**
BEN-HUR. A TALE OF THE CHRIST. BY LEW WALLACE. WITH ILLUSTRATIONS. LONDON: FREDERICK WARNE AND CO., (189–?). XI, 447p. + 4p. pub. cat.: front., 6 plates, some by W.S. Stacey. Bound in green cloth with coloured pictorial/decorative cover and spine, with gilt edges. Originally published 1880.
C 823.8 WAL

1812 **WALTON, AMY CATHERINE.**
AUDREY, OR CHILDREN OF LIGHT. BY MRS. O.F. WALTON. LONDON: THE RELIGIOUS TRACT SOCIETY, (188–?). 127p.: front., 5 plates. Bound in green cloth with pictorial/decorative cover and decorative spine.
C 823.8 WAL

1813 **WALTON, AMY CATHERINE.**
CHRISTIE, THE KING'S SERVANT. A Sequel to "Christies' Old Organ" by MRS O.F. WALTON. LONDON: THE RELIGIOUS TRACT SOCIETY, (1898). 162p.: col. front. ill. Bound in green cloth with coloured pictorial cover and spine, and coloured pictorial paper dust jacket.
C 823.8 WAL

1814 **WALTON, AMY CATHERINE.**
CHRISTIE'S OLD ORGAN OR "HOME SWEET HOME". BY MRS. O.F. WALTON. LONDON: THE RELIGIOUS TRACT SOCIETY, (188–?). 127p.: front., 2 plates, headpieces and tailpieces. Bound in blue cloth with coloured pictorial cover and decorative spine.
C 823.8 WAL

1815 **WALTON, AMY CATHERINE.**
LITTLE DOT. THE RELIGIOUS TRACT SOCIETY, (187–?). 64p.: col. front. Bound in blue cloth with embossed decorative cover, with inserted coloured paper vignette.
C 823.8 WAL

1815A **WALTON, AMY CATHERINE.**
MRS. CHRISTIE'S NEXT THINGS. BY THE AUTHOR OF "MRS. MORSE'S GIRLS". LONDON: THE RELIGIOUS TRACT SOCIETY, (189–?). 192p.: front., 2 plates. Bound in blue cloth with coloured pictorial cover and spine.
C 823.8 WAL

1816 **WALTON, AMY CATHERINE.**
MY LITTLE CORNER. A Book for Cottage Homes. BY MRS. O.F. WALTON. LONDON: THE RELIGIOUS TRACT SOCIETY, (188–?). 160p.: front., 3 plates, headpieces and tailpieces.
C 823.8 WAL

1817 **WALTON, AMY CATHERINE.**
MY MATES AND I. BY MRS. O.F. WALTON. LONDON: THE RELIGIOUS TRACT SOCIETY, (187–?). 160p.: front., 2 plates by Whymper. Bound in brown cloth with pictorial/decorative cover and decorative spine.
C 823.8 WAL

1817A **WALTON, AMY (CATHERINE).**
"A PAIR OF CLOGS": AND OTHER STORIES FOR CHILDREN. BY AMY WALTON. ILLUSTRATED. LONDON: BLACKIE AND SON, LIMITED, 192p. + 32p. ill. pub. cat.: front., 2 plates. Bound in red cloth with pictorial/decorative cover and decorative spine.
C 823.8 WAL

1818 **WARNER, ANNE (BARTLETT).**
STORIES OF VINEGAR HILL. BY THE AUTHOR OF "SUNDAY ALL THE WEEK", "LITTLE JACK'S FOUR LESSONS", "ELLEN MONTGOMERY'S BOOKSHELF", ETC. LONDON: THE LI-QUOR TEA COMPANY, 1879. 361p. + 12p. pub. cat.: col. front., 1 col. plate. Bound in brown cloth with decorative cover and spine. Originally published 1872.
C 813.4 WAR

1819 **(WARNER, SUSAN BOGERT).**
CARL KRINKEN; OR, THE CHRISTMAS STOCKING. LONDON: FREDERICK WARNE AND CO., (187–?). 153p. + 6p. col. front. Bound in blue cloth with embossed decorative cover and spine. ROUND THE GLOBE LIBRARY. Short stories, originally published 1854.
C 813.4 WAR

1820 **(WARNER, SUSAN BOGERT).**
DAISY IN THE FIELD, CONTINUED FROM "DAISY" AND "MELBOURNE HOUSE". BY THE AUTHOR OF "WIDE, WIDE WORLD", "QUEECHY", ETC. LONDON: WARD, LOCK AND CO. LIMITED, (189–?). 352p.: front. Bound in green cloth, with coloured pictorial/decorative cover and spine. Cover author: E. WETHERELL (Elizabeth Wetherell, pseud.). Originally published 1868.
C 813.4 WAR

1821 **Another copy.**
LONDON: RICHARD EDWARD KING, (191–?). 332p.: front. Bound in green cloth. Cover author: WETHERELL (Elizabeth Wetherell, pseud.).
YSC 813.4 WET

1822 **WARNER, SUSAN BOGERT.**
THE GOLDEN LADDER. STORIES ILLUSTRATIVE OF THE EIGHT BEATITUDES. BY SUSAN AND ANNA WARNER. LONDON: FREDERICK WARNE AND CO., (189–?). IX, 479p. + 8p. pub. cat.: Bound in green cloth with embossed decorative covers and spine.
C 823.8 WAR

1823 **(WARNER, SUSAN BOGERT).**
THE OLD HELMET. BY THE AUTHOR OF "THE WIDE, WIDE WORLD" WITH COLOURED ILLUSTRATIONS. LONDON: JAMES NISBET AND CO., 1867. 608p. + 16p. pub. cat.: col. front., 5 col. plates, some by J.D.W. engraved by B.D. and E. Evans. Bound in green cloth with embossed decorative cover and spine. Originally published 1863.
CBD 813.4 OLD

1824 **Another copy.**
MANCHESTER: John Heywood, (189–?). 437p.: Bound in buff cloth with decorative cover and spine.
C 813.4 WAR

1825 **(WARNER, SUSAN BOGERT).**
QUEECHY, BY ELIZABETH WETHERELL (pseud.). COMPLETE AND UNABRIDGED EDITION. LONDON: WARD, LOCK AND CO., (187–?). 448p. + 16p. pub. cat.: col. front. Bound in brown cloth with embossed decorative cover and spine. THE GOOD TONE LIBRARY. Originally published 1853.
C 813.4 WAR

1826 **Another copy.**
LONDON: HUMPHREY MILFORD, OXFORD UNIVERSITY PRESS, (1919). IV, 250p.: col. front., decorative title page, pictorial endpapers. Bound in cream cloth, with coloured pictorial paper label on cover. Herbert Strang's Library. Abridged version.
YSC 813.4 WAR

1827 **(WARNER, SUSAN BOGERT).**
THE WIDOW AND HER DAUGHTER. BY THE AUTHOR OF "THE WIDE, WIDE WORLD" ETC. ETC. WITH COLOURED FRONTISPIECE. LONDON: GEORGE ROUTLEDGE AND SONS, (188–?). 147p. + 8p. pub. cat.: col. front. Bound in blue cloth with embossed decorative cover with coloured paper vignette inserted, and spine.
C 813.4 WAR

1828 **WATERWORTH, E.M.**
HARRY'S HOLIDAYS. BY E.M. WATERWORTH. LONDON: THE RELIGIOUS TRACT SOCIETY, (188–?). 64p.: col. front., vignette on title page, headpieces and tailpieces. Bound in red cloth with decorative cover and inserted coloured paper vignette. Little Dot Series.
C 823.8 WAT

1829 **THE WEAVER BOYS OF BRUGES.**
THE BRAVE BOY OF HAARLEM. LONDON: THE RELIGIOUS TRACT SOCIETY, (188–?). 64p.: col. front. Bound in purple paper with decorative cover.
C 823.8 WEA

1830 **WEBB, MRS.**
MY LIFE IN THE PRAIRIE. BY MRS. WEBB. ILLUSTRATED. LONDON: GROOMBRIDGE AND SON, (187–?). Unpaginated: front., 3 plates, ill. Bound in blue cloth with decorative cover and spine and inserted coloured paper vignette. Includes also The Little Trapper: a tale of the coal mine by W. Heard Hillyard.
C 823.8 WEB

1831 **WENTWORTH, WALTER.**
THE DRIFTING ISLAND OR The Slave-Hunters of the Congo. BY WALTER WENTWORTH. LONDON: THOMAS NELSON AND SONS, 1891. 331p. + 4p. pub. cat.: front., additional vignette title page. Bound in blue cloth with coloured pictorial cover and spine.
C 823.8 WEN

1832 **WEST, THERESA CORNWALLIS J.**
FRYING PAN ALLEY. BY MRS. F. WEST. LONDON: S.W. PARTRIDGE AND CO., (1880). 77p. + 16p. pub. cat.: front., 5 plates, headpieces and tailpieces. Bound in brown cloth with embossed decorative cover.
C 823.8 WES

1833 **WEST, THERESA CORNWALLIS J.**
STELLA'S NOSEGAY AND OTHER TALES. BY MRS. F. WEST. LONDON: S.W. PARTRIDGE AND CO., (1884). 64p. + 8p. pub. cat.: front., 3 plates. Bound in brown cloth, with coloured decorative cover.
YSC 823.8 WES

1834 **WESTON, JAMES.**
A NIGHT IN THE WOODS AND OTHER Tales and Sketches. BY JAMES WESTON WITH FIFTY ILLUSTRATIONS . . . LONDON: SAMPSON LOW, MARSTON AND COMPANY LIMITED. (189–?). 96p.: col. front., 7 col. plates, 2 plates, ill. Bound in brown cloth with coloured pictorial cover.
CBD 823.912 WES

1835 **WEYMAN, STANLEY JOHN.**
UNDER THE RED ROBE. BY STANLEY J. WEYMAN. WITH TWELVE ILLUSTRATIONS BY R. CATON WOODVILLE. THIRTEENTH EDITION. LONDON: METHUEN AND CO., 1898. VI, 357p. +40p. pub. cat.: front., 11 plates. Bound in red cloth. Originally published 1894.
YSC 823.8 WEY

1836 **WHISHAW, FRED.**
BORIS THE BEAR-HUNTER. A Tale of Peter the Great and His Times. LONDON: T. NELSON AND SONS, 1895. 376p. + 8p. pub. cat.: front., additional vignette title page, 4 plates by Walter S. Stacey. Bound in brown cloth with embossed decorative/pictorial cover and spine.
C 823.8 WHI

1837 **WISHAW, FRED.**
HAROLD THE NORSEMAN, A Tale of Harold Haardraada, King of Norway. BY FRED WHISHAW. WITH SIX ILLUSTRATIONS BY W.H.M. LONDON: T. NELSON AND SONS, 1897. 396p., 4p. front., 5 plates. Bound in blue cloth with coloured pictorial/decorative cover and spine.
C 823.8 WHI

1837A **(WHITAKER, EVELYN).**
TIP CAT. BY THE AUTHOR OF "MISS TOOSEY'S MISSION", "LADDIE", AND "LITTLE ANN" WITH TWO ILLUSTRATIONS BY RANDOLPH CALDECOTT. ENGRAVED BY J.D. COOPER. LONDON: WALTER SMITH, 1886. VIII, 336p.: front. vignette title page. Bound in blue cloth with coloured pictorial cover and decorative end papers.
C 823.8 WHI

1838 **WHITNEY, ADELINE DUTTON.**
THE GAYWORTHYS, A Story of Threads and Thrums. BY THE AUTHOR OF "A SUMMER IN LESLIE GOLDTHWAITE'S LIFE", ETC., ETC. LONDON: WARD, LOCK, AND CO., (189–?). 358p. + 20p. pub. cat. Bound in coloured decorative paper covers.
YSC 813.4 WHI

1839 **WHITNEY, ADELINE DUTTON.**
WE GIRLS: A Home Story. BY ADELINE D.T. WHITNEY. New Edition. LONDON: SAMPSON LOW, MARSTON, SEARLE, AND RIVINGTON, LIMITED, 1888. 271p. Bound in red cloth, with coloured decorative cover and spine.
YSC 813.4 WHI

1840 **WHO ARE THE HAPPY ONES?**
OR HOME SKETCHES. BY THE AUTHOR OF "QUIET THOUGHTS FOR QUIET HOURS", AND "THE PEARL FISHER'S BASKET". With Illustrations by John Absolon. LONDON: WARD, LOCK, AND TYLER, (187–?). 247p. + 8p. pub. cat.: front., 4 plates, engraved by E. Evans. Bound in red cloth with embossed decorative cover and spine.
C 823.8 WHO

1841 **WHYMPER, ALFRED.**
TAKEN UP. A Tale FOR BOYS AND GIRLS. BY ALFRED WHYMPER. With Illustrations. LONDON: WILLIAM P. NIMMO, 1878. 200p.: front., 3 plates. Bound in blue cloth with embossed decorative cover and spine, with gilt edges.
C 823.8 WHY

1842 **WIDOW TANNER'S CACTUS.**
BY THE AUTHOR OF "MARY CLOUDSDALE". LONDON: SOCIETY FOR PROMOTING CHRISTIAN KNOWLEDGE, (188–?). 124p. + 4p. pub. cat.: front. Bound in green cloth, with coloured decorative covers and spine.
YSC 823.8 WID

1843 **WILBERFORCE, SAMUEL.**
AGATHOS AND OTHER SUNDAY STORIES. BY SAMUEL WILBERFORCE M.A. FIFTH EDITION. LONDON: R.B. SEELEY AND W. BURNSIDE, 1841. X, 166p. + 1p. pub. cat.: front., 3 plates. Bound in brown cloth with embossed decorative cover, spine repaired.
C 823.8 WIL

1844 **(WILCOX, E.G.).**
(EVIE) (BY E.G. WILCOX). Title page missing. LONDON: GARDNER, DARTON AND CO., (188–?). 124p. Bound in pink cloth, with coloured pictorial cover and spine.
YSC 823.8 WIL

1845 **WILFORD, FLORENCE.**
TRIED AND TRUE. BY FLORENCE WILFORD. LONDON: SOCIETY FOR PROMOTING CHRISTIAN KNOWLEDGE, (189–?). 222p. + 2p. pub. cat.: front., 2 plates. Bound in blue cloth with coloured pictorial cover.
C 823.8 WIL

1846 **WILLIE'S LESSON; AND OTHER TALES.**
LONDON: JAMES BLACKWOOD AND CO., (188–?). 94p.: front., vignette on title page, 3 plates, ill. Bound in brown cloth with embossed decorative cover and spine.
C 823.8 WIL

1847 **WOOD, FRANCES HARRIETT.**
TEN-MINUTES TALES FOR EVERY SUNDAY. BY FRANCES HARRIETT WOOD. Illustrated by I. Nash. LONDON: SOCIETY FOR PROMOTING CHRISTIAN KNOWLEDGE, 1891. IV, 210p. + 6p. pub. cat. Bound in green cloth with pictorial/decorative cover and spine.
C 823.912 WOO

1848 **WOOD, MRS. HENRY.**
ROLANDE YORKE. A Sequel to "THE CHANNINGS". BY MRS. HENRY WOOD. LONDON: RICHARD BENTLEY AND SON., 1886. IV, 467p.: front. Bound in blue cloth with embossed decorative cover and spine.
C 823.8 WOO

1849 **WOOD, KATE.**
A WAIF OF THE SEA. BY KATE WOOD. ILLUSTRATED. LONDON: BLACKIE AND SON., (189–?). 224p. + 32p. pub. cat.: front., 3 plates. Bound in green cloth with coloured/pictorial decorative cover and spine.
C 823.8 WOO

1850 **WORBOISE, EMMA JANE.**
EVELYN'S STORY; Or, Labour and Wait. BY EMMA JANE WORBOISE. ELEVENTH EDITION. LONDON: WM. ISBISTER LIMITED, 1885. VIII, 490p.: front. Bound in green cloth, with embossed decorative cover and spine, and gilt edges. Originally published in 1864 as Labour and wait, or Evelyn's story.
YSC 823.8 WOR

1851 **WRIGHT, MARIA.**
THE HAPPY VILLAGE, AND HOW IT BECAME SO. BY MARIA WRIGHT. NEW EDITION. LONDON: JARROLD AND SONS, (187–?). 214p. + 2p. pub. cat.: front., 3 plates, engraved by W. Cheshire. Bound in blue cloth, with embossed decorative covers and spine. Originally published 1873.
YSC 823.8 WRI

1852 **(WYSS, JOHANN DAVID).**
THE SWISS FAMILY ROBINSON. A TRANSLATION FROM THE ORIGINAL GERMAN. EDITED BY W.H.G. KINGSTON. WITH SIX COLOURED AND SEVENTY-FOUR OTHER ILLUSTRATIONS BY H. KLEY. LONDON: ERNEST NISTER, (189–?). 291p.: col. front., 5 col. plates, ill. Bound in brown cloth, with coloured pictorial cover and spine. Originally published 1813.
C 833.6 WYS

1853 **Another copy.**
WITH ILLUSTRATIONS IN COLOUR AND IN BLACK AND WHITE BY CHARLES FOLKARD. LONDON: J.M. DENT AND SONS LTD., 1910. VIII, 454p.: col. front., 11 col. plates, ill., pictorial endpapers. Bound in beige cloth, with coloured pictorial cover and spine.
C 833.6 WYS

1853A **WYSS, JOHANN DAVID.**
THE SWISS FAMILY ROBINSON BY JOHANN DAVID WYSS. ILLUSTRATIONS BY T.H. ROBINSON. LONDON: HUMPHREY MILFORD, OXFORD UNIVERSITY PRESS, n.d. XII, 431p.: col. front., 19 col. plates with pictorial endpapers. Bound in red cloth with decorative pictorial cover and spine and gilt top.
C 833.6 WYS

1854 **(WYSS, JOHANN DAVID).**
THE SWISS FAMILY ROBINSON, OR ADVENTURES IN A DESERT ISLAND. LONDON: GEORGE ROUTLEDGE AND SONS, (187–?). 410p. + 28p. pub. cat.: 1 map. Bound in green cloth, with pictorial/decorative cover and spine.
YSC 833.6 WYS

1855 **(WYSS, JOHANN DAVID).**
THE SWISS FAMILY ROBINSON; OR, THE ADVENTURES OF A SHIPWRECKED FAMILY ON AN UNINHABITED ISLAND NEAR NEW GUINEA. NEW AND UNABRIDGED TRANSLATION FROM THE ORIGINAL BY MRS. H.B. PAULL. WITH ORIGINAL ILLUSTRATIONS. LONDON: FREDERICK WARNE AND CO., (189–?). XVI, 562p. + 6p.: col. front., 4 col. plates, 17 plates, ill. Bound in olive cloth with coloured pictorial cover and spine and gilt edges.
C 833.6 WYS

1856 **(WYSS, JOHANN DAVID).**
THE SWISS FAMILY ROBINSON: OR, ADVENTURES OF A SHIPWRECKED FAMILY ON A DESOLATE ISLAND. LONDON: T. NELSON AND SONS, 1873. 337p. + 8p. pub. cat.: additional col. pictorial title page, 5 col. plates. Bound in brown cloth, with coloured pictorial paper label on cover, embossed decorative covers and spine, and gilt edges.
YSC 833.6 WYS.

1857 **Another copy.**
A New and Unabridged Translation. WITH AN INTRODUCTION FROM THE FRENCH OF CHARLES NODIER. LONDON: T. NELSON AND SONS, 1885. 690p. + 6p. pub. cat.: front., additional vignette title page, ill. Bound in blue cloth, with coloured pictorial cover and spine.

1857A **Y., R.A.**
THE STORY OF THE RED CROSS KNIGHT FROM SPENSER'S FAIRY QUEEN. BY R.A.Y. LONDON: T. NELSON AND SONS, 1887. 144p.: front., additional vignette title page, 9 plates. Bound in blue cloth with pictorial cover and spine.
C 823.8 STO

1858 **YONGE, CHARLOTTE MARY.**
THE CHAPLET OF PEARLS. BY CHARLOTTE M. YONGE. ILLUSTRATED BY W.J. HENNESSY. LONDON: MACMILLAN AND CO. LIMITED, 1889. XIV, 364p. + 8p. pub. cat.: front., vignette title page, 2 plates. Bound in blue cloth. Originally published 1868.
YSC 823.8 YON

1859 **YONGE, CHARLOTTE MARY.**
THE DOVE IN THE EAGLE'S NEST. BY CHARLOTTE M. YONGE. ILLUSTRATED BY W.J. HENNESSY. LONDON: MACMILLAN AND CO. LIMITED, 1890. XIII, 293p. + 6p. pub. cat.: front., vignette title page, 2 plates. Bound in blue cloth. Originally published 1866.
YSC 823.8 YON

1860 **YONGE, CHARLOTTE MARY.**
GRISLY GRISELL; OR, THE LAIDLY LADY OF WHITBURN, A TALE OF THE WARS OF THE ROSES. BY CHARLOTTE M. YONGE. LONDON: MACMILLAN AND CO., SECOND EDITION, 1894. VI, 300p. + 8p. ill. pub. cat. Bound in blue cloth. Originally published 1893.
YSC 823.8 YON

1861 **YONGE, CHARLOTTE MARY.**
THE LANCES OF LYNWOOD. BY THE AUTHOR OF "THE HEIR OF REDCLYFFE", ETC. WITH ILLUSTRATIONS BY J.B. LONDON: MACMILLAN AND CO. LIMITED, 1891. VI, 264p.: front., 7 plates, engraved by Dalziel Brothers. Bound in blue cloth. Originally published 1855.
YSC 823.8 YON

1862 **Another copy.**
LONDON: J.M. DENT AND SONS, 1911. XV, 314p. + 4p. about Everyman's Library: decorative front. and title page, 18 plates by Dora Curtis. Bound in brown quarter leather. EVERYMAN'S LIBRARY FOR YOUNG PEOPLE.
C 823.8 YON

1863 **(YONGE, CHARLOTTE MARY).**
THE LITTLE DUKE, RICHARD THE FEARLESS. BY THE AUTHOR OF "THE HEIR OF REDCLYFFE", ETC.

WITH ILLUSTRATIONS. LONDON: MACMILLAN AND CO. LIMITED, 1891. 223p.: front., 4 plates. Bound in red leather, with embossed decorative spine. Originally published 1854.
YSC 823.8 YON

1864 **Another copy.**
LONDON: G. BELL AND SONS LTD., 1930. VII, 166p. + 2p. pub. cat.: col. front., vignette title page, 7 col. plates, by H.R. Millar, pictorial endpapers. Bound in brown cloth, with pictorial/decorative cover and spine.
C 823.8 YON

1865 **YONGE, CHARLOTTE MARY.**
THE PILGRIMAGE OF THE BEN BERIAH. BY CHARLOTTE M. YONGE. LONDON: MACMILLAN AND CO. LIMITED, 1899. IX, 321p. + 6p. pub. cat.: 4 plates. Bound in blue cloth. Originally published 1897.
YSC 823.8 YON

1866 **YONGE, CHARLOTTE MARY.**
THE PRINCE AND THE PAGE, A STORY OF THE LAST CRUSADE. BY THE AUTHOR OF "THE HEIR OF REDCLYFFE", ETC. WITH A FRONTISPIECE BY ADRIAN STOKES. LONDON: MACMILLAN AND CO. LIMITED, 1891. VIII, 259p. + 8p. ill. pub. cat.: front. Bound in blue cloth. Originally published 1865.
YSC 823.8 YON

1867 **YONGE, CHARLOTTE MARY.**
P's and Q's; OR, THE QUESTION OF PUTTING UPON; AND Little Lucy's Wonderful Globe. BY CHARLOTTE M. YONGE. LONDON: MACMILLAN AND CO. LIMITED, 1891. XIII, 288p. + 2p. pub. cat.: front., vignette title page, 4 plates, by C.O. Murray, 23 plates by L. FR. Bound in blue cloth, with coloured decorative cover and spine, and gilt edges. Originally published 1872.
YSC 823.8 YON

1868 **(YONGE, CHARLOTTE MARY, EDITOR).**
SARAH WATKINS; OR, CRUMBS FOR THE BIRDS. EDITED BY THE AUTHOR OF "THE HEIR OF REDCLYFFE". WITH COLOURED FRONTISPIECE. LONDON: FREDERICK WARNE AND CO., (188–?). Unpaginated: col. front. Bound in beige cloth with coloured decorative cover.
C 823.8 YON

1869 **(YONGE, CHARLOTTE MARY).**
STRAY PEARLS; MEMOIRS OF MARGARET DE RIBAUMONT, VISOUNTESS OF BELLAISE. ILLUSTRATED BY W.J. HENNESSY. LONDON: MACMILLAN AND CO. LIMITED, 1889. XVI, 424p. + 8p. pub. cat.: front., vignette title page, 2 plates. Bound in blue cloth. Originally published 1872.
YSC 823.8 YON

1870 **(YONGE, CHARLOTTE MARY).**
UNKNOWN TO HISTORY, A STORY OF THE CAPTIVITY OF MARY OF SCOTLAND. ILLUSTRATED BY W. HENNESSY. LONDON: MACMILLAN AND CO. LIMITED, 1883. XIII, 589p. + 6p. pub. cat.: front., vignette title page, 2 plates. Bound in blue cloth. Originally published 1882.
YSC 823.8 YON

1871 **(THE YOUNG ARTIST).**
(LONDON: GROOMBRIDGE, n.d.). Title page missing. 46p.: 1 plate, ill., engraved by E. Whimper. Bound in blue cloth, with embossed decorative cover.
YSC 823.8 YOU

1871A **THE YOUNG OFFICER.**
AND OTHER Select Stories for the Young. With Illustrations. EDINBURGH: W.P. NIMMO, HAY AND MITCHELL, 1884. 120p.: col. front., 1 plate ill. Bound in red cloth with decorative cover and spine.
C 823.8 YOU

## 18 STORIES 1900–1939

1872 **ADAMS, ELLINOR DAVENPORT.**
May, Guy, and Jim, WITH OTHER STORIES FOR BOYS AND GIRLS BY ELLINOR DAVENPORT ADAMS. ILLUSTRATED BY JOHN H. BACON. NEW EDITION. LONDON: BLACKIE AND SON LIMITED, 1904. 192p. + 32p. ill. pub. cat.: front., 1 plate. Bound in green cloth, with decorative cover and spine.
C 823.912 ADA

1873 **ADVENTURES IN THE SOUTH PACIFIC.**
BY ONE WHO WAS BORN THERE. WITH COLOURED AND OTHER ILLUSTRATIONS BY LANCELOT SPEED. LONDON: THE RELIGIOUS TRACT SOCIETY, (190–?). 228p.: col. front., 5 plates. Bound in green cloth, with coloured pictorial cover and spine.
C 823.912 ADV

1874 **ALDEN, ISABELLA.**
CHRISTIE'S CHRISTMAS. BY PANSY. (Pseud. for Mrs Isabella Alden). LONDON: WARD, LOCK AND CO. LIMITED, (192–?). 256p.: Bound in brown cloth, with coloured pictorial paper label on cover.
YSC 813.4 PAN

1875 **A.L.O.E.** *(Pseud.).*
THE STORY OF A NEEDLE. BY A.L.O.E. (A LADY OF ENGLAND, pseudonym for Charlotte Maria Tucker). LONDON: THOMAS NELSON AND SONS. (191–?). 160p.: 3 col. plates by Rosa C. Petherick. Bound in brown cloth with decorative cover and spine.
C 823.8 ALO

1875A **A.L.O.E.** *(Pseud.).*
THE YOUNG PILGRIM. By A.L.O.E. LONDON: COLLINS' CLEAR-TYPE PRESS, (190–?). 190p.: front., 3 plates. Bound in red cloth, with coloured pictorial cover and spine.
C 823.012 ALO

1876 **ARMSTRONG, FRANCES.**
THE GENERAL AND HIS DAUGHTER, BY FRANCES ARMSTRONG, ILLUSTRATED BY HAROLD PIFFARD. LONDON: SOCIETY FOR PROMOTING CHRISTIAN KNOWLEDGE. (1907). 384p.: col. front., 3 col. plates: Bound in green cloth with pictorial cover and spine.
C 823.8 ARM

1877 **ARTHUR, FRANCES BROWNE** *(Pseud.).*
Mother Maud. BY MRS. ARTHUR. Illustrated by ROSA C. PETHERICK. LONDON: THOMAS NELSON AND SONS, (1904). 374p.: pub. cat.: front., additional ill. title page, ill. Bound in blue cloth, with coloured pictorial cover and spine.
C 823.912 ART

1878 **ASHFORD, DAISY.**
THE YOUNG VISITERS; OR, MR SALTEENA'S PLAN. BY DAISY ASHFORD. WITH A PREFACE BY J.M. BARRIE. LONDON: CHATTO AND WINDUS, 1919. 85p.: front. Bound in black cloth, with coloured decorative covers.
YSC 823.912 ASH

1879 **ATTERIDGE, HELEN.**
THE MYSTERY OF MASTER MAX AND The Shrimps of Shrimpton. BY H. ATTERIDGE. ILLUSTRATED. LONDON: CASSELL AND COMPANY LIMITED, 1900. 222p. + 2p. pub. cat.: front., 4 plates. Bound in beige cloth, with coloured pictorial cover and spine.
C 823.8 ATT

1880 **AUSTIN, CAROLINE.**
HUGH HERBERT'S INHERITANCE. BY CAROLINE AUSTIN. ILLUSTRATED BY C.T. GARLAND. LONDON: BLACKIE AND SON LIMITED, (190–?). 287p.: front., 3 plates. Bound in blue cloth with pictorial cover and spine.
YSC 823.8 AUS

1881 **AUSTIN, STELLA.**
RAGS AND TATTERS. A STORY FOR BOYS AND GIRLS. LONDON: WELLS GARDNER, DARTON AND CO., 11th EDITION, 1901. 192p. + 1p. pub. cat.: front., 2 plates by W.H.C. Groome. Bound in green cloth with coloured pictorial cover and spine.
YSC 823.912 AUS

1882 **AVERY, CHARLES HAROLD.**
THE CHARTERED COMPANY, A TALE OF CAILTHORPE COLLEGE. BY HAROLD AVERY. LONDON: THOMAS NELSON AND SONS, (1915). 334p.: col. front., 5 col. plates. Bound in green cloth, with coloured pictorial cover and spine.
C 823.8 AVE

1883 **AVERY, CHARLES HAROLD.**
In Days of Danger, A Tale of the Threatened French Invasion. By HAROLD AVERY. LONDON: THOMAS NELSON AND SONS, (1909). 396p. + 4p. pub. cat.: col. front., 3 col. plates. Bound in brown cloth, with coloured, pictorial cover and spine.
C 823.912 AVE

1884 **AVERY, CHARLES HAROLD.**
SALE'S SHARPSHOOTERS, The Historical Records of a very Irregular Corps. BY HAROLD AVERY. ILLUSTRATED BY ROSA C. PETHERICK. LONDON: THOMAS NELSON AND SONS, 1903. 316p. + 4p. pub. cat.: front., additional ill. title page, ill. Bound in red cloth, with coloured pictorial covers and spine.
C 823.8 AVE

1885 **BAGNOLD, ENID.**
ALICE AND THOMAS AND JANE. BY ENID BAGNOLD. ILLUSTRATED BY THE AUTHOR AND LAURIAN JONES. (LONDON: W. HEINEMANN, 1930). 172p.: front., ill. title page, 4 plates, ill. Bound in grey cloth with coloured pictorial and decorative cover and spine.
C 823.912 BAG

1886 **BAKER, MARGARET.**
A Matter of Time. By MARGARET BAKER. Pictures by MARY BAKER. OXFORD: BASIL BLACKWELL, (193–?). 32p.: 2 plates in silhouette, ill. Bound in black cloth, with pictorial paper label on cover.
YSC 823.912 BAK

1887 **BAKER, MARGARET.**
PATSY AND THE LEPRECHAUN. BY MARGARET BAKER. PICTURES BY MARY BAKER. ABRIDGED AND SIMPLIFIED. OXFORD: BASIL BLACKWELL, (1936). 47p.: pictorial title page, 6 plates in silhouette, ill. Bound in orange cloth, with pictorial cover.
YSC 823.912 BAK

1888 **BAKER, MARGARET.**
PEACOCK EGGS. BY MARGARET BAKER. PICTURES BY MARY BAKER. ABRIDGED AND SIMPLIFIED. OXFORD: BASIL BLACKWELL, (1936). 48p.: pictorial title page, 9 plates in silhouette, ill., Bound in blue cloth, with pictorial cover.
YSC 823.912 BAK

1889 **BAKER, MARGARET.**
TOMSON'S HALLOWE'EN. BY MARGARET BAKER. PICTURES BY MARY BAKER. ABRIDGED AND SIMPLIFIED. OXFORD: BASIL BLACKWELL, (1936). 46p.: vignette title page, 11 plates in silhouette, ill. Bound in green cloth, with pictorial cover.
YSC 823.912 BAK

1890 **BAKER, MARGARET.**
A wife for the Mayor of Buncastle. By MARGARET BAKER. Pictures by MARY BAKER. OXFORD: BASIL BLACKWELL, (193–?). 32p.: 4 plates in silhouette, ill. Bound in black cloth, with pictorial paper label on cover.
YSC 823.912 BAK

1891 **BALDWIN, MAY.**
THE FOLLIES OF FIFI. By MAY BALDWIN. WITH SIX ILLUSTRATIONS by A.S. Boyd. LONDON: W. AND R. CHAMBERS LIMITED, 1907. 352p.: front., 5 plates. Bound in mustard cloth, with coloured pictorial cover and spine.
C 823.912 BAL

1892 **BALDWIN, MAY.**
The Girls of St. Gabriel's or, Life at a French School. By MAY BALDWIN. WITH SIX ILLUSTRATIONS by Percy Tarrant. LONDON: W. AND R. CHAMBERS LIMITED, 1905. 296p. + 32p. ill. pub. cat.: front., 5 plates. Bound in blue cloth with coloured pictorial cover and spine.
C 823.912 BAL

1893 **BALDWIN, MAY.**
Holly House and Ridges Row, a Tale of London old and new. By May Baldwin. Illustrated by M.V. Wheelhouse. LONDON: W. AND R. CHAMBERS LTD., 1908. 339p.: col. front., pictorial title page, 11 col. plates, ill. Bound in red cloth, with coloured pictorial dust jacket.
YSC 823.912 BAL

1894 **BALDWIN, MAY.**
A Popular Girl, A TALE OF SCHOOL LIFE IN GERMANY. BY MAY BALDWIN. WITH SIX ILLUSTRATIONS BY JESSIE WILSON. LONDON, W. AND R. CHAMBERS LIMITED, (1901). 301p.: front., 5 plates. Bound in pink cloth, with coloured pictorial cover and decorative spine.
C 823.912 BAL

1895 **BALDWIN, MAY.**
SIBYL; or Old School Friends, A SEQUEL TO "A POPULAR GIRL". BY MAY BALDWIN. WITH SIX ILLUSTRATIONS BY W. RAINEY, R.I. LONDON: W. AND R. CHAMBERS, 1903. 310p. + 32p. ill. pub. cat.: front., 5 plates. Bound in blue cloth, with coloured pictorial cover and spine.
C 823.912 BAL

1896 **BALLANTYNE, ROBERT MICHAEL.**
THE CANNIBAL ISLANDS, CAPTAIN COOK'S ADVENTURES IN THE SOUTH SEAS. BY R.M. BALLANTYNE. LONDON: JAMES NISBET AND CO. LIMITED, (190–?). 116p. + 32p. pub. cat.: col. front. Bound in blue cloth, with coloured pictorial label and decorative spine.
C 823.8 BAL

1897 **BALLANTYNE, ROBERT MICHAEL.**
Erling the Bold, A Tale of the Norse Sea-Kings. BY R.M. BALLANTYNE. LONDON: BLACKIE AND SON LIMITED, (191–?). 270p.: col. front., 3 col. plates by T.H. Robinson. Bound in blue cloth, with decorative cover and spine.
C 823.8 BAL

1898 **BALLANTYNE, ROBERT MICHAEL.**
FREAKS ON THE FELLS AND, WHY I DID NOT BECOME A SAILOR. BY R.M. BALLANTYNE. LONDON: THOMAS NELSON AND SONS, (190–?). 364p. + 6p. pub. cat.: col. front., 3 col. plates by Arch. Webb. Bound in pink cloth, with coloured pictorial cover and spine. Originally published 1865.
C 823.8 BAL

1898A **BALLANTYNE, ROBERT MICHAEL.**
Gascoyne. The Sandal-wood Trader. By R.M. Ballantyne. LONDON: BLACKIE AND SON LIMITED, (190–?). 252p. + 4p. pub. cat.: col. front., 3 plates by Jas. F. Sloane. Bound in red cloth with embossed decorative cover and spine.
C 823.8 BAL

1899 **BALLANTYNE, ROBERT MICHAEL.**
THE GIANT OF THE NORTH OR POKINGS ROUND THE POLE. BY R.M. BALLANTYNE. With Illustrations. LONDON: JAMES NISBET AND CO. (190–?). VI, 432p. + 32p. pub. cat.: front., vignette title page, 4 plates, map. Bound in green cloth with coloured pictorial cover and spine. Originally published 1881.
823.8 BAL

1900 **BALLANTYNE, ROBERT MICHAEL.**
THE GORILLA HUNTERS, A Tale of the Wilds of Africa. By Robert Michael Ballantyne. NEW EDITION. LONDON: T. NELSON AND SONS, 1901. 328p. + 8p. pub. cat.: col. front., additional col. vignette title page. Bound in blue cloth, with pictorial/decorative cover and spine, and gilt edges.
C 823.8 BAL

1901 **Another copy.**
1904. vii, 328p. + 8p. pub. cat.: col. front., 7 col. plates by W.H.C. Groome. Bound in blue cloth, with pictorial cover and spine.

1902 **BALLANTYNE, ROBERT MICHAEL.**
HUDSON BAY. BY R.M. BALLANTYNE. LONDON: THOMAS NELSON AND SONS LTD., (1904?). XV, 202p. + 6p. pub. cat.: col. front., 3 col. plates by W.H.C. Groome. Bound in blue cloth, with decorative cover and spine. Originally published 1850.
C 823.8 BAL

1903 **BALLANTYNE, ROBERT MICHAEL.**
HUNTED AND HARRIED, A TALE OF THE SCOTTISH COVENANTERS. BY R.M. BALLANTYNE. With Illustrations. LONDON: JAMES NISBET AND CO. LIMITED, (190–?). 195p. + 32p. pub. cat.: front., 3 plates, 2 by Arthur W. Burton. Bound in grey cloth, with coloured pictorial cover and spine.
C 823.8 BAL

1904 **BALLANTYNE, ROBERT MICHAEL.**
HUNTING THE LIONS, THE LAND OF THE NEGRO + THE PIONEERS, A TALE OF THE WESTERN WILDERNESS. BY R.M. BALLANTYNE. LONDON: JAMES NISBET AND CO. LIMITED, (191–?). 116p. + 122p. + 8p. pub. cat.: col. fronts. by Arthur Twidle and Henry Austin. Bound in green cloth, with coloured pictorial/decorative cover and spine. THE PIONEER LIBRARY.
C 823.8 BAL

1905 **BALLANTYNE, ROBERT MICHAEL.**
The Lighthouse. BY R.M. BALLANTYNE. Illustrated by E.S. Hodgson. LONDON: BLACKIE AND SON LIMITED, (191–?). 248p.: col. front., 3 col. plates. Bound in red cloth, with decorative cover and spine.
C 823.8 BAL

1906 **BALLANTYNE, ROBERT MICHAEL.**
MARTIN RATTLER. BY R.M. BALLANTYNE. LONDON: J.M. DENT AND SONS LTD., 1907. ix, 266p. Rebound in brown leather and brown cloth (quarter leather). EVERYMAN'S LIBRARY FOR YOUNG PEOPLE, No. 246. Originally published 1858.
C 823.8 BAL

1907 **BALLANTYNE, ROBERT MICHAEL.**
TALES OF ADVENTURE IN FOREST AND FLOOD. Includes THE CANNIBAL ISLANDS. CAPTAIN COOK'S ADVENTURES IN THE SOUTH SEAS. CHASING THE SUN OR RAMBLES IN NORWAY. LOST IN THE FOREST OR WANDERING WILL'S ADVENTURES IN SOUTH AMERICA. BY R.M. BALLANTYNE. LONDON: JAMES NISBET AND CO. (191–?). 116p., 120p., 120p., + 8p. pub. cat.: 2 fronts., by Matt B. Hewerdine. Bound in blue cloth with coloured pictorial labels on cover and spine.
C 823.8 BAL

1907A **BALLANTYNE, ROBERT MICHAEL.**
UNDER THE WAVES, DIVING IN DEEP WATERS. BY R.M. BALLANTYNE. With Illustrations. LONDON: JAMES NISBET AND CO. LIMITED (190–?). 414p. + 32p. pub. cat.: front., 3 plates engraved by Pearson. Bound in red cloth with coloured pictorial cover and spine. Originally published 1876.
C 823.8 BAL

1908 **BALLANTYNE, ROBERT MICHAEL.**
THE WILD MAN OF THE WEST, A TALE OF THE ROCKY MOUNTAINS. BY R.M. BALLANTYNE. LONDON: THOMAS NELSON AND SONS (190–?). 395p. + 4p. pub. cat.: col. front., 3 col. plates by Arch. Webb. Bound in red cloth with pictorial cover and spine. First published 1863.
C 823.8 BAL

1909 **BARING, MAURICE.**
THE STORY OF FORGET-ME-NOT AND LILY OF THE VALLEY. BY MAURICE BARING. ILLUSTRATED BY S.B. LONDON: JAMES NISBET AND CO. LIMITED, (1909). 120p.: col. front., col. vignette on title page, col. ill. Bound in green cloth, with coloured pictorial label on cover.
C 823.912 BAR

1910 **BARING-GOULD, SABINE.**
THROUGH ALL THE CHANGING SCENES OF LIFE. BY S. BARING-GOULD. LONDON: SOCIETY FOR PROMOTING CHRISTIAN KNOWLEDGE, (190–?). 159p. + 8p. pub. cat.: front., 10 plates, ill. Bound in blue cloth with coloured pictorial cover and decorative spine.
C 823.8 BAR

1911 **BARNE, KITTY.**
SHE SHALL HAVE MUSIC. (BY) KITTY BARNE. ILLUSTRATED BY RUTH GERVIS. LONDON: J.M. DENT AND SONS LTD., 1938. X, 261p.: front., ill. Bound in blue cloth, with coloured pictorial dust jacket.
YSC 823.912 BAR

1914 **BARRIE, JAMES MATTHEW.**
J.M. BARRIE'S PETER PAN AND WENDY. DECORATED BY GWYNNEDD M. HUDSON. LONDON: HODDER AND STOUGHTON, LIMITED, (193–?). 272p.: col. ill. Bound in blue cloth with coloured pictorial cover.
CBD 823.912 BAR and C 823.912 BAR

1915 **BARRIE, JAMES MATTHEW.**
J.M. BARRIE'S PETER PAN AND WENDY. RETOLD BY MAY BYRON FOR BOYS AND GIRLS, WITH THE APPROVAL OF THE AUTHOR. Pictures by MABEL LUCIE ATTWELL. LONDON: HODDER AND STOUGHTON LTD., (1925). IX, 144p.: col. front., vignette title page, 6 col. plates, ill. Bound in green cloth, with green pictorial paper jacket.
823.912 BAR

1916 **Another copy.**
1938. 188p.: col. front., ill. title page, 11 col. plates, ill. Pictorial endpapers. Bound in blue cloth, with pictorial cover and spine, and with pictorial green paper jacket.

1919 **BARRIE, JAMES MATTHEW.**
PETER AND WENDY. BY J.M. BARRIE. ILLUSTRATED BY F.D. BEDFORD. LONDON: HODDER AND STOUGHTON, (1911). VII, 267p.: front., pictorial title page, 11 plates. Bound in green cloth with decorative cover and spine.
CBD 823.912 BAR

1920 **BARRIE, JAMES MATTHEW.**
PETER PAN AND WENDY. BY J.M. BARRIE. WITH THE ORIGINAL ILLUSTRATIONS BY F.D. BEDFORD. AUTHORIZED SCHOOL EDITION. LONDON: HUMPHREY MILFORD, OXFORD UNIVERSITY PRESS, 1934. 127p.: front., 6 plates (1 missing). Bound in green cloth, with pictorial cover.
YSC 823.912 BAR

1921 **BARRIE, JAMES MATTHEW.**
PETER PAN IN KENSINGTON GARDENS. BY J.M. BARRIE WITH DRAWINGS BY ARTHUR RACKHAM. LONDON: HODDER AND STOUGHTON, (1906). VII, 126p.: col. front., vignette on title page, 15 col. plates. Bound in red cloth with embossed decorative/pictorial cover.
CBD 823.912 BAR

1921A **BARRIE, JAMES MATTHEW.**
The Peter Pan Picture Book. By ALICE B. WOODWARD AND DANIEL O'CONNOR. LONDON: G. BELL AND SONS, LTD., 1911. X, 64p.: col. front., 27 col. plates by Alice B. Woodward. Musical score. Bound in brown paper, with coloured pictorial paper label on cover. Barrie's stories retold by Daniel O'Connor.
C 823.912 WOO

1922 **BARTER-SNOW, LAURA A.**
AGNES DEWSBURY, Or "He Led Them on Safely". By LAURA A. BARTER-SNOW. WITH SIX ILLUSTRATIONS. LONDON: S.W. PARTRIDGE AND CO. LTD., (190–?). 332p. + 32p. pub. cat.: front., 5 plates by Adolf Thiede. Bound in red cloth, with coloured pictorial cover and decorative spine.
C 823.912 BAR

1923 **BAYLY, ELISABETH BOYD.**
UNDER THE SHE-OAKS. By ELISABETH BOYD BAYLY. SECOND EDITION. LONDON: THE RELIGIOUS TRACT SOCIETY, (190–?). 383p. + 16p. pub. cat.: front., 6 plates by J. Macfarlane. Bound in blue cloth with pictorial and decorative cover and spine.
C 823.8 BAY

1924 **BEALE, ANNE.**
BELLE AND DOLLY. By ANNE BEALE. WITH COLOURED ILLUSTRATIONS BY ARTHUR TWIDLE. LONDON: THE RELIGIOUS TRACT SOCIETY, (191–?). 317p. + 2p. pub. cat.: col. front., 2 col. plates. Bound in green cloth, with coloured pictorial cover and spine.
C 823.912 BEA

1924A **BECKE, GEORGE LOUIS.**
The Settlers of Karossa Creek AND OTHER STORIES OF AUSTRALIAN BUSH LIFE: BY LOUIS BECKE. WITH THREE ILLUSTRATIONS BY J. FINNEMORE. LONDON: THE RELIGIOUS TRACT SOCIETY, (1907). 204p. + 16p. pub. cat.: front., 1 plate. Bound in blue cloth, with coloured pictorial cover and spine. Includes BELLA OF BARINA and 'SONNY'.
C 823.8 BEC

1925 **BECKE, GEORGE LOUIS.**
TOM WALLIS, A TALE OF THE SOUTH SEAS. BY LOUIS BECKE. WITH ELEVEN ILLUSTRATIONS BY LANCELOT SPEED. LONDON: THE RELIGIOUS TRACT SOCIETY, (190–?). 320p.: front., 10 plates. Bound in blue cloth, with coloured pictorial cover and spine.
C 823.8 BEC

1925A **BEDFORD, FRANCIS DONKIN.**
A NIGHT OF WONDERS BY FRANCIS D. BEDFORD. (LONDON): E. GRANT RICHARDS, (1906). 124p.: col. front., col. pictorial title page, 23 col. plates, ill. Bound in buff cloth with coloured pictorial cover with pictorial endpapers.
M 823 BED CHILDREN'S COLLECTION

1926 **BEVAN, TOM.**
THE BAYMOUTH SCOUTS, A Story of the Napoleon Scare. By TOM BEVAN. WITH COLOURED ILLUSTRATIONS BY GORDON BROWNE, R.I., R.B.A. LONDON: THE RELIGIOUS TRACT SOCIETY, (191–?). 281p. + 6p. pub. cat.: col. front., 2 col. plates. Bound in red cloth, with coloured pictorial cover and spine.
C 823.912 BEV

1927 **BEVAN, TOM.**
The Chancellor's Spy, A Vivid Picture of Life in the Reign of Henry the Eighth. By TOM BEVAN. LONDON: THOMAS NELSON AND SONS, (1909). 263p. + 8p. pub. cat.: col. front., 1 col. plate by Richard Tod. Bound in blue cloth, with coloured pictorial cover and spine.
C 823.912 BEV

1928 **BEVAN, TOM.**
The Fen Robbers. By TOM BEVAN. LONDON: THOMAS NELSON AND SONS, (1906). 280p.: col. front., 1 col. plate. Bound in brown cloth, with coloured pictorial/decorative cover and coloured pictorial spine.
C 823.912 BEV

1929 **BEVAN, TOM.**
A HERO IN WOLF-SKIN, A Story of Pagan and Christian. By TOM BEVAN. LONDON: THE RELIGIOUS TRACT SOCIETY, (192–?). 320p.: col. front., 6 col. plates. Bound in green cloth with coloured pictorial cover and spine.
C 823.912 BEV

1930 **BIRD, RICHARD.**
The Big Five at Ellerby, And Other School Stories. BY RICHARD BIRD (Pseud. for WALTER BARRADELL-SMITH). Illustrated by Frank Wright. LONDON: BLACKIE AND SON LIMITED, (1926). 256p.: front., 5 plates. Bound in green cloth, with coloured pictorial cover and spine.
C 823.912 BAR

1930A **BIRD, RICHARD.**
PLAY THE GAME, TORBURY! BY RICHARD BIRD. Illustrated by H.M. Brock, R.I. LONDON: BLACKIE AND SON LIMITED, (193–?). 255p.: front., 5 plates. Bound in buff cloth with coloured pictorial cover and spine.
C 823.912 BIR

1930B **BIRD, RICHARD.**
The Ryecroft Rivals. BY RICHARD BIRD. Illustrated by H.M. Brock, R.I. LONDON: BLACKIE AND SON, LIMITED, (1923). 256p.: front., 5 plates. Bound in beige cloth with coloured pictorial cover and spine.
C 823.912 BAR

1931 **BLACKWOOD, ALGERNON.**
The Fruit Stones. By Algernon Blackwood. OXFORD: BASIL BLACKWELL, (193–?). 32p.: 3 plates, ill., by Marian Allen. Bound in blue cloth, with coloured pictorial paper label on cover.
YSC 823.912 BLA

1932 **BLACKWOOD, ALGERNON.**
THE PARROT AND THE CAT! By ALGERNON BLACKWOOD. Pictures by Cecil G. Trew AND TALKS IN THE LARDER. By DOROTHY ARMSTRONG. Pictures by Phyllis Jerrola. OXFORD: BASIL BLACKWELL; (193–?). 32p. + 4p. pub. cat.: 2 plates, ill. Bound in orange paper, with coloured pictorial paper label on cover.
YSC 823.912 BLA

1934 **BLYTON, ENID.**
FIVE-MINUTE TALES, SIXTY SHORT STORIES FOR CHILDREN. BY ENID BLYTON. LONDON: METHUEN AND CO. LTD., 1933. VII, 182p. + 8p. pub. cat. Bound in brown cloth, with decorative cover and spine.
C 823.912 BLY

1935 **BOLTON, F.H.**
INTO THE SOUNDLESS DEEPS, A Tale of Wonder and Invention. By F.H. BOLTON. LONDON: "THE BOY'S OWN PAPER" OFFICE, (192–?). 391p.: col. front., 2 col. plates by George Soper. Bound in grey cloth, with coloured pictorial cover and spine.
C 823.912 BOL

1936 **BONE, FLORENCE.**
The Wonderful Gate. BY FLORENCE BONE. LONDON: THE RELIGIOUS TRACT SOCIETY, 1911. 191p. + 16p. pub. cat.: col. front. by Victor Prout. Bound in green cloth, with coloured pictorial cover and spine.
C 823.912 BON

1937 **BRAMAH, ERNEST.**
KAI LUNG'S GOLDEN HOURS. BY ERNEST BRAMAH. WITH A PREFACE BY HILAIRE BELLOC. LONDON: GRANT RICHARDS LTD., 1922. VII, 312p. Bound in green cloth, with decorative cover.
C 823.912 BRA

1938 **BRAMSTON, MARY.**
BARBARA'S BEHAVIOUR, A STORY FOR GIRLS.

BY M. BRAMSTON. ILLUSTRATED BY HAROLD PIFFARD. LONDON: SOCIETY FOR PROMOTING CHRISTIAN KNOWLEDGE. (190–?). 222p. + 16p. pub. cat.: col. front., 2 col. plates. Bound in brown cloth with coloured pictorial cover and spine.
C 823.8 BRA

1939 **BRAZIL, ANGELA.**
CAPTAIN PEGGIE. BY ANGELA BRAZIL. Illustrated by W.E. Wightman. LONDON: BLACKIE AND SON LIMITED, (1924). 319p.: front., 5 plates. Bound in blue cloth, with coloured pictorial jacket.
C 823.912 BRA

1939A **BRAZIL, ANGELA.**
The Fortunes of Philippa. A School Story. BY ANGELA BRAZIL. LONDON: BLACKIE AND SON LIMITED, (192–?). 208p.: col. front. by Arthur A. Dixon, 3 plates by John Campbell. Bound in green cloth with coloured pictorial cover.
M 823 BRA CHILDREN'S COLLECTION

1940 **BRAZIL, ANGELA.**
A Fourth Form Friendship. A School Story. BY ANGELA BRAZIL. ILLUSTRATED BY FRANK E. WILES. LONDON: BLACKIE AND SON LIMITED, (192–?). 255p.: col. front., 4 plates. Bound in green cloth, with coloured, pictorial cover and spine.
C 823.912 BRA

1941 **BRAZIL, ANGELA.**
The Girls of St. Cyprian's, A Tale of School Life. BY ANGELA BRAZIL. Illustrated by Stanley Davis. LONDON: BLACKIE AND SON LIMITED, (191–?). 288p.: front., 5 plates. Bound in grey cloth, with coloured, pictorial cover and spine.
C 823.912 BRA

1941A **BRAZIL, ANGELA.**
A HARUM-SCARUM SCHOOLGIRL. BY ANGELA BRAZIL. Illustrated by John Campbell. LONDON: BLACKIE AND SON LIMITED, (192–?). 288p.: front., 3 plates. Bound in green cloth with coloured pictorial cover.
M 823 BRA CHILDREN'S COLLECTION

1941B **BRAZIL, ANGELA.**
The Jolliest Term on Record. A Story of School Life. BY ANGELA BRAZIL. Illustrated by Balliol Salmon. LONDON: BLACKIE AND SON LIMITED, (192–?). 288p.: front., 5 plates. Bound in blue cloth with coloured pictorial cover and spine.
M 823 BRA CHILDREN'S COLLECTION

1942 **BRAZIL, ANGELA.**
MONITRESS MERLE. BY ANGELA BRAZIL. Illustrated by Treyer Evans. LONDON: BLACKIE AND SON LIMITED, (1922). 256p.: front., 5 plates. Bound in brown cloth, with pictorial cover and spine.
C 823.912 BRA

1943 **BRAZIL, ANGELA.**
A Pair of Schoolgirls, A Story of School Days. BY ANGELA BRAZIL. ILLUSTRATED BY JOHN CAMPBELL. LONDON: BLACKIE AND SON LIMITED, (191–?). 256p.: col. front., 4 plates. Bound in red cloth, with coloured pictorial cover and spine.
YSC 823.912 BRA

1944 **BRAZIL, ANGELA.**
A Patriotic Schoolgirl. BY ANGELA BRAZIL. Illustrated by Balliol Salmon. LONDON: BLACKIE AND SON LIMITED, (1918). 288p.: front., 5 plates. Bound in grey cloth, with coloured pictorial cover and spine.
C 823.912 BRA

1944A **BRAZIL, ANGELA.**
The Princess of the School. BY ANGELA BRAZIL. Illustrated by Frank Wiles. LONDON: BLACKIE AND SON LIMITED, (192–?). 288p.: front., 3 plates. Bound in buff cloth with coloured vignette on cover.
M 823 BRA CHILDREN'S COLLECTION

1941B

1944B **BRAZIL, ANGELA.**
The School in the South. BY ANGELA BRAZIL. Illustrated by W. Smithson Broadhead. LONDON: BLACKIE AND SON LIMITED, (192–?). 287p.: front., 3 plates. Bound in buff cloth with coloured vignette on cover and spine.
M 823 BRA CHILDREN'S COLLECTION

1944C **BRAZIL, ANGELA.**
SCHOOLGIRL KITTY. BY ANGELA BRAZIL. (193–?). Illustrated by W.E. Wightman. LONDON: BLACKIE AND SON, LIMITED, (193–?). 320p. front., 5 plates. Bound in green cloth, with coloured vignettes on cover and spine.
M 823 BRA CHILDREN'S COLLECTION

1944D **BRAZIL, ANGELA.**
The Youngest Girl in the Fifth. A School Story. BY ANGELA BRAZIL. ILLUSTRATED BY STANLEY DAVIS. LONDON: BLACKIE AND SON LIMITED, (192–?). 296p.: front., 4 plates. Bound in green cloth with pictorial cover and spine.
M 823 BRA CHILDREN'S COLLECTION

1945 **BRENT-DYER, ELINOR M.**
THE CHALET SCHOOL AND JO. BY ELINOR BRENT-DYER. LONDON: W. AND R. CHAMBERS, LTD. (193–?). 285p. Bound in blue cloth.
YSC 823.912 BRE

1946 **BRENT-DYER, ELINOR M.**
THE PRINCESS OF THE CHALET-SCHOOL. BY ELINOR M. BRENT-DYER. LONDON: W. AND R. CHAMBERS, LTD., (1927). 304p. Bound in green cloth.
YSC 823.912 BRE

1947 **BRENT-DYER, ELINOR M.**
THE RIVALS OF THE CHALET SCHOOL. BY ELINOR M. BRENT-DYER. LONDON: W. AND R. CHAMBERS, LTD., (192–?). 272p. Bound in blue cloth.
YSC 823.912 BRE

1948 **BRERETON, FREDERICK SADLEIR.**
The Armoured-car Scouts, A Tale of the Campaign in the Caucasus. BY CAPTAIN F.S. BRERETON. Illustrated by Arch. Webb. LONDON: BLACKIE AND SON LIMITED, 1918. 384p.: front., 5 plates + 1 map. Bound in beige cloth, with coloured pictorial jacket.
C 823.912 BRE

1949 **BRERETON, FREDERICK SADLEIR.**
At Grips with the Turk, A Story of the Dardanelles Campaign. BY CAPTAIN F.S. BRERETON. Illustrated by Wal Paget. LONDON: BLACKIE AND SON LIMITED, 1916. 352p.: sepia front., 5 sepia plates + 1 map. Bound in olive cloth, with coloured pictorial cover and spine.
C 823.912 BRE

1950 **BRERETON, FREDERICK SADLEIR.**
The Dragon of Pekin, A Tale of the Boxer Revolt. BY CAPTAIN F.S. BRERETON. ILLUSTRATED BY WILLIAM RAINEY, R.I. NEW EDITION. LONDON: BLACKIE AND SON LIMITED, 1910. 352p. + 16p. pub. cat.: front., 5 plates + 1 map. Bound in green cloth, with coloured pictorial cover and spine.
C 823.912 BRE

1951 **BRERETON, FREDERICK SADLEIR.**
Foes of the Red Cockade, A Story of the French Revolution. BY LT.-COL. F.S. BRERETON. Illustrated by W. Rainey, R.I. LONDON: BLACKIE AND SON LIMITED, (191–?). 375p.: front., 5 plates. Bound in green cloth with coloured pictorial cover and spine.
C 823.912 BRE

1952 **BRERETON, FREDERICK SADLEIR.**
The Great Aeroplane, A Thrilling Tale of Adventure. BY CAPTAIN F.S. BRERETON. ILLUSTRATED BY EDWARD S. HODGSON. LONDON: BLACKIE AND SON LIMITED, 1911. 396p.: sepia front., 7 sepia plates. Bound in blue cloth, with coloured pictorial cover and spine and coloured pictorial paper dust cover.
C 823.912 BRE

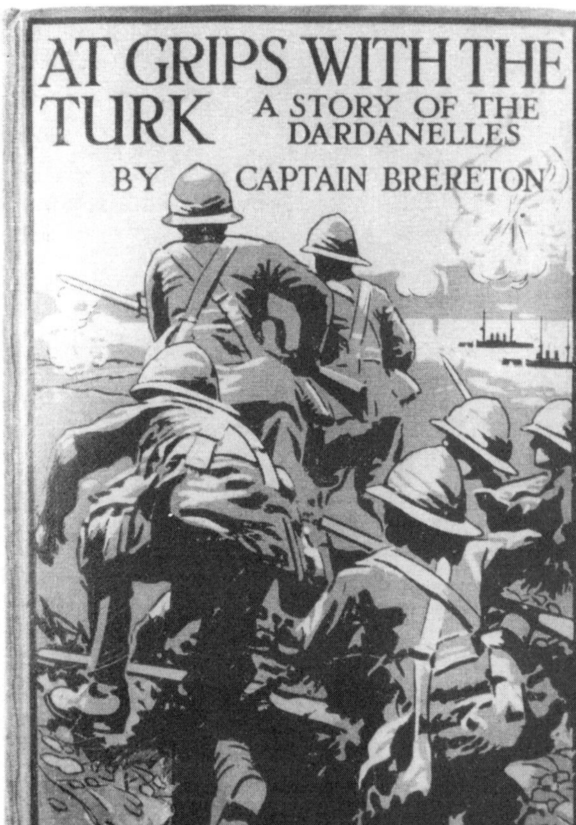


1949

1954 **BRERETON, FREDERICK SADLEIR.**
The Great Airship, A Tale of Adventure. BY CAPTAIN F.S. BRERETON. ILLUSTRATED BY C.M. PADDAY. LONDON: BLACKIE AND SON LIMITED, 1914. 360p.: sepia front., 5 sepia plates. Bound in blue cloth, with coloured pictorial cover and spine.
C 823.912 BRE

1955 **BRERETON, FREDERICK SADLEIR.**
A Hero of Lucknow, A Tale of the Indian Mutiny. BY CAPTAIN F.S. BRERETON. ILLUSTRATED BY WILLIAM RAINEY, R.I. LONDON: BLACKIE AND SON LIMITED, 1905. 336p. + 32p. ill. pub. cat.: front., 5 plates. Bound in green cloth, with coloured pictorial cover and spine.
C 823.912 BRE

1956 **BRERETON, FREDERICK SADLEIR.**
The Hero of Panama, A Tale of the Great Canal. BY CAPTAIN F.S. BRERETON. ILLUSTRATED BY WILLIAM RAINEY, R.I. LONDON: BLACKIE AND SON LIMITED, (191–?). 384p.: col. front., 7 col. plates. Bound in olive cloth, with coloured pictorial cover and spine.
C 823.912 BRE

1957 **BRERETON, FREDERICK SADLEIR.**
A Hero of Sedan. A Tale of the Franco-Prussian War. BY CAPTAIN F.S. BRERETON. ILLUSTRATED BY STANLEY L. WOOD. LONDON: BLACKIE AND SON LIMITED, 1910. 384p. + 16p. pub. cat.: col. front., 7 col. plates. Bound in blue cloth, with coloured pictorial cover and spine.
C 823.912 BRE

1958 **BRERETON, FREDERICK SADLEIR.**
How Canada was Won, A Tale of Wolfe and Quebec. BY CAPTAIN F.S. BRERETON. ILLUSTRATED BY WILLIAM RAINEY, R.I. LONDON: BLACKIE AND SON LIMITED, 1909. 391p. + 16p. pub. cat.: front., 7 plates + 3 maps. Bound in blue cloth, with coloured pictorial cover and spine.
C 823.912 BRE

1959 **BRERETON, FREDERICK SADLEIR.**
In the Grip of The Mullah, A Tale of Adventure in Somaliland. BY CAPTAIN F.S. BRERETON. ILLUSTRATED BY CHARLES M. SHELDON AND WITH A MAP. NEW EDITION. LONDON: BLACKIE AND SON LIMITED, 1912. 347p. + 16p. pub. cat.: front., 5 plates + 1 map. Bound in blue cloth, with coloured pictorial cover and spine.
C 823.912 BRE

1960 **BRERETON, FREDERICK SADLEIR.**
In the King's Service, A Tale of Cromwell's Invasion of Ireland. BY LT.-COLONEL F.S. BRERETON. Illustrated by Stanley L. Wood. LONDON: BLACKIE AND SON LIMITED, (191–?). 352p.: front., 5 plates. Bound in blue cloth, with coloured pictorial cover and spine.
C 812.912 BRE

1960A **BRERETON, FREDERICK SADLEIR.**
INDIAN AND SCOUT, A Tale of the Gold Rush in California. BY CAPTAIN F.S. BRERETON. ILLUSTRATED BY CYRUS CUNEO. LONDON: BLACKIE AND SON, LIMITED, 1911. 368p.: col. front., 6 col. plates. Bound in red cloth with coloured pictorial cover and spine, with coloured edges.
C 823.912 BRE

1960B **BRERETON, FREDERICK SADLEIR.**
John Bargreave's Gold. A Tale of Adventures in the Caribbean. BY CAPTAIN F.S. BRERETON. ILLUSTRATED BY CHARLES M. SHELDON. LONDON: BLACKIE, 1910. 356p. + 16p. pub. cat.: col. front., 5 col. plates. Bound in green cloth with coloured pictorial jacket and spine and blue pictorial dust cover and tinted edges.
C 823.912 BRE

1961 **BRERETON, FREDERICK SADLEIR.**
Jones of the 64th, A Tale of the Battles of Assaye and Laswaree.

BY CAPT. F.S. BRERETON. ILLUSTRATED BY W. RAINEY, R.I. LONDON: BLACKIE AND SON LIMITED, 1908. VIII, 341p. + 16p. pub. cat.: front., 5 plates + 2 maps. Bound in red cloth, with coloured pictorial cover and spine.
C 823.912 BRE

1962 **BRERETON, FREDERICK SADLEIR.**
On the Road to Bagdad, A Story of the British Expeditionary Force in Mesopotamia. BY CAPTAIN F.S. BRERETON. Illustrated by Wal Paget. LONDON: BLACKIE AND SON LIMITED, 1917. 384p.: front., 5 plates. Bound in beige cloth, with coloured pictorial cover and spine.
C 823.912 BRE

1963 **BRERETON, FREDERICK SADLEIR.**
ROGER THE BOLD. A TALE OF THE CONQUEST OF MEXICO. BY LT.-COLONEL F.S. BRERETON. ILLUSTRATED BY STANLEY L. WOOD. LONDON: BLACKIE AND SON LIMITED, (190–?). 381p.: front., 5 plates + 2 maps. Bound in green cloth, with coloured pictorial cover and spine.
C 823.912 BRE

1963A **BRERETON, FREDERICK SADLEIR.**
Rough Riders of the Pampas. A Tale of Ranch Life in South America. BT LT.-COLONEL F.S. BRERETON. ILLUSTRATED BY STANLEY L. WOOD. LONDON: BLACKIE AND SON LIMITED (1908). 366p.: front., 5 plates. Bound in brown cloth with coloured pictorial cover and spine.
C 823.912 BRE

1963B **BRERETON, FREDERICK SADLEIR.**
Scouts of the Baghdad Patrols. By Lieut-Colonel F.S. Brereton. With four illustrations in colour and Black and White by Stanley L. Wood. LONDON: CASSELL AND COMPANY LIMITED, NEW ED, 1931. 306p.: col. front., 3 plates. Bound in brown cloth with coloured pictorial label on cover.
C 823.912 BRE

1964 **BRERETON, FREDERICK SADLEIR.**
Tom Stapleton, The Boy Scout. BY CAPTAIN F.S. BRERETON. ILLUSTRATED BY GORDON BROWNE, R.I. LONDON: BLACKIE AND SON LIMITED, (191–?). 287p.: col. front., 6 plates. Bound in blue cloth, with coloured pictorial cover and spine.
C 823.912 BRE

1965 **BRERETON, FREDERICK SADLEIR.**
UNDER FOCH'S COMMAND, A Tale of the Americans in France. BY CAPTAIN F.S. BRERETON. Illustrated by Wal Paget. LONDON: BLACKIE AND SON LIMITED, (191–?). 287p.: front., 5 plates. Bound in beige cloth with coloured pictorial cover and spine.
C 823.912 BRE

1966 **BRERETON, FREDERICK SADLEIR.**
Under French's Command, A Story of the Western Front from Neuve Chapelle to Loos. CAPTAIN F.S. BRERETON. Illustrated by Arch. Webb. LONDON: BLACKIE AND SON LIMITED, (191–?). 336p.: front., 5 plates. Bound in brown cloth, with coloured pictorial cover and spine.
C 823.912 BRE

1967 **BRERETON, FREDERICK SADLEIR.**
Under Haig in Flanders, A Story of Vimy, Messines and Ypres. BY CAPTAIN F.S. BRERETON. Illustrated by J.E. Sutcliffe. LONDON: BLACKIE AND SON LIMITED, (191–?). 286p.: front., 5 plates. Bound in pink cloth, with coloured pictorial cover and spine.
C 823.912 BRE

1967A **BRERETON, FREDERICK SADLEIR.**
Under the Chinese Dragon. A Tale of Mongolia. BY CAPTAIN F.S. BRERETON. ILLUSTRATED BY CHARLES M. SHELDON. LONDON: BLACKIE AND SON, LIMITED, 1912. 363p.: col. front., 5 col. plates. Bound in orange cloth with coloured pictorial cover and spine, with tinted edges.
C 823.912 BRE

1967B **BRERETON, FREDERICK SADLEIR.**
Under the Spangled Banner. A Tale of the Spanish American War. BY CAPTAIN F.S. BRERETON. ILLUSTRATED BY C.M. PADDAY. LONDON: BLACKIE, NEW ED. (1913). 352p.: sepia front., 5 sepia plates. Bound in grey cloth with coloured pictorial cover and spine.
C 823.912

1967C **BRERETON, FREDERICK SADLEIR.**
With Allenby in Palestine. A Story of the Latest Crusade. BY LT. COL. F.S. BRERETON. Illustrated by Frank Gillett, R.I. LONDON: BLACKIE AND SON LIMITED, (1919). 287p.: front., 3 plates. Bound in buff cloth with pictorial cover and spine.
C 823.912 BRE

1968 **BRERETON, FREDERICK SADLEIR.**
WITH FRENCH AT THE FRONT. A Story of the Great European War down to the Battle of the Aisne. BY CAPTAIN F.S. BRERETON. Illustrated by Archie Webb. LONDON: BLACKIE AND SON LIMITED, (192–?). 292p.: front., 5 plates. Bound in buff cloth with coloured pictorial cover and spine.
C 823.912 BRE

1969 **BRERETON, FREDERICK SADLEIR.**
With Joffre at Verdun, A Story of the Western Front. BY LT.-COL. F.S. BRERETON. Illustrated by Arch. Webb. LONDON: BLACKIE AND SON LIMITED (191–?). 288p.: front., 5 plates + 2 maps. Bound in beige cloth, with coloured pictorial cover and spine.
C 823.912 BRE

1970 **BRERETON, FREDERICK SADLEIR.**
With Rifle and Bayonet, A Story of the Boer War. BY CAPTAIN F.S. BRERETON. WITH EIGHT ILLUSTRATIONS BY WAL PAGET. LONDON, BLACKIE AND SON LIMITED, 1901. 352p. + 32p. ill. pub. cat.: front., 7 plates. Bound in green cloth, with coloured pictorial cover and spine.
C 823.912 BRE

1971 **BRERETON, FREDERICK SADLEIR.**
WITH ROBERTS TO CANDAHAR, A TALE OF THE THIRD AFGHAN WAR. BY CAPTAIN F.S. BRERETON. ILLUSTRATED BY WILLIAM RAINEY, R.I. LONDON: BLACKIE AND SON LIMITED, 1907. 352p. + 16p. ill. pub. cat.: front., 5 plates. Bound in green cloth, with coloured pictorial cover and spine.
YSC 823.912 BRE

1972 **BRERETON, FREDERICK SADLEIR.**
With Shield and Assegai, A TALE OF THE ZULU WAR. BY CAPTAIN F.S. BRERETON. WITH SIX ILLUSTRATIONS BY STANLEY L. WOOD. LONDON: BLACKIE AND SON LIMITED, (190–?). 320p. + 16p. ill. pub. cat.: front., 5 plates. Bound in green cloth, with coloured pictorial cover and spine.
C 823.912 BRE

1973 **BRERETON, FREDERICK SADLEIR.**
WITH THE ALLIES TO THE RHINE, A Story of the Finish of the War. BY LT.-COLONEL F.S. BRERETON. Illustrated by Frank Gillett, R.I. LONDON: BLACKIE AND SON LIMITED, (191–?). 288p.: front., 5 plates. Bound in brown cloth, with coloured pictorial cover and spine.
C 823.912 BRE

1974 **BRERETON, FREDERICK SADLEIR.**
With The Dyaks of Borneo, A Tale of the Head Hunters. BY CAPTAIN F.S. BRERETON. ILLUSTRATED BY FRITZ BERGEN. LONDON: BLACKIE AND SON LIMITED, (190–?). 384p. + 16p. pub. cat.: front., 7 plates. Bound in green cloth, with coloured pictorial cover and spine.
C 823.912 BRE

1975 **Another copy.**
ILLUSTRATED BY WILLIAM RAINEY, R.I. NEW EDITION. LONDON: BLACKIE AND SON LIMITED (191–?). 384p. + 16p. pub. cat.: front., 5 plates. Bound in red cloth, with coloured pictorial cover and spine.

1977 **BRERETON, FREDERICK SADLEIR.**
With Wolseley to Kumasi, A Tale of the First Ashanti War. BY CAPTAIN F.S. BRERETON. ILLUSTRATED BY GORDON BROWNE, R.I. LONDON: BLACKIE AND SON LIMITED, 1908. VIII, 373p. + 16p. pub. cat.: front., 7 plates + 1 map. Bound in red cloth, with coloured pictorial cover and spine.
C 823.912 BRE

1977A **BRUCE, DORITA FAIRLIE.**
THAT BOARDING-SCHOOL GIRL. By DORITA FAIRLIE BRUCE. Illustrated by R.H. BROCK. LONDON: OXFORD UNIVERSITY PRESS, 1929. 190p.: col. front., 4 plates. Bound in red cloth with coloured pictorial paper dust jacket.
C 823.912 BRU

1978 **BRUCE, MARY GRANT.**
POSSUM. BY MARY GRANT BRUCE. LONDON: WARD LOCK AND CO. LIMITED, 1917. 312p. + 8p. pub. cat.: front., 7 plates, by J. Macfarlane. Bound in green cloth, with coloured pictorial cover and spine, and coloured pictorial label on cover.
YSC 823.912 BRU

1979 **BUCHAN, JOHN.**
THE FOUR ADVENTURES OF RICHARD HANNAY. LONDON: HODDER AND STOUGHTON, 1930, X, 1204p.: Bound in maroon cloth with pictorial paper jacket. Contains the Thirty Nine Steps, Greenmantle, Mr. Standfast, the Three Hostages.
YSC 823.912 BUC

1980 **BURCH, HARRIETTE E.**
WIND AND WAVE, A STORY OF THE SIEGE OF LEYDEN, 1574. BY H.E. BURCH. LONDON: THE RELIGIOUS TRACT SOCIETY, (190–?). 284p.: front., 14 plates. Bound in green cloth, with coloured pictorial cover and spine.
C 823.8 BUR

1981 **BURNETT, FRANCES HODGSON.**
THE SECRET GARDEN. BY FRANCES HODGSON BURNETT. ILLUSTRATED BY CHARLES ROBINSON. LONDON: WILLIAM HEINEMANN LTD., 1911. VIII, 306p. + 6p. pub. cat.: col. front., decorative title page, 7 col. plates, pictorial endpapers. Bound in green cloth with pictorial cover and decorative spine.
C 813.4 BUR

1982 **BURNETT, FRANCES HODGSON.**
TWO LITTLE PILGRIMS' PROGRESS. A Story of the City Beautiful. BY FRANCES HODGSON BURNETT. WITH ILLUSTRATIONS BY R.W. MACBETH, R.A. LONDON: FREDERICK WARNE AND CO., (191–?). 215p.: front., 3 plates, ill. Rebound in blue cloth. Originally published 1895.
YSC 813.4 BUR

1983 **BURRAGE, EDWIN HARCOURT.**
Carbineer and Scout, A Story of the Great Boer War. BY E. HARCOURT BURRAGE. WITH FOUR PAGE ILLUSTRATIONS BY N. TÈSTELIN. LONDON: BLACKIE AND SON LIMITED, (190–?). 240p. + 16p. pub. cat.: front., 3 plates. Bound in blue cloth with coloured, pictorial cover and spine.
C 823.912 BUR

1984 **BUTCHER, J. WILLIAMS.**
THE SENIOR PREFECT AND OTHER CHRONICLES OF ROSSITER. BY J. WILLIAMS BUTCHER. ILLUSTRATED BY B. HUTCHINSON. LONDON: CHARLES H. KELLY, 1913. 356p.: front., 5 plates. Bound in green cloth, with coloured pictorial cover and spine.
C 823.912 BUT

1985 **CAINE, OLIVER VERNON.**
IN THE YEAR OF WATERLOO. BY O.V. CAINE. LONDON: JAMES NISBET AND CO. LIMITED, (190–?). 365p. + 16p. pub. cat.: col. front., 3 col. plates by Chris Hammond, + 1 map. Bound in green cloth, with coloured pictorial labels on cover and spine. The Holiday Library.
C 823.8 CAI

1986 **CALLWELL, J.M.**
A Little Irish Girl. BY J.M. CALLWELL. ILLUSTRATED BY HAROLD COPPING. LONDON: BLACKIE AND SON LIMITED, (1902). 240p. + 16p. pub. cat.: front., 3 plates. Bound in green cloth, with coloured pictorial cover and spine.
C 823.912 CAL

1987 **CARR, KENT.**
RIVALS AND CHUMS. A Public School Story. By KENT CARR. WITH EIGHT ILLUSTRATIONS by Harold C. Earnshaw. LONDON: W. AND R. CHAMBERS LIMITED, (1908?). 307p.: front., 7 plates. Bound in red cloth, with coloured, pictorial cover and spine.
C 823.912 CAR

1988 **CARROLL, LEWIS.**
ALICE'S ADVENTURES IN WONDERLAND BY LEWIS CARROLL. WITH FORTY-TWO ILLUSTRATIONS BY JOHN TENNIEL. LONDON: MACMILLAN AND CO. LIMITED, 1904. VIII, 183p. + 8p. pub. cat.: front., ill. Bound in blue cloth with decorative spine. Originally published 1865.
C 823.8 CAR

1989 **Another copy.**
ILLUSTRATED BY ARTHUR RACKHAM, WITH A POEM BY AUSTIN DOBSON. LONDON: WILLIAM HEINEMANN, LTD., 1907. 162p.: col. front., decorative title page, 12 col. plates, 3 plates, ill., pictorial endpapers. Bound in blue cloth with coloured pictorial dust cover.
CBD 823.8 CAR

1989A **Another copy.**
With eight coloured plates and one hundred and twelve other illustrations by Charles Robinson. LONDON: CASSELL AND COMPANY, LTD., 1907. VII, 179p.: col. front., col. decorative title page, 7 col. plates, ill. Bound in blue cloth with decorative cover and spine.
M 823 CAR CHILDREN'S COLLECTION

1990 **Another copy.**
WITH 48 COLOURED PLATES BY MARGARET W. TARRANT. LONDON: WARD LOCK AND CO: LIMITED, 1922. 332p. + 12p. pub. cat.: col. front., 43 col. plates. Coloured pictorial endpapers. Bound in beige cloth, with coloured pictorial label on cover, and decorative spine.
C 823.8 CAR

1991 **Another copy.**
ILLUSTRATED BY SIR JOHN TENNIEL. LONDON: MACMILLAN, ST. MARTIN'S PRESS, 1927. XI, 206p.: col. front., vignette title page, 15 col. plates, ill. Coloured pictorial endpapers. Bound in green linson with embossed pictorial cover partly in red, pictorial paper jacket.
YSC 823.8 CAR

1992 **Another copy.**
ALICE IN WONDERLAND. BY LEWIS CARROLL. Illustrated by DUDLEY JARRETT. LONDON: THE READERS LIBRARY PUBLISHING COMPANY LTD. (193–?). 253p.: front., vignette title page, 13 plates, ill. Pictorial endpapers. Bound in purple cloth, with decorative cover and spine.
C 823.8 CAR

1993 **Another copy.**
FULLY ILLUSTRATED IN LINE AND COLOUR BY HARRY ROUNTREE. GLASGOW: THE CHILDREN'S PRESS, (193–?). 135p.: col. front., 3 col. plates. Bound in cream paper with coloured pictorial covers and matching dust cover.
CBD 823.8 CAR

1994 **CHADWICK, WILLIAM EDWARD.**
IN FELLOWSHIP, A STORY FOR YOUNG MEN. BY W.E. CHADWICK. WITH ILLUSTRATIONS BY J.

FINNEMORE. LONDON: THE SUNDAY SCHOOL UNION, (190–?). 403p.: front., 6 plates. Bound in blue cloth, with coloured pictorial cover and spine.
C 823.8 CHA

1995 **CHAFFEE, ALLEN.**
SULLY JOINS THE CIRCUS. BY ALLEN CHAFFEE. ILLUSTRATED BY ALBERT CARMEN. LONDON: THE CENTURY CO., 1926. X, 270p.: front., 3 plates. Bound in brown cloth, with coloured pictorial cover and spine.
C 813.52 CHA

1996 **CHAPPELL, JENNIE.**
Oughts and Crosses. BY JENNIE CHAPPELL. New Edition. LONDON: JOHN F. SHAW AND CO. (190–?). 128p., col. front. Bound in brown cloth with coloured pictorial cover and decorative spine.
C 823.8 CHA

1997 **CHESTERMAN, HUGH.**
Seven for a Secret. By HUGH CHESTERMAN. Pictures by the Author. OXFORD: BASIL BLACKWELL, (193–?). 31p.: 3 plates, ill. Bound in brown cloth, with coloured pictorial label and cover. Contains also THE WOLF, THE HARE AND THE HEDGEHOG. By Valery Carrick.
YSC 823.912 CHE

1998 **CHESTERTON, ALICE M.**
WHITTENBURY COLLEGE, A SCHOOL STORY FOR GIRLS. BY ALICE M. CHESTERTON. LONDON: THOMAS NELSON AND SONS, (192–?). 378p.: col. front., 5 col. plates, by Ethel Everett. Bound in blue cloth, with coloured pictorial cover and spine.
C 823.912 CHE

1999 **CHILDERS, ERSKINE.**
THE RIDDLE OF THE SANDS, A RECORD OF THE SECRET SERVICE. BY ERSKINE CHILDERS. SCHOOL EDITION. LONDON: EDWARD ARNOLD AND CO., 1931. VIII, 289p. + 1p. pub. cat.: 1 double map, 3 maps. Bound in blue cloth, with vignette on cover. Originally published 1903.
YSC 823.912 CHI

2000 **CLARE, AUSTIN.**
ANOTHER MAN'S BURDEN, A TALE OF LOVE AND DUTY. BY AUSTIN CLARE. ILLUSTRATED BY H.M. PAGET. LONDON: SOCIETY FOR PROMOTING CHRISTIAN KNOWLEDGE, (191–?). 380p. + 4p. pub. cat.: front., 3 plates. Bound in brown cloth, with coloured pictorial cover and spine.
C 823.8 CLA

2001 **CLARKE, COVINGTON.**
ACES UP. By COVINGTON CLARKE. LONDON: JOHN HAMILTON LIMITED, (192–?). 255p. + 1p. pub. cat.: col. front., 4 plates + 8 diagrams, by Johns. Bound in blue cloth, with coloured pictorial jacket.
C 823.912 CLA

2002 **CLARKE, COVINGTON.**
FOR VALOUR. By COVINGTON CLARKE. LONDON: JOHN HAMILTON LTD., (192–?). 254p. + 1p. pub. cat.: col. front., 4 plates + 8 diagrams, by Johns. Bound in blue cloth, with coloured pictorial jacket.
C 823.912 CLA

2003 **CLARKE, MRS. HENRY.**
A TRUSTY REBEL; OR, A FOLLOWER OF WARBECK. BY MRS. HENRY CLARKE. LONDON: THOMAS NELSON AND SONS, (190–?). 340p.: col. front., 5 col. plates, by Walter G. Grieve. Bound in brown cloth, with pictorial cover and spine.
C 823.912 CLA

2004 **CLEAVER, HYLTON.**
BROTHER O'MINE, A SCHOOL STORY. BY HYLTON CLEAVER. ILLUSTRATED IN COLOUR BY H.M. BROCK. LONDON: HUMPHREY MILFORD, OXFORD UNIVERSITY PRESS, 1920. 265p.: col. front., 3 col. plates. Bound in blue cloth, with coloured pictorial cover and spine.
C 823.912 CLE

2005 **CLEAVER, HYLTON.**
THE HARLEY FIRST XI. BY HYLTON CLEAVER. ILLUSTRATED IN COLOUR BY C.E. BROCK. LONDON: HUMPHREY MILFORD, OXFORD UNIVERSITY PRESS, 1922. 272p.: 3 plates. Bound in red cloth with decorative cover and spine and coloured pictorial labels on cover and spine.
C 823.912 CLE

2006 **CLEAVER, HYLTON.**
ROSCOE MAKES GOOD, A STORY OF HARLEY. BY HYLTON CLEAVER. WITH ILLUSTRATIONS BY H.M. BROCK. LONDON: HUMPHREY MILFORD, OXFORD UNIVERSITY PRESS, 1921. 296p.: col. front., 4 plates. Bound in brown cloth, with coloured pictorial cover and spine.
C 823.912 CLE

2007 **COBB, JAMES FRANCIS.**
THE WATCHERS ON THE LONGSHIPS, A TALE OF THE LAST CENTURY. BY JAMES F. COBB. TWENTY-SEVENTH EDITION. LONDON: WELLS GARDNER, DARTON AND CO. LTD., (190–?). X, 282p. + 1p. pub. cat.: front., 3 plates. Bound in red cloth, with coloured pictorial cover and pictorial spine.
C 823.8 COB

2008 **COBB, THOMAS.**
THE CASTAWAYS OF MEADOW BANK. BY THOMAS COBB. WITH FOUR ILLUSTRATIONS BY A.H. BUCKLAND. LONDON: METHUEN AND CO., (190–?). VI, 191p.: front., 3 plates. Bound in blue cloth, with pictorial cover and decorative spine. THE LITTLE BLUE BOOKS FOR CHILDREN.
C 823.912 COB

2008A **COKE, DESMOND.**
YOUTH, YOUTH! By DESMOND COKE. With Illustrations by H.M. Brock. LONDON: CHAPMAN AND HALL LTD., 1919. 304p.: front., pictorial title page, 7 plates, ill. Bound in blue cloth with pictorial cover and spine.
C 823.912 COK

2008B **COLLINGWOOD, HARRY.**
The Adventures of Dick Maitland. A Tale of Unknown Africa. BY HARRY COLLINGWOOD (pseud. for WILLIAM JOSEPH COZENS LANCASTER). ILLUSTRATED BY ALEC BALL. LONDON: BLACKIE AND SON LIMITED, 1912. 288p.: 5 sepia plates. Bound in green cloth with coloured pictorial cover and spine and tinted edges.
C 823.912 COL

2008C **COLLINGWOOD, HARRY.**
The Log of a Privateersman. BY HARRY COLLINGWOOD. ILLUSTRATED BY W. RAINEY, R.I. LONDON: BLACKIE AND SON LIMITED, NEW ED., 1910. 384p. + 16p. pub. cat.: front., 5 plates. Bound in blue cloth with coloured pictorial cover and spine.
C 823.912 COL

2009 **COLLINGWOOD, HARRY.**
The Log of the "Flying Fish", A Story of Aerial and Submarine Peril and Adventure. BY HARRY COLLINGWOOD. ILLUSTRATED BY GORDON BROWNE. LONDON: BLACKIE AND SON LIMITED, (190–?). 384p.: col. front., 4 plates. Bound in blue cloth, with coloured pictorial cover and spine.
C 823.912 COL

2010 **COLLINGWOOD, HARRY.**
A Middy in Command, A Tale of the Slave Squadron. BY HARRY COLLINGWOOD. ILLUSTRATED BY EDWARD S. HODGSON. LONDON: BLACKIE AND SON LIMITED, 1909. 384p. + 16p. pub. cat.: front., 7 plates. Bound in green cloth, with coloured pictorial cover and spine.
C 823.912 COL

2011 **COLLINGWOOD, HARRY.**
The Rover's Secret, A Tale of the Pirate Cays and Lagoons of Cuba. BY HARRY COLLINGWOOD. Illustrated by W. Christian Symons. LONDON: BLACKIE AND SON LIMITED, (190–?). 352p.: front., 2 plates. Bound in red cloth, with coloured pictorial cover and spine.
C 823.912 COL

2011A **COLLINGWOOD, HARRY.**
The Strange Adventures of Eric Blackburn. BY HARRY COLLINGWOOD. Illustrated by C. M. Padday, R.O.I. LONDON: BLACKIE AND SON LIMITED, (1922). 317p.: front., 5 plates. Bound in blue cloth with pictorial cover and spine.
C 823.912 COL

2011B **COLLINGWOOD, HARRY.**
A Strange Cruise. A Tale of Piracy on the High Seas. BY HARRY COLLINGWOOD. ILLUSTRATED BY ARCHIBALD WEBB. LONDON: BLACKIE AND SON LIMITED, (1912). 296p.: sepia front., 5 sepia plates. Bound in grey cloth with coloured pictorial cover and spine.
C 823.912 COL

2012 **COLLINGWOOD, HARRY.**
Two Gallant Sons of Devon, A Tale of the Days of Queen Bess. BY HARRY COLLINGWOOD. ILLUSTRATED BY EDWARD S. HODGSON. LONDON: BLACKIE AND SON LIMITED, 1913. 364p.: col. front., 5 col. plates. Bound in blue cloth, with coloured pictorial cover and spine.
C 823.912 COL

2013 **COLLODI, CARLO.**
PINOCCHIO, THE TALE OF A PUPPET. BY C. COLLODI (pseud. for CARLO LORENZINI). TRANSLATED FROM THE ITALIAN BY M.A. MURRAY. Illustrated by CHARLES FOLKARD. LONDON: J.M. DENT AND SONS LTD., 1911. XVI, 268p.: col. front., col. title page, 11 col. plates, ill., pictorial endpapers. Bound in cream cloth, with coloured pictorial and decorative cover and spine.
C 853.8 LOR

2014 **Another copy.**
LONDON: J.M. DENT AND SONS, LTD., 1914. 128p.: col., front., 7 plates by Charles Folkard. Bound in cream cloth with inserted coloured pictorial label on cover.
C 853.8 COL

2015 **Another copy.**
LONDON: J.M. DENT AND SONS LTD., 1939. XIX, 276p.: 24 plates, ill. by Charles Folkard. Bound in green cloth.
YSC 853.8 COL

2016 **COMFORT, JOHN.**
THE RIVER TRAMP. BY JOHN COMFORT. ILLUSTRATED BY WAL PAGET. LONDON: SOCIETY FOR PROMOTING CHRISTIAN KNOWLEDGE, (191–?). 223p. + 16p. pub. cat.: col. front., 2 col. plates. Bound in brown cloth, with coloured pictorial cover and spine.
C 823.912 COM

2017 **COOLIDGE, SUSAN.**
What Katy Did at School. BY SUSAN COOLIDGE, (pseud. for Sarah (Chauncey) Woolsey). LONDON: BLACKIE AND SON LIMITED, (191–?). 192p. + 8p. pub. cat.: front. by P.H. Bound in blue cloth, with coloured decorative cover and spine. Originally published 1886.
YSC 813.4 COO

2018 **COOPER, JAMES FENIMORE.**
THE LAST OF THE MOHICANS. BY FENIMORE COOPER. WITH ILLUSTRATIONS BY H.M. BROCK. AND AN INTRODUCTION BY MOWBRAY MORRIS. LONDON: MACMILLAN AND CO. LIMITED, 1900. XXVII, 398p. + 8p. pub. cat.: front., 24 plates. Bound in green cloth, with coloured pictorial cover and spine. Originally published 1826.
C 813.2 COO

2019 **Another copy.**
THE LAST OF THE MOHICANS, A NARRATIVE OF 1757. BY JAMES FENIMORE COOPER. LONDON: CHARLES H. KELLY, (191–?). VIII, 443p.: sepia front., 4 plates, by Henry Evison. Bound in green cloth, with coloured pictorial cover and spine.
YSC 813.2 COO

2020 **COOPER, JAMES FENIMORE.**
THE PIONEERS, OR THE SOURCES OF THE SUSQUEHANNA. A DESCRIPTIVE TALE. BY FENIMORE COOPER. WITH ILLUSTRATIONS BY H.M. BROCK. LONDON: MACMILLAN AND CO., LIMITED, 1901. VIII, 455p. + 4p. pub. cat.: front., 24 plates. Bound in red cloth with embossed pattern on covers. Originally published 1832.
CBD 813.2 COO

2021 **COOPER, MRS.**
TOM'S FIRST FRIEND. By Mrs. Cooper. LONDON: RELIGIOUS TRACT SOCIETY, (191–?). 61p., col. front., title page decorated in colour. Bound in brown paper with coloured pictorial cover.
C 823.912 COO

2022 **COWPER, EDITH E.**
The Girl from the North-West. BY E.E. COWPER. Illustrated by H. Coller. LONDON: BLACKIE AND SON LIMITED, (190–?). 319p.: front., 5 plates. Bound in grey cloth, with coloured pictorial cover and spine.
C 823.912 COW

2023 **COWPER, EDITH E.**
The Haunted Trail. BY E.E. COWPER. Illustrated by H. Coller. LONDON: BLACKIE AND SON LIMITED, (190–?). 224p.: front., 3 plates. Bound in blue cloth, with coloured pictorial cover and spine.
C 823.912 COW

2024 **COWPER, EDITH E.**
THE MYSTERY OF SAFFRON MANOR. BY E.E. COWPER. Illustrated by Gordon Browne, R.I. LONDON: BLACKIE AND SON LIMITED, (190–?). 284p.: front., 5 plates. Bound in green cloth, with coloured pictorial cover and spine.
C 823.912 COW

2025 **COX, M.B.**
THE ROYAL PARDON. A Tale for Village Lads. By M.B. COX (NOEL WEST). ILLUSTRATED BY W.S. STACEY. LONDON: SOCIETY FOR PROMOTING CHRISTIAN KNOWLEDGE. (190–?). 157p. + 16p. pub. cat.: front., 2 plates. Bound in green cloth with coloured pictorial cover and spine.
C 823.8 COX

2026 **CRAIK, DINAH MARIA.**
JOHN HALIFAX, GENTLEMAN. BY MRS. CRAIK. LONDON: W. NICHOLSON AND SONS, LIMITED, (190–?). 374p. + 10p. pub. cat. Bound in blue cloth, with embossed decorative covers and spine.
YSC 823.8 CRA

2026A **CRESWICK, PAUL.**
HASTING THE PIRATE by PAUL CRESWICK. ILLUSTRATIONS BY T.H. ROBINSON. LONDON: ERNEST NISTER (1902), 303p. + 8p. pub. cat.: front., 7 plates, ill. Bound in purple cloth with coloured pictorial cover and spine.
C 823.912 CRE

2027 **CRESWICK, PAUL.**
IN A HAND OF STEEL, OR The Great Thatchmere Mystery. BY PAUL CRESWICK. SIX ILLUSTRATIONS BY MURRAY URQUHART. LONDON: T.C. AND E.C. JACK, 1907. VIII, 243p.: front., 5 plates. Bound in beige cloth, with coloured pictorial cover and spine.
C 823.912 CRE

2028 **CRICHTON, FRANCES ELIZABETH.**
PEEP-IN-WORLD. BY F.E. CRICHTON. LONDON: EDWARD ARNOLD, 1908. VI, 258p. + 2p. pub. cat.: front., 3 plates by Harry Rountree. Bound in green cloth, with coloured pictorial cover and spine.
C 823.912 CRI

2028A **CROCKETT, SAMUEL RUTHERFORD.**
RED CAP TALES, STOLEN FROM THE TREASURE CHEST OF THE WIZARD OF THE NORTH. WHICH THEFT IS HUMBLY ACKNOWLEDGED BY S.R. CROCKETT. LONDON: ADAM AND CHARLES BLACK, 1904. XII, 413p. + 2p. pub. cat.: col. front., 15 col. plates by Simon Harman Vedder. Bound in yellow cloth with coloured pictorial cover and spine. Includes tales from Waverley, Guy Mannering, Rob Roy and the Antiquary by Sir Walter Scott.
C 823.8 CRO

2029 **CROCKETT, SAMUEL RUTHERFORD.**
SIR TOADY CRUSOE. BY S.R. CROCKETT. ILLUSTRATED BY GORDON BROWNE. LONDON: WELLS, GARDNER, DARTON AND CO. LTD., 1905. XII, 406p. + 6p. pub. cat.: front., vignette title page, 18 plates, ill. Bound in blue cloth, with coloured pictorial covers and spine.
C 823.912 CRO

2030 **CROCKETT, SAMUEL RUTHERFORD.**
Strong Mac. BY S.R. Crockett. Illustrated by Maurice Greiffenhagen. U.S.A., NEW YORK: DODD, MEAD AND COMPANY, 1904. IV, 399p.: front., 7 plates. Bound in green cloth, with coloured pictorial cover.
YSC 823.912 CRO

2030A **CROMPTON, RICHMAL.**
JUST-WILLIAM. BY RICHMAL CROMPTON. ILLUSTRATED BY THOMAS HENRY. LONDON: GEORGE NEWNES LIMITED, 1922. 187p.: front., ill. Bound in red cloth with coloured pictorial paper dust cover.
C 823.912 CRO

2031 **CROMPTON, RICHMAL.**
SWEET WILLIAM BY RICHMAL CROMPTON. ILLUSTRATED BY THOMAS HENRY. LONDON: GEORGE NEWNES, LIMITED, 1936. 252p.: front., 11 plates, ill. Bound in red cloth.
C 823.912 CRO

2031A **CROMPTON, RICHMAL.**
WILLIAM AGAIN. ILLUSTRATED BY THOMAS HENRY. LONDON: GEORGE NEWNES LIMITED, 1923. 251p.: front., ill. Bound in red linson.
C 823.912 CRO

2032 **CROMPTON, RICHMAL.**
WILLIAM AND A.R.P. BY RICHMAL CROMPTON. ILLUSTRATED BY THOMAS HENRY. LONDON: GEORGE NEWNES, LIMITED, 1939. 256p.: front., 1 plate, ill. Bound in red cloth.
C 823.912 CRO

2032A **CROMPTON, RICHMAL.**
WILLIAM THE CONQUEROR. BY RICHMAL CROMPTON. ILLUSTRATED BY THOMAS HENRY. LONDON: GEORGE NEWNES LIMITED, 1926. 252p.: front., 4 plates, ill. Bound in red cloth.
M 823 CRO CHILDREN'S COLLECTION

2033 **CROMPTON, RICHMAL.**
WILLIAM THE DICTATOR, BY RICHMAL CROMPTON. ILLUSTRATED BY THOMAS HENRY. LONDON: GEORGE NEWNES, LIMITED, 1938. 256p.: front., 8 plates, ill. Bound in red cloth.
C 823.912 CRO

2034 **CROMPTON, RICHMAL.**
WILLIAM THE GANGSTER. BY RICHMAL CROMPTON. ILLUSTRATED BY THOMAS HENRY. LONDON: GEORGE NEWNES LTD., 1934. 252p.: front., 3 plates, ill. Bound in red cloth.
C 823.912 CRO

2034A **CROMPTON, RICHMAL.**
WILLIAM – THE PIRATE. BY RICHMAL CROMPTON. ILLUSTRATED BY THOMAS HENRY. LONDON: GEORGE NEWNES LIMITED, 1932. 252p.: front., ill. Bound in red linson.
C 823.912 CRO

2035 **CROMPTON, RICHMAL.**
WILLIAM – THE REBEL, BY RICHMAL CROMPTON. ILLUSTRATED BY THOMAS HENRY. LONDON: GEORGE NEWNES, LIMITED, 1933. 256p. front., 6 plates, ill. Bound in red cloth.
C 823.912 CRO

2036 **CROMPTON, RICHMAL.**
WILLIAM – THE SHOWMAN, BY RICHMAL CROMPTON. ILLUSTRATED BY THOMAS HENRY. LONDON: GEORGE NEWNES, LIMITED, 1937. 253p.: front., 3 plates, ill. Bound in red cloth.
C 823.912 CRO

2037 **CROMPTON, RICHMAL.**
WILLIAM'S CROWDED HOURS, BY RICHMAL CROMPTON. ILLUSTRATED BY THOMAS HENRY. LONDON: GEORGE NEWNES, LIMITED, 1931. 250p.: front., 10 plates, ill. Bound in red cloth.
C 823.912 CRO

2038 **CURTIS, ALBERT CHARLES.**
THE VOYAGE OF THE "SESAME". BY A.C. CURTIS. ILLUSTRATED IN COLOUR BY W. HERBERT HOLLOWAY. LONDON: HENRY FROWDE, HODDER AND STOUGHTON, 1910. 351p. + 16p. pub. cat.: col. front., 5 col. plates, 1 map + 1 plan. Bound in grey cloth, with coloured pictorial cover and spine.
C 823.912 CUR

2039 **DALGLEISH, FLORENCE.**
THE MIGHTY PAST, A Tale of the Plagues of Egypt for Boys and Girls. BY FLORENCE DALGLEISH. LONDON: J.W. BUTCHER, (190–?). 200p. + 16p. ill. pub. cat.: front.: 1 plate, ill. Bound in blue cloth, with coloured pictorial cover and spine.
C 823.912 DAL

2040 **DARTON, F.J. HARVEY.**
Tales of the Canterbury Pilgrims. Retold from Chaucer and Others by F.J. Harvey Darton, with Introduction by F.J. Furnivall and Illustrations by Hugh Thomson. LONDON: WELLS, GARDNER, DARTON AND CO., 1904. XXIV, 365p. + 24p. ill. pub. cat. 16 plates, ill. Bound in black cloth with decorative cover and spine.
CBD 821.1 DAR

2041 **DEHN, OLIVE.**
The Basement Bogle. By OLIVE DEHN. OXFORD: BASIL BLACKWELL, (193–?). 30p.: 1 plate, ill., by Harry Rountree. Bound in purple cloth, with coloured pictorial paper label on cover.
YSC 823.912 DEH

2042 **DE LA MARE, WALTER JOHN.**
ANIMAL STORIES, chosen, arranged, and in some part rewritten by WALTER DE LA MARE. LONDON: FABER AND FABER LIMITED, 1939. LVI, 420p.: ill. Bound in red and black patterned cloth.
C 823.912 DEL

2043 **DE LA MARE, WALTER JOHN.**
BROOMSTICKS AND OTHER TALES. BY WALTER DE LA MARE WITH DESIGNS BY BOLD. LONDON: CONSTABLE AND COMPANY LTD., 1925. 378p.: front., vignette on title page, 12 plates, head and tail pieces. Bound in brown cloth with pictorial cover.
CBD 823.912 DEL

2044 **DE LA MARE, WALTER JOHN.**
THE LORD FISH. (BY) WALTER DE LA MARE. Illustrated by REX WHISTLER. LONDON: FABER AND FABER (1933). 289p.: col. pictorial title page, 3 col. plates, headpieces, pictorial endpapers. Bound in purple cloth with pictorial cover and decorative spine. Includes 7 short stories.
CBD 823.912 DEL and C 823.912 DEL

2045 **DE LA MARE, WALTER JOHN.**
LUCY. BY WALTER DE LA MARE. Pictures by Hilda T. Miller. OXFORD: BASIL BLACKWELL, (192–?). 40p.: 4 plates, ill. Bound in grey paper, with coloured pictorial paper label on cover.
YSC 823.912 DEL

2046 **DE LA MARE, WALTER JOHN.**
MISS JEMIMA. By WALTER DE LA MARE. ILLUSTRATED BY ALEC BUCKELS. OXFORD: BASIL BLACKWELL, (192–?). 36p.: 3 plates. Bound in grey paper, with coloured pictorial paper label on cover.
YSC 823.912 DEL

2047 **DE LA MARE, WALTER JOHN.**
OLD JOE. By WALTER DE LA MARE. Pictures by C.T. Nightingale. OXFORD: BASIL BLACKWELL, (192–?). 29p.: 3 plates, ill. Bound in grey paper, with coloured pictorial paper label on cover.
YSC 823.912 DEL

2048 **DE LA MARE, WALTER JOHN.**
SEVEN SHORT STORIES BY WALTER DE LA MARE CHOSEN FROM The Connoisseur and Other Stories, Broomsticks and Other Tales, The Riddle and Other Stories. WITH ILLUSTRATIONS BY JOHN NASH. LONDON: FABER AND FABER LIMITED, 1931. 196p.: col. front., vignette on title page, 7 col. plates, tailpiece. Bound in red cloth with pictorial cover.
CBD 823.912 DEL

2049 **DE LA PASTURE, MRS. HENRY.**
THE UNLUCKY FAMILY, A BOOK FOR CHILDREN. BY MRS. HENRY DE LA PASTURE. ILLUSTRATED BY CHARLES E. BROCK. LONDON: HENRY FROWDE, HODDER AND STOUGHTON, 1914. 284p. + 16p. pub. cat.: col. front., 5 col. plates. Bound in brown cloth, with coloured pictorial cover and spine.
C 823.912 DEL

2049A **DICKENS, CHARLES.**
BARNABY RUDGE. RETOLD FOR CHILDREN BY ALICE F. JACKSON. ILLUSTRATED IN COLOUR BY F.M.B. BLAIKIE. LONDON: T.C. and E.C. JACK, (191–?). 165p.: col. front., col. pictorial title page, 7 col. plates. Bound in brown cloth with coloured pictorial label on cover. Collection includes a similar edition of A Tale of Two Cities.
C 823.7 DIC

2050 **DICKENS, CHARLES.**
CHILD CHARACTERS FROM DICKENS. Retold by L.L. Weedon with 6 Colour Plates and 70 Half-Tone illustrations by Arthur A. Dixon. LONDON: ERNEST NISTER. (190–?). 32p., col. front., 5 col. plates, 12 plates, ill., pictorial decorative endpapers. Bound in green cloth with coloured pictorial/decorative cover and spine.
C 823.8 WEE

2051 **DICKENS, CHARLES.**
The HOLLY-TREE and Other Christmas Stories. By CHARLES DICKENS. Illustrated by Ernest H. Shepard. LONDON: W. PARTRIDGE AND CO. LTD., (192–?). 192p.: col. front., decorated title page, 30 sepia plates. Bound in beige cloth, with pictorial cover and spine. Includes also: THE SEVEN POOR TRAVELLERS, THE POOR RELATION'S STORY and THE HAUNTED HOUSE.
C 823.8 DIC

2052 **DIXIE, FLORENCE.**
The Two Castaways or ADVENTURES IN PATAGONIA. BY LADY FLORENCE DIXIE. With Illustrations. NEW EDITION. LONDON: JOHN F. SHAW AND CO., (190–?). 384p. + 8p. pub. cat.: front., 4 plates by H. PETHERICK. Bound in green cloth with coloured pictorial cover and spine, with gilt edges.
C 823.8 DIX

2053 **DOYLE, ARTHUR CONAN.**
The Adventures of SHERLOCK HOLMES. BY SIR ARTHUR CONAN DOYLE. LONDON: JOHN MURRAY, 1917. 292p. Bound in red linson with pictorial paper jacket. Originally published 1892.
YSC 823.912 DOY

2054 **DOYLE, ARTHUR CONAN.**
THE LOST WORLD BEING AN ACCOUNT OF THE RECENT AMAZING ADVENTURES OF PROFESSOR E. CHALLENGER, LORD JOHN ROXTON, PROFESSOR SUMMERLEE AND MR. ED. MALONE OF THE "DAILY GAZETTE". BY SIR ARTHUR CONAN DOYLE. LONDON: JOHN MURRAY, 1934, reprinted 1960. V, 213p. Bound in red linson with pictorial paper jacket. Originally published 1912.
YSC 823.912 DOY

2055 **DOYLE, A. CONAN.**
THE RETURN OF SHERLOCK HOLMES. LONDON: HODDER AND STOUGHTON, (192–?). 316p. Bound in red cloth. Originally published 1905.
YSC 823.912 DOY

2056 **DOYLE, ARTHUR CONAN.**
SHERLOCK HOLMES. HIS ADVENTURES. MEMOIRS. RETURN. HIS LAST BOW AND CASE-BOOK. THE COMPLETE SHORT STORIES. BY SIR ARTHUR CONAN DOYLE. LONDON: JOHN MURRAY, 1928, reprinted 1971. XI, 1336p. Bound in red linson with blue pictorial paper jacket.
YSC 823.912 DOY

2057 **DUFFIN, EMMA S.**
THE TALE OF LI-PO AND SU-SU. Written and Illustrated by E.S. DUFFIN, "Blackbird". LONDON: THOMAS NELSON AND SONS LTD., (192–?). 96p.: col. front., ill. Bound in paper-covered boards, with coloured pictorial cover and spine.
C 823.912 DUF

2058 **DUNLOP, MARION WALLACE.**
THE MAGIC FRUIT GARDEN. BY MARION WALLACE DUNLOP. LONDON: ERNEST NISTER, (192–?). 95p.: front., vignette title page, 4 plates, ill. Bound in brown cloth, with coloured pictorial cover, and gilt top.
YSC 823.912 DUN

2059 **EDGEWORTH, MARIA.**
POPULAR TALES WITH AN INTRODUCTION BY ANNE THACKERAY RITCHIE. ILLUSTRATED BY CHRIS HAMMOND. LONDON: MACMILLAN AND CO., LIMITED, 1903. XIX, 508p. + 4p. pub. cat.: front. 22 plates, ill. Bound in red cloth with decorative cover and spine.
CBD 823.7 EDG

2060 **ELLIOT, GERALDINE.**
THE LONG GRASS WHISPERS. By GERALDINE ELLIOT. ILLUSTRATED BY SHEILA HAWKINS. LONDON: ROUTLEDGE AND KEGAN PAUL LTD., 1939. VII, 132p.: vignette title page, 15 plates, ill. Bound in grey linson with pictorial cover and endpapers.
YSC 823.912 ELL

2061 **ELLIS, EDWARD SYLVESTER.**
BLAZING ARROW. A TALE OF THE FRONTIER. BY EDWARD S. ELLIS. LONDON: CASSELL AND COMPANY LIMITED, 1901. IV, 289p. + 16p. pub. cat.: front., 3 plates by Brinkman. Bound in brown cloth, with coloured pictorial cover and decorative spine.
C 813.4 ELL

2062 **ELLIS, EDWARD SYLVESTER.**
THE CHIEFTAIN AND THE SCOUT. A TALE OF THE FRONTIER. BY EDWARD S. ELLIS. WITH FOUR ILLUSTRATIONS. LONDON: CASSELL AND COMPANY LIMITED, 1901. IV, 296p. + 4p. pub. cat.: front. by Stanley S. Wood, 3 plates by Brinkman. Bound in blue cloth, with coloured pictorial cover and decorative spine.
C 813.4 ELL

2062A **ELLIS, EDWARD SYLVESTER.**
COWMEN AND RUSTLERS. A STORY OF THE WYOMING CATTLE RANGES. BY EDWARD S. ELLIS. LONDON: CASSELL AND COMPANY LTD, (192–?). IV, 322p.: col. front. by Dudley Tennant, 4 plates. Bound in green cloth with pictorial cover and spine.
C 813.4 ELL

2062B **ELLIS, EDWARD SYLVESTER.**
The Cruise of the Deerfoot. BY EDWARD S. ELLIS.

LONDON: CASSELL AND COMPANY LTD (191–?). 285p.: col. front. by Dudley Tennant, 4 plates. Bound in yellow cloth with coloured pictorial cover and spine.
C 813.4 ELL

2063 **ELLIS, EDWARD SYLVESTER.**
DEERFOOT ON THE PRAIRIES. BY EDWARD S. ELLIS WITH A COLOUR FRONTISPIECE AND FOUR BLACK-AND-WHITE ILLUSTRATIONS. NINETEENTH THOUSAND. LONDON: CASSELL AND COMPANY LIMITED, (190–?). 366p.: col. front., 4 plates by J. Steeple Davis. Bound in blue cloth, with coloured pictorial cover and spine.
C 813.4 ELL

2064 **ELLIS, EDWARD SYLVESTER.**
FIRE, SNOW AND WATER, OR LIFE IN THE LONE LAND. BY EDWARD S. ELLIS. ILLUSTRATED BY LOUIS R. DOUGHERTY. LONDON: CASSELL AND COMPANY LIMITED, 1908. 324p. + 4p. ill. pub. cat.: front., 3 plates. Bound in green cloth, with coloured pictorial cover and spine.
C 823.912 ELL

2065 **ELLIS, EDWARD SYLVESTER.**
Lost in the Wilds. BY EDWARD S. ELLIS. WITH FOUR FULL-PAGE ILLUSTRATIONS. SEVENTEENTH THOUSAND. LONDON: CASSELL AND COMPANY LTD., 1910. 331p. + 8p. ill. pub. cat.: front., 3 plates. Bound in grey cloth, with coloured pictorial cover and spine.
C 813.4 ELL

2065A **ELLIS, EDWARD SYLVESTER.**
THE LOST TRAIL, BY EDWARD S. ELLIS. LONDON: CASSELL AND COMPANY LTD (191–?). 378p.: col. front. by Stanley S. Wood, 4 plates. Bound in green cloth with coloured pictorial cover and spine.
C 813.4 ELL

2066 **ERCKMANN-CHATRIAN.**
THE GREAT INVASION OF 1813–14; OR AFTER LEIPSIG. BY MM. ERCKMANN-CHATRIAN. LONDON: WARD, LOCK AND TYLER, (191–?). 284p. + 4p. pub. cat. Bound in pictorial paper cover. Beetens Library.
C 823.8 ERC

2067 **EVERETT-GREEN, EVELYN.**
FALLEN FORTUNES. Being the Adventures of a Gentleman of Quality in the Days of Queen Anne. BY E. EVERETT-GREEN. LONDON: THOMAS NELSON AND SONS, 1903. 386p.: front., 3 plates by W.H. Margetson. Bound in blue cloth, with coloured pictorial cover and spine.
C 823.912 EVE

2068 **EVERETT-GREEN, EVELYN.**
The Young Pioneers, or WITH LA SALLE ON THE MISSISSIPPI. BY EVELYN EVERETT-GREEN. LONDON: THOMAS NELSON AND SONS, 1907. 534p. + 8p. pub. cat.: additional portrait title page. Bound in brown cloth, with coloured pictorial cover and spine.
C 823.912 EVE

2069 **FARJEON, ELEANOR.**
And I Dance Mine Own Child. By ELEANOR FARJEON. OXFORD: BASIL BLACKWELL, (193–?). 32p.: 2 plates, ill. by Irene Mountfort. Bound in green cloth, with coloured pictorial paper label on cover.
YSC 823.912 FAR

2070 **FARJEON, ELEANOR.**
A BAD DAY FOR MARTHA. By ELEANOR FARJEON. Pictures by Eugenie Richards. OXFORD: BASIL BLACKWELL, (192–?). 29p.: 1 plate, ill. Bound in grey paper, with coloured pictorial paper label on cover.
YSC 823.912 FAR

2071 **FARJEON, ELEANOR.**
KALEIDOSCOPE. By ELEANOR FARJEON. LONDON: W. COLLINS SONS AND CO. LTD., 1928. VIII, 239p. Bound in blue cloth.
C 823.912 FAR

2072 **FARJEON, ELEANOR.**
THE KING'S DAUGHTER CRIES FOR THE MOON. By ELEANOR FARJEON. Illustrated by May Smith. OXFORD: BASIL BLACKWELL, (193–?). 31p.: 2 plates, ill. Bound in grey paper, with coloured pictorial paper label on cover.
YSC 823.912 FAR

2073 **FARJEON, ELEANOR.**
MARTIN PIPPIN IN THE APPLE-ORCHARD. By ELEANOR FARJEON. Illustrated by C.E. Brock, R.I. LONDON: W. COLLINS SONS AND CO. LTD., 1921. XVIII, 376p.: col. front., 4 col. plates. Bound in brown cloth, with pictorial cover and spine.
C 823.912 FAR

2073A **FARJEON, ELEANOR.**
PALADINS IN SPAIN by ELEANOR FARJEON. Illustrated by Katharine Tozer. LONDON: THOMAS NELSON AND SONS, LTD. 1937. 168p.: col. front., 5 plates. Bound in green cloth. Horizon Books.
C 823.912 FAR

2073B **FARJEON, ELEANOR.**
Perkin the Pedlar, by Eleanor Farjeon with illustrations by Clare Leighton. LONDON: FABER AND FABER LIMITED, 1932. 206p.: col. front., 7 col. plates, 21 plates, ill. Bound in blue cloth with pictorial covers.
C 823.912 FAR

2074 **FARJEON, ELEANOR.**
TOM COBBLE. By ELEANOR FARJEON. ILLUSTRATED BY M. DOBSON. OXFORD: BASIL BLACKWELL, (192–?). 43p.: 6 plates, ill. Bound in grey paper, with coloured pictorial paper label on cover.
YSC 823.912 FAR

2075 **FARJEON, ELEANOR.**
WESTWOODS. By ELEANOR FARJEON. Pictures by May Smith. OXFORD: BASIL BLACKWELL, (193–?). 32p.: 4 plates, ill. Bound in green paper, with coloured pictorial paper label on cover.
YSC 823.912 FAR

2076 **FARJEON, ELEANOR.**
THE WONDERFUL KNIGHT. By ELEANOR FARJEON. Pictures by Doris Pailthorpe. OXFORD: BASIL BLACKWELL, (192–?). 31p.: 3 plates, ill. Bound in beige paper, with coloured pictorial paper label on cover.
YSC 823.912 FAR

2077 **FARRAR, FREDERIC WILLIAM.**
ST. WINIFRED'S; OR, THE WORLD OF SCHOOL. BY FREDERIC W. FARRAR. LONDON: A. AND C. BLACK, 1904. IX, 536p. + 16p. ill. pub. cat.: front. by W.J. Hennessy. Vignette title page. Bound in blue cloth, with coloured pictorial cover and spine. Originally published 1862.
YSC 823.8 FAR

2078 **FARRAR FREDERIC WILLIAM.**
THE THREE HOMES. BY FREDERIC W. FARRAR. WITH A FRONTISPIECE IN COLOUR AND FOUR BLACK-AND-WHITE PLATES. LONDON: CASSELL AND COMPANY LIMITED, 1911. VIII, 389p.: col. front., 4 plates by Stanley L. Wood. Bound in green cloth, with coloured pictorial cover and spine.
C 823.8 FAR

2079 **FENN, GEORGE MANVILLE.**
BLUE JACKETS, OR THE LOG OF THE TEASER. BY G. MANVILLE FENN. NEW EDITION. ILLUSTRATED IN COLOUR BY W.B. HANDFORTH. LONDON: HENRY FROWDE, HODDER AND STOUGHTON, (191–?). 284p. + 16p. pub. cat.: col. front., 3 col. plates. Bound in red cloth, with coloured pictorial labels on cover and spine.
C 823.8 FEN

2080 **FENN, GEORGE MANVILLE.**
CHARGE! A Story of BRITON AND . . . BOER . . . BY G. MANVILLE FENN. ILLUSTRATED BY W.H.C. GROOME. LONDON: W. & R. CHAMBERS, LIMITED, 1900. 391p. + 32p. ill. pub. cat.: front., 7 plates. Bound in red cloth with coloured pictorial cover and spine.
C 823.9 FEN

2081 **FENN, GEORGE MANVILLE.**
CORMORANT CRAG, A Tale of the Smuggling Days. BY GEO. MANVILLE FENN. ILLUSTRATED BY W. RAINEY, R.I. THIRD EDITION. LONDON: S.W. PARTRIDGE AND CO. (190–?). 416p. + 32p. pub. cat.: front., 5 plates, ill. Bound in brown cloth with coloured pictorial cover and spine.
C 823.8 FEN

2081A **FENN, GEORGE MANVILLE.**
DEAD MAN'S LAND. Being the Voyage to Zimbambangwe of certain and uncertain Blacks and Whites. By G. Manville Fenn. LONDON: S.W. PARTRIDGE AND CO., (1906). 410p. + 32p. pub. cat.: col. front., 7 col. plates. Bound in brown cloth with coloured pictorial cover and spine.
C 823.8 FEN

2082 **FENN, GEORGE MANVILLE.**
DEVON BOYS, A Tale of the North Shore. BY GEO. MANVILLE FENN. With Illustrations in Colour by Gordon Browne, R.I. LONDON: BLACKIE AND SON LIMITED, (190–?). 384p.: col. front., 3 col. plates. Bound in red cloth, with decorative cover and spine.
C 823.8 FEN

2083 **FENN, GEORGE MANVILLE.**
Dick o' the Fens, A Tale of the Great East Swamp. BY G. MANVILLE FENN. ILLUSTRATED BY FRANK DADD. LONDON: BLACKIE AND SON LIMITED, 1906. 383p. + 16p. pub. cat.: front., 11 plates. Bound in red cloth with coloured pictorial cover and spine.
C 823.8 FEN

2084 **FENN, GEORGE MANVILLE.**
The Golden Magnet, A Tale of the Land of the Incas. BY GEO. MANVILLE FENN. ILLUSTRATED. LONDON: BLACKIE AND SON LIMITED, (190–?). 384p.: col. front., 4 plates. Bound in red cloth with coloured pictorial cover and spine.
C 823.8 FEN

2085 **FENN, GEORGE MANVILLE.**
IN HONOUR'S CAUSE, A Tale of the Days of George the First. BY GEO. MANVILLE FENN. ILLUSTRATIONS BY LANCELOT SPEED. LONDON: S.W. PARTRIDGE & CO., (190–?). 416p. + 28p. pub. cat.: front., 3 plates, ill. Bound in red cloth with coloured pictorial cover and spine.
C 823.8 FEN

2085A **FENN, GEORGE MANVILLE.**
King Robert's Page. By G. Manville Fenn. Illustrated by G.C. Glover. LONDON: ERNEST NISTER, 1900. 72p., front., 4 plates, ill. Bound in cream cloth with pictorial paper covers.
C 823.8 FEN

2085B **FENN, GEORGE MANVILLE.**
The King's Sons. BY G. MANVILLE FENN. ILLUSTRATED BY T.H. ROBINSON. LONDON: ERNEST NISTER, 1901. 48p.: front., 3 plates, ill. Bound in blue cloth with coloured pictorial cover.
C 823.8 FEN

2086 **FENN, GEORGE MANVILLE.**
MARCUS: THE YOUNG CENTURION. BY G. MANVILLE FENN. ILLUSTRATED BY ARCHIBALD WEBB. LONDON: ERNEST NISTER, (191–?). 392p. + 8p. pub. cat.: front., 7 plates. Bound in green cloth, with coloured pictorial cover and spine.
C 823.8 FEN

2087 **FENN, GEORGE MANVILLE.**
NAT THE NATURALIST or, A Boy's Adventures in the Eastern Seas. BY GEO. MANVILLE FENN. WITH EIGHT FULL-PAGE ILLUSTRATIONS BY GORDON BROWNE. NEW EDITION. LONDON: BLACKIE AND SON LIMITED, 1905. 320p. + 32p. ill. pub. cat.: front., 7 plates. Bound in red cloth with coloured pictorial cover and spine.
C 823.8 FEN

2088 **FENN, GEORGE MANVILLE.**
NEPHEW JACK, HIS CRUISE FOR HIS UNCLE'S CRAZE. BY G. MANVILLE FENN. Illustrated by W.S. Stacey. LONDON: SOCIETY FOR PROMOTING CHRISTIAN KNOWLEDGE, (190–?). 508p. + 1p. pub. cat.: front., 4 plates. Bound in brown cloth, with coloured pictorial cover and spine.
C 823.912 FEN

2089 **FENN, GEORGE MANVILLE.**
THE SILVER CAÑON, A TALE OF THE WESTERN PLAINS. BY G. MANVILLE FENN. LONDON: SAMPSON LOW, MARSTON, AND COMPANY, LTD., (190–?). 318p. Bound in red cloth with pictorial design on cover and spine.
C 823.8 FEN

2090 **FENN, GEORGE MANVILLE.**
"TENTION!" A STORY OF BOY-LIFE DURING THE PENINSULAR WAR. BY G. MANVILLE FENN. WITH EIGHT ILLUSTRATIONS BY C.M. SHELDON. LONDON: W. AND R. CHAMBERS, 1906. 411p. + 48p. ill. pub. cat.: front., 7 plates. Bound in red cloth with coloured pictorial cover and spine.
C 823.8 FEN

2091 **FENN, GEORGE MANVILLE.**
TRAPPED BY MALAYS, A TALE OF BAYONET AND KRIS. By G. MANVILLE FENN. WITH ILLUSTRATIONS by Steven Spurrier. LONDON: W. & R. CHAMBERS, LIMITED, 1907. 420p.: front., 7 plates. Bound in red cloth with coloured pictorial cover and spine.
C 823.8 FEN

2092 **FENN, GEORGE MANVILLE.**
TRAPPER DAN, A Story of the Bushwoods. BY GEO. MANVILLE FENN. WITH EIGHT ILLUSTRATIONS BY WAL PAGET. LONDON: S.W. PARTRIDGE AND CO. (190–?). 424p. + 32p. pub. cat.: front., 7 plates. Bound in red cloth with coloured pictorial cover and spine.
C 823.8 FEN

2093 **FENN, GEORGE MANVILLE.**
UNCLE BART, THE TALE OF A TYRANT. BY G. MANVILLE FENN. Illustrated by W.S. Stacey. LONDON: SOCIETY FOR PROMOTING CHRISTIAN KNOWLEDGE, (190–?). 502p. + 8p. pub. cat.: front., 4 plates. Bound in brown cloth with coloured pictorial cover and decorative spine.
C 823.8 FEN

2094 **FENN, GEORGE MANVILLE.**
WALSH THE WONDER-WORKER. BY GEORGE MANVILLE FENN. EIGHT ILLUSTRATIONS BY W.H.C. GROOME, R.B.A. LONDON: W. & R. CHAMBERS, LIMITED, 1903. VI, 407p.: front., 7 plates. Bound in brown cloth with pictorial cover and spine.
C 823.8 FEN

2095 **FINDLATER, MARY.**
CROSSRIGGS. (BY) MARY AND JANE FINDLATER. LONDON: T. NELSON AND SONS, (193–?). 380p. + 2p. pub. cat.: front. by W.E. Hebster, decorative title page. Bound in red cloth.
YSC 823.912 FIN

2096 **FINDLATER, MARY.**
PENNY MONEYPENNY. BY MARY AND JANE FINDLATER. LONDON: THOMAS NELSON AND SONS LTD., (192–?). 384p. Bound in blue cloth, with decorative spine.
YSC 823.912 FIN

2097 **FINNEMORE, EMILY PEARSON.**
THE ORDEAL OF SUSANNAH VENTHAM. BY EMILY PEARSON FINNEMORE. ILLUSTRATED BY HAROLD PIFFARD. LONDON: SOCIETY FOR PROMOTING CHRISTIAN KNOWLEDGE, (190–?). 381p. + 16p. pub. cat.: col. front., 3 col. plates. Bound in blue cloth, with coloured pictorial cover and spine.
C 823.912 FIN

2098 **FINNEMORE, JOHN.**
HIS FIRST TERM, A STORY OF SLAPTON SCHOOL. By JOHN FINNEMORE. WITH EIGHT COLOURED ILLUSTRATIONS. By W.H.C. Groome. LONDON: W. AND R. CHAMBERS LIMITED, (191–?). VIII, 422p.: col. front., 7 col. plates. Bound in brown cloth, with coloured pictorial cover and spine.
C 823.8 FIN

2099 **FINNEMORE, JOHN.**
Teddy Lester's Schooldays. BY J. FINNEMORE. WITH SIX COLOURED ILLUSTRATIONS by W. Rainey. LONDON: W. AND R. CHAMBERS, (191–?). VIII, 376p.: col. front., 5 col. plates. Bound in red cloth, with coloured pictorial cover and spine.
C 823.8 FIN

2100 **FINNEMORE, JOHN.**
THREE SCHOOL CHUMS. By JOHN FINNEMORE. WITH SIX ILLUSTRATIONS by Harold Copping. LONDON: W. AND R. CHAMBERS LIMITED, (190–?). VIII, 318p.: front., 5 plates. Bound in grey cloth, with coloured pictorial cover and spine.
C 823.912 FIN

2101 **FINNY, VIOLET G.**
A DAUGHTER OF ERIN. BY VIOLET G. FINNY. WITH FOUR ILLUSTRATIONS BY G. DEMAIN HAMMOND. LONDON: BLACKIE AND SON, LIMITED, (190–?). IV, 224p. + 32p. ill. pub. cat.: front., 3 plates. Bound in grey cloth with decorative coloured cover and spine.
C 823.8 FIN

2102 **FLEMING, W.M.**
THE HUNTED PICCANINNIES. By W.M. FLEMING. ILLUSTRATED BY KAY EDMUNDS. LONDON: J.M. DENT AND SONS LTD., 1927. V, 185p.: col. front., vignette title page, 6 col. plates, ill. Bound in grey cloth, with coloured pictorial cover and spine.
C 823.912 FLE

2103 **FLETCHER, JOSEPH SMITH.**
Anthony Everton. BY J.S. FLETCHER. BEING THE PLAIN STORY OF AN EPISODE IN THE LIFE OF THOMAS WENTWORTH, EARL OF STRAFFORD, LORD PRESIDENT OF THE COUNCIL OF THE NORTH . . . WITH FRONTISPIECE BY D. MURRAY SMITH. LONDON: W. AND R. CHAMBERS LIMITED, 1903. 205p. + 2p. pub. cat.: front. Bound in blue cloth, with coloured pictorial cover and spine.
C 823.912 FLE

2104 **FLETCHER, JOSEPH SMITH.**
In the Days of Drake. Being the Adventures of HUMPHREY SALKELD . . . RETOLD BY J.S. FLETCHER. ILLUSTRATED BY W.S. STACEY. LONDON: BLACKIE AND SON LIMITED, (191–?). 192p.: front., 2 plates. Bound in grey cloth, with coloured pictorial cover and spine.
C 823.8 FLE

2105 **FORDE, H.A.**
ACROSS TWO SEAS: A New Zealand Tale. BY H.A. FORDE. ILLUSTRATED. LONDON: WELLS GARDNER, DARTON, AND CO., 1902. VI, 188p. + 4p. pub. cat.: front., 10 plates. Bound in blue cloth, with coloured pictorial cover and spine.
C 823.912 FOR

2106 **FORESTER, F.B.**
HARTER'S RANCH. BY F.B. FORESTER. ILLUSTRATED BY HAROLD PIFFARD. LONDON: SOCIETY FOR PROMOTING CHRISTIAN KNOWLEDGE, (190–?). 252p. + 16p. pub. cat.: front., 2 plates. Bound in beige cloth with coloured pictorial cover and spine.
C 823.8 FOR

2107 **FRASER, CHELSEA CURTIS.**
AROUND THE WORLD IN TEN DAYS. BY CHELSEA CURTIS FRASER. LONDON: THOMAS NELSON AND SONS, LTD., (192–?). IX, 310p.: col. front., 3 col. plates by Howard L. Hastings, 1 plate + 1 map. Bound in grey cloth, with coloured pictorial cover and spine.
C 823.912 FRA

2108 **FREEBORN, M.E.**
SENANIZA THE FAITHFUL KAFFIR, A Story of South African Life. BY MRS. A.C.R. FREEBORN. ILLUSTRATIONS BY GORDON BROWNE. THIRD EDITION. LONDON: THE SUNDAY SCHOOL UNION, (191–?). 96p.: front., 1 plate, ill. Bound in blue cloth, with coloured decorative cover and spine.
C 823.912 FRE

2108A **FYLEMAN, ROSE.**
THE RAINBOW CAT AND OTHER STORIES. BY ROSE FYLEMAN. SECOND EDITION. LONDON: METHUEN AND CO. LTD., 1924. 119p.: Bound in yellow cloth with decorative cover.
C 823.912 FYL

2109 **GEORGE, SIDNEY CHARLES.**
THE RED GODDESS. By FLIGHT LIEUT. S.C. GEORGE. LONDON: FREDERICK WARNE AND CO. LTD., 1939. 256p.: front. Bound in orange cloth, with coloured pictorial paper jacket.
C 823.912 GEO

2110 **GERARD, MORICE.**
PRINCE KARL, A Story of the Black Forest. BY MORICE GERARD. LONDON: THOMAS NELSON AND SONS, 1900. 172p. + 4p. pub. cat.: front., additional vignette title page. Bound in blue cloth, with pictorial cover and decorative spine.
C 823.912 GER

2111 **GIBBON, FREDERICK P.**
The Disputed V.C., A Tale of the Indian Mutiny. BY FREDERICK P. GIBBON. ILLUSTRATED BY STANLEY L. WOOD. NEW EDITION. LONDON: BLACKIE AND SON LIMITED, 1909. 352p. + 16p. pub. cat.: front., 5 plates. Bound in red cloth, with coloured pictorial cover and spine.
C 823.912 GIB

2112 **GIBERNE, AGNES.**
GWENDOLINE. BY AGNES GIBERNE. With three illustrations by J. Finnemore. LONDON: RELIGIOUS TRACT SOCIETY, (190–?). 249p. + 10p. pub. cat.: front., 2 plates. Bound in blue cloth, with coloured pictorial cover and decorative spine.
C 823.8 GIB

2113 **GIBERNE, AGNES.**
SWEETBRIAR, DOINGS IN PRIORSTHORPE MAGNA. BY AGNES GIBERNE. LONDON: JAMES NISBET AND CO. LIMITED, (190–?). 332p. + 16p. pub. cat.: front. Bound in green cloth, with coloured decorative cover and spine.
C 823.8 GIB

2114 **GILLIE, E.A.**
BARBARA IN BRITTANY. BY E.A. GILLIE. Illustrated by FRANK ADAMS. LONDON: COLLINS' CLEAR TYPE PRESS, (190–?). 192p. + 16p. pub. cat.: col. front., col. vignette on title page, 3 col. plates, col. pictorial endpapers. Bound in blue cloth, with coloured pictorial cover and spine and gilt edges.
C 823.912 GIL

2115 **GILSON, CHARLES.**
ACROSS THE CAMEROONS, A Story of War and Adventure. BY CAPTAIN CHARLES GILSON. ILLUSTRATED BY ARCH. WEBB. LONDON: BLACKIE AND SON LIMITED, (191–?). 254p.: col. front., 4 plates. Bound in green cloth, with coloured pictorial cover and spine.
C 823.912 GIL

2116 **GILSON, CHARLES.**
A Motor-Scout in Flanders, Or, Held by the Enemy. BY CAPTAIN CHARLES GILSON. Illustrated by F. Gillett. LONDON: BLACKIE AND SON LIMITED, (192–?). 255p.: col. front., 4 sepia plates. Bound in olive green with pictorial cover and spine.
C 823.912 GIL

2116A **GILSON, CHARLES.**
THE PIRATE AEROPLANE. BY CAPTAIN GILSON. ILLUSTRATED IN COLOUR BY CHRISTOPHER CLARK, R.I. LONDON: O.U.P. (1920). 327p.: col. front., 5 col. plates. Bound in blue cloth with coloured pictorial cover and spine. Originally published 1913.
C 823.912 GIL

2117 **GILSON, CHARLES.**
THE RACE ROUND THE WORLD. Being the Account of the Contest for the £100,000 Prize offered by the Combined Newspaper League, of the Invention of Methylite, and certain passages in the life of Mr. Wang. BY CAPTAIN CHARLES GILSON. ILLUSTRATIONS BY CYRUS CUNEO. LONDON: HENRY FROWDE, HODDER AND STOUGHTON, 1914. 283p. + 4p. pub. cat.: col. front., 5 col. plates + 1 map. Bound in blue cloth, with coloured pictorial cover and spine.
C 823.912 GIL

2117A **GILSON, CHARLES.**
SUBMARINE U93. A Tale of the Great War, of German Spies, and Submarines, of Naval Warfare and all manner of Adventures. BY CAPTAIN CHARLES GILSON. LONDON: "THE BOY'S OWN PAPER OFFICE" (1916). 295p.: col. front., col. title page with vignette, 6 col. plates by George Soper. Bound in beige cloth with pictorial cover and spine.
823.912 GIL

2117B **GILSON, CHARLES.**
The Treasure of the Red Tribe. By Major Charles Gilson. With Four Illustrations in Colour and Black-and-White by JOHN DE WALTON. LONDON: CASSELL AND COMPANY LIMITED. 1926. 216p.: col. front., 3 plates. Bound in brown cloth with coloured pictorial paper label.
C 833.912 GIL

2118 **GOLDEN GORSE.**
MOORLAND MOUSIE. By GOLDEN GORSE. Plates Drawn by LIONEL EDWARDS. LONDON: COUNTRY LIFE LTD., 1929. VIII, 106p.: front., 15 plates. Bound in green cloth and brown paper-covered boards.
C 823.912 GOL

2119 **GOLDEN GORSE.**
OLDER MOUSIE. By GOLDEN GORSE. Plates by LIONEL EDWARDS. LONDON: COUNTRY LIFE LTD., 1934. VIII, 102p.: front., 15 plates. Bound in green cloth.
C 823.912 GOL

2120 **GOLDING, HARRY.**
200 DAYS. BY HARRY GOLDING. WITH 48 COLOUR PLATES BY MARGARET W. TARRANT. SECOND EDITION. LONDON: WARD, LOCK AND CO. LIMITED, (191–?). 334p. + 10p. pub. cat.: col. front., 43 col. plates, col. pictorial endpapers. Bound in brown cloth, with coloured pictorial paper label on cover.
C 823.912 GOL

2121 **GRAHAME, KENNETH.**
THE GOLDEN AGE. BY KENNETH GRAHAME. ILLUSTRATED BY MAXFIELD PARRISH. LONDON: JOHN LANE, THE BODLEY HEAD, 1900. 252p. + 2p. pub. cat.: front., pictorial title page, 17 plates. Bound in green cloth, with coloured decorative cover. Originally published 1895.
C 823.912 GRA

2122 **Another copy.**
With Illustrations and Decorations by ERNEST H. SHEPARD. LONDON: THE BODLEY HEAD, fourth edition, 1930. X, 176p.: front., 10 plates, ill. Bound in grey linson with green and black pictorial jacket.
YSC 823.912 GRA

2123 **Another copy.**
With nineteen illustrations by R.J. Enraght-Moony. LONDON: JOHN LANE, THE BODLEY HEAD, 1915. 243p., col. front.: 18 col. plates. Rebound in blue cloth.

2124 **Another copy.**
LONDON: THOMAS NELSON AND SONS, (192–?). 287p. + 1p. pub. cat.: front. Bound in blue cloth with decorative cover and spine, and gilt top.
YSC 823.912 GRA

2125 **GRAHAME, KENNETH.**
THE HEADSWOMAN. By KENNETH GRAHAME. With Illustrations in Colour and Woodcuts by MARCIA LANE FOSTER. LONDON: JOHN LANE THE BODLEY HEAD LIMITED, 1921. 53p.: col. front., 7 col. plates, headpieces. Bound in cream cloth and green decorative paper. Originally published 1898.
CBD 823.8 GRA

2126 **GRAHAME, KENNETH.**
The Kenneth Grahame Book: THE GOLDEN AGE, DREAM DAYS, THE WIND IN THE WILLOWS. LONDON: METHUEN AND CO. LTD., 1932. VIII, 402p.: front. port. Bound in red cloth.
C 823.8 GRA

2127 **GRAHAME, KENNETH.**
The Reluctant Dragon and other stories from THE GOLDEN AGE and DREAM DAYS by KENNETH GRAHAME. LONDON: METHUEN AND CO. LTD., 1936. VII, 152p. Bound in green linson with pictorial cover.
YSC 823.912 GRA

2128 **GRAHAME, KENNETH.**
THE WIND IN THE WILLOWS. BY KENNETH GRAHAME. WITH A FRONTISPIECE BY GRAHAM ROBERTSON. Second Edition. LONDON: METHUEN AND CO., 1908. 302p.: front. Bound in blue cloth with pictorial cover and spine, with gilt top. Originally published 1908.
C 823.912 GRA

2129 **GRAHAME-WHITE, CLAUDE.**
The Invisible War-Plane. A Tale of Air Adventure in the Great Campaign. BY CLAUDE GRAHAME-WHITE AND HARRY HARPER. Illustrated by John de G. Bryan. LONDON: BLACKIE AND SON LIMITED (1915). 3p. + 272p.: 5 sepia plates. Bound in beige cloth with coloured pictorial cover and spine.
C 823.912 GRA

2130 **GRIFFITH, HELEN SHERMAN.**
A WILFUL GIRL. BY HELEN SHERMAN GRIFFITH. LONDON: THE PILGRIM PRESS, (190–?). VIII, 279p.: col. front. by Savile Lumley, 3 plates by Ida Waugh. Bound in blue cloth, with coloured pictorial cover and spine.
C 823.912 GRI

2132 **GROVES, JOHN PERCY-.**
The War of the Axe, Adventures in South Africa. BY J. PERCY-GROVES. ILLUSTRATED BY JOHN SCHÖNBERG. NEW EDITION. LONDON: BLACKIE AND SON LIMITED, 1904. 224p. + 32p. ill. pub. cat.: front., 2 plates. Bound in red cloth, with coloured pictorial cover and spine.
C 823.8 GRO

2133 **HADATH, GUNBY.**
THE OUTLAWS OF ST. MARTYN'S, OR THE SCHOOL

ON THE DOWNS. BY GUNBY HADATH. LONDON: S.W. PARTRIDGE AND CO., 1931. 384p.: col. front., 4 plates by Arch. Webb. Bound in green cloth, with pictorial cover and spine. Originally published 1915.
C 823.912 HAD

2134 **HAGGARD, HENRY RIDER.**
Morning Star. BY H. RIDER HAGGARD. LONDON: CASSELL AND COMPANY LTD., 1912. X, 308p. Bound in red cloth.
YSC 823.8 HAG

2135 **HAGGARD, HENRY RIDER.**
SHE AND ALLAN. By H. RIDER HAGGARD. WITH EIGHT ILLUSTRATIONS BY MAURICE GREIFFENHAGEN, A.R.A. THIRD EDITION. LONDON: HUTCHINSON AND CO., (192–?). 303p.: front., 7 plates. Bound in red cloth. Originally published 1921.
YSC 823.8 HAG

2136 **HAGGARD, HENRY RIDER.**
SWALLOW, A TALE OF THE GREAT TREK. BY H. RIDER HAGGARD. NEW IMPRESSION. LONDON: LONGMANS, GREEN AND CO., 1901. VIII, 348p.: front., 7 plates, by Maurice Greiffenhagen. Bound in red cloth. Originally published 1899. THE SILVER LIBRARY.
YSC 823.8 HAG

2137 **HAGGARD, HENRY RIDER.**
Wisdom's Daughter, The Life and Love Story of She-Who-Must-be-Obeyed. By H. RIDER HAGGARD. SECOND EDITION. LONDON: HUTCHINSON AND CO., (192–?). 288p. Bound in green cloth. Originally published 1923.
YSC 823.8 HAG

2138 **HALES, ALFRED GREENWOOD.**
TELEGRAPH DICK, A LONDON LAD'S ADVENTURES IN AFRICA. BY A.G. HALES. LONDON: CASSELL AND COMPANY LIMITED, 1907. VIII, 244p. + 8p. ill. pub. cat.: front., 7 plates by F.W. Boyington. Bound in grey cloth, with coloured pictorial cover and spine.
C 823.912 HAL

2139 **HANDASYDE.**
THE FOUR GARDENS, BY HANDASYDE. ILLUSTRATED BY CHARLES ROBINSON. LONDON: WILLIAM HEINEMANN, 1912. 161p.: col. front., pictorial title page, 7 col. plates, decorative initials and tailpieces, pictorial endpapers. Bound in purple cloth with decorative cover and spine.
CBD 823.912 HAN

2140 **HARDING, EMILY GRACE.**
A NOBLE SACRIFICE. BY EMILY GRACE HARDING. WITH ILLUSTRATIONS BY T. EYRE MACKLIN. FORTY-THIRD THOUSAND. LONDON: THE WALTER SCOTT PUBLISHING CO. LTD., (190–?). 387p. + 16p. pub. cat.: front., 4 plates. Bound in red cloth, with coloured decorative cover and spine, and gilt edges. Originally published 1897.
C 823.8 HAR

2141 **HARKER, L. ALLEN.**
A ROMANCE OF THE NURSERY. WRITTEN BY L. ALLEN HARKER. ILLUSTRATIONS BY KATHARINE M. ROBERTS. LONDON: JOHN LANE, THE BODLEY HEAD, 1903. XII, 333p. + 2p. pub. cat.: front., 7 plates. Bound in red cloth, with embossed decorative cover and spine.
C 823.912 HAR

2143 **HARRISON, FREDERICK.**
WYNPORT COLLEGE, A STORY OF SCHOOL LIFE. BY FREDERICK HARRISON. WITH EIGHT ILLUSTRATIONS BY HAROLD COPPING. LONDON: BLACKIE AND SON LIMITED, 1900. 351p. + 32p. ill. pub. cat.: (front. missing), 7 plates. Bound in green cloth, with coloured pictorial cover and spine.
C 823.912 HAR

2144 **HART, ELIZABETH ANNA.**
DAISY'S DILEMMAS. BY MRS. HART. ILLUSTRATED. LONDON: CASSELL AND COMPANY LIMITED, 1900. 224p. + 24p. ill. pub. cat.: front., 5 plates by W.S. Stacey. Bound in brown cloth, with coloured pictorial cover and spine.
C 823.912 HAR

2144A **(HART, ELIZABETH ANNA).**
THE RUNAWAY. A Victorian Story for the Young. Reissued with Illustrations by G. RAVERAT. LONDON: GERALD DUCKWORTH AND CO., LTD, 1936. VI, 209p.: front., vignette on title page, ill. Bound in blue cloth with vignette on cover. Originally published 1872.
M 823 HAR CHILDREN'S COLLECTION

2145 **HASSALL, JOHN.**
CHUMS. BY JOHN HASSALL. (LONDON): THOMAS NELSON AND SONS, (190–?). Pictorial title page, 24 col. plates by John Hassall. Bound in paper-covered boards, with coloured pictorial cover.
C 823.912 HAS

2146 **HAVERFIELD, ELEANOR LUISA.**
Queensland Cousins. By E.L. HAVERFIELD. LONDON: THOMAS NELSON AND SONS, LTD., (190–?). 238p.: col. front., 1 col. plate, by A.H. Jenkins. Bound in brown cloth, with coloured pictorial paper label on cover.
YSC 823.8 HAV

2147 **HAVERFIELD, ELEANOR LUISA.**
STANHOPE: A Romance of the Days of Cromwell. BY E.L. HAVERFIELD. LONDON: THOMAS NELSON AND SONS, (190–?). 351p. + 3p. pub. cat.: col. front., 3 col. plates by R.H. Bound in brown cloth, with coloured pictorial cover and spine. NELSON'S GIRLS' LIBRARY.
C 823.8 HAV

2148 **HAYCRAFT, MARGARET S.**
"LIKE A LITTLE CANDLE", OR Bertrande's Influence. BY MARGARET S. HAYCRAFT. NEW EDITION. LONDON: S.W. PARTRIDGE AND CO., (190–?). 160p. + 32p. pub. cat.: front., vignette on title page, 4 plates. Bound in green cloth, with coloured pictorial cover and decorative spine.
C 823.8 HAY

2148A **HAYENS, HERBERT.**
BESET BY SAVAGES. BY HERBERT HAYENS. LONDON: JAMES NISBET AND CO. LIMITED, 1910. 336p.: col. front., 3 plates by Arthur Twidle. Bound in blue cloth with coloured pictorial paper labels on cover and spine.
C 823.912 HAY

2149 **HAYENS, HERBERT.**
THE BRITISH LEGION, A TALE OF THE CARLIST WAR. BY HERBERT HAYENS. LONDON: THOMAS NELSON AND SONS, (191–?). 413p. + 4p. pub. cat.: col. front., 3 col. plates. Bound in green cloth, with decorative cover and spine.
C 823.912 HAY

2149A **HAYENS, HERBERT.**
THE GAYTON SCHOLARSHIP. A SCHOOL STORY. BY HERBERT HAYENS. LONDON: THOMAS NELSON AND SONS, 1911. 204p. + 4p. pub. cat.: col. front. by E.H. Stewart. Bound in blue cloth with coloured pictorial cover and spine.
C 823.912 HAY

2149B **HAYENS, HERBERT.**
THE MYSTERY OF THE AMAZON. BY HERBERT HAYENS. ILLUSTRATED BY ARCHIBALD WEBB. LONDON: COLLINS CLEAR TYPE PRESS, (1919). 318p. + 2p. pub. cat.: col. front., 2 col. plates. Bound in blue cloth with coloured pictorial cover and spine.
C 823.912 HAY

2150 **HAYENS, HERBERT.**
One of The Red Shirts, A Story of Garibaldi's Men. By Herbert Hayens. LONDON: JAMES NISBET AND CO. LIMITED, (190–?). VI, 368p. + 32p. pub. cat.: front., 3 plates, by Matt. B. Hewerdine. Bound in green cloth, with embossed decorative cover and spine, and gilt edges.
C 823.912 HAY

2151 **HAYENS, HERBERT.**
"PLAY UP, GREYS!" BY HERBERT HAYENS. ILLUSTRATED BY GORDON BROWNE, R.I. LONDON: COLLINS' CLEAR-TYPE PRESS, (191–?). 318p. + 2p. pub. cat.: col. front., 2 plates. Bound in blue cloth, with coloured pictorial cover and spine.
C 823.912 HAY

2152 **HAYENS, HERBERT.**
"PLAY UP, KINGS!" BY HERBERT HAYENS. ILLUSTRATED BY GORDON BROWNE, R.I. LONDON: COLLINS' CLEAR-TYPE PRESS, (191–?). 328p. + 8p. pub. cat.: col. front., 2 plates. Bound in blue cloth, with coloured pictorial cover and spine.
C 823.912 HAY

2152A **HAYENS, HERBERT.**
THE TIGER OF THE PAMPAS. LONDON: THOMAS NELSON AND SONS, LTD., (193–?). 373p.: front.: 3 plates. Bound in buff cloth with coloured pictorial cover and spine.
C 823.912 HAY

2152B **HAYENS, HERBERT.**
A Vanished Nation. By HERBERT HAYENS WITH SIX ILLUSTRATIONS BY W.B. WOLLEN, R.I. LONDON: THOMAS NELSON AND SONS, 1907. 412p. + 4p. pub. cat.: front., additional vignette title page, 4 plates. Bound in green cloth with pictorial cover and spine.
C 823.912 HAY

2153 **HAYENS, HERBERT.**
WITH SWORD AND SHIP. BY HERBERT HAYENS. WITH COLOURED ILLUSTRATIONS AND NUMEROUS BLACK AND WHITE ENGRAVINGS. LONDON: COLLINS' CLEAR-TYPE PRESS, (190–?). 416p. + 32p. pub. cat.: col. front., 6 double col. plates. 2 double plates, 7 plates. Bound in blue cloth, with coloured pictorial cover and spine.
C 823.912 HAY

2153

2154 **HAYENS, HERBERT.**
Ye Mariners of England. A Boy's Book of the Navy. By HERBERT HAYENS. LONDON: THOMAS NELSON AND SONS, 1908. 328p. + 8p. pub. cat.: front., 5 plates, 4 by Arch. Webb. Bound in blue cloth, with coloured pictorial cover and spine. "ACTIVE SERVICE" SERIES.
C 823.912 HAY

2155 **HEDDLE, ETHEL F.**
Strangers in the Land. BY ETHEL F. HEDDLE. ILLUSTRATED EDITION, with Eight Full-Page Plates by HAROLD COPPING. LONDON: BLACKIE AND SON LIMITED, 1904. X, 383p.: front., 7 plates. Bound in green cloth, with coloured pictorial cover and spine.
C 823.912 HED

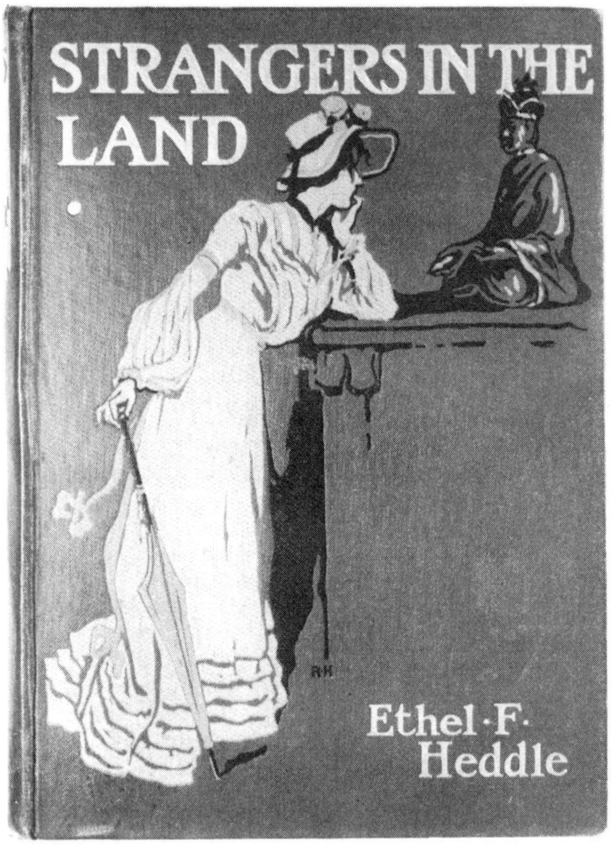

2155

2156 **HEGAN, ALICE CALDWELL,** *(afterwards Rice)*.
MRS. WIGGS OF THE CABBAGE PATCH. BY ALICE CALDWELL HEGAN. WITH SIX ILLUSTRATIONS BY HAROLD COPPING. LONDON: HODDER AND STOUGHTON, 1902. 201p.: front., 5 plates. Bound in green cloth, with coloured pictorial cover.
C 823.912 HEG

2156A **Another copy.**
ILLUSTRATED BY HAROLD COPPING. LONDON: HODDER AND STOUGHTON (1902), 208p.: col. front., col. vignette on title page. 17 col. plates, 16 plates. Bound in grey cloth.
M 813 RIC CHILDREN'S COLLECTION

2157 **HEMING, BRACEBRIDGE.**
COMBAT IN THE AIR. BY BRACEBRIDGE HEMING. LONDON: SAMPSON LOW, MARSTON AND CO. LTD., (191–?). VI, 250p.: front. Bound in red cloth, with pictorial cover and spine.
C 823.912 HEM

2158 **HENDERSON, J.E.**
DAYBREAK, A STORY. BY J.E. HENDERSON. ILLUSTRATED BY HAROLD PIFFARD. LONDON: SOCIETY FOR PROMOTING CHRISTIAN KNOWLEDGE, (190–?). 159p. + 16p. pub. cat.: col. front., 2 col. plates. Bound in grey cloth, with coloured pictorial cover and decorative spine.
C 823.912 HEN

2159 **HENTY, GEORGE ALFRED.**
Both Sides the Border. A Tale of Hotspur and Glendower. BY G.A. HENTY. ILLUSTRATED BY RALPH PEACOCK. NEW EDITION. LONDON: BLACKIE AND SON LIMITED, 1907. 384p. + 16p. ill. pub. cat.: front., 7 plates. Bound in red cloth, with coloured pictorial cover and spine.
C 823.8 HEN

2161 **HENTY, GEORGE ALFRED.**
By Right of Conquest; OR, With Cortez in Mexico. BY G.A. HENTY. ILLUSTRATED BY W.S. STACEY. LONDON: BLACKIE AND SON LIMITED, (191–?). 384p.: col. front., 4 plates, 2 maps. Bound in green cloth, with coloured pictorial cover and spine.
YSC 823.8 HEN

2162 **HENTY, GEORGE ALFRED.**
By Sheer Pluck, A Tale of the Ashanti War. BY G.A. HENTY. Illustrated by Gordon Browne. LONDON: BLACKIE AND SON LIMITED, (191–?). 352p. + 2p. pub. cat.: col. front., 4 plates. Bound in red cloth, with coloured pictorial cover and spine.
YSC 823.8 HEN

2163 **HENTY, GEORGE ALFRED.**
In the Hands of the Malays, and other stories. BY G.A. HENTY. ILLUSTRATED BY J. JELLICOE. LONDON. BLACKIE AND SON, LIMITED, (191–?). 176p.: front., 1 plate. Bound in blue cloth with coloured pictorial cover and spine. Includes also On the Track and A Frontier Girl.
C 823.8 HEN

2164 **HENTY, GEORGE ALFRED.**
In the Irish Brigade, A Tale of War in Flanders and Spain. BY G.A. HENTY. Illustrated. LONDON: BLACKIE AND SON LIMITED, (190–?). 384p.: col. front., 4 plates by Chas. Sheldon. Bound in green cloth, with coloured pictorial cover and spine.
C 823.8 HEN

2164A **HENTY, GEORGE ALFRED.**
IN TIMES OF PERIL. (BY) G.A. HENTY. LONDON: HENRY FROWDE, HODDER AND STOUGHTON, (191–?). 368p. + 16p. pub. cat.: col. front. Bound in green cloth with embossed cover and spine and pictorial end papers. Originally published 1881.
C 823.8 HEN

2165 **HENTY, GEORGE ALFRED.**
Redskin and Cowboy, A Tale of the Western Plains. BY G.A. HENTY. ILLUSTRATED BY ALFRED PEARSE. LONDON: BLACKIE AND SON LIMITED, (190–?). 384p.: col. front., 4 plates. Bound in blue cloth, with coloured pictorial cover and spine.
C 823.8 HEN & YSC 823.8 HEN

2167 **HENTY, GEORGE ALFRED.**
True to the Old Flag, A Tale of the American War of Independence. BY G.A. HENTY. ILLUSTRATED. LONDON: BLACKIE AND SON LIMITED, (190–?). 390p. + 2p. pub. cat.: front., 4 plates, 3 by Chas. Sheldon, 6 maps. Bound in green cloth, with coloured pictorial cover and spine. Originally published 1884.
C 823.8 HEN

2168 **HENTY, GEORGE ALFRED.**
WITH BULLER IN NATAL; OR, A BORN LEADER. BY G.A. HENTY. WITH TEN ILLUSTRATIONS BY W. RAINEY, R.I., AND A MAP. LONDON: BLACKIE AND SON LIMITED, (190–?). 384p. + 32p. ill. pub. cat.: front., 9 plates, map. Bound in blue cloth, with coloured pictorial cover and spine.
YSC 823.8 HEN

2169 **HENTY, GEORGE ALFRED.**
WITH CLIVE IN INDIA; OR, THE BEGINNINGS OF AN EMPIRE. BY G.A. HENTY. WITH TWELVE FULL-PAGE ILLUSTRATIONS BY GORDON BROWNE. LONDON: BLACKIE AND SON LIMITED, (190–?). 382p. + 32p. ill. pub. cat.: front., 11 plates, map. Bound in blue cloth, with coloured pictorial cover and spine.
C 823.8 HEN

2170 **HENTY, GEORGE ALFRED.**
WITH ROBERTS TO PRETORIA, A TALE OF THE SOUTH AFRICAN WAR. BY G.A. HENTY. WITH TWELVE ILLUSTRATIONS BY WILLIAM RAINEY, R.I. AND A MAP. LONDON: BLACKIE AND SON LIMITED, 1902. 384p. + 32p. ill. pub. cat.: front., 11 plates + map. Bound in red cloth, with coloured pictorial cover and spine.
C 823.8 HEN

2171 **HENTY, GEORGE ALFRED.**
WON BY THE SWORD, A TALE OF THE THIRTY YEARS' WAR. BY G.A. HENTY. WITH TWELVE ILLUSTRATIONS BY CHARLES M. SHELDON. AND FOUR PLANS. LONDON: BLACKIE AND SON LIMITED, 1900. 383p. + 32p. ill. pub. cat.: front., 11 plates, 4 plans. Bound in green cloth, with coloured pictorial cover and spine.
YSC 823.8 HEN

2172 **HINKSON, HENRY ALBERT.**
The King's Liege, A Story of the Days of Charles the First. BY H.A. HINKSON. ILLUSTRATED BY A.A. DIXON. LONDON: BLACKIE AND SON LIMITED, 1910. 224p. + 16p. pub. cat.: col. front., 3 plates. Bound in blue cloth, with coloured pictorial cover and spine.
C 823.912 HIN

2173 **HOFFMANN, ALICE SPENCER.**
THE CHILDREN'S SHAKESPEARE, BEING STORIES FROM THE PLAYS WITH ILLUSTRATIVE PASSAGES. TOLD AND CHOSEN BY ALICE SPENCER HOFFMANN. WITH MANY COLOURED ILLUSTRATIONS BY CHARLES FOLKARD. LONDON: J.M. DENT AND SONS, 1911. VIII, 472p.: col. front., 20 col. plates. Bound in green cloth, with coloured pictorial cover and decorative spine.
C 823.912 HOF

2174 **HOLLIS, GERTRUDE.**
BETWEEN TWO CRUSADES, A TALE OF A.D. 1187. BY GERTRUDE HOLLIS. ILLUSTRATED BY ADOLF THIEDE. LONDON: SOCIETY FOR PROMOTING CHRISTIAN KNOWLEDGE, (190–?). 247p. + 8p. pub. cat.: col. front., 2 col. plates. Bound in grey cloth, with coloured pictorial cover and spine.
C 823.912 HOL

2175 **HOLMES, FREDERICK MORELL.**
Brave Sidney Somers; Or, The Voyage of the Eastern Adventurer. BY F.M. HOLMES. ILLUSTRATED BY VICTOR PROUT. LONDON: BLACKIE AND SON LIMITED, (190–?). 260p.: 4 plates. Bound in green cloth with coloured pictorial cover and spine.
C 823.8 HOL

2176 **HOLMES, FREDERICK MORRELL.**
The Firebrands of the Caspian. The story of a bold enterprise. By F.M. Holmes. WITH SIX ILLUSTRATIONS. LONDON: S.W. PARTRIDGE AND CO. (191–?). 332p. + 32p. pub. cat.: front., 3 plates. Bound in red cloth with coloured pictorial cover and spine.
C 823.912 HOL

2177 **HOME, ANDREW.**
The Boys of Badminster, A School Tale By ANDREW HOME. ILLUSTRATED by C.M. Sheldon. LONDON: W. and R. CHAMBERS LIMITED, (191–?). VI, 398p.: front., 7 plates. Bound in blue cloth, with coloured pictorial cover and spine.
C 823.912 HOM

2178 **HORSLEY, REGINALD.**
IN THE GRIP OF THE HAWK, A Story of the Maori Wars. BY REGINALD HORSLEY. SIX ILLUSTRATIONS BY W. HERBERT HOLLOWAY. LONDON: T.C. AND E.C. JACK, 1907. XI, 243p.: front., 4 plates + map. Bound in beige cloth, with coloured pictorial cover and spine.
C 823.912 HOR

2179 **HOUSMAN, LAURENCE.**
COTTON WOOLLEENA. By LAURENCE HOUSEMAN. Pictures by Marian Allen. OXFORD: BASIL BLACKWELL, (193–?). 36p.: ill. Bound in orange paper, with coloured pictorial paper label on cover.
YSC 823.912 HOU

2180 **HOUSMAN, LAURENCE.**
THE OPEN DOOR. By LAURENCE HOUSMAN. Illustrated by Alec Buckels. AND TOFFEE BOY. By MABEL MARLOWE. Illustrated by D. Hutton. OXFORD: BASIL BLACKWELL, (192–?). 32p.: 6 plates, ill. Bound in grey paper, with coloured pictorial label on cover.
YSC 823.912 HOU

2181 **HUDSON, WILLIAM HENRY.**
MARY'S LITTLE LAMB. BY W.H. HUDSON. ILLUSTRATED BY ROBERTA F.C. WAUDBY. LONDON: J.M. DENT AND SONS, LTD., 1929. 28p.: front., vignette on title page, 4 plates, headpiece, tailpiece. Bound in yellow card with pictorial front cover.
CBDP 828.808 HUD

2182 **HULL, KATHARINE.**
THE FAR-DISTANT OXUS. by KATHARINE HULL AND PAMELA WHITLOCK. Illustrations by PAMELA WHITLOCK. Introduction by ARTHUR RANSOME. LONDON: JONATHAN CAPE, 1937. 351p.: front., vignette on title page, 25 plates, tailpieces, ill., col. maps on endpapers. Bound in red cloth.
C 823.912 HUL

2183 **HULME BEAMAN, SYDNEY GEORGE.**
TALES OF TOYTOWN. Written and Illustrated by S.G. HULME BEAMAN. LONDON: GEOFFREY CUMBERLEGE, OXFORD UNIVERSITY PRESS, 1928. 158p.: col. front., 5 col. plates, 3 plates, ill. Bound in blue cloth with coloured pictorial paper jacket.
C 823.912 HUL

2184 **HULME BEAMAN, SYDNEY GEORGE.**
WIRELESS IN TOYTOWN. By S.G. HULME BEAMAN. Illustrated by THE AUTHOR. (LONDON): COLLINS CLEAR-TYPE PRESS, 1938. V, 184p.: front., decorative title page. 13 plates, ill. Bound in green cloth. The Laurel and Gold Series, vol. 64.
YSC 823.912 HUL

2186 **HUNTER, NORMAN.**
THE BAD BARONS OF CRASHBANIA. By NORMAN HUNTER. Pictures by Eva Garnett. KINGS AND QUEENS. By GERTRUDE MONRO HIGGS. Pictures by Thomas Derrick. OXFORD: BASIL BLACKWELL, (193–?). 31p.: 3 plates, ill. Bound in red paper, with coloured pictorial paper label on cover.
YSC 823.914 HUN

2187 **HUTCHESON, JOHN CONROY.**
THE PENANG PIRATE AND THE LOST PINNACE. BY JOHN C. HUTCHESON. ILLUSTRATED. LONDON: BLACKIE AND SON LIMITED, (1912). 192p. + 32p. ill. pub. cat.: front., 2 plates. Bound in blue cloth, with pictorial/decorative cover and spine.
C 823.8 HUT

2188 **INMAN, HERBERT ESCOTT.**
DAVID CHESTER'S MOTTO "Honour Bright", A Boy's Adventures at School and at Sea. By H. ESCOTT-INMAN (sic.) WITH ORIGINAL ILLUSTRATIONS. LONDON: FREDERICK WARNE AND CO., (190–?). 371p. + 4p. pub. cat.: front., 15 plates. Bound in brown cloth, with coloured pictorial cover and spine.
C 823.912 INM

2189 **INMAN, HERBERT ESCOTT.**
The Second Form Master of St. Cyril's. By H. ESCOTT-INMAN (sic.) WITH ORIGINAL ILLUSTRATIONS BY RAYMOND POTTER. LONDON: FREDERICK WARNE AND CO., (190–?). 383p.: front., 15 plates. Bound in brown cloth, with coloured pictorial cover and spine.
C 823.912 INM

2190 **IRVING, WASHINGTON.**
The Legend of SLEEPY HOLLOW by WASHINGTON IRVING. Drawings by ARTHUR I. KELLER. INDIANAPOLIS, U.S.A.: THE BOBBS-MERRILL COMPANY, 1906. 92p.: col. front., title page decorated in colour, 13 col. plates, col. ill. Bound in green cloth with coloured pictorial/decorative cover and spine.
YSC 813.2 IRV and CBD 813.2 IRV

2191 **IRVING, WASHINGTON.**
TALES BY WASHINGTON IRVING. SELECTED AND EDITED BY H.A. TREBLE, M.A. LONDON: OLIVER AND BOYD, (193–?). VI, 98p.: front., by R.W.M., ill. Bound in brown cloth. Contains Rip Van Winkle; The Belated Travellers; Legend of the Moors Legacy; Dolph Heyliger's Adventures.
YSC 813.2 IRV

2192 **JACBERNS, RAYMOND.**
A BAD THREE WEEKS. BY RAYMOND JACBERNS. ILLUSTRATED BY A. TALBOT SMITH. LONDON: WELLS GARDNER, DARTON AND CO. LTD., 1907. IX, 248p.: front., 7 plates. Bound in grey cloth, with coloured pictorial cover and spine.
C 823.912 JAC

2193 **JACBERNS, RAYMOND.**
CRAB COTTAGE, A Girls' Story. BY RAYMOND JACBERNS. WITH SIX ILLUSTRATIONS by J. Menzies. LONDON: W. AND R. CHAMBERS LIMITED, 1905. 285p. + 40p. ill. pub. cat.: front., 5 plates. Bound in brown cloth, with coloured pictorial cover and spine.
C 823.912 JAC

2194 **JACBERNS, RAYMOND.**
POOR UNCLE HARRY. BY RAYMOND JACBERNS. WITTH SIX COLOURED ILLUSTRATIONS by Hilda Cowham. LONDON: W. AND R. CHAMBERS LIMITED, 1910. 275p.: col. front., 5 col. plates. Bound in red cloth, with pictorial cover and spine.
C 823.912 JAC

2195 **JACKSON, ALICE F.**
THE TOWER OF LONDON RETOLD FOR BOYS AND GIRLS. BY ALICE F. JACKSON. ILLUSTRATED BY T.H. ROBINSON. LONDON: T.C. AND E.C. JACK, (191–?). 196p.: front., vignette on title page, 7 plates. Bound in orange cloth, with vignette on cover.
C 823.912 JAC

2196 **JAMES, GEORGE PAYNE RAINSFORD.**
ARABELLA STUART; OR, THE DAYS OF JAMES I. BY G.P.R. JAMES. WITH AN INTRODUCTION. LONDON: GEORGE ROUTLEDGE AND SONS LIMITED, (190–?). 379p. Bound in blue cloth, with coloured, pictorial cover and spine. Originally published 1844.
C 823.8 JAM

2197 **JAMES, GEORGE PAYNE RAINSFORD.**
DARNLEY; OR, THE FIELD OF THE CLOTH OF GOLD. BY G.P.R. JAMES. WITH AN INTRODUCTION. LONDON: GEORGE ROUTLEDGE AND SONS LIMITED, (190–?). 392p. Bound in blue cloth, with coloured pictorial cover and spine. Originally published 1830.
C 823.8 JAM

2198 **JAMES, GEORGE PAYNE RAINSFORD.**
FOREST DAYS; OR, ROBIN HOOD. BY G.P.R. JAMES. WITH AN INTRODUCTION. LONDON: GEORGE ROUTLEDGE AND SONS LIMITED, (190–?). 382p. Bound in blue cloth, with coloured pictorial cover and spine. Originally published 1843.
C 823.8 JAM

2199 **JAMES, GEORGE PAYNE RAINSFORD.**
GOWRIE; OR, THE KING'S PLOT. BY G.P.R. JAMES. WITH AN INTRODUCTION. LONDON: GEORGE ROUTLEDGE AND SONS, LIMITED, (190–?). 432p. Bound in blue cloth, with coloured pictorial cover and spine. Originally published 1847.
C 823.8 JAM

2200 **JAMES, GEORGE PAYNE RAINSFORD.**
JOHN MARSTON HALL, A ROMANCE OF THE DAYS OF JAMES II. BY G.P.R. JAMES WITH AN INTRODUCTION. LONDON: GEORGE ROUTLEDGE AND SONS LIMITED, (190–?). 448p. Bound in blue cloth, with coloured pictorial cover and spine.
C 823.8 JAM

2201 **JAMES, GEORGE PAYNE RAINSFORD.**
THE KING'S HIGHWAY; OR, THE AGE OF WILLIAM III. BY G.P.R. JAMES. WITH AN INTRODUCTION. LONDON: GEORGE ROUTLEDGE AND SONS LIMITED, (190–?). 384p. Bound in blue cloth, with coloured pictorial cover and spine. Originally published 1840.
C 823.8 JAM

2202 **JAMESON, ELAINE MARY.**
THE PENDLETON TWINS. By E.M. JAMESON. ILLUSTRATED BY S.B. PEARSE. LONDON: HENRY FROWDE, HODDER AND STOUGHTON, 1909. 303p. + 16p. pub. cat.: col. front., 5 col. plates. Bound in green cloth, with coloured pictorial cover and spine.
C 823.912 JAM

2203 **JEANS, THOMAS TENDRON.**
On Foreign Service; Or, The Santa Cruz Revolution. BY STAFF SURGEON T.T. JEANS, R.N. ILLUSTRATED BY WILLIAM RAINEY, R.I. LONDON: BLACKIE AND SON LIMITED, 1911. 381p.: sepia front., 7 sepia plates. Bound in blue cloth, with coloured pictorial cover and spine.
C 823.8 JEA

2204 **JEFFERIES, RICHARD.**
BEVIS, THE STORY OF A BOY. BY RICHARD JEFFERIES. WITH AN INTRODUCTION BY E.V. LUCAS. LONDON: DUCKWORTH AND CO., 1910. XVI, 464p.: map. Bound in blue cloth. Originally published 1882.
YSC 823.8 JEF

2205 **JENKINSON, MAYSEL.**
BEYOND THE HILLS. By Maysel Jenkinson. Illustrated by REGINALD MILLS. LONDON: FREDERICK WARNE AND CO. LTD., (1926). VII, 248p.: front., vignette title page, 9 plates, pictorial end papers. Bound in brown cloth, with embossed vignette on cover.
YSC 823.912 JEN

2205A **JOHNS, WILLIAM EARL.**
BIGGLES FLIES SOUTH. (BY) CAPTAIN W.E. JOHNS. Illustrated by Jack Nicolle. LONDON: OXFORD UNIVERSITY PRESS, 1938, 255p. 5 plates, 2 maps. Bound in green linson.
C 823.912 JOH

2205B **JOHNS, WILLIAM EARL.**
BIGGLES TAKES A HOLIDAY. LONDON: HODDER AND STOUGHTON, (193–?). 191p.: front., title page missing, 7 col. plates. Bound in red linson with coloured pictorial paper dust cover.
C 823.912 BIG

2206 **JOHNS, WILLIAM EARL.**
THE SPY FLYERS. BY CAPTAIN W.E. JOHNS. ILLUSTRATED BY HOWARD LEIGH. LONDON: JOHN HAMILTON LTD., 1933. 256p.: col. front. 4 plates. Bound in blue cloth.
C 823.912 JOH

2207 **JOHNSTON, WILLIAM.**
TOM GRAHAM, V.C., A TALE OF THE AFGHAN WAR. BY WILLIAM JOHNSTON. LONDON: THOMAS NELSON AND SONS, (190–?). 360p.: front., 5 plates by George Soper and Emily A. Cook. Bound in blue cloth, with coloured pictorial cover and spine.
C 823.912 JOH

2207A **KAYE-SMITH, SHEILA.**
The Children's Summer, by SHEILA KAYE-SMITH ILLUSTRATED BY NORAH RONEY. LONDON: CASSELL AND COMPANY, LIMITED, 2ND ED., 1933. 311p.: vignette on title page, 4 col. plates, headpieces and tailpieces to chapters. Bound in green cloth with vignette on cover.
M 823 KAY CHILDREN'S COLLECTION

2208 **KEEN, J. OSBORNE.**
TOM SHARMAN AND His College Chums. BY J.O. KEEN, D.D. LONDON: S.W. PARTRIDGE AND CO., (190–?). 319p. + 20p. pub. cat.: front. Bound in brown cloth, with coloured decorative cover and spine.
C 823.8 KEE

2209 **KELLY, WILLIAM PATRICK.**
THE STONE-CUTTER OF MEMPHIS. BY WILLIAM PATRICK KELLY. WITH EIGHT PLATES BY J. AYTON SYMINGTON. LONDON: GEORGE ROUTLEDGE AND SONS LIMITED, 1904. XI, 371p.: front., 7 plates. Bound in orange cloth with pictorial cover and spine.
C 823.912 KEL

2210 **KEN, ELIZABETH.**
THE LOST WILL. BY ELIZABETH KEN. ILLUSTRATED BY OSCAR WILSON. LONDON: SOCIETY FOR PROMOTING CHRISTIAN KNOWLEDGE, (190–?). 150p. + 8p. pub. cat.: sepia front., 2 sepia plates. Bound in green cloth, with coloured pictorial cover and spine.
C 823.8 KEN

2211 **KENDREW, MARY E.**
WILLIE'S BATTLES AND HOW HE WON THEM. BY MARY E. KENDREW. FULLY ILLUSTRATED. LONDON: S.W. PARTRIDGE AND CO. LTD., (190–?). 96p. + 32p. pub. cat.: front., 3 plates. Bound in brown cloth, with coloured pictorial/decorative cover and spine.
C 823.8 KEN

2212 **KENYON, EDITH C.**
THE HEROES OF MOSS HALL SCHOOL, A Public School Story. By E.C. KENYON. WITH COLOURED AND BLACK ILLUSTRATIONS. LONDON: THE RELIGIOUS TRACT SOCIETY, (190–?). 383p. + 16p. pub. cat.: col. front., 2 col. plates, 4 plates by A. Pearse. Bound in green cloth, with coloured cover and spine.
C 823.9 KEN

2213 **KER, DAVID.**
THE LAST OF THE SEA-KINGS. BY DAVID KER. LONDON: THOMAS NELSON AND SONS, (191–?). 318p.: col. front., 3 col. plates by Malcolm Patterson. Bound in blue cloth, with decorative cover and spine.
C 823.8 KER

2213A **KINGSLEY, CHARLES.**
HEREWARD THE WAKE. RETOLD FOR BOYS AND GIRLS BY ALICE F. JACKSON. ILLUSTRATED BY MONRO S. ORR. LONDON: T.C. and E.C. JACK, (191–?). 196p.: col. front., col. pictorial title page. 7 col. plates. Bound in buff paper with coloured pictorial label on cover.
C 823.7 KIN

2214 **KINGSTON, WILLIAM HENRY GILES.**
Captain Mugford; or, Our Salt and Fresh Water Tutors. EDITED BY W.H.G. KINGSTON. LONDON: THOMAS NELSON AND SONS, (191–?). 371p. + 12p. pub. cat.: col. front., 3 col. plates by Holloway. Bound in green cloth, with coloured pictorial cover and spine.
C 823.8 KIN

2215 **KINGSTON, WILLIAM HENRY GILES.**
THE CRUISE OF THE "MARY ROSE", Or Here and There in the Pacific. By WILLIAM H.G. KINGSTON. NEW EDITION. LONDON: THE RELIGIOUS TRACT SOCIETY, (190–?). 269p. + 6p. pub. cat.: front., 16 plates. Bound in grey cloth with coloured pictorial cover and spine.
C 823.8 KIN

2216 **KINGSTON, WILLIAM HENRY GILES.**
FROM POWDER MONKEY TO ADMIRAL. A STORY OF NAVAL ADVENTURE. BY W.H.G. KINGSTON. WITH AN INTRODUCTION BY DR. MACAULAY, FOUNDER AND FIRST EDITOR OF "THE BOY'S OWN PAPER." NEW EDITION. ILLUSTRATED IN COLOUR BY ARCHIBALD WEBB. LONDON: HUMPHREY MILFORD, OXFORD UNIVERSITY PRESS, 1918. XIV, 400p.: col. front., 3 col. plates. Bound in pink cloth, with coloured pictorial labels on cover and spine.
C 823.8 KIN

2217 **KINGSTON, WILLIAM HENRY GILES.**
THE HEIR OF KILFINNAN. A TALE OF THE SHORE AND OCEAN. BY WILLIAM H.G. KINGSTON. LONDON: THOMAS NELSON AND SONS, (191–?). IV, 335p.: col. front., 3 col. plates by Holloway. Bound in green cloth, with coloured pictorial cover and spine.
C 823.8 KIN

2218 **KINGSTON, WILLIAM HENRY GILES.**
IN THE ROCKY MOUNTAINS. BY W.H.G. KINGSTON. LONDON: THOMAS NELSON AND SONS LTD., (190–?). 254p. + 6p. pub. cat.: col. front., 3 col. plates. Bound in pink cloth, with coloured pictorial label on cover.
C 823.8 KIN

2219 **KINGSTON, WILLIAM HENRY GILES.**
IN THE WILDS OF FLORIDA. A Tale of Warfare and Hunting. By W.H.G. KINGSTON, WITH THIRTY-SEVEN ENGRAVINGS. LONDON: T. NELSON AND SONS, 1901. 461p.: col. front., additional col. vignette title page, 28 plates, ill. Bound in brown cloth with embossed decorative/pictorial cover and spine.
C 823.8 KIN

2220 **KINGSTON, WILLIAM HENRY GILES.**
MANCO THE PERUVIAN CHIEF: or an Englishman's Adventures in the Country of the Incas. By William H.G. Kingston. Eight Coloured Illustrations. LONDON: COLLINS' CLEAR-TYPE PRESS, (190–?). 304p.: col. front., 7 col. plates by Stanley Berkeley. Bound in green cloth, with coloured pictorial cover and spine.
C 823.8 KIN

2222 **KINGSTON, WILLIAM HENRY GILES.**
MY FIRST VOYAGE TO SOUTHERN SEAS. By W.H.G. KINGSTON. LONDON: THOMAS NELSON AND SONS, (191–?). 412p. + 4p. pub. cat.: col. front., additional col. vignette title page, 4 col. plates by A. Pearse. Bound in red cloth, with coloured pictorial cover and spine.
C 823.8 KIN

2223 **KINGSTON, WILLIAM HENRY GILES.**
OLD JACK. By W.H.G. KINGSTON. LONDON: THOMAS NELSON AND SONS, (190–?). 472p.: col. front., additional col. vignette title page, 4 col. plates by W.H.C. Groome. Bound in olive cloth, with coloured pictorial cover and spine.
C 823.8 KIN

2224 **Another copy.**
OLD JACK, A TALE FOR BOYS. BY W.H.G. KINGSTON. ILLUSTRATED BY HENRY AUSTIN. LONDON: WARD, LOCK AND CO. LIMITED (191–?). 433p. + 14p. pub. cat.: front., 3 plates. Bound in blue cloth, with embossed decorative cover and spine.

2225 **KINGSTON, WILLIAM HENRY GILES.**
ON THE BANKS OF THE AMAZON. By W.H.G. KINGSTON. LONDON: THOMAS NELSON AND SONS, (190–?). 411p.: col. front., additional col. vignette title page, 3 col. plates by W.H.C. Groome. Bound in blue cloth, with coloured pictorial cover and spine, and gilt edges.
C 823.8 KIN

2226 **KINGSTON, WILLIAM HENRY GILES.**
OWEN HARTLEY; OR, UPS AND DOWNS, A TALE OF THE LAND AND SEA. BY WILLIAM H.G. KINGSTON. ILLUSTRATED BY ERNEST PRATER. LONDON: THE SHELDON PRESS, (192–?). 255p. + 16p. pub. cat.: col. front. Bound in grey cloth, with coloured pictorial/decorative cover and spine.
C 823.8 KIN

2227 **KINGSTON, WILLIAM HENRY GILES.**
PADDY FINN. BY W.H.G. KINGSTON. NEW EDITION. ILLUSTRATED IN COLOUR BY ARCHIBALD WEBB. LONDON: HENRY FROWDE, HODDER AND STOUGHTON, (191–?). VI, 430p.: col. front., 3 col. plates. Bound in pink cloth, with coloured pictorial labels on cover and spine.
C 823.8 KIN

2227A **KINGSTON, WILLIAM HENRY GILES.**
ROGER WILLOUGHBY. (BY) W.H.G. KINGSTON. LONDON: OXFORD UNIVERSITY PRESS, 1923. VI, 402p.: col. front. Bound in red cloth with embossed decorative cover and spine and pictorial endpapers.
C 823.8 KIN

2228 **KINGSTON, WILLIAM HENRY GILES.**
SAVED FROM THE SEA. BY W.H.G. KINGSTON. LONDON: THOMAS NELSON AND SONS LTD., (190–?). 317p.: col. front., 4 col. plates by Cyrus Cuneo. Bound in blue cloth, with vignette on cover and spine.
C 823.8 KIN

2229 **KINGSTON, WILLIAM HENRY GILES.**
THE SOUTH SEA WHALER. By W.H.G. KINGSTON. LONDON: THOMAS NELSON AND SONS, (191–?). 304p.: col. front., 4 col. plates, 3 and front. by W.H.C. Groome, 1 by W.S. Stacey. Bound in red cloth, with coloured pictorial cover and spine.
C 823.8 KIN

2230 **KINGSTON, WILLIAM HENRY GILES.**
TRUE BLUE. BY W.H.G. KINGSTON. LONDON: WARD, LOCK AND CO. LIMITED, 1910. 379p. + 4p. pub. cat.: front., 3 plates by Victor Prout. Bound in green cloth, with embossed decorative cover and spine.
C 823.8 KIN

2231 **KINGSTON, WILLIAM HENRY GILES.**
TWICE LOST. By W.H.G. KINGSTON. LONDON: THOMAS NELSON AND SONS, (190–?). 396p. + 4p. pub. cat.: col. front. by W.S. Stacey, additional col. vignette title page, 4 col. plates by C.J. Staniland. Bound in blue cloth, with coloured pictorial cover and spine.
C 823.8 KIN

2231A **KINGSTON, WILLIAM HENRY GILES.**
THE TWO SHIPMATES. BY THE LATE WILLIAM H.G. KINGSTON. LONDON: SOCIETY FOR PROMOTING CHRISTIAN KNOWLEDGE, (190–?). 160p. + 16p. pub. cat.: front., 2 plates. Bound in green cloth with coloured pictorial cover and spine.
C 823.8 KIN

2232 **KINGSTON, WILLIAM HENRY GILES.**
THE WANDERERS. By W.H.G. KINGSTON. LONDON: THOMAS NELSON AND SONS, (190–?). 332p. + 3p. pub. cat.: col. front., 4 col. plates. Bound in green cloth, with coloured pictorial cover and spine.
C 823.8 KIN

2233 **KINGSTON, WILLIAM HENRY GILES.**
WILL WEATHERHELM, THE YARN OF AN OLD SAILOR. BY W.H.G. KINGSTON. NEW EDITION. WITH ILLUSTRATIONS IN COLOUR BY ARCHIBALD WEBB. LONDON: HENRY FROWDE, HODDER AND STOUGHTON, 1915. 469p. + 16p. pub. cat.: col. front., 4

col. plates. Bound in grey cloth, with coloured pictorial cover and spine.
C 823.8 KIN

2234 **KINGSTON, WILLIAM HENRY GILES.**
THE YOUNG LLANERO. By W.H.G. KINGSTON. LONDON: THOMAS NELSON AND SONS, (190–?). 368p.: col. front., by W.S. Stacey, additional vignette title page, 4 col. plates by S. Paget. Bound in green cloth, with coloured pictorial cover and spine.
C 823.8 KIN

2234A **KINGSTON, WILLIAM HENRY GILES.**
THE YOUNG RAJAH. LONDON: THOMAS NELSON AND SONS (1903). 291p. + 4p. pub. cat.: front., 7 plates by W.H.C. Groome. Bound in blue cloth with embossed decorative cover and spine.
823.8 KIN

2235 **KIPLING, RUDYARD.**
ACTIONS AND REACTIONS. BY RUDYARD KIPLING. COPYRIGHT EDITION. GERMANY LEIPZIG: BERNHARD TAUCHNITZ, 1909. 294p.: col. decorative endpapers. Bound in red cloth.
YSC 823.8 KIP

2236 **KIPLING, RUDYARD.**
THE JUNGLE BOOK BY RUDYARD KIPLING. WITH ILLUSTRATIONS IN COLOUR BY MAURICE AND EDWARD DETMOLD. LONDON: MACMILLAN AND CO., LIMITED, 1908. XI, 314p. + 2p. pub. cat.: col. front., 15 col. plates, headpieces. Bound in red cloth with decorative cover. Originally published 1894.
CBD 823.8 KIP

2237 **KIPLING, RUDYARD.**
Just So Stories For Little Children. By Rudyard Kipling. Illustrated by the Author. LONDON: MACMILLAN AND CO. LIMITED, 1902. 249p. + 1p. pub. cat.: 22 plates, decorative initials to chapters. Bound in red cloth, with pictorial/decorative covers and spine.
C 823.8 KIP

2238 **Another copy.**
COPYRIGHT EDITION. ILLUSTRATED BY THE AUTHOR. GERMANY, LEIPZIG: BERNHARD TAUCHNITZ, 1902. 254p. + 32p. pub. cat.: 21 plates, map. Bound in paper. COLLECTION OF BRITISH AUTHORS, TAUCHNITZ EDITION, VOL. 3615.
YSC 823.8 KIP

2239 **KIPLING, RUDYARD.**
PUCK OF POOK'S HILL. BY RUDYARD KIPLING. LONDON: MACMILLAN AND CO. LIMITED, 1908. X, 306p.: decorative front. and title page, 20 plates by H.R. Millar. Bound in red leather, with embossed vignette on cover and embossed decorative spine. Originally published 1906.
YSC 823.8 KIP

2240 **KIPLING, RUDYARD.**
REWARDS AND FAIRIES. BY RUDYARD KIPLING. WITH ILLUSTRATIONS BY FRANK CRAIG. LONDON: MACMILLAN AND CO. LIMITED, 1910. XII, 338p., 4 plates. Rebound in blue check cloth.
YSC 823.8 KIP

2242 **KIPLING, RUDYARD.**
"THEY". BY RUDYARD KIPLING. WITH ILLUSTRATIONS BY F.H. TOWNSEND. LONDON: MACMILLAN AND CO. LIMITED, 1905. 80p.: col. front., 14 col. plates. Bound in white cloth.
YSC 823.8 KIP

2243 **LAMB, CHARLES.**
MRS LEICESTER'S SCHOOL, or The History of Several Young Ladies related by themselves. By CHARLES AND MARY LAMB. With Drawings by Charles E. Brock. LONDON: WELLS, GARDNER, DARTON and Co., (1904). 125p.: front., pictorial title page, 4 plates. Bound in blue cloth with pictorial cover and spine.
C 823.7 LAM

2244 **LAMPEN, CHARLES DUDLEY.**
THE STRANDING OF THE "WHITE ROSE". A Story of Adventure. BY C. DUDLEY LAMPEN. ILLUSTRATED BY ERNEST PRATER. LONDON: SOCIETY FOR PROMOTING CHRISTIAN KNOWLEDGE, (190–?). 221p. + 16p. pub. cat.: front., 1 plate. Bound in brown cloth, with coloured pictorial cover.
C 823.8 LAM

2245 **LAMPREY, L.**
IN THE DAYS OF THE GUILDS. BY L. LAMPREY. WITH FOUR ILLUSTRATIONS IN COLOUR BY FLORENCE GARDINER, AND NUMEROUS LINE DRAWINGS BY MABEL HATT. LONDON: GEORGE G. HARRAP AND CO. LTD., 1919. 282p. + 4p. pub. cat.: col. front., vignette title page, 3 col. plates, 9 plates. Bound in red cloth.
YSC 823.912 LAM

2246 **LANG, LEONORA BLANCHE.**
THE ALL SORTS OF STORIES BOOK. BY MRS. LANG. EDITED BY ANDREW LANG. WITH 5 COLOURED PLATES AND NUMEROUS OTHER ILLUSTRATIONS BY H.J. FORD. LONDON: LONGMANS, GREEN, AND CO., 1911. XVI, 377p.: col. front., vignette title page, 4 col. plates, 13 plates, ill. Bound in maroon cloth, with embossed decorative cover and spine, and gilt edges.
C 823.8 LAN

2247 **LE FEUVRE, AMY.**
His Little Daughter. BY AMY LE FEUVRE. With Three Illustrations by W.H.C. Groome. FIFTH IMPRESSION. LONDON: R.T.S. (RELIGIOUS TRACT SOCIETY), (190–?). 192p.: front., 2 plates. Bound in brown cloth, with pictorial cover and spine.
C 823.912 LEF

2248 **LE FEUVRE, AMY.**
"PROBABLE SONS". BY AMY LE FEUVRE. LONDON: THE RELIGIOUS TRACT SOCIETY, (190–?). 132p. + 16p. pub. cat.: front., 2 plates by Harold Copping. Bound in mustard cloth, with pictorial cover and spine.
C 823.912 LEF

2249 **LEIGHTON, ROBERT.**
CAP'N NAT'S TREASURE, A TALE OF OLD LIVERPOOL. BY ROBERT LEIGHTON. EIGHT ILLUSTRATIONS BY J.B. GREENE. LONDON: S.W. PARTRIDGE AND CO., (191–?). 422p. + 32p. pub. cat.: front., 5 plates. Bound in green cloth, with coloured pictorial cover and spine.
C 823.8 LEI

2250 **LEIGHTON, ROBERT.**
COO-EE! A STORY OF PERIL AND ADVENTURE IN THE SOUTH SEAS. BY ROBERT LEIGHTON. LONDON: C. ARTHUR PEARSON LTD., 1911. 256p.: front., 7 plates. Bound in buff cloth with coloured pictorial paper cover.
C 823.8 LEI

2250A **LEIGHTON, ROBERT.**
DREADNOUGHTS OF THE DOGGER. A Story of the War on the North Sea. LONDON: WARD, LOCK AND CO. LIMITED, 1916. 304p. + XVIp. pub. cat.: front., 12 plates in blue monochrome by Watson Charlton. Bound in buff cloth with coloured pictorial cover and spine.
C 823.8 LEI

2251 **LEIGHTON, ROBERT.**
The Golden Galleon, BEING A NARRATIVE OF THE ADVENTURES OF MASTER GILBERT OGLANDER . . . BY ROBERT LEIGHTON. ILLUSTRATED BY WILLIAM RAINEY, R.I. LONDON: BLACKIE AND SON LIMITED, (190–?). 352p. + 16p. pub. cat.: front., 7 plates. Bound in green cloth, with coloured pictorial cover and spine.
C 823.8 LEI

2252 **LEIGHTON, ROBERT.**
IN THE LAND OF JU-JU, A Tale of Benin, the City of Blood. BY ROBERT LEIGHTON. WITH ILLUSTRATIONS BY CECIL SCRUBY. LONDON: ANDREW MELROSE, (190–?). VIII, 343p.: front., 5 plates. Bound in red cloth, with coloured pictorial cover and spine.
C 823.8 LEI

2252A **LEIGHTON, ROBERT.**
A JEWEL OF THE SEAS. By ROBERT LEIGHTON. LONDON: JOHN F. SHAW (1928) AND CO., LTD., (192–?). 315p.: front., 2 plates. Bound in blue cloth with decorative covers.
C 823.8 LEI

2253 **LEIGHTON, ROBERT.**
The Thirsty Sword, A Story of The Norse Invasion of Scotland (1262–1263). BY ROBERT LEIGHTON. WITH ILLUSTRATIONS BY ALFRED PEARSE. LONDON: BLACKIE AND SON LIMITED, (191–?). 352p. + 16p. pub. cat.: col. front., 3 plates, + 1 map. Bound in blue cloth, with coloured pictorial cover and spine.
C 823.8 LEI

2254 **LESLIE, EMMA.**
CAUGHT IN THE TOILS, A STORY OF A CONVENT SCHOOL. BY EMMA LESLIE. FOURTH EDITION. LONDON: THE SUNDAY SCHOOL UNION, (190–?). 171p. + 12p. pub. cat.: front., 5 plates. Bound in green cloth, with coloured pictorial/decorative cover and spine.
YSC 823.8 LES

2255 **LESLIE, EMMA.**
THAT SCHOLARSHIP BOY. BY EMMA LESLIE. LONDON: THE RELIGIOUS TRACT SOCIETY, (190–?). 129p. + 16p. pub. cat.: col. front. by Leonard Skeats, col. decorative border on title page. Bound in brown cloth, with coloured pictorial/decorative cover and spine.
C 823.8 LES

2256 **LEWIS, CAROLINE.**
CLARA IN BLUNDERLAND. BY CAROLINE LEWIS, (pseud. for M.H. Temple and Harold Begbie.) WITH FORTY ILLUSTRATIONS BY S.R. LONDON: WILLIAM HEINEMANN, 1902. XVI, 150p.: front., 3 plates, ill. Bound in green cloth, with coloured pictorial cover. A parody of Alice in Wonderland which satirises politics and politicians.
C 823.912 LEW

2257 **LEWIS, HILDA.**
The Ship that Flew. (BY) HILDA LEWIS. Illustrated by NORA LAVRIN. LONDON: OXFORD UNIVERSITY PRESS, GEOFFREY CUMBERLEGE, 1939. 320p.: front., vignette title page, 2 plates, ill. Bound in green cloth, with coloured pictorial dust jacket.
YSC 823.8 LEW

2258 **LOFTING, HUGH.**
DOCTOR DOLITTLE IN THE MOON. Told and Illustrated by HUGH LOFTING. LONDON: JONATHAN CAPE LTD., 1929. 319p.: col. front., pictorial title page, 70 plates. Bound in black quarter leather.
YSC 823.912 LOF

2259 **LOFTING, HUGH.**
DOCTOR DOLITTLE'S CIRCUS. TOLD AND ILLUSTRATED BY HUGH LOFTING. LONDON: JONATHAN CAPE, 1925. 320p.: col. front., decorative title page, 79 plates. Bound in black quarter leather.
YSC 823.912 LOF

2260 **LOFTING, HUGH.**
DOCTOR DOLITTLE'S POST OFFICE. WRITTEN AND ILLUSTRATED BY HUGH LOFTING. LONDON: JONATHAN CAPE, 1924. 320p.: col. front., decorative title page, 76 plates. Bound in black quarter leather.
YSC 823.912 LOF

2261 **LOFTING, HUGH.**
DOCTOR DOLITTLE'S ZOO. WRITTEN AND ILLUSTRATED BY HUGH LOFTING. (LONDON): JONATHAN CAPE, 1926. 319p.: col. front., decorative title page, 88 plates, col. pictorial endpapers. Bound in grey cloth.
C 823.912 LOF

2262 **LOFTING, HUGH.**
THE Story of DOCTOR DOLITTLE, BEING THE HISTORY OF HIS PECULIAR LIFE AT HOME AND ASTONISHING ADVENTURES IN FOREIGN PARTS. NEVER BEFORE PRINTED. TOLD BY HUGH LOFTING. ILLUSTRATED BY THE AUTHOR. LONDON: JONATHAN CAPE, 1924. 223p.: col. front., decorative title page, 11 plates, ill., col. pictorial endpapers. Bound in blue cloth, with coloured pictorial dust jacket. Originally published 1922.
C 823.912

2263 **LOFTING, HUGH.**
THE VOYAGES OF DOCTOR DOLITTLE. BY HUGH LOFTING, ILLUSTRATED. LONDON: JONATHAN CAPE, 1923. 320p.: col. front., 19 plates, one col. Bound in blue linson with decorative cover, coloured pictorial endpaper and coloured pictorial paper jacket.
YSC 823.912 LOF

2264 **LONDON, JOHN GRIFFITH.**
THE CALL OF THE WILD By JACK LONDON. Illustrated by Philip R. Goodwin and Charles Livingstone Bull. LONDON: WILLIAM HEINEMANN, 1904. 231p.: col. front., pictorial title page, 10 col. plates, 7 plates, ill., some col. Bound in black cloth with coloured decorative cover and spine. Originally published 1903.
CBD 813.52 LON

2265 **LOW, ARCHIBALD MONTGOMERY.**
ADRIFT IN THE STRATOSPHERE. BY PROFESSOR A.M. LOW. LONDON: BLACKIE AND SON LIMITED, 1937. 224p.: front., 2 plates. Bound in green cloth.
C 823.912 LOW

2266 **LUCAS, EDWARD VERRALL.**
ANNE'S TERRIBLE GOOD NATURE AND OTHER STORIES FOR CHILDREN. BY E.V. LUCAS. WITH 12 ILLUSTRATIONS BY A.H. BUCKLAND. LONDON: CHATTO AND WINDUS, 1908. VIII, 262p.: front., 11 plates, col. pictorial endpapers by F.D. Bedford. Bound in cream cloth, with coloured pictorial cover and spine.
C 823.912 LUC

2267 **LUMSDEN, ALEC.**
BUMPY FLIGHT. BY ALEC LUMSDEN. LONDON: THE POPULAR LIBRARY, (193–?). 216p.: front., 3 plates by Stanley Bradshaw. Bound in red cloth, with coloured pictorial dust jacket.
C 823.912 LUM

2268 **LYNN, ESCOTT.**
COMRADES EVER! BY ESCOTT LYNN. Illustrated by PERCY TARRANT. LONDON: W. AND R. CHAMBERS LIMITED, 1921. 351p.: front., 5 plates. Bound in orange cloth, with coloured pictorial cover and spine.
C 823.912 LYN

2269 **LYSAGHT, ELIZABETH. J.**
REX SINGLETON OR THE PATHWAY OF LIFE. BY MRS. LYSAGHT. Illustrated. SECOND EDITION. LONDON: WELLS GARDNER, DARTON AND CO. (19–?). IV, 183p. + 16p. pub. cat.: front., 5 plates. Bound in brown cloth with coloured pictorial cover and spine.
C 823.8 LYS

2270 **MACDONALD, ALEXANDER.**
Through the Heart of Tibet. BY ALEXANDER MACDONALD, F.R.G.S. Illustrated by William Rainey, R.I. LONDON: BLACKIE AND SON LIMITED, (1910). 384p.: front., 5 plates. Bound in green cloth, with coloured pictorial cover and spine.
C 823.912 MAC

2270A **MACDONALD, ALEXANDER.**
THE WHITE TRAIL. A Story of the Early Days of Klondike.

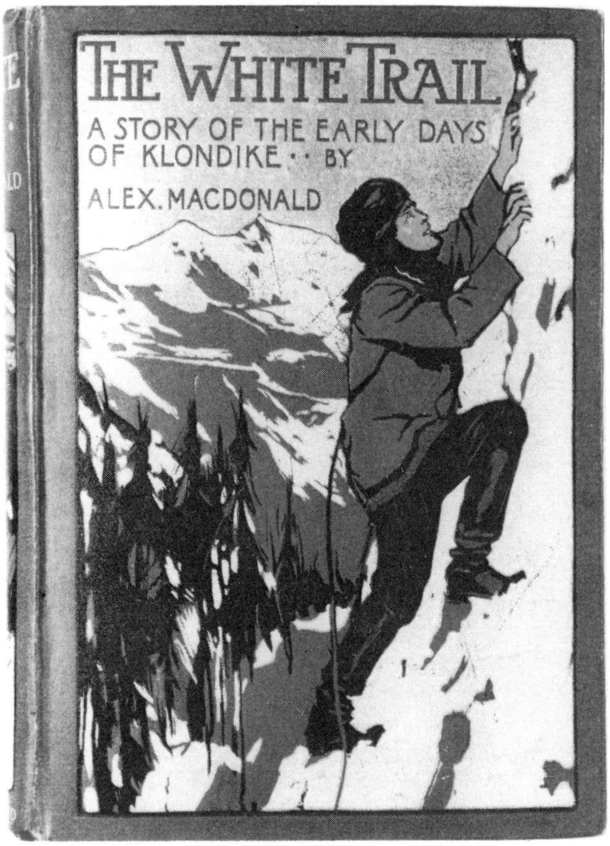

2270A

BY ALEXANDER MACDONALD, F.R.G.S. ILLUSTRATED BY WILLIAM RAINEY, R.I. LONDON: BLACKIE AND SON, LIMITED, 1909. 392p. + 16p. pub. cat. Bound in blue cloth with coloured pictorial cover and spine, with coloured edges.
C 823.912 MAC

2271 **MACDONALD, GEORGE.**
Ranald Bannerman's Boyhood. BY GEORGE MACDONALD. WITH THIRTY-SIX ILLUSTRATIONS BY ARTHUR HUGHES AND COVER-DESIGN BY LAURENCE HOUSMAN. LONDON: BLACKIE AND SON LIMITED, (190–?). VII, 299p. + 16p. pub. cat.: front., 23 plates, engraved by Dalziel Brothers. Bound in blue cloth with coloured pictorial/decorative cover and decorative spine. Originally published 1871.
C 823.8 MAC

2272 **MACDONALD, MARGARET P.**
Trefoil, The Story of a Girls' Society. By M.P. MACDONALD. With Six Illustrations by W.H. Margetson. LONDON: THOMAS NELSON AND SONS, 1902. 364p. + 4p. pub. cat.: front., 5 plates. Bound in brown cloth, with coloured pictorial vignette on cover and coloured decorative cover and spine.
C 823.912 MAC

2273 **MACDONALD, ROBERT M.**
The Great White Chief. A Story of Adventure in Unknown New Guinea. BY ROBERT M. MACDONALD. ILLUSTRATED BY W. RAINEY, R.I. LONDON: BLACKIE AND SON LIMITED, 1908. XI, 367p. + 16p. pub. cat.: front., 8 plates + map. Bound in red cloth, with coloured pictorial cover and spine.
C 832.912 MAC

2274 **McKEAN, D.G.**
THE STORY OF JOHNNY BERTRAM. BY D.B. McKEAN. Illustrated by W.H.C. GROOME. LONDON: WELLS GARDNER, DARTON & CO. 1900. 137p. + 15p. pub. cat.: front., 3 plates. Bound in green cloth with decorative cover and spine. CHATTERBOX LIBRARY.
C 823.8 MAC

2275 **MACKENZIE, COMPTON.**
THE ADVENTURES OF TWO CHAIRS. By COMPTON MACKENZIE. Illustrated by A.H. WATSON. OXFORD: BASIL BLACKWELL, (193–?). 31p.: 3 plates, ill. Bound in brown paper, with coloured pictorial paper label on cover.
YSC 823.912 MAC and C 823.912 MAC

2276 **MACKENZIE, COMPTON.**
THE ENCHANTED BLANKET. By COMPTON MACKENZIE. Pictures by A.H. Watson. OXFORD: BASIL BLACKWELL, (193–?). 28p.: 3 plates, ill. Bound in beige cloth, with coloured pictorial paper label on cover.
YSC 823.912 MAC

2277 **MACKENZIE, COMPTON.**
The Stairs that kept on Going Down. By COMPTON MACKENZIE. Pictures by A.H. WATSON. OXFORD: BASIL BLACKWELL, (193–?). 31p.: 6 plates. Bound in blue cloth, with coloured pictorial paper label on cover.
YSC 823.912 MAC

2278 **MACLEOD, MARY.**
THE SHAKESPEARE STORY BOOK BY MARY MACLEOD WITH INTRODUCTION BY SIDNEY LEE. ILLUSTRATIONS BY GORDON BROWNE. LONDON: WELLS, GARDNER, DARTON AND CO., 1902. XXI, 460p.: front., illustrated title page in 2 colours, 12 plates, ill. Bound in blue cloth with pictorial cover and decorative spine.
YSC 823.8 MAC and C 823.8 MAC

2279 **MACLEOD, MARY.**
STORIES FROM THE FAERIE QUEENE. BY MARY MACLEOD. WITH INTRODUCTION BY JOHN W. HALES. DRAWINGS BY A.G. WALKER, Sculptor. LONDON: WELLS GARDNER, DARTON & CO. LTD., FOURTH EDITION, NOVEMBER 1906. XX, 395p. + 24p. pub. cat.: front., vignette on title page, 42 plates, ill. Bound in brown cloth with yellow pictorial cover and spine.
C 823.8 MAC

2280 **MALET, LUCAS.**
LITTLE PETER. A CHRISTMAS MORALITY FOR CHILDREN OF ANY AGE. BY LUCAS MALET. NEW EDITION. WITH ILLUSTRATIONS IN COLOUR BY CHARLES E. BROCK. LONDON: HENRY FROWDE, 1909. 175p.: col. front., title page in red and black, 7 col. plates. Bound in cream cloth with coloured pictorial/decorative cover and spine.
CBD 823.8 MAL

2281 **MANIFOLD, AMY.**
THE ODD LITTLE GIRL; OR, BESSIE DREW. BY AMY MANIFOLD. LONDON: S.W. PARTRIDGE AND CO. LTD., (192–?). 122p. + 1p. pub. cat.: col. front., 3 plates by H.R. Bound in red linen, with pictorial cover and decorative spine.
YSC 823.8 MAN

2282 **MANWELL, M.B.**
THE BOYS OF MONK'S HAROLD, A TALE OF ADVENTURE. BY M.B. MANWELL. With Original Illustrations by J.R. BURGESS. LONDON: FREDERICK WARNE AND CO., (190–?). VI, 378p.: front., 15 plates. Bound in brown cloth, with coloured pictorial cover and spine.
C 823.8 MAN

2283 **MARC, ELIZABETH.**
Lost in the Arctic. By Elizabeth Marc. With Four Illustrations in Colour and Black-and-White. By ARCHIBALD WEBB. LONDON: CASSELL AND COMPANY LIMITED, 1926. XII, 211p.: col. front., 3 plates. Bound in brown cloth, with coloured pictorial cover and spine.
C 823.912 MAR

2284 **MARCHANT, BESSIE.**
ATHABASCA BILL, A Tale of the far West. BY BESSIE MARCHANT (MRS. J.A. COMFORT). ILLUSTRATED BY HAROLD PIFFARD. LONDON: SOCIETY FOR PROMOTING CHRISTIAN KNOWLEDGE, (190–?). 220p. + 16p. pub. cat.: col. front., 2 col. plates. Bound in brown cloth, with coloured pictorial cover and spine.
C 823.8 MAR

2285 **MARCHANT, BESSIE.**
A Courageous Girl; A STORY OF URUGUAY. BY BESSIE MARCHANT. ILLUSTRATED BY W. RAINEY, R.I. LONDON: BLACKIE AND SON LIMITED, 1909. 287p. + 16p. pub. cat.: front., 5 plates. Bound in green cloth, with coloured pictorial cover and spine.
YSC 823.912 MAR

2286 **MARCHANT, BESSIE.**
The Ferry House Girls, An Australian Story. BY BESSIE MARCHANT. ILLUSTRATED BY W.R.S. STOTT. LONDON: BLACKIE AND SON LIMITED, (191–?). 283p.: front., 5 plates. Bound in blue cloth, with coloured pictorial cover and spine.
YSC 823.912 MAR

2287 **MARCHANT, BESSIE.**
A Girl Munition Worker, The Story of a Girl's Work during the Great War, BY BESSIE MARCHANT. Illustrated by J.E. Sutcliffe. LONDON: BLACKIE AND SON LIMITED, (191–?). 288p.: front., 5 plates. Bound in grey cloth, with coloured pictorial cover and spine.
C 823.912 MAR

2288 **MARCHANT, BESSIE.**
Three Girls on a Ranch, A Story of New Mexico. BY BESSIE MARCHANT. ILLUSTRATED BY W.E. WEBSTER. LONDON: BLACKIE AND SON LIMITED, (190–?). 240p. + 16p. pub. cat.: front., 3 plates. Bound in red cloth, with coloured pictorial cover and spine.
C 823.912 MAR

2289 **MARLOW, KEITH.**
ROY CARPENTER'S LESSONS. BY KEITH MARLOW. WITH FOUR ILLUSTRATIONS. LONDON: S.W. PARTRIDGE AND CO. LTD., (191–?). 64p. + 32p. pub. cat.: front., 3 plates. Bound in red cloth, with coloured pictorial/decorative cover.
C 823.912 MAR

2290 **MARLOWE, FRANCIS.**
THE SUNSET EXPRESS, A STORY OF CANADIAN RAILWAY LIFE FOR BOYS. LONDON: THOMAS NELSON AND SONS LTD., (192–?). 328p. + 3p. pub. cat.: front. Bound in brown cloth, with coloured pictorial cover and spine.
C 823.912 MAR

2291 **MARRYAT, FREDERICK.**
The LITTLE SAVAGE by CAPTAIN MARRYAT. LONDON: J.M. DENT AND SONS LTD., 1907. VIII, 269p. + 2p. pub. cat.: decorative title page. Bound in red cloth. Everyman's Library, edited by Ernest Rhys for young people. Originally published 1848.
YSC 823.7 MAR

2292 **Another copy.**
LONDON: J.M. DENT & CO. (191–?). 269p. Rebound in quarter brown leather, brown cloth. EVERYMAN'S LIBRARY FOR YOUNG PEOPLE.
C 823.8 MAR

2292A **MARRYAT, FREDERICK.**
PETER SIMPLE. BY CAPTAIN MARRYAT. LONDON: CASSELL AND COMPANY LIMITED, 1909. 436p. Rebound in red cloth. THE PEOPLE'S LIBRARY. Originally published 1834.
YSC 823.8 MAR

2292B **Another copy.**
WITH A PORTRAIT AFTER JOHN SIMPSON, TWENTY-ONE COLLOTYPE PLATES OF ETCHINGS AND DRAWINGS BY R.W. BUSS AND A BIOGRAPHICAL ESSAY BY MICHAEL SADLEIR. IN TWO VOLUMES. LONDON: CONSTABLE AND CO., LTD., 1929. LXII, 359p., XI, 379p.: fronts., 20 plates. Bound in red cloth with embossed decorative covers.
CBD 823.8 MAR

2293 **MARRYAT, FREDERICK.**
The Settlers in Canada. Written for Young People BY CAPTAIN MARRYAT. LONDON: BLACKIE AND SON LIMITED (190–?). 265p.: col. front., 3 col. plates by A. Pearse. Bound in blue cloth with embossed decorative cover and spine. Originally published 1844.
C 823.8 MAR

2294 **MARSHALL, EMMA.**
OVER THE DOWN; OR, A Chapter of Accidents. By MRS. EMMA MARSHALL. LONDON: T. NELSON AND SONS, 1904. 126p.: col. front., additional col. vignette title page. Bound in blue cloth, with coloured pictorial cover and decorative spine.
C 823.8 MAR

2295 **MARSHALL, EMMA.**
PENSHURST CASTLE IN THE TIME OF SIR PHILIP SIDNEY. BY EMMA MARSHALL. Sixth Thousand. LONDON: SEELEY AND CO. LIMITED, 1900. 325p. + 18p. pub. cat.: front., 7 plates. Bound in red cloth, with vignette on covers.
C 823.8 MAR

2296 **MARTIN, MRS. HERBERT.**
The Two Dorothys, A TALE FOR GIRLS. BY MRS. HERBERT MARTIN. ILLUSTRATED BY GORDON BROWNE. LONDON: BLACKIE AND SON LIMITED, (191–?). 224p. + 16p. pub. cat.: front., 3 plates. Bound in grey cloth, with coloured decorative cover and spine.
C 823.912 MAR

2297 **MARTINEAU, HARRIET.**
FEATS ON THE FIORD OR Rolf and Oddo among the Pirates. BY HARRIET MARTINEAU. ILLUSTRATED. LONDON: GALL AND INGLIS, (190–?). 208p.: col. front. Bound in cream cloth with coloured pictorial cover and decorative spine. Originally published 1841.
CBD 823.8 MAR

2298 **MARTINEAU, HARRIET.**
FEATS ON THE FJORD and MERDHIN. By HARRIET MARTINEAU. LONDON: J.M. DENT AND SONS, LTD., 1910. XI, 239p.: decorative front. and title page, 11 plates by A. Rackham. Bound in blue cloth. EVERYMAN'S LIBRARY FOR YOUNG PEOPLE, NO. 429.
YSC 823.8 MAR

2299 **MARX, WILLIAM JAMES.**
THE GOLDHUNTERS BY WILLIAM JAMES MARX. LONDON: THE SHELDON PRESS, (192–?). 248p. + 4p. pub. cat.: col. front. Bound in brown cloth with coloured pictorial cover.
C 823.912 MAR

2300 **MASEFIELD, JOHN.**
MARTIN HYDE, THE DUKE'S MESSENGER. BY JOHN MASEFIELD. With Illustrations by T.C. DUGDALE. LONDON: WELLS GARDNER, DARTON AND CO. LTD., 1910. VII, 303p.: front., 15 plates. Bound in green cloth, with coloured pictorial cover and spine.
C 823.912 MAS

2301 **MAYO, ISABELLA FYVIE.**
A Daughter of the Klephts; OR A GIRL OF MODERN GREECE. BY ISABELLA FYVIE MAYO (EDWARD GARRETT). WITH SIX ILLUSTRATIONS BY W. BOUCHER. LONDON: W. AND R. CHAMBERS LIMITED, (190–?). 358p. + 32p. ill. pub. cat.: front., 5 plates. Bound in blue cloth, with coloured pictorial cover and spine.
C 823.8 MAY

2302 **MEADE, L.T.**
BEYOND THE BLUE MOUNTAINS. BY L.T. MEADE. (Pseud. for ELIZABETH THOMASINA SMITH). WITH COLOUR FRONTISPIECE BY HELEN JACOBS. LONDON: CASSELL AND COMPANY LTD., (192–?). VI, 280p.: col. front. Bound in beige cloth, with coloured pictorial paper label on cover, and coloured decorative spine.
YSC 823.912 MEA

2302A **MEADE, L.T.**
The Court-Harman Girls. By L.T. MEADE. ILLUS-

TRATED BY W. RAINEY, R.I. LONDON: W. & R. CHAMBERS, LIMITED, (192–?). 415p.: front., 5 plates. Bound in blue cloth.
C 823.912 MEA

2303 **MEADE, L.T.**
DADDY'S GIRL. BY L.T. MEADE. WITH THIRTY-SEVEN ILLUSTRATIONS BY GORDON BROWNE. LONDON: GEORGE NEWNES LIMITED, 1902. VII, 340p. + 1p. pub. cat.: front., ill. Bound in blue cloth, with embossed decorative cover and spine, and gilt top edge.
C 823.912 MEA

2304 **MEADE, L.T.**
The Daughter of a Soldier. BY L.T. MEADE. WITH SIX ILLUSTRATIONS by Gordon Browne. LONDON: W. AND R. CHAMBERS LIMITED, (191–?). 331p.: col. front., 5 col. plates. Bound in brown cloth, with coloured pictorial cover and spine.
C 823.912 MEA

2305 **MEADE, L.T.**
THE DOCTOR'S CHILDREN. BY L.T. MEADE. WITH SIX ILLUSTRATIONS by A.S. Boyd. LONDON: W. AND R. CHAMBERS LIMITED, (191–?). 296p.: front., 5 plates. Bound in red cloth, with coloured pictorial cover and spine.
C 823.912 MEA

2306 **MEADE, L.T.**
DUMPS: A Plain Girl. By L.T. MEADE. WITH SIX ILLUSTRATIONS by R. Lillie. LONDON: W. AND R. CHAMBERS, LIMITED, (190–?). 316p.: front., 5 plates. Bound in blue cloth, with coloured pictorial cover and spine.
C 823.912 MEA

2306A **MEADE, L.T.**
THE GIRLS OF MERTON COLLEGE. WITH SIX COLOURED ILLUSTRATIONS BY W. RAINEY. LONDON: W. AND R. CHAMBERS, (1911). 286p.: col. front., 5 col. plates. Bound in blue cloth with coloured pictorial cover and spine.
C 823.912 MEA

2306B **MEADE, L.T.**
Peter the Pilgrim. BY L.T. MEADE. ILLUSTRATED BY HAROLD COPPING. LONDON: W. & R. CHAMBERS LIMITED, 1921. VI, 296p.: front., 3 plates. Bound in orange cloth with pictorial cover and spine.
C 823.912 MEA

2306C **MEADE, L.T.**
POLLY A NEW-FASHIONED GIRL. BY L.T. MEADE. WITH FOUR FULL-PAGE COLOURED PLATES BY A.E. JACKSON. LONDON: CASSELL AND COMPANY, LTD, (192–?). VII, 284p.: col. front., 3 col. plates. Bound in blue cloth, with coloured pictorial paper vignette on cover and coloured decorative spine.
M 823 MEA CHILDREN'S COLLECTION

2307 **MEADE, L.T.**
PRETTY-GIRL AND THE OTHERS. BY L.T. MEADE. WITH SIX ILLUSTRATIONS by Percy Tarrant. LONDON: W. AND R. CHAMBERS LIMITED, (190–?). 301p.: front., 5 plates. Bound in brown cloth, with coloured pictorial cover and spine.
C 823.912 MEA

2308 **MEADE, L.T.**
The Rebel of the School. BY L.T. MEADE. WITH EIGHT ILLUSTRATIONS BY W. RAINEY. LONDON: W. AND R. CHAMBERS LIMITED, 1902. 378p. + 32p. ill. pub. cat.: front., 7 plates. Bound in blue cloth, with coloured pictorial cover and decorative spine.
C 823.912 MEA

2308A **METCALFE, WILLIAM CHARLES.**
All Hands on Deck! ILLUSTRATED BY WILLIAM RAINEY, R.I. LONDON: BLACKIE AND SON LIMITED, (1903). 287p. + 16p. pub. cat.: col. front., 3 plates. Bound in blue cloth with coloured pictorial cover and spine.
C 823.8 MET

2309 **MILNE, ALAN ALEXANDER.**
A GALLERY OF CHILDREN. BY A.A. MILNE. Illustrated by A.H. WATSON. LONDON: HARRAP, 1939. 143p.: front., 11 plates, ill. Bound in brown linson, with coloured pictorial paper jacket.
YSC 823.912 MIL

2310 **MILNE, ALAN ALEXANDER.**
The House at Pooh Corner with decorations by E.H. SHEPARD. LONDON: METHUEN AND CO. LTD., 1928. XI, 176p.: front., ill. pictorial endpapers. Bound in blue linson with pictorial cover and a pictorial paper jacket.
YSC 823.912 MIL

2311 **MILNE, ALAN ALEXANDER.**
ONCE UPON A TIME. By A.A. MILNE. DECORATED BY CHARLES ROBINSON. LONDON: HODDER AND STOUGHTON, (1917). 269p.: col. front., pictorial title page, ill., pictorial endpapers. Bound in blue cloth with coloured pictorial cover and spine.
CBD 823.912 MIL

2312 **MILNE, ALAN ALEXANDER.**
WINNIE-THE-POOH. BY A.A. MILNE. WITH DECORATIONS BY ERNEST H. SHEPARD. LONDON: METHUEN AND CO. LTD., 1926. Second Edition. XI, 158p.: vignette title page, 11 plates, ill., pictorial endpapers. Bound in green cloth, with embossed pictorial cover and gilt top. Originally published 1926.
C 823.912 MIL

2313 **MOCKLER, GERALDINE.**
The Best of Intentions, A Story of a Brother and Sister. BY GERALDINE MOCKLER. ILLUSTRATED BY HAROLD COPPING. LONDON: BLACKIE AND SON LTD. (190–?). 160p.: front., 1 plate. Bound in red cloth with coloured decorative cover and spine. Sage Series.
C 823.8 MOC

2314 **MOCKLER, GERALDINE.**
Nell, Edie, and Toby, THEIR STRANGE ADVENTURES BY GERALDINE MOCKLER. ILLUSTRATED. LONDON: BLACKIE AND SON LIMITED (190–?). 123p. + 16p. pub. cat.: col. front., 1 plate, by H.M. Brock. Bound in blue cloth, with coloured pictorial cover and spine.
C 823.8 MOC

2315 **MOLESWORTH, MARY LOUISA.**
THE CUCKOO CLOCK. BY MRS MOLESWORTH. ILLUSTRATED BY WALTER CRANE. LONDON: MACMILLAN & CO. LTD. 1908. 242p. + 6p. pub. cat.: front., vignette, 7 plates. Bound in blue cloth with green decorative cover and spine. Originally published 1877.
YSC 823.8 MOL

2315A **Another copy.**
Illustrated with Drawings by C.E. Brock. LONDON: MACMILLAN AND CO. LIMITED, 1931. VIII, 196p. + 2p. pub. cat.: col. front., 15 col. plates, ill. Bound in green and red cloth with pictorial cover and spine and coloured pictorial endpapers.
C 823.8 MOL

2315B **MOLESWORTH, MARY LOUISA.**
The House that Grew. (Abridged). By MRS MOLESWORTH. Illustrated by ALICE B. WOODWARD. LONDON: MACMILLAN AND CO. LTD., (191–?). 64p.: Limp bound in green paper with decorative cover. The Children's Classics. INTERMEDIATE 1 (Ages 8–10). No. 30.
CP 823.8 MOL

2316 **MOLESWORTH, MARY LOUISA.**
THE LITTLE GUEST, A STORY FOR CHILDREN. BY MRS. MOLESWORTH. WITH ILLUSTRATIONS BY GERTRUDE DEMAIN HAMMOND. LONDON: MACMILLAN AND CO. LIMITED, 1907. VII, 221p. + 2p. pub. cat.: front., 7 plates. Bound in orange cloth, with decorative cover and spine.
C 823.8 MOL

2317 **MOLESWORTH, MARY LOUISA.**
THE MAN WITH THE PAN-PIPES AND OTHER STORIES. BY MRS MOLESWORTH. ILLUSTRATED BY W.J. MORGAN. LONDON: SOCIETY FOR PROMOTING CHRISTIAN KNOWLEDGE, (190–?). 96p.: col. pictorial title page, col. ill., col. headpieces to chapters, ill., engraved by Edmund Evans. Bound in orange brown cloth with coloured pictorial cover. Originally published 1892.
CBD 823.8 MOL

2318 **MOLESWORTH, MARY LOUISA.**
Miss Bouverie. BY MRS. MOLESWORTH. WITH EIGHT ILLUSTRATIONS BY LEWIS BAUMER. LONDON: W. AND R. CHAMBERS, LIMITED, (192–?). 323p.: front., 7 plates. Bound in purple cloth with coloured pictorial cover and spine. Originally published 1880.
CBD 823.8 MOL

2319 **MOLESWORTH, MARY LOUISA.**
'My-Pretty' and her little brother 'Too' and other stories, by Mrs. Molesworth. Illustrated by Lewis Baumer. LONDON: W. AND R. CHAMBERS, 1901. 229p. + 52p. ill. pub. cat.: front., 11 plates, ill. Bound in blue cloth with pictorial cover and spine.
C 823.8 MOL

2320 **MOLESWORTH, MARY LOUISA.**
The Old Pincushion. BY MRS. MOLESWORTH. WITH EIGHT COLOURED ILLUSTRATIONS by Mabel L. Attwell. LONDON: W. AND R. CHAMBERS LIMITED, 1910. 271p.: col. front., 7 col. plates. Bound in blue cloth, with coloured pictorial cover and spine. Originally published 1889.
C 823.8 MOL

2320A **MOLESWORTH, MARY LOUISA.**
THE RECTORY CHILDREN. ILLUSTRATED BY WALTER CRANE. LONDON: MACMILLAN AND CO., LIMITED, 1903. X, 212p. + 4p. pub. cat.: front., vignette on title page, 7 plates. Bound in blue cloth with decorative cover and spine.
C 823.8 MOL

2321 **MOLESWORTH, MARY LOUISA.**
THE RUBY RING. BY MRS. MOLESWORTH. WITH ILLUSTRATIONS BY ROSIE M.M. PITMAN. LONDON: MACMILLAN AND CO. LIMITED, 1904. VII, 213p. + 2p. pub. cat.: front., 7 plates. Bound in orange cloth, with decorative cover and spine.
C 823.8 MOL

2322 **MOLESWORTH, MARY LOUISA.**
THE TAPESTRY ROOM, A Child's Romance. BY MRS. MOLESWORTH. ILLUSTRATED BY WALTER CRANE. LONDON: MACMILLAN AND CO. LIMITED, 1906. VIII, 237p. + 2p. pub. cat.: front., vignette title page, 6 plates engraved by Swain. Bound in blue cloth with decorative cover. Originally published 1879.
C 823.8 MOL

2323 **MOLESWORTH, MARY LOUISA.**
The Three Witches by Mrs. Molesworth, illustrated by Lewis Baumer. LONDON: W. & R. Chambers Ltd., 1900. 278p. + 2p. pub. cat.: front., 13 plates, ill. Bound in blue cloth with coloured pictorial cover and spine.
C 823.8 MOL

2324 **MONTGOMERY, LUCY MAUD.**
ANNE'S HOUSE OF DREAMS. BY L.M. MONTGOMERY. LONDON: GEORGE G. HARRAP AND CO. LTD., 1926. 436p. Bound in green cloth.
YSC 813.52 MON

2325 **MONTGOMERY, LUCY MAUD.**
THE STORY GIRL. By L.M. MONTGOMERY. With frontispiece and cover in colour by GEORGE GIBBS. LONDON: SIR ISAAC PITMAN AND SONS LTD., 1911. VI, 365p. + 24p. pub. cat.: col. front. Bound in red cloth, with coloured pictorial paper label on cover.
YSC 813.52 MON

2326 **MOORE, DOROTHEA.**
Knights of the Red Cross. BY DOROTHEA MOORE. LONDON: THOMAS NELSON AND SONS, 1912. 197p. + 6p. pub. cat.: col. front., ill. Bound in blue cloth, with coloured pictorial cover and spine.
C 823.912 MOO

2327 **MOORE, DOROTHEA.**
UNDER THE WOLF'S FELL, A STORY OF THE "FIFTEEN". BY DOROTHEA MOORE. LONDON: S.W. PARTRIDGE AND CO. LTD., (190–?). 384p.: col. front., vignette title page, 4 col. plates by C. Clark. Bound in red cloth, with coloured decorative cover and spine.
C 823.8 MOO

2328 **MOORE, HENRY CHARLES.**
Britons at Bay, THE ADVENTURES OF TWO MIDSHIPMEN IN THE SECOND BURMESE WAR. BY HENRY CHARLES MOORE. ILLUSTRATED BY J. JELLICOE. LONDON: WELLS GARDNER, DARTON AND CO. LTD., 1906. X, 346p. + 34p. pub. cat.: front., 19 plates. Bound in beige cloth, with coloured pictorial cover and spine.
C 823.912 MOO

2329 **MORRISON, ARTHUR.**
ADVENTURES OF MARTIN HEWITT. THIRD SERIES. BY ARTHUR MORRISON. ILLUSTRATED BY T.S.C. CROWTHER. LONDON: WARD, LOCK AND CO. LIMITED, (190–?). 333p. + 10p. pub. cat.: 18 plates, ill. Bound in blue cloth with embossed vignette on cover and spine.
YSC 823.8 MOR

2330 **MOWBRAY, JOHN.**
Dismal Jimmy of the Fourth. By JOHN MOWBRAY. With Four Illustrations in Colour and Black-and-White by H.M. BROCK, R.I. LONDON: CASSELL AND COMPANY LTD., 1928. 215p.: col. front., 3 plates. Bound in brown cloth, with coloured pictorial label on cover.
C 823.912 MOW

2331 **MUNRO, NEIL.**
The Daft Days. BY NEIL MUNRO. POPULAR EDITION. LONDON: WILLIAM BLACKWOOD AND SONS, 1924. 281p. Bound in blue cloth.
C 823.912 MUN

2332 **MUNROE, KIRK.**
SNOW-SHOES AND SLEDGES; A SEQUEL TO "THE FUR-SEAL'S TOOTH". BY KIRK MUNROE. ILLUSTRATED. LONDON: EDWARD ARNOLD, (190–?). VIII, 340p.: front., 11 plates by W.A. Rogers. Bound in green cloth, with coloured pictorial cover and spine, and gilt edges.
C 823.8 MUN

2333 **MUSGRAVE, MRS. H.**
A Little Hero. BY MRS. MUSGRAVE. ILLUSTRATED. LONDON: BLACKIE AND SON LIMITED (190–?). 95p. + 12p. ill. pub. cat.: col. front. by H.M. Brock. Bound in red cloth with coloured pictorial cover and spine.
C 823.8 MUS

2334 **NESBIT, EDITH.**
The Enchanted Castle. BY E. NESBIT. (Pseud. for EDITH NESBIT BLAND.) WITH 47 ILLUSTRATIONS BY H.R. MILLAR. LONDON: T. FISHER UNWIN, 1907. 352p.: front., 46 plates. Bound in red cloth, with pictorial cover and spine and gilt top.
C 823.912 NES

2335 **NESBIT, EDITH.**
THE HOUSE OF ARDEN, A STORY FOR CHILDREN. BY E. NESBIT. ILLUSTRATED BY H.R. MILLAR. LONDON: T. FISHER UNWIN, 1908. 349p. + 2p. pub. cat.: front., 32 plates. Bound in red cloth with pictorial cover.
C 823.912 NES

2336 **NESBIT, EDITH.**
THE MAGIC CITY. BY E. NESBIT. WITH ILLUSTRATIONS BY H.R. MILLAR. LONDON: MACMILLAN AND CO. LIMITED, 1910. XIV, 333p. + 2p. pub. cat.:

"IT'S THE ENTRANCE TO THE ENCHANTED CASTLE," SAID KATHLEEN.

2334

front., 26 plates. Bound in red cloth with pictorial cover and spine.
C 823.912 NES

2337 **NESBIT, EDITH.**
THE MAGIC WORLD. BY E. NESBIT. WITH ILLUSTRATIONS BY H.R. MILLAR AND SPENCER PRYSE. LONDON: ERNEST BENN LIMITED, 1930. VIII, 280p. front., 23 plates. Bound in blue cloth, with embossed pictorial cover. Originally published 1912.
YSC 823.8 NES

2338 **NESBIT, EDITH.**
New Treasure Seekers. BY E. NESBIT. ILLUSTRATED BY GORDON BROWNE AND LEWIS BAUMER. LONDON: T. FISHER UNWIN, 1904. 328p. + 8p. pub. cat.: front., 32 plates. Bound in red cloth, with pictorial cover.
C 823.912 NES

2338A **NESBIT, EDITH.**
OSWALD BASTABLE And Others. BY E. NESBIT. ILLUSTRATED BY CHARLES E. BROCK AND H.R. MILLAR. LONDON: WELLS, GARDNER, DARTON AND CO. LTD., 1905. X, 369p. + 9p. pub. cat.: front., pictorial title page, 20 plates, ill. Bound in maroon cloth with pictorial cover and spine.
C 823.8 NES

2339 **NESBIT, EDITH.**
The Story of the Amulet. BY E. NESBIT. WITH 48 ILLUSTRATIONS BY H.R. MILLAR. LONDON: T. FISHER UNWIN, 1906. 374p. + 8p. pub. cat.: front., 47 plates. Bound in red cloth, with pictorial spine and gilt top.
C 823.912 NES

2340 **NESBIT, EDITH.**
The Would-Be-Goods. By E. Nesbit. (LONDON): (T. FISHER UNWIN), (1901). 331p.: front., additional ill. title page, (title page missing), 17 plates by Arthur H. Buckland and others. Bound in red cloth with pictorial cover, and gilt top.
C 823.912 NES

2341 **O'BYRNE, W. LORCAN.**
The Knight of the Cave; Or, The Quest of the Pallium. BY W. LORCAN O'BYRNE. ILLUSTRATED BY PAUL HARDY. LONDON: BLACKIE AND SON LIMITED, 1906. 248p. + 16p. ill. pub. cat.: front., 5 plates. Bound in green cloth, with coloured pictorial cover and spine.
C 823.912 OBY

2342 **OVERTON, ROBERT.**
SATURDAY ISLAND: OR FUN, FRIENDSHIP AND ADVENTURE AT AN ELEMENTARY COUNCIL SCHOOL. BY ROBERT OVERTON. LONDON: SAMPSON LOW, MARSTON AND COMPANY LIMITED, (191–?). 308p.: col. front., 9 plates, 8 by A.P., 1 by C.H. Phelp. Bound in green cloth, with coloured pictorial cover and spine.
C 823.912 OVE

2343 **OXENHAM, ELSIE JEANETTE.**
THE ABBEY GIRLS WIN THROUGH. By ELSIE J. OXENHAM. LONDON: COLLINS, 1938. 315p.: col. front. Bound in orange cloth.
YSC 823.912 OXE

2344 **OXENHAM, ELSIE JEANETTE.**
GIRLS OF THE HAMLET CLUB. By ELSIE JEANETTE OXENHAM. WITH FOUR COLOURED ILLUSTRATIONS by Harold C. Earnshaw. LONDON: W. AND R. CHAMBERS LIMITED, 1914. 324p.: col. front., 3 col. plates. Bound in green cloth, with coloured pictorial cover and spine.
C 823.912 OXE

2345 **OXENHAM, ELSIE JEANETTE.**
Rosaly's New School. BY ELSIE JEANETTE OXENHAM. WITH FOUR COLOURED ILLUSTRATIONS by T.J. Overnell. LONDON: W. AND R. CHAMBERS LIMITED, 1913. 303p.: col. front., 3 col. plates. Bound in blue cloth, with coloured pictorial cover and spine.
C 823.912 OXE

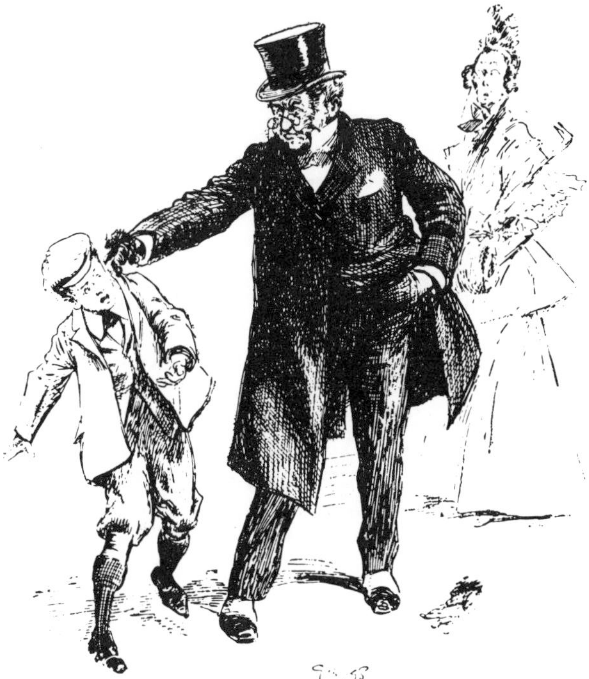

*"The old gentleman caught him by the collar, and called him a young thief."*

2338

2346 **OXLEY, J. MACDONALD.**
TERRY'S TRIALS AND TRIUMPHS. BY J. MACDONALD OXLEY. LONDON: T. NELSON AND SONS, 1903. 186p. + 6p. pub. cat.: front., 4 plates by W. Thomas Smith. Bound in blue cloth with coloured pictorial cover and spine.
C 823.912 OXL

2348 **PANTING, J. HARWOOD.**
THE BOYS OF BLAIR HOUSE. By J. HARWOOD PANTING. WITH EIGHT FULL-PAGE ILLUSTRATIONS. LONDON: "SUNDAY CIRCLE" OFFICE, 1904. 415p.: front., 7 plates by Ray Potter. Bound in red cloth with pictorial/decorative cover.
C 823.912 PAN

2349 **PANTING, J. HARWOOD.**
The Two Runaways. By J. HARWOOD PANTING. WITH SIXTEEN ORIGINAL ILLUSTRATIONS BY ERNEST HASSELDINE. LONDON: FREDERICK WARNE AND CO. (190–?). VIII, 344p.: front., 15 plates. Bound in red cloth, with pictorial cover and spine.
C 823.912 PAN

2350 **PARRY, DAVID HENRY.**
A Loyal Young Rebel. By D.H. Parry. With Four Illustrations in Colour and Black-and-White by C.E. BROCK, R.I. LONDON: CASSELL AND COMPANY, LIMITED, 1925. 216p.: col. front., 3 plates. Bound in brown cloth with coloured pictorial label on front cover.
C 823.912 PAR

2351 **PARRY, DAVID HENRY.**
Sabre and Spurs! A TALE OF THE PENINSULAR WAR. By D.H. PARRY. With Four illustrations in Colour and Black-and White by ARCHIBALD WEBB. LONDON: CASSELL AND COMPANY, LIMITED, 1926. 216p.: col. front., 3 plates. Bound in brown cloth with coloured pictorial label.
C 823.912 PAR

2352 **PARRY, DAVID HENRY.**
THE SCARLET SCOUTS. A STORY OF THE GREAT WAR. BY D.H. PARRY. WITH FOUR ILLUSTRATIONS IN COLOUR BY DUDLEY TENNANT. LONDON: CASSELL AND COMPANY, LTD., (192–?). VII, 312p.: col. front., 3 col. plates. Bound in blue cloth with coloured pictorial cover and spine.
C 823.912 PAR

2353 **PARRY, DAVID HENRY.**
THE TALE OF A TAMBOUR AND HOW HE MADE SOME NOISE IN THE WORLD. BY D.H. PARRY. ILLUSTRATED BY W. RAINEY, R.I., COLOURED FRONTISPIECE BY CHRISTOPHER CLARK, R.I. LONDON: HENRY FROWDE, HODDER AND STOUGHTON, 1913. 181p.: col. front., 10 plates. Bound in red cloth with coloured pictorial cover.
C 823.912 PAR

2354 **PARRY, DAVID HENRY.**
WITH HAIG ON THE SOMME. BY D.H. PARRY. WITH FOUR COLOUR PLATES BY ARCHIBALD WEBB. LONDON: CASSELL AND COMPANY LTD., 1917. VI, 301p.: col. front., 3 col. plates. Bound in blue cloth, with coloured pictorial cover and spine.
C 823.912 PAR

2354A **PARRY, EDWARD ABBOTT.**
GAMBLE GOLD. BY HIS HONOUR JUDGE EDWARD ABBOTT PARRY. With Illustrations by HARRY FURNISS. LONDON: HUTCHINSON AND CO., 1907. VIII, 248p.: front., 12 plates, ill. Bound in red cloth with pictorial cover and spine with gilt edges.
C 823.8 PAR

2355 **PARRY, EDWARD ABBOTT.**
KATAWAMPUS ITS TREATMENT AND CURE, AND THE FIRST BOOK OF KRAB, BY HIS HONOUR JUDGE EDWARD ABBOTT PARRY. ILLUSTRATED BY ARCHIE MACGREGOR. LONDON: WILLIAM HEINEMANN LTD., (191–?). 240p., ill. Bound in green cloth. Katawampus first published 1895.
YSC 823.8 PAR

2356 **PAYNE-GALLWEY DOROTHY.**
THE GYPSY PRINCESS, A TALE FOR CHILDREN. BY DOROTHY PAYNE-GALLWEY. ILLUSTRATED BY W.S. STACEY. LONDON: SOCIETY FOR PROMOTING CHRISTIAN KNOWLEDGE, (191–?). 215p. + 16p. pub. cat.: col. front., 2 col. plates. Bound in green cloth, with coloured pictorial cover and spine.
C 823.8 PAY

2356A **PEMBERTON, MAX.**
THE IRON PIRATE. A PLAIN TALE OF STRANGE HAPPENINGS AT SEA. WITH ILLUSTRATIONS BY ELLIS SILAS. LONDON: ASSOCIATED NEWSPAPERS LTD, 1935. 310p.: col. front., 3 plates. Bound in blue cloth with coloured pictorial cover and spine. Originally published 1893.
C 823.912 PEM

2357 **PHILLIPPS-WOLLEY, CLIVE.**
Gold, Gold in Cariboo! A Story of Adventure in British Columbia. BY CLIVE PHILLIPPS-WOLLEY. Illustrated by Godfrey C. Hindley. LONDON: BLACKIE AND SON LIMITED, (192–?). 288p.: front., 3 plates. Bound in beige cloth, with coloured pictorial cover and spine. Originally published 1894.
C 823.912 PHI

2358 **PICKERING, EDGAR.**
THE ADVENTURES OF DAVID OLIPHANT. BY EDGAR PICKERING. WITH ORIGINAL ILLUSTRATIONS BY LANCELOT SPEED. LONDON: FREDERICK WARNE AND CO., 1904. VI, 335p. + 8p. pub. cat.: front., 6 plates. Bound in blue cloth, with coloured pictorial cover and spine.
C 823.8 PIC

2359 **PICKERING, EDGAR.**
TRUE TO THE WATCHWORD. A STORY OF ADVENTURE FOR BOYS. BY EDGAR PICKERING. ILLUSTRATED BY LANCELOT SPEED. LONDON: FREDERICK WARNE AND CO., 1902. 300p. + 4p. pub. cat.: front., vignette on title page, 6 plates, ill., headpieces. Bound in red cloth with coloured pictorial cover and spine.
C 823.8 PIC

2360 **POCOCK, ROGER.**
JESSE OF CARIBOO. BY ROGER POCOCK. LONDON: JOHN MURRAY, 1911. VIII, 285p. + 2p. pub. cat. Bound in red cloth, with coloured pictorial vignette on cover.
C 823.8 POC

2361 **POLLARD, ELIZA FANNY.**
For the Emperor. LONDON: THOMAS NELSON AND SONS, (190–?). 312p. + 8p. pub. cat.: col. front., 1 col. plate by Richard Tod. Bound in blue cloth, with coloured pictorial cover and spine.
C 823.8 POL

2361A **POLLARD, ELIZA FANNY.**
The Little Chief. A Story of the Pilgrim Fathers by Eliza F. Pollard. Illustrated by T.H. Robinson. LONDON: ERNEST NISTER, (1901). 236p. + 8p. pub. cat.: front., 5 plates. Bound in blue cloth with coloured pictorial cover and spine.
C 823.8 POL

2362 **POLLARD, ELIZA FANNY.**
TRUE UNTO DEATH, A Story of Russian Life. BY ELIZA F. POLLARD. LONDON: S.W. PARTRIDGE AND CO., (191–?). 320p. + 32p. pub. cat.: front., 7 plates, 4 + front. by W.B. Wollen. Bound in blue cloth, with coloured pictorial cover and decorative spine.
C 823.8 POL

2363 **POYNTER, H. MAY.**
A FAIR JACOBITE. A Tale of the Exiled Stuarts. BY H. MAY POYNTER. LONDON: THOMAS NELSON AND

SONS, 1904. 296p.: col. front., additional col. vignette title page, by Walter C. Grieve. Bound in green cloth, with coloured pictorial label on cover and coloured decorative cover and spine.
C 823.912 POY

2364 **A RACE FOR LIFE AND OTHER TALES.**
WITH COLOURED AND OTHER ILLUSTRATIONS. LONDON: THE RELIGIOUS TRACT SOCIETY, (190–?). 316p.: col. front., 1 col. plate, 5 plates. Bound in green cloth with coloured pictorial cover and spine. Contains nine stories.
C 823.912 RAC

2365 **RAIFE, RAYMOND.**
THE QUEST FOR THE ARCTIC POPPY, A TALE OF THE GREAT ICE-WASTES OF THE FAR NORTH. BY RAYMOND RAIFE. WITH SIX FULL-PAGE ILLUSTRATIONS BY ARTHUR TWIDLE. LONDON: THE "BOY'S OWN PAPER" OFFICE, (190–?). 311p.: front., 5 plates. Bound in blue cloth, with coloured pictorial cover and spine.
C 823.912 RAI

2366 **RANSOME, ARTHUR.**
COOT CLUB. By ARTHUR RANSOME. LONDON: JONATHAN CAPE, 1934. 351p.: front., vignette title page, 21 plates, ill. (by the author), endpaper maps. Bound in green cloth.
YSC 823.912 RAN

2367 **RANSOME, ARTHUR.**
PIGEON POST by ARTHUR RANSOME. LONDON: JONATHAN CAPE, 1936. 384p.: front., 21 plates, ill. (by the author), endpaper maps. Bound in green cloth with pictorial green and white paper jacket.
Y 823.912 RAN

2368 **RANSOME ARTHUR.**
SWALLOWDALE by ARTHUR RANSOME. LONDON: JONATHAN CAPE, 1931. 453p.: front, 27 plates (by the author), ill., endpaper maps. Bound in green cloth with pictorial green and white paper jacket.
YSC 823.912 RAN

2369 **RANSOME, ARTHUR.**
SWALLOWS AND AMAZONS by ARTHUR RANSOME. Illustrated by the Author with help from Miss Nancy Blackett. LONDON: JONATHAN CAPE, 1930. 351p., front., 23 plates, map and endpaper maps by Steven Spurrier, ill. Bound in green cloth with pictorial green and white paper jacket.
YSC 823.912 RAN

2370 **RANSOME, ARTHUR.**
WE DIDN'T MEAN TO GO TO SEA by ARTHUR RANSOME. LONDON: JONATHAN CAPE, 1937. 351p.: front., 33 plates (by the author), endpaper maps. Bound in green cloth with green and white pictorial paper jacket.
YSC 823.912 RAN

2371 **RAY, ANNA CHAPIN.**
Half a Dozen Girls. BY ANNA CHAPIN RAY. Illustrated BY FRANK T. MERRILL. NEW EDITION. LONDON: JOHN F. SHAW AND CO. LTD., (191–?). 147p. + 32p. ill. pub. cat.: col. front. Bound in maroon cloth, with coloured pictorial label on cover, and decorative cover and spine.
C 823.912 RAY

2372 **RAY, ANNA CHAPIN.**
NATHALIE'S CHUM. BY ANNA CHAPIN RAY. ILLUSTRATED BY DUDLEY TENNANT. LONDON: HENRY FROWDE, HODDER AND STOUGHTON, 1910. 280p. + 16p. pub. cat.: col. front., 5 col. plates. Bound in blue cloth, with coloured pictorial cover and spine.
C 823.912 RAY

2373 **READE, F.E.**
HOW SANDY LEARNED THE CREED. BY F.E. READE. ILLUSTRATED BY J. NASH. LONDON: SOCIETY FOR PROMOTING CHRISTIAN KNOWLEDGE, (191–?). 158p. + 1p. pub. cat.: front., 2 plates. Bound in grey cloth, with coloured pictorial cover and decorative spine.
C 823.912 REA

2374 **REANEY, MRS. GEORGE SALE.**
MOLLY BROWN, A Girl in a Thousand. By MRS. G.S. REANEY. With Coloured Illustrations by Alfred Pearse. LONDON: THE RELIGIOUS TRACT SOCIETY, (190–?). 311p. + 8p. pub. cat.: col. front., col. decorative border on title page, 2 col. plates. Bound in green cloth, with coloured pictorial cover and spine.
C 823.912 REA

2375 **REASON, JOYCE.**
BRAN THE BRONZE-SMITH, A Tale of the Bronze-Age in the British Isles (by) J. Reason. LONDON: J.M. DENT AND SONS LTD., 1939. X, 310p.: ill. Bound in green linson.
YSC 823.912 REA

2376 **REDLICH, MONICA.**
JAM TOMORROW; A NOVEL FOR GIRLS. By MONICA REDLICH. Illustrated by Jack Matthew. LONDON: THOMAS NELSON AND SONS LTD., 1937. V, 330p.: col. front., 2 plates, ill. Rebound in maroon cloth.
YSC 823.912 RED

2377 **REED, TALBOT BAINES.**
The Adventures of a Three Guinea Watch. By TALBOT BAINES REED. LONDON: THE RELIGIOUS TRACT SOCIETY (190–?). 340p. + 12p. pub. cat.: front., 4 plates, ill. by Lancelot Speed. Bound in blue cloth with coloured pictorial cover and spine.
C 823.8 REE

2378 **REED, TALBOT BAINES.**
A Dog with a Bad Name. BY TALBOT BAINES REED. WITH SEVEN ILLUSTRATIONS BY ALFRED PEARSE. LONDON: THE RELIGIOUS TRACT SOCIETY (190–?). 320p. + 8p. pub. cat.: front., 6 plates. Bound in blue cloth with coloured pictorial cover and spine.
C 823.8 REE

PEARL DIVING

2369

2379 **REED, TALBOT BAINES.**
THE WILLOUGHBY CAPTAINS, A SCHOOL STORY. BY TALBOT BAINES REED. WITH TWELVE ILLUSTRATIONS BY ALFRED PEARSE. FIFTEENTH THOUSAND. LONDON: HODDER AND STOUGHTON, 1904. IV, 442p. + 2p. pub. cat.: front., 11 plates. Bound in grey cloth, with coloured pictorial/decorative cover and spine.
C 823.8 REE

2380 **REID, THOMAS MAYNE.**
Popular Adventure Tales. COMPRISING THE YOUNG VOYAGEURS; OR, THE BOY HUNTERS IN THE NORTH. THE FOREST EXILES; OR, ADVENTURES AMID THE WILDS OF THE AMAZON. THE BUSH BOYS; OR, ADVENTURES IN THE WILDS OF SOUTHERN AFRICA. BY CAPTAIN MAYNE REID. ILLUSTRATED. LONDON: SIMPKIN, MARSHALL, HAMILTON, KENT & CO. (190–?). XII, 468p.: front., ill. Bound in maroon cloth with decorative spine.
C 823.8 REI

2381 **REID, THOMAS MAYNE.**
THE RIFLE RANGERS; OR, ADVENTURES IN SOUTHERN MEXICO. BY CAPTAIN MAYNE REID. Illustrated by J.B. GREENE. LONDON: COLLINS' CLEAR-TYPE PRESS, (190–?). 296p.: col. front., 7 col. plates. Bound in red cloth, with coloured pictorial cover and spine.
C 823.8 REI

2382 **RENDEL, HUBERT P.**
Under Which King? A Story of Peace and War. By Hubert Rendel. LONDON: THOMAS NELSON AND SONS, 1904. 368p.: col. front., additional col. vignette title page, by Robert Hope. Bound in brown cloth, with coloured pictorial cover and spine.
C 823.912 REN

2383 **REYNOLDS, M.C.**
The Strange Adventures of Mr. Francis. BY M.C. REYNOLDS. Illustrated by John Cameron. LONDON: BLACKIE AND SON LIMITED, (191–?). 255p.: front., 5 plates. Bound in green cloth, with coloured pictorial cover and spine.
C 823.912 REY

2384 **RHOADES, WALTER C.**
For the Sake of his Chum. A SCHOOL STORY. BY WALTER C. RHOADES. ILLUSTRATED BY N. TENISON. LONDON: BLACKIE AND SON LIMITED, 1909. 288p. + 16p. pub. cat.: front., 5 plates. Bound in green cloth, with coloured pictorial cover and spine.
C 823.912 RHO

2385 **ROBINSON, PHILIP STEWART.**
Bubble and Squeak; Some Calamitous Stories. By Phil Robinson. With Illustrations by Cecil Aldin and J.A. Shepherd. LONDON: ISBISTER AND CO. LTD., 1902. VIII, 230p.: 15 plates, ill. Bound in green cloth, with vignette on cover and spine and gilt top.
C 823.912 ROB

2385A **ROBINSON, W. HEATH.**
BILL THE MINDER. Written and illustrated by W. HEATH ROBINSON. LONDON: CONSTABLE AND CO. LTD., 1912. XVI, 256p.: col. front., decorative/pictorial title page. 15 col. plates, 17 plates, ill. Bound in green cloth with coloured pictorial cover and decorative spine.
C 823.912 ROB

2386 **ROCHESTER, GEORGE E.**
THE SKY BANDITS. BY GEORGE E. ROCHESTER. LONDON: THE ACE PUBLISHING CO., (193–?). 223p.: front., 3 plates. Bound in red cloth.
C 823.912 ROC

2387 **ROPES, MARY EMILY.**
Wild Meg and Wee Dickie. BY MARY E. ROPES. (190–?). 160p. + 32p. ill. pub. cat.: front., 1 plate by A.P. Bound in blue cloth, with coloured decorative cover and spine.
C 823.8 ROP

2388 **SALTEN, FELIX.**
BAMBI, A LIFE IN THE WOODS. By FELIX SALTEN. Translated from the German by WHITTAKER CHAMBERS. With a foreword by JOHN GALSWORTHY. LONDON: JONATHAN CAPE, 1928. 223p.: ill., coloured pictorial endpapers. Bound in turquoise cloth, with cream dust jacket with pictorial cover.
C 833.912 SAL

2389 **SAND, GEORGE.**
THE WINGS OF COURAGE. By GEORGE SAND. (Pseud. for AMANDINE AURORE LUCILE DUDEVANT). LONDON: BLACKIE AND SON LTD., (192–?). 173p.: col. front., decorative title page, 7 col. plates, by Frank C. Pape. Bound in grey cloth, with coloured decorative cover and spine.
YSC 843.8 SAN

2389A **SCAMPERS AND SCRAPES.**
With Ten Coloured Pictures by John Hassall. LONDON: THOMAS NELSON AND SONS, 1905. 10p.: col. front., pictorial title page, 9 col. plates. Bound in blue cloth with coloured pictorial paper covers.
C 823.912 SCA

2390 **SCOTT, MICHAEL.**
The Cruise of the Midge. BY MICHAEL SCOTT. LONDON: BLACKIE AND SON LIMITED, (190–?). 256p. + 32p. pub. cat.: front. by W.S. Stacey. Bound in olive cloth, with coloured decorative cover and spine.
C 823.912 SCO

2391 **SCOTT, SIR WALTER.**
Guy Mannering; or The Astrologer. By Sir Walter Scott, Bart. Abridged, with Introduction and Notes by Y.W. Cann, M.A. LONDON: MACMILLAN AND CO., LIMITED, 1930. XIV, 193p. + 4p. pub. cat.: front. Bound in red cloth. English Literature Series. No. 126.
YSC 823.7 SCO

2391A **SCOTT, SIR WALTER.**
RED GAUNTLET. Retold for Boys and Girls. By ALICE F. JACKSON. Illustrated by MONRO S. ORR. LONDON: T.C. & E.C. JACK (191–?). 197p.: col. front., pictorial title page, 6 col. plates. Collection also includes similar editions of Ivanhoe, Peveril of the Peak, The Talisman and Waverley.
C 823.7 SCO

2392 **SEARCHFIELD, EMILY.**
THE HEIRESS OF WYVERN COURT. BY E. SEARCHFIELD. ILLUSTRATED. LONDON: CASSELL AND COMPANY LIMITED, 1900. 157p. + 2p. pub. cat.: front., 3 plates, by W.H.C. Groome. Bound in green cloth, with coloured pictorial cover and spine.
C 823.8 SEA

2393 **SEREDY, KATE.**
THE GOOD MASTER. WRITTEN AND ILLUSTRATED BY KATE SEREDY. LONDON: GEORGE G. HARRAP AND COMPANY LTD., 1937. 210p.: col. double front., vignette title page, 19 plates, ill., endpaper maps. Bound in yellow cloth, with blue dust jacket with coloured decorative cover.
YSC 813.52 SER

2394 **SETON, ERNEST THOMPSON.**
TWO LITTLE SAVAGES. Being the ADVENTURES of Two BOYS Who Lived as INDIANS and What They LEARNED. WITH OVER THREE HUNDRED DRAWINGS. Written and Illustrated By ERNEST THOMPSON SETON. LONDON: ARCHIBALD, CONSTABLE AND CO. LTD., 1911. 552p.: vignette title page, 29 plates, ill., pictorial endpapers. Bound in grey cloth, with embossed decorative cover and spine. Originally published in U.S.A. in 1903.
YSC 813.52 SET

2395 **SEWELL, ANNA.**
BLACK BEAUTY, The Autobiography of a Horse. By ANNA SEWELL. LONDON: PLANET PRESS, 1932.

128p.: Bound in cream paper, with coloured pictorial cover. Originally published 1877.
YSC 823.8 SEW

2396 **Another copy.**
Illustrated by Eighteen Plates in Colour specially drawn for this edition by CECIL ALDIN. LONDON: JARROLDS LTD. for BOOTS THE CHEMISTS (1932). VIII, 291p.: col. front., 17 col. plates. Bound in blue cloth, with pictorial cover.
CBD 823.8 SEW

2397 **SHAW, FRANK H.**
WITH JELLICOE IN THE NORTH SEA. BY CAPTAIN FRANK H. SHAW. WITH FOUR COLOUR PLATES BY J. MASON. LONDON: CASSELL AND COMPANY, LTD., 1916. VII, 311p.: col. front., 3 col. plates. Bound in blue cloth, with coloured pictorial cover and spine.
C 823.912 SHA

2398 **SHERWOOD, MARY MARTHA.**
MARGOT AND THE GOLDEN FISH. BY MRS. SHERWOOD. RE-TOLD BY AMY STEEDMAN. PICTURES BY M.D. SPOONER. LONDON: T.C. & E.C. JACK (190–?). 96p.: col. front., vignette, 7 col. plates. Bound in blue with coloured pictorial cover and reinforced spine. GRANDMOTHER'S FAVOURITES.
YSC 823.8 SHE

2399 **SILKE, LOUISA C.**
MARGARET SOMERSET, An Historical Tale. BY LOUISA C. SILKE. LONDON: THE RELIGIOUS TRACT SOCIETY, (191–?). 288p. + 16p. pub. cat.: col. front., col. vignette title page by Leonard Skeats. Bound in green cloth, with coloured pictorial cover and spine.
C 823.912 SIL

2400 **SILKE, LOUISA C.**
STEADFAST AND TRUE. A Tale of the Huguenots. BY LOUISA C. SILKE. With Coloured Illustrations. LONDON: THE RELIGIOUS TRACT SOCIETY, (191–?). 315p. + 20p. pub. cat.: col. front., 6 col. plates by J.F. Bound in beige cloth, with coloured pictorial cover and spine.
C 823.8 SIL

2401 **SITWELL, SYDNEY MARY.**
THE HERMIT OF HILLSIDE TOWER. BY MRS. ISLA SITWELL. With illustrations by E. STUART HARDY. LONDON: ERNEST NISTER (191–?). 256p. + 8p. pub. cat.: front., decorative title page, 7 plates, ill. Bound in grey cloth, with coloured pictorial cover and spine.
YSC 823.912 SIT

2402 **SLADE, GURNEY.**
A NORTH SEA QUEST. By GURNEY SLADE. ILLUSTRATED BY ERNEST RATCLIFF. LONDON: OXFORD UNIVERSITY PRESS. HUMPHREY MILFORD, 1935. 256p.: col. front., 6 plates. Bound in blue cloth, with coloured pictorial dust jacket.
C 823.912 SLA

2403 **SNOW, LAURA A. BARTER.**
HONOR'S QUEST; OR, HOW THEY CAME HOME. BY LAURA A. BARTER SNOW. LONDON: THE RELIGIOUS TRACT SOCIETY, (190–?). VI, 252p. + 16p. pub. cat.: front., 2 plates, by Oscar Wilson. Bound in green cloth, with coloured pictorial cover and spine.
C 823.8 SNO

2404 **SPRING, HOWARD.**
Darkie and Co. (BY) HOWARD SPRING. Illustrated by NORMAN HEPPLE. (LONDON): GEOFFREY CUMBERLEGE, OXFORD UNIVERSITY PRESS, 1932. 288p.: vignette title page, 8 plates. Bound in brown cloth, with pictorial cover.
C 823.912 SPR

2405 **SPRING, HOWARD.**
SAMPSON'S CIRCUS. By HOWARD SPRING. With illustrations by STEVEN SPURRIER. LONDON: FABER AND FABER LIMITED, 1936. 325p.: vignette title page, 6 plates, ill. Bound in maroon cloth, with yellow dust jacket, with pictorial cover and spine.
YSC 823.912 SPR

2406 **SPRINGS, ELLIOTT WHITE.**
CONTACT, A Romance of the Air. BY ELLIOTT WHITE SPRINGS. LONDON: JOHN HAMILTON, (193–?). 273p. Bound in blue cloth, with coloured pictorial dust jacket.
C 813.52 SPR

2407 **SPYRI, JOHANNA.**
HEIDI BY JOHANNA SPYRI. LONDON: J.M. DENT AND SONS, LTD., (1910). 262p. ill. Quarter rebound in brown leather. Everyman's Library edited by Ernest Rhys for young people. Originally published 1880.
C 823.8 SPY

2408 **STABLES, WILLIAM GORDON.**
ALLAN ADAIR; OR, HERE AND THERE IN MANY LANDS. BY DR. GORDON STABLES, R.N. WITH TEN ILLUSTRATIONS BY ALFRED PEARSE. SECOND EDITION. LONDON: THE RELIGIOUS TRACT SOCIETY, (190–?). 287p.: front., 9 plates. Bound in blue cloth, with coloured pictorial cover and spine.
C 823.8 STA

2409 **STABLES, WILLIAM GORDON.**
THE CRUISE OF THE SNOWBIRD, A Story of Arctic Adventure. BY GORDON STABLES, M.D., R.N. With Nine Illustrations. THIRTEENTH THOUSAND. LONDON: HODDER AND STOUGHTON, 1902. VI, 366p. + 2p. pub. cat.: front., 8 plates. Bound in brown cloth, with coloured pictorial/decorative cover and spine.
C 823.8 STA

2409A **STABLES, WILLIAM GORDON.**
The Cruise of the 'Vengeful'. A Story of the Royal Navy. BY GORDON STABLES. LONDON: JOHN F. SHAW AND CO., (1902) 268p. + 20p. pub. cat.: front., 3 plates. Bound in red cloth with coloured pictorial cover and spine and with gilt edges.
C 823.8 STA

2409B **STABLES, WILLIAM GORDON.**
ENGLAND'S HERO PRINCE. BY GORDON STABLES M.D. C.M. LONDON: JOHN F. SHAW, NEW ED. (1900). 378p. + 6p. pub. cat.: front., 5 plates. Bound in blue cloth with coloured pictorial cover and spine, with gilt edges.
C 823.8 STA

2410 **STABLES, WILLIAM GORDON.**
A FIGHT FOR FREEDOM, A STORY OF THE LAND OF THE TSAR. BY GORDON STABLES, M.D., C.M. WITH ILLUSTRATIONS. LONDON: JAMES NISBET AND CO. LIMITED, (190–?). VIII, 328p. + 8p. pub. cat.: front., 5 plates by C. Whymper. Bound in green cloth, with coloured decorative cover and spine.
C 823.8 STA

2410A **STABLES, WILLIAM GORDON.**
FOR CROSS OR CRESCENT. THE DAYS OF RICHARD THE LION-HEARTED. A ROMANCE. BY GORDON STABLES, M.D., R.N. LONDON: DEAN AND SON, LTD. (193–?). 247p.: col. front. by Noel Syers. Bound in blue cloth.
C 823.8 STA

2410B **STABLES, WILLIAM GORDON.**
For Life and Liberty. A Story of Battle by Land and Sea. BY GORDON STABLES, M.D. R.N. ILLUSTRATED BY SIDNEY PAGET. NEW EDITION. LONDON: BLACKIE AND SON LIMITED, 1911. 352p. + 16p. pub. cat.: front., 5 plates, double plate map. Bound in blue cloth with coloured pictorial cover and spine.
C 823.8 STA

2411 **STABLES, WILLIAM GORDON.**
"FROM GREENLAND'S ICY MOUNTAINS". A Tale of the Polar Seas. BY GORDON-STABLES, (sic) M.D., C.M. ILLUSTRATED BY W.H. OVEREND. LONDON: SOCIETY FOR PROMOTING CHRISTIAN KNOWLEDGE, (190–?). 224p. + 16p. pub. cat.: sepia front., 2 sepia plates. Bound in green cloth, with coloured pictorial cover.
C 823.8 STA

2412 **STABLES, WILLIAM GORDON.**
FROM PLOUGHSHARE TO PULPIT. BY GORDON STABLES, M.D., C.M. LONDON: JAMES NISBET AND CO. LIMITED, (191–?). VIII, 310p. + 18p. pub. cat.: col. front. by W. Lance. Bound in blue cloth, with coloured pictorial cover and spine.
C 823.8 STA

2413 **STABLES, WILLIAM GORDON.**
FROM POLE TO POLE, A TALE OF THE SEA. BY GORDON STABLES, M.D., R.N. NEW EDITION. ILLUSTRATED IN COLOUR BY ARCHIBALD WEBB. LONDON: HENRY FROWDE, HODDER AND STOUGHTON, 1909. VII, 388p. + 16p. pub. cat.: col. front., 5 col. plates. Bound in red cloth, with coloured pictorial cover and spine.
C 823.8 STA

2414 **STABLES, WILLIAM GORDON.**
In Quest of the Giant Sloth. A Tale of Adventures in South America. BY DR. GORDON STABLES, R.N. WITH SIX ILLUSTRATIONS BY J. FINNEMORE, R.I., R.B.A. LONDON: BLACKIE AND SON LIMITED, (190–?). 288p. + 16p. ill. pub. cat.: front., 5 plates. Bound in green cloth, with coloured pictorial cover and spine.
C 823.8 STA

2414A **STABLES, WILLIAM GORDON.**
In Ships of Steel. A Tale of the Navy Today. BY GORDON STABLES. LONDON: JOHN F. SHAW AND CO., (1902). 316p. + 4p. pub. cat.: front., 3 plates by H.E. Butler. Bound in blue cloth with coloured pictorial cover and spine and decorative endpapers.
C 823.8 STA

2414B **STABLES, WILLIAM GORDON.**
IN THE LAND OF THE GREAT SNOW-BEAR. A Tale of Love and Heroism. BY GORDON STABLES. WITH ILLUSTRATIONS BY GORDON BROWNE. LONDON: THE SUNDAY SCHOOL UNION, 4TH ED. (190–?). 268p.: front., 7 plates, ill. and decorative headpieces and tailpieces to chapters. Bound in red cloth with pictorial cover and decorative endpapers.
823.8 STA

2415 **STABLES, WILLIAM GORDON.**
THE IVORY HUNTERS; A Story of Wild Adventure by Land and Sea. BY DR. GORDON STABLES, R.N. ILLUSTRATED. LONDON: WARD, LOCK AND CO. LIMITED, 1909. 320p.: front., 3 plates, by A.P. Bound in pink cloth, with coloured pictorial paper label on cover, and decorative cover and spine.
YSC 823.8 STA

2416 **STABLES, WILLIAM GORDON.**
Kidnapped by Cannibals. BY GORDON STABLES, M.D., C.M. ILLUSTRATED BY J. FINNEMORE, R.B.A. LONDON: BLACKIE AND SON LIMITED, (191–?). 287p.: front., 5 plates. Bound in blue cloth, with coloured pictorial cover and spine.
YSC 823.8 STA

2416A **STABLES, WILLIAM GORDON.**
Midshipmite Curly. And other stories BY DR. GORDON STABLES, R.N. LIEUT.-COLONEL JOHN MACGREGOR, EDWARD TEBBUTT. LONDON: JOHN F. SHAW AND CO., (1903). 192p.: front. by Stewart Browne, plate by Stanley L. Wood. Bound in brown cloth with pictorial cover and spine.
C 823.8 MID

2417 **STABLES, WILLIAM GORDON.**
OFF TO KLONDYKE. BY GORDON STABLES, M.D., C.M. LONDON: JAMES NISBET AND CO. LIMITED, (190–?). VI, 327p. + 1p. pub. cat.: col. front., 3 col. plates. Bound in green cloth, with coloured pictorial label on cover and spine.
C 823.8 STA

2417A **STABLES, WILLIAM GORDON.**
ON SPECIAL SERVICE. A TALE OF LIFE AT SEA. BY GORDON STABLES, C.M., M.D., R.N. NEW EDITION. ILLUSTRATED IN COLOUR BY S.H. VEDDER. LONDON: HENRY FROWDE HODDER AND STOUGHTON, 1910. 362p. + 16p. pub. cat.: col. front., 5 col. plates. Bound in blue cloth with coloured pictorial cover and spine, with coloured edges.
C 823.8 STA

2418 **STABLES, WILLIAM GORDON.**
ON WAR'S RED TIDE, A TALE OF THE BOER WAR. BY GORDON STABLES, M.D., C.M. LONDON: JAMES NISBET AND CO. LIMITED, 1900. VIII, 328p. + 16p. pub. cat.: front., 5 plates, by Matt. B. Hewerdine. Bound in red cloth, with coloured decorative cover and spine and gilt edges. THE BOY'S HOLIDAY LIBRARY.
C 823.8 STA

2419 **STABLES, WILLIAM GORDON.**
OUT IN THE SILVER WEST. A Story of Struggle and Adventure. BY GORDON STABLES, M.D., R.N. WITH ILLUSTRATIONS BY ALFRED PEARSE. LONDON: THE RELIGIOUS TRACT SOCIETY, (190–?). 287p. + 8p. pub. cat.: front., 11 plates. Bound in blue cloth, with coloured pictorial cover and spine.
C 823.8 STA

2420 **STABLES, WILLIAM GORDON.**
THE SHELL-HUNTERS, THEIR WILD ADVENTURES BY SEA AND LAND. BY GORDON STABLES, M.D., R.N. SIXTH IMPRESSION. LONDON: THE RELIGIOUS TRACT SOCIETY, (190–?). 255p. + 16p. pub. cat.: col. front., by A. Pearse, 1 col. plate. Bound in green cloth, with coloured pictorial label on cover and coloured decorative cover and spine.
C 823.8 STA

2420A **STABLES, WILLIAM GORDON.**
SWEEPING THE SEAS. A TALE OF THE ALABAMA. BY GORDON STABLES, M.D. (SURGEON ROYAL NAVY). ILLUSTRATED BY ARCHIBALD WEBB. LONDON: ERNEST NISTER, (1902). 375p. + 8p. pub. cat.: front., 7 plates. Bound in blue cloth with coloured pictorial cover and spine.
C 823.8 STA

2420B **STABLES, WILLIAM GORDON.**
TO GREENLAND AND THE POLE. A STORY OF ADVENTURES IN THE ARCTIC REGIONS BY GORDON STABLES, M.D., C.M. NEW YORK, U.S.A.: A.L. BURT COMPANY, (191–?). 437p. + 6p. pub. cat.: front. Bound in blue cloth with coloured pictorial cover and spine.
C 823.8 STA

2421 **STABLES, WILLIAM GORDON.**
'Twixt Daydawn and Light. A TALE OF THE TIMES OF Alfred the Great. BY GORDON-STABLES (sic.). LONDON: JOHN F. SHAW AND CO., (190–?). XVI, 379p. + 4p. pub. cat.: front., 3 plates. Bound in blue cloth, with coloured pictorial cover and spine, and gilt edges.
C 823.8 STA

2421A **STABLES, WILLIAM GORDON.**
'TWIXT SCHOOL AND COLLEGE. A Tale of Self-Reliance. BY GORDON STABLES, C.M., M.D., R.N. ILLUSTRATED BY W. PARKINSON. LONDON: BLACKIE AND SON LIMITED (190–?). 352p. + 16p. pub. cat.: front., 5 plates. Bound in red cloth with coloured pictorial cover and spine.
C 823.8 STA

2422 **STABLES, WILLIAM GORDON.**
WILD ADVENTURES ROUND THE POLE; OR, THE Cruise of the "Snowbird" Crew in the "Arrandoon." BY GORDON STABLES, M.D., R.N. With Eight Illustrations. THIRTEENTH EDITION. LONDON: HODDER AND STOUGHTON, 1906. VIII, 333p. + 10p. pub. cat.: front., 7 plates. Bound in green cloth, with coloured pictorial/decorative cover and spine, and gilt edges.
C 823.8 STA

2423 **STABLES, WILLIAM GORDON.**
WILD LIFE IN SUNNY LANDS, A ROMANCE OF BUTTERFLY HUNTING. BY W. GORDON STABLES, M.D., R.N. WITH SEVEN ILLUSTRATIONS BY ALFRED PEARSE. LONDON: THE RELIGIOUS TRACT SOCIETY, (190–?). 325p. + 10p. pub. cat.: front. 6 plates. Bound in red cloth, with coloured pictorial cover and spine.
C 823.8 STA

2423A **STABLES, WILLIAM GORDON.**
YOUNG PEGGY McQUEEN, BY GORDON STABLES WITH ORIGINAL ILLUSTRATIONS. LONDON: COLLINS CLEAR-TYPE PRESS, (191–?). 190p. + 1p. pub. cat.: col. front. 2 col. plates by Warwick Goble. Bound in red cloth with coloured pictorial cover and spine.
C 823.8 STA

2424 **STEAD, RICHARD.**
ADVENTURES ON THE GREAT RIVERS, ROMANTIC INCIDENTS AND PERILS OF TRAVEL, SPORT, AND EXPLORATION THROUGHOUT THE WORLD. BY RICHARD STEAD, B.A. WITH SIXTEEN ILLUSTRATIONS. LONDON: SEELEY AND CO. LIMITED, 1907. 339p. + 28p. pub. cat.: front., 15 plates, 7 by Ernest Prater. Bound in blue cloth, with embossed pictorial and coloured decorative cover and spine. Contains 29 stories.
C 823.912 STE

2425 **STEAD, RICHARD.**
Grit will Tell. BY R. STEAD. ILLUSTRATED BY D. CARLETON SMYTH. LONDON: BLACKIE AND SON LIMITED, (191–?). 238p.: 3 plates. Bound in blue cloth with coloured pictorial cover and spine.
C 823.8 STE

2426 **STEVENSON, JOHN GILCHRIST.**
THE CHALLENGE, AND OTHER TALKS WITH BOYS AND GIRLS. BY REV. J.G. STEVENSON. WITH EIGHT ORIGINAL ILLUSTRATIONS BY T.H. ROBINSON. LONDON: JAMES CLARKE AND CO., 1906. 226p. + 32p. pub. cat.: front., 7 plates. Bound in brown cloth, with pictorial cover.
C 809.9331 STE

2426A **STEVENSON, ROBERT LOUIS.**
THE BLACK ARROW. A TALE OF THE TWO ROSES (by) ROBERT LOUIS STEVENSON ILLUSTRATED BY N.C. WYETH. LONDON: CASSELL AND CO. LIMITED, 1916. X, 296p.: col. pictorial title page, 13 col. plates. Bound in green cloth with coloured pictorial label on cover.
C 823.8 STE

2427 **STEVENSON, ROBERT LOUIS.**
FOUR STEVENSON STORIES. Edited by S.F. MOSCROP, M.A. LONDON: THOMAS NELSON AND SONS LTD., 1931. 239p. Bound in blue cloth. Includes The Sire de Malétroit's Door; Will O'the Mill; The Strange Case of Dr. Jekyll and Mr. Hyde; The Bottle Imp.
YSC 823.8 MOS

2428 **STOOKE, ELEANORA H.**
MOUSEY; OR, COUSIN ROBERT'S TREASURE. BY ELEANORA H. STOOKE. SECOND IMPRESSION. LONDON: S.W. PARTRIDGE AND CO. LTD., (190–?). 168p. + 32p. pub. cat.: front., 2 plates, by M.A. Boole. Bound in red cloth, with coloured pictorial cover and decorative spine.
C 823.912 STO

2429 **STOOKE, ELEANORA H.**
SALOME'S BURDEN; OR, THE SHADOW ON THE HOMES. BY ELEANORA H. STOOKE. WITH FOUR ILLUSTRATIONS. LONDON: S.W. PARTRIDGE AND CO., (190–?). 168p. + 32p. pub. cat.: front., 3 plates by C. Howard. Bound in red cloth, with coloured pictorial cover and spine.
C 823.912 STO

2430 **STRANG, HERBERT.**
THE ADVENTURES OF DICK TREVANION, A STORY OF EIGHTEEN HUNDRED AND FOUR. BY HERBERT STRANG (Pseud. for GEORGE HERBERT ELY AND JAMES L'ESTRANGE) ILLUSTRATED BY W. RAINEY, R.I. LONDON: HENRY FROWDE, HODDER AND STOUGHTON, 1911. 399p. + 16p. pub. cat.: col. front., 7 col. plates. Bound in red cloth, with coloured pictorial cover and spine.
C 823.912 STR

2431 **STRANG, HERBERT.**
The Adventures of Harry Rochester, A Tale of the Days of Marlborough and Eugene. BY HERBERT STRANG. NEW EDITION. LONDON: HUMPHREY MILFORD, OXFORD UNIVERSITY PRESS, 1922. VII, 417p.: col. front., 4 plates by W. Rainey, map, plan. Bound in olive cloth, with coloured pictorial vignette on cover and coloured decorative spine.
C 823.912 STR

2432 **STRANG, HERBERT.**
THE AIR PATROL, A STORY OF THE NORTH-WEST FRONTIER. BY HERBERT STRANG. ILLUSTRATED BY CYRUS CUNEO. LONDON: HENRY FROWDE, HODDER AND STOUGHTON, (191–?). 442p.: col. front., 7 col. plates. Bound in mustard cloth, with coloured pictorial cover and spine.
C 823.912 STR

2432A **STRANG, HERBERT.**
BARCLAY OF THE GUIDES. A STORY OF THE INDIAN MUTINY. BY HERBERT STRANG. ILLUSTRATED IN COLOUR BY H.W. KOEKKEK. LONDON: HODDER AND STOUGHTON, (1909). 392p.: col. front, 5 col. plates, double page map. Bound in red cloth with coloured pictorial cover and spine and tinted edges.
C 823.912 STR

2432B **STRANG, HERBERT.**
BROWN OF MOUKDEN. A Story of the Russo-Japanese War. BY HERBERT STRANG. Illustrated by William Rainey, R.I. LONDON: BLACKIE AND SON LIMITED, (1905). IX, 370p. pub. cat.: sepia front., 5 sepia plates, 3 maps. Bound in blue cloth with coloured pictorial cover and spine, with tinted edges.
C 823.912 STR

2432C **REPRINTED AS.**
JACK BROWN IN CHINA. A Story of the Russo-Japanese War. BY HERBERT STRANG. LONDON: NEW ED. OXFORD UNIVERSITY PRESS, 1938. VIII, 370p.: col. front. Bound in yellow paper with coloured pictorial cover and spine, New Ensign Series.

2433 **STRANG, HERBERT.**
THE CRUISE OF THE GYRO-CAR. BY HERBERT STRANG. ILLUSTRATED BY A.C. MICHAEL. LONDON: HENRY FROWDE, HODDER AND STOUGHTON, 1911. 243p.: col. front., 3 col. plates, map. Bound in red cloth, with coloured pictorial cover and spine.
C 823.912 STR

2433A **STRANG, HERBERT.**
THE FLYING BOAT. A STORY OF ADVENTURE AND MISADVENTURE BY HERBERT STRANG. ILLUSTRATED BY T.C. DUGDALE. LONDON: HODDER AND STOUGHTON, 1912. 271p.: col. front. 5 col. plates. Bound in blue cloth with coloured pictorial cover and spine and tinted edges.
C 823.912 STR

2433B **STRANG, HERBERT.**
A GENTLEMAN-AT-ARMS. BEING PASSAGES IN THE LIFE OF SIR CHRISTOPHER RUDD, KNIGHT, AS RELATED BY HIMSELF IN THE YEAR 1651 AND NOW SET FORTH. BY HERBERT STRANG. LONDON: OXFORD UNIVERSITY PRESS, 1914. 387p.: col. front. by Cyrus Cuneo, 3 plates and ill. by T.H. Robinson. Bound in buff paper with coloured pictorial cover and spine. New Ensign Series.
C 823.912 STR

2434 **STRANG, HERBERT.**
A HERO OF LIEGE, A STORY OF THE GREAT WAR. BY HERBERT STRANG. ILLUSTRATED BY CYRUS CUNEO. LONDON: HENRY FROWDE, HODDER AND STOUGHTON, 1914. 250p. + 6p. pub. cat.: col. front., 3 col. plates. Bound in blue cloth, with coloured pictorial cover and spine.
C 823.912 STR

2434A **STRANG, HERBERT.**
HUMPHREY BOLD. HIS CHANCES AND MISCHANCES BY LAND AND SEA. A STORY OF THE TIME OF BENBOW. BY HERBERT STRANG. ILLUSTRATED IN COLOUR BY W.H. MARGETSON. LONDON: HODDER AND STOUGHTON, 1909. 419p. + 12p. pub. cat.: col. front., 7 col. plates. Bound in red cloth with coloured pictorial paper label on cover.
C 823.912 STR

2434B **STRANG, HERBERT.**
JACK HARDY, or A Hundred Years Ago. By HERBERT STRANG. ILLUSTRATED BY WILLIAM RAINEY, R.I. LONDON: HODDER AND STOUGHTON, (1906). VIII, 232p.: sepia front., 3 sepia plates. Bound in red cloth with coloured pictorial cover and spine.
C 823.912 STR

2435 **STRANG, HERBERT.**
KING OF THE AIR; Or, To Morocco on an Airship. By HERBERT STRANG ILLUSTRATED IN COLOUR BY W.E. WEBSTER. LONDON: HENRY FROWDE, HODDER AND STOUGHTON, 1908. 272p. + 8p. pub. cat.: 3 col. plates. Bound in red cloth, with coloured pictorial cover and spine.
C 823.912 STR

2435A **STRANG HERBERT.**
KOBO. A Story of the Russo-Japanese War. BY HERBERT STRANG. Illustrated by William Rainey, R.I. LONDON: BLACKIE AND SON LIMITED, 1905. XI, 370p. + 72p. pub. cat.: sepia front., 5 sepia plates, 1 map, 1 plan. Bound in red cloth with coloured pictorial cover and spine and tinted edges.
823.912 STR

2436 **STRANG, HERBERT.**
LORD OF THE SEAS, A Story of a Submarine. By HERBERT STRANG. ILLUSTRATED IN COLOUR BY C. FLEMING WILLIAMS. LONDON: HENRY FROWDE, HODDER AND STOUGHTON, (191–?). 238p.: col. front., 3 col. plates. Bound in green cloth, with coloured pictorial label on cover and spine.
C 823.912 STR

2436A **STRANG, HERBERT.**
MARTIN OF OLD LONDON. By HERBERT STRANG. LONDON: OXFORD UNIVERSITY PRESS, 1930. 192p. col. front., 4 plates. Bound in blue cloth, with embossed pictorial cover and spine.
C 823.912 STR

2437 **STRANG, HERBERT.**
The MOTOR SCOUT. (BY) HERBERT STRANG. LONDON: HUMPHREY MILFORD, OXFORD UNIVERSITY PRESS, 1917. 303p.: col. front. by Cyrus Cuneo, pictorial endpapers. Bound in brown cloth, with embossed decorative covers and spine.
C 823.912 STR

2437A **STRANG, HERBERT.**
ON LONDON RIVER. A Story of the Days of Queen Elizabeth. By HERBERT STRANG. LONDON: OXFORD UNIVERSITY PRESS, (1929). 303p.: col. front. by T. Cuneo. Bound in red cloth with embossed decorative cover and spine.
C 823.912 STR

2437B **STRANG, HERBERT.**
ROB THE RANGER. A STORY OF THE FIGHT FOR CANADA. BY HERBERT STRANG. ILLUSTRATED IN COLOUR BY W.H. MARGETSON. LONDON: HODDER AND STOUGHTON, (1908). 406p.: col. front. 7 col. plates, 1 map, 1 plan, 1 double page plan. Bound in beige cloth with coloured pictorial cover and spine.
C 823.912 STR

2437C **STRANG, HERBERT.**
ROGER THE SCOUT. A STORY OF THE REIGN OF GEORGE THE SECOND. BY HERBERT STRANG AND GEORGE LAWRENCE. LONDON: HODDER AND STOUGHTON, 1911. 152p. + 8p. pub. cat.: col. front., 3 plates by Archibald Webb, 1 plan. Bound in red cloth with coloured pictorial cover and spine and pictorial end paper.
C 823.912 STR

2438 **STRANG, HERBERT.**
ROUND THE WORLD IN SEVEN DAYS. BY HERBERT STRANG. ILLUSTRATED BY A.C. MICHAEL. LONDON: HENRY FROWDE, HODDER AND STOUGHTON, (191–?). 295p.: col. front., 5 col. plates, map. Bound in blue cloth, with coloured pictorial cover and spine.
C 823.912 STR

2438

2438A **STRANG, HERBERT.**
SAMBA. A Story of the Rubber Slaves of the Congo. By HERBERT STRANG. ILLUSTRATED BY WILLIAM RAINEY, R.I. LONDON: HODDER AND STOUGHTON, (1906). XII, 342p. + 6p. pub. cat.: front. 7 plates. Bound in red with tinted edges.
C 823.912 STR

2438B **STRANG, HERBERT.**
TRUE AS STEEL. BY HERBERT STRANG. ILLUSTRATED BY C.E. BROCK. LONDON: OXFORD UNIVERSITY PRESS (1923). 284p.: col. front., 8 plates, ill. Bound in blue paper with coloured pictorial cover and spine. New Ensign Series.
C 823.912 STR

2438C **STRANG, HERBERT.**
WINNING HIS NAME. A Romance of Stuart Days. BY HERBERT STRANG. ILLUSTRATED BY C.E. BROCK.

LONDON: OXFORD UNIVERSITY PRESS (1922). 412p.: col. front., 10 plates. Bound in green paper with coloured pictorial cover and spine.
C 823.912 STR

2438D **STRANG, HERBERT.**
WITH DRAKE ON THE SPANISH MAIN BY HERBERT STRANG. ILLUSTRATED IN COLOUR BY ARCHIBALD WEBB. LONDON: HODDER AND STOUGHTON, (1907). 367p. + 16p. pub. cat.: col. front., 5 col. plates, 2 maps. Bound in green cloth with coloured pictorial cover and spine, with tinted edges.
C 823.912 STR

2439 **STRETTON, HESBA.**
THE LORD'S PURSE-BEARERS. BY HESBA STRETTON. LONDON: THE RELIGIOUS TRACT SOCIETY, (190–?). VI, 149p. + 20p. pub. cat.: front. by Lancelot Speed. Bound in blue cloth, with coloured decorative cover and spine.
YSC 823.8 STR

2440 **STRONG, L.A.G.**
THE OLD ARGO. By L.A.G. STRONG. Pictures by Ruth Cobb. OXFORD: BASIL BLACKWELL, (193–?). 28p.: 3 plates, ill. Bound in grey paper, with coloured pictorial paper label on cover.
YSC 823.912 STR

2441 **STUDDERT, A.F.**
UNTRUE STORIES. By A.F. STUDDERT. Illustrated by E.M. BALL. LONDON: HUMPHREY MILFORD, OXFORD UNIVERSITY PRESS, 1938. 190p.: col. front., 10 plates. Bound in red cloth, with decorative cover. Contains six stories.
YSC 823.912 STU

2442 **TARN, WILLIAM WOODTHORPE.**
THE TREASURE OF THE ISLE OF MIST. BY W.W. TARN. WITH SIX ILLUSTRATIONS BY SOMERLED MACDONALD. LONDON: PHILIP ALLAN AND CO., 1919. 163p.: front., 5 plates. Bound in green cloth.
C 823.912 TAR

2443 **TAYLOR, IRENE E. STRICKLAND.**
DIANA OR CHRIST, A TALE OF THE DAYS OF MARCUS AURELIUS. BY IRENE E. STRICKLAND TAYLOR. LONDON: THE RELIGIOUS TRACT SOCIETY, 1911. 221p. + 2p. pub. cat.: col. front., by Victor Prout. Bound in green cloth, with coloured pictorial cover and spine.
C 823.8 TAY

2444 **THACKERAY, WILLIAM MAKEPEACE.**
The History of Henry Esmond, Esq. By William Makepeace Thackeray. Abridged and Edited by A.C. Mackenzie. LONDON: MACMILLAN AND CO. LIMITED, 1929. XVI, 342p. + 4p. pub. cat.: front., 1 plate, by Hugh Thomson. Bound in red cloth. English Literature Series. No. 111. Originally published 1852.
YSC 823.8 THA

2445 **TIDDEMAN, LIZZIE ELLEN.**
Celia's Conquest. BY L.E. TIDDEMAN. WITH FOUR ILLUSTRATIONS BY J. WILSON. LONDON: W. AND R. CHAMBERS LIMITED, 1900. 286p.: front., 3 plates. Bound in blue cloth, with coloured pictorial/decorative cover and spine.
YSC 823.8 TID

2446 **TIDDEMAN, LIZZIE ELLEN.**
Little Ladybird, A STORY FOR GIRLS. BY L.E. TIDDEMAN. LONDON: BLACKIE AND SON LIMITED (190–?). 96p. +12p. ill. pub. cat.: col. front. Bound in green cloth, with coloured pictorial cover and spine.
C 823.8 TID

2447 **TIDDEMAN, LIZZIE ELLEN.**
ROBINETTA; OR, THE LIGHT OF HIS EYES. BY L.E. TIDDEMAN. LONDON: THOMAS NELSON AND SONS LTD., (192–?). 304p. + 3p. pub. cat.: col. front. Bound in orange cloth, with pictorial cover and spine.
YSC 823.8 TID

2448 **TREANOR, THOMAS STANLEY.**
HEROES OF THE GOODWIN SANDS. By the Rev. THOMAS STANLEY TREANOR, M.A. With Coloured and other Illustrations. LONDON: THE RELIGIOUS TRACT SOCIETY, (190–?). 250p. + 4p. pub. cat.: col. front., col. decorative title page, 15 plates, ill. Bound in green cloth, with coloured pictorial cover and spine.
C 823.8 TRE

2449 **TRITTEN, CHARLES.**
HEIDI GROWS UP. By CHARLES TRITTEN. (JOHANNA SPYRI'S Translator). Illustrated by PELAGIE DOANE. LONDON: COLLINS, 1939. 256p.: col. front., 19 plates, ill., pictorial endpapers. Bound in green cloth, with coloured pictorial dust jacket.
C 823.912 TRI

2450 **TURLE, JOSEPHINE.**
THE SQUIRE'S GRANDCHILDREN. BY JOSEPHINE TURLE. Illustrated by J. AYTON SYMINGTON. LONDON: WELLS GARDNER, DARTON AND CO. LTD., (190–?). IV, 124p.: front., 3 plates. Bound in green cloth, with coloured pictorial/decorative cover and spine.
C 823.912 TUR

2451 **TURLEY, CHARLES.**
A Scout's Son. By CHARLES TURLEY. LONDON: THOMAS NELSON AND SONS, (191–?). 325p. + 3p. pub. cat.: col. front., 3 col. plates by A.T. Smith. Bound in green cloth, with coloured pictorial cover and spine.
C 823.912 TUR

2452 **UTTLEY, ALISON.**
The Story of Fuzzypeg The Hedgehog, by Alison Uttley. Pictures by Margaret Tempest. LONDON: WILLIAM HEINEMANN, LTD., NEW EDITION 1934. 98p.: 23 col. plates, pictorial end papers. Bound in buff linson with pictorial cover.
YSC 823.912 UTT

2452A **UTTLEY, ALISON.**
Tales of the Four Pigs and Brock the Badger, by ALISON UTTLEY, illustrated by ALEC BUCKELS. LONDON: FABER AND FABER, 1939. 246p. front., 13 plates, ill. Bound in yellow buckram.
C 823.914 UTT

2453 **UTTLEY, ALISON.**
A TRAVELLER IN TIME, by ALISON UTTLEY. Illustrated by PHYLLIS BRAY. LONDON: FABER AND FABER, 1939. 331p.: ill. Bound in green linson with brown and black paper jacket.
YSC 823.912 UTT

2454 **VAIZEY, MRS. GEORGE DE HORNE.**
About Peggy Saville. BY MRS. GEORGE DE HORNE VAIZEY. LONDON: THE RELIGIOUS TRACT SOCIETY, (191–?). 255p. + 16p. pub. cat.: front., vignette title page, 2 plates. Bound in red cloth, with coloured pictorial cover and spine.
C 823.8 VAI

2455 **VAIZEY, MRS. GEORGE DE HORNE.**
A COLLEGE GIRL. BY MRS. GEORGE DE VAIZEY. LONDON: THE RELIGIOUS TRACT SOCIETY, 1913. 416p. + 16p. pub. cat.: col. front., 3 col. plates by W.H.C. Groome. Bound in green cloth, with coloured pictorial cover and spine.
C 823.912 VAI

2456 **VAIZEY, MRS. GEORGE DE HORNE.**
ETHELDREDA THE READY, A SCHOOL STORY. BY MRS. G. DE HORNE VAIZEY WITH FOUR FULL PAGE ILLUSTRATIONS IN COLOUR BY CHARLES HORRELL. LONDON: CASSELL AND COMPANY LTD., 1911. 316p.: col. front., 3 col. plates. Bound in blue cloth, with coloured pictorial cover and spine.
C 823.912 VAI

2457 **VAIZEY, MRS. GEORGE DE HORNE.**
THE INDEPENDENCE OF CLAIRE. BY MRS. GEORGE DE HORNE VAIZEY. WITH COLOURED ILLUSTRATIONS. LONDON: THE RELIGIOUS TRACT SOCIETY, (191–?). 380p. + 4p. pub. cat.: col. front., 1 col. plate. Bound in green cloth with coloured pictorial cover and spine.
C 823.912 VAI

2457A **VAIZEY, MRS. GEORGE DE HORNE.**
More About Peggy. BY MRS. GEORGE DE HORNE VAIZEY. WITH ILLUSTRATIONS BY M.E. EDWARDS. LONDON: RELIGIOUS TRACT SOCIETY, (1901). 287p. + 16p. pub. cat.: front. 3 plates. Bound in green cloth with pictorial cover and spine.
C 823.912 VAI

2458 **VAIZEY, MRS. GEORGE DE HORNE.**
MORE ABOUT PIXIE. By MRS. GEORGE DE HORNE VAIZEY. FOURTH IMPRESSION. WITH ILLUSTRATIONS BY W.H.C. GROOME. LONDON: THE RELIGIOUS TRACT SOCIETY, (190–?). 319p. + 16p. pub. cat.: front., 6 plates. Bound in blue cloth, with coloured pictorial cover and spine.
C 823.912 VAI

2459 **VALLINGS, HAROLD.**
THE SMUGGLERS OF HAVEN QUAY. BY HAROLD VALLINGS. ILLUSTRATED BY LANCELOT SPEED. LONDON: FREDERICK WARNE AND CO., 1911. VII, 306p. + 6p. pub. cat.: col. front., 3 col. plates, 4 plates, 1 plan. Bound in green cloth, with coloured pictorial label on cover, and pictorial spine.
C 823.912 VAL

2461 **VERNE, JULES.**
AMONG THE CANNIBALS, A Sequel TO "THE MYSTERIOUS DOCUMENT" AND "ON THE TRACK". BY JULES VERNE. LONDON: RICHARD BUTTERWORTH AND CO., (191–?). Bound in green cloth, with decorative cover and spine. Originally published 1868.
YSC 843.8 VER

2462 **VERNE, JULES.**
DICK SANDS, THE BOY CAPTAIN. BY JULES VERNE. TRANSLATED BY ELLEN F. FREWER. ILLUSTRATED. NEW EDITION. LONDON: SAMPSON LOW, MARSTON AND COMPANY LTD., (190–?). IV, 316p.: col. front., 8 plates by H. Meyer, engraved by Charles Barbant. Bound in red cloth, with coloured pictorial label on cover and pictorial/decorative spine. Originally published 1879.
C 843.8 VER

2463 **VERNE, JULES.**
DROPPED FROM THE CLOUDS. By JULES VERNE. Translated from the French by W.H.G. KINGSTON. LONDON: J.M. DENT AND SONS LTD., 1909. XIV, 240p.: decorative front. and title page, 50 plates by P. Ferat, engraved by Charles Barbant. Quarter bound in brown leather. EVERYMAN'S LIBRARY FOR YOUNG PEOPLE. Originally published 1875.
C 843.8 VER

2464 **VERNE, JULES.**
THE FIELD OF ICE. BY JULES VERNE. LONDON: GEORGE ROUTLEDGE AND SONS LTD., (191–?). 190p.: front. by H.L. Shindler. Bound in blue cloth, with coloured pictorial/decorative cover and spine. Originally published 1876.
YSC 843.8 VER

2465 **VERNE, JULES.**
THE FUR COUNTRY; OR, SEVENTY DEGREES NORTH LATITUDE. BY JULES VERNE. LONDON: SAMPSON LOW, MARSTON AND CO. LTD., (190–?). 334p.: front., 7 plates by P. Ferat. Bound in red cloth, with coloured pictorial cover and spine.
C 843.8 VER

2466 **VERNE, JULES.**
GODFREY MORGAN, A CALIFORNIAN MYSTERY. BY JULES VERNE. ILLUSTRATED. AUTHOR'S COPYRIGHT EDITION. LONDON: SAMPSON LOW, MARSTON AND COMPANY, (190–?). V, 272p. + 16p. pub. cat.: col. front., 6 col. plates, pictorial endpapers. Bound in green cloth, with coloured pictorial label on cover and decorative cover and spine. Originally published 1883.
C 843.8 VER

2467 **VERNE, JULES.**
HECTOR SERVADAC. BY JULES VERNE. ILLUSTRATED. Author's Copyright Edition. LONDON: SAMPSON LOW, MARSTON AND CO. LIMITED, (191–?). 370p.: 12 plates. Bound in red cloth, with coloured pictorial cover and spine. Originally published 1877.
YSC 843.8 VER

2468 **VERNE, JULES.**
THE LOTTERY TICKET, AND THE BEGUM'S FORTUNE. BY JULES VERNE. Numerous Illustrations. AUTHOR'S COPYRIGHT EDITION. LONDON: SAMPSON LOW, MARSTON AND COMPANY LIMITED, (191–?). 192p., IV, 239p.: front., 11 plates. Bound in green cloth, with coloured pictorial cover and spine. Originally published 1887.
YSC 843.8 VER

2469 **VERNE, JULES.**
THE MOON-VOYAGE. CONTAINING "FROM THE EARTH TO THE MOON", AND "ROUND THE MOON." BY JULES VERNE. ILLUSTRATED BY HENRY AUSTIN. LONDON: WARD, LOCK AND CO. LIMITED, (190–?). 132p., 147p. + 12p. pub. cat. Bound in green cloth, with coloured pictorial cover and spine.
C 843.8 VER

2470 **VERNE, JULES.**
THE MYSTERIOUS DOCUMENT. BY JULES VERNE. LONDON: RICHARD BUTTERWORTH, AND CO., (191–?). 192p. Bound in green cloth, with decorative cover and spine. Originally published 1868.
YSC 843.8 VER

2471 **VERNE, JULES.**
THE PURCHASE OF THE NORTH POLE, A SEQUEL TO "FROM THE EARTH TO THE MOON". BY JULES VERNE. ILLUSTRATED. LONDON: SAMPSON, LOW, MARSTON AND COMPANY LIMITED, (1919). 143p.: front., 3 plates. Bound in green cloth, with coloured pictorial cover and spine. Originally published 1889.
YSC 843.8 VER

2472 **VERNE, JULES.**
THE TOUR OF THE WORLD IN EIGHTY DAYS. BY JULES VERNE. LONDON: R.E. KING LIMITED, 1900. 184p.: front., 1 plate. Bound in blue cloth, with coloured pictorial cover and spine. Spine title: AROUND THE WORLD IN EIGHTY DAYS. Originally published 1873.
YSC 843.8 VER

2472A **W., M.C.E.**
"All About All of Us". Some Higgledy-Piggledy memories of a Happy Childhood, written for children, from a child's Point of View. By M.C.E.W. With Four Illustrations by H.M. Brock. LONDON: J.M. DENT and Co., 1901. 89p.: front., 3 plates. Bound in pale blue cloth with decorative cover and gilt top.
C 823.912 MCE

2473 **WALKER, ROWLAND.**
BY AIRSHIP TO THE TROPICS, The Amazing Adventures of Two Schoolboys. BY ROWLAND WALKER. LONDON: WARD, LOCK AND CO. LIMITED, (193–?). 256p.: front. Bound in red cloth, with pictorial cover.
C 823.912 WAL

2474 **WALMSLEY, LEO.**
THE SILVER BLIMP, A STORY OF ADVENTURE IN THE TROPICS. BY LEO WALMSLEY. LONDON: THOMAS NELSON AND SONS LTD., (192–?). 320p.: front., 7 plates by A.S. Forrest. Bound in green cloth, with coloured pictorial cover and spine.
C 823.912 WAL

2475 **WALPOLE, HUGH.**
A STRANGER. By HUGH WALPOLE. Illustrated by Roy Meldrum. RED PEPPER. By THOMAS QUAYLE. Illustrated by J.R. Monsell. OXFORD: BASIL BLACKWELL, (192–?). 31p.: 4 plates, ill. Bound in grey paper, with coloured pictorial paper label on cover.
YSC 823.912 WAL

2476 **(WALSHE, ELIZABETH HELY).**
CEDAR CREEK. A Tale of Canadian Life. WITH ILLUSTRATIONS BY SIR JOHN GILBERT. LONDON: THE RELIGIOUS TRACT SOCIETY, (190–?). 383p. + 12p. pub. cat.: col. front., 14 plates. Bound in brown cloth with coloured pictorial cover and spine. Originally published 1863.
C 823.8 WAL

2477 **WALTON, AMY CATHERINE.**
A Peep Behind the Scenes. BY MRS. O.F. WALTON. LONDON: THE RELIGIOUS TRACT SOCIETY, (190–?). 192p. + 12p. pub. cat.: front., vignette title page, 6 plates by Sydney Cowell. Bound in green cloth, with coloured pictorial label on cover and coloured decorative cover and spine. Originally published 1897.
C 823.8 WAL

2478 **Another copy.**
(192–?). 264p.: col. front. by Holloway. Bound in blue cloth, with pictorial cover and spine.
YSC 823.8 WAL

2479 **(WARNER, SUSAN BOGERT).**
(A RED WALLFLOWER). (LONDON: NISBET, (190–?)). Title page missing. 499p. + 16p. pub. cat. Bound in cream cloth, with coloured decorative cover and spine.
YSC 813.4 WAR

2480 **WATSON, FREDERICK.**
THE GHOST ROCK; OR, WHITE MAN'S GOLD. BY FREDERICK WATSON. LONDON: JAMES NISBET AND CO. LIMITED, 1912. VIII, 280p.: col. front., 4 plates by John Cameron. Bound in blue cloth, with coloured pictorial label on cover and decorative cover and spine.
C 823.912 WAT

2481 **WATSON, HELEN H.**
WHEN THE KING CAME SOUTH, A Romance of Borwick Hall. BY HELEN H. WATSON. LONDON: THE RELIGIOUS TRACT SOCIETY, (191–?). 369p.: col. front. by Victor Prout. Bound in brown cloth, with coloured pictorial cover and spine.
C 823.912 WAT

2482 **WESTERMAN, JOHN F.C.**
A MYSTERY OF THE AIR, BY JOHN F.C. WESTERMAN. ILLUSTRATED BY A. MASON TROTTER. LONDON: HUMPHREY MILFORD OXFORD UNIVERSITY PRESS, 1931. 253p.: col. front., 4 plates. Bound in blue cloth with coloured pictorial cover.
C 823.912 WES

2483 **WESTERMAN, JOHN F.C.**
PETER GARNER'S LUCK. BY JOHN F.C. WESTERMAN. LONDON: WARD, LOCK AND CO., LIMITED, 1934. 256p.: front., 3 plates by W. Edward Wigfull. Bound in brown cloth, with coloured pictorial dust jacket.
C 823.912 WES

2484 **WESTERMAN, PERCY FRANCIS.**
THE AMIR'S RUBY. BY PERCY F. WESTERMAN. Illustrated by W. Edward Wigfull. LONDON: BLACKIE AND SON LIMITED, (192–?). 224p.: front., 3 plates. Bound in brown cloth, with coloured pictorial cover and spine.
C 823.912 WES

2485 **WESTERMAN, PERCY FRANCIS.**
ANDY-ALL-ALONE. BY PERCY F. WESTERMAN. Illustrated by D.L. Mays. LONDON: BLACKIE AND SON LIMITED, (193–?). 255p.: front., 5 plates. Bound in blue cloth, with coloured pictorial dust jacket.
C 823.912 WES

2485A **WESTERMAN, PERCY FRANCIS.**
BILLY BARCROFT R.N.A.S. A STORY OF THE GREAT WAR. BY PERCY F. WESTERMAN. LONDON: S.W. PARTRIDGE AND CO. LTD., (1918). 416p.: col. front., 5 col. plates. Bound in brown cloth with coloured pictorial cover and spine.
C 823.912 WES

2486 **WESTERMAN, PERCY FRANCIS.**
CAPTAIN CAIN. BY PERCY F. WESTERMAN. LONDON: DEAN AND SON, LTD., (193–?). 248p.: col. front. Bound in blue cloth, with coloured pictorial dust jacket.
C 823.912 WES

2487 **WESTERMAN, PERCY FRANCIS.**
Captured at Tripoli. A Tale of Adventure. BY PERCY F. WESTERMAN. Illustrated by Charles M. Sheldon. LONDON: BLACKIE AND SON, LIMITED. 256p.: front., 3 plates. Bound in blue cloth with coloured pictorial cover and spine.
C 823.912 WES

2488 **WESTERMAN, PERCY FRANCIS.**
The Dispatch-Riders, The Adventures of Two British Motorcyclists in the Great War. BY PERCY F. WESTERMAN. Illustrated by F. Gillett. LONDON: BLACKIE AND SON LIMITED, (191–?). 288p.: front., 2 plates. Bound in blue cloth, with coloured pictorial cover and spine.
C 823.912 WES

2489 **WESTERMAN, PERCY FRANCIS.**
THE DREADNOUGHT OF THE AIR. BY PERCY F. WESTERMAN. LONDON: S.W. PARTRIDGE AND CO., 1914. 382p.: col. front. Bound in blue cloth, with pictorial spine.
C 823.912 WES

2490 **WESTERMAN, PERCY FRANCIS.**
The Fight for Constantinople. A Story of the Gallipoli Peninsula. BY PERCY F. WESTERMAN. Illustrated by W.E. Wigfull. LONDON: BLACKIE AND SON LIMITED, (191–?). 256p.: col. front., 4 plates. Bound in blue cloth, with coloured pictorial cover and spine.
C 823.912 WES

2490A **WESTERMAN, PERCY FRANCIS.**
The Junior Cadet. BY PERCY F. WESTERMAN. Illustrated by Rowland Hilder. LONDON: BLACKIE AND SON LIMITED, (1928). 255p.: front., 5 plates. Bound in beige cloth with coloured pictorial cover and spine.
C 823.912 WES

2491 **WESTERMAN, PERCY FRANCIS.**
A Lad of Grit, A Story of Adventure on Land and Sea in Restoration Times. BY PERCY F. WESTERMAN. ILLUSTRATED BY EDWARD S. HODGSON. LONDON: BLACKIE AND SON LIMITED, (192–?). 240p.: front., 3 plates. Bound in green cloth, with coloured pictorial cover and spine.
C 823.912 WES

2491A **WESTERMAN, PERCY FRANCIS.**
Leslie Dexter, Cadet. BY PERCY F. WESTERMAN. Illustrated by Norman Hepple. LONDON: BLACKIE AND SON LIMITED, (1930). 255p. front., 5 plates. Bound in black cloth with coloured pictorial cover and spine.
C 823.912 WES

2492 **WESTERMAN, PERCY FRANCIS.**
Midshipman Raxworthy. BY PERCY F. WESTERMAN. Illustrated by E.S. Hodgson. LONDON: BLACKIE AND SON LIMITED, (193–?). 208p.: front., 2 plates. Bound in blue cloth.
C 823.912 WES

2492A **WESTERMAN, PERCY FRANCIS.**
A Mystery of the Broads BY PERCY F. WESTERMAN. Illustrated by E.A. Cox. LONDON: BLACKIE AND SON LIMITED, (1930). 223p.: front., 3 plates. Bound in blue cloth with coloured pictorial cover and spine and coloured pictorial paper dust cover.
C 823.912 WES

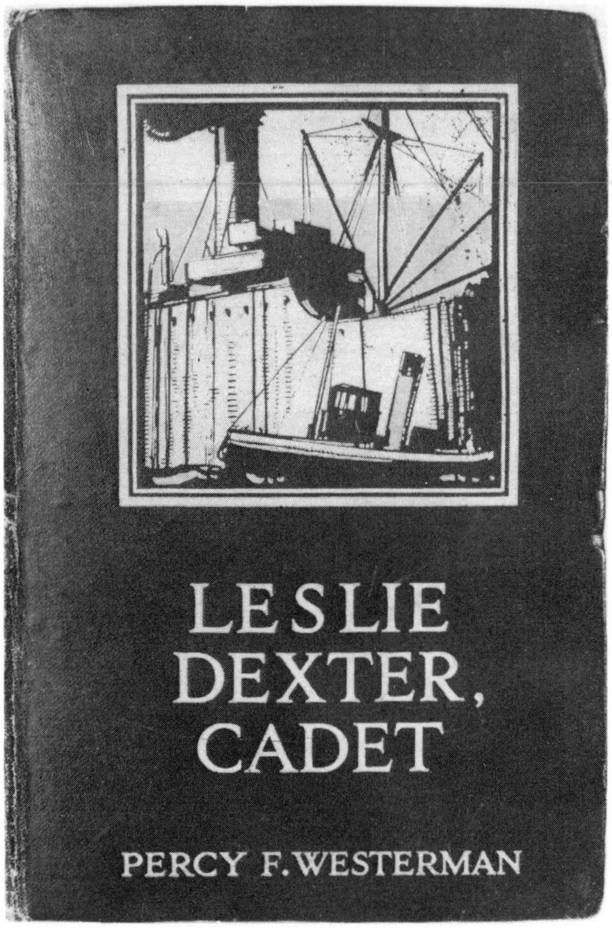


2491A

2492B **WESTERMAN, PERCY FRANCIS.**
THE PERCY WESTERMAN OMNIBUS. Three Famous Books. THE PIRATE SUBMARINE, CAPTAIN CAIN, THE FLYING SUBMARINE. LONDON: NISBET AND CO. LTD., (1933). VIII, 296, 284, 288p. Bound in brown cloth.
823.912 WES

2493 **WESTERMAN, PERCY FRANCIS.**
THE RIVAL SUBMARINES. BY PERCY F. WESTERMAN. ILLUSTRATED BY C. FLEMING WILLIAMS. THIRD IMPRESSION. LONDON: S.W. PARTRIDGE AND CO. LTD., (191–?). 432p.: front., 5 plates. Bound in red cloth, with coloured pictorial cover and spine.
C 823.912 WES

2493A **WESTERMAN, PERCY FRANCIS.**
THE SECRET BATTLEPLANE BY PERCY F. WESTERMAN. ILLUSTRATED BY ERNEST PRATER. LONDON: S.W. PARTRIDGE AND CO., (1916). 254p. front., 3 plates. Bound in red cloth with coloured pictorial cover and spine.
C 823.912 WES

2494 **WESTERMAN, PERCY FRANCIS.**
A SUB AND A SUBMARINE. The Story of H.M. Submarine R19 in the Great War. BY PERCY F. WESTERMAN. Illustrated by E.S. Hodgson. LONDON: BLACKIE AND SON, LIMITED. (192–?). 256p.: col. front., 4 plates. Bound in green cloth with coloured pictorial cover and spine.
C 823.912 WES

2495 **WESTERMAN, PERCY FRANCIS.**
The Submarine Hunters, A Story of Naval Patrol Work in the Great War. BY PERCY F. WESTERMAN. Illustrated by E.S. Hodgson. LONDON: BLACKIE AND SON LIMITED, (191–?). 288p.: front., 5 plates. Bound in blue cloth, with coloured pictorial cover and spine.
C 823.912 WES

2496 **WESTERMAN, PERCY FRANCIS.**
THE THIRD OFFICER, A Present-day Pirate Story. BY PERCY F. WESTERMAN. Illustrated by E.S. Hodgson. LONDON: BLACKIE AND SON LIMITED, (192–?). 288p.: front., 3 plates + 2 plans. Bound in blue cloth, with coloured pictorial cover and spine.
C 823.912 WES

2496A **WESTERMAN, PERCY FRANCIS.**
THE TREASURE OF THE "SAN PHILIPO" BY PERCY F. WESTERMAN. LONDON: THE BOY'S OWN PAPER OFFICE, (1916). 248p. + 8p. pub. cat. for Religious Tract Society: front. Bound in olive cloth with coloured pictorial cover and spine.
C 823.912 WES

2497 **WESTERMAN, PERCY FRANCIS.**
UNDER KING HENRY'S BANNERS, A STORY OF THE DAYS OF AGINCOURT. By PERCY F. WESTERMAN. WITH ILLUSTRATIONS BY JOHN CAMPBELL. LONDON: THE PIGRIM PRESS, (191–?). VIII, 310p. + 2p. pub. cat.: col. front., 4 plates. Bound in red cloth, with coloured pictorial cover and spine.
C 823.912 WES

2498 **WESTERMAN, PERCY FRANCIS.**
A WATCH-DOG OF THE NORTH SEA, A NAVAL STORY OF THE GREAT WAR. BY PERCY F. WESTERMAN. LONDON: S.W. PARTRIDGE AND CO., 1916. VII, 375p.: col. front., 7 col. plates. Bound in brown cloth, with coloured pictorial cover and spine.
C 823.912 WES

2499 **Another copy.**
ILLUSTRATED BY C.M. PADDAY. LONDON: S.W. PARTRIDGE AND CO. LTD., (192–?). VII, 375p.: col. front., 5 col. plates. Bound in blue cloth, with coloured pictorial cover and spine.

2500 **WESTERMAN, PERCY FRANCIS.**
WILMSHURST OF THE FRONTIER FORCE. BY PERCY F. WESTERMAN. LONDON: PARTRIDGE, (193–?). 252p.: front. by Ernest Prater. Bound in red linson, with pictorial cover and spine.
C 823.912 WES

2501 **WESTERMAN, PERCY FRANCIS.**
With Beatty off Jutland, A Romance of the Great Sea Fight. BY PERCY F. WESTERMAN. Illustrated by Frank Gillett, R.I. LONDON: BLACKIE AND SON LIMITED, (191–?). 284p.: front., 5 plates. Bound in blue cloth, with coloured pictorial cover and spine.
C 823.912 WES

2502 **WEVILL, LILIAN F.**
Betty's Next Term. BY LILIAN F. WEVILL. ILLUSTRATED BY A.A. DIXON. LONDON: BLACKIE AND SON LIMITED, 1912. 288p.: front., 5 plates. Bound in green cloth, with coloured pictorial cover and spine.
C 823.912 WEV

2502A **WHISTLER, CHARLES W.**
A Sea Queen's Sailing. By CHARLES W. WHISTLER M.R.C.S. LONDON: THOMAS NELSON AND SONS, (1910). 368p.: col. front., title page printed in red and black, 3 col. plates by W.H.C. Groome. Bound in brown cloth with coloured pictorial cover and spine.
823.912 WHI

2503 **WHITFELD, J.M.**
GLADYS AND JACK. (BY) J.M. WHITFELD. LONDON: HENRY FROWDE, HODDER AND STOUGHTON, (192–?). 318p. + 2p. pub. cat.: col. front. by N. Tenison, decorative title page, pictorial endpapers. Bound in brown cloth, with embossed decorative covers and spine. Originally published 1914.
YSC 823.912 WHI

2504 **WHITFELD, J.M.**
TOM WHO WAS RACHEL. BY J.M. WHITFELD. ILLUSTRATED IN COLOUR BY N. TENISON.

LONDON: HENRY FROWDE, HODDER AND STOUGHTON, 1911. 317p.: col. front., 5 col. plates. Bound in brown cloth, with coloured pictorial cover and spine.
YSC 823.912 WHI

2505 **WHITING, MARY BRADFORD.**
A THORNY WAY. (BY) MARY B. WHITING. LONDON: THOMAS NELSON AND SONS LTD., (191–?). 279p. + 3p. pub. cat.: col. front., 3 col. plates by E.F. Skinner. Bound in grey cloth, with coloured pictorial/decorative cover and spine. NELSON'S LIBRARY FOR GIRLS.
C 823.912 WHI

2506 **WHYTE-MELVILLE, GEORGE JOHN.**
THE QUEEN'S MARIES. (BY) G.J. WHYTE MELVILLE. ILLUSTRATED BY I.J. SYMES. LONDON: COLLINS' CLEAR-TYPE PRESS, (193–?). 475p.: front., pictorial/decorative title page, 4 plates. Bound in red cloth, with decorative cover and spine. Originally published 1862.
YSC 823.8 WHY

2507 **WIGGIN, KATE DOUGLAS.**
THE BIRDS' CHRISTMAS CAROL. BY KATE DOUGLAS WIGGIN. Two hundred and fifty-seventh thousand. LONDON: GAY AND HANCOCK LTD., 1910. 66p.: front., vignette title page, 4 plates, ill., by H.R.H. Bound in beige cloth, with pictorial/decorative cover.
YSC 813.52 WIG

2508 **WIGGIN, KATE DOUGLAS.**
THE DIARY OF A GOOSE GIRL. BY KATE DOUGLAS WIGGIN. With Illustrations by CLAUDE A. SHEPPERSON. U.S.A., BOSTON: HOUGHTON, MIFFLIN AND COMPANY, 1902. 117p.: front., ill. Bound in cream cloth, with coloured pictorial cover and spine.
C 813.52 WIG

2509 **WIGGIN, KATE DOUGLAS.**
MOTHER CAREY'S CHICKENS. BY KATE DOUGLAS WIGGIN. U.S.A., NEW YORK: GROSSET AND DUNLAP, (1911). V, 355p. + 4p. pub. cat.: front., decorative title page, 6 plates (1 missing), by Alice Barber Stephens. Bound in green cloth, with coloured pictorial/decorative cover and spine.
YSC 813.52 WIG

2510 **WIGGIN, KATE DOUGLAS.**
Penelope's English Experiences, BEING EXTRACTS FROM THE COMMONPLACE BOOK OF PENELOPE HAMILTON. BY KATE DOUGLAS WIGGIN. ILLUSTRATED BY CHARLES E. BROCK. LONDON: GAY AND BIRD, 1904. XII, 174p.: front., 15 plates, ill. Bound in green cloth, with embossed decorative cover and spine, and gilt edges. Cover title: PENELOPE'S EXPERIENCES: ENGLAND.
C 823.912 WIG

2511 **WIGGIN, KATE DOUGLAS.**
Penelope's Experiences in Scotland, BEING EXTRACTS FROM THE COMMONPLACE BOOK OF PENELOPE HAMILTON. BY KATE DOUGLAS WIGGIN. ILLUSTRATED BY CHARLES E. BROCK. LONDON: GAY AND BIRD, 1900. XII, 301p.: front., 13 plates, ill. Bound in green cloth, with embossed decorative cover and spine, and gilt edges.
C 823.912 WIG

2512 **WIGGIN, KATE DOUGLAS.**
Penelope's Irish Experiences. BY KATE DOUGLAS WIGGIN. ILLUSTRATED BY CHARLES E. BROCK. LONDON: GAY AND BIRD, 1902. XIV, 335p.: front., 12 plates, ill. Bound in green cloth, with embossed decorative cover and spine, and gilt edges. Cover title: PENELOPE'S EXPERIENCES: IRELAND.
C 823.912 WIG

2513 **WIGGIN, KATE DOUGLAS.**
REBECCA of Sunnybrook Farm. BY KATE DOUGLAS WIGGIN. LONDON: ADAM AND CHARLES BLACK, new edition, 1929. 276p. Bound in red linson with coloured pictorial paper jacket. Originally published 1903.
YSC 813.52 WIG

2514 **WILSON, THEODORA WILSON.**
The Children of Trafalgar Square. BY THEODORA WILSON WILSON. Illustrated by Gordon Browne, R.I. LONDON: BLACKIE AND SON LIMITED, (191–?). 256p.: (front. missing), 4 plates. Bound in olive cloth, with coloured pictorial cover and spine.
C 823.912 WIL

2515 **WINDER, F.H.**
With the Sea Kings. A Story of the Days of Lord Nelson. By F.H. WINDER. WITH FOUR ILLUSTRATIONS BY W.S. STACEY. NEW EDITION. LONDON: BLACKIE AND SON LIMITED, 1904. 320p. + 32p. ill. pub. cat.: front., 3 plates. Bound in green cloth with coloured pictorial cover and spine.
C 823.8 WIN

2516 **WODEHOUSE, PELHAM GRENVILLE.**
THE WHITE FEATHER. BY P.G. WODEHOUSE. CONTAINING TWELVE FULL-PAGE ILLUSTRATIONS BY W. TOWNEND. LONDON: ADAM AND CHARLES BLACK, 1907. 284p.: (front. missing), 11 plates. Bound in mustard cloth, with coloured pictorial cover and spine.
C 823.912 WOD

2517 **WOOD, FRANCES HARIOTT.**
THE OLD RED SCHOOL-HOUSE, A Canadian Bush Tale. BY FRANCES HARIOTT (sic.) WOOD. FULLY ILLUSTRATED. LONDON: S.W. PARTRIDGE AND CO. LTD., (191–?). 160p. + 32p. pub. cat.: front., 3 plates, 2 by Harold Copping. Bound in red cloth, with coloured pictorial cover and decorative spine.
C 823.912 WOO

2519 **WOTTON, MABEL E.**
THE LITTLE BROWNS. BY MABEL E. WOTTON. ILLUSTRATED BY H.M. BROCK. LONDON: BLACKIE AND SON LTD., 1900. 216p.: col. front., pictorial/decorative title page, 7 plates, ill., decorative endpapers. Bound in grey cloth, with coloured pictorial/decorative cover and spine, and gilt edges.
C 823.912 WOT

2519A **WRIGHT, WALTER P.**
AN OCEAN ADVENTURER, or, The Cruise of the Orb. WITH FOUR ILLUSTRATIONS BY PAUL HARDY. LONDON: BLACKIE AND SON LIMITED, (1900). 240p. + 32p. pub. cat.: front., 3 plates. Bound in blue cloth with coloured pictorial cover and spine.
C 823.912 WRI

2520 **WYNNE, MAY.**
A HEATHER HOLIDAY. BY MAY WYNNE. Illustrated by Thos. Somerfield. LONDON: BLACKIE AND SON LIMITED, (192–?). 208p.: front., 3 plates. Bound in green cloth, with coloured pictorial cover and spine.
C 823.912 WYN

2521 **YONGE, CHARLOTTE MARY.**
A Book of Golden Deeds of all Times and all Lands. GATHERED AND NARRATED BY CHARLOTTE M. YONGE. LONDON: BLACKIE AND SON LIMITED, (191–?). 352p. + 2p. pub. cat.: col. front., 2 col. plates, by Paul Hardy, 1 col. plate. Bound in brown cloth, with coloured decorative cover and spine. Originally published 1864.
YSC 823.8 YON

2522 **YOUNG, EGERTON RYERSON.**
ON THE INDIAN TRAIL, And Other Stories of Missionary Work among the Cree and Saulteaux Indians. By EGERTON R. YOUNG. LONDON: THE RELIGIOUS TRACT SOCIETY, (190–?). 278p.: front., 14 plates, 8 by J.E. Laughlin. Bound in green cloth, with coloured pictorial cover and spine.
C 823.8 YOU

2523 **YOUNG, EGERTON RYERSON.**
THREE BOYS IN THE WILD NORTH LAND. BY EGERTON R. YOUNG. LONDON: ROBERT CULLEY, (190–?). IX, 311p.: col. front., 5 col. plates, ill. Bound in brown cloth, with coloured pictorial cover and spine.
C 823.8 YOU

# 19 ANTHOLOGIES OF STORIES BY DIFFERENT AUTHORS

2524 **ALL THE FUN OF THE FAIR.**
A PICTURE BOOK FOR LITTLE FOLKS. LONDON: CASSELL AND COMPANY LTD., (191–?). Unpaginated: col. front. by Mabel Lucie Attwell, decorative title page, 24 col. plates, 22 plates, ill. Bound in green cloth, with coloured pictorial cover.
C 823.01 ALL

2525 **ASQUITH, CYNTHIA** *(Editor).*
Sails of Gold Edited by Lady Cynthia Asquith. LONDON: JARROLDS PUBLISHERS LTD., (192–?). 166p.: col. front., 3 col. plates, 11 plates, ill., decorative endpapers, by A.K. Macdonald. A.H. Watson, Daphne Jerrold, Hugh Lofting and Denis Mackail. Bound in red cloth, with coloured pictorial dust jacket. Includes stories by John Buchan, Hilaire Belloc, and A.A. Milne.
C 820.809282 SAI

2526 **AVERY, CHARLES HAROLD.**
GUNPOWDER TREASON AND PLOT, And Other Stories for Boys. BY HAROLD AVERY, FRED WHISHAW AND R.B. TOWNSHEND. WITH FOURTEEN ILLUSTRATIONS. LONDON: THOMAS NELSON AND SONS, 1907. 195p. + 6p. pub. cat.: front., 13 plates. Bound in blue cloth, with coloured pictorial cover and spine.
C 823.912 AVE

2526A **THE BIG CHRISTMAS WONDER BOOK.**
Edited by JOHN R. CROSLAND AND J.M. PARISH. LONDON: ODHAMS PRESS LTD., (1936). 768p.: col. front., pictorial title page, 4 col. plates, 8 col. plates as souvenir of Coronation of Edward VIII, 1936, ill. Bound in red cloth with embossed pictorial cover and spine. Includes contributions by prominent authors such as Rudyard Kipling and H.G. Wells.
C 820.809282 BIG

2527 **BLACKIE'S BOYS' STORY BOOK.**
LONDON: BLACKIE AND SON LIMITED, (193–?). VI, 198p.: col. front., pictorial title page, 8 plates, ill. Bound in brown cloth, with coloured pictorial cover. Contains nineteen stories.
C 823.91208 BLA

2528 **A BOOK OF NONSENSE: VERSE, PROSE AND PICTURES.**
COLLECTED BY ERNEST RHYS. LONDON: J.M. DENT AND SONS LTD., 1927. XIV, 283p.: 1 plate, ill. Bound in green cloth, with pictorial/decorative dust jacket. Includes work by Edward Lear, Lewis Carroll, and others.
C 808.803 BOO

2529 **CLARKE, J. ERSKINE** *(Editor).*
ANNIE BOURNE AND OTHER TALES. SELECTED AND EDITED BY J. ERSKINE CLARKE, M.A. LONDON: WELLS GARDNER, DARTON AND CO., 1898. 48p., 36p., 36p. + 4p. pub. cat.: front., 2 plates, ill. Bound in blue cloth, with pictorial/decorative cover and spine. Contains four stories.
C 823.8 ANN

2530 **THE COLLEEN'S CHOICE AND OTHER STORIES FOR GIRLS.**
BY M.B. MANNELL, IDA LEMON, EDITH HENRIETTA FOWLER, HARRY DAVIES, K.E. VERNHAM, LUCY HARDY AND OTHERS. LONDON: THE RELIGIOUS TRACT SOCIETY, (190–?). 224p. + 16p. pub. cat. Bound in blue cloth with decorative cover and inserted coloured pictorial paper label.
YSC 823.8 MAN

2531 **DAYS OF GRACE.**
SELECTED READING FOR OLD AND YOUNG. 26 ILLUSTRATIONS. GLASGOW: THE PUBLISHING OFFICE (OF "THE WITNESS"), (188–?). 144p., ill. Bound in brown cloth with decorative cover.
YSC 052 DAY

2532 **FENN, GEORGE MANVILLE** *(Editor).*
THE WORLD OF WIT AND HUMOUR. EDITED BY GEORGE MANVILLE FENN. LONDON: CASSELL, PETTER AND GALPIN, (187–?). XV, 480p.: front., vignette title page, 9 plates, ill. Half bound in leather, with embossed decorative spine.
C 827.8 FEN

2534 **FULLER, ALFRED J.** *(Editor).*
IN STORYLAND. A Volume of original Pictures, Stories and Verses written by G.A. Henty, L.T. Meade, G. Manville Fenn etc. etc. And illustrated by Ada Dennis, E. Stuart Hardy, E. Lane, Hilda Robinson and others. Edited and arranged by Alfred J. Fuller. LONDON: ERNEST NISTER, (1905). 144p. 10 col. plates, 9 plates, ill. Bound in green cloth with coloured pictorial paper cover.
YSC 372.4 HEN

2535 **THE GIRLS' BUDGET.**
LONDON: BLACKIE AND SON LIMITED, (192–?). 128p.: col. front., 2 plates, ill., by e.g. Gordon Browne, Frank Gillett and H.R. Millar. Bound with paper-covered boards, with coloured pictorial cover and spine. Contains sixteen stories.
C 823.912 GIR

2535A **GOOD AFTERNOON CHILDREN.**
Edited by COLUMBUS. Wireless Stories and plays from the Children's Hour. Illustrations by MORTON-SALE. LONDON: HODDER AND STOUGHTON, (193–?). 267p.: col. front., 3 col. plates, 15 plates, ill. Bound in yellow cloth with pictorial cover and spine and yellow pictorial paper dust cover.
C 820.809282 GOO

2536 **HENTY, GEORGE ALFRED** *(Editor).*
Yule-Tide Yarns. Edited by G.A. Henty. With Forty-five Illustrations. REISSUE. LONDON: LONGMANS, GREEN AND CO., 1899. XI, 370p.: front., vignette title page, 20 plates, ill. Bound in brown cloth, with coloured pictorial/decorative cover and spine, and gilt edges. Contains ten stories.
C 823.8 YUL

2537 **A HUNDRED ANECDOTES OF ANIMALS.**
WITH PICTURES BY PERCY J. BILLINGHURST. LONDON: JOHN LANE, THE BODLEY HEAD, 1901. VIII, 202p. + 2p. pub. cat.: front., decorative title page, 100 plates. Bound in blue cloth, with coloured pictorial cover and spine.
C 808.83936 HUN

2538 **KINGSTON, WILLIAM HENRY GILES.**
HOLIDAY STORIES BY W.H.G. KINGSTON, MRS. S.C. HALL AND OTHER AUTHORS. ILLUSTRATED. LONDON: GROOMBRIDGE AND SONS, 1879. Unpaginated, 4p. pub. cat.: col. front. by F. Lydon, 5 plates, ill. Bound in brown cloth, with decorative cover and spine, and gilt edges. Contains ten stories.
C 823.8 KIN

2539 **KINGSTON, WILLIAM HENRY GILES.**
Popular School Tales. BY W.H.G. KINGSTON, Rev. WILLIAM ADAMS, M.A., E.J. MAY. SECOND EDITION. ILLUSTRATED. LONDON: SIMPKIN, MARSHALL, HAMILTON, KENT, AND CO., (191–?). 466p. front., 15 plates. Bound in blue cloth, with decorative spine. Contains three stories: Ernest Bracebridge at School, by Kingston; The Cherry Stones, by Adams; and Louis' School Days, by May.
C 823.91208 KIN

2540 **LAMBORN, E.A. GREENING** *(Editor).*
PRESENT-DAY PROSE. LONDON: SIDGWICK AND JACKSON, LTD., 1928. XII, 244p. Bound in maroon paper.
YSC 828 LAM

2541 **LANG, ANDREW** *(Editor).*
THE ANIMAL STORY BOOK. EDITED BY ANDREW LANG. WITH NUMEROUS ILLUSTRATIONS BY H.J. FORD. NEW IMPRESSION. LONDON: LONGMANS, GREEN AND CO., 1908. XIV, 400p.: front., vignette title

page, 29 plates, ill. Bound in blue cloth, with embossed pictorial cover and spine, and gilt edges. Contains sixty-five stories.
C 823.008036 LAN

2542 **LUCAS, EDWARD VERRALL** *(Editor).*
FORGOTTEN TALES OF LONG AGO. SELECTED BY E.V. LUCAS. WITH ILLUSTRATIONS BY F.D. BEDFORD. LONDON: WELLS, GARDNER, DARTON AND CO. LTD., (190–?). XVIII, 424p. + 7p. ill. pub. cat.: col. front., col. pictorial title page, 22 plates. Bound in cream cloth, with coloured pictorial cover and spine. Twenty stories mainly from the late eighteenth and early nineteenth century.
C 823.008 FOR

2543 **LUCAS, EDWARD VERRALL** *(Editor).*
OLD FASHIONED TALES, SELECTED BY E.V. LUCAS WITH ILLUSTRATIONS BY F.D. BEDFORD. LONDON: WELLS, GARDNER, DARTON & CO. LTD. (1905). XXVI, 390p.: col. front., decorative coloured title page, 38 plates and decorations. Bound in blue cloth with pictorial cover and spine. A selection of stories by late eighteenth and early nineteenth century authors.
C 808.899282 OLD

2544 **(MACKARNESS, MATILDA ANNE)** *(Editor).*
THE MAGNET STORIES FOR SUMMER AND WINTER NIGHTS. BY THE AUTHOR OF "A TRAP TO CATCH A SUNBEAM" (i.e. Matilda Anne Mackarness), FRANCES BROWNE, L.A. HALL, EMILY TAYLOR, H.J. WOOD, W.H.G. KINGSTON, THE AUTHOR OF "THE HEIR OF REDCLYFFE" (i.e. CHARLOTTE MARY YONGE). LONDON: GROOMBRIDGE AND SONS, (186–?). 334p.: 13 plates, ill., by D.H. Friston, engraved by E. Whimper. Rebound in green cloth. Contains seven stories.
C 823.8008 MAC and C 823.8 MAC

2545 **MARRIOTT, J.W.** *(Editor).*
SHORT STORIES OF TODAY. SELECTED BY J.W. MARRIOTT. LONDON: GEORGE G. HARRAP AND CO. LTD., 1924. 295p. Bound in buff cloth.
YSC 823.01 MAR

2546 **MILES, ALFRED H.** *(Editor).*
CAPTURED BY THE NAVAJOS INDIANS, and other thrilling Stories of Captivity and Escape among Indians, Arabs, Ladrones, etc. By Capt. Charles Curtis, U.S.A., Capt. Glasspool, Gen. Leon de Narischkin and other Writers. EDITED BY ALFRED H. MILES. LONDON: R.A. EVERETT AND CO., (190–?). VI, 291p.: front., 2 plates. Bound in blue cloth, with coloured pictorial cover and spine.
C 823.912 CAP

2547 **MILES, ALFRED H.** *(Editor).*
FIFTY-TWO EXCELSIOR STORIES FOR BOYS. BY G. MANVILLE FENN, H.J.A. HERVEY, CHARLES E. PEARCE . . . AND OTHER WRITERS. EDITED BY ALFRED H. MILES. ILLUSTRATED. LONDON: HUTCHINSON AND CO., (1907). 456p.: front., 3 plates. Bound in green cloth, with coloured pictorial cover and spine, and gilt edges.
C 823.808 FIF

2548 **MILES, ALFRED H.** *(Editor).*
FIFTY-TWO OTHER STORIES FOR BOYS. BY GEORGE A. HENTY, . . . and other writers. EDITED BY ALFRED H. MILES. WITH ILLUSTRATIONS. LONDON: HUTCHINSON AND CO., (1892). 450p.: front., 5 plates. Bound in pink cloth with decorative cover and spine, with gilt edges.
C 823.8 FIF

2549 **MILES, ALFRED H.** *(Editor).*
FIFTY-TWO OTHER STORIES FOR GIRLS. BY MRS. G. LINNAEUS BANKS, ROSA MULHOLLAND, LUCY C. LILLIE, SUSAN COOLIDGE, SIDNEY DAYRE, DAVID KER, LIEUT.-COL. A.J. MACPHERSON, AND OTHER WRITERS. EDITED BY ALFRED H. MILES. WITH ILLUSTRATIONS. LONDON: HUTCHINSON AND CO., (189–?). 464p.: front., 4 plates. Bound in red cloth, with coloured pictorial cover and spine, and gilt edges.
C 823.808 FIF

2550 **THE SPLENDID ADVENTURE BOOK FOR BOYS.**
LONDON: THOMAS NELSON AND SONS LTD., (193–?). 95p.: col. front., by Harold C. Earnshaw, 2 plates, ill., by H.M. Talintyre. Bound with coloured pictorial paper-covered boards. Contains six stories.
C 823.91208 SPL

2550A **STATHAM, E.P.** *(Editor).*
FIFTY-TWO STORIES OF THE SEA. BY FRANK T. BULLEN, HAROLD BINDLOSS, FRANK SHAW, THE EDITOR, ETC. EDITED AND COMPILED BY COMMANDER E.P. STATHAM, R.N. ILLUSTRATED. LONDON: HUTCHINSON AND CO., (191–?). 512p.: front., 7 plates. Bound in blue cloth, with coloured pictorial cover and spine, and gilt edges.
C 823.912 FIF

2551 **STRANG, HERBERT** *(Editor).*
THE BIG BOOK FOR BOYS. EDITED BY HERBERT STRANG (Pseud. for GEORGE HERBERT FLY AND JAMES L'ESTRANGE). LONDON: HUMPHREY MILFORD, OXFORD UNIVERSITY PRESS, (1929). Unpaginated: col. front., pictorial title page, 3 col. plates, 7 plates, ill. Bound with coloured pictorial paper-covered boards. Includes stories and informative articles.
C 823.91208 BIG

2552 **STRANG, MRS. HERBERT** *(Editor) (Pseud).*
The VIOLET BOOK for GIRLS. EDITED BY MRS. HERBERT STRANG. LONDON: HENRY FROWDE, HODDER AND STOUGHTON, (191–?). Unpaginated: col. front., decorative title page, 11 col. plates, 2 plates, ill. Bound in violet cloth, with coloured pictorial label on cover and decorative covers and spine.
C 823.912 VIO

2553 **STRANGE TALES OF PERIL AND ADVENTURE.**
With Twenty-three Full-page Illustrations. LONDON: THE RELIGIOUS TRACT SOCIETY, (190–?). 332p.: front., vignette title page, 22 plates. Bound in grey cloth, with coloured pictorial cover and spine. Contains nineteen stories.
C 823.8 STR

2554 **TALES OF THE WILD.**
LONDON: JOHN F. SHAW AND CO. LTD., (193–?). Unpaginated: col. front., vignette title page, 3 col. plates, ill. Bound in coloured pictorial covers, with coloured pictorial dust jacket.
C 823.01 TAL

2555 **TUER, ANDREW W.** *(Editor).*
STORIES FROM OLD-FASHIONED CHILDREN'S BOOKS. (BY) ANDREW W. TUER. LONDON: EVELYN ADAMS AND MACKAY LTD., 1969. XV, 439p.: front., additional decorative title page, 250 woodcuts. Bound in blue cloth, with coloured pictorial dust jacket. Facsimile reprint of a compilation of stories and rhymes from 1770 to the 1820s, originally published 1899.
C 823.7 TUE

2556 **WOOD, WALTER** *(Editor).*
THE BOYS' ALL-ROUND BOOK OF STORIES, SPORTS, AND HOBBIES. EDITED BY WALTER WOOD. LONDON: THOMAS NELSON AND SONS LTD., (193–?). 360p.: col. front., vignette title page, 6 plates, ill. Bound in mustard cloth, with coloured pictorial cover and spine.
C 823.91208 BOY

2557 **YATES, M.T.** *(Editor).*
Graphic Stories OF Authors. EDITED BY M.T. YATES, LL.D. COLOURED ILLUSTRATIONS. LONDON: WILLIAM COLLINS, SONS, AND CO. LTD., (189–?). 256p. + 16p. pub. cat.: col. front., 7 col. plates, 10 plates, ill. Bound in green cloth, with coloured decorative cover and spine. Cover title: GRAPHIC STORIES FROM GREAT AUTHORS.
C 808.899282 GRA

## 20 PERIODICALS AND ANNUALS

2558 **THE ADVISER, A BOOK FOR YOUNG PEOPLE.**
GLASGOW: SCOTTISH TEMPERANCE LEAGUE. IV, 140p. + 2p. pub. cat.: 12 plates, ill. Bound in brown cloth, with coloured pictorial paper label on cover, and gilt edges. Published monthly at ½d. Library has one copy for 1878. Includes stories and poetry, mostly on the theme of temperance. Indexed.

2559 **ATALANTA.**
LONDON: HATCHARDS. Published monthly from October 1887 to September 1898 by various publishers. Editors: L.T. Meade; Alicia Amy Leith; John C. Staples; Alexander Balfour Symington; and Edwin Oliver. On the recto of the frontispiece of the first number: EVERY GIRL'S MAGAZINE, NEW SERIES. Volumes 7 to 9 subtitled THE VICTORIAN MAGAZINE. Ill. Bound in black half-leather. Library has complete set, v. 1–11. Contributions from outstanding writers of the day, including ROBERT LOUIS STEVENSON, CHRISTINA ROSSETTI, R.D. BLACKMORE, ETC. Includes fiction, poetry and informative articles. Index at beginning of each volume.

2560 **AUNT JUDY'S CHRISTMAS VOLUME FOR 1879.**
EDITED BY H.K.F. GATTY. WITH A COLOURED FRONTISPIECE AND NUMEROUS ILLUSTRATIONS BY R. CALDECOTT, CHARLES GREEN, F. FLINZER, AND OTHER ARTISTS. LONDON: GEORGE BELL AND SONS, 1879. VI, 761p. + 8p. pub. cat.: col. front. by R. Caldecott, ill. Bound in mauve cloth, with gilt embossed decorative cover and spine, and gilt edges. Includes fiction, poetry, songs and informative articles.

2561 **BEETON'S ANNUAL.**
A Book for the Young. LONDON: FREDERICK WARNE AND CO., 1866. WITH ILLUSTRATIONS PRINTED IN COLOURS, AND MANY WOODCUTS FROM ORIGINAL DESIGNS BY EMINENT ARTISTS. Fourth edition edited by S.O. Beeton and the Rev. J.G. Wood. 491p. + 2p. pub. cat.: col. front., ill. some col. Bound in red cloth, with gilt embossed decorative cover and spine, and gilt edges. Illustrators include Gustave Doré and Harrison Weir. Stories by Harriet Elizabeth Beecher Stowe, and Mayne Reid, Countess de Ségur, and others.

2562 **BLACKIE'S BOYS' ANNUAL.**
Authors: PERCY F. WESTERMAN, RICHARD BIRD, JOHN EASTON, JEFFREY HAVILTON, A.W. SEYMOUR, and others. Artists: E.S. HODGSON, H.M. BROCK, R.I., ERNEST PRATER, D.C. EYLES, REGINALD CLEAVER, and others. LONDON: BLACKIE AND SON LIMITED. 288p.: col. front., 3 col. plates, 8 plates, ill. Bound in paper-covered board, with coloured pictorial cover and pictorial spine. Library has one volume, (192–?). Includes stories and informative articles.

2562A **THE BOYS' JOURNAL.**
A Magazine of LITERATURE, SCIENCE, ADVENTURE AND AMUSEMENT. SUPERBLY ILLUSTRATED. LONDON: HENRY VICKERS. 444p.: front., plates, ill. Bound in red cloth. Library has one vol. for 186–?
C 052. BOY

2563 **THE BOY'S OWN ANNUAL.**
AN ILLUSTRATED VOLUME OF PURE AND ENTERTAINING READING. EDITED BY JAMES MACAULAY. LONDON: "LEISURE HOUR" OFFICE. Published weekly under the title: "The Boy's Own Paper". Ceased publication after February 1967. Library has: v.1–63, 1879–1941; v.68, 1945–1946; v.71–77, 1949–1955; v.82–85, 1959–1963. Edited by G.A. Hutchison, from 1879 to 1912, Arthur Lincoln Haydon, from 1913 to 1924, Geoffrey Pocklington, from 1925 to 1933, G.J.H. Northcroft, from 1934 to 1935, and Robert Harding from 1936. Jack Cox was editor 1946–1967. Includes stories, serials, hobbies, puzzles and informative articles. All volumes indexed to v.63, 1940–1941, except v.59 and 60. Subsequent volumes not indexed.

2564 **THE BOY'S OWN VOLUME.**
OF Fact, Fiction, History, and Adventure. ILLUSTRATED BY SEPARATE PLATES AND NUMEROUS WOODCUTS INSERTED IN THE TEXT. EDITED BY THE PUBLISHER. LONDON: S.O. BEETON. Published monthly from 1855 to 1870, with a second new series from 1870 to 1874. Bound in green cloth, with embossed decorative cover and spine, and gilt edges. Library has ten volumes: Midsummer 1863, Christmas 1863, Midsummer 1864, Christmas 1864, Midsummer 1865, Christmas 1865, Midsummer 1866 (2 copies), Christmas 1866, Midsummer 1867, Christmas 1867. Includes stories, poetry, puzzles and informative articles. All volumes, except for one copy of Midsummer 1866, are indexed.

NO. 15 OF CURRENT VOLUME.]
Full No. 1669.—Vol. XXXIII.
SATURDAY, JANUARY 7, 1911.
Price One Penny.
[ALL RIGHTS RESERVED.]

2563

2565 **BRIGHT EYES.**
An Annual for Young Folks. LONDON: CHARLES TAYLOR. 252p.: vignette on title page, 25 plates, some tinted, ill. Bound in paper-covered boards, with coloured pictorial cover. Library has one volume, (190–?). Includes fiction, poetry, informative articles and puzzles.

2566 **THE BRITISH GIRL'S ANNUAL.**
COMPILED BY THE EDITOR OF "THE GIRL'S REALM" AND CONTAINING CONTRIBUTIONS BY E.E. COWPER, BESSIE MARCHANT, DOROTHEA MOORE, RALPH SIMMONDS, MRS. G. DE HORNE VAIZEY, LILLIAN F. WEVILL, BELLA SIDNEY WOOLF, AND OTHER LEADING WRITERS FOR GIRLS. With Eight Full-page Colour Plates and a large number of Black-and-White Illustrations. LONDON: CASSELL AND COMPANY LTD. VIII, 230p.: col. front., 7 col. plates, 17 plates. Bound in grey cloth, with coloured pictorial cover and spine. Library has one volume for 1911. Includes stories, drama and articles on hobbies, pets.

2567 **BUBBLES ANNUAL.**
LONDON: AMALGAMATED PRESS LTD. Ill., some col. Bound in paper-covered boards, with coloured pictorial cover. The annual derives from the weekly paper, "Bubbles", from the same publishers. Library has 4 volumes: 1930, 1932, 1933, and 1934. Includes fiction, puzzles, games, model-making and poetry.

2568 **THE CAPTAIN.**
A Magazine for Boys and "Old Boys". LONDON: GEORGE NEWNES LIMITED. Published monthly. Library has v. 1–35, 1899–1916; v.37/38, 1917–1918; v.41–50, 1919–1923/24. Illustrators include Henry Matthew Brock, Charles Edmund Brock, Thomas Heath Robinson, and Harry Rountree. Includes fiction, sport and hobbies. Had editors for Philately, Athletics (C.B. Fry in 1920), Cycling and natural history (Edward Step in 1920). Volumes indexed.

2569 **CHATTERBOX.**
EDITED BY J. ERSKINE CLARKE. LONDON: WILLIAM MACINTOSH. Ill., some col. Annual volumes of the halfpenny weeklies, published from 1866 to 1956 by William Macintosh, later by Wells Gardner, Darton and Co., and Dean and Son Ltd. Library has 29 volumes: 1869–70; 1885; 1893; 1896–99; 1901; 1903; 1905–16; 1919; 1922–23; 1925; 1928; 3 undated volumes. Founded by the Rev J. Erskine Clarke as an antidote to the penny dreadfuls. Includes fiction, poetry, informative articles and puzzles. All volumes indexed apart from two later undated volumes which merely list contents.

2570 **THE CHICKS' OWN ANNUAL.**
LONDON: AMALGAMATED PRESS LTD. 100p.: ill., some col. Bound in paper-covered boards, with coloured pictorial cover. The annual derived from the weekly paper, "Chicks' Own", from the same publisher. Library has one volume for 1929. Includes fiction, poetry and puzzles intended for young children.

2571 **THE CHILDREN'S FRIEND.**
A Penny monthly begun in 1824 and first edited by the Rev. William Carus Wilson. Library has v.5–7, 1865–67, v.17, v.39–40, 1899–1900, v.44, 1905 and three loose numbers for Dec. 1909, Jan. 1912, and April 1912. Bound volumes are published by Seeley and Co., Seeley, Jackson and Halliday, and S.W. Pàrtridge and Co. and contain short stories, serials, poetry, songs, and engravings by, e.g., Harrison Weir, Dalziel Brothers and Birket Foster. Two page index at beginning of early volumes. Loose numbers published by S.W. Partridge and Co. and contain short stories, serials, verse, puzzles, and black and white illustrations. The number for Dec. 1909 is a Christmas double number and cost 2d. The numbers for Jan. and April 1912 have coloured pictorial covers and include a Play-Hour Supplement containing readers' contributions.

2571A **THE CHILDREN'S PRIZE.**
EDITED BY J. ERSKINE CLARKE, M.A. LONDON: WILLIAM MACINTOSH, 1867. 187p.: pictorial/decorative title page. ill. 12 monthly parts at one penny bound together with decorative red covers.

2572 **THE CHILDREN'S TREASURY OF PICTURES AND STORIES.**
LONDON: THOMAS NELSON AND SONS. 128p.: 18 plates, ill. Bound in paper-covered boards, with coloured pictorial cover. Library has one volume for 1899. Includes stories, poetry and anecdotes of a religious cast.

2573 **THE CHILD'S COMPANION AND JUVENILE INSTRUCTOR.**
LONDON: THE RELIGIOUS TRACT SOCIETY. Monthly. Library has 9 volumes: 1859–1863, 1881–1882, (1896), (1909). Volumes from 1859 to 1863 contain stories, poetry, serials, Scripture articles, and puzzles. Illustrated with black and white engravings and coloured plates by Kronheim and Co. Volumes from 1881 in larger format, and contain stories, poetry, serials, informative and handicraft articles, and puzzles. Latest volume "profusely illustrated with coloured pictures". All volumes indexed.

2573A **THE CHILD'S PICTORIAL.**
A MONTHLY COLOURED MAGAZINE (Annual Volume). LONDON: SOCIETY FOR PROMOTING CHRISTIAN KNOWLEDGE. Library has January–December 1894, 192p. ill., some col., engraved and printed by Edmund Evans. Bound in buff cloth with coloured decorative cover. Includes stories, nursery rhymes and informative articles for young children.
C 823.8 CHI

2574 **THE CHRISTIAN MISCELLANY, AND FAMILY VISITOR.**
LONDON: WESLEYAN CONFERENCE OFFICE. Monthly. Col. front., ill. Bound in half leather. Spine title: FAMILY VISITOR. Library has 3 volumes: Second series, v.13, 1867; third series, v.1, 1877; third series, v.2, 1878. Incudes stories, poetry and informative articles of interest to Methodists. Volumes indexed.

2575 **CHUMS.**
An Illustrated Paper for Boys. LONDON: CASSELL AND COMPANY LIMITED. Published as a weekly paper from 1892 to 1934, continuing as an annual until 1941. Edited first by Max Pemberton and from 1894 to 1907 by E. Foster. Library has 37 volumes: v.1–16, 1892–1908; v.27, 1919; vols. 1922–1941. Contributors include Robert Louis Stevenson and George Alfred Henty.

2576 **COLLINS' BOY SCOUTS' ANNUAL.**
STORIES BY Alfred Noyes, H. Mortimer Batten, T.C. Bridges, W.H. Davies, Geoffrey Prout. LONDON: COLLINS' CLEAR-TYPE PRESS. 224p.: col. front., col. vignette title page, 6 plates, ill., coloured pictorial endpapers. Bound in cream cloth, with coloured pictorial paper cover. Library has one volume for (193–?). Includes stories, poetry and articles on nature, sports, camping, etc.

2576A **COLLINS SCHOOLGIRL'S ANNUAL.**
LONDON: COLLINS CLEAR TYPE PRESS. Col. plates, Library has 1 volume (193–?). Mainly fiction.

2577 **THE EMPIRE ANNUAL FOR BOYS.**
EDITED BY J. BURNETT KNOWLTON. TALES OF ADVENTURE, SPORT, DISCOVERY, SCHOOL-LIFE AND MANY PLATES IN COLOUR AND PHOTOGRAVURE. LONDON: THE "BOY'S OWN PAPER" OFFICE. 288p.: col. front., vignette title page, 3 col. plates, 4 plates. Bound in blue cloth, with coloured pictorial cover and spine. Library has v.11, 12, 23 for 1919, 1920, and 1931. Ceased publication in 1933.

2578 **THE EMPIRE ANNUAL FOR GIRLS.**
EDITED BY A.R. BUCKLAND, M.A. With Contributions by Mrs. G. de Horne Vaizey, Dr. Gordon Stables . . . etc. With . . . Coloured Plates and Sixteen Black and White Illustrations. LONDON: (THE "BOY'S OWN PAPER" OFFICE). Bound in green cloth, with coloured pictorial cover and spine. Library has two volumes: 1909; (191–?). Includes stories and informative articles.

2579 **FAITHFUL WORDS FOR OLD AND YOUNG.**
LONDON: ALFRED HOLNESS. 188p.: vignette title page, 19 plates, ill. Bound in blue cloth, with decorative cover and spine. Annual. Library has one volume for (188–?). Contains short stories of a religious cast. Indexed.

2580 **THE FAMILY FRIEND.**
With Illustrations by (many) popular artists. Published fortnightly. Library has nine volumes: v.2, 1850, published by HOULSTON AND STONEMAN; v.3, published by S.W. PARTRIDGE; 1872–1875, 1878, 1882–1883, 1886, + 3 loose numbers for Dec. 1908, June 1910, and Feb. 1911. Includes stories, poetry, music, and informative articles on many subjects. Bound volumes indexed.

2580A **FATHER TUCK'S ANNUAL.**
Stories and Poems by Annie Matheson, Clifton Bingham, Felix Leigh etc. etc. Illustrated by Hilda Cowham, Mabel Lucie Attwell, M. & A.L. Bowley, Agnes Richardson and others. Edited by EDRIC VREDENBURG. LONDON: RAPHAEL TUCK AND SONS, LTD. Col. front., 5 col. plates, ill. Bound in buff cloth with coloured pictorial cover by Mabel Lucie Attwell. Library has one volume for 1913. Contains stories, poetry and nature notes for young children.

2581 **FLIP THE FROG ANNUAL.**
LONDON: DEAN AND SON LIMITED. Col. front., 3 col. plates. Bound in paper covered boards, with coloured pictorial covers. Library has one volume for 1920. Comic strip stories about the frog and other animals.

2582 **FRIENDLY GREETINGS.**
ILLUSTRATED READINGS FOR THE PEOPLE. PROFUSELY ILLUSTRATED BY THE BEST ARTISTS. LONDON: THE RELIGIOUS TRACT SOCIETY. Weekly. Library has three volumes: XIX, (188–?), XXXIV, (189–?), and New Series IV, (191–?). Includes stories, verse and articles, all of a religious nature. Indexed.

2583 **THE GEM LIBRARY.**
LONDON: HOWARD BAKER PRESS LIMITED. Facsimile reprints of The GEM LIBRARY OF SCHOOL AND SPORTING STORIES. Library has two volumes, originally published in single weekly issues: v.1, 1971, (originally published July 8th to Aug. 19th 1922); v.2, 1972, (originally published Dec. 5th, 12th 1925 and Aug. 11th to Sept. 1st 1928). Includes two stories by Martin Clifford: "D'Arcy the Runaway", and, "The Rebel of St. Jim's".

2584 **THE GIRL'S OWN ANNUAL.**
LONDON: "THE LEISURE HOUR" OFFICE. Cover title varies between "GIRL'S OWN PAPER" and "GIRL'S OWN ANNUAL". Later numbers, from 1915, assume the title "WOMAN'S MAGAZINE" in greater prominence than "GIRL'S OWN". Annual volumes of the weekly numbers were published from 1880 to 1948 with various changes of name. Volumes from 1913 to 1926 edited by Flora Klickmann; v.56 edited by Gladys M. Spratt. Library has 31 volumes: v.2–4, 1881–1882/3; v.6, 1884/85; v.8, 1886/87; v.9, 1887/88; v.13– 16, 1891/92–1894/95; v.18–20, 1896/97–1898/99; v.23, 1901–02; v.35, 1913; v.37–44, 1915–22; v.46, 1924; v.48, 1926; v.50, 1928; v.56, 1934–35; + vol. containing special summer and Christmas nos., 1884–1894. v.8 has a coloured frontispiece drawn by Kate Greenaway. There is increasing use of coloured illustrations in later volumes. Contributors include E. Nesbit and W.B. Yeats. Includes short stories and serials. Earlier volumes contain articles on cookery, needlework, music, sketching, and a correspondence column, all appealing to teenagers. Later volumes gradually appeal to older readers, until by the twenties they are women's magazines with articles on homemaking, fashion, motoring, etc. By the thirties it has become a schoolgirls' magazine again. All volumes indexed except v.3, v.6 and the special volume, 1884–1894.

2585 **THE GIRL'S REALM ANNUAL.**
BY CHARLOTTE M. YONGE, L.T. MEADE, FRANCES HODGSON BURNETT . . . AND OTHER POPULAR WRITERS. WITH UPWARDS OF 1200 ILLUSTRATIONS BY . . . EMINENT ARTISTS. LONDON: HUTCHINSON AND CO. LATER CASSELL AND COMPANY LTD. Col. front., ill. Bound in red cloth, with embossed decorative cover. Monthly. Library has volumes for 1899, 1913, 1914 and 1915. Includes stories, poetry, puzzles and articles on fashion, sport, hobbies, careers, etc. Indexed.

2586 **THE GOLDEN ANNUAL FOR GIRLS.**
LONDON: THE AMALGAMATED PRESS LTD. 191p.: col. front., ill. title page, 12 plates, ill. Bound in cloth, with coloured pictorial paper cover. Library has one volume for 1934. Annual of school and other stories for girls.

2587 **GOOD WORDS.**
EDITED BY DONALD MACLEOD, D.D., ONE OF HER MAJESTY'S CHAPLAINS. LONDON: ISBISTER AND COMPANY LIMITED. VIII, 860p.: front., ill. Bound in grey cloth, with embossed decorative cover and spine, and gilt edges. Monthly. Library has one volume: v.32, 1891. Includes stories, serials, poetry and articles on, e.g., art, biography, travel, and the Bible. Indexed.

2588 **THE GUIDE.**
The Official Organ of the Girl Guides. LONDON: HARRISON AND SONS LTD. A weekly publication, continued under the title "Today's Guide". Library has one volume: v.1, April 23rd 1921–April 15th 1922. Includes stories, serials, puzzles, articles on, e.g., nature, cookery, camping.

2589 **HARPER'S YOUNG PEOPLE.**
Library has: v.3–6, 1882–1885, published in New York by Harper and Brothers; v.6, 1890, published in London by Sampson Low, Marston, Searle and Rivington. Bound in green or brown cloth with coloured decorative cover and spine. An illustrated weekly, including stories, serials, poetry, puzzles and informative articles on, e.g., handicrafts, natural history and sport. Contributors include Louisa M. Alcott and Howard Pyle. All volumes indexed.

2590 **HERBERT STRANG'S ANNUAL.**
Col. front., col. plates, plates, ill., photographs. Bound in cloth, with coloured pictorial paper cover and coloured pictorial spine. Herbert Strang is a pseudonym used by George Herbert Ely and James L'Estrange. Library has volumes for 1910 and 1920, published in 1910 by Henry Frowde and Hodder and Stoughton, and in 1920 by OXFORD UNIVERSITY PRESS, both of London. Stories for boys illustrated by, e.g. H.M. Brock, Cyrus Cuneo, Gordon Robinson, T.H. Robinson, Archibald Webb. Continued by: Oxford Annual for Boys (q.v.).

2591 **HULLO BOYS!**
A BUDGET OF GOOD THINGS BY THE UNCLES ON THE WIRELESS. LONDON: CECIL PALMER. 160p.: front., vignette title page, 12 col. plates, 13 plates, including one by Jessie M. King, ill., decorative endpapers. Bound in red cloth with pictorial cover. Library has one volume for 1925. Includes stories and informative articles.

2592 **HULLO GIRLS!**
A BUDGET OF GOOD THINGS BY THE AUNTIES ON THE WIRELESS. LONDON: CECIL PALMER. 160p.: front., vignette title page, 16 col. plates, including two by Jessie M. King, 5 plates, ill., decorative endpapers. Bound in blue cloth, with pictorial cover. Library has one volume for 1924. Contains twenty stories for girls.

2593 **INFANTS' MAGAZINE.**
LONDON: S.W. PARTRIDGE AND CO. LTD. Bound in blue cloth with decorative cover. Published from 1866 to 1931, and "conducted by the Editor of The Children's Friend". Library has v.9., 1874. No. 568, April 1913, and annual for 1916, containing the monthly parts for 1915. Stories and verse for young children illustrated by, e.g., Harry Rountree, R.H. Brock, and Charles Folkard.

2594 **THE JOY BOOK, A PICTURE AND STORY ANNUAL FOR LITTLE FOLK.**
MANCHESTER: ALLIED NEWSPAPERS LIMITED. 151p.: col. front., col. pictorial title page, 4 col. plates, ill. Bound in paper-covered boards, with coloured pictorial cover.

Library has one volume for 1929. Contains stories and verse about fairies, animals and children.

2595 **JOY STREET: A MEDLEY OF PROSE AND VERSE FOR BOYS AND GIRLS.**
OXFORD: BASIL BLACKWELL. Ill., some col. Annual. Library has 9 volumes; Numbers 1–4 (1923–1926); numbers 6 and 7 (1928 and 1929); number 9 (1931), number Twelve "A", (1934); number 14 (1936). Includes stories by Eleanor Farjeon, G.K. Chesterton, Walter De La Mare, A.A. Milne and other important children's authors.

*Number One Joy Street*

*A Medley of Prose & Verse for Boys and Girls*

*By*

WALTER DE LA MARE
ELEANOR FARJEON
HILAIRE BELLOC
MADELEINE NIGHTINGALE
B. KATHLEEN PYKE
LAURENCE HOUSMAN
MABEL MARLOWE
HALLIWELL SUTCLIFFE
EDITH SITWELL
HUGH CHESTERMAN
ROSE FYLEMAN

*BASIL BLACKWELL*
*Broad Street, Oxford*
MD · CCCC · XXIII

2595

2596 **KIND WORDS.**
A Magazine for Young People. NEW SERIES. LONDON: HENRY HALL (SUNDAY SCHOOL UNION). Library has six volumes: v.1–6, 1871–76. Includes stories, informative articles, poetry, puzzles and music. Serial contributed by W.H.G. Kingston. Index missing from volumes 1 and 2. Continued by: Young England (q.v.).

2597 **LITTLE FOLKS.**
A Magazine for the Young. LONDON: CASSELL, PETTER, AND GALPIN. Published from 1871 to 1933 in weekly numbers, monthly parts, and half-yearly volumes. Bound in green and brown cloth with decorative cover and spine. Library has 27 volumes: 1871–72; 1874(?); 1880–81; 1890–92; 1894–98; 1900–01; 1903; 1910–15; 1919–20, and one part for April 1917. Volumes for 1920 edited by Herbert D. Williams. Includes stories, poetry, puzzles and informative articles, illustrated by eminent artists, e.g. Kate Greenaway, Arthur Rackham, Harry Rountree, Mabel Lucie Attwell. Indexed.

2597A **THE LITTLE MAGAZINE FOR YOUNG READERS OF EVERY DENOMINATION.**
LONDON: SAMUEL GILBERT, 1841. 368p.: front., 8 plates, ill. Quarter bound in brown calf and green cloth. A mixture of information including an almanack, fables, poetry and religious stories. Miniature size.

2598 **LITTLE WIDE-AWAKE.**
AN ILLUSTRATED MAGAZINE FOR CHILDREN. EDITED BY MRS. SALE BARKER. ILLUSTRATED BY GORDON BROWNE (and others). LONDON: GEORGE ROUTLEDGE AND SONS. 376p. col. front., vignette title page, 52 plates, ill. Bound in brown cloth, with embossed pictorial/decorative cover and spine. Published monthly from 1875 to 1892. Library has one volume for 1886. Includes stories, serials, poetry and puzzles. Indexed.

2599 **THE MAGNET.**
LONDON: HOWARD BAKER PRESS LIMITED. Facsimile reprints in bound volumes of numbers originally published in single weekly issues at 2d. Coloured cover, ill. Library has 13 volumes: v.1 (2 copies), v.2–4, v.7–8, v.10, v.12–14, v.17, v.21, published from 1969 to 1973, originally published from 1925 to 1938. Stories about the boys of Greyfriars School by Frank Richards (pseud. for Charles Hamilton).

2600 **THE MANCHESTER CHRISTMAS ANNUAL.**
EDITED BY FRED M. HYMAN. 76p., 102p., 94p.: fronts., 12 plates, ill. Bound in green cloth. Library has one volume containing the annuals for 1882, 1883 and 1884. Includes stories, poetry, songs and informative articles.

2601 **MINE: A MAGAZINE FOR ALL WHO ARE YOUNG.**
EDITED BY STEPHEN KING-HALL. LONDON: C. ARTHUR PEARSON LTD. Col. plates; ill., diagrs. Bound in maroon leather. Published monthly from April 1935 – June 1936. Library has three volumes: v.1., April–July 1935; v.2., August–Nov. 1935; v.3., Dec. 1935–March 1936. Includes articles on hobbies, current affairs, art, sport, as well as stories and verse. Illustrations include coloured plates. Indexed.

2602 **MRS HIPPO'S ANNUAL.**
A BOOK OF JOLLY PICTURES AND STORIES FOR BOYS AND GIRLS OF ALL AGES. LONDON: AMALGAMATED PRESS LTD. 71p.: col. front., col. title page, 3 col. plates, ill. Bound in green cloth, with coloured pictorial cover. Annual derived from the weekly picture paper 'The Playbox'. Library has one volume for 1932. Includes stories, puzzles and verse.

2604 **MRS. STRANG'S ANNUAL FOR GIRLS.**
LONDON: HUMPHREY MILFORD. OXFORD UNIVERSITY PRESS. 160p.: col. front., decorative title page, 5 col. plates, 3 plates, ill., decorative endpapers. Bound in brown cloth, with coloured pictorial cover and spine. Library has one volume for 1926. Includes stories, poetry and informative articles.

2605 **MY MAGAZINE.**
THE MONTHLY COMPANION OF THE CHILDREN'S NEWSPAPER. EDITED BY ARTHUR MEE. LONDON: "MY MAGAZINE". Illustrated in black and white with some coloured illustrations. Library has 12 volumes: v.8–12, 1914–1918; v.18–24, 1922–1928. Contains mainly informative articles on, e.g. Science, art, nature, biography, as well as stories, poetry and puzzles. A war-time supplement called "The Little Paper" was printed as part of "My Magazine" from July 1917 to June 1918. Volumes 8 to 12 not indexed.

2606 **NEW BUFFALO BILL LIBRARY.**
Price 1d.
LONDON: ALDINE PUBLISHING COMPANY LIMITED (191–?).
40p. each issue with coloured pictorial covers.
Library has Nos. 50, 58, 63, 64 and 73.

2607 **THE NEW PENNY MAGAZINE.**
CASSELL AND COMPANY LIMITED. Published weekly at 1d. Library has: v.1, nos. 1–13; v.2, nos. 14–25; v.3, nos. 27–39, v.4, nos. 40–52; v.5, nos. 53–65; v.6, nos. 66–78; v.7, nos. 79–91; v.8, nos. 92–104. Volumes 1 and 2, 3 and 4, 5 and 6, 7 and 8 rebound together. There is a separate copy of v.7 in original red pictorial binding dated 1900. Includes stories and informative articles on foreign customs, biography, nature, etc. Illustrated in black and white. Intended for all ages.

2608 **NISTER'S HOLIDAY ANNUAL FOR 1898.**
With Stories by Geo. Manville Fenn, Mrs Molesworth, E. Nesbit, etc. etc. Edited and arranged by Robert Ellis Mack and Alfred J. Fuller. LONDON: ERNEST NISTER. 128p.: col.

front., pictorial title page, 5 col. plates, 13 plates, ill. Bound in green cloth, with coloured pictorial cover. Library has one volume for 1898. Includes stories, poetry, games and puzzles, for younger children.

2609 **OUR GIRLS.**
LONDON: "OUR GIRLS". Newspaper format illustrated. Bound in red cloth. Originally issued in 1d. parts. Library has seven volumes: nos. 1–164, 1915–1918. Includes serials, stories and articles on, e.g., fashions, films, etiquette, etc.

2609A **OUR JABBERWOCK.**
EDITED BY BRENDA GIRVIN. LONDON: CHAPMAN AND HALL. Ill. Bound in red cloth with pictorial cover and gilt edges. Published monthly. Library has two Christmas volumes for 1906 and 1907. 1906 volume partially indexed. Includes stories, serial, drama, poetry, puzzles and articles on hobbies, handicrafts, cookery, sport, nature, etc.

2610 **OUR OWN GAZETTE.**
YOUNG WOMEN'S CHRISTIAN ASSOCIATION NEWS. EDITED BY MRS. STEPHEN MENZIES. LONDON: S.W. PARTRIDGE AND CO. Ill. One vol. has pictorial/decorative cover. Issued in monthly parts at 1d. Library has v.3–10, 1886–1893. Includes stories, serials and articles on subjects of interest to young women, e.g. needlework, cookery, nature, jobs, etc. Indexed.

2611 **OUR OWN MAGAZINE.**
(A MONTHLY PAPER FOR YOUNG PEOPLE). Edited by T.B. BISHOP. LONDON: CHILDREN'S SPECIAL SERVICE MISSION. Ill. Published monthly at 1d. Library has two volumes, v.XXVI, 1905 and v.XXVII, 1906. Includes stories and anecdotes of a religious cast. Indexed.

2612 **THE OXFORD ANNUAL FOR BOYS.**
25TH YEAR. EDITED BY HERBERT STRANG (Pseud. for George Herbert Ely and James L'Estrange). LONDON: HUMPHREY MILFORD, OXFORD UNIVERSITY PRESS. 292p.: col. front., vignette title page, 5 col. plates, 12 plates. Bound in cream cloth, with coloured pictorial cover and spine. Library has one volume for 1933. Includes stories, poetry and informative articles.

2613 **THE OXFORD ANNUAL FOR SCOUTS.**
EDITED BY HERBERT STRANG (pseud. for George Herbert Ely and James L'Estrange). 13TH YEAR. LONDON: HUMPHREY MILFORD, OXFORD UNIVERSITY PRESS. 196p.: col. front., col. vignette title page, 6 plates, ill. Coloured, pictorial cover and spine. Library has one volume for 1931. Contains stories, verse and articles of interest to scouts. Continues: Herbert Strang's Annual (q.v.)

2614 **PETER PARLEY'S ANNUAL.**
A CHRISTMAS AND NEW YEAR'S PRESENT FOR YOUNG PEOPLE. LONDON: DARTON AND CO. Ill., some col. Library has 10 vols: 1849, 1851, 1854, 1856, 1859, 1862, 1867, 1874, 1881 and 1888. The title pages of the volumes for 1859, 1862 and 1867 bear the editor's name, William Martin. The volume for 1849 is entitled Peter Parley's MAGAZINE. It is probable that the magazine was published from 1840 to 1863: the annuals continued until 1892. The volumes for 1874–1888 were published by Ben. George. Includes stories, poetry and informative articles on, e.g., natural history, geography, biography.

2615 **PIP AND SQUEAK ANNUAL.**
Third Year. Edited by "Uncle Dick". LONDON: THE DAILY MIRROR. 207p.: col. front., 3 col. plates, ill. Bound in red cloth, with coloured pictorial cover. Library has one volume for 1925. Includes stories, verse and puzzles.

2616 **THE PLAYBOX ANNUAL.**
A Picture and Story Book for Children. LONDON: THE AMALGAMATED PRESS LIMITED. Ill., some col. Bound in green cloth, with coloured pictorial cover. Annual derived from the weekly picture-paper "The Rainbow". Library has five volumes: v.13, 1921; v.17, 1925; v.19, 1927; v.22, 1930; v.27, 1935. Includes stories, verse, games, puzzles, riddles, etc.

2617 **THE POP ANNUAL.**
LONDON: DAILY SKETCH AND SUNDAY HERALD LTD. 96p.: Ill., some col. Bound in blue cloth, with coloured pictorial covers. Library has one volume for (192–?). Comic strip annual.

2618 **THE PRIMITIVE METHODIST JUVENILE MAGAZINE.**
LONDON: THOMAS HOLLIDAY. IV, 330p.: ill. Bound in half leather. Published monthly. Library has: v.1 and 2, 1852 and 1853, bound together. Includes stories, poetry, biographical sketches, Sunday school lessons and articles on missionary work. Illustrated with engravings. Indexed.

2619 **THE PRIZE FOR GIRLS AND BOYS.**
LONDON: WELLS GARDNER, DARTON, AND CO. LIMITED. Col. plates, ill. Published monthly from 1876 to 1931. Library has five volumes: 1908, 1910, 1911, 1915, 1919, and 1 volume published by SIMPKIN MARSHALL LTD.: v.65, (192–?). Founded by Rev. J. Erskine Clarke, under the original title "The Children's Prize". Includes stories, poetry, puzzles and informative articles intended for younger children. Indexed.

2621 **THE QUIVER.**
An Illustrated Magazine FOR SUNDAY AND GENERAL READING. LONDON: CASSELL AND COMPANY LIMITED. Ill. Library has 5 volumes: v.21, 1886; (new series) 1888; 1892; 1893, 1895. Includes stories, poetry, hymns, Scripture lessons and articles of a religious or moral cast. Indexed.

2622 **THE ROUND ROBIN.**
A GATHERING OF Fact, Fiction, Incident and Adventure. EDITED BY OLD MERRY. WITH ORIGINAL ILLUSTRATIONS BY BIRKET FOSTER AND J.D. WATSON. Printed in colour by Edmund Evans, AND NUMEROUS WOODCUTS BY H.D. FRISTON, J.A. PASQUIER, W.G.R. BROWNE, etc. etc. LONDON: FREDERICK WARNE AND CO. VIII, 960p.: col. front., 3 col. plates, 20 plates, ill. Bound in maroon cloth, with embossed decorative cover and spine, and gilt edges. Annual. Library has one volume for 1872. Includes stories by, e.g. R.M. Ballantyne and W.H.G. Kingston, poetry, puzzles and informative articles. Indexed.

2623 **ROUTLEDGE'S EVERY BOY'S ANNUAL.**
AN ENTERTAINING Miscellany of Original Literature. EDITED BY EDMUND ROUTLEDGE. With illustrations. LONDON: GEORGE ROUTLEDGE AND SONS. Ill., some col. Annual volumes of EVERY BOY'S MAGAZINE, published 1862–64, continued as ROUTLEDGE'S MAGAZINE FOR BOYS, 1865–68: the YOUNG GENTLEMAN'S MAGAZINE, 1869–73; and EVERY BOY'S MAGAZINE, 1874–89, when it was incorporated with the BOY'S OWN PAPER. Library has nine volumes: 1869 (2 copies) – 1872; 1876–1877; 1881; 1886. Title pages for 1881 and 1886 read: EVERY BOY'S ANNUAL. Contains stories by R.M. Ballantyne, W.H.G. Kingston and Jules Verne. Includes also puzzles, and articles on sports, handicrafts.

2624 **ROUTLEDGE'S EVERY GIRL'S ANNUAL.**
Edited by MISS ALICIA A. LEITH. ILLUSTRATED. (LONDON): GEORGE ROUTLEDGE AND SONS. Col. plates, ill. Bound in blue cloth, with coloured pictorial/decorative cover and spine and gilt edges. Annual volumes of EVERY GIRL'S MAGAZINE, a monthly published from 1878 to 1888. Library has three volumes: 1882; 1883; 1884. Later volumes entitled: EVERY GIRL'S ANNUAL. Includes stories, poetry, drama, puzzles and articles on cookery, needlework, hobbies and sports. Indexed.

2625 **ST. NICHOLAS: AN ILLUSTRATED MAGAZINE FOR YOUNG FOLKS.**
U.S.A. NEW YORK: THE CENTURY CO. LONDON: FREDERICK WARNE AND CO. Col. plates by Arthur Rackham, ill. Monthly: Annual volumes bound in red cloth with embossed decorative covers and spines. Library has:
V. 37 Part II May–Oct. 1910,

V. 38 Part I Nov. 1910–Apr. 1911
V. 39 Part II May–Oct. 1912
V. 40 Part I Nov. 1912–Apr. 1913
V. 40 Part II May–Oct. 1913
V. 41 Part I Nov. 1913–Apr. 1914
V. 41 Part II May–Oct. 1914
V. 42 Part I Nov. 1914–Apr. 1915
V. 42 Part II May–Oct. 1915
V. 43 Part I Nov. 1915–Apr. 1916
Includes stories, information, music, competitions.

2626 **THE SCHOOLGIRLS' OWN ANNUAL.**
LONDON: THE AMALGAMATED PRESS LTD., LATER THE OFFICES OF "THE SCHOOLGIRLS' OWN". Col. plates, ill. Bound in brown cloth with coloured pictorial cover. Annual derived from the weekly story-paper "THE SCHOOL GIRLS' OWN". (Edited by Flora Klickman.) Library has 6 volumes: v. 1, 1923; v. 5 and 6, 1927 and 1928: v. 10 and 11, 1932 and 1933; v. 14, 1936. Contains stories and articles on, e.g. games, needlework, camping.

2627 **THE SUNDAY AT HOME.**
A FAMILY MAGAZINE FOR SABBATH READING. (LONDON THE RELIGIOUS TRACT SOCIETY). 752p.: col. front., ill., some col. Bound in red cloth. Published weekly at 1d. Library has two volumes: Jan 6th 1883–Nov. 24th 1883 and 1889, No. 1810, 5 Jan. to No. 1852, 26 October. Includes stories, Scriptural puzzles, articles on Scripture and church history, missionaries, etc.

2628 **SUNDAY READING FOR THE YOUNG.**
ILLUSTRATED BY GORDON BROWNE, A.G. WALKER (SCULPTOR), HELEN MILES, G.E. ROBERTSON, ETC. LONDON: WELLS, GARDNER, DARTON AND CO. LTD. Col. front., ill. Pictorial cover. Published weekly at ½d. Library has 6 volumes for 1891, 1900, 1903, 1906, 1907, 1911. Includes fiction, poetry and informative articles. There are two copies of 1906 with different covers. Indexed.

2629 **SUNSHINE.**
"FOR THE HOME, THE SCHOOL, AND THE WORLD". CONDUCTED BY W. MEYNELL WHITTEMORE, D.D. LONDON: WILLIAM POOLE. IV, 188p.: vignette title page, ill. Bound in blue cloth, with embossed decorative covers and spine. Published monthly at 1d. Library has one volume: Nos. 217–228, 1880. Includes stories, poetry and puzzles. Indexed.

2631 **TIGER TIM'S ANNUAL.**
A Picture and Story Book for Boys and Girls. LONDON: THE AMALGAMATED PRESS LTD. Ill., some col. Coloured pictorial cover. Annual derived from the picture paper "Tiger Tim's Weekly", later "The Rainbow". Library has four volumes: 1931, 1934, 1951, 1953. Includes stories, verse, tricks and puzzles.

2632 **TIM, TOOTS AND TEENY ANNUAL.**
ANOTHER WHOLE YEAR OF ADVENTURE WITH THE FAMOUS PETS. LONDON: GEORGE NEWNES LIMITED. 127p.: ill. Bound in red cloth, with coloured pictorial cover. Annual. Library has one volume for 1932. A picture story annual.

2633 **TINY TOTS: A PICTURE STORY BOOK FOR LITTLE PEOPLE.**
LONDON: THE AMALGAMATED PRESS LTD. Col. plates, ill. Bound in red cloth, with coloured pictorial cover and spine. Annual derived from the weekly paper "Tiny Tots". Library has three volumes: 1930, 1931, 1932. Stories, verse, puzzles and games for younger children.

2634 **TOBY'S ANNUAL.**
EDITED BY G. HEATH ROBINSON. Containing many illustrations in colours and black and white. LONDON: G. HEATH ROBINSON AND J. BIRCH, LTD. Ill., some col. Bound in blue cloth, with coloured pictorial vignette on cover. Published monthly. Library has: v.1, 1922. Includes stories and articles on, e.g. drawing and model-making. Indexed.

2635 **THE TRACT MAGAZINE AND CHRISTIAN MISCELLANY.**
CONTAINING VARIOUS PIECES OF PERMANENT INTEREST. LONDON: THE RELIGIOUS TRACT SOCIETY. IV, 332p., ill. Half bound in leather. Published monthly. Library has one volume for 1863–1864. Includes stories, poetry and anecdotes of a religious cast.

2636 **UNCLE DICK'S ANNUAL.**
Packed with Thrilling Adventure Stories and many Novel Competitions in which Hundreds of Prizes are offered to Boys and Girls of all ages. PAGES of PICTURES OF PIP, SQUEAK AND WILFRED. Col. plates, ill. Bound in green cloth, with coloured pictorial cover. Library has one volume for 1931. Includes stories and puzzles.

2637 **UNCLE OOJAH'S BIG ANNUAL.**
LONDON: DAILY SKETCH AND SUNDAY GRAPHIC LIMITED. 128p.: col. plates, ill. Coloured pictorial cover and spine. Annual. Library has one volume for 1929. Includes stories, games, puzzles and things to make, for younger children. Printed by ALLIED NEWSPAPERS LIMITED, Withy Grove, Manchester.

2638 **THE UNION JACK.**
A MAGAZINE OF HEALTHY, STIRRING TALES OF ADVENTURE BY LAND AND SEA. EDITED BY G.A. HENTY. LONDON: SAMPSON LOW, MARSTON, SEARLE AND RIVINGTON. Published weekly at 1d, monthly at 6d. Col. plates, ill. Library has one volume: v.2, Oct. 7th 1880–Sept. 29th 1881. Founded by W.H.G. Kingston, it contains adventure stories for boys by, e.g. Jules Verne, George Manville Fenn and the editor. Indexed.

2639 **THE WESLEYAN JUVENILE OFFERING.**
A MISCELLANY OF MISSIONARY INFORMATION FOR YOUNG PERSONS. LONDON: WESLEYAN MISSION HOUSE. 139p.: front., 12 plates. Bound in purple cloth, with embossed decorative cover and spine. Published monthly. Library has one volume: v.10, New Series, 1876. Contains articles on missionary work in various countries, particularly China and India. Indexed.

2640 **THE WILD WEST LIBRARY.**
LONDON: JAMES HENDERSON AND SONS, (192–?). 24p. each. Bound with coloured pictorial paper covers. 1d. Library has Nos. 11, 31, 32, 188 + 7 unnumbered parts without covers. Consists of individual stories such as Buffalo Bill to the rescue, the Woman with the iron hand, The Creeping Terror, the Black Spider of the Shoshones. The seven copies without covers are stories by Charlton Lea.

2641 **WONDERLAND TALES.**
EVERY FRIDAY. LONDON: AMALGAMATED PRESS LIMITED. Coloured pictorial magazine of 24 pages. Library has No. 16 (1 Nov. 1919?). Includes stories and cartoons for younger children.

2642 **THE WORLD'S BEST BOYS' ANNUAL.**
Sport, Travel, and Adventure in Many Lands. MANCHESTER: ALLIED NEWSPAPERS LIMITED. 211p.: col. front., vignette title page, 3 col. plates, ill. Coloured pictorial cover and spine. Library has one volume for (193–?). Stories of sport, space, school life etc. for boys.

2643 **YOUNG ENGLAND.**
An illustrated Magazine for Boys THROUGHOUT THE ENGLISH-SPEAKING WORLD. LONDON: THE SUNDAY SCHOOL UNION. Ill., some col. Published monthly. Library has 10 volumes: v.19–24, 1898–1903; v.26, 1905; v.33, 1911/12; v.39, 1918; v.52, 1931. (2 copies of v.24). Volumes 39 and 52 published at the Pilgrim Press. Includes stories, verse and articles on hobbies, sport, pets, etc.

## 21 MISCELLANY

2644 **BALLANTYNE, ROBERT MICHAEL.**
AN AUTHOR'S ADVENTURES, OR PERSONAL REMINISCENCES IN BOOK-MAKING. BY R.M. BAL-

LANTYNE. LONDON: JAMES NISBET AND CO. LIMITED, (190–?). 238p. + 8p. pub. cat.: front., 2 plates. Bound in red cloth, with coloured pictorial cover and spine.
C 823.8 BAL

2645 **THE BEEHIVE.**
Large loose sheets of sugar paper held in maroon filing box, unpaginated. Dated items cover years 1830–1890. An example of a loose leaf scrapbook of mounted cuttings, prints, pictures and letter headings from the nineteenth century.
YSC 00 080 BEE (Grille)

2646 **BOWMAN, ISA.**
THE STORY OF LEWIS CARROLL. TOLD FOR YOUNG PEOPLE BY THE REAL ALICE IN WONDERLAND, MISS ISA BOWMAN, WITH A DIARY AND NUMEROUS FACSIMILE LETTERS WRITTEN TO MISS ISA BOWMAN AND OTHERS. ALSO MANY SKETCHES AND PHOTOS BY LEWIS CARROLL AND OTHER ILLUSTRATIONS. LONDON: J.M. DENT AND CO., 1899. VII, 132p.: front., 6 plates. Bound in blue cloth, with vignette on cover and gilt top.
C 828.809 CAR/BOW

2647 **EXERCISE BOOK COLLECTION.**
This group of manuscript books came chiefly from a private collection from a family in the Glossop area and date back to the 1840–1888 period.

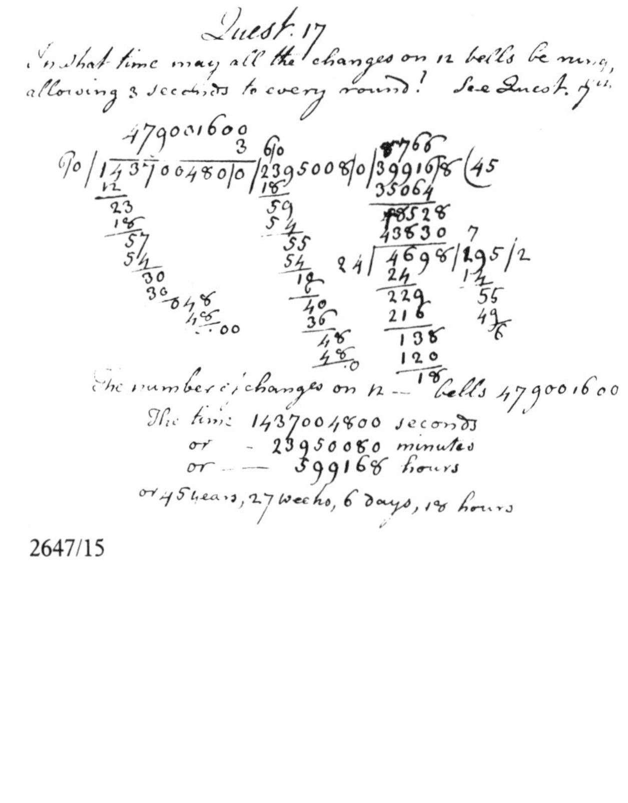
Quest: 17
In what time may all the changes on 12 bells be rung, allowing 3 seconds to every round? See Quest. 7th.

The number of changes on 12 bells 479001600
The time 1437004800 seconds
or 23950080 minutes
or 399168 hours
or 45 years, 27 weeks, 6 days, 18 hours

2647/15

1 H.A. Kershaw. March 23rd 1848. Grammar Book.
2 H.A. Kershaw. 1849. Grammar.
3 Miss Mary Bullass. Midsummer 1847. Maps of individual countries.
4 Miss Mary Bullass. Midsummer 1848. Book containing MS Hemispheres of the world.
5 A Juvenile Atlas consisting of 41 Outline Maps drawn by Elizabeth Officer at Miss Brinton's School, Kidderminster, June 1867.
6–10 Harriett Anne Kershaw. Historical notebooks, in chronological order from the Creation onwards to 1800.
11 E. Schofield. Arithmetic Exercise Book. n.d.
12 Mensuration of superfices. n.d.
13 Mensuration of solids continued. n.d.
14 Of bricklayers work – the mathematical principles of tiling, walling and chimney work.
15 Book of mathematical problems with worked examples. c. 1850.
16 Ethel Derbyshire. Writing book in which part of Alice's Adventures in Wonderland is transcribed with an illustration of the White Rabbit. 1888.
17 Writing book as used in Askern College near Doncaster. c. 1850.
18 Master Fred Taylor. Black and white pencil sketch book as used in J. Farrar's Commercial Classical and Mathematical Academy. Park Place, Halifax. December 1875.
19 Mr Wrigley's Academy, Bolton. Arithmetic practice books in copper plate hand giving examples. Used by Miss Mellor in 1869. 2 vols. Bound in red calf with coloured covers.
YRB BOX 371.3078 EXE

2648 **GATTY, HORATIA K.F.**
JULIANA HORATIA EWING AND HER BOOKS. BY HORATIA K.F. GATTY WITH A PORTRAIT BY GEORGE REID, R.S.A. SIXTEEN ILLUSTRATIONS FROM SKETCHES BY J.H. EWING, AND A COVER DESIGNED BY RANDOLPH CALDECOTT. LONDON: SOCIETY FOR PROMOTING CHRISTIAN KNOWLEDGE, 1885. 88p.: front., vignette on title page, ill. Bound in grey paper with pictorial cover.
YSC 920 EWI

2649 **MILNE, ALAN ALEXANDER.**
The CHRISTOPHER ROBIN BIRTHDAY BOOK. Compiled by A.A. Milne. Decorated by E.H. Shepard. LONDON: METHUEN AND CO. LTD., 1930. VII, 215p.: decorated title page, ill. Bound in red cloth, with embossed vignette on cover.
C 823.912 MIL

## GENERAL INDEX TO AUTHORS, TITLES, EDITORS, TRANSLATORS AND SERIES.

# INDEX TO ILLUSTRATORS, ENGRAVERS AND LOCAL PUBLISHERS